THE MARSHALL CAVENDISH
ILLUSTRATED ENCYCLOPEDIA OF

WORLD
WAR I

VOLUME ELEVEN
1919–21

THE MARSHALL CAVENDISH ILLUSTRATED ENCYCLOPEDIA OF

WORLD WAR I

Editor-in-Chief
Brigadier Peter Young
Editorial Board
Lt.-Col. A. J. Barker; Dr. John Bradley
Professor John Erickson; Lt.-Cdr. Peter Kemp
John Keegan; Kenneth Macksey; S. L. Mayer
Lt.-Col. Alan Sheppard; Norman Stone
Revision Editor
Mark Dartford

MARSHALL CAVENDISH
NEW YORK, LONDON, TORONTO

Editorial Staff

Editor	Brigadier Peter Young
Deputy Editor	Kenneth Macksey
Co-ordinating Panel	Lt.-Col. A. J. Barker
	Dr. John Bradley
	Prof. John Erickson
	Lt.-Cdr. Peter Kemp
	John Keegan
	S. L. Mayer
	Lt.-Col. Alan Sheppard
	Norman Stone
Military Consultants	Capt. Sir Basil Liddell-Hart
	Barrie Pitt
Executive Editor	Patrick Scrivenor
Assistant Editors	Chris Chant
	Carolyn Rutherford
	Bruce French
	Rose Thomson
	Margaret Burnley
Design Consultants	Peter Dunbar Associates
Art Director	Liam Butler
Art Editor	Brigit Webb
Cartographers	Gatrell
	Dunbar, Harison & Rees
	Alan Robertson
Technical Artist	John Batchelor
Picture Director	Robert Hunt

Reference Edition Published 1986

Published by Marshall Cavendish Corporation
147 West Merrick Road
Freeport, Long Island
N.Y. 11520

Printed and Bound in Italy by L.E.G.O. S.p.a. Vicenza.

Library of Congress Cataloging in Publication Data

Main entry under title:

The Marshall Cavendish encyclopedia of World War One.

  Bibliography:
  Includes index.
  1. World War, 1914–1918—Chronology. I. Marshall Cavendish Corporation.
D522.5.M39 1984   940.3   83-20879
ISBN 0-86307-181-3 (set)
    0 86307 192 9 vol

British Library Cataloguing in Publication Data

The Marshall Cavendish illustrated encyclopedia of World War One.
  1. World War, 1914–1918
  I. Young, Peter, *1915–*   II. Pitt, Barrie
  III. Dartford, Mark
940.3   D521

  ISBN 0-86307-181-3 (set)
      0 86307 192 9 vol

New Edition Staff

Revision Editor	Mark Dartford
Editorial Consultants	Randal Gray
	David Rosser-Owen
Project Executive	Robert Paulley
Designer	Trevor Vertigan
Indexers	F & K Gill
Production Manager	Dennis Hovell
Production Assistant	Richard Churchill

Contents of Volume 11

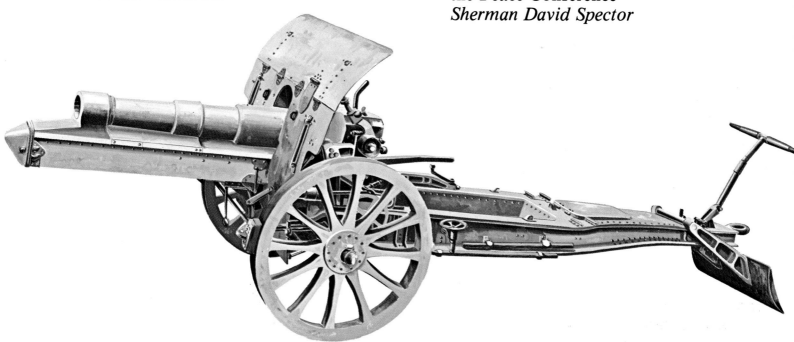

1918

NOV	**1**	Serbians recapture Belgrade.
	3	Austrians accept Serbian terms. French and American forces drive Germans from the Meuse-Argonne. Austria surrenders.
	4	Austrians sign armistice with Italy. Revolt spreads throughout Germany.
	7	German armistice commission meets Foch. Armistice signed at 5 am. Firing ceased 11.00 hrs.
	21	German High Seas Fleet surrenders to British at Scapa Flow.
DEC	**4**	Kingdom of Yugoslavia created.
	14	Portuguese President Paes assassinated.

1919

JAN	**5**	National Socialist Party formed in Germany.
FEB	**23**	Mussolini founds Italian Fascist Party.
MAR		Influenza epidemic rages in Europe.
JUN	**14**	Alcock and Brown fly Atlantic.
JUL	**31**	Weimar Republic founded in Germany.
NOV	**28**	Lady Astor becomes first female Member of Parliament in U.K.

1920

JAN	**16**	Prohibition in U.S.
JUN	**25**	International Court of Justice established at The Hague.
DEC	**2**	Woodrow Wilson and Leon Bourgeois win Nobel Prize.
	23	Government of Ireland Act divides country.

1921

FEB	**18**	U.S. Representative recalled from Reparations Committee.
	27	Communists and Fascists clash in Italy.
MAR	**4**	President Harding inaugurated in U.S.
	8	French troops occupy Ruhr.

Italy's international position on the eve of the Paris Peace Conference was mainly determined by the secret Treaty of London of April 26, 1915, which had laid down the terms on which Italy entered the war. It committed Britain, France and Russia to ensuring that when victory had been won, Italy would achieve certain precisely defined aims. First, she would obtain from Austria-Hungary the Trentino, Trieste and the Istran peninsula, which were inhabited by 'unredeemed' Italians. This would mean the completion of Italy's national unity. Second, she would secure more easily defended frontiers by extending her territory northwards and north-eastwards to the Alpine watershed. Thirdly, she would annex a large part of Dalmatia, together with most of its islands, and establish a foothold at Valona in Albania. This would increase her naval power and give her dominion of the Adriatic. Fourthly, she would keep the Dodecanese which she had 'temporarily' occupied in 1912. And lastly, if Britain and France increased their colonial territories in Africa or partitioned Turkey in Asia as a result of the war, Italy would get 'equitable compensation' in Africa or 'a just share of the Mediterranean region adjacent to the province of Adalia'. Her aims were, therefore, in part irredentist, in part strategic and in part imperialist.

When the terms of the Treaty came to be known generally in the last year of the war, it seemed to many Italians that because the world had changed greatly since 1915, some of its clauses were outdated. One great change was brought about by the intervention of the United States of America in 1917. Its militantly liberal President, Woodrow Wilson, declared that the war was a war for democracy and national self-determination, and against imperialism, colonialism and secret treaties. The 9th Point of Wilson's 14 Points of January 1918, in which he defined US peace aims, proposed that 'a readjustment of the frontiers of Italy should be effected along clearly recognisable lines of nationality'. But the northern frontier promised in the Treaty of London carried Italy up to the Brenner Pass, engulfing 250,000 Germans in the south Tyrol on the way and totally ignoring 'the recognisable line of nationality'. And the promised north-eastern frontier, which gave Italy the whole of the Istran peninsula with its mixed Italian and Slav population, together with the annexation of a large portion of Dalmatia, would bring 750,000 Southern Slavs under Italian rule. In short, the Treaty of London and the 14 Points were irreconcilable.

Another great change, which was of enormous importance to Italy, was the disintegration in defeat of her historic enemy and oppressor, Austria-Hungary. This destroyed the European framework into which the Treaty of London was intended to fit. Instead of a multi-national Austria-Hungary as neighbour, Italy now found she had Southern Slavs – Croats and Slovenes – clamouring in the name of self-determination for union with Serbia in a single great Yugoslav state. But such a state, if created, could never tolerate Italy's annexation of the Slav portion of Istra and a large part of Dalmatia, the cradle of the Yugoslav movement. Moreover, President Wilson had towards the end of the war announced US support for the Yugoslav cause. In Britain and France, too, there

ITALY
walk-out and disappointment

Italy had entered the war in 1915 to gain the specific territorial advantages promised her in the Treaty of London. But when the Peace Conference convened, Italy found that a totally unforeseen series of conditions had made her demands impossible – to the US. *Christopher Seton-Watson*

had been clear signs of growing sympathy and many Italians began to wonder whether their Allies were not contemplating evasion of their obligations under the Treaty of London.

Italo-Yugoslav antagonism, which smouldered during the war, exploded as soon as the armistice of November 3, 1918, was signed. Already on October 29 a Yugoslav National Committee at Zagreb had proclaimed the independence of the Croats and Slovenes. The Italians lost no time in moving their troops and ships to occupy all territories within the lines laid down in the Treaty of London, as authorised by the Allied armistice agreements. Tension, hatred and sometimes violence followed the arrival of the Italians, especially in Dalmatia. The Italians answered with repression and behaved as if the occupied zones belonged to Italy already.

Fiume: the beginning of an obsession
It was at Fiume that the tension was greatest. Fiume had not been promised to Italy in the Treaty of London, but was left to be 'assigned by the four Allied Powers to Croatia'. The town of Fiume had an Italian majority, but if its twin, Sušak, separated by only a narrow river, was counted in, the majority became Slav. The surrounding countryside was incontestably Slav and a wide belt of Slav territory cut Fiume off from Italy. Fiume had figured rarely in irredentist programmes before 1914. But during the war, as expectations of the rewards of victory escalated, it became added to the list. When Hungarian authority collapsed in October 1918 troops loyal to the Zagreb National Council took over. The Italians of Fiume then set up their own National Council which proclaimed the annexation of their town to Italy on October 31. Next day Orlando, the Italian Prime Minister, told the assembled Allied leaders in Paris that 'Fiume is more Italian than Rome'. When he heard that a Serbian battalion was on the way he authorised the landing of Italian troops. This act was in breach of the armistice. The crisis was solved with difficulty by an agreement whereby Serbian and Croat troops withdrew and Fiume was occupied by Allied and Italian troops under the command of an Italian

general. This was the beginning of an obsession with Fiume that plagued the Italians throughout the Peace Conference.

These events antagonised Italy's allies and led to much tension in the Adriatic, where the French forces of occupation favoured the Yugoslav cause. They also intensified the long-standing divisions within Italy. Her intervention in 1915 had been the work of a powerful and committed minority and it had split not only the nation but also the ruling class. Victory failed to heal the breach. The bitter divisions of 1915 within the ruling Liberal Party between neutralists, led by the great old man of politics, Giolitti, and interventionists, led first by Salandra, then Boselli, then Orlando, persisted after the war. Orlando's government in 1918 was predominantly interventionist but it was at the mercy of a parliament with a neutralist majority. The growing Socialist Party, which had opposed the war and sometimes actively sabotaged it, had been carried away by Bolshevik and 'soviet' hysteria and was playing a largely destructive political rôle. It looked to Moscow and ignored the Paris Peace Conference. Endless strikes and disorders were a prominent feature of the postwar months in Italy. The economy had been disrupted by the war and the financial position of the country was desperate, even with massive American credits and loans. Internal divisions, economic crisis and social disruption, which a weak government found difficult to control, seriously undermined Italy's credit abroad and the effectiveness of the Italian delegation in Paris.

When the time came for Italy to formulate her claims for the Conference, three broad attitudes emerged. The first was that of Sonnino, Foreign Minister since 1914, supported by powerful conservative forces. Sonnino had been the chief architect of the Treaty of London in 1915 and clung to it with an obduracy which, as his critics liked to say, rivalled that of Shylock over his bond. In November 1918 he dissuaded Orlando from proclaiming the annexation of Fiume because such an act would have violated the Treaty on which Italy depended. Every suggestion that it should be modified or in part renounced in the light of changed circumstances left him unmoved. Orlando, a liberal rather than a conservative, had unlike Sonnino shown sympathy with the Yugoslav cause during the war and, left to himself, might well have been willing to renounce Dalmatia in exchange for Fiume. But he was a weak man. Not only was he incapable of standing up to Sonnino; he also succumbed in turn to the pressures of the other two political groups, the Democrats and the Nationalists.

The Democrats were led by Bissolati, ex-socialist and one of the first interventionists in 1914. His views were based on Mazzini's doctrine of nationality and his concept of Italy's mission to lead the subject nationalities of Austria-Hungary to liberation. He revived Mazzini's battle cry *Delenda Austria* ('Austria must be destroyed'). Bissolati and his followers had the courage and integrity to apply their principles impartially to the Treaty of London. They consequently advocated the renunciation of Dalmatia and Eastern Istra to the Slavs, the German areas of South Tyrol to the Austrians, the Dodecanese to the Greeks and Valona to the

3253

The proclamation in Fiume of the Italian Regency of the area on September 9, 1920

Vittorio Orlando, Italy's Prime Minister

Albanians. But he also supported Fiume's plea to be annexed to Italy.

The Nationalists preached the doctrine that Italy, economically weak and over-populated, was a 'proletarian nation' morally entitled to colonial territory where Italian emigrants could live under the Italian flag. They dreamt of an enlarged empire in Africa, of making the Adriatic a wholly Italian sea and of restoring to reality the ancient Roman concept of the Mediterranean as *mare nostrum*. They were the first to note the power vacuum created by the collapse of the Russian, Austro-Hungarian and German Empires and be-lieved that a virile and aggressive Italy could fill it. They approved of the Treaty of London, but only as a minimum, a base for further expansion in the Balkans, Asia Minor and Africa. And they clamoured for Fiume and all Dalmatia. Whereas the Democrats wished to win Yugoslav friend-ship and had worked hard for it in the last year of the war, the Nationalists regarded Yugoslavs as Italy's bitterest enemies, and potential rivals in the Adriatic.

D'Annunzio the demagogue

The best-known Nationalist was D'Annun-zio, not a politician but a poet, dramatist and novelist, the prophet of national great-ness and now a war hero. He had played a big part in 1915 in inflaming the masses with the passion of war. In 1919, fresh from spectacular feats on sea and in the air, he returned to the political fray. Victory was being mutilated by weak politicians, he declared, and called for the immediate seizure of Fiume and all Dalmatia.

Bissolati had been a Minister since 1916 but resigned on December 27, 1918 be-cause the intransigence of his colleague Sonnino had become intolerable to him. He was by then the leading advocate in Italy of Wilsonian principles. But from the day of his resignation his influence and that of his followers declined. Throughout the period of the Peace Conference the Nation-alists were the dominant political force. Bissolati was reviled as a 'renouncer' and on January 11, 1919 his speech on the League of Nations in the Scala Opera House in Milan was broken up by a band of hooligans which included Mussolini. This was a foretaste of fascism.

The flag of the new Free State of Fiume, a state only until Mussolini's takeover in 1924

The area of Italy's main territorial interests

The Peace Conference opened formally on January 18, 1919. The Italians were at once worried by an early decision of the directing Council of Ten (composed of two representatives from each Great Power: USA, Britain, France, Italy and Japan) that the German treaty should be given priority of consideration by the Council. For the Italians Germany had always been the second enemy, Austria-Hungary the first; and it was the treaties with Austria and Hungary, now separate states, that mainly concerned them. The Italian delegates therefore played little part in the main work of the Conference in the first two months. Orlando and Sonnino sat in the Council of Ten but made only sporadic contributions. Their main concern was to prevent recognition by the Conference of the united Kingdom of the Serbs, Croats and Slovenes which a joint declaration of the Serbian Government and the Yugoslav National Council had brought into existence on December 1, 1918. The Italians objected passionately to the inclusion of Croats and Slovenes—to them still enemies —in the Serbian delegation and did their best to silence the Yugoslav representatives in the Council and its committees. On the main economic and territorial committees the Italian representatives lost no opportunity of obstructing any decision favourable to the Yugoslavs (or Greeks). Harold Nicolson, who as a junior member of the British Peace Delegation watched them in action, called them 'sulky children'.

On February 7 the Italians presented an official statement of their claims. These included all that had been promised in the Treaty of London, together with a further wedge of territory round Tarvisio on the north-eastern frontier designed to keep the Trieste-Vienna railway out of Yugoslav territory; and Fiume, claimed on the very ground of self-determination that the Treaty of London violated. On that same day the US government announced its recognition of the Yugoslav state. This turned the Italo-Yugoslav dispute into a dispute between Italy and the USA. The Yugoslavs countered the Italian statement with their own, which they presented to the Council on February 18. On that occasion Orlando and Sonnino absented themselves for reasons of national dignity.

The Yugoslavs claimed the whole of Istra and Trieste. 'They are idiots', commented Harold Nicolson. The two delegations thus made public their respective intransigent and irreconcilable positions. Italian claims were not discussed again until April 3.

Behind the scenes, however, unofficial discussions were almost continuous. In January Orlando and Sonnino had sounded President Wilson and his chief adviser, Colonel House, Lloyd George and his Foreign Secretary, Balfour, and Clemenceau, French Prime Minister and chairman of the Conference. For the Italians it had been a painful process. Wilson made it brutally clear that he was totally unconcerned with the Treaty of London and intended to insist on the application of his principles in any Adriatic settlement. At the outset he weakened his moral position by agreeing too easily, and probably out of ignorance, to Italy's northern frontier on the Brenner. Perhaps this made him all the more adamant on Dalmatia, the north-eastern frontier in Istra and Fiume which, because it was the essential commercial outlet for Yugoslavia and Central Europe, he was determined should not fall 'into Italian hands. On the question of the Dodecanese Wilson and his advisers were equally intransigent: the American representatives on the Greek territorial committee refused to recognise the Treaty of London and urged the cession of the Dodecanese to Greece. The position of Britain and France was very different. They were tied by the Treaty of London but now found its non-ethnic clauses extremely embarrassing. Their policy in the Adriatic and Dodecanese questions was therefore passive: to let Wilson carry the burden, hoping that he would negotiate a compromise and so get them out of the mess.

The Wilson Line rejected

The first attempt at an Italo-Yugoslav compromise occurred early in February. The initiative came from the American delegation. Their plan was to extract from the Yugoslavs a statement of their minimum terms, present them to Wilson and if he thought them just, to ask him to impose them on the Italians. The problem that worried the Americans most, apart from Fiume, was the north-eastern frontier. With the help and consent of Yugoslav delegates the American experts worked out an alternative to the Treaty of London line which would run down the central watershed of the Istran peninsula. This would give two-thirds of Istra to Italy and one-third to Yugoslavia. It would also give to Yugoslavia the belt of Slovene territory which divided Italy from Fiume. This line was presented to Wilson who approved it and it became known as the Wilson Line. It was then arranged that Wilson should see Trumbić, leader of the Yugoslavs in exile during the war and now Yugoslav Foreign Minister. Trumbić proposed that the whole Adriatic dispute be referred to the President for arbitration. This proposal came before the Council of Ten on February 17. Orlando had already made it known that the Wilson Line was totally unacceptable to Italy, both because militarily it was less defensible than the Treaty of London Line and because it isolated Fiume. In the Council Sonnino commented pithily that the Italian government could not accept any proposal for arbitration on any question affecting Italy that was before the

Conference. This killed the idea of arbitration. Orlando meanwhile returned to Rome for a brief visit to resume contact with parliament. On March 1, in the presence of his cabinet, he reasserted in the Chamber of Deputies that Fiume was *italianissima*.

The Adriatic question simmered throughout March. Innumerable private meetings and discussions took place, mainly between American and Italian experts and delegates. The Yugoslavs kept silent, counting on Wilson to safeguard their interests. No progress was made towards a solution until the first fortnight of April when Orlando had a series of private meetings with Lloyd George, Clemenceau and Wilson. The meeting with Lloyd George was amicable but those with Wilson painful and stormy. On April 17 Wilson's expert advisers urged him not to yield: 'The President is given the rare privilege of going down in history as the statesman who destroyed, by a clean-cut decision against an infamous arrangement, the last vestige of the old order'. On April 19 the Council of Four (Wilson, Lloyd George, Clemenceau and Orlando), which had replaced the Council of Ten, took up the Adriatic question. It was a tense and unhappy meeting. Wilson yielded nothing as regards the Treaty of London but he did accept the possibility of making Fiume a free port under the League of Nations, rather than giving it to the Yugoslavs. Orlando repeated all the old arguments, including the superiority of Italian culture in Dalmatia. Wilson dismissed Italy's strategic argument on the ground that 'under the régime of the League of Nations he could not conceive of a Yugoslav fleet which could threaten Italy'. Sonnino commented, 'How can we put our trust in the League of Nations until it has proved itself fully capable?' After three hours of discussion the problem was not an inch nearer solution. That evening the Italian delegation had a long, bitter, stormy debate. 'We are at a turning-point in Italy's history', declaimed Crespi, the economic expert of the delegation. It was resolved to fall back on the Treaty of London. Orlando read out the delegation's resolution to the Council of Four next morning. When he had finished speaking, the minutes record, 'he sobbed for a long while'. It seemed that the Adriatic question was back where it started.

On April 21 Lloyd George, Clemenceau and Orlando, with their respective Foreign Ministers, met without Wilson as signatories of the Treaty of London. Lloyd George took a conciliatory line and begged Orlando not to withdraw from the Conference as it had been rumoured that he intended to do. Lloyd George and Clemenceau made it quite clear that on Fiume they were wholly in agreement with Wilson. 'We cannot break our word to the Croats', said Clemenceau. 'We must have Fiume', retorted Orlando and added, not for the first time, that if he went back to Italy with 'Wilson's peace', there would be a revolution. The meeting ended without a decision.

Lloyd George persisted in his efforts for conciliation over the next two days and devised an embryo compromise: Fiume to be under League of Nations administration; four Dalmatian towns, Zara (Zadar), Traù (Trogir), Sebenico (Sibenik) and Spalato (Split) to be free cities under League of Nations administration, pending a plebiscite; and all but one of the Dalmatian islands to go to Italy. This scheme was dis-

The Treaty of Rapallo, November 11, 1920. Signing it is Sforza's Prime Minister, Giolitti of Italy

cussed in the Council of Four on April 23. But Wilson had by now lost his patience. That same afternoon he published a manifesto to the Italian people. It was intended to clarify the situation and bring the Italians to reason; instead it made a rupture inevitable. With Lloyd George still working on his compromise and appealing to the Italians to stay, Orlando left for Rome on the night of April 24. He had no alternative but to 'go back to the source of my authority', the Italian Parliament, and by securing its support demonstrate to the world the failure of what Italian opinion, despite Wilson's denial, was bound to interpret as an attempt to undermine his position at home.

As he was leaving Paris Orlando was asked whether and when he would return. He replied that that depended on how he fared in Rome. At first he fared very well, far above his expectations. His progress from the frontier to Rome was that of a victorious hero. Italians almost unanimously applauded his gesture, rallying behind him from a sense of injured national pride. Not even Bissolati and his followers spoke up for Wilson. The manifesto turned out to have been a psychological blunder. Orlando responded to the euphoria. 'Italy knows poverty and hunger: she does not know dishonour', he told the huge crowd awaiting his arrival. His reception in parliament was delirious. D'Annunzio and Mussolini urged the immediate annexation of Fiume and Dalmatia. D'Annunzio denounced the Peace Conference as powerless against 'the most victorious of nations, the nation that has saved all nations'. The press excelled itself in vituperation against the Allies, the Peace Conference and Wilson personally. Rome experienced again the atmosphere of May 1915.

But the mood soon changed. Orlando waited for an invitation to return but it never came. Very soon Crespi, who had been left behind in Paris with a watching brief, was telegraphing frantic appeals to come back. In Italy's absence Wilson, Clemenceau and Lloyd George allotted all the mandates over Germany's African colonies to Britain and France and the reparation clauses of the German treaty were amended to Italy's detriment. It was further made known to the Italians that if

they had no representative at the meeting on May 7 at which the treaty was to be presented to the German representatives, Italy would be deemed by her Allies to desire a separate peace and the Treaty of London would become null and void. By May 5 the seriousness of the situation in Paris had become apparent even to Sonnino. On the morning of May 7 he and Orlando were back.

Negotiations were immediately resumed and dragged on for the rest of the month. First Colonel House and other leading members of the US delegation had a try; then came the French in the person of Tardieu, Clemenceau's confidant. Orlando also authorised direct political negotiations between the economic experts of the Italian and Yugoslav delegations. In the process of negotiation the area of disagreement did eventually narrow. The Italians were now prepared to accept for Fiume the status of free state under the League of Nations, provided it was Italian in character and contiguous with Italy; and they reduced their demands in Dalmatia to the towns of Zara and Sebenico and the islands. But Wilson, who kept aloof but maintained his power of veto, stuck to the Wilson Line and insisted that whatever form the free state of Fiume might take, it must reflect the Slav majority of the surrounding region. A solution still evaded the Conference.

In April two other problems deeply affecting the Italians came to the fore: Asia Minor and African colonies. In both cases Italy had only the imprecise clauses of the Treaty of London to rely on: the larger promises regarding Asia Minor, including Smyrna, which Sonnino had extracted from his allies in 1917, had been declared invalid at the end of the war by Britain and France on the legalistic ground that Russia had never approved them. Early in April Sonnino, fearing that the Greeks were about to steal a march on him, decided to stake Italy's claim by force. Italian marines were landed at Adalia and two warships despatched to Smyrna. This action, which he ordered without even consulting Orlando, added to the irritation of the British and French and precipitated the very event that it was intended to prevent. On May 5 Lloyd George, with the approval of Wilson and Clemenceau, in-

vited the Greek Prime Minister, Venizelos, to send an expeditionary force immediately to Smyrna. Sonnino, on his return, resenting the *fait accompli*, retaliated by ordering further landings and on May 15 Italian troops reached Scalanova, only 40 miles from Smyrna. It looked as if an armed clash between Greek and Italian troops was inevitable.

Italy's right, by the terms of the Treaty of London, to 'equitable compensation' in Africa was dealt with by a special Anglo-Franco-Italian Committee on which Crespi was the chief Italian representative. It met four times in May. In North Africa the Italians asked only for an expansion of the frontiers of Libya. In East Africa they were more ambitious, hoping to acquire British and French Somaliland as a link between Eritrea and Italian Somaliland and a base for establishing an Italian protectorate over Ethiopia. The British and French ruled out such big demands, and also Crespi's request for a mandate over Togoland, as being beyond the terms of the clause in the Treaty of London. All that the Italians achieved was a promise from the British Colonial Secretary, Lord Milner, of the oasis of Jarabub on the border of Egypt and of Jubaland, the north-eastern province of Kenya.

Brief triumph
Orlando and his delegation never recovered from the humiliation of their return to Paris. Only the acquisition of Fiume could have restored their credit. Their voice in the Council of Four carried less weight than ever before. Over Fiume and Dalmatia, Smyrna and East Africa, there had been nothing but disappointment. The only consolation came from the treaty with Austria. Not only did it confirm the Brenner frontier, but thanks to the stubbornness of Sonnino the wedge of Slovene-inhabited territory round Tarvisio was also ceded to Italy, beyond the Treaty of London line, so that the railway from Trieste to the Austrian frontier was kept out of Yugoslav territory. Italy was also allotted the greater part of the Austro-Hungarian merchant marine network. The text of the treaty was presented to the Austrian representatives at St Germain on June 2 and the Italian delegation had a brief moment of triumph. 'Italy has achieved all her war aims as regards Austria', Orlando told Crespi. But this success passed almost unnoticed in Italy. In Rome there was a growing conviction that only a new team could end the Adriatic deadlock. Economic crisis, food shortages and persistent strikes and disorders created a rising wave of discontent for which the government was made the scapegoat. Orlando himself was almost prostrate with nervous exhaustion and from within the cabinet Crespi was pressing for resignation. On June 19 the government was defeated in Parliament by a large majority and resigned.

Orlando's successor was Nitti, Sonnino's was Tittoni. Nitti, although a lukewarm interventionist with a well-merited reputation for defeatism, had been Orlando's Minister of Finance from October 1917 to his resignation in January 1919. His main preoccupation on taking power was not a glorious or imperialist peace, about which he was highly cynical, but Italy's precarious economic and financial situation. The threat of 'national starvation' loomed large in his mind. His foreign policy was determined by his knowledge that Italy depended on the US and Britain for credits and vital supplies. In that context Fiume and Dalmatia seemed trivialities. Tittoni, a veteran diplomat and former Foreign Minister, agreed with Nitti that Italy's future foreign policy should be unambitious and conciliatory. His intention was to negotiate a general agreement with Britain and France covering Asia Minor and Africa as well as the Adriatic: concessions in one region might then be compensated by gains in another. If good relations could be restored with the two Allies, he hoped that Wilson might accept such a general agreement as better than no agreement at all.

Tittoni had hardly had time to make his first soundings in Paris, where he had received a cool welcome, when Fiume threw up a new crisis. On July 6 the last of a series of clashes between the French garrison and the local population led to the lynching of nine French soldiers by a mob which included uniformed Italians. The Council of Four sent an Allied military mission to enquire and accepted its recommendations on August 26. The most important was the creation of an Allied police force to replace the existing Italian garrison in maintaining order. This proposal aroused rebellious sentiments in some units of the Italian army and a small group of mutinous young officers sent a deputation to D'Annunzio to ask him to lead them. On September 12 D'Annunzio drove into Fiume at the head of 1,000 men, meeting no resistance from the Allied or Italian garrisons, and was proclaimed dictator by the National Council.

D'Annunzio's action was a challenge to his own government, the Peace Conference, President Wilson and the Yugoslavs. For that very reason it aroused enthusiasm not only among the nationalists but over a wide range of Italian opinion. The Chamber of Deputies passed a motion affirming the Italian character ('italianità') of Fiume. Even Bissolati and the democrats felt bound to condone his purpose. Volunteers flocked to Fiume and by the end of the month D'Annunzio had 8,000 'Legionaries' under his command. Like Orlando in April, Nitti came under great pressure to proclaim annexation, but he refused, arguing that it might well lead to war with Yugoslavia and would certainly destroy all that was left of Allied goodwill. To eject D'Annunzio by force was impossible because Nitti knew that he could not rely on the army to carry out his order. There was therefore nothing to be done but wait on events. The Peace Conference deplored the episode but it too was impotent.

Between September and November 1919 Tittoni produced a series of proposals for solving the Adriatic deadlock. None of them were accepted by the Conference and in November he resigned, from weariness and frustration. Scialoja, who had been his deputy, succeeded him and carried his work on into 1920. Nitti himself played an active part and was responsible for one of the many compromises put forward. By 1920 Dalmatia had lost most of its importance in the controversy because the Italians had reduced their demands to one town, Zara, and an acceptably small number of islands. But Fiume remained an intractable obstacle to agreement.

Tittoni, Nitti and Scialoja all aimed at

Gabriele D'Annunzio, the dictator of Fiume

Benito Mussolini, the voice of chauvinism

persuading their Allies to accept an arrangement whereby the Italian town of Fiume would acquire an autonomous status of its own as a small Free State, with a narrow strip of coastal territory to give it contiguity with Italy. It was clearly the Italians' calculation that such an arrangement would facilitate eventual annexation. For that very reason Wilson passionately opposed it. On October 29 he wrote peremptorily to Nitti: 'You know that my views on the problem of Fiume are not susceptible of modification.' But Wilson no longer spoke with his old authority, either in Europe or in his own country. The decline of US influence also tempered the Yugoslavs' intransigence. Britain and France began to ignore the President's reprimands and moved closer to the Italian position. This trend was reinforced in Britain's case by Nitti's firm support of the conciliatory European policy of Lloyd George, with whom he established close and friendly relations.

In January 1920 the two Allies accepted the essence of the Italian proposals, despite Wilson's protests. Once again general approval was lacking, this time owing to a last display of obstinacy by the Yugoslavs. In May Scialoja met Trumbić and his Prime Minister, Pašić, and the last phase, direct negotiations between Italy and Yugoslavia, began. Nitti's fall in June left it to his successor, the veteran Giolitti, arch-neutralist and symbol of the old pre-war liberal régime, to tie up the loose ends. In November 1920 his Foreign Minister, Sforza, after tough bargaining signed the Treaty of Rapallo. It gave Italy an excellent strategic north-eastern frontier, far to the east of the Wilson Line and even a little east of the Treaty of London line; Zara and four Dalmatian islands; and a small autonomous Free State of Fiume contiguous with Italy. Sforza declared, 'Italy's unity has been completed with perfect frontiers.' There remained D'Annunzio. On Christmas Day 1920 Giolitti ordered the army to move into Fiume. With Giolitti's firm hand in control it obeyed. D'Annunzio fled and the Free State was established by Italian arms.

Italy's new conciliatory policy also bore fruit in regions other than the Adriatic. In July 1919 Tittoni made an agreement with Venizelos, Prime Minister of Greece, whereby the Greeks made concessions favourable to the Italians in Albania and the Italians in return promised, on certain conditions, to cede the Dodecanese. Those conditions were, in fact, never fulfilled and the Dodecanese remained Italian until 1943. Tittoni also reached an understanding with Venizelos over zones of occupation in Asia Minor. But during 1919 an unforeseen factor, a formidable Turkish national resistance under Kemal, appeared on the scene. Sforza wisely decided to withdraw and in June 1921 the last Italian troops evacuated Adalia. In Africa Milner's promises were carried out after much delay: Jubaland was annexed to Italian Somaliland in 1924 and Jarabub to Libya in 1925.

Mussolini had the last say in the Adriatic situation. He had had no influence over the peace settlement in 1919-20 beyond adding to the shrill voice of chauvinism in his paper Il Popolo d'Italia. He raised large sums for D'Annunzio in Fiume but, unlike D'Annunzio, accepted the Treaty of Rapallo. In 1924 as Prime Minister he agreed with Yugoslavia to the incorporation of the Fiume Free State in Italy.

The final peace settlement, once the wild nationalist dreams had been abandoned, gave Italy 14 years of security and stability. It was Mussolini's revival of those dreams after 1934 that brought his country to ruin.

Further Reading
Mayer, Arno J., Politics and Diplomacy of Peace-making (Weidenfeld & Nicolson 1968)
Nicolson, Harold, Peacemaking 1919 (Methuen)
Albrecht-Carrié, R., Italy at the Paris Peace Conference (New York 1938)
Lederer, Ivo J., Yugoslavia at the Paris Peace Conference (Yale University Press 1963)

CHRISTOPHER SETON-WATSON was born in London in 1918. He served from 1939 to 1945 in the Royal Horse Artillery, mostly overseas, and ended the war in Italy, a country for which he has developed a lasting affection. In 1946 he became a Fellow of Oriel College and University Lecturer in Politics at Oxford University and has since published a study of modern Italy.

AUSTRIA
ANSCHLUSS OR REPUBLIC

In 1914 Austria had led a great empire into the war. In 1918 she was struggling to keep the shattered remnants, but was indeed lucky to hang on to her own integrity, even as a republic, in face of internal and external strife. *A. Wykes*

Karl, Emperor of Austria and King of Hungary since 1916, went into exile on November 11, 1918. He was 31 years old, a gentle Christian idealist, the last of the Habsburg rulers. His departure with the Empress Zita and their five children was hurried and ignominious. They left the Schönbrunn Palace, Vienna, by the tradesmen's entrance and stowed themselves into two ordinary taxicabs. It was dusk, and behind them the 1,400 rooms of the palace were in darkness. At the front gates there was an angry mob of unemployed steel workers from the nearby Florisdorf foundries who were beating at the palace railings and shouting for food, work, justice and peace.

The Emperor's deposition and flight marked the dissolution of the Austro-Hungarian Empire. Two days later the National Assembly declared German Austria—all that was left of the ramshackle empire that for 600 years had been under the dynastic rule of the Habsburgs—a republic. They did so in a document of only three sentences: 'German Austria is a democratic republic. All power emanates from the people. The German-Austrian Republic is an integral part of the German Republic.'

It was a simple declaration to make and without doubt had the approval of the majority of the war-torn and starving nation. But the union with Germany, the *Anschluss,* was not to be so easily achieved. At that time there was not even an established German Republic to unite with. The National Constituent Assembly convened to establish one did not begin its deliberations at Weimar until February 1919, at a time of revolutionary outbreaks throughout the country. However, the Weimar Constitution that was eventually hammered out there eagerly anticipated the *Anschluss.* 'It is comforting', wrote Friedrich Ebert, the elected President, 'that in the midst of insurrection . . . there is a calm untroubled wish on the part of Austria to unite with the German nation, and on our part to return that wish for unity'. Article 61 of the Constitution declared 'German Austria after its union with the German Reich will receive the right of participation in the Reichsrat'.

The desire by both nations for the *Anschluss* was not surprising. Before 1914 the dual monarchy of Austria-Hungary had depended largely on the alliance with Germany. Indeed, Germany's support in crushing Serbia after the assassination of the Archduke Franz Ferdinand in Sarajevo in June 1914 had brought the rest of Europe tumbling into the maelstrom of war. Also, Germany herself had gained great advantage from the economic progress of Austria from 1900 to 1910.

The statesmen of the victorious Allies, however, were by no means unanimous in their view that there should be an *Anschluss.* They were not, in fact, unanimous about anything. They had begun to assemble in Paris in December 1918 for the Peace Conference that would ultimately, after six months' wrangling, hesitation, bitterness and innumerable meetings by innumerable committees, sub-committees, and sub-sub-committees, bring forth the Hydra-headed Treaty of Versailles.

Austria's plight

The Conference was the brainchild of the United States' President, Woodrow Wilson, an idealist scathingly referred to as 'all buck teeth and high principles'. The Wilsonian ideals had been textually expressed in the famous 14 Points and Four Principles at the beginning of 1918; and the second of the Principles stated: 'Peoples and provinces shall not be bartered from sovereignty to sovereignty as if they were but chattels or pawns in a game'.

Regrettably, many of the 70 delegates of the 27 Allied nations represented at the Conference were more concerned with territorial gains and the removal of threats to their boundaries than with ideals. With regard to Austria they had at first given little thought to her plight—or, indeed, to her future status. Her plight was in fact that of all the defeated nations: economic collapse, rebellion, starvation. Immense imports into Germany of American wheat, flour, meat and coffee were, it was supposed, implementing the compassionate decision of the victors not to let the vanquished starve; and as for economics and internal politics—they would have to take care of themselves in due course. The business of the Conference was to forge permanent peace from the insanity of war, not to worry about trifles like nations attempting to determine their own future—in which contemptuous attitude the Conference appears to have forgotten Wilson's other principle that 'peoples shall be free to form their own nations on the basis of self-determination'. (Ironically, had the Habsburg Empire survived intact 'self-determination' would have been the last thing it wanted, since that would have meant giving autonomy to, among other states, Serbia, Croatia, Hungary and Slovakia—all Habsburg territories.)

To begin with, the formation of a Danubian Confederation, which would include Austria, had been proposed. But France, whose Prime Minister Georges Clemenceau presided over the Conference and was pathological in his hatred of Germany, saw nothing in the proposed confederation but a potential threat—since, he said, Austria could quite easily lead the confederation into union with Germany in the future. An *Anschluss* of Germany and Austria was one thing; a confederation of all the Danubian States was quite another. It constituted a potential of vast forces that could be led against France. Clemenceau having alarmed everybody with the intensity of his denunciation, the confederation idea was abandoned. That left Italy free to grasp at the South Tyrol, which by an astonishing *volte face* on Wilson's part was given to her—thus cutting Austria down to a territorial size that harboured a mere 6,000,000 people, of whom more than a third were in the *Land* (Province) of Vienna.

But notwithstanding this small population, the problem still had to be dealt with. Shamed by their own violation of the Wilsonian principle of 'self-determination' the Allies now had to paste over this particular crack—one of many that would continue to appear in Versailles' edifice. They did so with a compromise, ordering Germany to give Austria strict independence inside frontiers that were to be fixed in peace negotiations separate from the main Paris discussions.

These negotiations began at St Germain-en-Laye, a dozen miles west of Paris, on May 14. It was a town with historic precedent in the matter of peace negotiations. Charles IX and the Huguenots had come to terms here in 1570 and the treaty between France and Brandenburg was signed in the famous château in 1679.

The Austrian delegation was headed by the Chancellor, Karl Renner, an intellectual who in prewar days had led the May Day procession of workers with red carnations in their buttonholes through the boulevards of Vienna. But this was no time for revolutionary action. Renner obsequiously kowtowed to the French, who in their turn were relatively gracious—in contrast to their attitude to the German plenipotentiaries at Versailles, whom Clemenceau in particular was determined to humiliate.

Vienna: 'a cripple with blatant sores'

Apart from the loss of the South Tyrol, which was all that remained of the prizes promised to Italy by the secret Treaty of London (1915) in return for entering the war on the Allies' side, the Austrian frontier remained intact. The draft Treaty was ready two weeks after the negotiations began. Renner scurried away with it, hardly satisfied but seeing in it the smallest of many possible evils. There was now no point in proceeding with the *Anschluss* discussions at Weimar and the Austrian delegates were summoned back to Vienna. They returned to that once beautiful city to find it in an even more deplorable state than when they had left it in February. It was the capital of a Republic that nobody wanted. In the *Ringstrasse* the cafés were in darkness, the theatres boarded up. The long midsummer evenings shed a merciless light on the litter that blew like spindrift along the boulevards with their ragged lawns and trampled flower beds. The remains of winter fires blackened the grass in the *Prater,* where starving refugees had huddled for warmth, bringing with them the

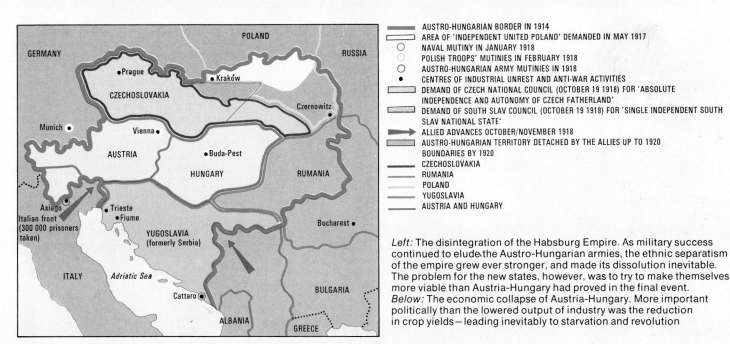

AUSTRO-HUNGARIAN BORDER IN 1914
AREA OF 'INDEPENDENT UNITED POLAND' DEMANDED IN MAY 1917
NAVAL MUTINY IN JANUARY 1918
POLISH TROOPS' MUTINIES IN FEBRUARY 1918
AUSTRO-HUNGARIAN ARMY MUTINIES IN 1918
CENTRES OF INDUSTRIAL UNREST AND ANTI-WAR ACTIVITIES
DEMAND OF CZECH NATIONAL COUNCIL (OCTOBER 19 1918) FOR 'ABSOLUTE INDEPENDENCE AND AUTONOMY OF CZECH FATHERLAND'
DEMAND OF SOUTH SLAV COUNCIL (OCTOBER 19 1918) FOR 'SINGLE INDEPENDENT SOUTH SLAV NATIONAL STATE'
ALLIED ADVANCES OCTOBER/NOVEMBER 1918
AUSTRO-HUNGARIAN TERRITORY DETACHED BY THE ALLIES UP TO 1920
BOUNDARIES BY 1920
CZECHOSLOVAKIA
RUMANIA
POLAND
YUGOSLAVIA
AUSTRIA AND HUNGARY

Left: The disintegration of the Habsburg Empire. As military success continued to elude the Austro-Hungarian armies, the ethnic separatism of the empire grew ever stronger, and made its dissolution inevitable. The problem for the new states, however, was to try to make themselves more viable than Austria-Hungary had proved in the final event.
Below: The economic collapse of Austria-Hungary. More important politically than the lowered output of industry was the reduction in crop yields—leading inevitably to starvation and revolution

Austrian Crop Yields
In thousands of doppelzentner
1 dz = 220 lbs
= 1/10 tons

Potatoes: 77 584 / 63 195 / 38 942
Sugar Beet: 67 748 / 46 187 / 44 945 / 28 925
Rye: 18 939 / 13 009 / 9 681 / 8 889
Wheat: 10 349 / 7 698 / 5 868 / 5 172
Barley: 12 728 / 6 474 / 6 982 / 3 928
Oats: 19 176 / 8 364 / 10 375 / 4 846

These figures relate only to the non-invaded areas of Austria.

No general figures are available for 1918, but other figures suggest that the yields declined still further.

Crop yields in Hungary also fell sharply, though the decline was not so marked as in Austria.

Austrian Industrial Production
In millions of doppelzentner

Lignite: 237·7 / 220·2 / 232·0 / 216·5 / 153·6 Jan to Sept
Pit Coal: 154·1 / 160·8 / 176·0 / 167·6 / 108·0 Jan to Sept
Sugar: 11·7 / 11·7 / 7·6 / 7·3 / 5·0
Pig Iron: 11·5 / 11·4 / 15·2 / 9·4
Iron Ore: 22·8 / 25·5 / 32·0 / 24·9
Raw Silk (thousands of kg): 157·8 / 133·8 / 113·3 / 87·7 / 120·7
1 kg = 2·205 lbs
Beer (millions of hectolitres): 178·8 / 128·3 / 23·2 / 16·9
1 hectolitre = 22 gallons
Locomotives (numbers): 273 / 273 / 395 / 398 / 463

Efforts were made to maintain or even increase the production of pit coal, iron ore and lignite, which were essential for carrying on the war. Other industries were allowed to decline. By 1918 total industrial production was about 20% below the pre-war level.

Note the increase in the production of locomotives. These were mainly used for military purpose.

Hungary had no industries of great importance.

1914 / 1915 / 1916 / 1917 / 1918

3259

Dr Renner arrives to sign Austria's peace

The Emperor Karl and his son Otto in exile

A demonstration in favour of union with Germany in front of Vienna town hall in February 1919

Versailles drew toward the conclusion of their Treaty, many of the sick and starving had been defeated finally by death. It was still not unusual to find corpses in shop doorways or crumpled against the plinths of statues. But the population problem had not vanished. As hundreds died or left the city other hundreds seemed to spring up in their place. Pillaging and drunkenness had faded out—there was little left to loot—but Austrian Communists had organised street fighting squads to encourage hunger riots and, they hoped, thereby topple the government. Renner combated these with his sparse police force aided by the *Volkswehr* ('People's Militia'); and by some miracle he contained them. But he could not contain the economic insurrection of inflation.

Chronic inflation

The whole Habsburg Empire had been an endless economic roundabout of 50 million customers; now, with every detached component part of the Empire raising its barriers against its former master state, Austria had ceased to be a viable economic unit. She lacked fuel for her factories and public services, food for her people, raw materials for her manufactures. Within a year inflation was to lead to the grotesque situation in which Germans—whose own inflation troubles were not far behind—crowded across the Bavarian border into Salzburg for the sake of buying a postage stamp or getting drunk at a fraction of the cost on their own side of the border. 'Every night,' Stefan Zweig recalled, 'the station was a veritable pandemonium of drunken, bawling, belching humanity; some of them, helpless from over-indulgence, had to be carried to the train on hand trucks, and then, with bacchanalian yelling and singing they were transported back to their own country. But we had our revenge when the Krone was stabilised and the Mark plunged below it in value; the stampede across the border was repeated, but this time in the opposite direction.'

The summer of 1919 faded into autumn. In Vienna the most brutal signs of defeat had been cleared away and a few shop windows had light restored to them. The giant wheel in the amusement park remained still, its cars rusting and swinging as autumn gales buffeted them. Emaciated people still thronged the streets, lining up with their ration tickets and hoping the bread would last till their turn. This was Vienna, the heart of Austria and the now demolished Empire of the Habsburgs, at the end of 1919; its benches lined with crumpled beggars, its fountains dry, its parks desolate. But as the winter snow begins to fall and whiten the faded spires and equestrian statues, 'the dignity of ghostliness' was caught again. But no one yet hears the fainter sound of ominously goose-stepping feet and an hysterical voice demanding a different kind of *Anschluss*.

leg of a chair or table as a contribution to the communal flames. In the old city inside the *Ringstrasse* the sewers had ceased to work through neglect. Filth oozed back up the drains and defiled the steps of St Stephen's Cathedral. 'Not even the dignity of ghostliness softens the city,' wrote the novelist Stefan Zweig. 'No strains of *Rosenkavalier* echo from the dead opera house. Vienna is ugly, a cripple with blatant sores, and one heartlessly longs for snow and darkness to cover it all.'

In the shabby parliament building Renner and the Assembly turned themselves to the problems of independence. 'We have been abandoned by all the States we have ruled,' he said in session, 'and we are unprepared for nationalism after 600 years at the heart of a mighty Empire with many languages.' The statement had about it a touch of self-pity, but it was true. Hungary had cut off her exports of wheat to her previous partner in the Dual Monarchy in a gesture of vicious punishment; American supplies were being hoarded by *Lander* which were to some extent self-supporting in the fear that the spectre of starvation would grope outwards from the capital; and the snowball of inflation had already begun.

But the worst problem of all was the enormously swollen and continually swelling population. On November 3, 1918 the Emperor Karl had been forced to sue for an armistice in the field. His crack Hungarian troops had mutinied and their defection had spread throughout the armies locked in hopeless battle with the Italians. The men were starving, ragged and ill with influenza and malaria. They flung down their arms at the first rumoured intimation of the armistice and headed for home. All the railway lines converged on Vienna and every train was stuffed with sick, tattered, famished troops. Many of them, unable to force their way into the carriages, whose windows and partitions they tore out, travelled on the roofs and hundreds of them fell to battered deaths in the alpine tunnels. Those who survived arrived in a city already stark and torn by angry mobs of unemployed workers and escaped Italian prisoners from the unguarded camps outside the city—most of them plundering the bars and hotels in search of insensibility in drunkenness. Soon they too had joined the looters and for weeks during the increasingly bitter weather Vienna was filled with mutinous drunken riff-raff smashing windows and falling upon the few remaining cab horses, which they clubbed to death and slashed into bloody strips of flesh to be borne off and roasted outside the government buildings in a mood of sullen reproach.

Now, in summer, as the peacemakers of

Further Reading
Taylor, Edmond, *The Fall of the Dynasties* (Weidenfeld & Nicolson)
Frischauer, Willi, *Twilight in Vienna* (Collins 1938)
Watt, Richard, *The Kings Depart* (Weidenfeld & Nicolson 1969)
Nicolson, Harold, *Peacemaking 1919* (Methuen)

[*For Alan Wykes' biography, see page 773.*]

CZECHOSLOVAKIA

CTK

Independence and Recognition

The most stable of the new states to emerge from the debris of the Habsburg Empire was Czechoslovakia, partly as a result of a strong and long-standing feeling of nationalism, and partly of quick recognition by the Allies. But even so, there remained the problems of the dissident minorities. *Dr J. F. N. Bradley. Above:* The streets of Prague as independence is declared in 1918

After the death of Franz Josef of Austria-Hungary in 1916 the new Emperor's liberal policies gave fresh hopes to his non-German subjects. However, ultimately they all proved counterproductive. Thus, although the Emperor released practically all political prisoners in several massive amnesties, these same immediately showed their gratitude by agitating against the Habsburgs, even in the *Reichsrat*. Almost all Slav political leaders began to put pressure on Karl by demanding greater autonomy for themselves; some asked for complete independence—the Czechs being among the foremost. The Emperor curtailed the powers of the German nationalists, but let loose all the others, for it was no longer only the Czechs and Slovaks in exile, Masaryk and his companions, who sought independence: they were joined by the Poles, Croats, Slovenes, Ruthenians and Rumanians. The Allies also finally realised the usefulness of nationalist propaganda against the Austro-Hungarian army, especially after the German spring offensive in 1918. In addition, the rôle played by the Czechoslovak Legion in Russia after the Bolshevik takeover in 1917 made of it a major asset for the cause of Czecho-Slovak independence, and *ipso facto* one of the causes of the destruction of the Habsburg Monarchy.

The Treaty of Brest-Litovsk early in 1918 was a mixed blessing as far as the Czechs were concerned. On the one hand it forced the Allies to reassess the position of the Czechoslovak Army Corps in Russia, but on the other hand it afforded a breath-ing space to the hard-pressed Habsburg Monarchy. Nonetheless it was not too long before a breakthrough in the Balkans occurred, and even the German element of the Monarchy saw the end coming. Events then took place at a breakneck speed. The Emperor had no time to implement his reforms; his Imperial Manifesto, prepared by Premier Hussarek and released on October 16, 1918, had been intended to satisfy legitimate demands for autonomy and self-determination, but instead, only helped to open the floodgates of separatism. Peace conditions, as proposed by President Wilson, brought about the collapse of the monarchy in the same month.

When the end came, the Czechs and Slovaks were in a much more privileged position than other national groups. The Czechoslovak Army Corps had been, since May 1918, fighting the Bolsheviks (and the Germans) in Russia on behalf of the Allies. Its revolt on the Trans-Siberian Railway, although it had surprised the Czechs and Slovaks, had been welcomed by the Allies and considered as their contribution to Allied victory. The Czechoslovaks in exile knew, therefore, that the Allies would favour the separatist aims of their country. The Czech political leaders at home had also an inkling of this and consequently acted in the calmest possible way. There was no outbreak of rioting, no chaos nor anarchy, only slight political tightening up. In fact, what remained to be done was to secure an agreement with the politicians in Prague to recognise the Czechoslovak National Council abroad.

Beneš arranged this at a series of meetings in Geneva between October 28 and 31, 1918. On October 28 national independence was proclaimed by the National Committee in Prague; the Allies immediately recognised this as a *fait accompli* and in their eyes the Czechoslovak National Council, under Professor Masaryk's leadership, became the Czechoslovak government *de facto*. The National Committee in Prague also recognised the émigré government. To everyone's satisfaction the Slovaks proclaimed their independence of Hungary on October 31, 1918 and opted to join the Czech provinces with which they had many links, particularly linguistic ones. But this Slovak declaration by Turčanský Svätý Martin was purely formal: the ultimate fate of Slovakia was settled by arms. The Buda-Pest government had been over the years far less lenient towards the Slovaks than the Vienna government towards the Czechs. The Slovaks were kept in undignified subjugation with only one national representative in the Hungarian parliament. Now it all backfired: when the one representative opted for Czechoslovakia, the whole Slovak nation opted so, too. But the Hungarians still had a few means of dissuasion, and the Slovaks appealed to the Czechs, who sent them *gendarmes* and later troops, thus asserting Slovak independence.

In the Czech provinces, Bohemia and Moravia, and in Prague, which became the capital, independence and changes were bloodless and smooth, particularly because of fears of a possible Bolshevik takeover

Left: Tomáš Masaryk signs the Declaration of Freedom and Co-operation of Middle European Nations in Philadelphia, USA, on October 26, 1918 — two days before the country he had been instrumental in creating declared itself an independent nation. Realising that he could achieve more by working with the Allies than by fomenting revolution at home, he inspired the declaration of independence from abroad, returning to take up the Presidency only in December 1918. *Above:* Masaryk's triumphal and hugely emotional arrival in Prague on December 21. *Above right:* Masaryk again. With his arrival in Prague, he could himself take up the reins of power which had been wielded, not entirely to Masaryk's satisfaction, by Dr Kramář. The latter was succeeded as Prime Minister by the Social Democrat Tusar. *Far right:* Dr Karel Kramář, the leader of the Czech right wing nationalist party. He ran foul of President Masaryk as a result of his economic policies and

if chaos was allowed to spread. The Czech *Reichsrat* deputies, after rounding off their numbers with co-opted representatives, declared themselves the Czechoslovak Parliament, the supreme representative body of national sovereignty. The National Assembly, as it called itself, then approved and thus legitimised the declaration of independence by the National Committee, appointed the émigré government as the constitutional government of Czechoslovakia, and elected Professor Masaryk, still in the United States, the first President. Beneš was confirmed as Foreign Minister, and he continued to represent the new country at international conferences, especially at the Peace Conference in Paris, where he was in residence.

A measure of unrest prevailed in the new state, especially in the first months of independence. The émigré leaders were slow in coming back and it was obvious that the armed forces of the new Republic would be most important for upholding the newly-gained independence. However, the new War Minister, Milan Štefánik, now promoted to General of the Czechoslovak Army, was not even in Europe. He was dealing with the difficulties of his troops, the Czechoslovak Legion, in Siberia, and neither he nor the troops would be available to Czechoslovakia for some time. After the elevation of Professor Masaryk to the Presidency the effective

power in the new state passed into the hands of the Prime Minister, Dr K. Kramář, the hero of the domestic resistance. He also was not leader of the majority party.

Constitutional niceties still seemed unimportant, for strictly speaking none of the Czechoslovak leaders had a clear democratic mandate for the position of power they came to occupy. The leaders had first to prove themselves in action, and the foremost task before them was the establishment of effective control over the territory that they considered as the Czechoslovak Republic. Next, they needed international recognition of the Republic and a clear definition of its frontiers. At the same time the Czechoslovak government had to secure

chauvinism. *Below left:* Part of the scene in the Old Town Square in Prague on November 8, 1918, as the Czech forces take their ceremonial oath of allegiance. Watching the ceremony are members of the government. *Below:* The latent desire for independence among all the national minorities of Austria-Hungary grew as the war progressed and conditions grew ever more difficult, but this latent feeling was exacerbated by the ruthless way in which the not infrequent army mutinies were suppressed. Below is the execution of the leaders of a mutiny in Rumburk in northern Bohemia in May 1918. *Below right:* The burial of the executed Czech mutineers at Rumburk. The fear of such treatment at the hands of the Austrian- and Hungarian-dominated army made many conscripts from the national minorities desert to the Allies, principally the Russians. It was in just such a way that the Russians were able to raise the Czechoslovak Army Corps

food supplies for the population and to keep the national economy going, in order to avoid the revolutionary collapse and chaos that was occurring in other parts of the former Monarchy and all over Central Europe. These were tremendous tasks, but a sense of historical achievement helped the Czechs on their way: at long last, after some 300 years of Habsburg rule, they were independent. The initial impressions of Czechoslovakia proved so attractive that it moved the Ruthenians to join the new Republic. The new state was admittedly a curious creation, similar in composition to the defunct Habsburg Monarchy, only on a microscopic scale. The bulk of the population of over $13\frac{1}{4}$ million was formed

by the Czechoslovaks (8,760,957), but 23.4% (3,123,448) were Germans, 5.6% Hungarians, 3.4% Ruthenians, 1.3% Jews, 0.6% Poles; and there were several other nationalities, with 238,943 resident foreigners as well. Soon the Slovaks began to emerge as a separate national group, and the power basis for Czech predominance was further diminished. However, from the beginning in 1918, it was obvious that minority problems and conflicts would be inherited from the Monarchy and national coexistence would therefore be the cornerstone for the existence of the new state.

Coinciding with the declaration of Czech and Slovak independence came that of the Germans in Bohemia and Moravia. The

two German districts which proclaimed themselves independent called themselves Deutschböhmen ('German Bohemia') and Sudetenland, and opted to join the Austrian Republic. But this was not a viable proposition, though no one doubted their right to self-determination and autonomy. The two districts were unconnected territorially and did not even border on Austria. The German leaders opted for Austria only because they knew that it was impossible to join the defeated Germany. The proclamation of independence was more a gesture of defiance than a practical policy; the Germans would continue to fight against Czech predominance even after the destruction of the Monarchy, for which they, incidentally, had never exhibited a great affection. The government in Prague had no choice but to take up this challenge; it sent troops into the separatist districts and, after minor bloodletting, the independent regions were reannexed. The Germans were too demoralised by defeat and subsequent prospects to put up effective resistance, though their wish to separate themselves from the new state, was almost unanimous. In Slovakia the circumstances were more complicated and the solution more bloody. The Slovaks had no autonomy and were ruled directly by Hungarian officials. But the demoralised administrators on the whole agreed to hand over to the Czechs or their Slovak agents the purely Slovak districts. The Slovak National Council, an *ad hoc* committee, therefore controlled only parts of Slovakia, and the mixed districts remained under Hungarian administration. Negotiations were proceeding about a peaceful transfer of these districts, when Béla Kun seized power in Hungary and his revolutionary armies invaded Slovakia in order to annex it to Hungary. The Czechoslovak government had rather hastily to organise new army units and then send them to Slovakia to rid the province of Hungarian invaders, and finally incorporate it in the Republic. The Czechoslovak army also established the new Slovak frontiers, as well as those of Transcarpathian Ruthenia. One more border conflict occurred before the Republic took its final shape. In November 1918 the Poles, who claimed for themselves the Těšín (Teschen) area of Moravia, occupied it with their armed forces. In January 1919 Czech army units invaded the disputed territory and drove the Poles out. For a time a full-scale conflict threatened to break out between Czechoslovakia and Poland, but in 1920 both sides accepted Allied arbitration: the area was divided between the new states, and there was no war. The conflict solved, Czechoslovakia's frontiers only awaited international recognition.

Success at Versailles

International recognition would inevitably come from the Peace Conference in Paris and would be solemnified in the peace treaties. This was so important for Czechoslovakia that its Prime Minister, Dr Kramář, hurried there to join Dr Beneš in the peace negotiations. Because of his wartime contacts and acquaintance with Allied statesmen Dr Beneš was extremely successful and obtained for his country almost everything he asked for. As regards Czechoslovakia, the principle of the historic frontiers was accepted at Versailles. This largely favoured Czechoslovaks, for many districts within the historic frontiers were completely germanised or Hungarian dominated. However, the Supreme Allied Council made three exceptions to this principle: two rectifications of the southern border at Austria's expense, and the cession by Germany of the Hlučín salient in western Silesia, where 80% of the population were Czech. Other rectifications proposed by the French expert, General Lerond, and accepted by Dr Beneš, would have reduced the number of Germans in the Republic by some 800,000, but they were rejected by the Supreme Council where Clemenceau rigidly insisted that Germany could not benefit from the war. Realism was rejected and Czechoslovakia retained its historical borders.

As subsequent events proved, the question of minorities was to be a burden that Czechoslovakia did not have time to solve. Of course, the adoption of purely ethnographic frontiers 'would have left the country so entirely defenceless as to be incapable of independent life'. But the inclusion of 3,000,000 Germans and 250,000 Magyars placed Czechoslovakia among the most vulnerable countries. In a memorandum of May 20, 1919 Dr Beneš undertook to make Czechoslovakia a sort of Switzerland in which the minorities, sharing with all the citizens universal and proportionate suffrage, would possess their own language in schools, local administration and courts of law. Czechoslovakia was also required by the Supreme Allied Council to sign a special minority treaty, which she did without protest, unlike Rumania, Poland and Yugoslavia. In 1920 a series of peace treaties was finally signed at Versailles, St Germain and Trianon, and internationally Czechoslovakia came into existence as a succession state to the Habsburg Monarchy.

Beneš and Masaryk, the makers of modern Czechoslovakia

In the meantime President Masaryk returned in triumph from America to Czechoslovakia in December 1918, and became the first constitutional, as well as effective, ruler of the new state. President Masaryk, already advanced in age, became the real successor of that other father figure, the Emperor Franz Josef, and even his paternalistic rule was similar to that of his imperial predecessor. Formally, supreme power resided in the bi-cameral parliament, the National Assembly, freely and secretly elected; but the President had great powers, too, the greatest of them that of appointing and dismissing governments. In emergencies, the President had direct executive powers. In addition, subsequent political development also increased his power: since there was no Czechoslovak party with a clear parliamentary majority, he acted as arbiter and created coalitions. This enabled him to have his personal nominees foisted on the coalition governments, and in several emergencies cabinets were responsible to himself and not to parliament. Although the presidential exercise of power created what became known as the castle clique (the President resided in the royal castle in Prague), President Masaryk never abused his power. In some cases he might have exceeded them, but the system was his own creation and, while obviously not perfect, it was the most constitutional and democratic in Central Europe.

The competition for power within the new system was lively, but always within the legal, and later on, constitutional framework. The few exceptions to this rule were extraordinary ones. President Masaryk found himself on his return saddled with a Premier whom he considered quite unsuitable for the post. Dr Kramář was not only not a majority leader, but in addition held nationalist views extreme enough to make him utterly unfit for such a powerful position in a multi-national Republic. He and his National Democratic Party believed in such absolute Czech predominance in the new state that they were even willing to compromise on their conservative principles in economics in order to achieve Czech domination. Though Dr Kramář and his party were trained financiers and entrepreneurs, they advocated the nationalisation of German economic and financial interests. In addition they held extreme and nationalist views on international affairs; they continued to look to Russian power and influence, as represented at the time by the White movement and armies. President Masaryk differed in everything from the Prime Minister; he was for national conciliation, opposed Czech chauvinism, and in foreign affairs sought Western alliances, not only because they were really responsible for the restoration of the Czechoslovak state, but also because the Western hegemony was the most favourable to the existence of Czechoslovakia. In 1919 President Masaryk solved these differences rather abruptly. When in a local government election the Social Democratic Party were victorious, the President dismissed Dr Kramář, who was at the time in Paris, and replaced him with a Social Democratic premier.

President Masaryk might have acted quite constitutionally had he waited for the results of the general election in 1920. The Social Democrats again emerged as the strongest party and its leader, Tusar, was reappointed Prime Minister. But the weakness of this socialist party rapidly became apparent: the party split into a left and a right wing and the Prime Minister was, in fact, a minority right-wing leader. The left wing, who came to call themselves Communists, objected to this anomaly and decided to take over the party organisation. But the right-wing leaders invoked the aid of the police and beat off the challenge. The infuriated left turned against the system and planned to seize power. They proclaimed a general strike, and hoped that in the resulting confusion they could carry out a *coup d'état*. However, they had miscalculated, for as soon as their plan became apparent President Masaryk dismissed Tusar, put in his place an experienced civil servant who had faced similar situations in the Habsburg Monarchy, and, by personally directing repressive actions, put down the general strike, and the Communist attempt with it. The Communists were so thoroughly beaten that they never renewed their challenge and in 1921 Czechoslovakia was able to return to parliamentary government.

In the same year Czechoslovakia was internationally recognised, well consolidated and on the way to its separate, independent national development. It was the only example of a succession state with political stability and continuing prosperity. And it was as a direct result of the war that a liberal democratic régime was established and continued to prosper in Central Europe.

Further Reading
Bradley, J. F. N., *Czechoslovakia: a History* (Edinburgh University Press 1971)
Macartney, C. A., *National States and National Minorities* (Oxford University Press 1934)
Krofta, K., *A Short History of Czechoslovakia* (Williams & Norgate 1934)

[*For Dr J. F. N. Bradley's biography, see page 97.*]

Tomáš Garrigue Masaryk, the first President of Czechoslovakia, was born into a Czecho-Slovak family at Hodonín on March 7, 1848. Masaryk's father was a coachman working on imperial estates and young Tomáš spent his childhood on various estates in southern Moravia. He was intended to become an artisan, possibly a smith, but when the local priest discovered that he was a bright boy, he persuaded his parents to send him instead to a grammar school, at Hustopeče and then Brno. The family was poor and Tomáš had to keep himself alive by giving tuition. He had the good fortune of becoming tutor to the son of the Brno police chief and remained with this family even when they moved out of Brno to Vienna. He graduated from the grammar school in Vienna and immediately entered Vienna University to study philosophy. Apart from a year which he spent at Leipzig University, Masaryk continued his studies under Professor F. Brentano and in 1876 he successfully defended his doctoral thesis on Plato's ideas of immortality. At Leipzig University he met an American student, Charlotte Garrigue, whom he later married. He decided on an academic career and spent the next six years preparing a larger doctoral thesis, *Habilitation,* which eventually procured him a university post. But his thesis was a sociological one, on suicide, and even when completed and successfully defended it brought no immediate post, which by then he desperately needed: he had married Charlotte and children began to arrive. Then in 1882, the new Czech university in Prague offered him a post as Lecturer in Philosophy. Masaryk's education was purely German and he had moved mainly in German society, but in 1882 the future president turned to Czech nationalism and departed for Prague.

In Prague Masaryk soon became involved in political struggle. With several university colleagues he joined the Young Czech Party and was elected to the *Reichstag.* He was an independent deputy who was really interested in the *Kulturkampf* ('conflict of beliefs' between Bismarck and the Roman Catholic Church) and soon was in conflict with the narrow-minded party leadership. He therefore left the Young Czechs and founded his own Realist Party. The party consisted mainly of Masaryk's university students and in the end had one representative in parliament, Professor Masaryk himself. However, Masaryk was a recognised political leader and though without a party machine and mass support, his actions caused the imperial authorities more anxiety than those of most of the Czech leaders. The foreign ministry watched him when he visited various Slavonic provinces of the Empire; diplomats reported on his visits to Russia. His university career suffered and the Emperor was determined to prevent such a man ever reaching any position of power. Right up to the outbreak of the First World War Professor Masaryk was a minor provincial leader who had to be watched.

When the war came Masaryk's sympathies were immediately with the Allies, in whose countries he had many academic friends and acquaintances. The possibility of Germany's victory frightened him. Through his friends he submitted a memorandum to the British government on the

Top: Tomáš Garrigue Masaryk, President of Czechoslovakia. *Above:* Dr Eduard Beneš

war and Austria-Hungary, and in 1915, to avoid arrest, he escaped from the Habsburg Monarchy and found political asylum in Switzerland. In Geneva he finally decided to launch an anti-Monarchy movement which would either result in the destruction of the Monarchy and in Czech independence, or end in exile for ever. At the same time he was joined by two students of his: Eduard Beneš, and Milan Štefánik, a Slovak, who launched the movement in Paris. Through his academic contacts Masaryk gradually brought his movement to the attention of Allied politicians; but it was an uphill struggle. Only in 1917, when Masaryk left for Russia to organise a Czechoslovak army there, did the émigrés gain limited recognition by the Allies. When in 1918 the Czechoslovak Legion revolted against the Bolsheviks and defeated them in Siberia, the recognition became more concrete, and when Austria-Hungary disintegrated after the armistice in November 1918, Czech independence

was automatic. On November 14, 1918, while Masaryk was still in exile in the United States, the Czechoslovak provisional parliament met in Prague and unanimously elected him President of the new state, Czechoslovakia. He returned to Czechoslovakia in triumph. In the government which was appointed at the same time, Štefánik became Defence Minister and Beneš Foreign Minister and Czechoslovak representative in Paris.

President Masaryk's most intimate collaborator, Dr Eduard Beneš, was a Czech from western Bohemia. He also came from a poor family and had to work hard to get through his schooling. In 1896, aided by his elder brother, young Eduard entered a grammar school in Prague, played football passionately and in 1904 graduated in order to register at the philosophy faculty of Prague University. There he attended Professor Masaryk's lectures and came under his influence. In 1905, on Masaryk's recommendation, Beneš departed for Paris University to work on a doctoral thesis. During his stay in France he was a special correspondent of several Czech and German journals; he also travelled widely in France, England and Germany and in 1908 passed an examination at Dijon University, which gave him the title of doctor. He returned to Prague, achieved a doctorate of philosophy there and through the political influence of the Realist Party, was appointed Lecturer at the College of Commerce in Prague. He continued his political and sociological research and aimed at an academic career, like his teacher and guide, Masaryk. In 1911 he went to do research in Paris and London, and on return he was appointed Lecturer in Sociology at Prague University. In the prewar years he associated politically with Professor Masaryk and his Realist Party, wrote articles for Realist journals, and became a friend of the Masaryk family. When the war broke out Masaryk confided to the young lecturer his ideas on the destruction of the Monarchy and Beneš passionately agreed with them. Beneš gave Masaryk money for the journey to Italy that ended in exile, and agreed to be his agent in Bohemia. He successfully maintained contact with Masaryk in Switzerland, and supplied him with political and intelligence materials. In 1915 Beneš decided that his place was abroad with Masaryk; he escaped to Switzerland to help in the organisation of the émigré movement. But his knowledge of France led to his appointment as Masaryk's representative in Paris, where he settled in September 1915 and remained until the end of the war. In 1916 he became Secretary General of Masaryk's Czechoslovak National Council and in this capacity he greatly aided the Slovak leader and politician, Milan Štefánik. With Štefánik's help Beneš met French politicians, explained the Czechoslovak case for independence to them, and in 1918 achieved the official recognition of his National Council as the Government of Czechoslovakia. When in 1918 the Czechoslovak parliament in Prague appointed him Foreign Minister of Czechoslovakia he was 34 years of age, and despite his youth and because of his wartime experience and contacts, he was able to contribute much to the new state, especially at the Peace Conference.

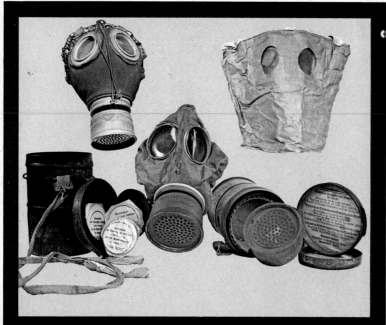

Top left: The German Model 1917 gas mask, made of heavily oiled leather. It was not proof against high concentrations of gas, however, and was stuffy, as the wearer had to breath both in and out through the drum containing the chemicals. *Above right:* The Italian Modello Piccolo No. 2 mask. *Above:* The German Model 1916 mask, made of rubberised fabric. It was again stuffy, and the eye pieces were prone to misting up

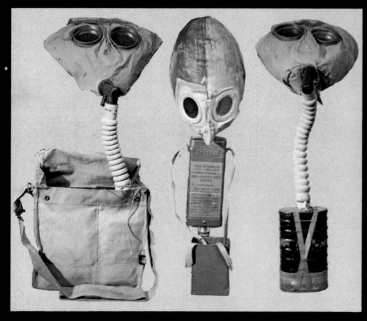

Left: The British 1917 pattern Small Box Respirator. This had splinterless eye pieces and a breath-outlet valve, and was therefore more comfortable to wear than its German counterpart. It was the best mask of the war, proof against all gases except, of course, mustard gas. *Centre:* The Russian box respirator, with the box attached to the nose piece. *Right:* The British 1916 Respirator, with an extra filter on the box

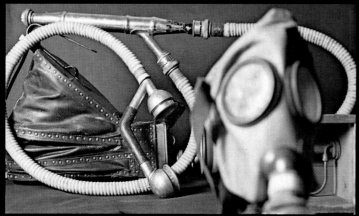

Above: A bellows-operated resuscitator. There was always the chance that if uncontaminated air could be given quickly to a man who had been only slightly gassed, he might make a far better recovery

GAS

Gas was introduced to the arsenal of the First World War in 1915, and quickly adopted by all the other belligerents. There were two methods of launching a gas attack, from cylinders or by projectiles. The cylinder attack entailed bringing a large number of cylinders of compressed gas up to the line, laying pipes from these as far forward into No-Man's Land as possible and releasing the gas in a dense cloud when the wind was from the right quarter to blow the cloud of gas down onto the enemy's front line. The need for the right wind was a distinct disadvantage for the Germans on the Western Front,

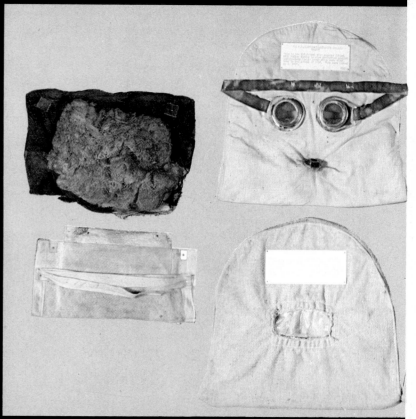

Top row left: The British 1915 Veil Respirator, an impregnated mouth pad. *Centre:* The British 1916/17 Phenate-Hexamine-Goggle helmet. *Right:* The British tank-crew respirator and goggles (left) and anti-lachrymator gas

THE ODOUR OF DEATH

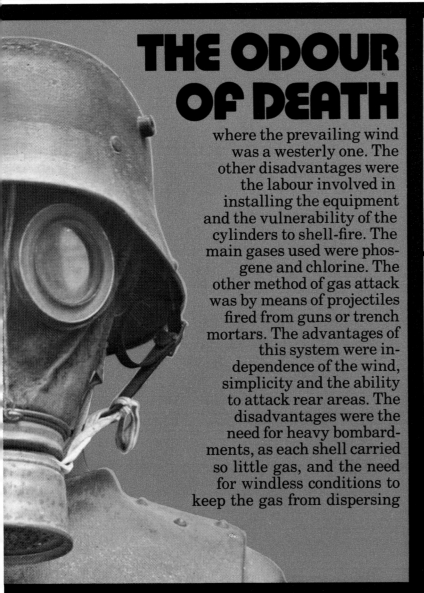

where the prevailing wind was a westerly one. The other disadvantages were the labour involved in installing the equipment and the vulnerability of the cylinders to shell-fire. The main gases used were phosgene and chlorine. The other method of gas attack was by means of projectiles fired from guns or trench mortars. The advantages of this system were independence of the wind, simplicity and the ability to attack rear areas. The disadvantages were the need for heavy bombardments, as each shell carried so little gas, and the need for windless conditions to keep the gas from dispersing

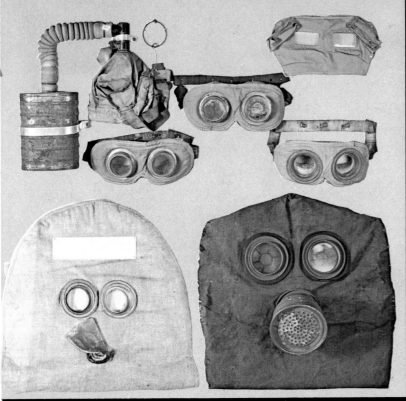

Chris Barker.

goggles (three on right). *Bottom row left:* The Maw civilian mask of 1917. *Centre left:* The British 1915 Hypo Helmet. *Centre right:* The British 1916 Phenate-Hexamine helmet. *Right:* An unrubberised German fabric helmet

British gas casualties in France, 1915–1918

from British official sources

	🧍	🧍
APRIL AND MAY 1915 Cloud attacks with chlorine	7 000 *	350 *
MAY 1915–JULY 1916 Lachrymator gas shell	?	—
DECEMBER 1915–AUGUST 1916 Cloud attacks	4 207	1 013
JULY 1916–JULY 1917 'Lethal' gas shell	8 806	532
JULY 1917–NOVEMBER 1918 (Mustard gas period) Gas shell	160 526	4 086
DECEMBER 1917–MAY 1918 PROJECTOR ATTACKS	444	81
TOTAL	180 983	6 062

German cloud gas attack April 30 1916

FRONT LINES
BRITISH
GERMAN
GAS STRONGLY FELT, HELMETS WORN
GAS SLIGHTLY FELT
PLACES WHERE CATTLE WERE KILLED
0   400 YARDS

🧍 CASUALTIES

🧍 DEATHS

* Approx figures for casualties admitted to medical units only; many died on the field or were taken prisoner.

Gas casualties in the First World War

	Non-fatal injuries 🧍	Deaths 🧍	Total
BRITISH EMPIRE	180 597	8 109	188 706
FRANCE	182 000	8 000	190 000
UNITED STATES	71 345	1 462	72 807
ITALY	55 373	4 627	60 000
RUSSIA	419 340	56 000	475 340
GERMANY	191 000	9 000	200 000
AUSTRIA-HUNGARY	97 000	3 000	100 000
OTHERS	9 000	1 000	10 000
TOTAL	1 205 655	91 198	1 296 853

Note: These figures, apart from the American ones, are only approximate. In many cases they differ from the official published figures, which, since they do not include men who died on the battlefield, tend to be far too low.

Production of poison gases during the First World War (in tons)

	Lachrymators	Acute Lung Irritants	Vesicants	Sternutators	Totals
BRITAIN	1 800	23 335	500	100	25 735
FRANCE	800	34 000	2 140	15	36 955
UNITED STATES	5	5 500	170	—	6 215
ITALY	100	4 000	—	—	4 100
RUSSIA	150	3 500	—	—	3 650
GERMANY	2 900	48 000	10 000	7 200	68 100
AUSTRIA-HUNGARY	245	5 000	—	—	5 245
TOTALS	6 000	123 335	13 350	7 315	150 000

Poison Gases used during the First World War

	date of introduction	approx concentration to incapacitate a man in a few secs. (in parts per 10m)	approx concentration which, if breathed for more than 1 or 2 mins, would cause death	used by: British / French / Germans / Austrians
ACUTE LUNG IRRITANTS				
Chlorine	1915	1 000	1 000	
Phosgene	1915	100	200	
Chlormethyl-chloroformate	1915	100	1 000	
Trichlormethyl-chloroformate	1916	50	200	
Chloropicrin	1916	50	200 ▲	
Stannic chloride	1916	—	1 000	
Phenyl-carbylamine-chloride	1917	50	1 000	
Cyanogen bromide	1918	—	300	
Dichlor-methyl-ether	1918	1 000	1 000	
LACHRYMATORS (tear producers)				
Benzyl bromide	1915	5	—	
Xylyl bromide	1915	5	—	
Ethyl-iodoacetate	1916	5 to 2	200	
Bromacetone	1916	5	1 000	
Monobrom-methyl-ethyl-ketone	1916	2	2 000	
Dibrom-methyl-ethyl-ketone	1916	2	2 000	
Acrolein	1916	—	—	
Methyl-chlorsulphonate	1915			
PARALYSANTS				
Hydrocyanic acid	1916	5 000 ●	5 000	
Sulphuretted hydrogen	1916	10 000 ●	1 000 ■	
STERNUTATORS (sensory irritants of eyes, nose and chest)				
Diphenyl-chlorarsine	1917	1	200	
Diphenyl-cyanarsine	1918	1	200	
Ethyl-dichlor-arsine	1918	20	500	
Ethyl-dibrom-arsine	1918	—	—	
N.ethyl carbazol	1918	—	—	
VESICANTS (blister producers)				
Dichlor-ethyl-sulphide (Mustard gas)	1917	—	10 ○	

▲ Cumulative   ● Immediately fatal   ■ Affects eyes and lungs   ○ With 60-minute exposure

Above: Gas casualties, production and types in the First World War. It is worth noting that the most effective type was not one of the so-called lethal types, but one of the incapacitators, mustard gas

REVOLUTION
in Hungary

KULTURA R.T.
LITH.MUINTÉZETE
BUDAPEST

The first and largest portion of the Habsburg Empire to break away was Hungary, but in front of her lay civil war between factions of the extreme right and left. *D. R. Shermer*

Left: Communism completes Károlyi's task of burying Austria-Hungary. *Above:* University militia

The Hungarian occupation of Fünfkirchen, 1920

In October 1918, the Austro-Hungarian Empire was disintegrating. The driving force behind this upheaval came from the discontent of the many minorities of the multi-national Empire. Allied war aims and the disastrous fortunes of war of the Central Powers accelerated the disruptive process. Within the Monarchy, South Slav and other nationalist elements saw impending defeat as their opportunity to seize the independence for which they longed. In the final months of the war, their task was made easier by the mood of shell-shocked apathy which had permeated the Habsburg domains. At the same time Magyar separatist nationalism, being all the more potent because long repressed, burst forth in revolt against the Austrian connection, which it somewhat illogically blamed for Hungarian involvement in the First World War.

During October 1918, a rapid succession of events completed the undermining of the Habsburg structure. By the middle of the month, the Hungarian Premier, Count Tisza, was forced to announce in Parliament that the war was lost. On October 16, the Emperor Karl appealed for the rebuilding of the Empire along federal lines, although 'the integrity of the lands of the Holy Crown of Hungary is not to be affected'. The minorities were unmoved. Later in the month, the American Secretary of State, Robert Lansing, informed Vienna that the independence of Czechs, Slovaks and South Slavs would have to be acknowledged. Meanwhile the final Italian offensive was in progress, and by November 3 the Habsburg representatives were forced to sign an armistice at Padua.

Emperor Karl's reservations about the Crown Lands of St Stephen matched the chauvinistic mood which was prevalent among many of the Magyars of the Dual Monarchy. The Hungarian gentry looked down upon non-Magyars as backward and less civilised than themselves. They believed that the historic mission of the Magyars was to assimilate these peoples, welding the whole into a Greater Hungary.

While the gentry indulged in this *folie de grandeur,* the Magyar people made their revolution on October 30, 1918. The popular upsurge was anti-Austrian and mainly anti-aristocratic; there were strong,

but unfounded, hopes that a new régime could make a peace with the Entente that would preserve Hungarian territorial integrity. A new government headed by Count Mihály Károlyi was sworn in. Károlyi, the former leader of the opposition in the Hungarian Parliament, was a convinced democrat, anglophile and germanophobe, ideas which were bizarre for one of his background, for Károlyi was a member of one of the oldest and most influential families of the Magyar aristocracy. He was immediately faced with the consequences of his first major false assumption, that the democrats could mollify the minorities and retain them within historic Hungary. Reality proved otherwise, and events outpaced each other. On November 16, Hungary proclaimed itself a republic, four days after Austria had done so.

The new republic coped as best it could with a myriad of problems, not the least of which was the arrival of many thousands of ethnic Magyars from neighbouring areas and of hundreds of thousands of exhausted soldiers from the front. Károlyi himself was too idealistic to be suited to the practicalities of ruling at such a difficult juncture, and he lacked the strength and determination to act against those who posed threats to his authority. The government, which was a coalition among Károlyi's own small Independence Party, the Social Democrats and the Radical Bourgeois Party, agreed to give priority to making peace. It hoped to appeal to the Entente for justice by emphasising its democratic and anti-authoritarian tendencies, assuming quite wrongly that because of its hasty divorce from Austria, the new Hungarian régime would be treated as part of the victorious anti-German crusade, not as an erstwhile enemy.

These early mistakes were compounded by others. Before the peace treaty was signed, the army was largely disbanded, yet France encouraged the Czechs, Serbs and Rumanians — all successors to the disintegrated Habsburg Empire — to occupy areas of Hungary far in excess of their legitimate ethnic claims. The Károlyi government was largely impotent to secure justice by its own endeavours, and the territorial settlement offered to Hungary

was worse than any one in the government had expected — yet still it satisfied none of the contending interest groups. The régime found itself in an impossible situation, since no government which accepted such injuries to the nation could then have remained in power. Not knowing what else to do, the government resigned. In this way the Hungarian Soviet Republic was born on March 21, 1919 — an experiment which lasted only 133 days and which proved as ineffective as its predecessor.

Repercussions of feudalism

The reasons for the failure of the Károlyi régime were many. To the lack of success in its foreign policy must be added its internal shortcomings. Károlyi and his followers were unable either to create a strong government or to establish truly representative institutions. Thus they demonstrated their weakness to the population. Attempts to hold elections were handicapped by the atmosphere of instability which pervaded a nation as yet without clearly defined boundaries or even electoral districts, and which was plagued by fear of the clamorous Soldiers' Councils and other groups. Moreover, the Social Democrats wanted a more liberal franchise before elections were held, and did much to frustrate the electoral process in the interim. Social and economic conditions were nightmarish. Much of the illiterate population was, for all practical purposes, in serfdom to the landowners. The tangled complexities of the nationalities problem defied reasonable solution. The Minister of Nationalities, Professor Oscar Jászi, favoured a federation of all the peoples of historic Hungary, while granting equality and autonomy to each. Yet the minorities sought, and obtained, nothing less than full independence and sovereignty — though whether they were to achieve true political and economic viability remained to be seen. This meant that a rump Hungarian state would emerge from the territorial negotiations of the Paris Peace Conference. Meanwhile the Károlyi government floundered in an atmosphere of procrastination, timidity and confusion.

Nor had the outgoing government settled the urgent question of land reform. Before the upheavals of the war, Hungary had

Left: One of the many executions that were so much a feature of the troubled birth of Hungary. Above: The Communist Party's May Day parade through Buda-Pest in 1919. On the right is a bust of Marx and a quotation from his *Das Kapital*. Above right: The crowd outside the Hungarian parliament after the establishment of the Hungarian Soviet

been a semi-feudal state in which an élite 4,000 of its population of over 18 million owned over half the land. In contrast, five and a half millions owned no land at all. In February 1919 Károlyi set an example by announcing the subdivision of part of his estates among the people. Other aristocrats remained reluctant toward the idea of land redistribution.

Perhaps the government could have survived all of its failures if only a less iniquitous social system had existed and if strong and stable parties had been well established. As it was, aristocrats, much of the military, Communists, and Social Democrats, though vehemently opposing each other, had this in common: each wanted Károlyi to fail, in order to assume power in his stead.

The largest of these groups was the Social Democrats, whose power base lay in the trade unions of the urban proletariat. Yet its effectiveness was severely limited by the deep divisions among both leadership and members. The most formidable challenge to the Social Democrats came from the Communists. The Communist Party had originated in Russia, where Hungarian POWs were susceptible to Bolshevik agitation promising greater equality and an end to the vile conditions of the prison camps. The Hungarian events of October to November 1918 were greeted by the Communists as the beginning of the world

revolution. By the middle of December, all the leaders except Tibor Szamuely had returned to Hungary and had established contact with groups opposing the Social Democrats. The Communists made some headway among the discontented majority in the unruly conditions of the time.

A crucial event for the Communists was a demonstration led by them in Buda-Pest on February 20, 1919. The demonstrators clashed with police, and between four and eight policemen were killed. Some historians maintain that the Social Democrats organised the provocation, while others have noted the influence of the German Spartacists. In any event, the violence forced the Károlyi government to take a strong stand against the Communists. A number of Party leaders, including Béla Kun, were arrested and imprisoned. Popular opinion became sympathetic towards the Communists' rôle as a result of newspaper accounts of police brutality and pictures of Kun's face swathed in bandages. And the government failed to enforce the ban against the Communist Party.

The situation in Hungary was rapidly deteriorating. Unemployment, hunger, and starvation were commonplace. The Czech armies were only 50 miles from Buda-Pest. Public hostility to the government was coupled with bitterness and mistrust towards the Allies. Any change appeared to be for the better. Strikes crippled the

capital in the absence of effective police or army units.

It was in these dire circumstances that on March 20 an Allied ultimatum was delivered by Lieutenant-Colonel Vyx of the French Military Mission in Buda-Pest. The Allies demanded the surrender within ten days of vast tracts of the Crown Lands, including Debrecen and Nagyvárad (Oradea), the second and third largest cities of Hungary. Vyx intimated that lack of co-operation might result in the resumption of Entente hostilities against Hungary. Furthermore, whatever borders emerged from a renewed conflict would probably be imposed as a *diktat* on the Hungarians.

Soviet Hungary

The Vyx ultimatum was the final humiliation which toppled the Károlyi régime. The General Staff insisted on the military impossibility of accepting such demands, and the coalition resigned. Although Károlyi hoped to be succeeded by a Social Democrat government, the party was too divided to assume power on its own. Thus even Károlyi's last gamble had failed, for apparently he had calculated that his Socialist successors would be able to control the remnants of the army and threaten to fight against the Allied demands. Kun, however, claimed that with himself in power, Russia would join forces with Hungary and repel an invasion. The Communists were not yet

PUSZTISATOK EL·A·ŐKET·1 HOGY·ROMJAIN FELEPITHES — SÜK·A·VILÁG NEMZETKÖZI KOMMUNISTA TARSADALMAT 1·9·1·9

Ullstein

Republic on March 23, 1919. The Republic had 133 days of chequered history before it. *Right:* Admiral Miklós von Nagybánya Horthy is sworn in as the Regent of Hungary after the defeat of the Kun régime. Horthy had commanded the Austro-Hungarian cruiser *Novara* in 1914, but rose to the command of the Austro-Hungarian navy by 1918

powerful enough to form a government, and thus a Communist-Socialist coalition emerged. Béla Kun, holding the Foreign Affairs portfolio, was the real power. In this way, highly unorthodox from a Marxist standpoint, the Hungarian Soviet Republic was established.

The establishment of the Kun régime was thus influenced in part by the presence of the Russian Red Army near the Hungarian borders at that time. Unfortunately for the Communists, however, the Bolsheviks suffered many setbacks that spring and summer, and hostile territory separated the sister revolutionary Soviets. Meanwhile the Hungarian Soviet Republic continued to play into the hands of anti-Communists by impractical actions and empty verbiage. It requested a treaty of alliance with Soviet Russia and hailed Lenin's unequivocal authority as 'the leader of the international proletariat'. The Republic sent 'greetings to the working classes' of Great Britain, France, Italy and the United States, and appealed to 'the workers and peasants of Bohemia, Rumania, Serbia and Croatia' to form 'an armed alliance against the boyars, estate-owners and dynasties'. This followed cease-less propaganda directed especially at the establishment of Communist régimes in Austria and Bavaria, where a shortlived Soviet had sprung up in April. Conditions were ripe for troublemaking, for as Alfred

Low has pointed out, Austria, like Hungary, was now 'an impoverished remnant of yesterday's imperial wealth and splen-dour, former co-ruler and now fellow-sufferer'. Kun claimed to foresee that 'our mere existence is a danger to the capitalists of the world', since the Hungarian pattern 'will be followed by the proletarians of the entire globe'. In com-munications to the Allied leaders, how-ever, he was more moderate. This merely increased the suspicions of everyone.

Kun's assumption of power rocked the Paris Peace Conference. Except for certain Italian representatives, all the Entente diplomatic missions were withdrawn. Al-though some French circles wanted an intervention in Hungary as a prelude to similar moves against Russia, in the end a diplomatic mission led by the South African general, Jan Smuts, and including Harold Nicolson, went to Buda-Pest. The purpose of this foray was decidedly obscure, al-though one of its aims was apparently to find out whether or not some communica-tion with Lenin could be established via Kun. No concrete benefits emerged for Hungary, both because of Kun's lack of diplomatic expertise and because of the rigid attitudes of the mission itself. Smuts was so determined to avoid giving Kun and his government even a modicum of Allied recognition, approval or acquies-cence that he did not leave the railway

station during his stay in Buda-Pest, although several times he consented to receive Kun on board his train!

These events were followed by Rumanian and Czech military activities against Hungary 'in the name of' the Allies, al-though the Peace Conference did not initi-ate these attacks. In May the Hungarians managed to rally around a combination of nationalist and Communist exhortations, and the defunct army was partly revital-ised. Within a few weeks the Rumanians were halted and the Czechs routed. For a brief period the Hungarians even managed to establish a Slovak Soviet régime.

The Allies intervene

Despite their mixed feelings towards the Czech-Rumanian assault, the Allies felt unable to abandon them, and French military aid and supplies began to pene-trate. On June 7 the Allies ordered Kun to cease hostilities: 'otherwise the Allied and Associated Governments are absolute-ly decided to have immediate recourse to extreme measures to oblige Hungary to cease hostilities and to bow to the unshake-able will of the Allies to make their in-junctions respected'. Hungary was to reply to this communication 'within 48 hours'.

The Allies reminded Hungary that at the time of the attack the Hungarians had been about to be invited to the Peace Con-ference. The implication was that when

Béla Kun

Béla Kun was born on February 20, 1886, the son of a lower-middle-class Transylvanian Jewish clerk, but despite this modest background he managed to enter the Calvinist *Kollegium,* an academically outstanding boarding school, at the age of ten. In 1902 Kun joined the Hungarian Social Democratic Party and was active in local politics.

In the autumn of 1904, Kun continued his education at the Kolozsvár Law Academy. With this background and aided by a certain inner dynamism, he had become editor of a small newspaper by the age of 20. After the newspaper went bankrupt, he obtained a position on an important daily newspaper in Buda-Pest, returning to Kolozsvár a few years later.

Shortly after the outbreak of the First World War, while he was employed as a clerk in the Workers' Accident and Disability Insurance Bureau in Kolozsvár, there were allegations that Kun had misappropriated a small sum of money, but the matter was dropped when he volunteered for the army. Early in 1916 he was taken prisoner by the Russians and, influenced by the underground revolutionary ideas of the time, he and a small group of junior officers started a Marxist study circle. Early in 1917 he somehow obtained permission to live outside the prison camp, and from there plunged into politics in neighbouring Tomsk. In April 1918 he was invited to join the Russian Social Democratic Workers' Party, and in Decem-

Béla Kun, the Communist ruler of Hungary for four months in 1919. He was defeated by his impractical and untutored approach to the practical difficulties of power as much as by the military intervention of the Allies

ber was sent to Petrograd, where he met Lenin. He worked with Karl Radek in the Commissariat for Foreign Affairs and became editor of *Nemzetközi Szocialista* ('International Socialist'), a vehicle of Soviet propaganda directed at Hungarian soldiers, and then also of *Fackel* ('Torch'), a German-language publication. Kun and several comrades had meanwhile organised a hardcore, Bolshevist leadership of the Hungarian POW movement; he himself had become one of the most influential foreign socialists in the embryonic Soviet state. He was aided by a boyish enthusiasm, a charming personality and a fine organisational ability, and by now was known as a dedicated worker and a competent orator and journalist.

On March 24, 1918, Kun and several comrades established the Hungarian Group of the Russian Communist Party in Moscow. Kun was elected chairman. The Group was the first foreign Communist organisation to be founded under full Bolshevik auspices. In late 1918, Kun and his circle returned to Hungary to take advantage of the chaos to further Bolshevist aims. Success came in 1919 – but it was ephemeral. After the fall of his Republic, Kun was interned by the Austrians, but returned to Russia in 1920. He became a high Comintern official and remained in prominent circles until spring 1937, when he was tried for alleged disrespect towards Stalin. Thereafter he disappeared from public view, and died on November 30, 1939.

fighting stopped, the followers of Kun, if not actually recognised, would at least be invited to state their case. On June 13 a further Allied ultimatum defined the new Hungarian boundaries to which the Entente insisted that Hungary begin withdrawal, 'within four days from midday on June 14'. Failing this, the Allies would 'hold themselves free to advance on Buda-Pest and to take such other steps as may seem desirable to secure a just and speedy peace'. In effect this meant that a joint Allied military intervention would take place. Kun had no choice but to accept, and withdrawal from Slovakia was ordered.

By now there was widespread criticism of the foreign policy of the Hungarian Soviet, both from the public and within the government itself. Amid the mounting dissatisfaction, an abortive coup by disillusioned soldiers and workers was attempted in Buda-Pest on June 24. Afterwards Kun was unable to regain the support of powerful nationalist elements, and could rely on the confidence of only a section of the Party and the army.

By early July, the Allies felt that Hungary was an economic danger to the rest of Central Europe, and the removal of the Kun régime was again mooted. Before any action was taken, on July 21 the Hungarians attacked the Rumanians on the Eastern Front, 'In the face of the attitude of the Rumanians who have been aggressive in defiance of the will of the Entente', as Kun somewhat ingratiatingly radioed to Clemenceau. The move was probably a desperate attempt by Kun to rally national support through a military success. There was also a desire to conquer at least part of Rumania and seize the proceeds of the harvest. In addition, the prestige of the Hungarian Soviet had been further under-

mined by another mismanaged coup on July 20 to 21, this time by dissident leftists.

However, the Hungarian offensive was hampered by low troop morale in the wake of the Slovak débâcle, as well as by severe lack of supplies. Rumania counterattacked and came within reach of Buda-Pest. As his government crumbled, Kun resigned on August 1 and went into exile with several associates. The Allies, still dithering about whether or not to intervene, were therefore spared the necessity of making a decision.

The Hungarian Soviet Republic was plagued with misfortune throughout its short life. Although the Bolsheviks had supported the Hungarian Communist Party since its inception, force of circumstances had left them in no position to supply concrete aid. Matters were not helped when, particularly in internal matters, the policies of Kun frequently ran counter to those of Russia and the Comintern. Because of practical difficulties, Moscow's main rôle became one of giving advice, encouragement, and also warnings. Russian aid of this nature may even have had a detrimental effect, since resounding declarations supporting Soviet Hungary helped convince other nations that the threat of Communism was immediate, dynamic, and worldwide.

Although the Hungarian Soviet fell as a result of external factors, a number of internal mistakes fatally weakened its position. At the beginning, nationalists had hoped to channel the revolutionary fervour of the Communists into actions serving the national interests of Hungary. The failure of the Slovak Soviet made these men implacable enemies of Kun. As soon as the Hungarian Soviet was inaugurated, the 'extreme right' of the Social Democrats had withdrawn, taking with

them a reservoir of experienced politicians and organisational experts. The Slovak failure further alienated important liberal Socialists. There were also endless ideological and factional disputes.

The biggest mistake of the Communists was their failure to divide the land among the peasantry. After nationalising the estates, Kun left them as *Kolkhozes,* often under the management of their former owners. He was also indiscreet enough 'not to conceal his intention to nationalise even the peasant holdings. The enraged peasants did everything they could to weaken the régime by cutting off urban food supplies. Government violence against them only exacerbated the situation. As early as May 5, Count Gyula Károlyi (not to be confused with Mihály Károlyi) and others had organised a counterrevolutionary government in Arad, then occupied by the French. On May 29 they were joined by General Béla Szombathelyi and others, and recruited a small army commanded by Admiral Horthy, the former Commander-in-Chief of the Austro-Hungarian navy.

In the chaos that was never absent during these months, labour discipline slackened, causing a serious fall in production. The peasants and most of the urban population refused to trade in the money printed by Soviet Hungary, and there was not enough old money in circulation to meet the demand. Furthermore, the Allied blockade of Hungary caused serious famine. Many shops closed through fear of nationalisation. Industries stood idle through lack of fuel. As if this were not enough, the virulent anti-semitism of wide sections of the population was aroused by an ill-timed anti-clerical campaign. In retaliation, the clergy did not hesitate to point out that in the Kun régime, Jewish intellectuals play-

JEGYEZZETEK·HADIKÖLCSÖNT

HOGY·MIELÖBB VISSZATÉRHESSENEK

Fegyverbe! Fegyverbe! Proletárok védjétek meg a tanácsköztársaságot Fegyverbe! Fegyverbe!

Victoria and Albert Museum

VÖRÖS KATONÁK ELÖRE!

ed the dominant rôle. This propaganda was effective, though no cause and effect relationship was established.

Nevertheless it must be said that the Communists tried hard to solve some of the problems of one of the most educationally and socially deprived areas of Europe. Reforms of education, health and sanitation were attempted, and the Soviet began a programme of welfare, food and attention for the children of poor families. Writers and artists received a great deal of encouragement. The Kun régime also proved that, at least sporadically, it could rally public support towards achieving remarkable military successes. However, perhaps the most telling factor against the success of both Károlyi and Kun is that their actions took place in a situation in which that most necessary of commodities, time, was in extremely short supply.

The Hungarian Soviet Republic left a firm imprint on the history of the region. The events of 1919 were used throughout the interwar period to justify the policies of the Horthy régime. In turn, the Russians used the oppressive nature of the Horthy era as an example of the fate awaiting Russia if Bolshevism were to falter.

The Kun régime was succeeded by an all-Socialist government headed by Gyula Peidl, a moderate. The Peidl government notified the Peace Conference that it would definitely co-operate with the Entente. Yet when Rumanian forces occupied Buda-Pest on August 4 under the banner of anti-Communism, the régime of Peidl staggered under the humiliation. Now, however, the Peace Conference promised that if Hungary complied with the Allied terms, the blockade would be raised, traffic on the Danube would not be impeded, and food surpluses from the Banat could be import-

ed. An Allied mission arrived in Buda-Pest to put the Rumanians on their best behaviour, although Rumania nonetheless presented such draconian terms to Peidl that on August 6, a bloodless coup returned Archduke Josef as head of state, with István Friedrich, a convinced conservative, as head of government. Rumanian marauding and terrorism was widely reported throughout this period.

On August 22 the Allies informed the Archduke that they could not negotiate peace with, nor economically support, a government established 'by a *coup d'état* carried out by a small body of police under the protection of a foreign army'. Archduke Josef complied with their suggestion that he resign so that an all-party government could appeal to the people, but Friedrich continued as Premier. Rumania was recalcitrant about withdrawal, managing to play off one power against another until November 1919. Early in that month they turned over the capital to Horthy. A new caretaker government, installed on November 24, was headed by Karl Huszár, a moderate clerical who gained the co-operation of some right-wing Socialists. Yet Huszár depended on the protection of Horthy and right-wing 'Whites' such as the Nationalists and Christian Socialists. Despite the objections of Huszár and others, Gyula Gömbös and Tibor Eckhardt conducted a horrific 'White Terror', of which Jews in particular were victims. Thousands of law-abiding Jews paid for the sins of the notorious Tibor Szamuely and his 'Red' atrocities. In December, further thousands of people were interned under a governmental authorisation supposedly preventing 'a danger to the public order'. The Social Democrats used this as an excuse to boycott the elections due to be

Above left: A wartime exhortation aimed at Hungary's women—'Buy war loans and bring the soldiers home'. But the continued lack of success of the armies sapped the morale of the Hungarian element and rendered it prone to disaffection when it returned home of its own accord. *Above:* The Communist call-to-arms: 'To arms! To arms! Proletarians, you must keep the people's state in arms! In arms! Red Soldiers Go Forward!' *Below:* The Communist warning to those 'in darkness, who disseminate false information and who are opposed to socialism'. · *Overleaf:* Hungary's heartfelt desire after four years of war: to plough up the battlefields

Te! sötétben bujkáló rémhír-terjesztő ellenforradalmár reszkess!

HOGY FELSZÁNTHASSUK
A HARCTEREKET –

JEGYEZZÜNK
HADIKÖLCSÖNT

held in January 1920.

The largest party to emerge from the campaign was the leftist United Agrarian Labourers' and Smallholders' Party of Nagyatádi Szabó. On March 14 a coalition of the left and certain right-ring elements of the Christian National Union formed a government under Simonyi-Semadam, and this government signed the Treaty of Trianon on June 14, 1920.

Earlier the Huszár government had proclaimed the definite dissolution of the link with Austria, while leaving to the future the practical consequences of the *de facto*

cessation of the functions of the monarch. In the meantime, a Regent was to exercise the duties of Head of State, and on March 1, 1920, Horthy was elected to this office. During the first few years of the Horthy régime, 5,000 people were executed and 75,000 jailed for their alleged connections with Kun, and over 100,000 people fled the country, the majority of them being liberal politicians, democratic intellectuals and urban middle-class Jews, whose skills were sadly missed. It was an inauspicious ending to the hopes of Hungarian progressivism.

Further Reading

Low, Alfred D., *The Soviet Hungarian Republic and the Paris Peace Conference* (Transactions of the American Philosophical Society (Philadelphia) vol 53, part 10, 1963)

Macartney, C. A., *October Fifteenth: A History of Modern Hungary* (Edinburgh University Press 1956)

Mayer, Arno J., *Politics and Diplomacy of Peacemaking* (Weidenfeld & Nicolson 1968)

Tökés, Rudolf L., *Béla Kun and the Hungarian Soviet Republic* (Pall Mall Press 1967)

[*For D. R. Shermer's biography, see page 407.*]

Left: Czechoslovakia, whose strong and able leadership was amply repaid in avoiding the worst of the evils that affected her neighbour Hungary. The one very dangerous moment was the establishment of the Slovak Soviet Republic. This was doomed, however, by the fact that it relied entirely on the failing Hungarian Soviet Republic to its south. *Below:* The military suppression of the Hungarian Soviet Republic

BORDERS IN 1914
DECLARATION OF INDEPENDENCE
COUNTRY INCORPORATED IN THE NEW STATE
PLACES IN WHICH SOVIET GOVERNMENTS WERE PROCLAIMED IN 1919
PLACES IN WHICH WORKERS SOVIETS HAD BEEN DECLARED BY THE END OF 1918
PLACES IN WHICH THE WORKERS TOOK OVER CONTROL DURING THE GENERAL STRIKE IN DECEMBER
AREAS AFFECTED BY GENERAL STRIKES IN 1919 AND 1920
MUTINIES BY SOLDIERS REPATRIATED FROM RUSSIA
FRONTIER OF THE SLOVAK REPUBLIC JUNE 16 1919
CZECHOSLOVAK-HUNGARIAN DEMARCATION LINE ACCORDING TO THE NOTE FROM THE ENTENTE – HANDED OVER DECEMBER 24 1918
FRONTIER OF THE HUNGARIAN SOVIET REPUBLIC APRIL 15 1919
DEMARCATION LINE ACCORDING TO CLEMENCEAU'S NOTE JUNE 7 1919
PROJECTED ADVANCE BY THE RED ARMY
DIRECTION & GAINS OF HUNGARIAN RED ARMY AGAINST CZECH FORCES (BY JUNE 11 1919)
HUNGARIAN RED ARMY'S COUNTERATTACKS ON THE TISZA REPULSED
POSITION OF HUNGARIAN RED ARMY APRIL 15 1919
SUPPRESSION OF ANTI-SOVIET RISINGS

CONCENTRATION AREAS OF 'INTERVENTION' ARMIES
CZECHOSLOVAK
SERBIAN, CROATIAN & SLOVENE (YUGOSLAV)
RUMANIAN
FRENCH
ADVANCES AND GAINS OF 'INTERVENTION' FORCES
CZECHOSLOVAK
SERBIAN, CROATIAN & SLOVENE
RUMANIAN
FRENCH
JUNCTION OF POLISH & RUMANIAN FORCES TO PREVENT RUSSIAN INTERVENTION
ACTIVITY BY ANTI-SOVIET GUERRILLAS (PETLYURA'S FORCES)

BORDERS IN 1923
CZECHOSLOVAKIA
YUGOSLAVIA
RUMANIA
POLAND
AUSTRIA AND HUNGARY

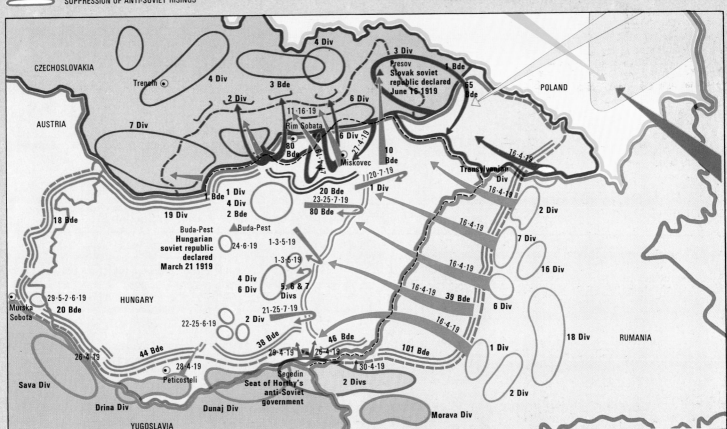

THE CREATION OF YUGOSLAVIA

Yugoslavia's problem at Paris was both simple and complicated. Simple because she wanted only her borders to be established, complicated because her wishes were opposed to Italy's. *Ivo Lederer. Below:* Yugoslavia's wartime legacy — one of Serbia's many dead

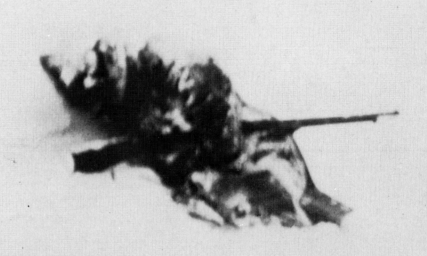

Yugoslavia, or the Kingdom of Serbs, Croats and Slovenes as it was then called, was one of the new political entities in Eastern Europe to emerge from the First World War. The new state became reality on December 1, 1918, nearly two months prior to the opening of the Peace Conference in Paris. Its geographical limits, however, were not finally set until the Treaty of Rapallo in November 1920. If victory had gone to the Central Powers, an independent Yugoslav state would probably not have emerged. While Allied victory was a precondition, though not the originating cause, of the new state, the Paris Peace Conference ratified the *fait accompli* and fixed its boundaries, thereby determining the new nation's ethnic composition, strategic position and economic situation.

On the eve of the war, the bulk of territory inhabited by Yugoslavs (literally, South Slavs) belonged to the Austro-Hungarian monarchy and the small independent states of Serbia and Montenegro. The predominantly Catholic, and culturally western-oriented, Slovenes and Croats were thus Habsburg subjects, as were the Moslems of Bosnia-Herzegovina, while the Orthodox, and eastern-oriented, Serbs, Montenegrins and Macedonians were not. Before 1918 these populations had never shared a common national home, and were further separated by different social systems, levels of economic development, cultural contexts, and historical experiences. Nevertheless, ethnic kinship, increasing cultural contact, and common aversion to the imperial rule and ambitions of Austria-Hungary, combined in the late 19th Century to generate a fairly strong movement for cultural and, increasingly, political co-operation among the South Slavs. The unification of Italy and then Germany led many intellectuals and some politicians to advocate the eventual formation of a Yugoslav state. By 1905 Serbia was seen in many circles as the 'Piedmont' of the South Slav world, while within the Croat and Slovene regions of the Habsburg empire 'Yugoslav' political conceptions began to take form.

The outbreak of war in 1914 crystallised the issue. Up to this point official Serbian nationalism had focused on advancing Serbian state interests, quite independently of the Habsburg Slavs, but now a new opportunity was perceived, in the event of Allied victory, of liberating the South Slav provinces from Habsburg control and joining them to Serbia. In December 1914 the Serbian government of Nikola Pašić and the *Skupština* adopted as their official war programme the goal of 'liberation and unification of all our Serb, Croat and Slovene brothers'. With the opening of hostilities, too, a number of Croat and Slovene leaders fled to the west where, under the guidance of Frano Supilo and Ante Trumbić, they established the Yugoslav Committee. In 1915 the Committee moved from Rome to London, where it remained until the end of the war. In 1915 Supilo, Trumbić and their colleagues issued a dramatic manifesto calling for the dissolution of the Habsburg Empire and the union of all Yugoslavs into a single sovereign state, and in 1916 to 1917 lobbied in Entente capitals, preparing British, French, American and Tsarist Russian opinion for this cause. Working through sympathetic Allied academic and journalistic circles — in Great Britain, for example,

with the crucial help of R. W. Seton-Watson and Wickham Steed of *The Times* — the Yugoslavs elicited first the private and eventually the public support of such Allied leaders as Lloyd George, Woodrow Wilson, Stephen Pichon and, albeit more tepidly, Vittorio Emanuele Orlando. Trumbić, who took over when Supilo died in 1917, conducted an articulate and effective campaign. Even before the dissolution of the Habsburg Empire became Allied policy in the late spring of 1918, the unification of all Yugoslavs was psychologically accepted in most official circles of the Entente.

Declaration of Corfu

The cause of Yugoslav union was also advanced by the Serbian government of Pašić, though its position was not so clear as that of the Committee, nor pursued with as much vigour. Pašić, above all a Serbian nationalist and patriot — and by now a septuagenarian, not prone to flexibility — contemplated the 'liberation' of the Habsburg Slavs under the aegis of Serbia. His

Greater Serbian conception did not envisage a Serbo-Croatian-Slovene-Montenegrin partnership, or federative arrangement, as advocated by Trumbić and his friends. In such a scheme Pašić feared the end of Serbian sovereignty and national unity, a dilution of Orthodox culture, and a potential surrender to Croatian Catholic central European values and influences. However, wartime exigency and the popularity of the 'Yugoslav' idea — especially among his Serbian political opposition — induced him to lend it his support. In 1915 and 1916 the Serbian government and the Yugoslav Committee did not act in concert. In July 1917, however, a frustrated Pašić joined with the Committee in the Declaration of Corfu which called for the establishment of a Yugoslav state. Thus, from mid-1917 onwards the Entente powers had to take into account a Yugoslav solution whenever they considered the postwar reorganisation of south-east Europe.

In Great Britain, France, Russia and, to a lesser extent, Italy, the Yugoslav pro-

gramme elicited sympathetic response, especially in certain influential academic circles. The governments, however, despite some benevolent interest, remained politically unresponsive. In order to bring Italy into the war on their side, in April 1915, London, Paris and Petrograd promised the Italians all of Istra, the principal Adriatic islands and the lion's share of Dalmatia. This arrangement, effected in the secret Treaty of London, was based on the assumption that while Austria-Hungary would survive the war Italy would become the dominant power in the Adriatic. That objective in fact dominated Italian policy and diplomacy, especially under Foreign Minister Baron Sidney Sonnino, and stood in the way of the Yugoslav territorial programme from 1915 to 1920. Bound by the 1915 treaty, the Allies during this period found their interests frequently at odds, particularly after Woodrow Wilson entered the picture in 1917.

The strains of war in central and southeastern Europe exacted a heavy toll. By late summer 1918 Austria-Hungary was on the verge of collapse; its armies dispirited and suffering a rapidly increasing rate of desertion among soldiers of Slavic nationality, the economy in disarray, the political framework of the empire disintegrating. Military collapse, beginning with the fall of Bulgaria and culminating in the armistice with Austria on November 3 (Germany, November 11, and Hungary, November 13), engendered a series of nationalist revolutions in the Habsburg lands. On October 29, six days before the Austrian armistice, Croat and Slovene leaders established a revolutionary government in Zagreb, the *Narodno Vijeće,* that quickly gained territorial control and proclaimed an independent state of Serbs, Croats and Slovenes in the former Habsburg lands. The Vijeće acted independently of the Serbian government or the Yugoslav Committee. Within less than a month, however, it became subsumed within the larger Yugoslav state that was proclaimed in Belgrade on December 1. In the interim, of course, little could be done about the economic chaos and financial depletions caused by the war. A good deal of energy was devoted by public authorities and the Serbian army that had now entered the former Habsburg domains in putting down the so-called Green Cadres, roving bands of deserters, perhaps 100,000 strong, who pillaged the countryside, settling scores with landowners, while indulging loosely in the rhetoric of social revolution under the influence of the Bolsheviks in Russia. The wartime loss of skilled labour, and professional and administrative personnel was quickly felt, as efforts were started to rekindle normal urban life and economic activity. Even more serious, however, was the condition of land and peasantry, the one ravaged and depleted, the other decimated by battle or disease. Political party life was in convulsion, too, as new coalitions were being formed and loyalists of the old régime were being weeded out.

In contrast to the western regions, Montenegro and especially Serbia suffered even greater damage as a result of the war. Serbia's losses are estimated at 330,000, and Montenegro's at some 20,000, or relatively over twice as high as those suffered by France. By late 1918 Serbia's economy was not only laid waste by the military occupation of Austria-Hungary and Bulgaria, but the population suffered from lack of food and health care, the breakdown of most services, and the virtual cessation of education for the young. Here, as elsewhere, exhaustion was profound and the end of war was greeted with euphoric relief.

Throughout the Yugoslav lands the future was being perceived with a mixture of enthusiasm and apprehension. The slogans of 'self-determination', 'agrarian reform' and 'democracy' had fired the popular mind, while the starkness of material conditions imposed evident restraints on public and private discussions. Nationalist fervour and, above all, excitement at the realisation of Yugoslav unity pervaded the entire country, though the crucial differences between Serb and Croat and Slovene party leaders began to shape as clouds on the horizon. The accession of Montenegro to the Yugoslav union on November 26, by resolution of the *Skupština* in Podgorica, and the proclamation of the overall national union on December 1 led to massive celebrations. Quickly, however, domestic and international politics sobered the national mood.

State without frontiers

December 1918 was spent on the formation of a national government, a difficult process made more difficult by the political differences and personal antipathies between Pašić and Trumbić. Their struggle, unhappily, personified wider Serbo-Croat divergences. The first Yugoslav cabinet, confirmed at the end of December, was not headed by the natural choice, Pašić, but by the Serbian Stojan Protić. The Slovene Antun Korošec became Deputy Prime Minister, and Trumbić Minister of Foreign Affairs. Pašić, the master mind of Serbian politics since 1903, was instead placed at the head of the Yugoslav peace delegation in Paris. Trumbić, as foreign minister, naturally went to Paris too. Their rivalry continued at the peace conference where it did not enhance the Yugoslav cause.

In January 1919 the Kingdom of Serbs, Croats and Slovenes began to function as a state, but it was a state without frontiers. Internal stability could not be ensured until that problem was resolved, if then. Meantime, how to deal with the territorial disputes that involved every adjacent state save Greece? Moreover, while Yugoslav interests stood a good chance of being advanced *vis-à-vis,* say Albania, Bulgaria and Hungary, how would they fare in relation to Italy which, as one of the principal powers, would sit in the inner councils of the peace conference? If Italian claims carried the day—and after the Armistice Italy occupied most of the territories it sought—the Yugoslav state would be mutilated and vulnerable, its population embittered and perhaps recklessly irredentist. Herein lay the major problem the Yugoslavs faced in Paris.

As soon as the peace conference opened, the Yugoslavs presented a territorial programme that envisioned the acquisition of all disputed territories from Istra to Albania in the south, and from Carinthia (Kärnten) to the Banat in the north. In the east, extensive frontier rectifications with Bulgaria were sought, largely on strategic considerations arising from Bulgaria's attacks on Serbia in 1913 and 1915. More specifically, the proposed national territory was to include Serbia, Montenegro, Bosnia, Herzegovina, Croatia and Slavonia (in-

Above: Serbian cavalry.
Left: A Serb infantryman. Serbia had been an Ally since 1914, and now became the nucleus of Yugoslavia, with the former Austro-Hungarian provinces of Croatia, Slovenia and Bosnia and Herzegovina added to her.
Right: Serbia, 1915, Mrs Stobart, one of the many British women serving with the Serb army, leads her column during the great retreat of 1915

Imperial War Museum

cluding Fiume [Rijeka] in the south and Medjumurje in the north), the Banat, Bačka and Baranja, Prekmurje, southern Styria, southern Carinthia, Carniola (Kranj), Istra and the Istran Isles, Trieste, Gorizia, Dalmatia and the Dalmatian archipelago. This programme essentially corresponded to the 1915 manifesto of the Yugoslav Committee; it called for a nation of 14 million people, including over 1,000,000 non-Slavs, and a territory of some 250,000 square kilometres, or somewhat less than half of France. On the Albanian side, the city of Scutari was sought on historic and economic grounds, with a contingency plan for gaining much of northern Albania if Italy were to dominate the rest. On the Bulgarian side, the Serbs asked for a strip of varying width running from the Rumanian frontier to that of Greece. The Yugoslavs also laid claim to the western and part of the central Banat—the region inhabited by Magyars, Germans, Serbs and Rumanians, which up to 1918 had belonged to Hungary—on

ethnic, strategic, economic and historic grounds, while Rumania claimed the entire Banat in fulfilment of the secret 1916 Treaty of Bucharest and on ethnic grounds as well. Bačka and Baranja, also to be ceded by Hungary, were ethnically mixed, but with a clear Slavic majority. The claimed parts of Styria and Carinthia corresponded roughly to a line of linguistic partition, except for four major towns with a German majority in 1919: Radkersburg, Marburg (Maribor), Villach and Klagenfurt. As for the division with Italy, the Yugoslavs drew an ethnic line slightly west of the River Isonzo, and claimed the whole Istran peninsula (including Trieste and Pula), the city of Fiume, plus all Dalmatia. With the exception of Trieste and the towns of Pula and Gorizia, the Slavic population was in clear majority everywhere. Fiume, one should note, was assigned by the Treaty of London to Croatia and was not claimed by Italy until 1918, and then apparently only for reasons of prestige.

The Yugoslav claims were based primarily on the principle of nationality, but also combined arguments of historical precedent, economic viability and military security. In some instances—for example, Trieste, Scutari, the city of Temesvar— their claims were excessive and indefensible from the point of view of nationality, thereby placing the Yugoslav peace delegation at a tactical disadvantage in Paris. Yet, the delegation had little choice. Mirroring the ethnic admixture of the new state, as well as the regional pressures, vanities and jealousies that were surfacing at home, it had to cater to every territorial demand as though it were a *sine qua non*, lest it be accused of betrayal or foul politics. For the Yugoslavs, the Paris conference setting now turned into an arena in which diplomacy and domestic politics became intertwined, and on occasion a hindrance to the conduct of effective negotiations. It was, in fact, something of a miracle—and testimony to the considerable talents of Trumbić, Pašić and the Yugoslav ambassador to France, Milenko Vesnić—that a façade of unity was maintained almost throughout and that most Allied statesmen were not aware of the bickering that was carried on.

As with the other lesser states, Yugoslavia was limited in its ability to influence, let alone determine, the outcome. Italian ambitions and claims, based on the 1915 Treaty of London, carried great weight, as of course did the powerful position of Italy in the European, Near Eastern and African arenas. Still, the Yugoslavs enjoyed certain vital advantages: Serbia had been the first victim of the war and fought a gallant fight; the Yugoslav idea had gained increasing currency between 1914 and 1918; the new state had many influential friends; and, as the overall Yugoslav case corresponded to the principles of nationality and self-determination, it found a sympathetic and vigorous champion in Woodrow Wilson. Wilson, among other things, considered the secret Treaty of London as repugnant and in consequence Italian claims to Dalmatia and some other Yugoslav territories as deficient in terms of moral legitimacy. The cause of the Southern Slavs, in short, quickly came to be transacted in the epicentre of the peace conference, and there to be determined by the larger European and extra-European issues that confronted the Big Four—a mixed blessing at best.

From the start Orlando and Sonnino succeeded in separating those Yugoslav issues that affected Italian interests. These were reserved for action by the Council of Four, to which the Yugoslavs did not have access. All other matters were to be scrutinised by the working committees and here, too, the Yugoslavs suffered an early setback. On January 31 the Council of Ten turned its attention to the Banat and, after a bitter clash between Ion Brătianu of Rumania and Milenko Vesnić, it assigned the problem to the territorial experts on the Commission on Rumanian and (as of this point) Yugoslav Affairs. But the heart of the issue did not revolve around ethnic and economic data; rather, it was political, centreing on the validity of the Compact of Bucharest of 1916. Thus Yugoslav fortunes dangled on the fate of the secret wartime treaties of London and of Bucharest, the one involving Croat and Slovene and the other primarily Serbian interests. That fate could only be resolved by Wilson, Lloyd George and Clemenceau. Meanwhile, under Italian pressure, the Allied powers had not yet granted diplomatic recognition to the Yugoslav state; while Dalmatia and other territories continued under Italian military occupation, with the rest under economic blockade.

Formal recognition
On February 1 Trumbić had a long interview with Secretary of State Robert Lansing; on February 7 he saw Wilson. He evidently made able representations, for hours after seeing Wilson the Americans

broke the diplomatic impasse and formally recognised the Kingdom of Serbs, Croats and Slovenes. That was the very day when the Italians had presented their official programme of claims, which included all the territories granted in the Treaty of London, plus Fiume. By demanding Fiume, on the grounds of self-determination, Orlando and Sonnino unwittingly weakened the validity of the Treaty of London, and by simultaneously insisting on the implementation of the treaty they provoked

Imperial War Museum

a conflict with Wilson. Indeed, the two events of February 7 transformed the Yugoslav-Italian conflict into an Italian-American confrontation. The Yugoslavs wisely stepped aside, counting on Wilson to materialise their dreams. The British and the French, embarrassingly tied down by the Treaty of London, also hoped that the American President would carry the ball and absolve them from having to face up to the Italians.

The Americans were not to have an easy time: the German settlement and the question of the League were clearly more important than Adriatic matters, yet now Italy might undermine Allied unity on larger issues; the Yugoslav case corresponded more closely to Wilsonian principles than the Italian case, yet London and Paris were treaty-bound to Rome; also, if a diplomatic solution could not be worked out, the harsh Italian military occupation in Yugoslav territories might lead to larger-scale fighting in Adriatic regions and develop into a serious crisis for the entire Paris conference. From mid-February to mid-April, therefore, there were countless meetings and exchanges in search of an acceptable compromise.

The first of several American initiatives, in early February, did not work. The idea was to have both contestants submit the Adriatic dispute to Woodrow Wilson for arbitration. Arthur Hugh Frazier and Douglas W. Johnson put it, at first obliquely, to Trumbić who liked the plan for several reasons. Firstly, Wilson was patently sympathetic to the Yugoslav cause, and if he imposed a compromise formula then

Wilson and not the Yugoslav delegation (or the government in Belgrade) would bear the blame. Furthermore, Pašić and the Serbs could not be accused of abandoning Croat and Slovene interests, nor could anyone be accused of having given in to the Serbs. Fearing the loss of Trieste and western Istra, however, two Slovene members of the delegation, Ivan Zölger and Otokar Ribarž, refused to agree. Pašić, in the circumstances, took refuge on the fence. The matter was finally refer-

red to Belgrade where the government, with noteworthy despatch, ruled in favour of submitting the Adriatic dispute to Wilson for arbitration. On February 10 the President sent a message to the Yugoslavs saying he was 'deeply moved' by their show of confidence and, next, tried to induce the Italians to follow suit. But the Italians, incensed, refused. Arbitration would surely have cost them Fiume and eastern Istra.

The Yugoslavs then agreed, under some American pressure, to a partition of Istra, by which the western two-thirds of the peninsula would go to Italy, as an American concession to Italian security arguments. The line of partition, running down the spine of Istra, east of the Treaty of London line, quickly became known as the 'Wilson Line'. The Yugoslavs accepted it because it was the next best thing 'to arbitration, and because they had no choice, if American sponsorship of their cause was to continue. On April 14, however, Orlando rejected the 'Wilson Line' out of hand, despite the additional American offer of a 'free city' status for Fiume which Wilson refused to grant outright to Italy as it was essential to Yugoslavia.

Wilson despairs
On April 16 Trumbić, with Pašić's support, proposed to Clemenceau, Lloyd George, Wilson and Orlando that all the territories in dispute with Italy be submitted to a plebiscite, an adroit initiative (cleared in advance with the American staff) which the Italians also turned down. Faced with such intransigence, and particularly repelled

3279

by the Treaty of London argument and Italian scepticism about the proposed League of Nations, Wilson lost all patience. Now he became adamant. On April 21 to 23 Lloyd George made several attempts to heal the rift, but without success. Late on April 23 Wilson issued a manifesto, in effect appealing to the Italian nation to bring their government to reason. But the intervention had the opposite effect. The following day Orlando left Paris in a huff. In Rome he quickly won parliamentary and, throughout Italy, national support. Wilson was confounded and the rupture seemed beyond repair.

The Yugoslavs were pleased, baffled, alarmed — but they remained sensibly quiet. There was not much that they could do. The crisis of the Italian boycott was not ended until May 7, when Orlando and Sonnino returned to Paris under the threat of seeing the Treaty of London nullified in their absence. For the rest of May and most of June negotiations continued, with scant results. The Italians did make concessions, agreeing to 'free city' status to Fiume (though closely bound to Italy) and a considerable narrowing of demands in Dalmatia; but still no overall Adriatic settlement was on the cards, by the time the German treaty was signed at Versailles on June 28.

In June the position in Paris changed dramatically. Unable to ensure success, and faced with a rebellious parliament in Rome, Orlando and Sonnino resigned on the 19th. Their fall closed an era, though their successors — Francesco Nitti and Tommaso Tittoni — did not resume negotiations on Adriatic matters for some time. On the Yugoslav side, word came on the 27th that in view of the deadlock Premier Protić, accompanied by several Cabinet members, would soon arrive in Paris to repair fissures within the delegations and explore prospects with Allied leaders. And finally, with the German treaty in hand, Woodrow Wilson, saddened among other things by his inability to forge an Adriatic settlement, left for home. Their patron gone, the Yugoslavs found themselves alone.

The focus now shifted to the Austrian frontiers, and in the autumn those involving Hungary and Bulgaria. Negotiations, begun before June, were complicated by outbursts of violence in Carinthia, Albania, Fiume and elsewhere. On the Austrian side, the Yugoslavs encountered determined Allied opposition, particularly Italian, to their demand for Carinthia (including the town of Klagenfurt); while they found Article 59 of the Austrian draft treaty highly objectionable. That article sought to safeguard the rights of the former Austro-Hungarian nationalities in all the successor states. In the case of Yugoslavia, Serbia had been a sovereign state and not part of the Dual Monarchy; hence, the Yugoslavs argued, it should not be treated the same as, say, Hungary. This view was not shared and heavy American, British and French pressure was applied. Still, the Yugoslavs would not give in because they argued, not unreasonably, that only territories acquired after 1914 ought to be subject to these treaty provisions, and not the lands annexed to Serbia in the Balkan wars. Domestic affairs dictated the taking of this line in Paris, much to the chagrin of the Allies. As neither side gave in the Yugoslavs refused to sign the Treaty

of St Germain on September 10, 1919. They finally yielded to threats that the Americans would abandon their Adriatic cause, and to the inter-Allied injunction that if they did not sign the Austrian treaty they would not be allowed to adhere to the Bulgarian settlement. Together with the Rumanians — who similarly resisted the minorities conventions in the two peace treaties — the Yugoslavs affixed their signatures to the Treaty of Neuilly with Bulgaria on November 27, and to the Austrian document on December 5, 1919. With these acts, the Yugoslav state gained several strategic salients in the east — in the Strumica valley, and in the Vranje, Tsaribrod and Negotino districts, but none around Vidin — amounting to some 960 square miles, and a Bulgarian population of some 100,000. On the Austrian side, however, the Yugoslavs suffered disappointment. The Allies divided the much desired Klagenfurt basin into two zones, with provision for a plebiscite in the southern (ethnically more Slav) zone, three months after the ratification of the Treaty of St Germain. The plebiscite, held on October 10, 1920, resulted in a vote (22,025 to 15,279) in favour of union with Austria; thus the entire Klagenfurt basin reverted to Austria.

D'Annunzio's Fiume
In the Adriatic regions, however, progress continued to elude all sides. The picture was greatly complicated when, in September 1919, the author-*condottiere* D'Annunzio invaded Fiume and had himself proclaimed Dictator. The 'rape of Fiume', as Lloyd George put it, worked Woodrow Wilson (now back in Washington) to 'such a pitch of indignation' that he never forgave the Italians. The Yugoslavs were similarly affected, but to little effect. In October and November 1919 a variety of proposals was put forward, mainly by the Italian side; none broke the deadlock, even though Tittoni had reduced Italian claims in Dalmatia. Fiume, as before, was the Gordian Knot. In late autumn, the frustrated Tittoni resigned and his successor, Scialoja, attempted several variations on the main theme of Italian 'needs'. The Dalmatian coastal demands were further reduced to the city of Zara (Zadar), plus several islands, but under no circumstances were the Italians willing to see Fiume turned over to Yugoslavia. The most they would concede was to turn Fiume into an independent state, that would evidently some day be absorbed.

Negotiations along the line dragged on into 1920, with the Yugoslavs steadily losing ground as a result of growing American preoccupation with presidential elections and Anglo-French impatience. In Belgrade, too, internal politics gradually overshadowed the diplomatic scene. In June 1920 Nitti fell and the new government of Giolitti and Sforza determined to bring Adriatic issues to a close. In a series of adroit manoeuvres, which the dispirited and isolated Yugoslavs could not effectively counter, Sforza brought about a direct Italo-Yugoslav conference at Rapallo in November 1920 and there, in effect, imposed a 'settlement' on Trumbić and the new Prime Minister, Vesnić. By the Treaty of Rapallo, Italy gained an advantageous strategic line — including Monte Nevoso, the dominant position in southern Istra — an independent state of Fiume contigu-

ous with Italy, Italian sovereignty in the Dalmatian city of Zara, and four of the more important Dalmatian islands. D'Annunzio was finally expelled from Fiume by the Italian government in late December 1920; the 'Free State' led an artificial existence until Mussolini annexed it to Italy in 1924, a fact formally accepted by the Belgrade government of the day, headed by Nikola Pašić.

The Yugoslavs, by the Treaty of Rapallo, at long last obtained concrete western frontiers and, thereby, a much needed measure of peace. True, with some 720,000 South Slavs left beyond national frontiers — of these about 480,000 in Italy alone — the combined territorial settlements (St Germain, Neuilly, Trianon and Rapallo) contravened the principles of nationality and self-determination and consequently engendered much irredentist feeling. Yet, the treaties also assigned some 230,000 Rumanians, 467,000 Magyars and 500,000 Germans to Yugoslavia and thereby aroused irridentist passions in adjacent states, while creating various internal problems for the Yugoslavs. Throughout the 1920's and 1930's the sword thus cut both ways.

On balance, the Yugoslavs could look on the proceedings of 1919 to 1920 with some, even if tempered, satisfaction. What in 1914 appeared to be a remote dream had turned into reality by 1918. By 1920 the new state had imperfect but viable frontiers, and general international recognition as well. Except on the side of Italy, Yugoslavia's frontiers represented a reasonable compromise between considerations of nationality, geography, economic viability and strategic security. Whether the Rapallo line in the north-west, coinciding so nearly with that of the Treaty of London line, and the Rapallo formula for Fiume, bespoke the surrender of wisdom to expediency, or not, is of course debatable. Whatever the case, the Treaty of Rapallo ensured little stability in this troubled zone of Europe; it engendered much bitterness and, during the following 20 years, fatally imbued the Yugoslavs with a determination to settle scores next time round.

Further Reading
Alatri, P., *Nitti, d'Annunzio e la Questione Adriatica* (Feltrinelli 1959)
Almond, N. & Lutz, R. H. (eds.), *The Treaty of St Germain: a Documentary History of its Territorial and Political Clauses* (Stanford University Press 1935)
Jelavich, C., *Nikola P. Pasic: Greater Serbia or Yugoslavia?* (Journal of Central European Affairs, volume 2, p. 133, 1951)
Johnson, D. W., 'Fiume and the Adriatic Problem', in E. M. House & C. Seymour's *What Really Happened at Paris* (Scribner's 1921)
Lederer, Ivo J., *Yugoslavia at the Paris Peace Conference* (Yale University Press 1963)

IVO J. LEDERER was born in Yugoslavia in 1929 and educated in Yugoslavia, Italy and the USA. After leaving Princeton University he taught at a number of American universities and is at present a Professor at Stanford University. He is a member of several professional societies and is on the board of directors of the American Association for the Advancement of Slavic Studies. Professor Lederer has written a number of books, including *Yugoslavia at the Paris Peace Conference*, and *The Foreign Policy of Opposition Parties in Eastern Europe, 1900-1914*.

CHINA AND THE FOURTH OF MAY MOVEMENT

When the Peace Conference failed to restore to China the Shantung territory for which she had entered the war, indignant students and intellectuals blamed their delegates in Paris, and not the Allied Powers who had imposed the ruling.
Ronald Ian Heiferman. Above: Chinese student demonstration

The decision of the Chinese government to enter the war against Germany in August 1917 was largely made on the assumption that by entering the war on the Allied side China would be guaranteed a platform at the immediate postwar peace conference from which she might gain redress of her grievances against Japan. The Japanese annexation of German leaseholds in Shantung and their presentation of the infamous 21 Demands to the government of Yuan Shih-k'ai threatened to turn China into an economic and political appendage of Japan. With no possibility, given the rampant warlordism of the period, of confronting Japan militarily, the Chinese government, or, to put it more accurately, Chinese political factions, adopted a policy designed to exploit world opinion as a device to force the Japanese to return their interests and former German holdings to Chinese sovereignty. Thus, when the government of the United States actively solicited the co-operation of neutrals in February 1917, the Peking régime not only severed relations with Germany but actually declared war on the Central Powers soon after.

China's rôle in the war was minimal. Except for the contribution of labour brigades, the Chinese played little part in the action and saw no military service. Nevertheless, the war in Europe was deemed vital to their interests and followed with eagerness and excitement by members of the Chinese intelligentsia and student community. The announcement of the Armistice on November 11 was greeted with spontaneous enthusiasm. The Peking government declared a three-day public holiday, and on November 17, 60,000 marchers in the Chinese capital celebrated the 'victory of democracy over absolutism'.

For leaders of the rival Peking and Canton governments, the end of the war

augured a new era and the opportunity to confront Japan at the conference table in Paris. The leaders of the rival northern and southern governments naïvely assumed that former German leaseholds in China would be returned to Chinese sovereignty and that the new diplomacy defined by Woodrow Wilson would force Japan to recognise the righteousness of Chinese grievances against her aggressive acts of 1915. Wilson's support of the Chinese position had already been made clear prior to the conference and, like many of their counterparts who were to represent nationalist movements and minor powers at the conference, the Chinese assumed that Wilson's messianic influence would not be lost on the other powers. Such, unfortunately, was not to be the case.

In preparation for the peace conference, both polities (Peking and Canton) appointed delegations to attend the conference in Paris. Although the conference recognised only one *de jure* delegation representing the Republic of China, there were in fact two delegations, one representing the Kuomintang régime based in Canton and the other representing the Peking clique. Despite the fact that representatives of both interests had broadly similar views as to what China should achieve at the conference, the many political differences and the long and bitter feud between the two régimes did not contribute to the most efficient presentation of the Chinese position. The conference rules provided for no distinction between the factions, demanding only that two members of the delegation be permitted to represent the country at any given time. The selection of the representatives was up to the delegates themselves.

The Peking régime was to be represented at Paris by Lu Cheng-hsiang, Foreign Minister of the Republic, while the Canton contingent was headed by C. T. Wang, Kuomintang party stalwart and former Minister of Agriculture. Serving as a political bridge between the two men and the factions they represented was V. K. Wellington Koo, Chinese Ambassador to the United States (Peking régime). Koo was to play a vital rôle as an intermediary between the two factions and, more important,

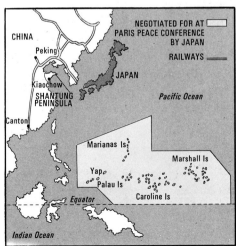

Above: Territory disputed by China and Japan at the Paris Peace Conference. *Left:* Peking police arguing with a group of lecturers campaigning for a boycott on Japanese goods. The May 4 Movement was led by intellectuals, who organised demonstrations and agitated for government reform, but the whole population rejected the Versailles settlement

though Wilson was not very optimistic about the possibility of achieving a 'just settlement' of the issue in Paris, the Chinese diplomat was buoyed up by Wilson's pledge of support for the Chinese.

On the way to Paris, the Chinese mission had a brief meeting with the Japanese delegates in Tokyo, which destroyed what unity the Chinese may have had. Charges and countercharges were made concerning the pro-Japanese sympathies of certain members of the delegation, particularly Lu Cheng-hsiang, the leader of the Peking contingent. When the delegation finally reached Paris, it was divided almost beyond repair. Throughout their time at the conference, rivalry and accusations continued between the factions. Even Wellington Koo, the one man most likely to stand between the factions as a 'mediator', was accused of pro-Japanese sympathies because of his engagement to the daughter of a Chinese official known for his reputed pro-Japanese leanings. It was in this spirit that the Chinese entered the negotiations.

Imperial War Museum

Above: A parade of Chinese labourers at Boulogne in 1917. Labour brigades were China's main contribution to the war, in which she took hardly any part. *Below:* Student demonstrators advertise their grievances. *Centre:* Group of Chinese students, among them Chou En-Lai and his wife. The students and the intelligentsia were the force behind the May 4 Movement and many worked hard to bring about wide-ranging reforms in the life of their country. *Opposite:* Chinese labourers loading sacks of oats in France in August 1917, soon after China entered the war. The problem of communication must have been considerable for the workers who found themselves transplanted to Europe as part of the token war effort which was all that China could manage. The British recruited 175,000 Chinese for service in several theatres, and many died on the Western Front

served as the chief spokesman for the Chinese position at the formal meetings of the conference at which the Chinese delegation was invited to contribute and participate. For this rôle he was eminently qualified, as a result of his legal training and diplomatic experience.

As the 60 odd members of the Chinese mission prepared to depart for Paris, Koo, in Washington DC, was granted an audience with Woodrow Wilson, who was preparing to leave for Europe with his entourage. At this brief session, which was held on November 26, 1918, the two men laid the groundwork for what they hoped would be a complementary Sino-American presentation of the Shantung question. Al-

The first session of the peace conference convened on January 18, 1919, but it was not until January 27 that the Shantung question was taken up. From the outset of the conference, however, it was clear that the Japanese had little inclination to consider seriously the immediate return of former German leaseholds to Chinese sovereignty, and, what was worse for the Chinese, representatives of the European powers were not prepared to force the Japanese to do so. The reason for this became abundantly clear when Baron Makino Nobukai, head of the Japanese delegation to the conference made his presentation on January 27 at the first plenary session of the Council of Ten.

Speaking bluntly

In his presentation, Baron Makino revealed for the first time to the Chinese and Americans the existence of secret agreements with Great Britain, France and Italy, concluded prior to the opening of the conference, which 'supported Japan's

claims in regard to the disposal of Germany's rights in Shantung'. Makino would have preferred not to make this stunning disclosure in the presence of the Chinese representatives but the American Secretary of State Lansing insisted that China's representatives be present at the meeting when the Shantung issue was to be introduced. The revelation dealt a heavy blow to China's hopes of securing some redress of her grievances against Japan. It caught the US and Chinese delegations off balance, and they never fully recovered.

Following their first encounter with the able Baron Makino, the leaders of the Chinese delegation, headed by Wellington Koo, talked with Wilson and his advisers, seeking to prepare for the Chinese presentation which was to be made the following day. On the advice of Wilson, it was agreed that Koo would speak bluntly for the Chinese position while his compatriots tested sentiments among the other delegations, particularly the British. The Chinese, in turn, requested that Wilson should add his view of the situation at the second session.

Unfortunately for the Chinese cause, on the eve of Koo's presentation the existence of secret loan agreements between China and Japan for purposes of financing railway construction in Shantung and a general accord reached between the Chinese and Japanese governments on the Shantung issue on September 24, 1918, were revealed for the first time to Wilson and many members of the Chinese mission. Indeed, Koo was obliged to confirm to

Wilson the existence of the agreements just as he was preparing to articulate his government's position. Had he not done so, Baron Makino would have done so in his response to Koo's appeal. When informed of the agreements, Wilson and his associates advised the Chinese that it would be difficult for the United States to continue to range themselves with the Chinese on the Shantung question unless China repudiated these Sino-Japanese agreements, which had yet to be ratified by the parliament in Peking. Among several suggestions made to the Chinese was that the agreements be immediately submitted to the Chinese parliament for a ratification vote. Since parliament would certainly reject them, the Japanese might not then be able to force the Chinese to acknowledge or honour the agreements. For some reason, however, no effort was made to initiate a ratification vote in Peking, or to postpone consideration of China's views on the Shantung question at the conference. Thus Koo's presentation on January 28 was made in the knowledge that the existence of the agreements with Japan would be revealed by the Japanese delegates. In such circumstances, the Chinese claims were doomed from the outset.

In his speech of January 28, Wellington Koo attempted to counter the Japanese assertion that the German leaseholds in Shantung were, by virtue of prior agreements with the Allies, to be given over to Japan. He pointed out that the original Sino-German arrangements had been concluded under duress and represented a series of wrongful acts. It would therefore be wrong to transfer the territory to another power. Invoking the principles of nationalism and territorial integrity, Koo argued that the Allied powers had no choice

but to return these areas to Chinese rule. Although grateful for the opportunity to present their grievances before the international tribunal in Paris, Koo pointed out that the Chinese delegation felt that they would be false to their duty to China and to the world if they did not object to paying their debts of gratitude by selling the birthrights of their countrymen and thereby sowing the seeds of discord for the future.

Makino replied that Japan's case was based on three agreements:
● the Sino-Japanese Treaty of May 25, 1915;
● the texts of the Tsinan-Shunteh and Kaomi-Hsü-chou railroad loan agreements; and
● the September 24, 1918, exchange of notes between China and Japan on the Shantung question. There was little that the Chinese could do to dispute this. Indeed, as Wunsz King, secretary of the Chinese delegation, later put it, 'The revelation of these agreements amounted virtually to a waiver on China's part of the right to protest Japanese annexations at the peace conference'. This being the case, there was little hope of salvaging the Shantung situation in the long run.

Whither Shantung?

On April 22, 1919, after a gap of nearly two months, the Shantung question was reopened for the last time. In a meeting of the representatives of the Three Powers (US, Great Britain and France) held at Wilson's Paris residence, the Chinese delegation made its last formal presentation. It offered little new information to support the Chinese position. Wilson told Clemenceau and Lloyd George that he was unable to persuade the Japanese to make any concessions on the matter of Shantung and

asked for their views. Lloyd George asked Chinese delegates whether they preferred to allow Japan to succeed to German rights in Shantung, as defined in Sino-German agreements, or to Japanese rights as stipulated in Sino-Japanese agreements. Koo's embarrassed response was that neither of these alternatives was acceptable but when pressed by the British Prime Minister to explain how it was that the Peking government, recognised by the Powers as the *de jure* government of China, had conceded Shantung interests to Japan in negotiations as recent as September 1918, Koo could offer no convincing answer. Wilson, always the patron of Chinese interests, had little choice but to agree with Lloyd George's suggestion that if the Chinese were permitted to abrogate a treaty which was not definitely negotiated under duress, the sanctity of any and every treaty between two sovereign states would be called into question. The sanctity of treaty commitments was, for Wilson, an issue which transcended the Shantung question. Thus, if the Japanese could not be persuaded to

C. T. Wang, leader of the Canton Chinese delegation in Paris. In 1922 he became director of the Sino-Japanese commission on Shantung

agree to an abrogation of the treaty, it would have to be recognised. On April 30, 1919, Wilson joined Lloyd George and Clemenceau in an agreement to transfer to Japan Germany's former Shantung interests. This agreement was eventually written into the final peace treaty (Section VIII, Articles 156-158).

The decision to confirm Japan's Shantung interests was given to the Chinese mission by Wilson's emissary, Ray Stannard Baker, on May 1. News of the impending tragedy for China was carried home from Paris by Chinese journalists and the letters of the delegation members, trigger-

ing a wave of reaction and criticism of the government in Peking and the 'traitors' who had compromised Chinese interests to serve their Japanese mentors.

On May 1 the Press confirmed the story of impending diplomatic disaster at Versailles and student groups in Peking prepared to demonstrate their opposition to the resolution of the Shantung affair and the conduct of the Chinese delegation at the conference. Their bitterness was everywhere to be seen in letters to newspapers, placards and posters. One student at Peking University aptly summed up the general disillusionment when he assessed the meaning of the situation at Paris in the following manner: *Throughout the world, like the voice of a prophet, has gone the word of Woodrow Wilson strengthening the weak and giving courage to the struggling. And the Chinese have been listening and they too have heard. . . . They have been told that in the dispensation which was to be made after the war, unmilitaristic nations like China would have an opportunity to develop their culture, their industry, their civilisation, unhampered. They have been told that secret covenants and forced agreements would not be recognised. They looked for this new era but no sun rose for China. Even the cradle of the nation was stolen.*

Meeting on May 1, 1919, a coalition of students representing the academic institutions in Peking called for a massive demonstration to protest against the events of the peace conference. Their original plans called for the demonstration to be held on May 7, the fourth anniversary of Japan's presentation of the 21 Demands to the government of Yuan Shih-k'ai in 1915. Already recognised as a 'day of national humiliation', the students deemed it a particularly appropriate occasion on which to demonstrate their opposition. However, due to rapidly rising public indignation over the solution of the Shantung affair and police preparations to crush and limit the demonstration, leaders of the effort met in an emergency session on the evening of May 3 and called for a march the following afternoon.

Square of the Heavenly Peace
On the eve of the May 4 demonstration, rumours spread rapidly through Peking. On the morning of the demonstration, however, students assembled peacefully at Peking University to plan their strategy for the day. At that session a five-point course of action was adopted, including a peaceful march to focus public attention on the crisis faced by China. Despite pleas and warnings from officials from the Ministry of Education and the police authorities in Peking, the students decided to rally their numbers at the T'ien An Gate (Square of the Heavenly Peace) and to march from there to the foreign legations and the offices and homes of government officials involved in the negotiations in Paris. The purposes of the demonstration were embodied in a manifesto adopted by the students at this meeting: *Japan's demand for Tsingtao and other rights in Shantung is now going to be acceded to in the Paris Peace Conference. Her diplomacy has secured a great victory; and ours has led to a great failure. The loss of Shantung means the destruction of the integrity of China's territory. Once the integrity of her territory is destroyed, China will soon be annihilated. Accordingly, we students today make a demonstration*

march to the Allied legations, asking the Allies to support justice. . . . Today we swear solemn oaths to our fellow countrymen: 1) China's territory may be conquered but it' cannot be given away; 2) the Chinese people may be massacred, but they will not surrender. Our country is about to be annihilated. Up, brethren!

The student demonstration was launched at 2 pm in an orderly fashion. However, as the afternoon wore on, the marchers became less disciplined. Refused entrance into the foreign legations, the students turned, instead, toward the residence of Ts'ao Ju-lin, a Chinese diplomat long active in Japan. After forcing their way into his home and finding that Ts'ao was not there, the students sacked his home and moved on to the homes of other Chinese officials. By late afternoon, the Peking authorities declared martial law, dozens of demonstrators were arrested, and the demonstration was temporarily crushed.

The May 4 incident, as the events referred to above are frequently described, sparked off similar demonstrations in other cities. Limited to student groups at first, these demonstrations were soon joined by merchants and urban workers. Within a month after the first demonstration, a boycott against Japanese goods had been organised, and all sections of the population had been mobilised in opposition to the Versailles settlement. Given this upsurge of popular sentiment, the Chinese government had little choice but to instruct its delegates to refuse to sign the treaty when it was formally presented on June 28, an action in which the delegates representing the Canton régime fully concurred. This did not, however, placate the students and intellectuals, who continued to press for government and cultural changes.

In the broadest sense, the May 4 incident symbolised a larger movement which had begun before the demonstrations in Peking and continued long after the student demonstrations of 1919 ended. As defined by Professor Chow Tse-tsung, the May 4 Movement was a combined socio-political and intellectual movement to achieve national independence, the emancipation of the individual, and a just society. It led to a complete re-examination of the cultural, political, philosophical and social traditions of China. Its members, as well as its leaders, had many different approaches, but a common aim in the creation of a new China. They worked to further new ideologies, such as Marxism or Bolshevism; some worked to spread literacy and to develop a new literature: others joined the Kuomintang cause and participated in Sun Yat-sen's attempt to unseat the Peking régime. By their refusal to cling to the mores and the ideologies of the past, those who took part in the movement forced China into the 20th Century.

Further Reading
Chow Tse-Tsung, *The May Fourth Movement* (Cambridge, Mass.: Harvard University Press 1961)
Hu Shih, *The Chinese Renaissance* (New York: Paragon Reprint 1968)
Li Chien-nung, *The Political History of China 1839-1928* (Englewood Cliffs, NJ: Prentice-Hall 1956)
Meisner, Maurice, *Li Ta-chao* (Cambridge, Mass.: Harvard University Press 1969)

[*For Ronald Ian Heiferman's biography, see page 1040.*]

JAPAN AT THE PEACE CONFERENCE

When negotiations began in Paris, Japan was already entangled in a complicated system of diplomatic relations which she had constructed in order to have the strongest possible support for her claims. It was a major failure on the part of Wilson that he did not observe the

It has been said that no country was so ill-prepared for the coming of peace in November 1918 as Japan. Her war industries were working round the clock; and her capitalists were investing in them as though the war would continue for at least another year. Nor were her politicians attuned to the ending of the war. They had not really taken seriously the 14 Points of President Wilson on which the Armistice turned out to be based. They would probably have preferred an outcome in which both sides emerged exhausted and no one was the winner. Instead they feared that the United States might have a dominant voice at the peace conference, since her military intervention had tipped the scales in favour of the Allies. In fact, the government of the day—the Hara cabinet, which had only been in office since September 29—was baffled by the prospect of peacemaking. It had no clear notion of what form the conference would take or how soon it would get under way. Moreover the cabinet was preoccupied with domestic crises: the summer of 1918 had been plagued with rice riots which had overturned the previous government and were still far from being solved.

But, if the Hara government was taken aback by the suddenness of the Armistice, it was not really ill-prepared. The Japanese, whose main contribution to the war had been in 1914 and whose involvement in it had since been limited, had been able to work out their strategy for the peace, confident that they would have a seat at the peace conference if the Allies were victorious. Since September 1915, a peace preparation committee, composed of officials from the various departments, had been reporting regularly, although no decisions had been taken on its findings. On the other

suggested scheme of procedure which would have made null and void all treaties concluded before the Armistice. As a result he was forced to give preference to the less soundly-based but more cleverly upheld claims of Japan over those made by China. *Ian Nish*

hand, Japan's war aims were openly discussed and fairly widely understood.

Japan was represented at the preliminary stages of the conference by her ambassadors in London and Paris, Chinda and Matsui. In Tokyo the Prime Minister had taken office too recently to be able to go overseas, while Foreign Minister Uchida was not in good health. Baron Makino was, therefore, chosen as delegate and took part in lengthy briefings before he set off via the United States on December 10. Makino was a politician, a former foreign minister and a liberal. He identified himself with the 'New Diplomacy' and advocated that Japan should accept the 14 Points and the concept of a league of nations. When, however, it was clear that other countries would be represented at the level of prime minister and president, Japan chose as chief delegate Prince Saionji Kimmochi, a veteran politician who had for five years been inactive in party affairs. He had been educated in France in the 1870s and claimed to have a long-standing friendship with Georges Clemenceau. Since he was appointed late and did not reach Paris until March 3, Saionji seems to have played largely a titular part.

The delegation was in any case kept on a tight rein by the Tokyo government. This was not only from the Foreign Ministry and the cabinet but also—and most significantly—from the Advisory Council on Foreign Affairs, a supra-party body whose purpose was to take foreign policy-making out of the party arena. In five long sessions in November and December, it discussed the mandate to be given to the delegates at the greatest length and in the utmost detail. Even after the negotiations began in Paris, the Advisory Council met regularly to debate the instructions to be given to Makino. For this reason, the Japanese delegates probably had less flexibility in their bargaining position than most other delegations in Paris.

Japan's basic demands were two. The first concerned the Japanese occupied area of Kiaochow. Japan could have demanded permanent occupation of the territory but she decided to ask for transfer of the German lease to her and to undertake to give the territory back to China in due course. At the same time she wanted to receive the unconditional surrender of German rights in Kiaochow and Shantung and to secure the transfer of railway and other rights from Germany in accordance with the Sino-Japanese treaties of 1915 and 1918, which she wanted the conference to endorse. Her second ambition was to acquire the German islands in the Pacific north of the equator which Japanese units had occupied in 1914. This was the demand in which the Japanese navy was most interested; but it was generally agreed that it could not be pursued independently and that Japan would have to act in line with the delegates of the British Empire, who were hopeful of gaining the German islands in the South Pacific and also German colonies in Africa. These were the over-riding Japanese demands.

It was also necessary for Japan to settle in advance her attitude towards any proposal that a league of nations should be built into the peace settlement. Most of Japan's leaders (except Makino) took the view that any league was likely to be restrictive and prejudicial to Japan's interests: it might act unfavourably against the yellow race; it might hinder Japan's military agreements such as the naval alliance with Britain. There was no real question of Japan not joining any world organisation which was ultimately set up; but she had no intention of doing anything positive to encourage it. Japan's instructions were that, if it came up for discussion, her delegates should try to defer any resolution for its practical accomplishment; but that, if it did come into being, they should seek suitable guarantees as far as circumstances permitted to prevent any damage to Japan which might result from racial considerations. On other matters, where Japan's interests were not affected, it was left to Makino to 'adapt to the circumstances of the conference'. One observer, Stephen Bonsal, has written of the Japanese delegates sitting through the stormy sessions 'calm and imperturbable like Buddha on his lotus throne'. At least, this calm—and apparent impartiality—where their interests were unaffected was authorised by Tokyo.

Preparing the ground

Japan realised that all her demands were controversial and would be challenged by one power or another. It was therefore necessary for her during the war years to prepare her ground as far as possible. With regard to her demands over Kiaochow, which were bitterly disputed in China and the United States, vigilance was doubly necessary. The countries which she approached in advance were Britain, her ally of two decades, and her wartime partners, France and Russia. When Britain was suffering from the German U-Boat menace towards the end of 1916, she asked for the assistance of Japanese cruisers for the western Indian Ocean and destroyers for the Mediterranean. Japan replied that this help might be more readily given if Britain could undertake to assist her in attaining her war aims. On February 16 Britain agreed to support at any peace conference Japanese claims to the disposal of Germany's rights in Shantung and possessions in islands north of the equator. Within six weeks France and Russia had followed suit with explicit offers of support. But the validity of these guarantees was open to question. In August 1917 China entered the war against Germany and abrogated all treaties and agreements existing between the two countries. It was arguable, therefore, that the British guarantee of February became null and void. Moreover there were rumours that China had only agreed to enter the war on receipt of guarantees from the Allies, promising their support to China at the peace conference. This was not so; but it certainly seemed plausible to contemporaries. Moreover the 1917 guarantees were general rather than specific: they offered support but did not ensure the successful outcome of Japanese ambitions. On all these counts Japan's leaders were doubtful as to whether or not the 1917 undertakings still held good; they were far from confident about this. When the delegates assembled in Paris in January 1919, early steps were taken to enquire whether Britain and France were inclined to stand by these undertakings; and the Japanese breathed a sigh of relief when the answer was favourable.

Japan's other anxiety was to prepare the way with China. We have seen (Volume 1, pp 313-19) how Japan had extracted certain legal assurances in the Sino-Japanese treaties of May 1915. These too were in doubt after China's entry into the war, one effect of which was that China *would* attend the peace conference. For the rest of the war the Peking government was the pliable government of Premier Tuan and President Hsu. It was with them that Japan entered into a further agreement on September 25, 1918 whereby China promised 'to give Japan the German rights and interests in Shantung Province when an agreement was reached between Japan and Germany' in return for a loan of 20,000,000 yen. When the Armistice was declared, Japan talked of China being represented at Paris by the Japanese delegation and of China and Japan making common cause. These illusions were seemingly affirmed by the visit to Tokyo of Lu Cheng-hsiang, the chief Chinese delegate, on his way to Paris. In his conversations with the Japanese foreign minister, an atmosphere of cordiality prevailed and Japan undertook to support China in her plea for the abolition of the unequal treaties, provided China supported Japan's Shantung demands. According to the Japanese record, this was readily accepted: thus, Peking and the chief Chinese delegate had evidently been in agreement. But Peking did not give the other members of the Chinese delegation in Paris a specific mandate over Shantung and they assumed that they were allowed discretion on the point. Moreover they did not acknowledge Lu's leadership when he joined them in Paris. So there soon developed a bitter confrontation between the two oriental neighbours over Germany's former lease. Of course Japan had certain shadowy offers of support from Britain and France. The fruits of her preliminary diplomacy, mainly in the form of secret treaties, were allowed to leak out in Paris; but Wilson announced that he could not be bound by them.

Surprises at Paris

From January 18 when the Paris conference opened, the Hinomaru flag flew outside the Hotel Bristol on one corner of the Place Vendôme. This provided accommodation for most of the Japanese delegation and served as their conference headquarters. It was the first truly international conference at which Japan had been represented. Certainly it was the first at which she had enjoyed such high status: she was recognised as one of the five great powers and was entitled to appoint five plenipotentiaries. Gradually, however, the decision-making rôle passed to the Council of Four and Japan was excluded. Prince Saionji, the head of delegation, was over 70 and was not really anxious to cut a public figure in Paris; indeed, he was said to spend all his time in his hotel suite. Following his lead, the Japanese tried to secure their ends by informal contacts with other delegations rather than by rhetoric at conference sessions. Nor did they feel it necessary to appeal to public opinion by wooing the press.

These tactics may have been influenced by the false assumption on Tokyo's part that its demands would not encounter much serious opposition. Instead, Japan's ambitions were harshly attacked from the start, especially by the Chinese, whom they thought had been won over in advance. The Japanese delegates were unequal to the challenge of Dr Wellington Koo, who gradually took over the effective leadership of the Chinese delegation in Paris. Makino, who bore the brunt of the appearances in the various conference committees, had an imperfect knowledge of English. Some writers speak of his halting and embarrassing presentation, although others, including the secretary of the British delegation, Maurice Hankey, praise him for the lucidity and brevity of his arguments. Even Ambassador Chinda, Makino's deputy, was less fluent and less skilful in answering questions than Koo. It was no surprise therefore that the Japanese chose to avoid confrontations by absenting themselves from sessions at which the Chinese were presenting their case.

The first of Japan's demands to come up was that for the Pacific islands. The initial scheme advanced by the powers (including Japan) that had occupied German territories outside Europe during the war, was for outright retention by the occupier. Japan made a brief statement to this effect for the German Pacific islands on January 27. But President Wilson had already convinced himself of the merits of a mandatory system, whereby acquired territories would be awarded as mandates of the League of Nations to certain countries who would be accountable to the League. It seems that Wilson was doubtful whether Japan could be permitted to acquire the Pacific islands, even in the capacity of a mandatory power. At a lengthy session of the Advisory Council on Foreign Affairs on February 3, the navy minister, Admiral Kato, remarked that the islands would lose their value if Japan was forbidden to fortify them as a condition of the mandate; while these islands could never have become naval bases, they could have carried small defence installations and it was a pity that these would be ruled out; their sole remaining value would be for signalling and communication. Nonetheless Japan accepted the broad principle of mandates. It was not until May 6 that the world leaders made the final allocations: the Pacific islands became class C mandates; the Japanese received the mandate for the islands north of the equator which they still occupied while the British Empire received the islands to the south of the equator under a similar dispensation. There was doubtless disappointment,

especially in naval circles, but Japan had to recognise that she had not been less favourably treated than Britain. Moreover, she had acquired – or so her delegates thought – mandatory rights over the most useful island of Yap.

Japan and the racial issue

The next issue which arose was that of the League of Nations, whose covenant dominated Japan's activities at the Paris peace conference in February and March. Although the Japanese were fundamentally suspicious and sceptical about the League organisation as it was taking shape, they discussed it very thoroughly. There was, as Premier Hara wrote, no question of Japan's remaining in isolation outside the League; she had to enter it. He devoted his attention to one aspect of the League, that is, Japan's desire to incorporate within the covenant words which would remove disadvantages arising from racial considerations. It was out of line with the Japanese government's accustomed policies to raise the racial issue so publicly. She had over the past two or three decades protested to powers who applied discriminatory policies; but she had been moderate in approach and had never carried her protests to extremes. Why then did she change her tactics in 1919? There were, of course, diplomatic reasons. An appeal against racial treatment was an issue on which she could make common cause with China. Also, further trouble with the United States over California was in the offing and Paris provided an opportunity to solve the matter once and for all. Then there were domestic reasons. Under the influence of Wilson's 14 Points, many societies sprang up, proclaiming that the Paris meetings should be used to abolish racial discrimination and that the drawing up of the League covenant should be used to provide a charter for coloured races. By February 1919 a powerful nationwide society for the removal of racial discrimination was organised, and so enthusiastically was it supported in the press that it caused the government some alarm. For these reasons the government was ready to include this demand as part of Japan's peace terms.

On February 13 Makino asked the commission on the drafting of the League

covenant that it should include a formula to eliminate the causes of racial disharmony. But this gambit was unsuccessful. At meetings of the Advisory Council in Tokyo, Makino's tactics were subjected to harsh criticisms for their moderation; and the delegates were positively instructed to raise the racial question again. They decided to approach informally the British Dominions, Australia and New Zealand, who had been major opponents of the earlier proposals. Despite mediation by various statesmen in the British delegation, by the end of March the Australian Premier still regarded the proposal as anathema. Failing to make headway along this tack, Makino proposed to the League commission on April 11 that the preamble to the covenant should recognise 'the principle of equality of nations and of just treatment of their nationals'. The Japanese insisted that a vote be taken; and 11 out of the 17 present supported the motion. But President Wilson interpreted the issue as one of principle which required a unanimous vote and declared from the chair that the resolution was lost. Dismayed but still full of resilience, Makino again gave vent to Japan's desire for some racial equality formula governing the League in an address to the plenary session on April 28. Although he did not press for another vote, he placed on record 'in the name of the Japanese government and people that they regretted their failure to have it adopted' and promised that Japan would in the future continue her efforts through the League of Nations to see this principle adopted. So ended discussion of one of the most explosive issues to come before the conference. In Japan generally, this was the issue which stimulated most criticism of the Allied leaders in Paris; and the press and interested associations had a field day in April, just when the most serious Japanese demand, that on Kiaochow, came up for settlement.

Kiaochow and Shantung

On January 27 Makino introduced what was unquestionably the most important of Japan's demands. He asked the Council of Ten that Germany should retrocede to Japan, without compensation, the leased territory of Kiaochow together with the rail and other rights which the Germans

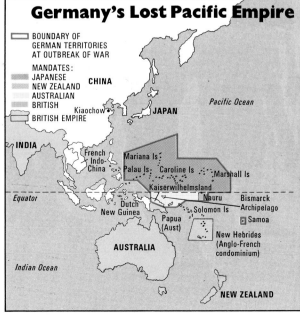

Germany's Lost Pacific Empire

BOUNDARY OF GERMAN TERRITORIES AT OUTBREAK OF WAR

MANDATES:
JAPANESE
NEW ZEALAND
AUSTRALIAN
BRITISH
BRITISH EMPIRE

CHINA
Kiaochow
JAPAN
Pacific Ocean
INDIA
French Indo-China
Mariana Is
Palau Is
Caroline Is
Marshall Is
Kaiserwilhelmsland
Equator
Dutch New Guinea
Nauru
Bismarck Archipelago
Papua (Aust)
Solomon Is
Samoa
New Hebrides (Anglo-French condominium)
AUSTRALIA
Indian Ocean
NEW ZEALAND

The German colonies in the Near North, or the territories immediately to the north of Australia and New Zealand, were tempting to the antipodean Dominions when the First World War broke out. While the Japanese soon seized the German islands north of the Equator, including the Marshalls, Marianas and Carolines, as well as Kiaochow, the German enclave in China, the Australians moved northward to capture what Germany owned south of the Equator. These islands included German Samoa, a few assorted islands, plus the Bismarck Archipelago and Kaiserwilhelmsland (north-east New Guinea). Within four months of the outbreak of the war Australasian and Japanese forces had completed their conquests. On August 30, 1914 New Zealand troops occupied Samoa, and on September 13 the Australians raised the British flag over German New Guinea after some intense fighting. The British and their Dominions were not pleased to watch the Japanese move so far south in their conquests, and once the German territories south of the Equator were secured, the Australasians were not inclined to give up what they had won so easily, particularly after so many of their troops had fallen on behalf of British interests in the Middle East, Gallipoli and elsewhere. After intense debate and argument at the Peace Conference, in a fight led by Australia's pugnacious Prime Minister, Billy Hughes, the conquests of Australia and New Zealand were legalised, within the framework of the mandate system, mostly to please Woodrow Wilson. When asked by Wilson whether the American missionaries would be prevented entry to New Guinea if Australia became the mandatory power, Hughes reputedly answered, 'Certainly not, Mr. President. I understand that these poor people often go for months at a time without enough to eat.'* Australia received the mandates for all German possessions south of the Equator, except for Samoa, which became a New Zealand mandate, and Naura which became a British one. The last was the only territory then thought valuable economically, because of its phosphate deposits.
*Wm Roger Louis, *Great Britain & Germany's Lost Colonies,* (Clarendon Press 1967)

Controllers of Japan's Peace Delegation: The Hara Cabinet

(Left to right) *Top:* Lieutenant-General Tanaka, Minister of War;
Mr Yamamoto, Minister of Agriculture and Commerce; Mr Noda, Minister
of Communications. *Centre:* Viscount Uchida, Minister of Foreign
Affairs; Mr Hara, Prime Minister and Minister of Justice; Mr Toko-
nami, Minister of Home Affairs. *Bottom:* Mr Nakahashi, Education;
Vice-Admiral Kato, Navy Minister; Baron Takahashi, Finance

had acquired in Shantung province. He based his plea on the wartime treaties of 1915 and 1918 and by implication sought the recognition of these by the conference. On the following day Dr Koo proposed that Germany should be required to hand over these rights directly to China. Since Japan had already promised to restore Kiaochow to China, he argued, it would be logical to make one bite of the cherry rather than two. To the Japanese, of course, this was a complete breach of faith. They tried to contact the chief Chinese plenipotentiary but he lay low. So Tokyo instructed its new minister in Peking to get China to accept the undertakings earlier given by Lu in Tokyo. While he extracted the assurance that the Chinese government wanted the fullest co-operation with Japan – all the more necessary because of Japan's continued military presence on Chinese soil – there is no sign that Peking tried to discipline its delegates in Paris. It must be realised that the Kiaochow issue was less important for the world powers than the developing dispute over Germany's colonies and that its great significance for East Asia was not appreciated.

After this brief foray, the question lapsed for three months, squeezed out by more pressing European problems. It was, however, raised again in mid-April by the Japanese, who announced that they must have a solution of the Shantung dispute before the completion – then imminent – of the German treaty. Implicit in this statement was the threat that Japan might not sign the treaty and consequently the covenant of the League, if her wishes were not met. This telling blackmail followed Japan's failure over the racial equality clause and coincided with the breach among the Big Four on account of Italy's Adriatic ambitions. The Japanese had, as one writer remarks, chosen their time 'with exquisite cunning'.

The matter came before the Council of Three on April 22, the day that the Japanese delegation received instructions that they were to defer signing the covenant of the League if Japan's demands concerning Shantung were not accomplished or if the territory were to be leased under mandatory arrangements. It is important to note that the Japanese were not told not to sign, although rumours to that effect circulated in Paris and may have been deliberately leaked. From Tokyo's point of view it was mainly a delaying operation. Later that day the Chinese delegation was heard, without the Japanese being present. It was generally conceded that the Sino-Japanese treaties of 1915 and 1918 could not be made void by the conference as the Chinese pleaded. Advice on the terms on which the territory was to be ceded to Japan was sought from an expert sub-committee, which consisted of three 'Old China hands', Jean Gout of France, E. T. Williams of the United States and Ronald Macleay of Britain. They reported without hesitation that it·was to China's advantage to accept Japan's succession to German rights as defined in the Sino-German agreement of 1898 rather than the one-sided treaties of 1915 and 1918. There can be little doubt about the wisdom of this advice: Japan had added to these rights considerably in her wartime agreements. But the recommendation was diametrically opposed to the lines along which the Chinese had been arguing.

At the Council of Three on April 24 this report was discussed and it was decided to ask A. J. Balfour to work out with the Japanese the terms on which they would ultimately hand Kiaochow back to China. Balfour met Makino and Chinda and received assurances that Japan would not interfere with Chinese sovereignty. The issue was discussed daily by the Council, as Wilson, in particular, tried to avoid giving the Japanese any pretext for retaining military forces in Shantung province. Eventually on April 30 it was agreed that German rights in China should be handed over, not to China, but to Japan, on certain strict conditions. These were stated to the Council by the Japanese, with the endorsement of the Advisory Council in Tokyo as follows: 'the policy of Japan is to hand back the Shantung Peninsula in full sovereignty to China, retaining only the economic privileges granted to Germany and the right to establish a settlement under the usual conditions at Tsingtao'. In addition, the Japanese railway authorities there would use special police (who would be Chinese) only to ensure security for traffic and certain Japanese instructors who would be appointed by the Chinese government. The Japanese delegates reported evasively to Tokyo that the meeting had agreed to their demands. As we have seen, this was true only in a superficial sense. Moreover, the conference did not recognise the Sino-Japanese treaties of 1915 and 1918, although it did not expressly repudiate them. It merely substituted a new formula which was devised privately with the Japanese.

No time-limit

The obvious shortcoming of the settlement was that it set no time-limit for Japanese withdrawal. It was indispensable for the Powers to get the Tokyo authorities to spell out their intentions publicly. But such statements as were made were vague and evasive. This naturally exasperated the Chinese who were already operating a boycott of Japanese goods. Late in May the Chinese government asked Japan to issue an explicit statement containing its programme for withdrawal from Shantung and details of commercial privileges sought, and threatened otherwise to abstain from signing the peace treaty. The Japanese, however, declined to be specific and could not be compelled to subscribe to the various undertakings which other delegates drafted for them. Since Japan had been putting pressure on Peking to sign the treaty, she was confident – falsely as it turned out – that this would present no problem.

The peace treaty with Germany was signed at Versailles on June 28. By its terms Germany granted Japan the unexpired portion of the lease of Kiaochow without compensation, together with such railway and mining rights as she had held. Thus, Japan had secured the major part of her major demand. Over racial equality she got nothing, although she had put her viewpoint on record. For the German islands in the Pacific, she got a class C mandate from the League of Nations, rather less than she had hoped. Her attainments were rather less than her aspirations; but this was true for all the victorious Powers who had been present at Paris. The Advisory Council on Foreign Affairs had often been critical of the actions of the Japanese delegates. And, when they returned home in August, they were given a mixed reception.

It was widely said that the Powers had leant towards Japan rather than China. It seemed as though Britain and France had been governed in their judgement by the 1917 undertakings and Wilson had reneged on his promises to China. But these judgements ignore the conditions on which Kiaochow had been granted to Japan – the 'small print' as it were of the Versailles treaty. It was not that Wilson, Lloyd George and Clemenceau were unsympathetic to China but that they found it legally difficult and politically impossible to resist the Japanese demands. Had time been adequate, it might have been possible to tie Japan down more effectively. But, as Hankey said, this Far Eastern imbroglio had been 'an almost intolerable strain to all concerned coming on top of the Italian claims and a spate of urgent questions pouring in about the compilation of the German treaty'. Within the context of the world-wide problems with which the leaders were dealing there was a limit to the time that could be devoted to the Far East. Instead, Britain and the United States decided to reopen the question as soon as the Versailles treaty was disposed of. In July pressure began in London and Washington to ensure that Japan should live up to her promise to return Kiaochow to China as soon as possible. It was hoped that this diplomatic pressure would redress the main shortcoming of the Versailles settlement for East Asia, namely the absence from the treaty of any specified date by which Japan would return Kiaochow to China. The American Senate's rejection of the Versailles treaty and China's refusal to negotiate with Japan spoiled this particular line of approach. But eventually by the Sino-Japanese treaty of February 1922, signed in Washington at the time of the international conference there, Japan gave up the lease of Kiaochow.

But there was one other gain which the Japanese reaped at Paris, the less tangible one of international prestige. When their chief delegate, Prince Saionji, returned to Tokyo in August, he presented the Emperor with an account of his stewardship which contains the following assessment of Japan's world position: 'the influence of the present conference on Japan's standing among the Powers will be very great; Japan now stands among the five great Powers in the world and has been allowed to take a share in the affairs of Europe; she has been granted an important place in the League of Nations and has acquired the right to become involved more and more in future in every aspect of affairs between east and west; it can be said that Japan is now entering a new period in her history.' If Japan's positive gains from the Paris settlement were short-lived, she gained immensely in international prestige.

Further Reading
Fifield, R. H., *Woodrow Wilson and the Far East: the diplomacy of the Shantung Question* (Hamden Conn: Archon 1965)
Hankey, M., *The Supreme Control at the Paris Peace Conference, 1919* (George Allen & Unwin 1963)
Nish, I. H., *Alliance in Decline* (Athlone Press, forthcoming)

[*For Ian Nish's biography, see page 319.*]

THE «CAT'S WHISKERS»
The Ultimate Aircraft of WWI

Had the war continued into 1919, there would have doubtless been great advances in the technology of war, but none so much as in aeronautics. By 1918, the Germans and the Allies had made enormous strides in basic design, engine power and in structures and materials

Double page, top: The classic two-seater of the First World War, the Bristol F2B fighter. The photograph shows four F2B's of 22 Squadron taking off in France in June 1918. *This page, top:* The Vickers FB 27 Vimy bomber, destined for a great future in 1919. *Centre left:* The Pfalz D XII fighter. Though overshadowed by the remarkable Fokker D VII, the D XII was nevertheless an excellent machine. *Above:* The Junkers CL I ground attack fighter, whose advanced features included cantilever monoplane wings and a metal skin. The gunner had a good field of fire and the pilot two machine guns, compared with the more standard one of most such machines. *Left:* The ultimate in the Sopwith stable of rotary-engined fighters, the 7F I Snipe. *Opposite page, top left:* The Junkers D I fighter, of which the CL I was a scaled-up version. This was the world's first all-metal service warplane, and proved very nimble and strong. *Top right:* The Pfalz D XV was fast and scheduled for large production in 1919. Note the fuselage mounted between the wings and the lack of exterior wires. *Centre left:* The Nieuport 29C 1 fighter. It was very fast (143 mph at sea level) and the first Nieuport fighter to have a stationary engine. *Centre right:* The Siemens-Schuckert D VI experimental fighter, featuring a parasol wing and a jettisonable belly tank for its fuel. *Bottom:* The Martinsyde F 4 fighter, the fastest Allied fighter of the war at 145 mph

Top: The **Bristol F2B** reconnaissance fighter. *Engine:* Rolls-Royce Falcon III, 275 hp. *Armament:* one fixed Vickers and one or two free Lewis guns plus 12 20-lb bombs. *Speed:* 123 mph at 5,000 ft. *Climb:* 11 mins 15 secs to 10,000 ft. *Ceiling:* 21,500 ft. *Endurance:* 3 hours. *Weight empty/loaded:* 1,934/2,779 lbs. *Span:* 39 ft 3 ins. *Length:* 25 ft 10 ins. *Above:* The **Siemens-Schuckert D IV** fighter, which had an incredible rate of climb. *Engine:* Siemens-Halske Sh IIIa, 200 hp. *Armament:* two Spandau machine guns. *Speed:* 119 mph. *Climb:* 13 mins to 16,400 ft. *Ceiling:* 26,240 ft. *Endurance:* 2 hrs. *Weight empty/loaded:* 1,190/1,620 lbs. *Span:* 27 ft 4¾ ins. *Length:* 18 ft 8½ ins

THE «CAT'S WHISKERS» The Ultimate Aircraft of WWI

Above: The **Fokker D VIII** fighter, possessed of good performance and quite outstanding manoeuvrability. *Engine:* Oberursel U II, 110 hp. *Armament:* two Spandau machine guns. *Speed:* 127½ mph at sea level. *Climb:* 10¾ mins to 13,120 ft. *Ceiling:* 19,680 ft. *Endurance:* 1½ hours. *Weight empty/loaded:* 893/1,334 lbs. *Span:* 27 ft 4⅜ ins. *Length:* 19 ft 2¾ ins.
Below: The **Handley Page V/1500** heavy bomber. *Engines:* four Rolls-Royce Eagle VIII, 375 hp each. *Armament:* up to five Lewis guns and 7,500 lbs of bombs. *Speed:* 97 mph at 8,750 ft. *Climb:* 18½ mins to 6,500 feet. *Ceiling:* 10,000 ft. *Endurance:* 14 hours. *Weight empty/loaded:* 16,210/29,230 lbs. *Span:* 126 ft. *Length:* 62 ft. By the end of the war, only three of these huge 'Berlin bombers' had been built, with three more by the end of the year

John Batchelor

ARABS

at the Peace Conference: Misgivings and Disillusion

The Arabs could not hope to achieve Arab unity on the strength of their own influence. They had to depend on the support of their allies — and it seemed that British and French altruism was not to be relied on. *Suleiman Mousa. Below:* Feisal and Lloyd George, with Allenby on the left, in London, 1919

During the First World War, the Arabs believed that the day which would see the setting of the Ottoman sun would also see the rising of the powerful Arab state to which they aspired. They relied on their natural right, on the pledges of Great Britain and on the principle of self-determination which was upheld by President Woodrow Wilson, which had greatly impressed their leaders.

As early as May 1917, Mark Sykes had informed Sherif Hussein that the administration of liberated territories would be 'according to the choice of the people'. And when General Allenby met Feisal at Damascus on October 3, 1918, he informed him that France and Great Britain had 'agreed to recognise the belligerent status of the Arab forces fighting in Palestine and Syria as allies against the common enemy'. Two weeks later, Allenby gave Feisal an official assurance that the Arabs would be represented at the Peace Conference and that 'the Allies are in honour bound to endeavour to reach a settlement in accord-

ance with the wishes of the peoples concerned'. Finally, there came the Declaration of November 7, 1918 in which Great Britain and France asserted that their object was 'the complete independence and definite emancipation of the peoples so long oppressed by the Turks, and the establishment of national governments and administrations deriving their authority from the initiative and free choice of the indigenous populations'.

Hopes and fears
In spite of these promises, however, the Arabs were torn between confidence in and fear of the future when the Armistice with Germany was concluded. Their fears were based on the fact that the British army was occupying Iraq, Palestine and Syria, and the French army the Syrian littoral.

Early in November, both Wingate (High Commissioner in Egypt) and Allenby recommended to their government that Sherif Hussein be invited to send a representative to the Peace Conference. Both

Press Association

recommended that Feisal should be that representative. Allenby added in his telegram that the 'Arabs trust implicitly in Great Britain. All confidence in good faith of Allies will be destroyed if our pledges are not kept'.

For some reason, T. E. Lawrence was given the privilege of conveying the message of invitation to Sherif Hussein, over the heads of both Wingate and Allenby. On November 10, Hussein received Lawrence's telegram inviting him in the name of the British government to send someone to represent him at Paris, with the recommendation that Feisal be charged with the mission. Hussein accepted and telegraphed Feisal in Aleppo, instructing him to proceed to Paris 'as a representative of Arab interests'. Hussein impressed upon Feisal the necessity of confining his discussions to British statesmen, on the ground that the Arabs were bound to Great Britain alone, and that Great Britain was responsible for safeguarding their interests.

Feisal left Syria for Europe, intending to offer the British government a treaty of alliance with the Arabs 'on condition that there be no connection with any other foreign power'. In return, the Arabs would give Britain preferential treatment in economic matters and would ask Britain to provide them with advisers, technicians, finance and arms on condition that the Arabs would enjoy full sovereignty and that they would not by doing this lose any degree of their independence.

During the war the feeling had grown among the Arabs that Britain was their natural ally, and at the same time they distrusted France, whose direct rule in North Africa, compared with the British style of indirect rule in Egypt, aroused their fears of French colonialism. Behind the insistence of the Arabs that their connection be with Britain only lay this fear of French ambitions. Feisal had established an Arab administration in the interior of Syria, but the French prevented him from extending it to the coast. The Arabs were intent on safeguarding their portion and extending their administration, while the French did not conceal their intention of controlling the interior of Syria on the lines of the Sykes-Picot Agreement.

Feisal arrived in France towards the end of November, at the head of a delegation of nationalists. A French delegation met Feisal and informed him that their government welcomed him as a distinguished guest and a comrade-in-arms, but did not recognise that he had any diplomatic status or that he was on an official mission. The French view was that the Allied Powers had never recognised an Arab kingdom and that, therefore, Feisal could represent only the Hejaz and not the Arab nation. The British government disagreed with this view and informed the French that they regarded Feisal 'as the representative of our co-belligerent and ally King Hussein sent to be present in Paris during the discussions of the Peace Conference to voice and look after his father's interests'.

Feisal spent two weeks in France, during which he did not take part in any political discussions. He left for London on December 10 and, on the following day, held a meeting with Mr Balfour, the Secretary of State for Foreign Affairs. He informed Mr Balfour that the Arabs wished to have connections with one Power only, namely Great Britain, and that they ex-

pected Britain's help in attaining this, especially as they saw France bent on 'swallowing up' the whole of Syria. Balfour replied that Great Britain wished to tear up the Sykes-Picot Agreement, but would prefer this to be done by the Peace Conference.

The desire to be free
On the eve of the Conference, Feisal left London for Paris, confidently relying on Britain and President Wilson. The Arabs at that time were only one of several weak nations that pinned their faith to the Wilsonian ideals and the principle of self-determination. On arriving in Paris, Feisal submitted a memorandum to the Allied Powers, requesting them to recognise him as the representative of the Arabs at the Conference. The French objected, but as a result of British support, the Allied Supreme Council (Great Britain, France, the United States of America, Italy and Japan) decided that the Arabs should be represented by two members. This episode strengthened Feisal's belief that the British were the real friends of the Arabs.

On January 30, 1919, the Allied Powers took an important decision by which Asian Arab countries were separated from Turkey and provisionally recognised as 'independent nations'. This recognition was made 'subject to rendering of administrative advice and assistance by a mandatory power until such a time as they are able to stand alone'. The decision stipulated that the 'wishes of these communities must be a principal consideration in selection of the mandatory power'.

On January 31, Feisal submitted another memorandum to the Peace Conference, in which he asked for recognition of the independence of all the Arabic speaking countries in Asia. Feisal based his demand on
- the ability of the inhabitants;
- the Arabic language;
- natural boundaries;
- the Semitic race;
- identity of economic interests; and
- the Arab effort during the War.
He informed the Conference that the Arabs would agree to Lebanon's independence. On Palestine, he said 'in view of its universal importance, I leave the question for the time being to the discretion of those concerned'.

Feisal presented the Arab case to the Supreme Council on February 6. He concluded his speech by saying 'We Arabs have tasted tyranny for so long . . . Our hearts are bleeding . . . We desire to be free, to live in peace and security . . . For these reasons, we do not accept the partition of our country, but want it to be united and independent.' Feisal asked that the big powers send a commission to ascertain the wishes of the inhabitants regarding their future government. President Wilson proposed on March 20 that an Allied commission of inquiry should be sent to Syria. Lloyd George agreed, but Clemenceau made his acceptance conditional on the inquiry being extended to include Palestine and Iraq. As a result, the British attempted to bring about an accord between Feisal and France. Feisal had several discussions with Clemenceau, but he refused to accept a French mandate for Syria. No progress was achieved and Feisal left Paris for Damascus, which he reached early in May.

The Arabs pinned their faith on the Commission, in the belief that the Allied Powers would be obliged to respect its findings. Above all, they trusted in the disinterested support of President Wilson. Feisal, however, approached the French again and held discussions with George Picot during May and June. He sought the support of France for the establishment of an Arab administration in a unified Syria, offering to cooperate with France in matters of finance and technical advice. He also sought French support for the unification of Palestine, Syria and Mosul, and for the obtaining of independence for Iraq. Apparently the French did not favour these proposals, while Feisal was still hoping to obtain 'a recognition of complete and unfettered independence'.

The political fight for Syria was the touchstone for determining the relationship between France, Great Britain and the Arabs. The Arabs were mainly concerned in preserving the unity which they had had under the Ottoman Turks. On May 24, their delegation to the Peace Conference stated that the Arabs wished 'that the whole of the Arab speaking countries should be placed under one mandatory and not divided up amongst two or three'. The answer of the head of the British delegation was that placing all the Arabs 'under one mandatory would be an almost impossible burden for the Power that was charged with it'.

During the meetings of the Council of Four on May 21 and 22, the question of the Commission of Inquiry was discussed. Clemenceau accused Lloyd George of breaking faith and declared that he would not send the French representatives 'to make an inquiry under the dictatorship of General Allenby'. The French Premier threatened that if the British representatives were sent to Syria before the withdrawal of British troops 'he would no longer associate with the British in this part of the world because the harm done to his country was too great'. Lloyd George immediately backed down and announced that he would not send his representatives if the French did not send theirs. The Italians followed suit, and it remained for the Americans to go alone.

Towards the end of May a Syrian Congress was convened to voice the public opinion of geographic Syria. At the same time President Wilson ordered the American members of the Commission to proceed, and they arrived in Palestine on June 10. Their arrival raised the hopes of the Arabs, who were still thinking that they might avoid British and French designs through American intervention. The Commission spent six weeks touring Palestine, Syria and Lebanon, meeting delegations and receiving petitions. On July 3, the Syrian Congress submitted to the Commission a resolution demanding the following concessions:
● recognition of the complete political independence of geographic Syria and Iraq;
● technical and economic assistance from the United States of America and, if she was unwilling, from Great Britain. French assistance was rejected; and
● rejection of Zionist claims in Palestine.

On July 10, the Commissioners sent a telegram to the Peace Conference, stating that they found 'intense desire for unity of all Syria and Palestine and for as early independence as possible'. With the exception of strong parties of Lebanese, they found determination 'against any kind of French mandate'.

After completing their tour, the Commissioners returned to Paris and handed over their report to the American delegation. But the report had no influence on the final settlement. It happened that the Americans soon afterwards refused to ratify the Versailles Treaty and followed a policy of isolation, while Italy had its own ambitions in other territories. Thus the door was left open to Great Britain and France to settle the question of the Arab countries to their own advantage.

The British change their ground

The Arab demand for the independence of Palestine and Iraq, and the lack of American support for Feisal, pushed British policy gradually nearer to the French viewpoint. We can find an indication of this trend in British policy in a telegram Lord Curzon sent to General Clayton on June 24, 1919, in which he stated that the 'spread into Mesopotamia of Feisal's propaganda for the complete independence of Arabia is causing considerable apprehension here and at Baghdad'.

Two days later (June 26) Balfour suggested that Syria be placed under French mandate, Iraq under British mandate and Palestine under American or British mandate. On August 11, Balfour recommended upholding the Sykes-Picot Agreement and Zionist policy in Palestine, on the grounds that Zionism was 'of far profounder import than the desires and prejudices of the 700,000 Arabs who now inhabit that ancient land'. Balfour added that he did not think 'that Zionism will hurt the Arabs'.

The final turning-point came in September when Lloyd George ignored his country's commitments to the Arabs and met the wishes of the French. The new trend in British policy materialised in a decision taken on September 10 to withdraw British troops from Syria and to hand over the Syrian interior to the Arabs, and the Syrian littoral to the French. Lloyd George informed those who were with him that Clemenceau had promised that the British should have the mandate for Palestine. It was, however, claimed that the British government by this decision would be able to meet 'its obligations, both to the French government and to the Arab State'. We may suppose that preliminary discussions between the British and French governments took place before the decision of withdrawal was taken. News of these discussions leaked out and must have reached the Arab delegation in Paris, who sent a memorandum to the British delegation on September 10 warning against 'deals' and 'arrangements' at the expense of the people concerned.

At the insistence of Allenby, Lloyd George invited Feisal to come to Paris at once, so that he might be informed in person of the new development. But before Feisal received the message, Lloyd George had delivered to Clemenceau, on September 13, an aide-mémoire, justifying the British decision on the grounds of American indecision regarding the mandates for Ottoman territories and the inability of the British to maintain an army of over 400,000 men to garrison those territories. On September 15, Lloyd George handed over copies of his aide-mémoire to the members of the Supreme Council. This document stated that British troops would commence the evacuation of Syria and Cilicia on November 1, and that these troops would remain in Palestine and Iraq. The Supreme Council took note of the arrangement, considering it a temporary measure which would not affect the final settlement of the mandates or frontiers. However, in his reply to the aide-mémoire, Clemenceau stated that the Sykes-Picot Agreement should be the only basis of understanding between Great Britain and France, that the position of France in Syria should be analogous to the position of Britain in Iraq, that France was prepared to give up Mosul and Palestine in return for similar concessions on the part of the British, that France was prepared to negotiate with Feisal if the British ceased to protect him and that France considered Britain's promise to uphold Feisal's independence in the Syrian interior as direct interference conflicting with the terms of the French mandate for Syria.

On receiving Lloyd George's telegram, Feisal sailed for Europe. At Marseilles, he was informed by a French officer that the French government had nothing to discuss with him and that, therefore, he had better go direct to London. Feisal arrived in London on September 18. He remained there for more than a month, during which he had several meetings with Lloyd George, Curzon and other British statesmen. Feisal tried to persuade the British to support the unity of the Arab countries instead of dividing them between two Powers. He even offered to accept French assistance exclusively in Iraq, Syria and Palestine. When this was rejected, he tried to persuade the British to delay their withdrawal until the Peace Conference decided on the final settlement. But the British held fast to their original decision and tried in turn to convince Feisal that the arrangement was a temporary measure. Feisal later suggested the cancellation of the Paris arrangement so that the Peace Conference might discuss the Syrian question and arrive at a final settlement, but Lloyd George refused to entertain this proposal and advised Feisal to go to Paris and endeavour to reach an understanding with the French.

There was no alternative left to Feisal. It was very clear that the withdrawal of the British meant, sooner or later, a clash with the French. The Arabs were not strong enough to fight the French successfully. It was his duty as a leader to reach a direct settlement with the French, especially as he felt that the Peace Conference and his British Allies had abandoned him. Feisal went to Paris, troubled and disgusted, but determined to explore all possibilities for a peaceful settlement. He sent a memorandum to Clemenceau, explaining his concern about the division of Syria and demanding the withdrawal of both French and British troops from the whole of the country. Feisal sought also the support of the American delegation, but the United States withdrew from the Peace Conference during November 1919 (as a result of the refusal of Congress to ratify the Versailles Treaty). As a result, Feisal lost the support on which he was counting.

On November 9 Clemenceau wrote to Lloyd George, thanking him for abandoning Feisal and saying that in future 'the Peace Conference will have nothing to do but to sanction our agreement for the

French mandate in Syria and the British mandate in Mesopotamia'.

Feisal was convinced more than at any time before that there was no alternative but to reach a settlement with the French. The outcome was a draft agreement, dated January 6, 1920, which stated that France would guarantee the independence of Syria and grant her assistance, and that Syria would accept French advisers and grant France absolute preference in business contracts and financial loans, in addition to recognising the political separation of the Lebanon. In deference to instructions from his father, Feisal did not sign the agreement but promised to urge the Syrians to accept it.

The sense of betrayal

When Feisal returned to Damascus in the middle of January 1920, he found that the political situation had changed considerably. There was bitterness, disappointment and frustration. *Le Temps* had published the outline of the draft agreement, the terms of which had aroused the indignation of public opinion in Damascus. Feisal himself was not happy with the 'agreement' and confided to a British officer that it was 'largely distasteful to him, and would be unpopular with his people but that the attitude of the British authorities gave him no choice and that he had been tied by feet and hands to the French'.

Feisal informed the Syrian leaders of the developments in the attitudes of Great Britain and France. He declared that 'Britain had abandoned us at the last moment to satisfy her ally, France', and that the proposed agreement with Clemenceau 'makes France an ally who guarantees the independence and unity of Syria, both in the interior and the littoral, with the exception of Mount Lebanon'. There was little response to this attempt to present France as a friend, and the French did not make matters easy for Feisal, because General Gouraud wanted to enter

RESULT OF TREATY OF SAN REMO, 1920
BRITISH MANDATE
FRENCH MANDATE

Above: The Arabs wanted a single Allied power to have the mandate over all the Arab countries. The solution was, as they had feared, that the mandate was split between Britain and France, with Syria going to France. *Below:* The Arab delegates to the Paris Peace Conference with their advisers. In front, the Emir Feisal with, left to right behind him, Mohammed Rustum Bey Haider of Baalbek; Brigadier-General Nuri Pasha Said; Captain Pisani; Colonel Lawrence; Captain Hassan Bey Kadri. Feisal found out the hard way that he could not trust the Allies

Damascus as a conqueror and Millerand, the new French Premier, was much less liberal than his predecessor, Clemenceau, had been.

Feisal was in a difficult position. On one hand, his father and the Syrian extremists wanted nothing short of complete independence while, on the other, French intransigence gave him no chance to convince his father and the nationalists of the benefits of a peaceful settlement. The extremists carried the day and the Syrian Congress proclaimed him, on March 8, 1920, King of geographic Syria.

The British government was surprised at this new development, and Lord Curzon informed Feisal that Great Britain and France did not recognise the decisions taken by the Damascus Congress and considered them 'null and void'. He urged him to return to Europe to place his case before the Peace Conference. Feisal replied that 'recognition of the principle of independence and United Syria', by Great Britain would enable him to go to Europe. Curzon replied that there should be no difficulty in recognising Feisal as the representative of the Arab peoples of Syria and Palestine, provided that he came 'to the Peace Conference with corresponding recognition of the special position of France in Syria and Lebanon and the British in Palestine, the latter including an obligation to provide a national home for Zionists in that country'.

Feisal was not prepared to accept these conditions, nor were the British and French governments ready to accept the Arab demands. The situation remained unsettled until the Supreme Council of the Allied Powers met at San Remo on April 18, 1920. Great Britain, France, Italy and Japan were represented at the Conference, but not the United States. On April 24, Great Britain and France signed an agreement on the Mosul oilfields by which France obtained a share of 25%. On the next day, the Conference decided on the distribution of mandates. The Allied Powers gave themselves the authority to select the mandatory power, and France was given the mandate for Syria (including Lebanon) and Great Britain was given the mandate for Iraq and Palestine. The Conference based its decisions on Article 22 of the Covenant of the League of Nations without, however, consulting the populations concerned as the same article stipulated. The San Remo decisions came as an affirmation of the secret agreements concluded during the War, as a co-ordination of the military occupation, and as the result of the political bargaining which began at the end of the war. The new system of mandates was, as Lloyd George himself said, no more than 'a substitute for old Imperialism'.

The relations between the Syrians and the French continued to deteriorate. Early in July Feisal decided to go to France for further discussions, but the French had by then decided to impose their will by force. On July 25, the troops of General Gouraud occupied Damascus after a sharp battle with the Syrians the day before.

That was how the Arabs discovered that the Peace Conference of Paris was merely a platform for delivering speeches, under cover of which the great powers acted with no concern for anything except self-interest. The experience of the Arabs in the Peace Conference was a bitter one and, when Damascus was lost to the French troops, the Arabs finally lost their faith in the platitudes of western civilisation. They realised that rights would be lost if not supported by strength, and that, in matters of justice, the strong did not see eye to eye with the weak.

Further Reading
Mousa, Suleiman, *The Arab Movement 1908-1924* (Beirut: Dar al-Nahar 1970)
Nevakivi, Jukka, *Britain, France and the Arab Middle East 1914-1920* (London: Athlone Press 1969)
Zeine, Zeine N., *The Struggle for Arab Independence* (Beirut: Khayat's 1960)

[*For Suleiman Mousa's biography see page 2407.*]

BRITAIN, INDIA AND THE AMRITSAR MASSACRE

In the atmosphere of spreading violence, which was a paradoxical though understandable consequence of Gandhi's campaign of passive resistance, the British in India were uncertain whether they faced insurrection or merely unrest. It was difficult to decide how firmly to deal with the situation. In this atmosphere an over-reaction like General Dyer's, apart from the appalling carnage which it caused, could start a revolution. *Michael Edwardes. Right:* Brigadier-General R. E. H. Dyer. *Below:* The ill-fated Jallianwala Bagh

The end of the war in November 1918 brought, for the combatants, a sense of release, and, for the victors, hopes of that better world for which, it was alleged, the war had actually been fought. But for those Indians—and there were many—who had shared such hopes, the peace brought with it unease, anger, and fear of what the future held in store. Four years previously, the declaration of war against Germany had been greeted in India with an outburst of loyalty and enthusiasm. Indian politicians, whom the British believed wanted only to undermine the *raj,* vied with each other in voicing 'their feelings of unswerving loyalty and enthusiastic devotion to their King-Emperor and . . . their unflinching support to the British Government'. But as the war dragged on, loyalty eroded and enthusiasm seeped away, leaving behind resentment and discontent. The war years gave Indians a new view of the realities of the world outside India which radically altered their attitude to Europe and its peoples. In particular, they learned to measure their British rulers against a new set of values—and found them wanting.

The Indian response to the declaration of war caught the British by surprise. The government of India, unused to displays of popularity, accepted the tribute and did nothing about it except call for recruits to fight overseas. The government in London, concerned only with the prosecution of the war, issued a number of vaguely promising statements about the possibility of political reforms—after the war was over. Indian nationalists believed, for a time at least, that in return for India's whole-hearted support for the war effort of the Empire, there would be tangible rewards in terms of a substantial measure of self-government within the Imperial system. They were supported in this belief by the praise lavished upon the services of Indian troops and India's financial contribution to the cost of the war. The praise was more than justified. In the autumn of 1914 an Indian Army corps had been sent to France to fill the gap until 'Kitchener's Army' could take the field. When Turkey entered the war on October 1914, Indian troops garrisoned the Suez Canal and drove off a Turkish attack. Later, Indian troops served in Macedonia and German East Africa and, above all, played a vital rôle in the campaigns in Iraq which led to the capture of Baghdad in 1917. They formed part of the Allied army that entered Jerusalem in the same year, and swept on to victory in 1918. India supplied over 1,200,000 volunteers for the armed forces, three-quarters of them combatants. It was obvious to all thinking Indians that, without India, the position of the Allies would have been considerably weakened, particularly in the Middle East.

But, like the Allies themselves, Indians had expected a short war, quick victory and large rewards. As the war dragged on without any precise commitments from the British government on political reform, the old suspicions re-emerged. As early as March 1915, when the House of Lords rejected a proposal for the creation of an executive council in the largest of the Indian provinces, it seemed that—if this was the attitude of British legislators towards Indians during the war, when their support was needed and appreciated—what would it be like after the war was over? 'They have been paying us high and extremely flattering compliments upon our loyalty and devotion to the British Crown,' said an Indian member of the Imperial Legislative Council, 'and yet in the same breath they tell us that we are in such a backward and primitive condition that even an executive council would be too good for us.'

The war, too, was having its material effect. Increasing pressure on the Indian economy led to inflation and steeply rising prices. Controls antagonised Indian businessmen and made them look more favourably on the demands of the nationalists. By 1917 these demands were being so forcibly expressed that the British government finally decided that some gesture must be made to appease them, especially since the collapse of Britain's ally, Tsarist Russia, seemed imminent. The result was a visit to India in October by Montagu, the Secretary of State for India.

The demand for reforms

The political scene presented to Montagu was one which showed all levels of opinion united behind a demand for self-government. The principal nationalist movement, the Indian National Congress, was now led by men who no longer asked for concessions but demanded rights. For the first time, nationalism also displayed a united front against the British. In 1916, Congress and the Muslim League had come together in what was called the Lucknow Pact. This alliance, which would have been unthinkable a year before, had come about because of growing Muslim unease over the war with Turkey, whose sultan was also the Caliph of Islam—the spiritual and temporal leader of the whole Muslim community. Fears that Congress, dominated as it was by Hindus, would discriminate against Muslims once it achieved self-government were softened by an agreement that Congress would no longer oppose separate electorates for Muslims under any new reforms that might be won.

There were many indications that substantial reforms would, after all, be granted. Before Montagu's visit, the British government had announced that changes were being considered 'with a view to the progressive realisation of responsible government in India'. The general climate, too, seemed to be in India's favour. While Montagu was in India, Russia, now in the hands of the Bolshevik revolutionaries, signed a separate peace with Germany. The overthrow of Tsarist tyranny appeared to be a triumph for liberalism. In Indian eyes, Russian and British despotism were often equated. If one despotism could fall, why not the other? An even more significant event followed the entry of the USA into the war. In January 1918 President Wilson enunciated his 14 Points. 'National freedom' and 'self-determination of peoples' were phrases which conjured up visions of a new world for the war-weary and the disillusioned. Britain had promised reforms in the spirit of the fundamental principles accepted by the Allies. Surely America would see that those promises were kept. The Indian image of Europe as

Above: Hall Gate, Amritsar, one of the gates encircling the centre of the town. *Right:* Bazaar leading to Jallianwala Bridge. It was impossible for the large crowd which collected in the Bagh to escape through the narrow streets and alleys surrounding it—those inside were mown down and the exits closed

India Office Library

India Office Library

be confined to provincial governments, while the central authority remained unchanged. Also criticised was an extension of the principle of separate electorates, which was now to include not only the large minority Muslim community, but the comparatively minute minorities of Indian Christians, Eurasians and Europeans. It seemed, on the whole, to be a classic example of 'divide and rule'. To add to Indian suspicions, it was soon made clear that though it would take years to implement the reforms, only months were needed to enact legislation giving the government of India the powers advocated in the Rowlatt report.

The passage of the security laws early in 1919 created widespread indignation. Even the government of India recognised its cause, and the powers were, in fact, never used. But the damage had been done. The government, like the Bourbons, had learned nothing. Neither, it appeared, had those British administrators who returned from war service with the conviction that they merely had to take up where they had left off. The frustration of the political classes and the economic distress of the masses united the Indian people as never before in a desire for change. Yet the old methods of protest no longer seemed relevant. The moderate approach, so much like that of a 'loyal opposition', had failed to change the nature of government. Terrorism, which in the early part of the century had seemed the road to revolution, had resulted only in oppression. In any case, such methods were confined to sophisticated minorities. What was needed was some new form of protest, and one that would provide the widest popular base for the expression of nationalist demands. The answer came from a 49-year-old lawyer named Mohandas Karamchand Gandhi.

Gandhi's reputation, such as it then was, was as a moderate in politics—even a loyalist, for in the latter stages of the war he had helped in recruiting campaigns for the Indian army. His political activities had not been in India at all but in South

morally superior had been destroyed in the holocaust of war. The values of the world had changed for the better—and America was their guarantor.

This belief did not last for long, for it was soon made clear that the government of India did not share it. The war had not expanded the government's horizons beyond those of paternalist autocracy. Convincing itself that the unease of the times was a prelude to violence, the government of India set up a commission under Mr Justice Rowlatt to recommend measures against subversion. The report was published in April 1918. It proposed that judges be given power to try political cases without a jury, and provincial governors, the authority to intern suspects without

trial. The acceptance of these recommendations by the government took the gloss off the proposals for reform announced three months later.

The reforms were, in fact, radical both in substance and intent. The British government not only accepted the principle of self-government for India but actually prepared for it. There was to be a considerable enlargement of the electorate, popular representation, and ministerial responsibility. Indians, examining the proposals in the light of the Rowlatt report, ignored their radical content and criticised the fact that ultimate power still remained where it had always been—with the British. The handing over of certain responsibilities to elected Indian ministers was to

Africa, where he had organised a passive resistance movement against the restrictions placed on Indians there. But his moderation was a reflection of his belief in the virtues of non-violence, and his support for recruiting had emerged from his conviction that the discipline of army life would prepare Indians for the kind of struggle he had in mind. His loyalty to the British, therefore, was conditional and, in his terms, purposeful. Gandhi's judgement of actions and events was wholly moral; everything was measured against his concept of truth. The Rowlatt Acts offended against those standards, and he believed that they could and should be condemned — not merely in words, but certainly not with violence. Gandhi had learned in South Africa that the mobilising of mass passive resistance could bring intense pressure to bear upon a government which at least paid lip service, if no more, to human rights. But the situation in India was not the same as it had been in South Africa. There, a minority had suffered precise and mainly economic discrimination. In India the discrimination, though real, was difficult to define to the illiterate masses, especially when the Hindu religion enjoined acceptance of one's lot, however hard, as part of the divine order. Gandhi's technique was to give a religious colour to the form of protest he had decided to adopt.

The action Gandhi proposed was a *hartal*, a kind of strike in which shops and businesses close as a sign of mourning. A *hartal* was not just a negative affair but a positive rededication of the spirit. Those taking part would take a ritual bath in the sea or river, fast and pray. The *hartal* was to be followed by civil disobedience, which would be demonstrated by refusal to obey the law, though 'only such laws . . . as easily lent themselves to being disobeyed by the masses', such as the salt tax. March 30, 1919 was first fixed as the day, but the date was changed to April 6. The *hartal* began prematurely in Delhi with vast processions and some police firing, but on April 6 the whole of India observed the

call. For the first time the nationalist movement, once the preserve of the upper classes, acquired significant and impressive populist overtones.

But the movement lacked discipline and there were men anxious to direct mass protest into violence. Mobs attacked police stations in Bombay and Ahmedabad. When Gandhi appeared in Bombay the

crowd hailed him as *Mahatma* ('Great Soul') — and went on throwing stones. In Ahmedabad martial law was declared after a policeman was killed. Gandhi, horrified at the spread of violence, called off his campaign. But it was like ordering the fire to stop burning. The flames spread, most destructively in the Punjab. There, tensions ran particularly high. Thousands of demobilised soldiers had returned home to find only unemployment and no hope for the future. A terrible epidemic of influenza had killed off hundreds of thousands. Altogether in India more people died than the total number who were killed in the war. The authorities in the Punjab believed themselves menaced by rebellion and thought Gandhi's non-violent cam-

Opposite: Amritsar — the narrow passage through which General Dyer entered the Bagh. *Above:* A leader of a German mission which failed to turn the Afghan Emir Habibullah against the British is taken away in handcuffs. *Left:* The pro-German Emir Amanullah (second from right), son and successor of the murdered Habibullah. His hopeless attempt to invade British India was soon suppressed

paign was merely a camouflage. The British in the Punjab had a long tradition of instant and crushing response to any sign of disorder, real or imagined. The situation was ripe for an explosion. It took place on April 13, 1919 in the town of Amritsar.

Amritsar was — and still is — the holy city of the Sikhs, a people who supplied some of the toughest of soldiers to the Indian Army. On April 10 the authorities arrested two nationalist leaders in the city, and rioting followed. A large crowd tried to enter the civil lines, that part of the city occupied by Europeans, but was turned back by armed police. The mob then moved into the city itself, attacking two banks and murdering some of the European staff. The railway station was set on fire and a European was killed. In another part of the city a European woman missionary was set upon and left for dead. The situation was soon out of police control and the army was called in.

In command was Brigadier-General Dyer, an Irishman born and educated in India, with strong racial antipathies.

Arriving in Amritsar the day after the rioting, he immediately prohibited all public meetings. The proclamation was made at various points throughout the city, verbally. No written declaration was posted at any spot where it might be read by the citizens of Amritsar. Large numbers of people journeyed from the surrounding countryside for the annual horse fair on April 13 and it is unlikely that many of them had heard of General Dyer's proclamation. At one o'clock on that day, Dyer was told at his headquarters that a public meeting had been called for half-past four on a large piece of waste land known as the Jallianwala Bagh.

'Bagh' means a garden, but a place less like one would have been difficult to find. There were a few stunted trees and large quantities of refuse. The space, roughly a square and quite large, was completely enclosed by houses. Access from the surrounding streets was by four narrow entrances only wide enough to allow three or four people to walk abreast.

Dyer decided to wait until the crowd had collected and then to make an example of those who had defied the proclamation. At four o'clock he was informed that a crowd estimated at between 5,000 and 20,000 had gathered in the Bagh and was being addressed by agitators. Dyer, a stranger to Amritsar, had no idea what the Bagh was like and did not inquire. His purpose, apparently — for he later made conflicting statements on his intention — was to disperse the crowd by firing over the people's heads and driving them along with the aid of two armoured cars.

Panic in the 'garden'

Dyer did not expect much trouble in dispersing a mob from what he obviously thought to be an open space, for he took with him only 90 Gurkha and Baluchi soldiers. Forty of the Gurkhas carried only *kukris,* their traditional curved daggers. Arriving at the Bagh, Dyer discovered that the armoured cars could not pass through the entrances. Proceeding on foot, he saw a vast crowd being harangued by speakers whose words he could not hear but which he was convinced were incitements to violence. Dyer undoubtedly panicked. He ordered his men to fire without warning directly into the crowd. As it broke, children were trampled underfoot, some women threw themselves down wells, men trying desperately to climb the walls were picked off as they did so. Using up all his ammunition — 1,650 rounds in all — Dyer withdrew, ordering the entrances to be blocked so that none could escape and no medical attention reach the wounded inside. Officially, 397 were killed and over 1,500 wounded.

Dyer went away from the massacre believing, or so he claimed later, that he had saved the Punjab from bloody revolution. His behaviour was supported and approved of by the provincial governor and, when they heard about it, by most of the British in India. But Dyer's action did not bring order to Amritsar. On April 15 martial law was declared and not lifted until June 9. During that period a number of punitive measures and humiliating orders were implemented by the army and the police. Anyone passing through the street where the woman missionary had been attacked was forced to crawl on all fours or be tied to a post and whipped. Public floggings were imposed for 'the contravention of the curfew order, failure to salaam to a commissioned officer, for disrespect to a European' and even for refusal to sell milk. By these methods the Punjab was subdued, and General Dyer went off to the Afghan war to the sound of praise from his fellow countrymen. As for Indians, the implications of what had taken place in the Punjab were not immediately realised. Strict censorship prevented much of the detail from swiftly reaching other parts of India. Everyone knew that the Punjab had a long history of violence, and the Punjab administration pointed to the trouble on the North-West Frontier as justification for its actions.

Through the Khyber Pass

It was true that the frontier situation was serious, and the government had no way of knowing that the Third Afghan War would turn out such a curiously abortive affair. For the first time in British-Indian history the Afghans were the aggressors. In February 1919 the pro-British ruler of Afghanistan, the Emir Habibullah, was murdered, and his successor, Amanullah — in order to divert attention from his seizure of the throne and to consolidate his position with those Afghans who had hated Habibullah's neutral attitude during the war — ordered Afghan troops to attack British India. The most direct threat came down the Khyber Pass. The initial British response was no masterpiece of military science, and a breakdown in medical services resulted in many deaths. But of two

actions fought at Bagh Springs on May 9 and 11, the second was a British victory, and troops pushing through the Khyber Pass soon threatened Jalalabad.

In the Kurram Valley a British force besieged by some 4,000 tribesmen in the fort at Thal was relieved by General Dyer on June 1. The Afghan commander, Nadir Khan, asking for a truce, received from Dyer the message: 'My guns will give an immediate reply.' Nadir Khan fled, abandoning his camp and supplies. On the southern front, the second strongest fort in Afghanistan, Spin Baldak, was taken on May 26 with the loss of 400 Afghans and 58 British. Amanullah had not realised the great technical changes that had taken place in warfare over the years of conflict in Europe. The British used aircraft and radio, the former with tremendous moral rather than material effect. When one lone—and obsolete—Handley Page aircraft appeared over the Afghan capital of Kabul and scored four direct hits on the ruler's palace, Amanullah's nerve gave way and he sued for peace. An armistice was agreed on June 3 and peace signed on August 8.

The Third Afghan War passed almost unnoticed in India. Its effect was mainly upon the behaviour of the frontier tribes, and the end of the war itself was followed by a number of punitive expeditions and a revision of frontier policies. One ripple, however, reached the hill station of Mussooree, where a comparatively unknown nationalist named Jawaharlal Nehru, staying fortuitously in the same hotel as an Afghan delegation discussing details arising out of the peace treaty, was visited by a superintendent of police. Nehru was asked to give an undertaking that he would not contact the delegation, refused—on principle only, as he had no intention of meeting the Afghans—and was ordered to leave the district within 24 hours.

During the Afghan War, the facts and the implications of the Amritsar affair had slowly leaked out, but it was not until

October 1919 that liberal opinion in Britain convinced the government that there should be an inquiry. A commission of four Indians and four Europeans presided over by a judge, Lord Hunter, was appointed. The questions it raised were simple but sensational. Was an act of terrorism justified if it helped to preserve British rule? Was an Indian life equal in value to a European? The controversy raged for months and was only intensified when the commission's report was published in the spring of 1920. Dyer's action was condemned, but the measure of that condemnation showed that the commission was divided upon racial lines. Dyer, instead of pleading the exigencies of the times, had boasted that his purpose had been to make an example so terrifying that it would have a moral effect upon the rest of the country. In saying so, he seemed to be expressing the opinion of the majority of his countrymen, though the government of India immediately repudiated Dyer's view of the use of force. Dyer was compelled to leave the army—rather feeble punishment for what most Indians believed to have been a crime. Worse still were the way in which he was greeted as a maligned hero by Members of Parliament in Britain, and the heavy subscriptions made to a fund to mark appreciation of his services to the Empire.

It was this obviously racial partiality which gave Gandhi his chance to take control of the nationalist movement. Sensing the mood of the times he declared that, though Congress had been willing to work the new reforms before, now 'co-operation in any shape or form with this satanic government is sinful'. India, tense with emotion, responded not to a rational politician but to a visionary and a man of feeling. The Gandhian reign of 28 years had begun. Under his leadership, Congress boycotted the elections for the new assemblies in 1920 and these met without any representation of the largest Indian political movement. 'The shadow of Amritsar,'

said the Duke of Connaught, when he inaugurated the new legislatures in 1921, 'lengthened over the fair face of India.' It was not to be lifted until India became independent 26 years later.

Further Reading
Report of a Committee appointed to Investigate Revolutionary Conspiracies in India Cmd 9190—report of the Rowlatt Committee (HMSO 1918)
Report on Indian Constitutional Reforms Cmd 9109 (HMSO 1918)
Report of the Hunter Committee Cmd 681—Report of the Inquiry into the Amritsar Massacre (HMSO 1920)
Curtis, Lionel, *Dyarchy* (Oxford University Press 1921)
Edwardes, Michael, *Nehru: A Political Biography* (Allen Lane: The Penguin Press 1971)
Molesworth, Lt-Gen. G. N., *Afghanistan 1919* (London: Asia Publishing House 1963)
Montagu, Edwin, *An Indian Diary* (Heinemann 1930)
O'Dwyer, Sir Michael, *India as I Knew It* (Constable 1925)
Payne, Robert, *The Life and Death of Mahatma Gandhi* (The Bodley Head 1969)
Sitaramayya, P., *The History of the Indian National Congress* (Bombay: Indian National Congress 1946)

MICHAEL EDWARDES is the author of a number of books on Indian history, including *A History of India, The Last Years of British India,* and *Nehru: A Political Biography.* He is a frequent commentator on Asian affairs on both radio and television in Britain, and one of his books, *British India 1772-1947,* was adapted for a British television series. It was subsequently reissued in paperback as *Raj.*

Opposite: Surrender of the wartime German mission to Afghanistan. In the words of the *Illustrated London News,* 'The German mission was part of a plan to capture Central Asia, Afghanistan and Persia for Germany, under the cloak of Mohammedanism.' By doing this, Germany hoped both to enlarge her own empire and to harass the British. *Below:* Map of the town of Amritsar as it was on April 13, 1919

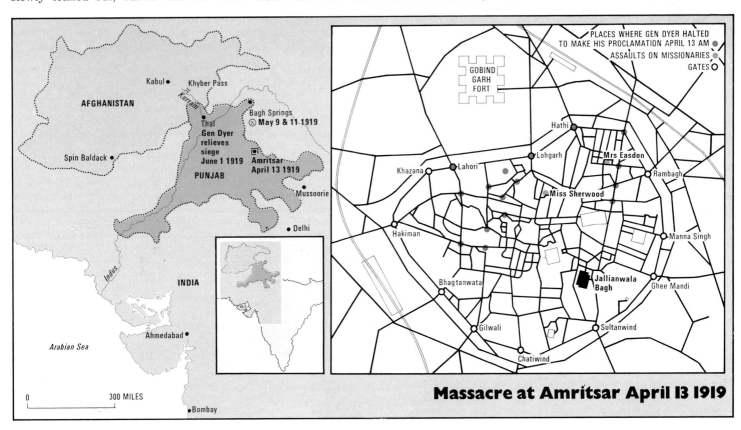

Massacre at Amritsar April 13 1919

GANDHI & THE ASIAN REVOLUTIONARIES

In Asia, by comparison with Europe, nationalism was a relatively new force during and after the First World War. As the peoples of the Indian and Far Eastern colonies gained confidence, single-minded political leaders emerged who were capable of concentrating the efforts of their supporters on one aim: self-government. *S. L. Mayer. Opposite, left to right:* Mahatma Gandhi, champion of the Indian people; Pandit Jawaharlal Nehru, Gandhi's disciple, and his successor as National Congress Party leader; Ho Chi Minh ('He who enlightens')

At the time of the Russo-Japanese War, Lord Curzon, the Viceroy of India, said, 'the reverberations of that victory have gone like a thunderclap through the whispering galleries of the East'. The myth of European invulnerability was broken. Throughout colonial Asia small groups of revolutionaries formed and began to organise nationalist movements. In India the Congress Party, whose ultimate aim was independence from the British *raj,* developed with a certain degree of success. When the First World War broke out many Indian nationalists saw this as a unique opportunity to gain concessions from the British which the British were not likely to make in peacetime.

From the collapse of the Indian mutiny in 1857-58, India had been politically stable and at peace. But toward the end of the 19th Century outbreaks of nationalist sentiment began to occur. From that point on the whole history of India was virtually the story of the conflict between the Indian National Congress, which comprised the main body of nationalist sentiment, and the constitutional concessions made by the British to pacify them. The Morley-Minto reforms represented the first major concession. Among other things they increased membership of the Central Legislative Council from 16 to 60, and of these, 27 were to be elected mainly from special interest groups, such as the enormous Muslim minority, which, for the first time, was officially recognised by the *raj* as the paramount special interest group. The reforms, as envisaged by Morley, '. . . were fundamentally designed to encourage support for the British régime, to create, in effect, that characteristically British institution, a Loyal Opposition'. Perhaps he should have said 'control the opposition', for loyal, in the fullest sense it was not and could not be. Nevertheless, when the First World War broke out Britain received a considerable degree of loyalty from many elements of Indian society.

There were, of course, those who attacked the Morley-Minto reforms from the outset. The moderate Indian leader, Gokhale, claimed that the reforms were a mere shadow of democratic government, which was a fair criticism. Nevertheless, the reforms did have a quieting effect upon many nationalists, and the outbreak of war brought a lull in the agitation. In fact, at the very start there was a burst of genuine pro-British enthusiasm. At the time most nationalists directed their demands toward achieving self-government within the British Empire. When the government asked for volunteers for the war effort, about 1,200,000 Indians answered the call, and many of these were to serve on various fronts, including the Western Front in France and Belgium as well as the Middle East. Voluntary contributions to war loans and other fund raising drives were also considerable. Ironically, two of the demands which nationalists had been making before 1914 were granted as a direct consequence of Britain's involvement in the war. They sought a reduction in British forces in India and higher promotion of Indians within the Civil Service. The exigencies of war forced the British to reduce their garrison to around 15,000 and the jobs of the many British administrators who fought in the war were filled by their Indian subordinates.

However, as the war continued, enthusiasm for the war effort waned and recruiting for the British army declined. This was partly a result of the government's inability to make use of its newly won popularity. Also the outbreak of the troubles in Ireland acted as an example to Indian nationalists. The concentration of British efforts in Europe and the Middle East led to increasing inefficiency within the Indian Empire. Restrictions were placed on Indian businessmen, and many drew the conclusion that in the interests of their own businesses, they ought to support the nationalist cause. In addition, the Indian forces in Mesopotamia encountered great difficulties in maintaining supply lines from India. This caused widespread dissatisfaction, even outside the ranks of those who were fighting. Another cause of dissent was that one of the Central Powers, the Ottoman Empire, was an Islamic state and, in fact, was the seat of the Caliphate. In 1916 the Muslim League was finally persuaded to join the Congress Party in the Lucknow Pact, which led to increased nationalist activity in India. Since no British troops could be spared to suppress these activities by force, persuasion was attempted.

Stepping into this increasingly dangerous set of circumstances was Mohandas K. Gandhi. In July 1914 his work in South Africa was finished, and although what he achieved there had no lasting effect on the position of Indians in South Africa, the struggle had already revealed his capacity for leadership and the potential of *satyagraha,* Gandhi's concept of non-violent resistance. After a stay in England, he returned to India, where his *satyagraha* campaign had aroused the keenest interest and admiration. He had already shown that his tactics could embarrass a modern, Western government, and his association with the indentured labourers had shown his capacity to win the hearts of the masses as well as a faithful élite who would act as his lieutenants. In South Africa he had above all acquired supreme self-confidence and a fanatical faith in the righteousness and practical uses of *satyagraha.* Upon his arrival in India in early 1915, Gandhi promised his political mentor, Gokhale, that he would spend a year travelling throughout India to gain experience, without expressing his political opinions.

Protector of the untouchables

This year, however, served to spread his already considerable popularity throughout the country and within nationalist circles. During that year he established an *ashram,* or hermitage, a centre of social and public service, near Ahmedabad, and allowed the so-called untouchables to the *ashram* even at the cost of losing financial support among his Brahmin followers and benefactors. Gandhi believed that handicraft and cottage industries, especially handloom weaving and hand-spinning of textiles, were a panacea for India's grinding poverty. He felt that this work would also combat idleness when villagers had little to do in the fields, and would supplement their meagre incomes. All of these notions became symbolic of the independence movement.

Soon after Gandhi's return to India, however, Gokhale died, which gave him his opportunity to gain control of the nationalist movements, and to put his *satyagraha* tactics into use at a time when outright repressive measures on the part of the British *raj* were becoming impractical. The difficulties of the tenant farmers of the Bihar indigo planters were the occasion for Gandhi's first conspicuous entrance on to the Indian political stage. Under the system then in force, the ten-

ants were required to plant indigo on 3/20ths of their land. The real grievances were the unlawful exactions and bullying by the landlords, both of which were widespread. When Gandhi entered Bihar to agitate against these practices he was treated by the authorities as an interfering busybody and was advised to leave at once. When he was served with an order to leave, he refused, and was therefore forced to stand trial for disobedience of a legal order. The trial gained considerable publicity; Gandhi pleaded guilty and read out a dignified statement to the magistrate explaining his reasons for having come to the district and for disobeying the order to leave it. The magistrate adjourned the case without passing judgement and before the date of the next hearing informed Gandhi that the case against him had been withdrawn by order of the provincial government. At the same time the collector of the district wrote to him saying that he was at liberty to conduct the inquiry which he had proposed and he could count on all the help he needed from local officials. The eventual outcome of this was the passing of legislation abolishing the system against which Gandhi had protested.

Those Indians who had considered Gandhi somewhat of a crank — and there were many — now took notice. They admired his resolute defiance of a foolish order, his systematic on-the-spot study of the peasants' grievances, and his readiness to face imprisonment. Among those who were impressed was Nehru, who was to become his chief aide in the years to come.

As Gandhi's fame spread from the Bihar episode, so, through Gandhi's agitation in his own region, the Gujarat, *satyagraha* began to take root in India. Through his actions he compelled the educated Indian élite to establish contact with the life of the peasantry and to work with them toward ultimate independence. 1917 saw the beginnings of a mass movement in India, and Gandhi's reputation within the country was firmly established. The outbreak of the Russian Revolution had the effect of enhancing Gandhi's power and encouraging the nationalist movement. And despite the ambivalence of the Muslims toward Turkey, the publication of Wilson's 14 Points created enthusiasm in nationalist circles and added fuel to the fire of opposition to Britain.

In the light of these developments, the British moved toward pacifying dissident elements. In August 1917 Edwin Montagu announced in the House of Commons that gradual development of self-governing institutions was well under way in India, and that this would lead to responsible government in India 'as an integral part of the British Empire'. Furthermore, Montagu announced that he was going to visit India for discussions with officials and representative members of the Indian community alike. This was the first time that a secretary of state had actually gone to India to seek out nationalist opinion on the spot. When he arrived, in October 1917, Montagu was received by some nationalists almost as a liberator.

Britain expresses her gratitude

The Montagu proposals, supported by Lord Chelmsford, the new Viceroy, were the great turning point in India's road toward self-government. Although bitterly opposed in the House of Lords, they showed Britain's gratitude for the support she had received in the war from much of the Indian population and from the troops who served so gallantly on several fronts. When the results of Montagu's inquiries were published in the summer of 1918, it still appeared that he had faith in India's ability to manage responsible self-government. Muslims still feared that representative government would submerge them, but to some extent these fears were calmed because in the Lucknow Pact Congress had agreed to separate Hindu and Muslim electorates. Montagu wanted to maintain separate electorates for only the Muslims and Sikhs, the largest minorities. However, when the reforms were finally put into law in 1919, separate electorates for Indian Christians, Anglo-Indians and Europeans were also established. The British moves served to fragment the nationalist movement and, above all, to keep it pacified throughout the First World War. When the war came to an end, the reforms had already been announced and vociferously debated. For in the period 1917-19 events moved quickly. The Government of India had begun to feel themselves under the threat of revolution, although this was largely an illusion created from efficient nationalist propaganda. Confidence was restored by the *raj* only as a result of

victory in the war and the return of old India hands to the subcontinent in 1919. But the moderates in the nationalist movement were checked throughout the war. During the period 1916-19 Gandhi himself climbed to leadership of the Congress over the head of Tilak, Gokhale's successor, while at the same time constantly praising the merits of the older man. The transformation of the outlook of the Congress was symbolised in this change from Tilak to Gandhi. Tilak was a man of the middle class, a Brahmin and an aristocrat in the Hindu sense. He appeared to the people as a superior, not as an equal and one of themselves. Remote and even Olympian in his manner to the masses, he played upon racial pride and talked of postponing social reform until 'after independence'. Gandhi, on the other hand, was by origin one of the common people. He was of low caste and therefore denied the respect which would be shown to one of the warrior or priestly caste. By 1921 he adopted the loincloth and *dhoti* of the peasant as his normal dress, but at the same time he understood the British mentality better than Tilak. It was Gandhi, almost alone, who converted Indian nationalism from a strictly middle class movement to a mass emotion shared by all castes and groups. Gandhi, perhaps better than anyone else, knew how to make the British feel uncomfortable by attacking them in the name of their own principles.

India passed through the First World War into the modern world. It is not surprising that Indian representatives were to be found at the Paris Peace Conference in 1919, demanding self-government in the name of the Wilsonian principles of national self-determination. The First World War had an unsettling effect on India and at its close many parts of the country were in a state of ferment. Had the war lasted only six months, as many had hoped, the government might have emerged stronger than before. But as it continued, enthusiasm turned to impatience and even bitterness. The promised reforms saved British India from real disturbances in India during the war, and since Britain emerged from it with her prestige not diminished and even enhanced, many British felt that things could return to the way they were before the war. But the war had diminished British capital.

Political power is intimately linked with economic strength and the British Empire had been built and maintained by Britain's financial and industrial dominance in the world. That position was shaken by the war, and therefore Britain's colonial hegemony was also damaged.

Although the position of the Dutch and French in South-East Asia cannot be compared with Britain's control over the Indian Ocean and her economic position in Eastern Asia, especially China, both nations were forced to respond to nationalist sentiment which was stirred up by the war. In the Dutch East Indies, the largest Asian colony controlled by Europeans excluding India, reforms had already been undertaken before the war began. The Netherlands remained neutral throughout the First World War, but nonetheless their economy was heavily affected be-

The Volksraad had no real legislative power, and only appeared to be a step towards representative government. But the government of the Indies had to consult the Volksraad in certain matters of finance, including the budget, and might take its advice on other matters, such as military defence. Although half of its members were Indonesian and were elected, many members of the Volksraad were, in effect, government nominees, although they were often free to criticise severely the government which they served. The practice of ensuring a European majority in the Volksraad was soon abandoned. These liberal measures encouraged extremists, including Marxists who moved into the islands during the war. In May 1918 the governor-general opened the Volksraad with a speech which anticipated a much greater degree of autonomy

good as that of Europe, except on a technical or industrial level. The policies of the governor-general, Sarraut, helped to keep French Indo-China relatively quiet during the First World War, but nationalist opinion gathered strength during the 1914-18 period. The forcible recruitment of nearly 100,000 Vietnamese for military service in Europe was widely resented, but it also brought many Vietnamese in closer contact with France, especially French socialists, who encouraged their drive toward self-determination. Among those who were affected in this way was Ho Chi Minh, who settled in Paris under the name of Nguyen Ai Quoc. When the war broke out Ho was 24, and he saw France, not as an apostle of a superior civilisation, but as yet another predator, which had replaced China as Vietnam's traditional enemy. Realising that only in France could he influence Vietnam's future, Ho left for Paris, with a long stopover in the United States. There he retouched pictures and contributed occasional articles to the Communist journal, *L'Humanité*, during the war, and was invited by Marx's grandson, Longuet, to contribute to *Le Populaire*. By the end of the war the Indo-Chinese nationalist and Marxist movement was still in its earliest stages of organisation, but resentment of the French was stronger than ever before. It is not insignificant that Ho Chi Minh, who became Vietnam's representative at the Paris Peace Conference, demanded national self-determination together with representatives from British India as well as from many of Britain's and France's African colonies.

As Japan had defeated Russia at its own game in the Russo-Japanese War, so the Asian revolutionaries adopted tactics calculated to undermine European self-confidence through a policy of confronting the colonial masters with their own supposedly liberal and democratic principles. But the First World War damaged European self-esteem more than any action of the Asian nationalists. It shook concessions out of the Western imperial powers which they would otherwise have been reluctant to grant, hastening by a generation the advance of national self-determination in Asia. It was embarrassing to defend the principle of self-rule for the peoples of Central and Eastern Europe and to deny it to Africans and Asians.

'Hunger is the argument that is driving India to the spinning wheel.' *Gandhi*
'Having become the centre of attraction for imperialist ambitions, the Pacific area and the neighbouring colonies are likely . . . to become the seat of a new world conflagration, whose proletariat will have to bear the burden.' *Ho Chi Minh*

cause of the blockade placed on Germany by the Allies and because of Holland's close links with Germany due to the position of the Netherlands at the mouth of the Rhine. The liberalising effect of the war generally was bound to influence Holland's greatest colony. Even before the war political parties which were nationalist in character had begun to emerge in the Indies. The National Indies Party, although supported by the sizeable Indo-European population, strongly influenced the course of Indonesian nationalism. It expressed the resentment felt by the so-called Inlanders against Europeans who went out to the Indies for some years, made their money, and then returned to Holland as soon as they had achieved financial success. Budi Utomo and Sarekat Islam, founded before the war, were more Indonesian in character, but they too shared resentment toward the Dutch and demanded some degree of self-government. The Indies Social Democratic Association, established in 1914, was growing more radical. Although the nationalist movement was not strong during the war, it increased its support partly because the Dutch were often either in tenuous contact or, from time to time, altogether out of touch with Batavia, the capital of the island empire, which gave the governor-general more independence from the home government than ever before.

In 1916 certain powers were transferred from the Netherlands to the Indies, and a Volksraad (Peoples' Council) was set up.

in the Indies than that permitted by the Act which instituted the Volksraad. One of the first acts of the Volksraad was to reject a proposal that a loyal cable should be addressed to Queen Wilhelmina, and the government was compelled to permit debates in the Indonesian language (Pasar Malayu, or Bahasa Indonesia), even though for many of its members this language was as foreign as Dutch. Ironically, the Dutch had always discouraged Indonesians from speaking Dutch to them, usually addressing them in Indonesian, which was considered by the Dutch to be an inferior language and the language of inferiors. By the end of 1918 Sarekat Islam was demanding major social reforms, and organised Marxism had received a major stimulus with the arrival in the Indies of Hendrik Sneevliet (or Maring, his Comintern code name). His arrest and exile in December 1918 did not prevent either revolutionary socialism or nationalism in general from continuing its progress. Although the Volksraad was basically a sounding board for indigenous opinion, it also tended to neutralise and channel nationalist sentiment for a time. Thus the Dutch took temporising measures vis-à-vis Indonesian nationalism in much the same manner as British India did during the war.

In French Indo-China the nascent nationalist movement was confined almost exclusively to the Vietnamese. They considered themselves to be superior to the other peoples of Indo-China and they felt that their Sinic culture was at least as

Further Reading
Benda, Harry J., *The Crescent and the Rising Sun* (The Hague and Bandung: van Hoeve 1958)
Buttinger, Joseph, *The Smaller Dragon* (New York: Praeger 1958)
Edwardes, Michael, *The Last Years of British India* (Cassell 1963)
Hall, D. G. E., *A History of South-East Asia* (Macmillan 1964)
Kahin, George McT., *Nationalism and Revolution in Indonesia* (Ithaca, NY: Cornell University Press 1952) and *Government and Politics of South-East Asia* (Ithaca, NY Cornell University Press 1959)
Lacouture, Jean, *Ho Chi Minh* (Pelican 1969)
Lancaster, Donald, *The Emancipation of French Indo-China* (Oxford University Press 1961)
Moon, Sir Edward Penderel, *Gandhi and Modern India* (English Universities Press 1958)
Spear, T. G. Percival, *Oxford History of Modern India* (Oxford University Press 1958)

[For S. L. Mayer's biography, see page 9.]

BRITAIN & THE IRAQ REVOLT

In Mesopotamia, nationalism, once channelled against Ottoman rule, was after the Armistice redirected against the British. Talk of British 'treachery' over Damascus and at San Remo, combined with innate dislike of an 'infidel' government and tribal resentment of tighter bureaucratic controls, in 1920 flared up into outright revolt. *General Sir John Glubb. Below: Part of the Sherifian army that took Damascus, headed by Feisal*

Below: The French colonial soldier in Syria, 1921. His equipment would have been identical to that of soldiers in France, but the material of which his uniform was made was light khaki drill, instead of wool. His topee was high in shape, like the German topee, and his puttees would have been made of dark khaki wool. The soldier in this picture carries a Lebel model 86 rifle, although several other types were used as well. *Right:* A British convoy of Ford trucks in the Iraqi desert. *Below right:* At a horse-racing meeting in Baghdad, 1918, later capital of independent Iraq

Before 1914, there was little general desire for independence in the Arab countries east of Sinai. Two potential sources of revolt against the Ottomans did, however, exist, entirely distinct from one another. The first of these movements was based on the nationalist sentiments current in Europe, and was largely limited to young intellectuals who had studied in Europe. The Ottoman government showed no sympathy with these aspirations, with the result that the young Arab nationalists went underground. In 1914, they had formed two small secret societies — *Al Fatat*, the youth movement, which was civilian, and *Al Ahad* ('the Pledge'), which consisted of young Arab officers in the Ottoman army. The general public was almost entirely unaware of these two groups, but there was a general feeling that control by the Ottoman Empire was no longer satisfactory. Considerable admiration was felt for the Western Powers although in a rather vague way. Britain was particularly admired, being considered to be honourable and honest, and to grant her subjects a liberal allowance of freedom.

The second group potentially hostile to Turkey was the tribes. The tribesmen had little or no feeling of nationality as it existed in the west, and were in general untouched by European influence. As Moslems, they generally professed loyalty to the Sultan, who was, in any case, so far away that he scarcely affected their lives. But the majority of the tribes had lived in independence or semi-independence for centuries. Ottoman authority was centred in the cities, where large military garrisons were located. The more rural areas occasionally suffered a punitive expedition, when their villages were burnt down and their flocks driven off, but normally there was little evidence of government interference in their lives, apart from the occasional tax-collector. Since the middle of the 19th Century, however, the Ottoman government had made attempts to introduce direct administration in tribal areas, a process which gave rise to increasing tribal resentment.

In November 1914, there were, therefore, two potentially subversive movements in the Arab world, the western-inspired nationalism of students and army officers, on the one hand, and the endemic rebelliousness of the tribes on the other. Sheriff Hussein of Mecca was familiar with both these worlds. In the Hejāz the Sheriff was a prince with a following of armed tribes, but Hussein had lived for many years in Istanbul, where he had observed western nationalism at close quarters. In 1908 he was made Sheriff of Mecca and left Istanbul to live in the Holy City, but his son Abdullah was made a member of the Ottoman Parliament and remained in Istanbul, where he was in touch with the Arab secret societies. In the correspondence which took place between the British High Commissioner in Egypt, Sir Henry McMahon, and Sheriff Hussein, in 1915 and 1916, Britain virtually pledged herself to grant independence to all Arabs east of Sinai after the war. Lebanon alone was excluded on the grounds that France claimed certain rights there. No formal agreement was signed, but Hussein trusted to the good faith of Britain.

Before committing himself, however, Sheriff Hussein decided to contact the Arab secret societies in Damascus. He sent his third son, Feisal, to carry out this task. Feisal reached Damascus and returned to Mecca with the draft demands to be made on Britain, drawn up by the secret societies. These terms gave Britain everything she wanted from the Arabs. But in May 1916 Britain signed the secret Sykes-Picot agreement with France, in which the two nations divided between them any benefits accruing from the Arab state, which Britain had promised to set up. The benefits foreseen were in enterprises and local loans and the supply of foreign advisers, at the request of the Arab state. Then, in June 1916, the Sheriff rebelled against Turkey and there ensued the campaigns of Feisal and Lawrence, terminating in the establishment of an Arab government in Damascus, with Feisal as *de facto* King.

Meanwhile, in November 1917, the British government had issued the Balfour Declaration, promising to assist in the establishment of a national home for the Jewish people in Palestine after the war — undoubtedly a breach of the agreement with Sheriff Hussein.

Noble sentiments — but no promises

On November 14, 1914, the 6th Indian Division had landed at the mouth of the River Shaṭṭ al 'Arab, south of Basra. Throughout the war, Anglo-Indian troops fought in Mesopotamia, until the Mosul area was occupied in October 1918. Whereas the operations in Palestine and Syria had been directed from London, the Mesopotamian campaign was conducted by the government of India. In Mesopotamia (known after 1921 as Iraq) no promises whatever were made to the Arabs, nor was Arab co-operation solicited, though it might well have been even more valuable than it was in Palestine and Syria. The south was inhabited by semi-independent tribes, who had been in frequent revolt against the Turks for centuries. Lines of communications in Mesopotamia were long and highly vulnerable, both sides using boats on the River Tigris to bring up supplies. If the banks of the river had been lined by insurgent tribes, the Turkish troops might have been almost immobilised, but no attempt to raise the tribes was ever made. On the other hand, the omission to solicit Arab co-operation meant that no promises were made, on which charges of breach of faith could subsequently have been based.

After the capture of Baghdad on March 11, 1917, however, General Maude issued a proclamation, promising that Britain did not intend to impose alien institutions, but desired 'that the Arab race may rise once more to greatness'. These sentiments were substantiated on November 8, 1918, in an Anglo-French declaration issued simultaneously in both Syria and Mesopotamia: 'The goal envisaged by France and Great Britain . . . is complete and final liberation of the peoples who have for so long been oppressed by the Turks, and the setting up of national governments and administrations that shall derive their authority from the free exercise of the initiative and choice of the indigenous populations.' President Woodrow Wilson's 14 Points had used similar language. Nevertheless, British desire to remain in an advisory capacity to the administrations of the provinces of Baghdad and Basra had been mentioned in the Hussein-McMahon correspondence; the Sheriff had made no objection to the idea. In so far as Mesopotamia was concerned, therefore, there were few concrete promises made. The Mesopotamian Arabs had no claim to the gratitude of Britain because they had not assisted in the military operations although sympathy was expressed with their nationalist objectives.

With an Arab government, under the Emir Feisal, now installed in Damascus, the French landed an army in Lebanon. Tension soon mounted between the French army in Lebanon and the Arab government in Syria, and on July 20, 1920 the French army invaded Syria. On July 25 it occupied Damascus, abolished the Arab state and set up direct French rule. Britain protested violently, alleging that the action of France was a breach of faith with the Arabs, but the French refused to withdraw. The Allies were already faced with innumerable problems and could not afford to fight one another, so the British eventually ceased their protests, but the French seizure of Syria inflicted on Anglo-French relations a deep wound, which remained open for many years.

Feisal's operations from 1916 to 1918 had been marked by the same dual character as other Arab movements of the time. The Arab army consisted, firstly, of 'regulars', officers and soldiers of Arab descent taken prisoner with the Turkish army and recruited from POW camps. Before the war, a considerable number of Mesopotamian Arabs had served as officers in the Ottoman army, although many of these had joined *Al Ahad,* the officers' secret society working for Arab independence. The second faction within Feisal's army was that of the desert tribes, relatively untouched by the concept of nationalism.

When the French took Damascus on July 25, 1920, and broke up Feisal's army, the Arab officers dispersed, the majority taking refuge in Mesopotamia, the land of their birth. Burning with indignation, they were convinced that Britain had secretly been a party to the French seizure of Syria. The most bitter recriminations were exchanged between France and Britain on the subject at Versailles. But the Arab officers fleeing from Damascus could not possibly appreciate the international situation at Versailles. They arrived in Mesopotamia, furiously denouncing British treachery in the betrayal of their Arab allies to France. Feisal himself, who was at Versailles, was aware of the real situation, but was out of touch with his officers, who set themselves to attack the British in Mesopotamia by every possible means.

The Government of India, which directed operations in Mesopotamia, held no romantic views regarding the rights of the Arabs, or the recovery of their former greatness. On the other hand, the Indian Civil Service were competent administrators, who found in Mesopotamia large areas of cultivated land, which had never been properly administered by the Ottomans — indeed, parts of the country had scarcely been controlled, much less policed. The civil servants set themselves to remedy the situation with the best of intentions. 'Political Officers' were posted over all the tribal areas. These were mostly army officers who had volunteered for the work and were not, like the senior administrators, members of the Indian Civil Service. Unable to speak Arabic, they depended on the honesty of their local interpreters and were often unable to penetrate below the surface, and find out what was really going on. Local men were enlisted as police, but office staff and junior technicians were Indians. Resistance seemed to the Arabs to be impossible, for a considerable Anglo-Indian army was in occupation. The tribes of Mesopotamia, like all tribes, did not feel the call of western nationalism, but they were deeply concerned to preserve their tribal independence and to keep government — any government — at arm's length.

The close administration introduced by the British was therefore unwelcome, not because it was British, but because it represented an attempt to control their movements.

In addition to the indignation roused by the army officers from Damascus and to tribal opposition the religious factor was a further source of discord. Islam is broadly divided into two divisions – the Sunnis and the Shiis – and the official religion of the Ottoman Empire was Sunnism; that of Persia was Shiism. The people of Mesopotamia, south of Baghdad, were Shiis; those north of the city and the nomads of the desert were Sunnis. Moreover the two most holy sanctuaries of the Shiis, An Najaf and Karbelā', to which tens of thousands of pilgrims resorted every year, lay south of Baghdad. In these cities lived the religious leaders of the Shii world.

When the insurrection took place in Mesopotamia in the second half of 1920, all the tribes which rose up were Shii. No Sunni tribe took up arms. It is, of course, true also that the southern or Shii tribes had been under close administration for two or three years, while the tribes north of Baghdad had not had time to experience it. In spite of this, however, there is no doubt that the insurgent Shii tribes had received considerable encouragement from their religious leaders in Karbelā' and An Najaf to oppose an 'infidel' government.

It is possible that no rebellion would ever have taken place if the British government had, in 1919, announced a constitution for Mesopotamia. But the authorities in London were overwhelmed with other problems, involving the peace negotiations at Versailles, the future of Germany, Bolshevik Russia, relations with France and the attitude of the USA and against these major problems a settlement in Iraq was low on the list of priorities. But there is no reason to doubt that the British government intended to fulfil its pledges in Mesopotamia. Soon after the Armistice, the Civil Commissioner, who was responsible for administration, received a questionnaire from London. In it, he was asked to record the wishes of Mesopotamians on the establishment of an Arab state, whether they would prefer British tutelage or that of some other power, and whether they desired an Arab ruler and, if so, who he should be. In May 1920, a year and a half after the Armistice, no statement of British policy towards Mesopotamia had been made, though the Civil Commissioner had begged for some statement of intention. Then, suddenly, the British government announced its acceptance of a mandate for Mesopotamia, as decided by the San Remo Conference between the western Allies. No one had any idea of the meaning of a mandate, but it appeared that the Allies had handed over Mesopotamia to Britain

Popperfoto

Above: McMahon, British High Commissioner for Egypt. The McMahon-Hussein correspondence stressed eventual Arab independence, but it came too late. *Below:* Beirut Harbour, scene of French landings in October 1918

without consideration for the feelings of the inhabitants. The use of such official phrases as mandate and tutelage conveyed an unpleasant suggestion of inferiority; more tactful wording, such as assistance in lieu of tutelage, might have sweetened the pill. Advice and assistance were, nevertheless, necessary, for all the senior officials and officers in Ottoman times had been Turks and had vanished with the retreating Ottoman army. It would have been very difficult for the Mesopotamians to set up an administration without outside aid.

In June 1920, tribal disorders broke out in Mesopotamia. In July the French occupied Damascus and the fugitive officers from Feisal's army arrived, loudly denouncing British treachery in Syria, and urging armed resistance in Mesopotamia. Nearly all the fighting was done by the Shii tribes, east of Baghdad on the River Diala, and south of Baghdad on the Lower Euphrates. Time was taken in recalling troops leaving for demobilisation or the insurrection could have been quickly suppressed. Its scope was meanwhile expanded by the disaster to the Manchester Column, south of Hillah. Most of the officers and men who had fought in the war were returned to England in the year after the Armistice and units in Mesopotamia were brought up to strength with young conscripts. Under pressure of tribal attack, the Column partly disintegrated and a number of British soldiers were captured and paraded round the tribal settlements, with the result that the rebellion spread rapidly. Fighting, however, was not very severe. Columns were sent up the Diala and down the Euphrates, transport and communications delaying the operations as much as the resistance of the rebels. Except for an incident in Tel Afar, west of Mosul, the officers from the Sherifian army did not take any part in the fighting, but their indignant remarks on the Syrian débâcle considerably inflamed resentment in Mesopotamia.

On October 1, 1920, when hostilities were virtually over, Sir Percy Cox arrived in Baghdad as British High Commissioner, having previously been Civil Commissioner in Mesopotamia from November 1914 to the spring of 1918. He spoke Arabic and was widely known and respected. A Council of State was set up under the presidency of the Naqib of Baghdad. But not until June 1921 did the British government make a statement of policy on Mesopotamia. Shortly afterwards the Emir Feisal, driven from Damascus by the French a year before, came to Mesopotamia and was accepted as king by a popular referendum. A constitution was drawn up, including parliamentary institutions. Ironically enough, when the rebellion was over, many tribes demanded a British administration, and opposed a Mesopotamian government.

Other tribes, thereupon, supported the nationalists and rejected the British; these intrigues were to cause disquiet for several years. In 1924, the Turkish Republic laid claim to Mosul, and the province remained unstable until 1926, when it was finally allotted to Mesopotamia. Without British intervention, Turkey would have occupied the area.

Further Reading
Glubb, Sir J. B., *Britain and the Arabs* (Hodder & Stoughton)
Glubb, Sir J. B., *A Soldier with the Arabs* (Hodder & Stoughton)

GENERAL SIR JOHN GLUBB was born in Preston in England and educated at Cheltenham College and at the Royal Military Academy. Having served in France and Belgium during the First World War, he went to Iraq in 1920 as a British army officer, but in 1926 accepted a civilian post as Administrative Inspector to the Iraqi government. From 1928 to 1930 he worked in the Southern Desert of Iraq, dealing with the problems of desert raiding, and in 1930 signed a contract with the government of Transjordan to put an end to desert raids in that area. For this achievement King Abdullah gave him the rank of colonel in the Arab Legion and in 1939 he was appointed Chief of Staff. Since his retirement in 1956 he has written many books on Arab affairs and lectured all over Britain, the United States and Europe.

PALESTINE

& THE LEVANT

With the end of Ottoman rule, the Middle East, a secondary front during the war, assumed a new importance for the Allies. But territorial settlements could only be complex and tentative, reflecting the divergent British, French, Arab and Jewish interests concentrated in the area. *Elie Kedourie. Top:* Abdullah (centre), ruler of mandatory Transjordan, with a British Agent. *Above left:* General Gouraud (seated centre), French C-in-C in Syria. *Above right:* Roots of a lasting conflict—Arab-Jewish disturbances in Jerusalem, May 1920

In the second half of September 1918 Allenby mounted his last great offensive against the Ottoman armies in the Levant. By the time the Armistice of Mudros between the Allies and the Ottoman Empire was signed at the end of October, the Egyptian Expeditionary Force was in full control of the territories which, after the war, were to be known as Palestine, Syria and Lebanon. As Commander-in-Chief Allenby exercised ultimate authority over the whole area. This authority he exercised through Chief Administrators whom he appointed to take charge in the Occupied Enemy Territory Administrations (OETA's). In the territory with which we are here concerned, there were three such OETA's: OETA (South) roughly corresponding to mandatory Palestine, OETA (West) including Beirut, Alexandretta and Mount Lebanon, and OETA (East) controlling Syria and Transjordan.

The significance of these divisions was not military or administrative, but primarily political. They reflected the various arrangements which Britain had made during the war with France and the Sheriff of Mecca for partitioning the Ottoman Empire, affected, however, by second thoughts which British ministers had come to have regarding the desirability of these arrangements, and the possibility of modifying them. Thus, under the tripartite agreement between Britain, France and Russia of 1916, commonly known as the Sykes-Picot agreement, a large part of Palestine was to be under international administration. But Lloyd George, who became Prime Minister at the end of 1916, was in favour of British annexation or control of Palestine; in April 1917, a Cabinet 'Committee on Territorial Terms of Peace', the chairman of which was Curzon, recommended that Palestine should come under exclusive British control. This aim seemed easier to realise when, at the end of 1917, Russia withdrew from the war, thus making it possible for the Sykes-Picot arrangements to be challenged and modified. When, almost simultaneously, Allenby occupied Jerusalem, the military administration which he set up was put under the supervision of Clayton, his Chief Political Officer. When his responsibilities grew later to be more extensive, Allenby appointed as Chief Administrator General Money. He was succeeded in turn by General Watson and General Bols. The latter handed Palestine over in 1920 to his civilian successor, Sir Herbert Samuel, who was appointed first British High Commissioner for the mandated territory of Palestine. Thus, British officers controlled OETA (South) all through and, despite their protests, the French were allowed no say in the administration of this territory.

In OETA (East) Allenby appointed as Chief Administrator Feisal, third son of Hussein, the Sheriff of Mecca, now King of the Hejāz. The territory of OETA (East) was in fact identical with those areas called A and B in the Sykes-Picot agreement, in which the signatories agreed that an Arab state or federation of states would be set up. Feisal was the commander of a small

Sherifian force, armed, supplied and financed chiefly by the British. After the capture of 'Aqaba in July 1917, this force came under Allenby's command and was styled the Northern Arab Army. On October 1, 1918, Allenby received two telegrams from the War Office which were the conclusion and culmination of exchanges which had been going on all through the previous summer. These two telegrams make it clear that it was the desire of the British Government that 'the authority of the friendly and allied Arabs should be formally recognised in any part of the Areas A and B [as defined in the Sykes-Picot agreement] where it may be found established, or can be established, as a result of the military operations now in progress' and that Allenby was 'authorised by His Majesty's Government to hoist the Arab flag in Damascus when you arrive there'. It was presumably in order to carry out these instructions that Allenby forbade all his troops, except for the Northern Arab Army, to enter Damascus. Feisal thus appeared as the conqueror of Damascus, and his authority was recognised and sanctioned by Allenby appointing him Chief Administrator in OETA (East). But from the start Feisal behaved as someone whose position was more exalted than that of an administrator subordinate to the Commander-in-Chief. The Sherifian flag was hoisted in his territory and his officers and officials behaved like the agents of an independent state rather than strictly temporary caretakers.

OETA (West) comprised territories which had been promised to France. But the Sherifians, perhaps with T. E. Lawrence's encouragement, thought to forestall the French by sending a small force to Beirut, and hoisting the Sherifian flag there. The flag was hoisted, but owing to Allenby's categorical objections, it had to be hauled down, and the Commander-in-Chief shortly afterwards appointed as Chief Administrator a French officer, Colonel de Piépape, commander of a French contingent landed in Beirut to affirm the French presence in the Levant.

These arrangements, it soon appeared, aroused tension and conflict between the French and the British, and in this Feisal and the Sherifians were directly involved. Feisal, as has been seen, was Chief Administrator in OETA (East), and thus directly responsible to the Commander-in-Chief. But OETA (East) included both Area A where the Sykes-Picot agreement recognised French predominance, and Area B where British predominance was conceded. In Area A therefore the French would expect to have the decisive say in the setting up and the functioning of that Arab state which, in the Sykes-Picot agreement they had pledged themselves to 'uphold'. But by virtue of his authority as Commander-in-Chief, Allenby could, and did, interpose himself between Feisal and the French Government. Allenby's stance, it soon became clear, went hand in hand with a British policy which aimed at preventing the French from establishing predominant influence in Syria. Thus, in

November 1918, without consulting or even informing the French, the British transported Feisal aboard a destroyer to France, where he was supposed to represent his father at the Peace Conference. Again, British troops remained stationed in Area A and there was no sign that Lloyd George would allow them to be withdrawn. At the Peace Conference acute disagreement over the Middle East settlement between Lloyd George and Clemenceau soon became evident. The deadlock continued throughout the spring and summer of 1919, the French claiming what they considered to be their rights under the Sykes-Picot agreement, and the British maintaining that the agreement had been rendered inoperative by the withdrawal of Russia, and the universal acceptance of President Wilson's principles. But towards the end of August, financial difficulties and public pressure in favour of demobilisation compelled Lloyd George to reconsider his Syrian policy. The price of carrying on the conflict with France was proving too high, and the issue was in any case secondary. Very quickly, Lloyd George jettisoned his original policy, informed the French that he would withdraw his troops from Syria, and advised Feisal to come to terms with them. By the end of 1919 British troops had evacuated the whole of the Levant north of Palestine.

Feisal was now in an awkward position. His whole policy of resisting the French demand for the predominant influence in Syria had rested on the belief that the British would stand by him. Suddenly deprived of their support, he did his best to come to some tolerable arrangement with the French. On his return to Syria in January 1920, he found that any such arrangement (to which he personally may have been resigned, as the best obtainable at the time) was unlikely to be accepted by his followers who seemed bent on a belligerent course. The French were reinforcing their troops in the Lebanon, and relations between them and the Sherifians became gradually more tense. There was friction over the Biqa' which the French wanted to annex to the Lebanon, and the Sherifians claimed to be part of Syria. There were incursions by armed bands from both sides of the frontiers; the French complained that the Sherifians were hampering their communications with Cilicia, which they had also occupied, and where they had now to withstand attacks by Turkish nationalist forces.

In April 1920, the Allied Supreme Council meeting at San Remo agreed, among other things, that France should become the mandatory for the Lebanon and for Syria, and that Britain should assume the mandate for Palestine. The idea of mandates had been put forward towards the end of the war by General Smuts, and incorporated in the Covenant of the League of Nations. According to this idea, certain territories not yet ripe for full independence would be entrusted for a period of time to a mandatory, responsible to the League of Nations, who would prepare the population concerned for self-government. In becoming the mandatories respectively of Palestine, and of Syria and the Lebanon, Great Britain and France satisfied their aims in the Levant. They did so, not through annexations or the establishment of protectorates (as had been contemplated in the Sykes-Picot agreement), but indirectly by means of this device of mandates. About this device there always was therefore an uncomfortable suggestion both of impermanence and of dishonesty which contributed subsequently to the discomfiture of the Powers who, in 1919, seemed utterly self-confident and indeed omnipotent.

The response in Damascus to the award of the Syrian mandate to France was uncompromising. In the summer of 1919, anticipating the visit of an inter-Allied Commission to investigate the wishes of the population, the Sherifian authorities had called together a Syrian Congress purporting to represent all the populations of the Levant. Owing to French objections which the British were unwilling to overrule, the inter-Allied Commission ended by being reduced to two US commissioners, King and Crane. These commissioners visited the Levant and subsequently submitted a report to President Wilson which, owing to his withdrawal from active negotiations at Paris, had no influence on subsequent developments. The Syrian Congress remained in being, and seemed indeed to embody the most uncompromising and intransigent opposition to France. Feisal, as has been said, may have favoured a moderate and conciliatory policy, but he was unable to impose his views. In March 1920, the Congress met and declared the independence of Syria 'within its natural boundaries', that is, including the Lebanon and Palestine. Of this state Feisal was proclaimed the constitutional sovereign. Britain and France refused to recognise this new kingdom, and indeed the arrangements on which they agreed at San Remo were quite at variance with it. Between the French in Beirut and Feisal's régime in Damascus a clash was therefore imminent. At the beginning of May new ministers took office in Damascus who pledged themselves, with the outspoken support of the Congress, to resist the San Remo decision. Relations with the French became very tense. At the end of May, General Gouraud, the French High Commissioner and Commander-in-Chief in the Levant, negotiated an armistice with the Turkish nationalist forces in Cilicia, and thus became able to exert a much greater pressure on Damascus. All through June attempts to bring the two sides to terms continued. But the French were adamant that their predominance should be acknowledged and accepted in Damascus, and Feisal's followers—or at any rate those of them who were then in the ascendant—equally adamant in resisting such pretensions. On July 14 Gouraud sent an ultimatum to Feisal demanding the acceptance of the French mandate, the disbanding of the Sherifian army and the dismissal of anti-French extremists. The ultimatum was to expire on July 18. Feisal, afraid that

his forces would be unable to resist the French, accepted the ultimatum at the last minute 'only in principle and in his personal capacity'. This became known in Damascus where disorders broke out, demonstrators looting the arsenal, breaking into prisons and even attacking Feisal's residence. They were dispersed by force and many killed. Gouraud deemed Feisal's answer unsatisfactory and extended the ultimatum to July 21. Feisal agreed to it on July 20, but Gouraud, alleging non-receipt, ordered his army to march on Damascus. On July 24 it clashed with, and routed, a detachment of Sherifian troops and of volunteers at Khan Maisalun. On the following day it entered Damascus, bringing the Sherifian régime to an end.

OETA (South), which by and large comprised the territory which was to become mandatory Palestine, was already under British military administration. Lloyd George was determined that in this area there would be no internationalisation (as had been agreed in the Sykes-Picot agree-

British support for Jewish ambitions in Palestine horrified the Arab majority, delighted the Jews. A Zionist Commission, headed by Weizmann *(right),* left for Palestine. *Below:* Weizmann fêted. *Far right:* Allenby and Weizmann (seated on platform)

ment), but that it should come, somehow or other, under sole British control. Clemenceau, representing France, the surviving partner in the Sykes-Picot agreement, agreed to this while on a visit to London early in December 1918. But in pursuit of this aim—British control of Palestine—the British Cabinet had earlier taken a fateful decision, the consequences of which are even now far from being fully worked out. Shortly before Allenby's capture of Jerusalem, they had authorised the issue of the Balfour Declaration by which they promised to 'use their best endeavours to facilitate' the establishment in Palestine of 'a national home for the Jewish people'. Support for Zionism—such

was the calculation—would in turn elicit Zionist support for British control of Palestine, and render French claims so much weaker. There seem to have been two other motives for the Declaration: one, the belief that the Germans and their Ottoman allies were themselves on the point of making some such declaration; and the belief that supporting the Zionists would induce them to use their influence with the Russian Jews—which was thought considerable—to induce them to endeavour to keep Russia in the war. Such a calculation was of course false, since the Zionists had little influence with the Russian Jews, and the Russian Jews were themselves in no position to influence Russian politics.

Though the Balfour Declaration was never officially published by the military authorities in OETA (South), its terms became quickly known to the population, who received it with some disquiet. The disquiet was understandable, since the terms of the Declaration were vague and nobody could tell exactly what it portended. The disquiet was increased by the arrival, at the beginning of 1918, of a Zionist Commission headed by Dr Weizmann, the functions and attributes of which were equally vague and mysterious. So long as the war lasted, OETA (South) was quiet. But after the Mudros armistice, and with the establishment of Feisal in Damascus, the situation became more fluid and unrest was henceforth a real possibility. There were many reasons for this: the Zionists and the small Jewish minority, taking the Balfour Declaration to mean that Palestine was now theirs, displayed their pride and self-confidence to a population which was overwhelmingly Moslem and had been accustomed to look upon Jews as subjects, not equals or rulers; again, propaganda for the Sherifian cause—now visibly triumphant at Damascus—had gone on during and after the war, and the Zionist vision was matched, among the Moslems, by the vision of a great Arab state of which they

would form a part; also, French agents were using Zionism in order to discredit Britain in the eyes of the Palestinians, and spreading the view that a French mandate would preserve the country from Zionism. All this effervescence came to a head in Easter 1920. The Moslem feast of Nabi Musa, traditional to Jerusalem, fell during this period, and the city was full of Moslems who had come in groups from various localities for the customary celebrations. A short while before, it will be remembered, Feisal had been proclaimed King in Damascus of a Syria which included Palestine, and emissaries of the Sherifian régime were busy in Jerusalem spreading propaganda in favour of this régime. They seem to have been left free to pursue their activities because the Chief Administrator and his Chief-of-Staff were themselves in favour of Feisal ruling over Palestine. On April 4 severe anti-Jewish riots broke out in Jerusalem in which many were killed and wounded. They showed what deep passions could be stirred among the native inhabitants by the attempt to establish Zionism in Palestine. Shortly after these riots, in pursuance of the San Remo decisions, the British Government announced the termination of military government and the appointment of Sir

Herbert Samuel as High Commissioner for the mandated territory.

Area A (as in the Sykes-Picot agreement) of OETA (East), where French influence was to be predominant, corresponded roughly to mandatory Syria; while Area B was to become the mandated territory of Transjordan, ruled by Abdullah, the second son of King Hussein. The creation of such a separate entity had never been contemplated. When accepting a mandate for Palestine in April 1920, the British Government had not yet worked out the precise boundaries of the mandated territory; at that time indeed Feisal still exercised authority in Damascus, and his writ was supposed to run east of the Jordan. The Zionists, it is true, assumed and declared that 'Palestine' embraced both sides of the Jordan, but this was only a claim which had not yet been accepted by their British patrons. As for Abdullah, when his younger brother was proclaimed King of Syria by the Syrian Congress in March 1920, a parallel Iraqi Congress had proclaimed him King of Iraq. Abdullah regarded himself as the real architect of the Arab Revolt; he had a high opinion of his own political abilities, and an Iraqi throne was the least to which he would have considered himself entitled.

When the French occupied Damascus and ejected Feisal in July 1920, the fate of the area east of the Jordan became problematic. The French began by trying to extend their authority there, but soon gave up such a pretension, recognising that the territory lay within the British zone. To the British it now represented a difficult and worrying problem. Though Feisal's writ was supposed to run in the area, in fact the authority of any government whatsoever was conspicuous only by its absence. In Ottoman times the territory had been notoriously under-administered, and the war and its aftermath now meant that insecurity and chaos ruled everywhere. There were no public services, and few officials or policemen; those that existed were strangers to the district, and disorientated by the disappearance of the Sherifian régime at Damascus which had been the source of such tenuous authority as they managed to exercise. Tribe fought against tribe, while the settled peasant and the townsman went in fear of the nomad and his depredations. Sir Herbert Samuel, the newly-appointed High Commissioner in Palestine, had to deal with the problem immediately upon his arrival in Jerusalem. He advised that the territory should be occupied by British troops so that an orderly administration could be established. But the authorities in London, faced with demands of financial retrenchment and reluctant to assume new military responsibilities, refused permission. Lord Curzon, the Foreign Secretary, informed Samuel that British policy was for the area to be independent 'but in closest relation with Palestine'. He instructed Samuel to send a few British political officers east of the Jordan 'provided that no military escorts are necessary to ensure their safety', to help the native population to set up institutions of local self-government and to encourage trade with Palestine.

Accordingly, the High Commissioner went to Es-Salt (north-west of 'Amman) on August 21, 1920, where he addressed a gathering of some 600 notables and informed them of the future régime of the territory as laid down by the British Government. Soon afterwards seven British officers were sent across the Jordan and stationed in the most important localities where they were supposed to carry out the instructions described above. One of these was Captain C. D. Brunton who eventually took up duties in 'Amman, and to whose initiative was due the foundation of the force which, in later years, became famous as the Arab Legion.

Opposite page, top: Sir Herbert Samuel, the British High Commissioner for Palestine from 1920 to 1925. *Bottom:* The Allied Supreme Council meet at San Remo, in April 1920, to discuss territorial settlements in the Levant. It was decided to make France the mandatory for Syria, Britain for Palestine. *Above:* General Allenby and, *below,* General Gouraud—officially allies but representatives of Powers whose interests in the Middle East frequently clashed

As may be expected, the stationing east of the Jordan of seven British political officers, who had no military or administrative support to fall back upon, was by no means sufficient to establish law and order. The situation was made worse by the fact that Sherifian supporters used the territory as a sanctuary from which to mount raids on the French. This led to strong protests from the French, which went virtually unheeded, since there was no organised military force to police the frontier. In the autumn of 1920 rumours began to reach Jerusalem that Abdullah, who was then his father's Foreign Minister, was setting out from Der'ā with an armed following, his object to attack the French in Syria in revenge for their treatment of his brother. Whether Abdullah was in earnest about such a plan, or what exactly he had in mind, is not known. The fact is that he arrived on November 21 at Ma'an, a station on the Hejāz railway, that with him was an armed following, and that he began sending proclamations in which he described himself as 'Vice-King of Syria' and called upon all troops and officers of the Syrian army to join him at Ma'an.

During the following months the situation remained both obscure and difficult. Sherifians were flocking to Abdullah, and with no force available to check or control his activities, he was becoming a power in the land. Towards the beginning of March 1921, news was received that he was now in 'Amman. At this juncture a Middle East Conference was on the point of assembling at Cairo under the chairmanship of Winston Churchill who had shortly before become Colonial Secretary and assumed responsibility for British interests in the Middle East. When the Conference ended Churchill went to Jerusalem where Abdullah was summoned to meet him on March 27. Abdullah, promising to cease his attacks on the French, made a good impression on the Colonial Secretary who decided to entrust Transjordan to him for a period of six months. During this period affairs in Transjordan did not improve. Abdullah proved incapable of maintaining public order, of repressing tribal quarrels, or of preventing raids into French-controlled territory. Both in Jerusalem and in the Colonial Office many were in favour of terminating this experiment and bringing the territory under direct British administration. T. E. Lawrence, then a member of the Middle East Department of the Colonial Office, was asked to visit Transjordan and advise. Towards the end of October 1921 Lawrence arrived in 'Amman, and shortly afterwards informed Churchill that he recommended that Abdullah should remain in charge for the time being. He repeated this advice in December, and in the following February Churchill wrote in a Minute: 'I do not want to change Abdullah or the policy followed during the last nine months.' Abdullah was to remain ruler, first of Transjordan and then of Jordan, until his murder in 1951.

When recommending that Abdullah should continue in Transjordan, Law- rence also recommended that the provision of the Palestine mandate requiring the Mandatory to facilitate Jewish settlement there should not apply to Transjordan and that this should be made public. This advice too Churchill accepted, and the mandate for Palestine approved by the Council of the League of Nations in July 1922 contained a provision, in article 25, to the effect that: 'In the territories lying between the Jordan and the eastern boundary of Palestine as ultimately determined, the Mandatory shall be entitled . . . to postpone or withhold application of such provisions of this mandate as he may consider inapplicable to the existing local conditions.' The article, as may be seen, is phrased in studiously general terms, and the name, Transjordan, is not even mentioned. But this provision nonetheless heralded the separation of this territory from that area where, as the preamble of the mandate for Palestine put it, the Mandatory was 'responsible for putting into effect' the Balfour Declaration. This became clear as early as December 1922 when, after a visit by Abdullah to London, the British Government entered into an agreement recognising 'the existence of an independent constitutional Government in Transjordan under the rule of His Excellency the Emir Abdullah ibn Hussein'.

With the establishment of Abdullah in Transjordan, the long and painful process of transition from war to peace in the Levant may be said to have been concluded. Many details of the settlement which took shape by 1922 have proved remarkably durable: the Lebanon, Syria and Transjordan (which changed its name to Jordan in 1950 when Abdullah annexed portions of Palestine to his kingdom) remain as internationally recognised entities, and no longer under mandate. Palestine, however, has been since 1948 the scene of an unresolved dispute between the Zionists, organised in the state of Israel, and their neighbours. This dispute too may be considered an outcome of this settlement.

Further Reading
Dann, Uriel, 'The Beginnings of the Arab Legion' in *Middle Eastern Studies,* volume 5, no 3 (Cass 1969)
Kedourie, Elie, *England and the Middle East: the Destruction of the Ottoman Empire 1914-1921* (Bowes & Bowes 1956)
Kedourie, Elie, *The Chatham House Version and Other Middle-Eastern Studies* (Weidenfeld & Nicolson 1970)
Klieman, Aaron S., *Foundations of British Policy in the Arab World: the Cairo Conference of 1921* (Johns Hopkins Press 1970)
Nevakivi, Jukka, *Britain, France and the Arab Middle East* (Athlone Press 1969)
Zeine, Zeine S., *The Struggle for Arab Independence* (Khayat 1960)

ELIE KEDOURIE is Professor of Politics at the London School of Economics in the University of London and editor of the journal *Middle Eastern Studies.* He has also taught, as a Visiting Professor, at the universities of Princeton and Harvard in the United States. He is particularly interested in the diplomatic history of the Middle East since the First World War and has written extensively on the subject.

Jan Christiaan Smuts

Of all the delegates at the Peace Conference, Smuts was the most cogent and outspoken critic of the terms presented to the Germans, and yet he signed a treaty which he knew well was fatal.

As the second representative of a minor power Smuts was under less pressure, both at the Conference and at home, than the major participants. He was therefore able to take a more dispassionate stand on points of principle. His weakness lay in the fact that he *was* merely the second representative of a minor power. Outside the British Empire Delegation, where he was only one of several delegates, his direct influence on events was confined to jogging Lloyd George's wayward conscience, and sometimes President Wilson's as well. He himself described his rôle as that of 'a still, small voice', and such was the strength of his reputation that Lloyd George found it an increasingly difficult voice to ignore.

Smuts' early hopes that the Conference would be a means of building a better world were soon dashed. On January 18, 1919, at the First Plenary Session of the Conference, he heard with a sinking heart the opening speech by President Poincaré. The President spoke about Justice, but it was clear from his repeated reference to war crimes that Justice, to the French, meant only the punishment of Germany.

Punitive clauses
The clauses that were to make up the draft Treaty were hammered out in innumerable committees and sub-committees. From February 11 to March 23 Smuts was absent from the Conference, a victim of the prevalent influenza. During his illness he grew more and more troubled about the course affairs in Paris were taking, and on his return he was horrified at the extent to which entirely punitive ideas governed the draft proposals. On March 26 he wrote to Lloyd George condemning the proposals as they stood as 'impossible' and conceived on a 'wrong basis'. His argument was this: Germany was by far the most important single power in Europe. If the stability of Germany were destroyed, the stability of Europe would be destroyed as well. Germany's potential power was such that, however deeply she was humiliated, the time would come when she would take her revenge. No permanent peace was possible, he declared, unless it recognised that Germany was a dominant factor in Europe. German goodwill and assistance should be solicited in rebuilding the world. Without German goodwill and approval nothing that the Conference did would be lasting. Smuts himself, of course, had been at the receiving end of both a galling defeat and a magnanimous peace. He had seen the value of treating a beaten enemy leniently.

Imperial War Museum

His warnings went unheeded. On May 7 the draft Treaty was presented to the Germans. Their first reaction was to deny sole responsibility for the war and to assert that the 14 Points should be binding to both sides. It was not until May 29 that the Germans submitted their counter-proposals. Their case was that they had agreed to an armistice to discuss peace on the basis of Wilson's notes of October and November 1918 (substantially, that is, on the 14 Points) and that the draft Treaty did not reflect this basis.

Between May 7 and 29 Smuts had continued his efforts to amend the draft Treaty. He saw with increasing clarity that the proposals would merely guarantee another war in as short a time as it took Germany to recover her economic position — in other words in about 20 years. On May 14 he wrote again to Lloyd George and Wilson, stressing the danger of a future war and urging that the German view be given a fair hearing. Wilson's reply to this appeal was cool, and dispelled the last hopes Smuts had of amending the draft by appealing to the President. He now saw clearly that the Treaty would go through,

and that the Germans would be compelled to sign it. In his view the terms were disastrous. His attempts to alter them had failed, and only one further opportunity lay open to him — the meeting of the British Empire Delegation on May 30. In the meantime he had to decide what his own attitude would be if the Treaty went through unaltered. In a letter to his wife on May 20 he announced his determination not to sign, and, if necessary, to abandon his political career in order to campaign against the Treaty. He called it a 'terrible document, not a peace treaty but a war treaty'.

A last chance
His last chance to alter it came when the Delegates of the British Empire met on May 30. If the British Empire Delegation could be persuaded to support Smuts' views, then the French would be compelled to make some alterations. In three meetings Smuts laid down his views and gained the sympathy of the meeting for many, if not all, of his proposals. But when the resolution of the meeting appeared, little mention was made of the dissenting views expressed at the meeting. It consisted mainly of a summary of Lloyd George's views. Smuts had been outwitted, and his last chance to alter the Treaty had been lost.

Between the Empire Delegation meetings and the signing of the Treaty on June 28 Smuts wavered. To sign or not to sign? As late as June 21 he telegraphed Botha announcing his intention not to sign, but on June 28, along with all the other delegates, Smuts added his name at the foot of the Treaty.

Why did he do it? The most outspoken critic of the Treaty, all of whose misgivings have been substantiated by later events, nonetheless signed the document which he clearly saw was merely a guarantee of another war. His reasons are not far to seek. Firstly, some formal peace, even a bad one, was essential if Europe was to escape from anarchy. Secondly, attached to the Treaty, bad though it might be, was the Covenant of the League of Nations. Thirdly, and most important of all, if South Africa refused to sign the Treaty she would forfeit South West Africa. There could be no question of this. If Smuts, therefore, declined to sign, it would be as a solitary personal gesture. He would have had to resign his post as a Union Minister, and rupture his association with Botha, an association on which South Africa had been built. The price was too high. In spite of his misgivings, Smuts had no choice but to sign the Treaty.

Further Reading
Hancock, W. K., *Smuts 1. The Sanguine Years* (Cambridge University Press 1962)

Mainstay of the Infantry: The Bolt-Action Rifle

Of the millions of men who fought in the First World War, the majority were infantrymen whose personal weapon was a rifle. The First World War was fought at a time when the bolt-action magazine rifle had reached a peak of development upon which no subsequent improvements have been made. From the comparatively crude Dreyse Needle Gun of the Austro-Prussian war, the modern rifle gradually took shape, but no improvements would have been possible without the one outstanding feature of the Needle Gun: the combination of projectile, propellant and detonator. From this improvement all others sprang.

The principle of the bolt action is as follows:

The bolt, in outline resembling an ordinary door bolt, contains a long, spring-loaded, firing pin. On sliding the bolt towards the breech, the bullet is inserted into the breech, the spring, making contact with the trigger mechanism via the cocking piece, is compressed, thus withdrawing the firing pin, and the bolt is locked into the breech mechanism. The most effective of the locking systems is by dual lugs which revolve into recesses in the breech; these can be either vertical or horizontal. Other locking systems are of a

wedge type in the breech or by a rear lug. This last system, which is employed in the British Short Magazine Lee-Enfield, has been subjected to criticism because it allows too much 'play' in the bolt and, in general, is not as strong as the front locking system. Various methods of triggering the mechanism to release the firing pin have been developed. Essentially, however, the process is the same — by squeezing the trigger the resistance to the cocking piece is released and the firing pin makes contact with the percussion cap. With a turn-bolt, the locking mechanism is engaged by turning the bolt handle down when the bolt has been fully pushed home. The straight-pull bolt has an internal spiral system which automatically revolves the lugs into place as the bolt slides forward.

The box magazine, variations of which were employed by the majority of rifles of the period, is an extremely simple mechanism; it consists of a metal box incorporating a spring-loaded platform. The magazine is situated, forward of the trigger guard, below the mechanism. The capacity of the various designs varied from 3 to 10 rounds. For the most part, the magazines were an integral part of the rifle but there were several removable designs. In some instances,

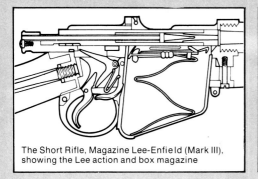

The Short Rifle, Magazine Lee-Enfield (Mark III), showing the Lee action and box magazine

The Russian M1891 Moisin-Nagant rifle with Moisin action and the Belgian Nagant magazine

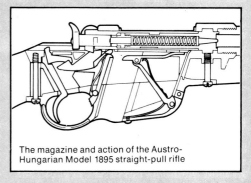

The magazine and action of the Austro-Hungarian Model 1895 straight-pull rifle

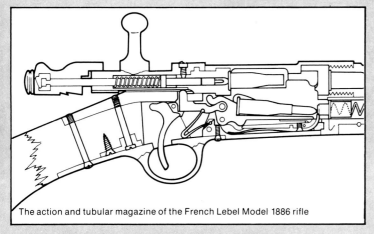

The action and tubular magazine of the French Lebel Model 1886 rifle

The action and magazine of the German Model 1898 rifle and carbine

the cartridges were staggered within the box, in others they were in-line. Cartridges were injected into the magazine by means of a clip. Clips assumed a variety of different shapes, but the principle was the same in all. They consisted of open-ended slides or cases within which a number of cartridges, 3, 5, or 6, were gripped whether by the spring metal of the case or a spring incorporated in the base. When the bolt was withdrawn, the clip was positioned between the bolt-head and the breech, and the cartridges were usually pressed down into the magazine by the thumb. The subsequent forward movement of the bolt ejected the clip and pushed the first round into the breech. The major deviation from this method was that adopted by Mannlicher for most of his designs. The Mannlicher system involved placing the clip with the cartridges into the magazine, a spring then pushing the cartridges up *within* the clip. When the last round was in the breech, the clip would fall through an aperture in the bottom of the magazine.

Without doubt the German contribution to small arms design has been the greatest. In particular the rifles of Peter Paul Mauser demonstrated a remarkable ingenuity and have influenced rifle design throughout the world. The Mauser Gewehr 98 was probably the most successful rifle of its kind ever designed.

Second only to Mauser was Mannlicher. A frequently under-estimated inventor, he was often badly used. It is significant, however, that his designs and elements of his designs have been incorporated in the weapons of many different countries.

The United States claims, with some justification, much credit for advances in small arms design. Most of these advances, however, applied to weapons of eras before and after that which concerns us here. The biggest single contribution from America was that of the Lee box magazine and Lee, although he worked in America, was born in Scotland.

Britain's contribution was in the field of rifling. Before the introduction of the smokeless 'cordite' propellant, the Metford system of rifling was general; the new propellant, however, necessitated a different system and the Enfield system was almost universally adopted and is still used. Illustrated overleaf are the genealogies of the major design features of the First World War's rifles and carbines, with the colour coding showing the provenance of each weapon's cartridge, bolt system and magazine. A few further points about some of the weapons follow. The Italian Mannlicher-Carcano is sometimes called the Mauser-Paravicino and has been described, erroneously, as dangerous to fire. The Mauser Gewehr 88 was Germany's answer to the French introduction of smokeless powder with the 1886 Lebel rifle. The Gewehr 98 was a development of this, and can be claimed to be the world's most successful bolt-action rifle ever. The Mauser M1889 was Belgium's first modern rifle, and was the first rifle to utilise the Mauser magazine charger. The Turkish M1893 rifle was basically the same as the Spanish 7-mm weapon of the same date. Both introduced the Mauser staggered-row magazine. The Springfield M1903 was an adaptation of the Mauser ▷

Mainstay of the Infantry:

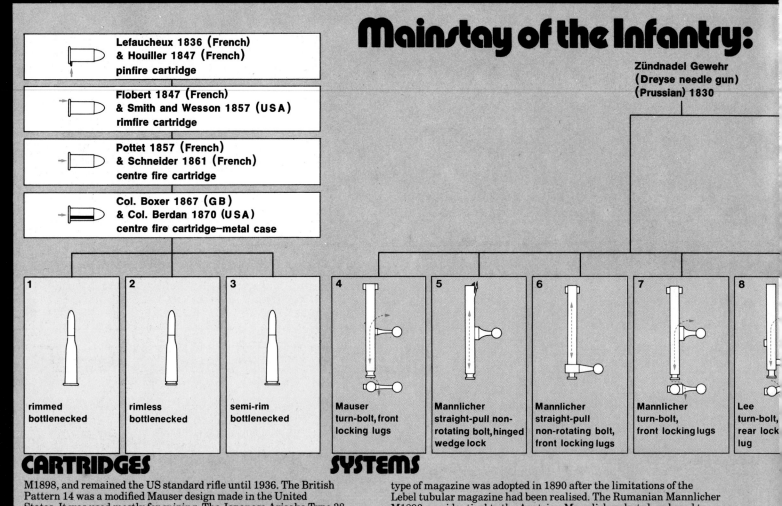

Zündnadel Gewehr (Dreyse needle gun) (Prussian) 1830

Lefaucheux 1836 (French) & Houiller 1847 (French) pinfire cartridge

Flobert 1847 (French) & Smith and Wesson 1857 (USA) rimfire cartridge

Pottet 1857 (French) & Schneider 1861 (French) centre fire cartridge

Col. Boxer 1867 (GB) & Col. Berdan 1870 (USA) centre fire cartridge—metal case

1 rimmed bottlenecked

2 rimless bottlenecked

3 semi-rim bottlenecked

4 Mauser turn-bolt, front locking lugs

5 Mannlicher straight-pull non-rotating bolt, hinged wedge lock

6 Mannlicher straight-pull non-rotating bolt, front locking lugs

7 Mannlicher turn-bolt, front locking lugs

8 Lee turn-bolt, rear lock lug

CARTRIDGES

SYSTEMS

M1898, and remained the US standard rifle until 1936. The British Pattern 14 was a modified Mauser design made in the United States. It was used mostly for sniping. The Japanese Arisaka Type 38 was introduced in 1905, and had a sliding bolt cover to keep the action clean. It was usually removed in action, however, as it made a great deal of noise. The Austrian Mannlicher M88/90 was introduced in 1890 to take advantage of the new and more powerful smokeless powder. Otherwise the rifle was identical to the Model 1886. An unusual feature was the fact that the magazine charger clip was ejected from the bottom of the magazine when the latter was empty. The M90 carbine introduced the rotating bolt to the Austrian army. The M95 was the main Austrian rifle of the First World War and was used also by the Italians, Bulgarians, Serbs and, to a lesser degree, by the Greeks. The Mannlicher-Berthier rifles were, with the Lebel, France's standard rifle until well into the 1930s. The Mannlicher

type of magazine was adopted in 1890 after the limitations of the Lebel tubular magazine had been realised. The Rumanian Mannlicher M1893 was identical to the Austrian Mannlicher, but chambered to take a Dutch round. The British Short Magazine Lee-Enfield No 1 Mark III was introduced in January 1907 and was the main infantry weapon used by the British in the First World War. The French Lebel was the world's first modern, mass-produced magazine rifle, and also introduced smokeless powder to the armies of the world. The Lebel's round was, however, of a design unsuitable for automatic weapons, and future French rifles reverted to a more conventional design of magazine and round. Finally, the Russian Moisin-Nagant, which was introduced in 1891. It was designed for a conical-nosed bullet, but the adoption of the Spitzer pointed round in 1908 necessitated no more than a change in the rear sight to accommodate the new ballistics. *Owen Wood*

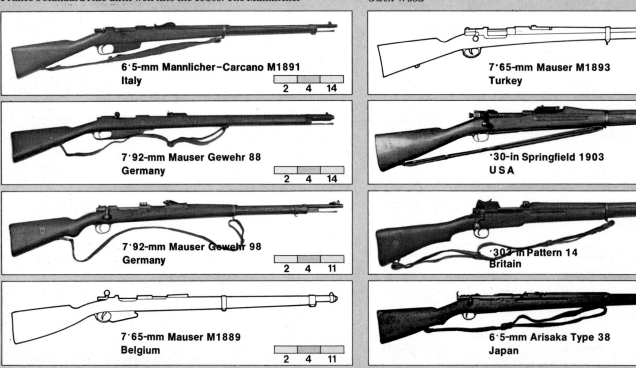

6·5-mm Mannlicher–Carcano M1891 Italy — 2 | 4 | 14

7·92-mm Mauser Gewehr 88 Germany — 2 | 4 | 14

7·92-mm Mauser Gewehr 98 Germany — 2 | 4 | 11

7·65-mm Mauser M1889 Belgium — 2 | 4 | 11

7·65-mm Mauser M1893 Turkey — 2 | 4 | 13

·30-in Springfield 1903 USA — 2 | 4 | 13

·303-in Pattern 14 Britain — 1 | 4 | 13

6·5-mm Arisaka Type 38 Japan — 3 | 4 | 13

The Bolt-Action Rifle

Lee box magazine 1879

Chassepot rifle (French) 1866

Gras rifle 1874

tubular magazine of a type used in many early repeating rifles

9
Moisin turn-bolt, horizontal front locking lugs

10
Lebel turn-bolt, front locking lugs

11
Lee box magazine, 10 rounds capacity

12
Nagant box magazine, 5 round capacity

13
Mauser box magazine, 5 round capacity

14
Mannlicher box magazine, 3, 5 & 6 round capacity

15
Lebel tubular magazine, 8 round capacity

FEED DEVICES

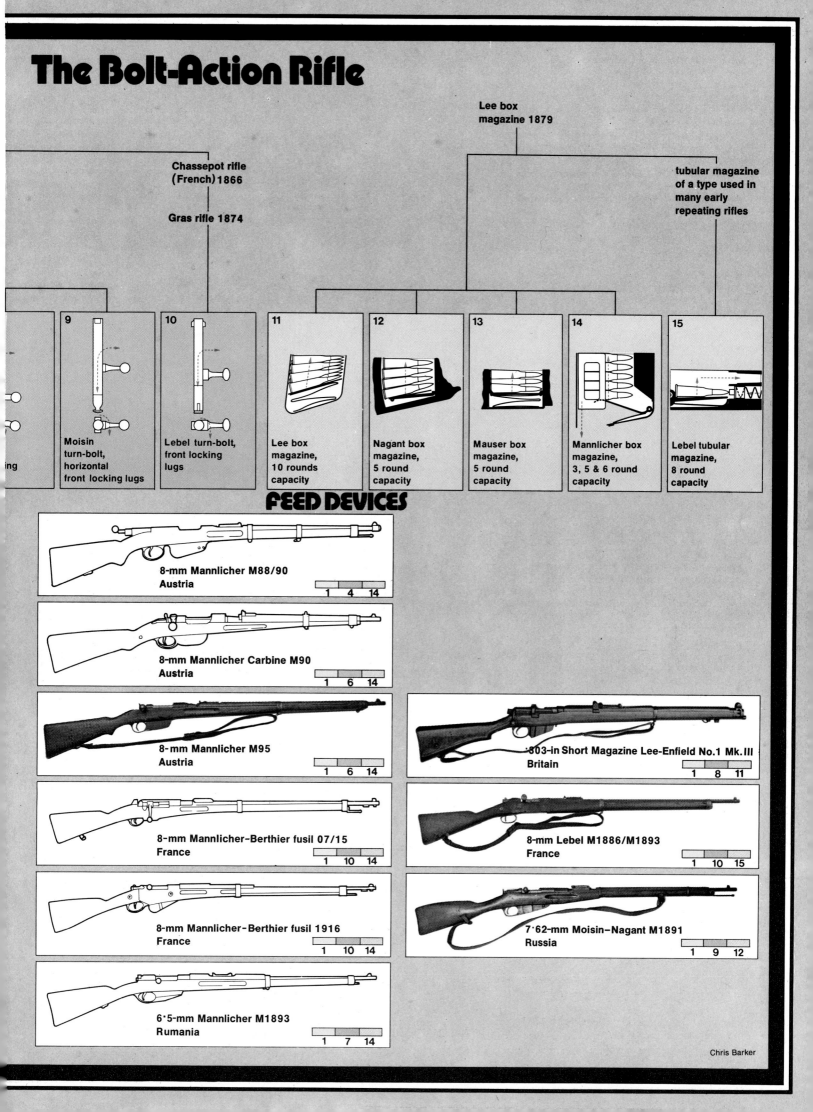

8-mm Mannlicher M88/90
Austria
`1  4  14`

8-mm Mannlicher Carbine M90
Austria
`1  6  14`

8-mm Mannlicher M95
Austria
`1  6  14`

8-mm Mannlicher–Berthier fusil 07/15
France
`1  10  14`

8-mm Mannlicher–Berthier fusil 1916
France
`1  10  14`

6·5-mm Mannlicher M1893
Rumania
`1  7  14`

·303-in Short Magazine Lee-Enfield No.1 Mk.III
Britain
`1  8  11`

8-mm Lebel M1886/M1893
France
`1  10  15`

7·62-mm Moisin–Nagant M1891
Russia
`1  9  12`

Chris Barker

UNREST
IN EGYPT

Egypt, occupied by Britain since 1882, was to the British
a vital link in the route to the Far East; with its
command over the Suez Canal it was inconceivable to the
Foreign Office in London that Britain should pull out.
But Egyptian nationalism, encouraged by the sympathetic
hearing that nationalist objectives were receiving at
the time, presented a growing challenge to British
sovereignty. In Sa'ad Zaghlul it found a forceful
spokesman and in the *Wafd* a powerful vehicle for the
expression of dissatisfaction at British procrastination
in granting independence. But with pleas for talks
rejected it seemed that only rioting and sabotage
would make the British listen. *Suleiman Mousa.*
Above: British remount depot exercising — evidence of the
military presence so detested by the nationalists.
Right: Anti-British demonstrations in Cairo, 1918.

Imperial War Museum

During the First World War, statements of lofty aims by the Allied Powers gave hope and encouragement to the Egyptian nationalists. Wilson's '14 Points' were considered a solemn undertaking and carried great weight in the East. The Anglo-French declaration promising freedom to the former vassals of the Ottoman Empire was published in Egypt on November 8, 1918. Five days later, an Egyptian delegation of three nationalists had an interview with Sir Francis Wingate, High Commissioner for Egypt. Sa'ad Zaghlul, the leader of the delegation, demanded independence, offering Britain a treaty of alliance and the right to reoccupy the Suez Canal, if necessary. Zaghlul suggested that he and his associates should go to London to discuss Egyptian affairs with the British Government. Wingate informed the Foreign Office; but he was told that the time was 'inopportune' and that the nationalists should not be permitted to leave Egypt. In answer, Zaghlul formed a political party, which became known as the *Wafd* ('delegation'), and issued a statement in which he declared that his object was 'to achieve the independence of Egypt by peaceful means'. The *Wafd* was destined to dominate Egypt's political arena as the most important party during the following 34 years — up to the revolution of 1952.

Zaghlul, who before the war had held the posts of Minister of Education and Minister of Justice, soon became the embodiment of Egyptian nationalism. Born an Egyptian peasant his background, allied to his religious education, enhanced his appeal to the rank and file in Egypt. He had proved himself an able statesman and an astute politician, and a man strong enough to lead the nationalist movement in his country.

The roots of the modern nationalist movement in Egypt go back to the years 1880-1882 when Arabi, himself of peasant stock, attempted to free the Egyptians from the autocratic rule of the Khedive and the Turco-Circassian élite. Arabi was defeated by a British army on September 13, 1882, and Egypt fell under British occupation (the British Government at the time declaring that they would withdraw their military forces 'as early as possible'). Egypt remained legally under the Sultan's sovereignty, but in fact his sovereignty was nominal. This contradictory state of affairs continued until December 18, 1914, when Britain proclaimed Egypt a Protectorate as a step in the prosecution of the war which had broken out with Turkey on October 29, 1914.

The Egyptians felt a genuine resentment towards British occupation. This resentment was aggravated by the severance of their country from the Ottoman Sultan, the recognised religious leader of all Moslems. Moreover in 1914 Britain undertook 'to bear the sole burden of the war without calling on Egypt for aid', but in spite of this undertaking the grain and livestock of the peasantry were requisitioned and a Labour Corps of 117,000 men was recruited to serve the needs of the British forces in France and Palestine. The methods applied intensified the resentment against the British. Although when the war ended the rules of martial law were relaxed, Zaghlul and his colleagues found the minds of their countrymen fertile ground; for the Egyptians, who believed themselves more advanced than the Arabs of Asia, felt

Above: Inauguration of the Egyptian Parliament. Centre — the king. Standing, reading — Zaghlul

Above: Sa'ad Zaghlul, twice deported for *Wafd* activities, but made Prime Minister in 1924

Above: British march past in Alexandria; reminder to the nationalists of British control

slighted when King Hussein of the Hejāz was invited to send a representative to the Peace Conference and their own request for representation at the Conference fell on deaf ears.

Meanwhile Lord Curzon, a former Viceroy of India, was controlling the day-to-day work of the Foreign Office in London. Britain's interest in Egypt traditionally concentrated on the vital artery of communications with the British Empire in Asia: the occupation in 1882 had taken place largely in order to safeguard the Canal. Foremost in Curzon's mind therefore was the safety of the Suez Canal and the route to the Far East. Wingate on the other hand was aware of the strength of Egyptian nationalist feelings. In January 1919 he went to Paris and London to point out the latent dangers and try to convince the government of the need for conciliation. He conveyed his warning to Lloyd George and Balfour in Paris, but he had to wait 14 days in London before Curzon would give him a hearing. On February 17, Curzon rejected Wingate's proposal that Zaghlul be invited to London. The Foreign Office invited an Egyptian ministerial deputation, but refused to entertain the idea of negotiating with the nationalists. The nationalists, however, were by then in complete control of the masses, and the ministers could not swim against the tide of nationalist opposition; they at once resigned, the situation began to deteriorate, and the result 'was a lifetime of Egyptian hostility' to Britain.

Zaghlul's attempts to frustrate the formation of a new Cabinet aroused British official anger. On March 8, he and three of his colleagues were arrested and deported to Malta. This was the spark which ignited the already inflammable situation. Revolt broke out throughout Egypt on the second day. There were strikes, riots and acts of sabotage from Alexandria to Luxor. Demonstrations by students continued for a week. Communications were attacked; Cairo was isolated from the rest of the country, and unrest spread rapidly to the provinces. British soldiers were assaulted and much public property was damaged. The revolt took the British Government by surprise. Lloyd George decided that a

strong man was needed to control the situation. His choice fell on General Allenby, who had defeated the Turks in Syria and had earned fame in the Middle East. Wingate was dismissed and Allenby appointed Special High Commissioner to restore law and order in Egypt and 'to administer in all matters as may be required by the necessity of maintaining the King's Protectorate on a secure basis'.

Egypt in those days was teeming with British soldiers and the March rebellion was soon controlled. Allenby decided to establish contact with the *Wafd* and recommended to his government the release of Zaghlul and his colleagues. On April 7 they were released and allowed to go to Paris, where the Peace Conference was in session. This step was greeted with great rejoicing by the Egyptians.

The rejoicing, however, was brief, because Lord Curzon promptly declared that the British Government would not negotiate with Zaghlul. This resulted in a strike of government officials and the resignation of the Egyptian Cabinet. Allenby was forced to restore martial law.

In Paris, the *Wafd* met with more disappointment. They were denied a hearing by the Peace Conference and were shocked when President Wilson recognised, on April 13, their country as a Protectorate of Great Britain. This was a severe blow to the *Wafd* and one which caused a split in its ranks, but Zaghlul managed to retain his leadership of the majority of the Egyptian people. Zaghlul was now determined to abolish the Protectorate while the British Government was as determined to maintain it.

To gain time, the British Government resorted to a device that has proved effective many times in similar circumstances. A Commission was appointed in May 1919 under the chairmanship of Lord Milner, Secretary of State for the Colonies. The terms of reference of the Commission stated that its purpose was: 'To inquire into the causes of the late disorders in Egypt, and to report on the existing situation in the country and the form of the Constitution which, under the Protectorate, will be best calculated to promote its peace and prosperity, the progressive development of

self-governing institutions and the protection of foreign interests.'

While the British Government considered these terms liberal and generous, the Egyptians thought them an insult, particularly as everything was to remain 'under the Protectorate'. The Commission did not arrive until December, enabling the *Wafd* to organise opposition to it. It was greeted with riots, demonstrations and a general boycott. In the face of all this, Milner issued a statement in which he declared that the object of his Commission was 'to reconcile the aspirations of the Egyptian people with the special interests which Great Britain has in Egypt'. This statement was welcomed by the *Wafd*'s Central Committee, whose members suggested direct negotiations between them and the Commission; but although, by that time, it was evident that the *Wafd* represented the majority in Egypt, the British Government were not yet ready to recognise that fact or to act accordingly.

A gulf too wide to bridge

The Commission spent three months in Egypt and, in spite of the boycott, was able to learn a good deal about Egyptian aspirations. When Milner was back in London, he decided that direct contact with the *Wafd* was after all necessary. Zaghlul was accordingly invited to London and, in the summer of 1920, informal talks took place between the two men. Milner wanted to find out if he could reach an agreement with Zaghlul that would be acceptable to the British Government. At the same time Zaghlul thought it possible to reach a settlement that would give Egypt genuine independence while safeguarding British interests. These talks resulted in what came to be known as the Milner-Zaghlul Agreement, which envisaged the conclusion of a treaty recognising Egypt's independence and safeguarding British interests through an Anglo-Egyptian alliance and an undertaking by Britain to defend Egypt. But although both parties were anxious to reach a satisfactory settlement, the gulf was still too wide to bridge. Milner was bound to a definite policy of the British Government, while Zaghlul wanted more than the semblance of independence. Their talks were suspended and the Commission submitted its report to the British Government in December 1920, recommending the conclusion of a bilateral agreement in a treaty of alliance 'by which Egypt, in return for Great Britain's undertaking to defend her integrity and independence, would agree to be guided by Great Britain in her foreign relations and would at the same time confer upon Great Britain certain definite rights in Egyptian territory'.

The report came as a shock to the Conservatives in Britain, who were primarily concerned about the safety of imperial communications. The British Cabinet did not accept Milner's recommendations, being of the opinion that he 'had far exceeded his terms of reference'. The British Government, however, persisted in its attempts to reach a negotiated agreement. They announced in February 1921 their readiness to abolish the Protectorate as the basis for negotiations over a treaty with Egypt. Negotiations with a governmental delegation started in London, but were broken off in the face of nationalist opposition. On December 23, 1921, Zaghlul and his leading colleagues were arrested

A riot breaks out in Cairo. Anti-British feeling took the form of demonstrations, sabotage, violent riots and severed communications

and deported to the Seychelles.

Allenby now took matters into his own hands. He set out to break the political power of the *Wafd* and to help the moderates earn the credit for obtaining for Egypt what the *Wafd* could not obtain. Terms were worked out, only to prove unacceptable to the Foreign Office. Allenby decided the situation could stand no more procrastination, and went himself to London in February 1922. He submitted a long memorandum to the Cabinet, and informed the Prime Minister that either his proposals or his resignation must be accepted. By the logic of his case and the strength of his personality, Allenby was able to obtain the acquiescence of the Cabinet. After his return to Cairo, he published, on February 28, the Declaration of Egyptian Independence, which terminated the Protectorate. Four points, however, were: . . . *absolutely reserved to the discretion of His Majesty's Government until such time as it may be possible by free discussion and friendly accommodation on both sides to conclude agreements in regard thereto between His Majesty's Government and the Government of Egypt:*

● *the security of the communications of the British Empire in Egypt;*
● *the defence of Egypt against all foreign aggression or interference, direct and indirect;*
● *the protection of foreign interests in Egypt and the protection of minorities;*
● *the Sudan*

Pending the conclusion of such agreement the status quo *in all these matters shall remain intact.*

The important factor that prevented the ultimate success of the new policy was that it was a unilateral action and not a negotiated agreement. The *Wafd* rejected the Declaration, considering it a national catastrophe and arguing that the reservations robbed the independence of its substance. Nevertheless, an Egyptian Ministry of Foreign Affairs was established and, on March 15, the Sultan assumed the title of King; a constitutional committee was established to draft a constitution and an electoral law.

The *Wafd,* however, remained opposed to the policy of the Declaration and Egypt was without a Cabinet for about 40 days. Troubles and assassinations took place and Allenby found it necessary to arrest the *Wafd*'s Central Committee. Nevertheless, the constitution was promulgated on April 19, 1923 and made electoral law on April 30. Martial law was abolished in July and Zaghlul returned from his banishment in September 1923. He was still the popular leader of Egypt. This was proved in the first elections held at the beginning of 1924, when, out of 214 members of the new parliament, 190 declared themselves supporters of Zaghlul, who became the first Prime Minister of the new Egypt. But formal recognition on the part of the Egyptians of the special position of Great Britain had to wait until the conclusion of the Treaty of Alliance on August 26, 1936.

Further Reading
Hurewitz, J. C., *Diplomacy in the Near and Middle East,* volume 2 (Princeton 1956)
Zayid Mahmud, Y., *Egypt's Struggle for Independence* (Khayats, Beirut 1965)

[*For Suleiman Mousa's biography, see page 2407.*]

Popperfoto

The Pan-African Movement

In February 1919 one more congress besides the Peace Conference was gathered in Paris. There were only 57 delegates and its aims were modest and conciliatory but it aroused an entirely new political force in the 20th Century – black nationalism. *Immanuel Geiss. Above:* The British in Nigeria – Government House, Lagos. *Right:* Nigerian troops, used by the British

The end of the war and the convening of the Paris Peace Conference had raised many hopes throughout the world. It was not only the many belligerent and the few remaining neutral nations that were looking to the French capital for a more permanent peace settlement. Members of the numerous colonial peoples in Asia and Africa, represented by their few intellectual leaders, also thought the day had come to voice their aspirations. The Great War had, after all, been waged against the autocratic Central Powers under the banner of liberty and self-determination for suppressed peoples, particularly after the United States of America had entered the war in spring 1917. Surely the victorious democratic Allied and Associated Powers would also give national self-determination to the colonial peoples? With this aim in view representatives of all shades converged on Paris to hover on the fringes of the International Peace Conference: delegations and individuals from Arab countries and India, and of the Zionist movement appeared to stand a better chance than others, since they spoke in the name of well-organised groups or princes. A shy and slim young man from Indo-China presented a petition to the Peace Conference. But he was shrugged off and drew the conclusion that organisation for revolution was the answer – the late Ho Chi Minh had made his entry into world politics, hardly noticed by his contemporaries. One of the more flamboyant attempts to capture the atten-

tion of the Peace Conference was made by a group that spoke for Africans and people of African descent, the early Pan-African movement. It held its first Congress in early 1919 in Paris which was covered by the press because of the novelty of about 60 Africans and Afro-Americans being assembled in a white man's capital. The direct political consequences to the Powers were slight after the First World War, but the first Pan-African Congress did mark a new stage in the development of Pan-Africanism, which later had a direct bearing on the emergence of African nationalism after the Second World War.

What, then, was the Pan-African movement in early 1919? Where did it come from? What was its social basis? The name 'Pan-African' dates back to 1900. It was coined in the course of preparations for the Pan-African Conference held in London in July 1900. The intellectual and political aspirations behind that name, however, can be traced back in their origins well into the 19th Century. Pan-African ideas, however vaguely articulated, came from small modernised groups of Africans and Afro-Americans in the United States and the British West Indies who had been cut off or alienated from their traditional background in Africa, almost completely in the case of America, and at least partly in Africa herself. These groups had sprung into existence as a by-product of the transatlantic slave trade and of slavery in the New World. They formed a conspicuous mulatto element, their white

fathers being involved in the slave trade along the West African coast, in particular the Gold Coast (Ghana), or in actual slavery in the New World. Their mothers were free African women on the West African Coast, who lived with the Europeans there, or enslaved African women in the New World.

From the late 18th Century communities of free Afro-Americans and educated Africans slowly developed and in America they began to organise themselves. In Africa they developed in two main centres – on the Gold Coast and in Sierra Leone. It was from Sierra Leone that after the abolition of slavery in the British Empire in 1834 groups of modernised and mostly Christianised ex-slaves, 'liberated Africans' or 'Sierra Leoneans', spread along the West African coast, especially to the coastal areas of Nigeria. They were the only major groups of Africans or Afro-Americans who were not predominantly mulattoes.

All these groups, scattered about on both sides of the Atlantic, took some more coherent form during the 19th Century. The various Protestant churches, above all the Methodists and the Anglicans, gave them the first introduction into more highly developed ways of life through schools, and the first chances of organising themselves in a more permanent way. By acquiring a modest share of wealth and a modern education (from the late 19th Century onwards also on the university level) their most progressive exponents developed a political consciousness of their

own. Generally, as unwanted products of European expansion overseas, they were also products of Europe in their political ideas. They reacted either in accordance with or in opposition to white domination, represented by European colonial rule in Africa and the 'white power structure' in America. During most of the 19th Century the African and Afro-American modern élites asked for nothing more than fair treatment and equality of opportunity, at least for the 'civilised members' of the 'Negro race'. But the end of the 19th Century saw a drastic change. White power and white racism triumphed with the completion of European colonial rule and the breakdown of reconstruction in North America. ·The much-dreaded colour bar spread from South Africa to East and West Africa, a particularly unpleasant shock to the modernised African élites in Sierra Leone, the Gold Coast and Nigeria, all the more because they had been accustomed to the humanitarian liberalism of the Victorian age. In America it was the formal establishment of the system of segregation and racial suppression in the South and the spread of lynching and urban riots in the North that, from 1890 onwards, aroused the small but growing groups of modernised intellectuals.

These experiences of shock on both sides of the Atlantic provoked two important movements—African nationalism and the Afro-American Civil Rights movement. Both met in Pan-Africanism. In 1897, W. E. B. Du Bois, one of the most im-portant Pan-African leaders, saw the Afro-Americans as 'the advance guard of the Negro people' and as 'the vanguard of Pan-Negroism'. His concept was to relieve the position of his own group in America by improving Africa's position in the world. In 1898, Henry Sylvester-Williams, a 30-year-old barrister from Trinidad, started to organise the first Pan-African Conference, which took place in London in July 1900. The conference was planned as a conscious reaction to the deterioration of the position of Africans and Afro-Americans in the preceding decade and as the first attempt to articulate their aims in the modern world. In the conference's pathetic appeal, *To the Nations of the World,* its author, Du Bois, struck a note which appears to us every day more and more realistic . . . *The problem of the 20th Century is the problem of the colour line, the question as to how far the differences of race, which show themselves chiefly in the colour of the skin and the texture of the hair, are going to be made, hereafter, the basis of denying to over half the world the right of sharing to their utmost ability the opportunities and privileges of modern mankind.*

The London Pan-African Conference had no direct political impact. It suffered from the disabilities common to struggling causes: poverty of finances, weakness of organisation, scarcity of genuinely African representation, lack of information. Nevertheless, a first Pan-African Association was founded, which met with some en-thusiastic echo in British West Africa. It was planned to have a Pan-African Congress every two years. But none of the far-flung hopes materialised: the Pan-African Association was stillborn and no Pan-African Congress took place before the First World War.

While the first Pan-African Association dissolved, however, Du Bois in America apparently acted according to his 'vanguard' concept of 1897. In organising the modern intelligentsia of Afro-Americans, 'the talented tenth', to a more militant resistance against white racism, in particular by the National Association for the Advancement of Coloured People (NAACP) in 1910, he maintained Africa in the perspectives of his followers. In 1915 he saw the war as a chance to do something for Africa and Afro-Americans at the same time: victory of the democratic principle would weaken the colonial system in Africa and racism in America. The large-scale use of African and Afro-American troops on French soil in the defence of democracy against the militarism of Germany, whose colonial record in Africa was notoriously bad amongst informed African and Afro-American intellectuals even before 1914, had put new political ideas into the heads of many black soldiers. The marked contrast between racial tolerance practised by large sections of the French population and the racial discrimination practised by the US Army in France, made many Africans and Afro-Americans more thoughtful than their white masters could have liked.

After the war their articulateness was increased by contact with Marxism in London or Paris.

It was in this ferment of political events and ideas that Du Bois arrived in Paris in December 1918. Originally, he had been charged by the NAACP to investigate complaints of Afro-American soldiers in France about racial discrimination in the US Army and to look after the interests of Africa in the broadest sense during the Peace Conference. Apparently, he came with the intention of organising a Pan-African Congress on the spot. In Paris he immediately established contact by letter with local groups in London, British humanitarians, the Anti-Slavery and Aborigines Protection Society, and the newly-founded African Progress Union. On December 28, Du Bois attended a public ceremony in Paris, during which Blaise Diagne, the black deputy of the Sénégal, was decorated with the cross of the Légion d'Honneur for having organised mass recruitment of African troops in French West Africa. Du Bois was moved to tears: 'Men of Africa! How fine a thing to be a black Frenchman in 1919 – imagine such a celebration in America!'

In Du Bois and Diagne we see the two main elements represented that made up early Pan-Africanism: the Afro-American intellectual, who had studied in American and European universities, at Harvard and Berlin, and who had started to organise his fellow-countrymen with an eye to Africa; and the African professional politician, with administrative practice in the French West Indies, who had organised his fellow-countrymen for war. Du Bois, the intellectual, and Diagne, the man of action, of unmingled African origin. Du Bois with a precarious mandate of his organisation, NAACP, which stood in internal opposition to official government; Diagne, with his parliamentary mandate and prestige of his war service for France.

The US: White opposition

Contact was soon followed by co-operation. In the first days of the new year 1919 Du Bois addressed Diagne in a memorandum, suggesting a congress be held in Paris in early February. Du Bois wanted to invite representatives of the whole 'Negro Race', from Africa, America and the West Indies, in particular from Abyssinia, Liberia and Haiti, but also from Japan, China and India. His idea was to analyse the position of the 'negro' and to advance demands to improve it, notably universal education, recognition of independence and territorial integrity of Abyssinia, Liberia and Haiti 'with their full natural boundaries' and the 'development of the former German colonies under the guarantees and oversight of the League of Nations'.

Du Bois' original grandiose scheme was impracticable in the given situation: the African, Haitian and Asian governments earmarked for participation were not interested politically. It was impossible to get together sufficiently qualified representatives from the various countries and territories, especially in view of the prevailing difficulties of transport and free movement at the end of the war. Furthermore, the United States Government, with its roots in the racist South, did everything to prevent the success of the Congress: national self-determination was meant for whites only. The American

government, therefore, stopped all Afro-Americans or white sympathisers who wanted to go to Paris for the Pan-African Congress. The British colonial governments followed suit, so that Africans from British colonies who wanted to go to Paris for the Pan-African Congress were denied the necessary travel papers. The US government even spread the (false) rumour that the French government would ban the Congress anyway. In spite of diplomatic pressure, the French did, however, allow the Congress to take place. The French Premier Georges Clemenceau is reported to have told Diagne: 'Don't advertise it, but go ahead.'

In view of the many obstacles, the first Pan-African Congress, as it opened on February 19, 1919, was greatly reduced in scope compared with Du Bois' first concept. Only 57 'delegates' assembled, none of them, of course, actually delegated for the Congress, because there would have been no time for such procedures. Most of them happened to be in France at the time for some reason or other. The 16 delegates from the USA and the 13 delegates from the French West Indies dominated clearly, strengthened by 7 Haitians. Those seven listed as coming from France may have been mostly African. In addition to them there were three delegates from Liberia, two from Spanish colonies and one each from Portuguese, British, French and Belgian colonies in Black Africa, Algeria, Egypt, Abyssinia, San Domingo and England. There were none from the British West Indies and apparently only one from Sierra Leone. The Congress, therefore, was as representative as it could be under the difficult political circumstances of early 1919. Its composition was also one-sided in another aspect: only the groups of modernised Africans and Afro-Americans were represented at the Congress: three members of the French National Assembly for the French West Indies (Candace, Boisneuf and Lagrossillière), their colleagues for the Sénégal, Diagne, and the Liberian President-elect, C. D. B. King. It was the modernised establishment of Africans and Afro-Americans that duly assembled in the 'Grand Hotel', Paris.

Two-fold weakness

Traditional Africa, however, was not and could not be present at the Paris Congress. The reason is suggested by the perceptive remark of the French Africanist Maurice Delafosse, one of the white sympathisers to observe the Congress: the traditional representatives of African tribes could not even have followed the proceedings without numerous interpreters and would have been completely unprepared for it intellectually. 'Most probably they would have expressed strange views, betraying their single-minded preoccupation with petty local problems and not the least concern for common interests of the race.' Such was the two-fold weakness of the Pan-African Congress in 1919 that made its deliberations largely academic: that the 'delegates' represented only their own small groups of modern intelligentsias or the middle class, who were mostly cut off from tribal, traditional Africa, which, in her turn, was unprepared, intellectually and politically, to make good the immediate claims of their learned spokesmen. This dilemma perhaps also explains why the sources on the proceedings of the

Congress are so poor and unsatisfactory. Apparently the Congress did not go very much beyond an uncertain attempt to take stock of the general situation and to make some cautious proposals. Diagne, presiding over the Congress in all its sessions, opened the proceedings with an eloquent praise of French colonial rule. The three French West Indian deputies harshly criticised the USA for her policy of racial discrimination, especially in view of the war, fought, ostensibly, for democracy and equality. William E. Walling, a white Liberal, meekly defended his country by pointing out that the United States were changing already and would have to give way to the pressure of world opinion in the long run, one of the many illusions of American liberals of the day. More directly apologetic were French, Belgians and Portuguese who gave glowing descriptions of the colonial policies of their respective countries. In the brow-beating presence of so many members of the colonialist 'motherlands' it is understandable that what was said on the situation as seen from the other side was neither disquieting nor revolutionary. Africans merely sketched their colonial situation under white rule.

In its final resolution the Congress pleaded above all for humanitarian reforms in the colonies: definite abolition of slavery, forced labour and flogging; protection against economic exploitation and confiscation of land. The one political point raised was carefully worded so as not to provoke hostile reactions from the colonial powers: *The natives of Africa must have the right to participate in the Government as fast as their development permits ... They shall at once be allowed to participate in local and tribal government according to ancient usage, and this participation shall gradually extend, as education and experience proceed to higher offices of state; to the end that, in time, Africa is ruled by consent of the Africans.*

It is not clear whether members of the Congress saw their dilemma themselves, because a kind of self-government, under the protection of the League of Nations and based on the principle of 'tribal government according to ancient usage', and put forward by modernised, de-tribalised African and Afro-American intellectuals, was bound to be unworkable in the modern world. The Paris formula of 1919 was also a retreat from the platform of the almost forgotten London Pan-African Conference of 1900, which had demanded 'self-government' for Africa. Thus, American and French observers could be satisfied that the demands of the Pan-African Congress had been so 'reasonable' and 'moderate'.

The composition of the Pan-African Congress and the structural weakness of its social basis explains why Du Bois failed in the short term. Only two years later, at the next Pan-African Congress, it became possible to find a permanent organisation of some sort, at least on paper, the (second) 'Pan-African Association'. Du Bois succeeded in carrying on for another two Congresses, the last one in New York in 1927. The direct results of his efforts were almost negligible, but he succeeded in creating a precedent, mobilised in later years to promote African national independence.

[For Immanuel Geiss' biography, see page 68.]

The African Settlement

In colonial Africa Britain, France and Germany were the major powers, but after the First World War France and Britain combined to oust Germany — ostensibly for humanitarian reasons. *W. R. Louis. Below:* Engine sabotaged by Germans on the way out

'There are but three powers in Africa: England, France and Germany, two of which must inevitably combine against the third.' So wrote the Director of the German Colonial Office in 1894. Exactly 20 years later the truth of that observation became manifest to the entire world. After the outbreak of the war, Germany's colonial empire fell like an imperial stack of cards, leaving the Germans with only one ace, German East Africa, where Lettow-Vorbeck held out in isolation until after the Armistice. As Bismarck had surmised, overseas colonies in wartime would be seized by the dominant power at sea. British and French colonial troops turned hesitantly and then ferociously against their German adversaries. In August 1914 the British seized Togoland, forcing the Germans to blow up the most powerful wireless station in colonial territory. In July of the next year the South Africans captured the first Germany colony, South West Africa. In the summer of 1916 the Cameroons fell before the onslaught of an Anglo-French contingent. However, in that most interesting of all the 'side shows', East Africa, the British found themselves outclassed and outmanoeuvred by the Germans and outwitted by their allies, the Belgians, who moved into the north-west part of the colony as the British drove the Germans southwards. The results of these military operations preordained the territorial settlement of 1919, France and Britain partitioning Togoland and the Cameroons, South Africa acquiring South West Africa, and Great Britain relinquishing the north-west part of German East Africa to Belgium.

The African campaigns are well known. The official histories and memoirs recount the battles in minute detail and popular histories and films such as the *African Queen* have established the East African struggle as an epic. Who can forget Lettow-Vorbeck's account of his trek across the deserts and swamps of 'German East', being chased (according to him) by countless British generals? In the realm of international politics the settlement of 1919 is usually held to be no less remarkable than the military exploits of Lettow-Vorbeck. For the Allied statesmen declined to annex the German colonies and decided instead to place them as mandates, 'sacred trusts of civilisation', under the supervision of the League of Nations — a triumph for international idealism. In the conventional historiography of the colonial era in Africa the African settlement of 1919 indicates a turning point towards a more humane and progressive period. Before the First World War European Powers regarded their African colonies as experiments; the metropolitan governments,

in fact, had little actual control over them and they expected them to be, above all, financially self-supporting. Before 1914 these Powers made their greatest mistakes: 'the delegation of governmental powers to chartered and concessionaire companies; the encouragement of planter-settlers, whose interests were bound to conflict with those of the indigenous peoples; the confiscation of African land; atrocities and military excesses committed in the course of occupation or in the repression of revolt'. After 1919 colonialism in Africa seemed to be less exploitative, less cruel, and certainly more paternalistically devoted to the welfare of the indigenous inhabitants. Article 22 of the League Covenant provided the moral tone of the inter-war years—helping Africans to stand on their own feet, the implicit premise being that the imperial powers would lead them to independence. But the war aims of the African powers, which can now be studied with the aid of historical evidence rather than propaganda, belie that assumption.

'Morality plus security'

As *The Times Literary Supplement* commented, the African settlement in 1919 amounted to little more than horse-swapping. From the beginning of the war the British and French 'imperialists' regarded Africa merely as part of a worldwide redivision of territory. It is indeed astonishing to review the bargaining of less than two generations ago, when Britain and France had barely patched up their own colonial quarrels. In March 1915 the British Colonial Secretary, Lewis Harcourt, wrote:

We want from France two things: their share of the Condominium in the New Hebrides; their small settlement of Jibuti opposite Aden, which controls the mischievous arms traffic to Abyssinia and Central Africa. To obtain these we can offer France three-quarters of the Cameroons (instead of one half), plus *our half share of Togoland; or, if we wish to retain all Togoland and acquire Dahomey, we can offer France all the Cameroons except Mount Cameroon and Duala, and in such a wide settlement we could throw in the Gambia, which is an object of great desire by the French; but the cession of the Gambia would be very unpopular in this country, and arouse much public and parliamentary criticism and agitation. Alternatively we might surrender to France our share of the New Hebrides Condominium as compensation, with nearly the whole of the Cameroons, for our possession of Togoland and Dahomey.*

The French put forward similar schemes, though the two powers never came to such a grandiose settlement as outlined by Harcourt. Nor were Britain and France the only ambitious powers. Belgium and Portugal were also out for what pickings they could get. The former wanted greater access to the mouth of the River Congo; the latter hoped to expand from Moçambique into the south of German East Africa. In government circles, officials secretly discussed these schemes in relation to national and imperial security; publicly they claimed that whatever 'territorial adjustments' might be made in Africa at the close of the war would be 'for the benefit of the natives'. True enough, ran the argument, the Allied powers did not invade the German colonies to free the natives. But, having freed them, why should they be handed back to the 'Huns'? In Lord Curzon's words, if the colonies were returned, there would be the 'certainty of the fearful vengeance that would be wreaked upon the wretched natives who have aided or abetted our cause. We may be sure that a carnival of blood would be inaugurated in every territory so restored.' This was a convincing statement. To return the colonies would be immoral. Indeed, some historians think that the moral revulsion against the Germans because of atrocities in places such as Belgium as well as Africa formed the overriding reason for denying Germany any colonies whatsoever: *The shock of the war gave birth in England to a great discovery: the discovery of the numerous and abominable crimes the Germans had committed in their colonies. This became the theme of an abundant literature. Everything pointed in the same direction: that the Germans were unworthy of having any colonies at all.* In addition to the morality of the issue, there were compelling strategic reasons why the colonies should be retained. According to one school of thought, submarine warfare had revolutionised the problem of imperial security. 'A base at Duala in the Cameroons, commanding the routes to South America and South Africa; one or more bases in the Pacific—once they are well organised the next war with the British Empire could be undertaken under far more favourable conditions.' Morality plus security added up to the Allied powers keeping the sum of the German colonies.

After the war the Germans became increasingly resentful at the charge that their colonies had been maladministered. Compared with the Congo Free State, the Portuguese colonies, the French Congo, and even, in some instances, the British colonies, the German overseas possessions had been, in the view of the colonial enthusiasts, models in development of resources, roadbuilding, administration of justice, and so on. There was some truth in this, and also truth in the German charge that the African settlement of 1919, by inventing mandates, merely camouflaged naked British, French and Belgian imperialism. By adhering to such an extreme position, the German critics of the mandates system made the same mistake as the British who denounced German colonialism as a threat to civilisation. The Germans failed to see that the mandates system did have substance, though some politicians used its idealistic rhetoric for their own purposes.

Like the story of the African campaigns, the history of the birth of the mandates system is well known. In brief, a certain group of left-wing British politicians, notably E. D. Morel, Ramsay MacDonald and Sidney Webb, believed that 'overseas imperialism' was one of the primary causes of the war and proposed that all colonies should be placed under the direct control of an international board, not merely under international supervision. This proposal was the subject of considerable ridicule until President Wilson proclaimed the 14 Points. He probably had no precise ideas about the future administration of the German colonies. And, according to Professor Arthur Link, he probably was not over-optimistic about American influence in the African settlement at the Peace Conference. Nevertheless, he insisted that the principle of self-determination be applied to the German as well as other conquered territories. The British, among others, thought this idea both mischievous and dangerous. How could head-hunters and cannibals be expected to vote in favour of the Empire? But the President would not yield. Wilson insisted that even 'black barbarians' (Balfour's description) should have some say in determining their own future. However, not for one moment did President Wilson contemplate the return of the German colonies or direct international administration. He merely wanted international supervision, and certain guarantees such as non-fortification and annual reports. In one of his first important speeches to the Peace Conference in January 1919, he stated that everyone agreed that the colonies could not be handed back to Germany. Yet he unalterably opposed annexation. Japan's acquisition of the Pacific islands north of the equator would bring her within striking distance of the United States; Britain and France's expansion into the Middle East might alter the balance of power in the Mediterranean; and the takeover of the German colonies in Africa symbolised the type of power politics or the techniques of the 'old diplomacy' against which the United States had, in part, gone to war. In 1919 these ideas were compelling. Wilson, Lloyd George and Clemenceau had to find answers to problems concerning different geographical locations and entirely different groups of indigenous inhabitants. Here arose, on a large scale, the question of 'race'. Some peoples of the world appeared to be at higher stages of civilisation than others. The delegates of the Peace Conference accordingly ranked them as 'A', 'B', or 'C'. The 'A' peoples were those closest to independence—the Arabs of the Middle East. The 'B' peoples were those of tropical Africa (Togoland, the Cameroons and German East Africa), who in some way had managed to civilise themselves more than those of the 'C' group of South-West Africa and the Pacific islands. General Smuts more than anyone else devised this formula, recognising that a 'C' mandate would give South Africa total control over South-West Africa, which became, in the phrase current at the time, a colony in all but name. Hughes of Australia also concurred: New Guinea might not be annexed, but Australia would have complete authority in commerce and immigration—two of the touchstones of colonialism. So the President got more or less what he wanted, a loose form of international control, by which each of the governing powers would merely submit a yearly report to the League and promise not to fortify the mandates. No doubt he would have preferred more, if only to curtail 'Japanese militarism' in the Pacific. But he achieved his purpose: idealism coupled with internal security. He was not 'bamboozled' by cunning European imperialists. Still, there is some truth in the following statement: 'Bamboozled though he was by the last clever manoeuvrings of the imperial camp—united at least against the self-determining outsider—Wilson had one final post-grave laugh. His warning about Japanese colonisation paid off: too late for those who died at Pearl Harbour . . . but in time to influence the second global carve-up.' In Africa, on the other hand,

AFRICA ON THE EVE OF THE WAR, 1913

- BRITISH
- FRENCH
- BELGIAN
- PORTUGUESE
- ITALIAN
- SPANISH
- GERMAN

POST WAR AFRICA

— INTERNATIONAL BOUNDARIES

— TERRITORIAL BOUNDARIES

0   500 MILES

SPANISH MOROCCO
MOROCCO
RIO DE ORO
TUNISIA
to Italy 1919
to Italy 1925
to Italy 1919
ALGERIA
LIBYA
EGYPT
ERITREA
FRENCH WEST AFRICA
French Mandate 1920
FRENCH EQUATORIAL AFRICA
FRENCH SOMALILAND
BRITISH SOMALILAND
GAMBIA
GUINEA
SIERRA LEONE
LIBERIA
Togoland
NIGERIA
French Mandate 1920
ANGLO-EGYPTIAN SUDAN
ABYSSINIA
GOLD COAST
British Mandate 1920
Cameroons
SPANISH GUINEA
UGANDA
KENYA
ITALIAN SOMALILAND
Jubaland to Italy 1925
to France 1919
Ruanda-Urundi Belgian Mandate 1920
BELGIAN CONGO
German East Africa
Tanganyika British Mandate 1920
CABINDA
Kionga to Portugal 1919
ANGOLA
N. RHODESIA
German South-West Africa
S. RHODESIA
NYASALAND
WALVIS BAY
BECHUANA-LAND
MOÇAMBIQUE
MADAGASCAR
South African Mandate 1920
SWAZILAND
UNION OF SOUTH AFRICA
BASUTOLAND

Above: Wounded Ndanda tribesmen in German East Africa—African casualties of a European war

the Wilsonian settlement remained intact, with the British, French, Belgians and South Africans still holding the territories they had won in 1919.

There is considerable reason to believe that Wilson had little objection to the South Africans simply annexing South West Africa, as they would greatly have preferred. As one South African observer accurately predicted at the time, the imposition of the mandates system would sow the seed of future trouble. Wilson certainly did not intend to cause difficulty for the South Africans, and probably assumed that they would prove themselves faithful 'guardians'; in any case the principle of self-determination would safeguard the interests of the Africans. Wilson respected General Smuts; there is no reason to believe that he feared the permanent annexation of South West Africa by South Africa and indeed he thought ultimately that absorption would be the best solution if the Africans voted in favour of union with South Africa. Wilson remained adamant on the question of South West Africa being included in the mandates system mainly because, if he yielded to South Africa, he would have less reason to insist that Japan place the Pacific islands under international supervision.

The Allies only reluctantly accepted the mandates scheme. The French Colonial Minister, Simon, stated categorically that France favoured outright annexation. Clemenceau, however, repudiated this stance, no doubt to win a bargaining point with Wilson and in the belief that international supervision would amount to very little anyway. The British calculations were more complex because of the ambitions of the Dominions. In January 1918 Lloyd George had publicly declared Great Britain in favour of the principle of self-determination, but the War Cabinet continued to scrutinise the wisdom of the proclamation. Balfour thought it preposterous that the self-determination principle be applied to 'black barbarians' who in some cases did not even know that the British were now their masters. Curzon, on the other hand, stated: 'I am inclined to value the argument of self-determination because I believe that most of the people would determine in our favour.' In Africa British and South African officials were appalled at the idea, but systematically set about gathering evidence that the natives favoured British and South African rule. By the time of the opening of the Peace Conference, the British had acquired ample photographic and legal evidence to prove that under no circumstances should the conquered territories be returned to Germany and also that the natives preferred British rule to any other.

Curiously enough, the major controversies in the territorial settlements did not arise between the two traditional colonial rivals in Africa—Britain and France—but between Britain and Belgium and Portugal. In 1916 Sir Edward Grey had 'sold out' (in Lewis Harcourt's phrase) to the French by giving them the better part of Togoland and no less than nine-tenths of the Cameroons—in return for nothing. To the Colonial Office, which had hoped to use the Cameroons as a basis for a worldwide settlement of colonial issues with the French, this constituted, again in Harcourt's words, no less than 'an imperial disaster'. Grey, on the other hand, had calculated that it was better to convince the French that the British Empire was not a land-devouring octopus grabbing overseas territories while France was paralysed in Europe. He had no intention of alienating Britain's ally by quarrelling over African jungles. His concession proved to be decisive. When the Peace Conference opened, only minor adjustments of the boundaries of these 'jungles' needed to be made, which Milner (now Colonial Secretary) and the French Colonial Minister accomplished easily in the tradition of imperial diplomacy.

Milner had much more trouble with the Belgians, whom he described as 'sitting' on British lines of communication in East Africa. In 1916 Belgian troops had overrun the German colony all the way to Lake Victoria and the rail centre of Tabora to the south. With an attitude of 'we hold what we have', the Belgians refused to listen to British arguments about the difficulty of administering the colony without the two most populous districts, Ruanda and Urundi. In fact, the Belgians recognised that the occupied territory constituted a valuable pawn. With it they hoped to bargain in order to acquire the southern bank of the mouth of the River Congo, without which, they feared, in the event of another war, the entire Congo could be paralysed if an enemy power occupied Northern Angola. If Belgium could acquire the southern Congo bank, Britain could have the occupied territory in East Africa, and Portugal could be compensated by part of the south of German East Africa, thus allowing her to extend the Moçambique colony. But the Portuguese refused to listen and indeed demanded the south of German East Africa anyway—as a mandate, on grounds merely that if Belgium were to have a mandate, Portugal should have one too. Milner thought this was absolutely preposterous. The Portuguese, who had been unable even to defend their own territory against Lettow-Vorbeck, now demanded a share of the spoils! Still, as a part of the settlement, the Portuguese received a slice of territory at the mouth of the River Rovuma, 'stolen' from them by the Germans. This was done, in Milner's words, 'as a matter of grace and convenience'. Belgium, failing to acquire the Congo bank, retained Ruanda and Urundi, thus creating a geographical and political anomaly that became the independent states of Rwanda and Burundi.

Italy also joined the scramble. When the Italians entered the war on the side of the Allies, the Allies promised that Italy would receive compensation if Britain and France extended their African possessions at the expense of Germany. The Italians accordingly drew up grandiose plans using as bases for expansion the colonies of Libya and Somaliland and also hoping for economic concessions in the Portuguese colonies. They then learned that France and Britain were prepared to yield only a fraction of their demands. After acrimonious negotiations Italy received from France a few oases in the Sahara and from Britain a slice of British East Africa called Jubaland, which Milner considered to be a great sacrifice because of its potential richness in cotton. When an Italian representative asked an Englishman at the Peace Conference the reason for this niggardly settlement, he got the response that France and Britain could not encourage

British police in Northern Rhodesia: their main concern safeguarding the Cape to Cairo route

Italy's imperialist aims 'because imperialism is dead'!

In the interests of the nation . . .

From the African point of view, Professor Roland Oliver has put forward the most persuasive argument concerning the general significance of the 1919 settlement: *After 1919 colonialism has so far seemed in comparison distinctly gentler and more law-abiding—its moral outlook conditioned by the mandates system, its new concern for the welfare of its African subjects expressed in a score of major reports and policy statements. The colonialism of the 1920's and 1930's has been seen as smug and paternalistic, and certainly as very unrealistic about the time at its disposal; but the people operating it have so far emerged as a decent and forward-looking lot, very different from the swashbucklers and scallywags of the Scramble.* Wilson, however, insisted that indigenous peoples should and would have to be consulted about their own fate and that eventually they would determine their own future— a view not shared by many of his European colleagues. Perhaps more important, the Wilsonian policy of dual concern for moderation of power politics and respect of non-western peoples heralded the United States's policy during the throes of European decolonisation—though many would argue that concern for national security dominated in both cases. And whatever might be said of the mandates system, instituted in Africa only at American insistence, it did cause the mandates to become the object of international publicity.

As far as the French and the Belgians were concerned their prime objective was national security, their main aim being to secure the mouth of the Congo to provide greater protection in the event of another war. For the French, acquisition of the German colonies would help to consolidate French colonial territory stretching from the Mediterranean to the Gulf of Guinea. And it is remarkable that the only colonial issue in which Clemenceau showed any real interest was what Lloyd George referred to as the French 'nigger army'. Clemenceau, who proved himself flexible on other African issues, would not budge for one moment on France's right to raise African troops in mandated territories in case of war. The other powers acquiesced, seeing the importance of France being able to defend herself against Germany.

For the British the key issues remained those of the 19th Century: the Cape to Cairo route and control over the sources of the Nile. Smuts and Amery, the great enthusiasts of the Cape to Cairo route at this time, foresaw the possibility of Germany in a future war gaining control of the seas and cutting off the dominions and colonies from the major theatre of war. They envisaged not only a railway but also an air route that would facilitate troop movements over land and in the air from the Cape to Cairo and on to Europe—at the same time connecting with routes running through the Middle East, India and on to Australasia. Smuts at the same time was interested in acquiring control of the minerals of Moçambique (if not Moçambique itself), but his primary concern was strategic. In regard to the control of the Nile, it can be argued that at heart the issue was pre-eminently economic since protection of the Nile would protect Egypt, and, by extension, India. But in Africa generally it is clear that British motives were predominantly strategic. According to Milner: 'We have one absolutely vital interest; it is to safeguard the head waters of the Blue Nile. When the time comes to liquidate the Abyssinian situation, we must be in a position to stipulate for the security of this water supply.' But it was Balfour who, with shrewd scepticism, realised the implicit dangers of imperialism: 'Every time I come to a discussion—at intervals of, say, five years—I find there is a new sphere which we have got to guard, which is supposed to protect the gateways of India. Those gateways are getting further and further from India.'

Further Reading
Beloff, Max, *Imperial Sunset* (Methuen 1969)
Fischer, Fritz, *Germany's Aims in the First World War* (Norton 1967)
Hall, H. Duncan, *Mandates, Dependencies and Trusteeship* (Carnegie Endowment 1948)
Louis, W. R., *Great Britain and Germany's Lost Colonies, 1914-1919* (Clarendon Press 1967)

W. R. LOUIS is Professor of History at the University of Texas. He is the author of *Great Britain and Germany's Lost Colonies, E. D. Morel's History of the Congo Reform Association* (with Jean Stengers), and *British Strategy in the Far East, 1919-1939*. With P. Gifford he has edited *Britain and Germany in Africa*.

Südd Verlag

POLAND: A NATION REBORN

In 1918 Poland emerged from two years of twilight as a client kingdom of Germany and Austria into the light of full independence. But she was immediately beset by problems: the need to obtain a port and the Polish ethnic areas of Germany and Austria, and to settle the Soviet threat both within and outside her borders. *Professor Dziewanowski*. *Left:* Joseph Piłsudski. *Above:* The Polish entry into Kiev in May 1920

3337

Top left: Jedrzej Moraczewski, who led Poland's fight to establish international control in the new state. His main achievement was the setting up of an efficient food distribution system, vital in the task of combating the inroads of Communist propaganda. *Top right:* Roman Dmowski, head of the Polish National Committee, which secured recognition of Poland at the Paris Peace Conference. Originally opposed to Piłsudski's Socialist government, Dmowski reached a compromise agreement with the latter in January 1919. *Left:* Polish peasants bury some of the corpses of the Battle of Limanowa-Lapanów in 1914. The ebb and flow of the war over this part of the new state of Poland led to great hardship, relief of which was the first priority of the government. *Below left:* Men of Piłsudski's small army, which despite its size was immediately sent into action against the Ukrainians. *Above:* Polish troops near Danzig. *Superimposed:* General Haller

The reconstruction of the Polish state in 1918/19 was a consequence of two sets of circumstances: of, first, the victory of the Entente over the Central Powers and, secondly, of a series of political as well as military efforts by the Polish people themselves.

Already on October 7, 1918, the Regency Council in Warsaw, anticipating the defeat of the Central Powers and defying their authority, proclaimed the independence of a United Poland. When, on November 10, Joseph Piłsudski returned from German captivity to the Polish capital, the Council handed its political power over to him and he became the first Head of State of a restored Poland.

The crumbling within about a year and a half of the Romanov, Habsburg and Hohenzollern Empires created a power vacuum in East Central Europe. The area

affected increased when, in accordance with Article 12 of the armistice agreement of November 11, the German forces began their gradual retreat from the 'Oberost' territories, East European lands which they had conquered. Behind the retreating Germans followed the detachments of the Red Army with their revolutionary slogans of the proletarian revolution. By January 5, 1919, the Bolshevik forces occupied Vilnyus. To the west of Poland, the German people were scarcely able to suppress their feelings of humiliation and hatred for the victors. In the east, on the territories of the former Tsarist Empire, the civil war was about to enter into a decisive phase and its outcome remained uncertain until the end of 1919. In the south the peoples of the Dual Monarchy were seething both with repressed resentment of the defeat, and from mutual animosities.

In these circumstances, the most important tasks for the leaders of the Polish Republic which was emerging from this chaos in November 1918 were not only to defend Poland's rights at the approaching peace conference, but to protect the new state from the effects of the civil war in the east, and secure for it the necessary degree of stability.

The need for stability
The problems facing Poland reborn were tremendous. In order to appreciate them one must remember that the state emerging from the war was a composite with no established frontiers. It consisted of the two former governor-generalships of Warsaw and of Lublin (which had formed the Austro-German sponsored Kingdom of Poland, proclaimed on November 6, 1916)

plus the former Austrian Galicia together with the tiny Silesian province of Teschen, the latter an object of dispute between the Poles and the Czechs. While, in the Lublin area, the Austrian forces had already been disarmed by the beginning of November 1918 and the administration taken over by the Poles without resistance, in the Warsaw area the disarming took place after November 11. The full regular Polish detachments were no match for them even with Joseph Piłsudski's Polish Military Organisation, now emerging from the underground and numbering around 30,000 men.

Furthermore, all of Western Poland (the provinces of Pomerania, Poznan and Silesia) was still controlled by the Germans who hoped to retain at least part of it, despite the defeat in the West. The German troops also controlled the outlet to the Baltic Sea and its entire south-eastern littoral as far as the Estonian capital of Tallin. Since November 1, Eastern Galicia, with its capital of Lvov (Lemberg), was engaged in a civil war between the Ukrainians and the Poles. The province and the city of Vilnyus were still in German hands, but menaced by the Bolshevik detachments already advancing from the east. In February 1919 the Red Army clashed for the first time with the units of the newly organised Polish armed forces.

In addition to the Red Army units there were cells of Communist agitators, originally mostly natives of Poland and the non-Russian borderlands, now eager to be planted as governments of their respective countries by the 'revolutionary intervention' and 'fraternal assistance' of their Soviet comrades. Some of these cells had at

their disposal some hastily organised armed units, like, for instance, the Western Rifle Division, composed partly of Polish Communists, partly of Poles from Russia, but largely of Russians simply assigned to it. The Communist agitation, following the Soviet military pressure, was dangerous because of the unsettled social and economic conditions in Poland. The external danger was coupled with the danger of internal upheaval preached and prepared for by the Communist Party of Poland (set up in December 1918), and now conspiring, eager to seize power at the approach of the Red Army.

The protracted, exhausting war, in which most of the Eastern Front was on Polish territory, left behind it devastation, dislocation and bitterness. With the end of hostilities, war industries were suddenly closed down, throwing masses of unemployed workers into the streets to demonstrate their wrath. Profiteering and the black market were rampant. Inflation sent prices soaring. The prolonged industrial unemployment resulted in appalling poverty and consequent radicalisation of the working class. Moreover, a large part of the labour force was still abroad, having been evacuated to Russia in 1915, or deported to Germany between 1916 and 1918. It was estimated, for instance, that in the autumn of 1918 over 3,000,000 Poles were in adjacent countries. Some of the workers returning from Russia were not only swelling the ranks of the unemployed, but were spreading Communist ideas as well. On their way home, millions of German, Austrian, Hungarian and Russian soldiers were passing through Poland. Some of them formed into armed bands ▷3341

Paderewski

Jan Paderewski, brilliant pianist and Poland's first Prime Minister and Foreign Minister, and one of Poland's signatories of the Treaty of Versailles. His contribution to the quick recognition of Poland was considerable, as a result of his wartime propaganda missions

Jan Ignacy Paderewski (1860-1941) was born on November 18, 1860 at Kurylowka in Russian Podolia, the son of a manager of a large landed estate. He studied from 1872 to 1876 at the Warsaw Conservatory of Music, where he also taught the piano for the next four years. In 1880 he married one of his students, Antonina Korsak, who died in childbirth one year later.

From 1884 to 1887 Paderewski studied in Vienna, while at the same time teaching at the Strasburg Conservatory. Between 1887 and 1891 he gave his first public piano concerts in Vienna, Paris, London and New York. Chopin, Bach, Beethoven and Schuman formed part of his repertoire. Soon he was recognised as the world's leading pianist. His personality was colourful, flamboyant and charming, and he had wide interests. He studied the history of music, edited many musical works, including those of Chopin; he also became friendly with many prominent personalities, including members of European royal families. He was a mesmerising lecturer and an inspired public speaker. In 1898 Paderewski settled at Rion Bosson, near Morges, in Switzerland, and in the following year married Helena Gorska, née Baroness von Rosen. In 1901 the Dresden Opera Company presented with great success his opera 'Manru' based upon the life of the Tatra mountaineers. In 1909 he was appointed Director of the Warsaw Conservatory of Music. The

same year his Symphony in B Minor was performed in Boston. His success was acclaimed throughout the world.

Paderewski was an ardent Polish patriot and throughout his life spent large sums of money on philanthropic causes. In 1910, on the 500th anniversary of the battle of Grünwald-Tannenberg, a great victory for Poland over the Teutonic Knights, the dominant military power of the late Middle Ages, he presented the city of Kraków with a commemorative monument. Later, during the First World War, he joined the Polish National Committee in Paris, and successfully represented it in the United States. Thanks to his personal friendship with President Wilson and Colonel House he managed to insert the 13th Point, concerning Poland, into the President's 14 Points speech of January 8, 1918.

In 1918 Paderewski visited France and Great Britain. In London A. J. Balfour suggested to him that he should return to Poland and 'unite Polish hearts', and create a government acceptable to the Entente. And indeed, in December 1918 he left for Poznan and Warsaw, and persuaded Pilsudski, then already Head of State, to replace the existing left-wing cabinet, which was not recognised by the Allies, with a coalition cabinet. On January 17, 1918, a coalition government was set up, with Paderewski as Prime Minister, Foreign Minister and Chief of the Polish

delegation to the Paris Peace Conference. In the latter capacity, together with Roman Dmowski, he signed the Treaty of Versailles on Poland's behalf.

Despite his considerable personal and diplomatic talents and his magnetic oratory, Paderewski was unable to cope with the host of complicated political and socio-economic problems, and on November 27, 1919 he resigned the premiership and retired to his villa at Rion Bosson. In 1921 Paderewski resumed his musical career, devoting a large proportion of his income to aid for war victims, and other humanitarian causes. After the outbreak of the Second World War, he became Chairman of the Polish National Council in Paris set up after the German invasion of Poland by the government in exile, headed by General Władysław Sikorski. After the capitulation of France Paderewski went to the United States and died there on June 29, 1941. By special permission of President Franklin D. Roosevelt his body was buried in Arlington National Cemetery.

Further Reading
Landau, Rom, *Paderewski* (1934)
Lawton, Mary, *The Paderewski Memoirs* (1939)
Opienski, Henryk, *I. J. Paderewski – esquisse de sa vie et de son oeuvre* (1948)

[*For Professor Dziewanowski's biography, see page 1834.*]

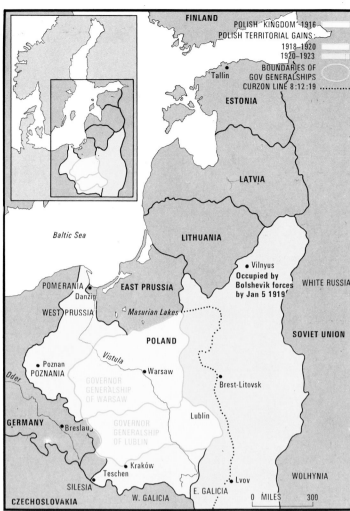

Above: The Russo-Polish Conference in Riga on October 9, 1920, in an attempt to halt the war between the two countries and settle their border disputes. *Above right:* The growth of emergent Poland between 1916 and 1923

who pillaged the countryside. Consequently, war-ravaged Poland was passing through a period of economic crisis and social conflict, in some ways not much less acute than that in Russia, Germany or Hungary.

Food before frontiers

In the political sphere the young Polish state had to face tremendous obstacles. The old political tradition, where not entirely destroyed, was preserved mainly in the province of Galicia, an autonomous part of the Habsburg monarchy since 1867. The many partitions which the country had suffered greatly affected the mentality of the people. Protracted subservience to foreign masters left deep marks on their attitudes and patterns of behaviour. Pre-occupied for over 100 years with the idea of regaining their freedom, many Poles were so used to resisting the partitioning powers that they tended to assume a negative attitude toward any authority.

Thus Poland was ripe for a proletarian upheaval. Consequently, the first tasks of the government in Warsaw led by a Socialist, Jedrzej Moraczewski, were to re-establish a semblance of order, to overcome the dislocation caused by the war, and initiate democratic reforms, including agrarian reform, to deal with rising unemployment and widespread starvation. The new administration had to combat rampant lawlessness and hooliganism to

bring the country back to more or less normal conditions. To cope with the tremendous difficulties the authorities had to mobilise all available resources. The government immediately decreed an eight hour working day. An extensive system of social security was soon introduced and a Ministry of Food was established; supplies were stored and distributed by the state. Considerable help was given by the American Relief Committee, headed by Herbert Hoover.

The re-establishment of order and legality based on the will of the people was an urgent necessity. The decree of November 29, 1918, provided that democratic elections to the Constituent Assembly should take place on January 26, 1919, in the territory of the former Congress Kingdom in Western Galicia. Eastern Galicia, where 'for the time being' elections could not take place, because of the Polish-Ukrainian hostilities, was to be represented by the deputies to the former Austrian Parliament. The decree promised also to summon to the Polish Constituent Assembly former representatives from Lithuania, Belorussia and Wolhynia. This, however, was never put into practice. Joseph Piłsudski, acting Head of State and Commander-in-Chief of the Armed Forces from November 19, 1918, was asked to continue in both his offices.

The Diet or *Sejm* which emerged from the elections was largely composed of the moderate right and the non-Communist left. The extremes were poorly represented, while the newly born Communist Workers' Party of Poland, having boycotted the election, had no parliamentary representation in the first Polish Parliament. The orderly elections consolidated the young Republic

internally and paved the way for its international recognition. The constitution of the Republic, modelled on the French charter of 1875, was finally voted in March 1921. Thus, by the middle of 1919 the domestic crisis had been eased to a certain extent.

Drawing the boundaries

Meanwhile the crucial problem of Poland's frontiers had to be faced. As far as the western frontiers were concerned they were determined by the Paris peace treaties and the series of plebiscites and compromises that followed. In the east the Poles had to face a protracted struggle against Soviet Russia.

In President Wilson's Fourteen Points was named, as one of the conditions of peace, the creation of an independent Polish state to include all the territories 'inhabited by indisputably Polish populations' and having 'a free and secure access to the sea'.

Owing to the activities of Roman Dmowski and the Polish National Committee in Paris, Poland was recognised by all the Entente Powers as 'an allied belligerent nation' on June 3, 1918. Meanwhile the Committee organised in France a Polish army of some six divisions, headed by General Joseph Haller. This meant that Poland would be represented at the Peace Conference as one of the victorious Allied states. The problem of the existence of two rival bodies, each claiming to represent the Polish people, the conservative Polish National Committee, headed by Dmowski, and the largely Socialist government in Warsaw, was settled by compromise in January 1919. Piłsudski was to remain Head of State, and a coalition cabinet

Piłsudski: 'A pronounced sceptic about orthodox methods, whether applied to military affairs or politics; he loves danger, his pulse only beating at a normal rate when he is in imminent personal peril. Next to danger, he is said to love intrigue — a revolutionary by temperament and circumstances, his ingrained proclivity is to the secret and indirect.' *(Lord D'Abernon).* 'A third rate Buonaparte.' *(Leon Trotsky)*

Above left, centre and far right: The Polish war effort before the establishment of a Polish state — service in other men's armies. Illustrated are Poles serving in the Russian cavalry, the Austrian lancers, and the French army. *Centre:* The Polish-American entente commemorated

nominated by him, with I. J. Paderewski as Prime Minister and Foreign Minister, was to rule in Poland, while the Committee was to represent Poland at the coming Paris Peace Conference. The Polish delegation at Versailles was to be headed by Paderewski and Dmowski.

While there were considerable disagreements, even among the Poles, what were 'indisputably' Polish territories in the east, in the west the situation was fairly clear. The German census of 1910 left no doubt that former West Prussia, or old Polish Pomerania, as well as Poznan, had preserved their Polish character despite over a century of German rule. This was true also of the northern part of Pomerania, or the strip of land which German propaganda had labelled as the 'Polish Corridor'. The only exception to the largely Slavic character of Poznan and Pomerania was the city of Danzig at the mouth of the Vistula, and a small strip of territory around it. The

George Washington

Woodrow Wilson

Kazimierz Pułaski

Walczmy Zjednoczeni za Wolność i Prawo!

I. J. Paderewski

Malcolm McGregor

Commission for Polish Affairs unanimously voted to restore Danzig to Poland for historic, strategic and economic reasons. As the US delegate to the commission, Professor Robert Howard Lord of Harvard, argued, to deprive Poland of the mouth of the Vistula would be to favour the interests of 200,000 Germans over those of 20,000,000 Poles; it would be like handing over the mouth of the Nile or the Mississippi to a foreign power. Upon the insistence of the British Prime Minister, Lloyd George, Danzig was declared a free city, with special rights reserved to Poland, especially in the harbour.

The German census of 1910 also made it clear that large stretches of Silesia, which Poland lost in the fourteenth century, still preserved their Slavic character. This was true of the southern fringes of East Prussia, or the district of the Masurian lakes, inhabited by Polish-speaking Lutherans. Also on the insistence of Great Britain, the

Conference reversed its initial decision and concluded that in both cases the controversies should be resolved by means of plebiscites. Three successive uprisings which took place in 1919, 1920 and 1921, led by a former Reichstag deputy Wojciech Korfanty, demonstrated the will of the Silesian masses to belong to Poland.

The plebiscites, in both cases conducted by the old German administration of the disputed lands, only partly satisfied Poland. In the case of East Prussia the plebiscite took place while the Red Army was at the gates of Warsaw. The Poles lost the Masurian district to Germany, and in the case of Upper Silesia most of the land as well as its industrial wealth was given to Poland by the League of Nations in 1921. The problem of the Teschen region was settled by a compromise which partitioned the area between Poland and Czechoslovakia, the latter obtaining the area south of the River Olza. Thus by the middle of 1921 the

frontiers of the Polish Republic were settled; they were formally recognised by the Council of Ambassadors in 1923.

Further Reading

Bromke, Adam, *Poland's Politics: Idealism versus Realism* (Harvard University Press 1967)

Conze, Werner, *Polnische Nation und Deutsche Politik im Ersten Weltkriege* (1958)

Dmowski, Roman, *Polish Policy and Rebuilding of the State* (in Polish 1925)

Dziewanowski, M. K., *Joseph Piłsudski, 1918-1922* (1969) and *The Communist Party of Poland* (Harvard University Press 1959)

Haskins, C. H., and Lord, R. H., *Some Problems of the Peace Conference* (1920)

Komarnicki, Tytus, *Rebirth of the Polish Republic* (1957)

Wandycz, Piotr, *France and her Eastern Allies, 1919-1925* (1962) and *Polish-Soviet Relations, 1917-1921* (1969)

[*For Professor Dziewanowski's biography, see page 1834.*]

THE BALTIC FRINGE

Unlike Poland, the Baltic States, when they achieved a form of independence in the aftermath of the First World War, had little or no history of independence, and no strong economic basis for survival. And so they were soon beset from all sides: Russia from the east, Germany and Poland from the south and Communists from within. *Richard Condon. Above:* German troops in action with Red Guards near Helsinki in 1919. *Right:* A Finnish White Guard parade in Helsinki. *Far right:* A Lithuanian patrol in Memel

Ullstein

Bundesarchiv

Südd Verlag

Among the new states to appear on the European map in the wake of the First World War were three which had never known independence, Finland, Estonia and Latvia, and one, Lithuania, which had been independent briefly in the Middle Ages. Finland had enjoyed a century of not uninterrupted autonomy as a Grand Duchy of Russia with her own constitution and military force and was therefore somewhat better prepared, at least domestically, for independence than the three Baltic States. That these peoples, with their tiny populations and little or no expertise in domestic or foreign affairs, should have attained statehood by war and diplomacy is one of the amazing facts of the period, even with the Wilsonian concept of national self-determination.

When war erupted in 1914, the national minorities of Russia loyally supported the Tsar, bravely marching off to stop the Germans. Since Finland, however, maintained

her own defence force which could not be incorporated into the Imperial Army, only volunteers joined the Russian ranks from Finland. Indeed, as a result of Finnish cultural affinity with Germany and dissatisfaction with Russian interference in Finnish affairs, 2,000 men were secretly sent for training and service with the German army until summoned home to fight the Red Guard in 1918. When the Revolution began in March 1917, the key demand of Finland and the unoccupied Baltic provinces was national autonomy within a reconstituted Russia. In Latvia and Estonia the nationalists' hatred of the Baltic Germans (Balts) was the strongest political factor because of the oppression they had suffered at the hands of the Balts, who had been given control of the land, economy and local governments in return for supporting the Russification programme. Since the provisional government on April 13 restored the Finnish constitution and repealed the oppressive laws of the previous decade, the Finns also adopted a conciliatory policy toward Petrograd.

In the areas occupied by Germany, Lithuania and Courland, a genuine independence movement got under way with the aid of the German military command. There were several reasons for this movement: first, Russian and Prussian Lithuania were united as a result of German successes, and, freed from the Tsar, might still succeed in breaking away from Germany too; secondly, in 1916, Lithuanians abroad formed a national council based in Switzerland to promote Lithuanian independence; finally, General Erich von Ludendorff, Commander of the East, who had annexationist desires in the East, saw the independence movement as a means of achiev-

ing *Lebensraum*, since the movement could succeed only with German agreement and would therefore be in Germany's debt. Ludendorff was further influenced by the fear that the Polish Kingdom, established by Germany in November 1916, would seek to incorporate Lithuania. He therefore urged his government to permit Lithuanian nationalists to operate within the province as a make-weight against the Poles. Consequently, the Lithuanian nationalists were allowed to bring their movement home.

The March Revolution added impetus to the Lithuanian independence movement. In May, Ludendorff's annexationist hopes were raised when he was allowed to establish a 'confidential council' in Lithuania which could be used as a ploy to incorporate the province into the Hohenzollern Empire. In September a Lithuanian National Diet met at Vilnyus and elected a 20-member *Taryba* (National Council) which mainly represented the bourgeoisie. The Diet also passed a resolution calling for independence on the basis of democratic principles and ethnological frontiers that took into consideration the interests of the nation's economic life. To this end, a democratically elected constituent assembly was to convene at Vilnyus. Article II called on Germany to recognise and defend Lithuanian independence and interests in the peace negotiations. If Germany did so, the Lithuanians admitted the possibility of future relations with her which would not prejudice Lithuania's free development. Thus set in motion, the Lithuanian movement in the ensuing months assumed a more independent attitude toward Germany.

In early November a Lithuanian conference met at Berne and approved the deci-

Above: White Guards in Helsinki, known as Helsingfors at the time. *Right:* April 1918. German troops from Count Rüdiger von der Goltz's force guard Finns awaiting deportation as Red sympathisers. The White Commander in Finland at the time, Mannerheim, had asked that the aid of German troops should not be requested, but he was over-ruled by the Svinhufud government

Right: Another example of the German presence in Finland. In this photograph, German troops are bringing refugees from the Red Guards' activities into the 'safety' of the area dominated by the Whites. Aided by the Germans, and with the majority of the population behind them, the Whites had little difficulty in putting down the Red uprising after a period of under four months

sions of the Vilnyus Diet, recognised the *Taryba* as the legitimate organ of the Lithuanians, fixed the boundaries of the state and declared that a port on the Baltic was a vital economic facility. Meanwhile the Lithuanian National Council, which had formed at Petrograd in March (the Bolsheviks having withdrawn in October), busily promoted independence. In December it, too, accepted the decisions of the Vilnyus Diet. On December 11 the *Taryba* declared Lithuania independent, proclaimed Vilnyus the capital, requested German assistance to defend Lithuanian interests at the Peace Conference and agreed to establish a permanent federal attachment with Germany.

The power of the peasants

Although slower to start, the independence movement in Estonia and Latvia soon caught up with that of Lithuania. On April 12 Estonia was allowed to establish local self-government for herself and the Estonian-speaking areas of Livonia and on the 21st was permitted to form an Estonian army. In reaction to Bolshevik agitation, the failure of the Russians to introduce the Estonian language in schools and government, and the continued presence of Russians in the bureaucracy, Estonia soon moved toward complete separation from Russia. The National Council, which first met on July 14, saw the usual class conflict develop between the bourgeois and socialist parties. Local councils, in the main Bolshevik dominated, called upon the peasants to seize estates and redistribute the land. On November 28, 1917, the Bolsheviks forced the National Council to disband, but not before it had declared Estonia independent and itself the supreme power in Estonia.

For the next three months the Bolsheviks did everything possible to gain power. When 70% of the returns in the elections for the Constituent Assembly in January 1918 had only brought the Bolsheviks less than a third of the votes, an immediate halt to the ballot was ordered and the Constituent Assembly forbidden to meet. This Bolshevik attempt to retain control failed when the Brest-Litovsk negotiations broke down and the Germans invaded Estonia.

Latvia did not fare as well as Estonia under the provisional government, which refused to grant autonomy to, or unification of, the Latvian-speaking territories. Taking matters into their own hands, the bourgeoisie formed local councils to maintain order but failed to include the landless peasants. At the same time they convoked a Congress for a United Latvia. The exclusion of the peasants was a major error since they were the back-bone of the Latvian battalions in the Russian army and were as land hungry as the Russian peasants. Thus, the landless peasants readily accepted the Bolshevik programme for land redistribution and the right of secession from Russia. In response to the peasants' needs, the Social Democrats established a council for the landless as an answer to the bourgeois Congress. Ultimately, the two groups merged when Kerensky's government decreed a temporary autonomous government for Latvia on July 5, 1917, and called for elections to a Latvian Provincial Council in September.

On July 30 representatives gathered at Riga and unanimously resolved the following: the Latvian people had a right to self-determination; Latvia was indivisible, including Southern Livonia, Courland and Latgale; Latvia was an autonomous republic within the Russian Republic. In conclusion the representatives protested against annexations and all attempts to determine the political frontiers of the state without consulting the people. These brave resolutions and the Council elected in September were to avail little in 1917, when the Germans began to invade the territory. As the Russian armies retreated, the Bolsheviks seized power and began a reign of terror. The bourgeois leaders fled to Petrograd soon after the election and initiated countermoves, including appeals to the Allied representatives in Petrograd. Moreover, a Latvian National Council was formed to promote Latvian independence. On November 18 it declared Latvia independent and sent a representative to speak to the Allies. Before anything came of this, however, Latvia was occupied by Germany.

In Finland events moved as swiftly. Because the Russian Provisional Government could not decide where the power of the Tsar-Archduke of Finland should reside, the Finnish Diet, controlled by the Social Democrats, seized the initiative on July 18 and declared itself supreme, except for military and foreign affairs. This decision was flatly rejected by Kerensky, who despatched more Russian troops to Finland and ordered the Diet dissolved and new elections held in October. By the time returns were in, the Social Democrats had lost eleven seats and the bourgeoisie were in the ascendant.

The election results reflected the uneasiness of the more conservative elements in Finland at the alarming number of recent strikes and the tendency toward violence by the Left during the summer and autumn. Since the Social Democrats had campaigned on a platform of autonomy within the Russian state, they were seriously compromised by the November Revolution. Nationalist aspirations were advanced by this event, and the bourgeois parties wasted no time in making the Diet active. On November 15 the Diet proclaimed that it held supreme power by virtue of the Constitution of 1772, which was a step beyond the July resolution. This declaration was followed by a period of violence, while the socialists called a general strike. Because of the terror tactics of the Red Guard, however, the strike was called off on November 20 and the initiative slipped from the hands of the Left. On December 6 the Diet declared Finland independent and proceeded to invite a German prince to occupy the vacated throne. The Soviet government recognised Finnish independence on January 1, 1918, and the rest of the world followed suit soon after.

The red and the white

Soviet recognition of the bourgeois government of Finland was due to political necessity. Too weak to oppose the Finns and beset by internal problems, the Soviet leaders hoped that a proletarian revolution in Finland would be carried out by the Social Democrats. The Russians made no effort to withdraw their 40,000 troops from Finland. At the same time existing tensions between the socialists and bourgeois camps were heightened by their armed forces, the Red and White Guard. The latter, organised during the summer of

1917 as a civil defence corps to maintain order and to control the Russian troops, were suspected by the Left of being counter-revolutionary. To balance the White Guard, the Social Democrats had organised their own force, the Red Guard, receiving arms and supplies from Russia, and they also established a revolutionary committee similar to that in Petrograd.

On January 28, 1918, the Reds struck, seized the government buildings in Helsinki and ordered Red units in other cities to do the same. Thereupon, Finland was declared a Socialist Workers' Republic, and the stage was set for civil war.

The White Government of Pehr Svinhufvud fled to Vaasa, where it called upon General Carl G. Mannerheim to organise the White forces and conduct the war. Mannerheim agreed on condition that German assistance should not be sought. His wishes were ignored, however, and German aid was enlisted, the troops arriving at Hanko in early April. Meanwhile, Mannerheim's forces succeeded in disarming the Russian troops in Western Finland and used their arms to equip themselves. Aided by the Finnish *Jäger* Battalion, which was recalled from Germany, the White forces were able to move on Tampere, the centre of Red resistance, on April 3. After three days of savage fighting, the city fell at the same time as the German expedition, under General Rüdiger von der Goltz, landed. While Mannerheim's troops cleared the north, the Germans moved on Helsinki, and the Red government fled. By May 15 all of Finland was in White hands and the Civil War was over.

The tide of Bolshevism

In the Baltic states the bourgeois governments established under German auspices came under Soviet attack when Germany collapsed in November. The Allies, faced with greater problems in the west and a power vacuum in the east, wrote Article 12 into the Armistice. This article insisted that German forces should remain in the Baltic area to stem the tide of Bolshevism. The German troops, however, were also in a revolutionary mood and for the most part refused to comply with the terms of the Armistice. Moreover, in the hasty withdrawal ordered by the German command, much of the arms and equipment needed by the inhabitants to fight the Bolsheviks was taken along. Consequently, in Latvia, where Bolshevism prevailed among the people, the bourgeois government was driven out of Riga by the Soviet Russian army shortly after New Year's Day, despite the presence of two British warships in the harbour. By January 10, 1919, most of Latvia was under Bolshevik control.

For Estonia the situation was equally critical. The German withdrawal, accompanied by the destruction of telephone and telegraph lines, the dumping of 15,000 rifles into the sea and the monopolisation of the railroad, left the Estonian government virtually unable to defend itself. Because money was in short supply and the Estonian army, dissolved by the Germans in April 1918, was not yet reorganised, there was no possibility of stopping the army of Estonian and Latvian Bolsheviks which advanced from Pskov in November. In the midst of this crisis the Red Army began an offensive from Petrograd. Within a short time Tartu (Dorpat) and Narva fell, and Tallin was in peril.

Above: General Yudenich, whose forces used the Baltic States as a springboard in their war with Soviet Russia. *Above right:* von der Goltz (left) and Mannerheim. *Below:* A German landing in central Finland. *Right:* The Baltic States

Imperial War Museum

Ullstein

An Estonian Soviet Republic was proclaimed in the occupied areas in December.

With the aid of Finnish volunteers, a British naval squadron and their own reorganised army, however, the Estonians were able to save Tallin from Red attack on December 14. By January the White Estonian forces, aided by the anti-Bolshevik Russian North Army, assumed the offensive; by February 24, 1919, they had driven the Red Army back into Russia.

Lithuania also attracted the attention of the Reds even though there was little understanding of, or sympathy for, the Soviet ideology there. After Brest-Litovsk the Communists began to circulate propaganda for their movement, and early in December, after the Germans withdrew, a provisional revolutionary government of Lithuania was formed to await the Red Army's conquest of the country. In January 1919, the Reds occupied the Vilnyus district, and the Soviet Republic of Lithuania was proclaimed. There was never any real hope for this government, however, because the Bolshevik following was small. In April the Poles captured Vilnyus, putting an end to the scheme for a Lithuania-White Russia federation attached to Soviet Russia.

The Latvian Soviet Republic lasted for five months, largely due to the popular support enjoyed by the Reds. The Latvian Soviet government was patterned on that of Soviet Russia. Meanwhile, the bourgeois government operating from Liepāja pleaded for help from the Allies and Germany. In January German officers began to train a White Latvian army. Volunteers recruited in Germany were promised land and Latvian citizenship. In February General von der Goltz arrived from Finland to take command and by March 18 most of Courland was in White hands.

However, Goltz's aim was to gain *Lebensraum* for Germany. In April the White Latvian government was overthrown and a government of which Goltz approved was installed. This government was pro-Balt and pro-Germany. At the request of the new government the German forces moved to take Riga and managed to capture it on May 23. By this time the Allies had recognised the danger of German operations in Latvia and the Baltic region. Accordingly, plans were made to replace the Germans with Baltic volunteers and to have Goltz recalled. Further complications arose, however, because the Russian White forces under General Yudenich wanted to use the Baltic States as a staging area for an attack upon Petrograd. To this end Russian White refugees were recruited and combined with

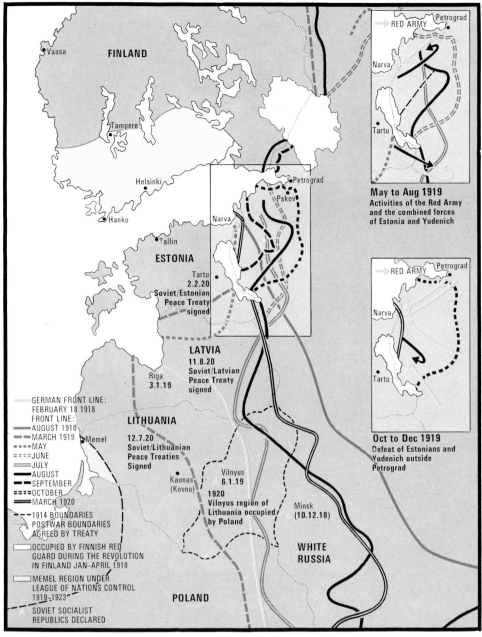

FINLAND

Vaasa

Tampere

Helsinki

Hanko

ESTONIA

Tallin

Narva

Tartu
2.2.20
Soviet/Estonian
Peace Treaty
signed

LATVIA
11.8.20
Soviet/Latvian
Peace Treaty
signed

Riga
3.1.19

LITHUANIA

Memel

12.7.20
Soviet/Lithuanian
Peace Treaties
Signed

Kaunas
(Kovno)

Vilnyus
6.1.19

1920
Vilnyus region of
Lithuania occupied
by Poland

Minsk
(10.12.18)

**WHITE
RUSSIA**

POLAND

Pskov

Petrograd

May to Aug 1919
Activities of the Red Army
and the combined forces
of Estonia and Yudenich

RED ARMY — Petrograd

Narva

Tartu

Oct to Dec 1919
Defeat of Estonians and
Yudenich outside
Petrograd

RED ARMY — Petrograd

Narva

Tartu

GERMAN FRONT LINE:
FEBRUARY 18 1918
FRONT LINE :
AUGUST 1918
MARCH 1919
MAY
JUNE
JULY
AUGUST
SEPTEMBER
OCTOBER
MARCH 1920

1914 BOUNDARIES
POSTWAR BOUNDARIES
AGREED BY TREATY
OCCUPIED BY FINNISH RED
GUARD DURING THE REVOLUTION
IN FINLAND JAN-APRIL 1918
MEMEL REGION UNDER
LEAGUE OF NATIONS CONTROL
1919-1923
SOVIET SOCIALIST
REPUBLICS DECLARED

the German forces. Instead of attacking Petrograd, however, they moved against Riga on October 8 on the grounds that the Latvian government, the earlier one restored at Allied insistence, was not honouring its commitment to grant citizenship to the German volunteers. The Latvian army held out until the Anglo-French Baltic Fleet arrived on the 15th and helped drive off the Russo-German force. The Germans were driven into Lithuania, from which they were expelled in December. The Russians were joined up again with Yudenich's forces in Estonia. From there they attacked Petrograd, only to be driven back and interned in Estonia.

Vilnyus tug-of-war

Lithuania faced a twofold threat to her independence from Soviet Russia and Poland and had to fight both powers simultaneously. Both Lithuania and Poland laid claim to Vilnyus; at the Paris Peace Conference the baffling question of Vilnyus was never fully resolved. While a sub-commission on Polish affairs studied the problem, the Lithuanians and Poles came to blows. Both states were in the process of expelling the Red Army; when their armies were about to meet, it appeared they would do so as enemies because the Poles had occupied Gardinas, a district claimed by Lithuania. On April 19 the Poles seized Vilnyus from the Reds just before the Lithuanians arrived, and refused to turn the city over to them. In June the Allied Supreme Council delineated a line beyond which the Polish army was not to pass. Disregarding this line, the Poles advanced and ignored an Allied request to withdraw. They made a further incursion into Lithuania, after which a new line was drawn, only to be violated again by the Poles.

With the collapse of the anti-Bolshevik Russian armies in the autumn of 1919, the three Baltic States at last began to negotiate a final settlement with the Soviet government. On December 2, 1919, Estonia and Russia agreed to an armistice and on February 2, 1920, signed the Peace of Tartu which recognised the independence of Estonia. Lithuania and Latvia followed suit and signed peace treaties at Tartu on July 12 and August 11 respectively.

In the Russian-Lithuanian treaty the Soviet government recognised Vilnyus as the Lithuanian capital. The city was still in Polish hands, with the Red Army advancing on it. The Poles offered to evacuate the city before the Reds arrived so that the Lithuanian army could occupy it. When the Lithuanian force appeared, however, it was attacked by the Polish army and held back so that the Reds entered the city first. Nevertheless, true to their agreement, the Russians turned the city over to the Lithuanians and the government was moved there. On October 7, 1920, the Poles recognised Vilnyus as the Lithuanian capital, and the very next day Piłsudski sent his confidant, General Zeligowski, to occupy the city. Zeligowski's 'free-booting' effort was successful and on October 9 the city was back in Polish hands, where it remained, as a cause of dissent between the two states.

At the end of 1920 Lithuania still had one problem outstanding. This was the Memel question. Memel, or Lithuania Minor, had been a part of Germany which was detached from her by the Allies in 1919. A French High Commissioner was appointed to administer the district until the Allies could decide how to dispose of it. Since a majority of the inhabitants were Lithuanian and Lithuania was granted recognition by the Allies in December 1922, it was hoped that the area would be incorporated with Lithuania. Since the Poles and the French were opposed to this solution, the inhabitants rebelled in January 1923 and overthrew the German directorate which had continued to function under the French High Commissioner.

Lithuania was accused of instigating the revolt and ordered to withdraw the insurgents. The Lithuanian government ordered all its volunteer nationals who had crossed the border to return and awaited the decision of the Allies concerning the district. On February 17, 1923, the ambassadors' conference decided to transfer the sovereignty of the district to Lithuania. This decision was confirmed by the Memel Convention which provided for a large measure of autonomy for the district and for the official use of both the Lithuanian and German languages. The port itself was recognised as being of international importance, and a three-member harbour board consisting of a representative from the Memel district, one from Lithuania and one from the League of Nations was established to manage it. Thus, the goal of a port on the Baltic which had been enunciated by the Lithuanians was finally realised.

Further Reading
Jurgela, Constantine R., *History of the Lithuanian Peoples* (New York: John Felsberg 1947)
King, J. C., *The First World War* (New York: Harper 1972)
Mazour, Anatol, *Finland between East and West* (Princeton, NJ: Van Nostrand 1956)
Nodel, Emmanuel, *Estonia: Nation on the Anvil* (New York: Bookman Associates 1963)
Page, Stanley, *The Formation of the Baltic States* (Cambridge, Mass: Harvard 1959)
Pusta, K. R., *The Soviet Union and the Baltic States* (New York: John Felsberg 1942)
Ruhl, A. B., *New Masters of the Baltic* (New York: Dutton 1921)
Smith, C. Jay., *Finland and the Russian Revolution 1917-1922* (Athens, Ga: University of Georgia Press 1958)

RICHARD W. CONDON was born in Chicago and received his education at Suomi College, Hancock, Michigan, the University of Nebraska at Omaha (BA and MA) and the University of Minnesota (PhD). His graduate work was in the history of Europe in the 20th Century, with particular emphasis on Finland during the Second World War. At present he is Chairman and Professor of the History Department at Mansfield State College, Mansfield, Pennsylvania.

THE END OF THE OTTOMAN EMPIRE

The hierarchical Ottoman Empire had been destroyed in the war. In its wake, despite the efforts of the Allies, Turkish nationalism grew and overthrew the centuries-old Ottoman régime. *Norman Itzkowitz. Below:* Turkish troops

THE PEACE QUEUE.

AUSTRIA (to Germany). "GET A MOVE ON!"
BULGARIA. "IT'S NO GOOD HAGGLING; WE'VE ALL GOT TO HAVE IT."
TURKEY. "WELL, I'M LAST, AND I DON'T CARE HOW LONG ANYBODY TAKES."

Left: A *Punch* cartoon of May 21, 1919, five weeks before the Treaty of Versailles was signed, exemplifying the British conservative view. By hanging back, however, the Bulgars and Turks were able to secure terms more favourable than those allowed to Germany and Austria. *Right:* The scene in Constantinople as the Allies hand over to the Kemalists. *Far right:* Mustapha Kemal (right), Turkey's nationalist leader. *Below:* The Serbian General Misič (left) with the British General Milne, before the latter's appointment in Constantinople

On March 16, 1920 the sound of marching feet reverberated through Constantinople as Allied troops under the command of General Sir George Milne occupied the Imperial City. In the face of Kemalist successes in Anatolia the Allies hoped through this action of theirs to bolster the rapidly diminishing authority of Sultan Mohammed VI. That enfeebled ruler, whose throne was being challenged by the tattered nationalist forces under the command of Mustapha Kemal, was the direct descendant of Bajazet I, the scourge of Europe, who in the late 15th Century had boasted that he would stable his horses at St Peter's altar. The last act in the long and often splendid drama of the Ottomans, an act that had commenced in 1914 when Enver Pasha and his colleagues in the ruling triumvirate had taken the Ottomans into the First World War on the side of Germany, was swiftly approaching its end.

On the outbreak of the First World War the Ottoman Empire, although racked by recent setbacks in the Balkans and in North Africa, was still formidable. The Empire contained a variety of peoples speaking many languages and professing many faiths. It was a non-national state in which an individual's identity was still determined primarily by his religious affiliation. Islam was the dominant religion, with the Moslems considering themselves as the *ummah,* that is, the people of Mohammed. The main minority religions had their own corporate communal organisations known as *millets.* Despite the reform movement initiated in 1839 the non-Moslems still complained that compared to their Moslem counterparts they were second-class citizens. But even within the Moslem community there were differences. The main distinction there was between the Ottomans and the non-Ottomans.

Initially, Ottoman was a dynastic term used to designate the ruling house of the Empire that was descendant from its late 13th-Century eponymous founder, Osman. Later, the term was applied to the Empire's ruling élite and their own form of High Islamic culture. In the 16th Century, as well as in the 19th and 20th, the true Ottomans were those men who served the state and the religion, and knew the Ottoman Way. In other words, they were the Moslem office holders in the military, bureaucratic and religious establishments who were fully at home in the use of Ottoman Turkish and whose daily lives conformed to the

Südd Verlag

mores of the society for which that language was the medium of expression. With elements of Arabic and Persian as well as Turkish, Ottoman Turkish was the language of court, government, scholarship and polite discourse. By means of the twin dividing lines of religion and education, the Ottomans were removed from the non-Moslems and from their fellow non-Ottoman Moslems as well. Members of the ruling élite identified themselves as Ottomans and not as Turks. As employed by the Ottomans, 'Turk' was a term of contempt. It was not until the late 19th Century that 'Turk' and 'Turkish' began to achieve respectability and only then under the influence of the virulent, hothouse nationalism that swept the Balkans and Anatolia.

Burgeoning nationalism

Nationalism was the force which gradually destroyed the *millet* structure that had bound the disparate elements of the empire together. Infused with romanticism and grounded in philological studies that served to resurrect forgotten glories and to idealise ancient pasts, the concept of nationality came to compete with religion as the basis of individual and group identity first among the non-Moslems, and then among the Turks in general. In the course of the 19th Century a number of nation states, including Greece, Bulgaria and Rumania, successfully separated themselves from the Ottoman Empire. That process often involved the protection of one or another of the great powers in the diplomatic game known to historians as the Eastern Question. The Ottomans were not unaware of the danger to their Empire inherent in nationalism. Upon the outbreak of the Greek rebellion the Ottoman government hanged both the patriarch of the Greek Orthodox Church and the Phanariot Greek who was the chief translator of the Porte. That was, however, a futile gesture and totally ineffective.

Similarly ineffective was their own countermovement of Ottomanism. That was a fore-doomed attempt to instil in all their inhabitants a new loyalty to an Ottoman constitutional monarch which would transcend religious ties or ethnic origins in return for full rights of citizenship. Ottomanism offered too little too late to the Sultan's non-Moslem subjects who were already committed to nationalist solutions to what they considered to be their intolerable plight.

As the Empire contracted in the late 19th Century, Anatolia became again the heart of the Empire, as it had been at the start. Anatolia's population was predominantly Moslem in religion and Turkish in language. After the Seljuks had defeated the Byzantines at the battle of Manzikert in 1071 permanent Turkish settlement replaced nomadic life in Anatolia. Under the frontier conditions existent in Anatolia the Turkish language quickly spread, and was often, but not always, accompanied by Islamisation. By the 19th Century, Turkish-speaking Moslems made up the bulk of the population in Anatolia. However, important enclaves of Greek Orthodox and Armenian Christians, whose language was often Turkish, still remained. After 1875 nationalism made its inroads among the minorities of Anatolia as well. The Greeks wished to establish a Greek Pontic state, and the Armenians too aspired to nationhood. Greeks and Armenians founded organisations dedicated to the realisation of their ambitions.

The Ottomans reacted with severity against what they conceived to be a dangerous ideology dedicated to their destruction and that of their Empire. Fear of Armenian involvement with Russia only intensified the Ottoman distrust of Armenian nationalism. What have come to be known as the 'Armenian Massacres', but which the Ottomans viewed as the pacification and elimination of internal rebels, served to increase the homogeneity of the area, largely Turkish speaking and Moslem in character.

It is understandable that with the high value placed on Ottoman culture Turkish nationalism would be the last in the Empire to develop. As the government sponsored ideologies of Ottomanism and then pan-Islam failed, the concept of 'Turkishness' and of 'Turkey for the Turks' began to take root and flourish. Late in the reign of Sultan Abdul Hamid II (1876-1909) several individual Ottomans began to extol the virtues of Turkishness. The origins of Turkish nationalism are still uncertain, but it is clear that like its counterparts in the Balkans it was a romantic movement based on western models. In 1897 an Ottoman, Mehmet Emin, produced a volume of poems in simple Turkish employing rhyme schemes of folk origin: 'I am a Turk. My religion and my race are great.'

For incipient Turkish nationalism to succeed in creating a Turkish state three conditions would have to be met. First, the true Ottomans would have to divest themselves of allegiance to their Ottoman status and Ottoman culture, and replace them with a sense of shared identity with the Anatolian Turks. Second, the Turkish speaking Muslim peasantry of Anatolia would have to come to value their own Turkishness and develop a loyalty for a Turkish nation as yet unborn. Third, the Ottoman Empire would have to disappear.

The rise of Kemal

The defeat of the Ottoman Empire in the First World War facilitated the realisation of all three conditions and prepared the ground for the emergence of the modern republic of Turkey. On October 30, 1918 the Mudros armistice was signed, putting an end to the Ottoman Empire's participation in the war. The armistice's terms were harsh, opening the Straits to the Allies and granting them permission to occupy any strategic area deemed necessary for their security. Weary of war and unable to resist further, the Ottoman army proceeded to demobilise in accordance with the terms of Mudros. Although defeated, the Sultan still reigned in Istanbul and what nationalist sentiment existed was local and poorly organised. It was primarily, if not solely, the landing of Greek troops at Smyrna on May 15, 1919 that galvanised the nationalist forces into action and brought Mustapha Kemal to the fore.

In Mustapha Kemal the nationalist movement found its embodiment and personification. He had achieved a brilliant military record during the war and was renowned for his defence of Gallipoli. No other Ottoman military commander had surpassed his achievements and few had equalled them. Moreover, none of the political responsibility for the Empire's defeat adhered to him as it did to other commanders who were intimately connected with the policies of the Young Turk party. More importantly, Mustapha Kemal had a keen mind, and he combined intelligence with will. His training had accustomed him to the responsibilities of command and the charismatic force of his personality attracted capable men to his side who followed his lead with fierce devotion.

Disillusioned with the Sultan's acquiescence in Allied policies, Mustapha Kemal had been in the process of having himself assigned to Anatolia as Inspector-General of the *Ninth Army* (later changed to the *Third*), ostensibly to put an end to the attacks of local Turks on Greek villages around the Black Sea port of Samsun. In reality, however, he was bent on the creation of a national movement of liberation. When the Greeks landed in Smyrna he hastened his departure in order to avoid detention by the British authorities. Leaving Istanbul on the evening of May 16 aboard the *Bandirma* he arrived at Samsun on May 19, 1919.

Resistance to Allied plans for the partition of Anatolia took the form of spontaneous local and regional organisation such as the Assembly for the Defence of the Rights of Eastern Anatolia, and the Ottoman Society for the Defence of the Rights of Smyrna. Mustapha Kemal realised that expulsion of the invaders required a national base and a single unified movement under his direction. It was not yet time for him to unfurl his own banner. Therefore, his public image was that of a

man seeking to save his people by means of a movement based in Anatolia while the Sultan remained a virtual prisoner and pawn in the hands of the Allies who had occupied Constantinople. Mustapha Kemal's programme was simply the creation of an independent Turkish nation with absolute sovereignty over its own internal and external affairs. Such an independent state would be firmly grounded in Turkish nationalism embracing all whose language was Turkish and whose religion Islam, from Ottoman army officer and bureaucrat to Anatolian peasant.

National liberation movement

Completely disregarding his orders, Mustapha Kemal set about organising an army and establishing his movement of liberation on a national basis. His programme was defined in a telegram sent on June 22, 1919 to all civil and military figures whom he considered to be reliable and whose assistance he wished to solicit. In it he said that national independence and integrity were in danger; the Constantinople government was unable to discharge its responsibilities. National independence could be achieved only through the efforts and will of the nation. A national committee must be established to review the situation. The telegram went on to call for a national congress to convene in Sivas. All provinces were asked to send delegates and to keep the matter secret.

In Constantinople the Sultan's government soon realised that Mustapha Kemal was using his authority as Inspector-General to undermine its position. He was ordered to return to Constantinople, a command he could not obey. Preferring to avoid any overt act of rebellion against the Sultan, Mustapha Kemal resigned his commission on July 8, 1919. At this juncture the Assembly for the Defence of the Rights of Eastern Anatolia centred in Erzerum provided him with an organisation for the furtherance of his own views. Under his chairmanship the society held a congress in Erzerum from July 23 to August 17. The Erzerum congress's resolutions spoke of national frontiers, national resistance to partition, the need for national forces to take the field, and a national assembly.

After Erzerum another congress, the one referred to in Kemal's initial telegram, met in Sivas from September 4 to September 14, 1919. Seeking to make the movement national in character, the Assembly for the

Imperial War Museum

Defence of the Rights of Eastern Anatolia was reorganised into the Assembly for the Defence of the Rights of Anatolia and Rumelia. A representative committee was elected with Mustapha Kemal as chairman to conduct the day-to-day affairs of the society. Kemal's movement still wished to avoid an open break with the Sultan whose dual status as Caliph continued to carry great weight with the people. The congress blamed the government for the country's ills and the present threat to its integrity and independence, but reaffirmed its loyalty to the Sultan. This and other pressures forced the resignation of the Damat Ferid Pasha cabinet which was replaced by that of Ali Riza Pasha who was somewhat more favourably disposed to the nationalists. In October conversations were held between the Istanbul government and Mustapha Kemal's representatives which resulted in the acceptance by Istanbul of the Sivas Congress resolutions and recognition of the legality of the Defence of Rights Organisation. New elections were then held for the Ottoman parliament in December 1919. Kemal's supporters and sympathisers were the dominant political group as the new parliament convened in Constantinople on January 12, 1920. On January 28 the National Pact, considered by many to be Turkey's Declaration of Independence, was passed. Based on the resolutions of the Erzerum and Sivas congresses, the National Pact restated Mustapha Kemal's programme for complete independence and total sovereignty in economic, judicial, political, and territorial matters.

Kemal's intransigence

Mustapha Kemal's intransigent position on independence, and the success of his troops against the French at Marash in south-eastern Anatolia, led to the Allied occupation of Constantinople on March 16, 1920. Parliament was dissolved and many deputies were interned in Malta. The Italians and the French privately made it known to Kemal that the occupation of Constantinople was not their idea. The Sultan's government declared the nationalists to be rebels and a religious decree was issued enjoining Moslems to kill them on sight as a religious duty. The alliance between the traditional forces and the Sultan did not go unnoticed by Kemal.

With Constantinople occupied and parliament dissolved, the nationalists proceeded to convert themselves into a separate govern-

ment. Kemal called for an assembly to convene in Ankara. Elections were held and on April 23, 1920 the Grand National Assembly was established in Ankara, and the next day Mustapha Kemal was elected its President. The Grand National Assembly assumed responsibility for the present and future of Turkey and notified the foreign powers that it alone spoke for the Turkish people. The Sultan then had more religious decrees issued against the nationalists whose leaders, including Mustapha Kemal, were condemned to death *in absentia*.

After the Sultan's government accepted the treaty of Sèvres on August 10, 1920, a sign of the Sultan's complete submission to the will of the Allies, public opinion began to shift in favour of the nationalists. In this period Kemal's overriding concern was with military matters. He had to contend with the troops sent against him by the Sultan, with uprisings of the Georgians and Armenians, and with the invading Greeks. By the end of 1920, the internal military situation had been resolved and Kemal could now concentrate on the Greek front. Here the nationalists made excellent use of military aid supplied by the Soviet government with whom a treaty of friendship was signed in March 1921. The following month Colonel Ismet defeated the Greeks near Inönü (Ismet later took Inönü for his family name). Another Greek offensive was halted at the Sakarya River on August 24. Military victory brought diplomatic fruits as the French reconciled their differences with the Ankara government by a treaty in October 1921. The Italians, who early befriended Kemal, also withdrew from Anatolia.

Militarily and diplomatically strengthened, Mustapha Kemal was now prepared for the final confrontation with Greece. At the second battle of the Sakarya in August 1922 the Turks threw the Greeks back and pursued them, remembering Kemal's exhortation that they should make the Mediterranean their goal. On September 9, 1919 the Turks retook Smyrna and drove the Greeks into the sea. Mustapha Kemal then tried to cross the Dardanelles in order to oust the Greeks from Thrace. The Allied force occupying that narrow neck of land barred his way. After the French and Italians withdrew, fighting almost broke out between the Turks and the British, but in the end the armistice signed at Mudanya on October 11, 1922 provided a settlement. Three days later the Greeks too accepted the armistice. On October 19, Lloyd George resigned. His support for Venizelos's dream of a Greek state in Anatolia had provided the impetus that enabled Turkey to rise from the ashes.

Mudanya was to be followed by a peace conference at Lausanne. The Allies, who still recognised the Sultan's government, invited them and the Ankara government to the conference. Mustapha Kemal was not going to let the great victory won by and in the name of the nation be snatched from his hands by the Sultan. He would have preferred to be rid of both sultanate and caliphate in one swoop, but he demonstrated his political astuteness by proceeding in stages so as not to arouse too much opposition. On November 1, 1922 the Grand National Assembly passed a resolution that abolished the sultanate, but ensured the continuance of the caliphate in the Ottoman dynasty. On November 12, 1922 Sultan Mohammed VI fled from

Constantinople on board a British warship. Thus, when the Lausanne conference opened, Turkey was represented by the nationalist government alone in the person of Ismet Inönü.

The Lausanne Treaty, signed on July 24, 1923, represented the realisation of Mustapha Kemal's vision of Turkey for the Turks. The borders were essentially those of the National Pact. The capitulations (the agreements by which nationals of other countries remained under the jurisdiction of their own countries while in Turkey) were abolished, and Turkish law was supreme at home. Turkey achieved complete independence and total sovereignty except for the régime established at the Straits, and that might work to Turkey's advantage. No other nation defeated in the First World War had fared as well and Turkey was the only one to negotiate a favourable peace.

Secure at home and recognised in the international community, Mustapha Kemal continued with his plan to break with the past. On October 29, 1923 Turkey was declared a republic and Mustapha Kemal was elected its first president. It was only a matter of time before the main remaining institutional link with the past, the caliphate, would join the sultanate in oblivion. When Caliph Abdul-mejid soon threatened to become the focus for the forces of reaction, Mustapha Kemal made his plans to abolish the office. On March 3, 1924 the Grand National Assembly deposed the Caliph, abolished the caliphate, and banished all members of the Ottoman dynasty from the country. The following day Abdul-mejid was sent into exile on the Orient Express.

In less than five years after his landing at Samsun on May 19, 1919 Mustapha Kemal had succeeded in creating a Turkish nation firmly rooted in nationalism. With sultanate and caliphate abolished, the new republic would have to demonstrate its ability to survive. The rest of Mustapha Kemal's life and career were dedicated to the modernisation of Turkey and Turkish society to ensure that survival.

Further Reading

Craig, Gordon A. and Felix Gilbert, *The Diplomats 1919-1939* (Princeton University Press 1936)

Kili, Suna, *Kemalism* (Robert College 1969)

Kinross, Lord, *Ataturk: The Rebirth of a Nation* (Weidenfeld and Nicolson 1964)

Lewis, B., *The Emergence of Modern Turkey* (Oxford University Press 1961)

Thomas, L. V., and R. N. Frye, *The United States and Turkey and Iran* (Harvard University Press 1951)

Young, T. Cuyler, *Near Eastern Society and Culture* (Princeton University Press 1951)

NORMAN ITZKOWITZ was born in New York in 1931 and educated there and at Princeton. He has held various academic posts, and has maintained his connection with Princeton, where he is currently Professor of Near Eastern Studies. In 1970 Dr Itzkowitz was a Visiting Professor at the Hebrew University of Jerusalem. He has written or contributed to a number of publications in the field of Turkish and Near Eastern history. Among them are his books *The Ottomans* and *The Ottoman Empire and Islamic Tradition*, published by Knopf. Dr Itzkowitz is married, with two children.

PLEBISCITES: SELF-DETERMINATION IN ACTION

Wilson had insisted on plebiscites, and now the question was the way in which the relevant areas would jump. *S. L. Mayer. Below:* Russian émigrés arrive to vote in the East Prussian plebiscite

Wilson's principles of national self-determination were to be carried out in at least one respect by the Paris Peace Conference. Although many territories were stripped from Germany, some of them German-speaking, and although Austria—the rump remaining from what was once a great empire—was specifically forbidden to become part of Germany even though its people wanted this *Anschluss* in 1919, other territories claimed by both Germany and her neighbours would be allowed to have plebiscites to determine their future. Peripheral areas of other defeated states would be allowed the same privilege. There were also many territorial claims presented to the Supreme Council, or Council of Ten, as it was known, by lesser powers including Greece, Denmark, Rumania, Yugoslavia, Czechoslovakia and Poland.

The first plebiscite to be formally considered by the Conference was the case of North Schleswig (or, as the Danes called it, Slesvig). Although not mentioned in the 14 Points, Schleswig had been in dispute between Denmark and Prussia (and later Ger-

many) since 1848. Although both Schleswig and Holstein had been seized in the Prusso-Danish War of 1864, after the Peace of Prague which ended the Austro-Prussian War both were annexed to the North German Confederation which later became the German Empire. A plebiscite was promised at that time, since in northern Schleswig most of the population was Danish, although in the rest of Schleswig and all of Holstein the population was German. Despite enormous emigration and massive Germanisation of the area, particularly since 1900, the 1905 census showed that out of the 148,000 people in northern Schleswig, 139,000 spoke Danish, which was even learned by a third of the German immigrants to the area. The total population of the whole of Schleswig-Holstein was 1.6 million. The Danish Minister at Paris formally raised the matter of northern Schleswig before the Council of Ten on February 21, 1919, and he requested plebiscites in the two most northern zones. These plebiscites were ordered, and German forces were asked to evacuate the area in preparation for the plebiscites. Both Denmark and Germany mounted massive propaganda campaigns, but the daily sight of automobiles coming over from Denmark laden with butter, pork, tea and coffee, and distributed free to the population was the best propaganda of all for an area which, like the rest of Germany, had been living at the edge of subsistence for months, especially during the blockade. Both Germany and Denmark shipped in hundreds of people qualified to vote but living outside Schleswig, many being members of the armed forces. On February 10, 1920, the first plebiscite was held, in the northernmost zone, under international auspices. Over 90% of eligible voters went to the polls, and the result was 75,431 for Denmark, 25,329 for Germany. This put great pressure on the voters in the second zone for the election of March 14, in

which more complex linguistic divisions were involved. In the west the people spoke Frisian, a Celtic tongue; in the centre, Danish and German; and in the east, around Flensburg, chiefly German. The result of the second plebiscite was 12,793 for Denmark, 51,820 for Germany, and in Flensburg 8,947 for Denmark, and 26,911 for Germany. Denmark was finally allotted the first zone, with minor border adjustments; the second zone remained German, and anyone over 18 or resident there since 1900 could opt for Denmark and leave. As a result the Schleswig Question, which caused three wars in the 19th Century, ceased to exist.

The eastern boundaries of Germany presented a far greater problem than those with Belgium, Denmark and France. The Poles were busily expanding their new state, and there seemed to be no

end to their demands for territory in every direction. With the French egging them on, the Poles advanced along the Russian frontier (until they were stopped), and they continued to make enormous demands upon a defeated Germany, alongside whom many Poles had fought when things had looked brighter for the Reich. Now their delegates at Paris, with Allied assistance, used the principle of national self-determination to acquire territory. There was no doubt that many formerly German areas had large minorities and in some places majorities of Polish-speaking people. Even the Germans did not contest the obvious. But in others an outcry was raised when it became known that Germany was to be divided in two (as, for example, Pakistan was) with a narrow band called the Polish Corridor running through the two sections. The Baltic seacoast had been German for centuries, including the port of Danzig, whose population included 308,000 Germans and only 16,000 Poles. The 1910 German census, generally reliable, indicates that in the areas to be ceded by Germany, 528,000 Poles and 385,000 Germans lived in West Prussia (most of the Germans near the Baltic), 15,000 Poles and 10,000 Germans in East Prussia, 1,273,000 Poles and 682,000 Germans in Posnania (Posen), 28,000 Poles and 10,000 Germans in Middle Silesia. Thus, out of the whole population ceded to Poland, 1,844,000 were Polish and 1,087,000 German. On the face of it, these figures seem to support Poland getting all the territory. Yet as the boundaries were drawn, over a million Germans became Polish overnight.

Self-determination in abeyance

The Corridor aroused most conflict, since it had been promised to Poland under the 14 Points, and this ran strictly counter to the principle of national self-determination. Recognising this anomaly, the Conference decided to award Danzig, the biggest prize in the Corridor, to the League of Nations, who would administer the territory. The Conference, especially the French and Poles, were afraid that if Danzig remained in Germany, the Germans could later block Poland's access to the Baltic. The existence of the Corridor also made it possible for Poland to create her own port right next to Danzig, which, in time, they did: this was Gdynia. But the Corridor was militarily indefensible, and no German government from 1919 onwards was prepared to accept that Germany should be arbitrarily divided contrary to the principle of national self-determination for the sake of Poland, who had already received so much territory from Germany and was working hard to gain more at the expense of all her new neighbours. The Corridor and Danzig remained a burning issue in Germany under every régime and was later the *casus belli* for the opening shots of the Second World War.

Despite French and Polish protests Wilson saw to it that other, less clearly defined areas were allowed to vote on their future. These areas were contiguous to those which Poland was to receive anyway, and fierce propaganda campaigns from both sides were soon mounted, although the German government was unwilling for plebiscites to be held at all in territory which had been German for many centuries. The 1910 census gives the following population figures for the plebiscite areas: in those in East Prussia, 268,000 Poles and 288,000 Germans (approximately 14% Catholic, 85% Protestant); in West Prussia 24,000 Poles and 114,000 Germans (40% Catholic, 60% Protestant); in Middle Silesia 3,000 Poles and 1,000 Germans (48% Catholic, 52% Protestant); in Upper Silesia 1,245,000 Poles and 672,000 Germans (85% Catholic, 15% Protestant). The figures for the religious division are approximate, since they take no account of the sizeable Jewish population. Nevertheless they are significant in view of the fact that Germany was still more than 50% Protestant, while Poland was predominantly Catholic. Many Protestant Poles would vote for Germany for that reason, although Catholic Germans would not opt for Poland, since they formed a large minority in Germany at that time.

In the Marienwerder and Allenstein plebiscites in East Prussia, held on July 11, 1920, the vote, as in the other plebiscite zones, had more than merely ethnic significance, since each area had a greater or lesser economic value for either Germany or Poland. Allenstein, for example, exported timber in large quantities, and Marienwerder was crossed by the Danzig-Mława railway, by far the shortest rail route between Danzig, the port Poland would use the most, and Warsaw. Since Danzig had a customs union with Poland rather than Germany, the railway was vital to Polish interests. Both areas would help to define the width of the Polish Corridor as well as its future defence. Despite the fact that roughly half the population of both Allenstein and Marienwerder were Polish speaking, most of these were Protestant, and the overwhelming majorities in favour of Germany also indicated a lack of confidence in the economic future of the new Polish state. Disappointing as this was for the French and Poles, Poland was given

Südd Verlag

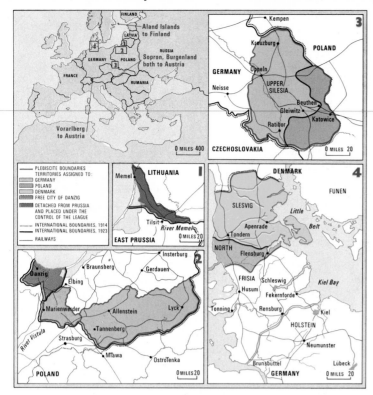

transit rights for the railway through Marienwerder, and, with a few minor border modifications, both areas went to Germany.

The plebiscite in Upper Silesia was probably the most important of all postwar plebiscites. Its valuable coal deposits were vital for German industry, but most of the coal areas were more than 50% Polish in character. Indeed, a large emigration out of Poland to the mines had gone on throughout the 19th Century. Yet, whereas both Posnania and West Prussia had been Polish during a large part of their history, Upper Silesia had been Austrian for centuries until Frederick the Great seized it for Prussia in the War of Austrian Succession (1740-48), and Prussia had developed the area economically ever since. The Polish that was spoken in the area was as diluted as the people's Polish character, and it is hard to see why this area was included for plebiscite except for its economic value to Poland. Nevertheless the Poles had a linguistic majority in the area according to the 1910 census – 1,245,000 Polish as against 672,000 German-speaking people. Upper Silesia, prior to the vote, was like a powder magazine ready to explode, and riotous political activity preceded the election. 75% of the total zinc ore of Germany was in Upper Silesia, as well as 23% of Germany's prewar output of coal, in addition to lead deposits of considerable size; this was a prize to be won at any cost. The plebiscite was finally held in March 1921, and the result, measured in individual votes, was about 6:4 in Germany's favour, again showing that little confidence was felt in the new Polish republic. Taken by communes, the vote was still 5:4 in favour of Germany.

Taken at face value, these results implied that the territory should be split roughly down the middle, but the question of where the frontier line should be drawn remained a problem. The pro-German communities and the pro-Polish areas were inextricably confused. The famous Industrial Triangle, where most of the mining areas were, was the furthest east in Germany and therefore the nearest to Poland. The German vote had been strongest in this area. Since most observers took it for granted that the Triangle could not be divided, the plebiscite had created as many problems as it solved, and Germany confidently demanded that the whole of the Triangle should be returned to German sovereignty. Britain and Italy suggested that Germany should get the lot, leaving Poland with a few country districts which could be easily detached. The French insisted that the whole Triangle, and about three-fifths of the rest of Upper Silesia, should go to Poland. The Poles claimed a still larger area, and in May 1921 attempted to occupy it by force. After weeks of fighting, order was restored by an international defence force after many lives on both sides and among the ranks of the soldiers were lost. The League of Nations settled the dispute in a manner which, inevitably, pleased no one. About two-thirds of the territory of Upper Silesia went to Germany and about three-fifths of its population as well. But the Triangle was divided, with Poland getting most of it, and almost all the mineral resources which were the major object of conten-

tion. In fact, the territory which Poland was granted by the League was close to what France had asked for on Poland's behalf earlier in the year. Poland and Germany, both unhappy with this, ratified the decision in 1922, the Reichstag draped in black for the occasion. The disappointment felt by the German public, however, was exacerbated by the popular press, who misrepresented the results of the plebiscite in order to make Germans feel that the whole area should have gone to them. But 350,000 of them found themselves in Poland after the Upper Silesia plebiscite and partition; 570,000 Poles remained in Germany. The collective effect of the decisions to partition Germany left over a million Germans in Poland after the war, and Poland received, in all, 8.53% of prewar Germany. Germany lost altogether about 13% of its former territory, and gained a legacy of bitterness which was to help Hitler's cause later on.

Europe patched together

Germany lost two additional bits of territory to other neighbours. Memel, a small area in the north-east of East Prussia, was detached from Germany, with its population of 150,000, about half of them German, most of whom lived in the Baltic city of Memel itself. Lithuania unsuccessfully claimed large areas west and south of the Niemen River, and the town of Memel was the only access to the sea for over two million Lithuanians. The Allied powers still had not decided the fate of Memel in 1923, when it was taken by a Lithuanian coup. Germany took it back in 1939. In addition Germany was forced to cede 122 square miles of Silesia to Czechoslovakia.

The cession of territory caused strong resentment in Germany throughout the interwar period. Yet the five plebiscites, with all their inequities, were the fairest way to handle complicated questions of nationality. Other territories in dispute after the war were dealt with in similar ways. For example, the Burgenland and Sopron were transferred from Hungary to Austria, partly with the help of a plebiscite. In Western Austria, the Vorarlberg, on the Swiss border adjacent to Lake Constance, was also given the right to choose its fate. The plebiscite held there in May 1919 resulted in a decision to join Switzerland. But the Swiss, as usual, remained neutral in the dispute, Austria put up a fight, and the area remained Austrian. The Aland Islands, 96% Swedish speaking, but near Finland, had a plebiscite, in which the people opted for Swedish nationality. But the League of Nations gave the islands to Finland anyway. There were other attempts at plebiscite during the immediate postwar period, for example in Vilnyus, where force of arms decided the matter in favour of the Poles, who seized the ancient Lithuanian capital city before a vote could be taken.

Germany's eastern boundaries were never accepted fully by any German government, but had plebiscites been held in the areas which were seized by force or which were simply given over to Poland at once at French insistence, the Polish Corridor might never have existed, and Germany's revenge might never have come to boiling point under Hitler. But, if national self-determination had won the day, Germany, though it would have lost territory to Denmark, probably France, and Poland, would have ended up larger than before the war, since there is little doubt that the greater part of Austria would have preferred to become German in 1919. The League often made an honest attempt to be fair, and there was bound to be bitterness after any plebiscite. But this acrimony would have subsided in time, as in Schleswig, if the settlements had been uniformly fair. In the cases where territory was ceded without plebiscite Poland always seemed to get the better of the bargain, with France consistently supporting her. Above all, it was probably Wilson's ill-conceived promise of an independent Poland with access to the Baltic, creating the problem of the Polish Corridor, which exacerbated other, less important questions. The League and the plebiscites cannot be blamed for the troubles which lay ahead. On the contrary, the five major plebiscites helped to improve a difficult situation. If national self-determination is still a universally-held ideal, then the plebiscite must remain as the fairest way to settle disputes of this kind.

Further Reading
Black, C. E., and Helmreich, E. C., *Twentieth Century Europe* (New York: Alfred A. Knopf 1966)
Temperley, H. W. V., *A History of the Peace Conference of Paris* Volumes II and VI (Oxford University Press for RIIA 1920)
Walters, F. P., *A History of the League of Nations* (Oxford University Press 1952)
Wambaugh, Sarah, *Plebiscites since the World War* Volumes I and II (Washington: Carnegie Endowment for International Peace 1933)

[*For S. L. Mayer's biography, see page 19.*]

RUMANIA AND BULGARIA

Litigants at the Peace Conference

Bulgaria had been one of the Central Powers, and Rumania one of the Allies, but the problem of their territorial adjustment was dealt with as a single question at the Paris Peace Conference. The difficulties presented were, superficially, minimal, as it was expected that the victor would be rewarded and the vanquished chastised. In fact, matters proved extremely difficult — the Americans suddenly developed an odd 'Bulgarophilia', and the Rumanians a stubborn intransigence about their claims. *S. D. Spector. Right:* Bulgaria and Rumania

BOUNDARY BEFORE 1919
RUMANIA BEFORE 1919
AREA ACQUIRED BY RUMANIA FROM THE
PARIS PEACE CONFERENCE, 1919
AREAS CEDED BY BULGARIA, 1919
BULGARIA AFTER CONFERENCE, 1919
RUMANIA/BULGARIA BOUNDARY AFTER 1919

The problem of Eastern Europe was a major concern of the Paris Peace Conference, consuming more time and creating more anxiety than the question of postwar Germany. Not only did the Bolshevik panic aggravate the Conference proceedings, but the need to trace viable frontiers also became quite obvious. The new or enlarged states of the region were viewed as potential allies in the new power structure, with Russia and Germany now considered as outcasts.

Two neighbours who were seldom on good terms, Rumania and Bulgaria, became litigants before the Peace Conference of the Allied and Associated Powers assembled in Paris to draft a general peace after the most devastating war fought up to that time. Both had negotiated with both sides, Entente and Triple Alliance, before entering the war, each holding out for the best possible gains with least sacrifice. But whereas Bulgaria in joining the Central Powers did not abandon any prewar alliances, Rumania, like Italy, did renege on her obligations in joining the Allies in August 1916. Ironically, however, the enemy state was to secure preferential treatment by the Allies, while the Allied power would run foul of the Conference's anger. Thus the two Balkan neighbours came before the Peace Conference with appeals for mercy, justice, forgiveness and real estate.

Neither nation achieved battle honours comparable with the heroism of the Belgians and Serbs, two smaller Allied powers who did not try to negotiate terms before entering the conflicts. Rumania and Bulgaria deliberately calculated their intervention, not realising, of course, that both would ultimately collide with Woodrow Wilson and the pious idealism which the American President introduced into the peace negotiations. Rumania came to Paris

with her secret Treaty of Bucharest (August 17, 1916) by which the four Allied powers (England, France, Italy and Russia) agreed to deliver large portions of Austria-Hungary to their new associate when the war ended in an Allied victory. Two years of haggling with both sides ended in this magnanimous gesture of awarding territory with no consideration given to the question of national self-determination for the non-Rumanians who were to be swallowed up by the projected postwar kingdom. Rumania was promised the entire Banat of Temesvar, all of Transylvania, most of Bukovina, and an equal voice at the Peace Conference. All the Central Powers would offer was Bessarabia from a defeated Russia. The choice was obvious. It was not a point of honourable commitment to an obligation contracted in 1883 when Rumania adhered to the Triple Alliance; now, in the midst of a great war, the question of national self-fulfilment outweighed the ethical issue.

Bulgaria, on the contrary, had very little to gain by joining the Allies, with whom, however, she did not hesitate to negotiate. A year of talks with both sides revealed Bulgaria's plight. Bristling with a spirit of revenge after having been thwarted in the Second Balkan War (1913), losing Adrianople, eastern Thrace, Kaválla, on the Aegean Sea, and southern Dobruja to Rumania, Bulgaria sought to regain the territory taken by her enemies in that war. Among the rewards promised in her alliance with the Central Powers of September 6, 1915, were Macedonia from Serbia, most of Dobruja if Rumania joined the Allies, and Kaválla in Thrace if Greece intervened on the Allied side. Dreams of resurrecting the ephemeral 'Greater Bulgaria' of the Treaty of San Stefano (1878) seized Bulgaria's leaders.

Rumania's military defeat in 1916 and her subsequent signing of the separate Peace of Bucharest (May 7, 1918) exacerbated the crisis caused by her entry into the war. Bulgaria, on the other hand, was tossed southern Dobruja by her wartime associates; but northern Dobruja, which she also coveted, was placed under the condominium of the four Central Powers, to ensure unrestricted access to the Danube delta. This state of affairs was to last only six months. Rumania's occupation of Bessarabia, 70% of whose population was Rumanian, in April 1918, while Russia was embroiled in her worst crisis, added yet another problem to the question of making peace. The success of the English and French in dragging Greece into the war afforded Bulgaria the chance to seize Kaválla, Drama and Sérrai in western Thrace, thus invalidating the Treaty of Bucharest (1913) and yielding to Sofia a larger area than had been envisaged by the Balkan League in 1912.

Allied advance

Bulgaria's territorial aggrandisement was short-lived, however, because the Allied offensive from Salonika during the summer of 1918 succeeded in knocking Bulgaria out of the war. The first of the four Central Powers to seek an armistice, Bulgaria agreed to a truce on September 30. The Bulgarian army was to be immediately demobilised and its equipment handed over to the Allied Army of the Orient. All occupied Greek and Serbian territory was to be evacuated, all means of transport placed at the disposal of the Allies, and Bulgarian territory made available for Allied operations. Allied troops marched north through Bulgaria, compelling King Ferdinand, ruler since 1887, to abdicate in favour of his son Boris on October 4. They then crossed the Danube into Rumania on November 10, and persuaded the Rumanian government to tear up the Peace of Bucharest and declare war on Germany one day prior to the latter's signing the armistice. Rumanian troops joined the westward march into Transylvania and would have seized Buda Pest if Hungary, which had split from Austria on November 1, had not sued for an armistice on November 3.

Four years of hostilities came to an end, but none of the belligerents was satisfied. A new conflict immediately arose – the war aims of the Allied secret treaties versus the idealism brought to foreign affairs by President Wilson. The forthcoming Peace Conference would be the arena where this battle would be waged. The four Allied powers had prepared studies during the war in defence of their aims and of national self-determination. But where the two collided, classic European *Realpolitik* would usually prevail. Allies and Central Powers alike paid lip-service to Wilson's 14 Points and Lloyd George's war aims address of January 1918. The irreconcilable conflict between realism and idealism was to bedevil the Peace Conference.

To her credit, Rumania did not make any territorial demands upon Bulgaria during the First World War. Retrocession of southern Dobruja, originally seized by Rumania in the Treaty of Bucharest (1913), was anticipated by Ion I. C. Brătianu (1864-1927), eleven times Liberal Party premier, and architect of 'Greater Rumania'. Although it had been suggested to Brătianu during the war that Rumania should restore southern Dobruja as the price for Bulgaria's entry on the Allied side, he brushed aside all such suggestions. At the opening of the Peace Conference in January 1919 no territorial claims appeared which could seriously affect the tracing of a postwar frontier between these two Balkan states. But Wilson's insistence upon a peace settlement based on the judicious reapportioning of territories would influence the tracing of frontiers here and in all other disputed areas.

Bulgarophobes and Bulgarophiles

Bulgaria, as a defeated state and a minor power, had little cause for optimism; the Allies were bound to be more indulgent to the claims of Greece and Yugoslavia, who had fought with them, and reports, during the war, of Bulgarian atrocities would not soften their attitude. But the Bulgarians had expectations. They hoped to regain many Bulgarian nationals living under alien rule. There was considerable irony in the fact that at the termination of hostilities Bulgaria should still clamour that to the vanquished belonged the spoils and demand that the Allies should give her, at the expense of their Greek and Serbian associates, the lands which she had hoped to gain by entering the war on the side of the Central Powers. On the other hand, Bulgaria and her powerful friends abroad regarded the Treaty of Bucharest (1913) as a perfidious iniquity – the partition of the Bulgarian nation at the hands of greedy neighbours. Therefore, when the Allies were about to trace the frontiers of a new Europe on the basis of national self-determination, the Bulgarians argued that it was only right that the 'shame of 1913' be undone, and that Bulgaria should be permitted to achieve national unity, as Greece, Rumania and Serbia were about

Right: In happier days – King Ferdinand of Bulgaria (centre) during a state visit to Vienna before the war. *Far right:* Ion Brătianu, the *eminence grise* of Rumanian politics and the architect of Rumania's change of allegiance to the Allied camp in 1915. Xenophobe and chauvinist, he placed his 'mission' of uniting all Rumanians into a single state above any other consideration in Paris. *Below left:* King Boris III of Bulgaria. He alone of the Central Powers' monarchs kept his throne after the war. *Below centre:* Aleksandr Stambulisky. *Below right:* General Coanda of Rumania

to do. The Bulgarians inundated the Peace Conference with propaganda about a century of instability in the Balkans if their claims were denied.

American experts arrived in Paris armed with cogent arguments in favour of permitting Bulgaria to retain southern Dobruja and secure access to the Aegean. Bulgaria had kept her envoy, Stefan Panaretov, in Washington throughout the war. The United States reciprocated and had preserved normal diplomatic relations. A curious Bulgarophilia among Americans resulted partly in a degree of indulgence towards the Bulgarians, which outraged the other Allied powers who had fought against them. If Bulgaria was the least troublesome of the states, Rumania was the most obstreperous and intransigent.

Brătianu lost no time in demanding the execution of the terms of the 1916 alliance. He spurned efforts to create a bloc comprising Rumania, the new Czech-Slovak republic, and the new Kingdom of the

Serbs, Croats and Slovenes (Yugoslavia), which could have presented a formidable challenge to the Conference's authority. When the Conference convened in January, Rumanian troops were already occupying all of the promised lands except the western region of the Banat, which had been seized by Yugoslav forces. The Conference was confronted with the task of drawing Rumania's new frontiers and forcing the Rumanians to evacuate territories assigned to other states.

Wily arrogance

The Rumanian premier, a xenophobic nationalist, did not understand vague moral aspirations, he considered the Americans and English undisguised hypocrites, and he did not conceal his disdain for the concept of a general association of nations. He was the only Allied statesman still in office who had taken his country into the war willingly and without previously being attacked by enemy forces. He was

now in Paris to collect the Allies' debts to Rumania.

Brătianu had two separate but related rôles in Paris. He attempted to get the best possible settlement for his own country in recognition of Rumania's joining the war on the Allied side, and at the same time he acted as unofficial spokesman for the disgruntled smaller powers, attacking the arrangement by which they were not even represented on the commissions responsible for tracing frontiers and drafting treaties for the protection of minority peoples.

In difficult meetings on January 31 and February 1 Brătianu put his claim to the Supreme Council. The present leaders had not negotiated the secret treaty of 1916, on which his demands were based, and did not feel bound by it, since Rumania had signed a separate peace in 1918. They also cast doubt on the votes of the national assemblies convened in Transylvania, the Banat, Bukovina and Bessarabia, which the wily Brătianu cited as evidence that the grant-

ing of these territories to Rumania would be in accordance with the principle of self-determination. The Council informed Brătianu that his claims would be examined by a mixed territorial commission.

The four Allied powers had arrived at the Conference with specific peace proposals designed to assist the chief peace-makers. But little attempt had been made prior to the Conference to reconcile the various Allied proposals. The Commission for the Study of Territorial Questions relating to Rumania and Yugoslavia began to work in February, and its activities were still unfinished when the Conference ended a year later. The Commission was not authorised to rule on the legality of the 1916 alliance, but its sanctity was defended by the Italians whose claims also depended on the validity of a secret treaty. The territorial experts were entrusted with the duty of submitting opinions on the ethnic, geographic and economic bases on which the new frontiers could be established. The experts ranged from the illiberal Americans to the more liberal British, the generous Italians, and the lavish French. The tedious activities of the Commission, whose schedule precluded the despatching of on-the-scene observers, involved the submission, on April 8, of a report which clearly revealed the different attitudes among the Allies—the French seeking to bolster Rumania as a counterweight to Germany and Russia, the Italians attempting to fish in the troubled waters of East Europe, the English looking to petroleum concessions and the Americans primarily concerned with fair play.

The Commission revised the frontier with Hungary specified in the 1916 alliance, assigning to Rumania 11 of the 15 counties comprising Transylvania and eastern Hungary. Although this included the whole of Transylvania, the new frontier still fell short of that promised in 1916, and it also violated ethnic principles by transferring several predominantly Hungarian urban centres to Rumania. Almost interminable discussions had ensued about the effects of this on the transport systems. The new frontier would leave Rumanians in Hungary and about 1.5 million Hungarians in Rumania.

Rumania received about two-thirds of the Banat of Temesvar, two major railway lines were severed and about 75,000 Rumanians were to be left in Yugoslavia. Most of Bukovina, with its considerable Ukrainian population, was also assigned to Rumania, and Bessarabia was vaguely mentioned as Rumanian property. Unfortunately, Russia was not consulted in the negotiations and never recognised the loss of Bessarabia. The question of the southern Dobruja, claimed by both Rumania and Bulgaria, was not resolved until the end of the Conference.

Of course, Brătianu could not be satisfied unless his claims were met in full. The establishment of Béla Kun's Hungarian Soviet Republic in March gave him a lever to use against the Allies, who felt the need to form a bloc of armed states to counter the spread of communism. Brătianu moved his army nearer Buda Pest, planning to eject the communists from Hungary. The Allies made no attempt at restraint.

Brătianu's revolt

On May 29, the terms of Austria's treaty were presented to the delegates. Brătianu

staged the famous 'revolt of the small powers', demanding to examine the treaty before approving it. The Supreme Council yielded, and naturally the disgruntled smaller states rejected the terms. Brătianu was angry at the news that Rumania would be denied a section of Bukovina which would have given her a common frontier with Poland, and that the Banat would be partitioned. But he was most incensed to learn that the Allies intended to impose Article 44 of the Treaty of Berlin (1878) which bound Rumania to grant alien minorities in her lands such security as the Allies would judge necessary. In view of Rumania's continuing anti-Semitism, the Allies intended to extract from Rumania a solid contract which would guarantee rights to the numerous minorities. Brătianu regarded this as unwarranted interference in his country's internal affairs, and refused to attend the plenary session when the treaty was presented to the Austrian delegation.

On June 10, at his last meeting with the Supreme Council, Brătianu was warned by the Allies against seizing unauthorised territories.

When, on June 11, Brătianu received the official recommendations for the new frontiers of Rumania, they had already been published in the newspapers. He realised that the Allies were seriously divided and too weak to enforce their treaty settlements. Feeling cheated and completely disillusioned, he returned to Rumania immediately after signing the Treaty of Versailles on June 28.

The question of Bulgaria was examined by three commissions, the Commission for the Study of Territorial Questions relating to Rumania and Yugoslavia, the Commission on Greek and Albanian Affairs and the Central Territorial Commission. The hard line adopted by Rumania made Bulgaria seem relatively co-operative by comparison, and the Allies regarded her claims favourably, partly as a result of this. Also, a Bulgarian republic had recently been proclaimed, led by Alexander Stambulisky, whose outspoken opposition to intervention had led to his imprisonment in 1915. Stambulisky's new régime had lost no time in signing the armistice and submitting to the Allies a memorandum containing territorial claims based on the Wilsonian formula which, however, conflicted with the claims put forward by Greece and Yugoslavia.

It was clear that Bulgaria would have to forfeit Macedonia, for which she had entered the war, and which she had held since 1915. Greece claimed not only this, but the whole Aegean coastline and western Thrace. This was a devastating blow, since it would deprive Bulgaria of access to the Aegean along the Marítsa river. President Wilson suggested that most of western Thrace should be included in the mandatory zone which the Allies proposed to set up round Constantinople, but England and France rejected this. In the end it was decided that Bulgaria's access would be secured by internationalising the Straits. Turkey objected strongly to this solution, to which she put an end in 1923. Strategic considerations, as well as the persuasiveness of the prime minister, Venizelos, caused the Allies to grant western Thrace to Greece. They felt it was in their interest to leave a barrier between Bulgaria and the Straits. Greece offered a trade outlet to the Aegean, but Bulgaria rejected this, feeling that it would cost too much to establish and maintain, and would weaken her bargaining position on the territorial claims.

Yugoslavia's claims were at first sight more modest, entailing chiefly some strategic boundary alterations. Her representatives persuaded the Allies that the transfer of these key areas would make it difficult for Bulgaria to fight another offensive war. In granting this territory, largely inhabited by Bulgarians, to Yugoslavia, the Allies showed that they were prepared to apply or ignore Wilson's principles as it suited them in any given instance. The territory consisted of four small but important salients with a total area of 975 square miles. These were Tsaribrod (with about 21,000 Bulgarian inhabitants and few Serbs), Bosilegrad (22,000 Bulgarians and almost no Serbs), the Strumitsa salient (25,000 inhabitants, mainly Bulgarians, but including Macedonians and a few Serbs), and a small area in the Timok valley in the north-west. With these, Yugoslavia would gain control of certain passes and push the Bulgarian frontier further east from the vital Belgrade-Salonika railway. The strategic value of these changes to the Allies was beyond dispute, since it had been through Tsaribrod that the Bulgarians had invaded Serbia in 1915. Now the frontier was to be brought within 35 miles of Sofia. The transfer of the Strumitsa salient put an end to Bulgaria's attempts to take over Macedonia, which had begun in 1870 with the creation of the Bulgarian Exarchate. The new frontiers of Bulgaria would leave outside about 1.5 million Bulgarians, and the Macedonian population problem was one of the most complex which confronted the Allies.

The Allies also found it impossible to reach agreement on Bulgaria's claim to Rumanian-occupied southern Dobruja, the Black Sea littoral province, which had considerable economic as well as strategic importance, with rich arable land producing good wheat crops. The Quadrilateral, as it was also known, was about 2,791 square miles in area. About one third of the population were Turks and Tatars. The Americans championed the Bulgarian cause as usual and held out on this demand until the end of the war. The Bulgarians ought perhaps to have been content with the provisions of the armistice, which forbade the occupation of their country by Greek, Rumanian or Serbian troops. Bulgaria was virtually the only state on the side of the Central Powers whose lands had not been occupied, invaded or devastated to any great extent.

While the Bulgarian delegation waited to see their draft treaty in Paris, the Rumanians were doing their best to create an upheaval in the Balkans. Having rejected the Treaty of St Germain and the partition of the Banat, Brătianu returned home determined to impose his own version of the peace terms. A succession of warning notes to Béla Kun failed to subdue him, and a confrontation between the Hungarians and the Rumanians seemed inevitable. On July 20 the Hungarians attacked the Rumanian lines. Kun attempted a defiant justification of his action by saying that he was forcing Rumania to conform with the will of the Allies. Within a week, however, Rumanian forces were in Buda Pest, Béla Kun had fled, and the 120-

day-old soviet republic had collapsed. Rumania had taken advantage of the obvious weakness and indecision of the Allies. This was the first successful attempt of an Allied power to resist her partners. Brătianu realised that, as the Allies had been unable to remove Béla Kun, so they could not force the Rumanians to withdraw. Instead of sending an army, the Conference could only manage an inter-Allied mission of four generals to ensure that they did not make off with everything portable. Brătianu was determined to compensate his country for losses sustained during the war. There was also a strong element of revenge for centuries of Magyar domination in Transylvania. He even worked out a plan for annexing Hungary.

Brătianu was, in a sense, carrying out the wishes of the Conference against its will. His activities seriously threatened their authority, but at the same time the Allies were anxious to eradicate Bolshevism in Hungary and provide a bulwark against a possible advance of the Red Army through the Ukraine into Central Europe. No other force of any consequence was available in the area to resist a Soviet offensive. The Conference decided to send Sir George Clerk to Bucharest on September 7. He was greeted on his arrival with the news of Brătianu's resignation, and the appointment of a non-party cabinet of army officers. Clerk learned in Bucharest that the main obstacle to a settlement was the treaty for the protection of the rights of minority groups, who would constitute almost one third of the population. Brătianu, who remained in power, though out of office, associated the treaty with Allied designs to seize more of Rumania's natural resources. When he tentatively agreed to evacuate Hungary, the Allies became afraid that an abrupt withdrawal would result in complete chaos.

In November, long overdue elections were held in Rumania, with surprising results. That they were not rigged was a novelty in the kingdom, and the National Party of Transylvania, together with the Peasant Party, won a majority. The nationalists hesitated to take office, unwilling to be seen to submit to the Allies. King Ferdinand was also doubtful about appointing a government whose leaders, Iuliu Maniu and Alexandru Vaida Voevod, had so recently become eligible for Rumanian citizenship.

Ultimatum

At the end of November the Paris Conference despatched an ultimatum demanding immediate compliance with orders to evacuate Hungary. If Rumania refused, diplomatic relations would be broken off, and she would be dismissed from the Allied circle. Maniu declined the premiership offered to him, and the King asked Vaida Voevod to form a new government. The ultimatum apart, the Allied attitude towards Rumania mellowed as a result of Brătianu's departure from active politics.

On November 19 a dangerous precedent was created. The United States Senate refused to ratify the Treaty of Versailles unless certain reservations were inserted. The Rumanians, and others, interpreted this as meaning that any government could refuse to sign or ratify treaties to which they objected. On November 27 the Rumanians refused to sign the Treaty of Neuilly.

In their anxiety for the Rumanians to

sign the treaty and evacuate Buda Pest, the Allies were now willing to agree to some modification to be made to the offending minority treaty. Pressure was brought to bear on the Americans, who, the day before they left Paris, agreed to sign a revised treaty, from which the so-called 'Jewish clauses' had been deleted. General Coandă, the Rumanian delegate, signed the Austrian, Bulgarian and minorities treaties on December 10, the day after the Allies, but the signature was antedated to December 9.

During the crisis in relations with Rumania, the Americans pressed harder for the transfer of southern Dobruja from Rumania to Bulgaria. The other Allies were still unwilling to sanction a settlement which involved an ally yielding territory to an enemy, so the Americans tried to insert a clause in Bulgaria's treaty providing for bilateral talks between the two claimants on the subject of ethnic divisions and a new boundary. No such clause appeared in the Treaty of Neuilly, and Rumania's 1913 acquisition of southern Dobruja was confirmed.

Stambulisky, leading a coalition government dominated by his own Agrarian Party, was anxious for Bulgaria to cooperate in the creation of a new order in the Balkans. Unable to achieve any substantial modifications of the Treaty of Neuilly, he and his delegation signed it on November 27. Three days later Stambulisky sent letters to the premiers of Greece, Rumania and Yugoslavia, proposing that the past should be forgotten, and suggesting that the Balkan governments should work together for the common security and the economic welfare of the peninsula. This helped to bring about subsequent population exchanges between Greece, Bulgaria and Turkey, which partly alleviated the unresolved problem of the minority groups.

Further Reading

Deak, Francis, *Hungary at the Paris Peace Conference* (New York: Columbia University Press 1942)

Lederer, Ivo J., *Yugoslavia at the Paris Peace Conference* (New Haven, Conn.: Yale University Press 1963)

Levin, N. Gordon, Jr., *Woodrow Wilson and World Politics* (New York: Oxford University Press 1968)

Mee C. L., *The end of order: Versailles 1919* (Secker & Warburg 1981)

Spector, Sherman D., *Rumania at the Paris Peace Conference* (New York: Bookman Associates 1962)

Temperley, H. W. V., *A History of the Peace Conference of Paris* (London: Oxford University Press for Royal Institute of International Affairs 1920-24, reprinted 1969)

SHERMAN DAVID SPECTOR was born in 1927. After naval service in the Second World War, he graduated with honours from Bowdoin College, earned a Master's degree and the Certificate of the Russian Institute at Columbia University, returned to active naval service during the Korean conflict, and was awarded his Doctor's degree at Columbia in 1960. His thesis, *Rumania at the Paris Peace Conference*, was published in 1962, and he has since written numerous articles. He has been Professor of History at Russell Sage College (Troy, New York) since 1968, and held a Fulbright-Hays professorship at the University of Bucharest where he researched a biography of Ion Brătianu. He has travelled widely in Eastern Europe, and has edited and translated René Ristelhueber's *A History of the Balkan Peoples* (New York: Twayne, 1971).

THE ARMENIANS AFTER THE WAR

Armenia became a state for 18 months after the war, but her fate was sealed from the first. *A. O. Sarkissian. Right:* Armenian refugees near Baku

At the end of the war the Armenian people were excited and expectant. This mood was felt by those then living in Constantinople and Smyrna – some 100,000 lucky ones who were spared deportation – and even by those fleeing their wartime captors, the Turks, and returning to their home towns in western Asia Minor, now under the occupation of the victorious powers. Such was also the prevailing mood among those in the Caucasus; though facing starvation in their war-ravaged patch of land there, most of them were optimistic about their future, for their friends as victors would not let them down. This naïve view was natural for a people unschooled in the devious turns and twists of international diplomacy, who had always expected Europe's aid in their struggle to better their unenviable lot under the Ottoman Turks. They felt that in the past they were not aided effectively by their friends in the west, but now events had decidedly taken a turn in their favour; their oppressors were crushed by the victors, and on these victors the Armenians pinned their hopes. In the defeat of the Turks they sought their salvation, and in the break-up of the Ottoman Empire they envisaged the realisation of their elusive national goal, the rebirth of an independent Armenian state in their historic homeland.

The overthrow of the Tsarist régime in Russia in 1917 brought about instantaneous and catastrophic changes in Transcaucasia. Soon after the success of the Bolsheviks the once large Russian army on the Transcaucasian Front became a disorganised, disorderly rabble. Field commanders could not maintain discipline and desertion by large numbers became frequent all along the 400-mile Russo-Turkish front. In the course of a few months Russia's fighting force there simply melted away and disappeared, as if it had been shifted suddenly and bodily to another front. Actually nearly all Russians left the front and went home. Many non-Russian elements in that army – the Azerbaijanis, Georgians and others – followed suit. The Armenian element, however, could not and would not do that, for their homes were behind that front and already endangered by the Turks.

The abandoning of the front by several hundred thousand Russian troops created a chaotic situation in the Caucasus. The entire region was in turmoil, and the Turks were quick to take advantage of this turmoil. By the Brest-Litovsk Treaty (signed between the Central Powers and the Soviets on February 9, 1918) the Turks were not to advance beyond certain lines on the Transcaucasian Front, but that front being disorganised, they were tempted to disregard any injunction and move on into areas beyond these lines deep into Russian Armenia. Facing them was an Armenian force of some 20,000 troops, ably led by veteran Armenian officers long in service under the Tsarist régime, but this force by itself alone could not halt or delay the onrushing and much larger Turkish force. Meanwhile Armenian leaders appealed to the Germans and the Soviets, hoping that they could and would restrain the Turks. But the latter were resentful of any outside interference in the movement of their forces on the Transcaucasian Front. The Armenians fell back until most of their land was lost and the Turks were within 20 miles of Erivan, their capital city. There on the plain of Sardarabad a decisive do-or-die battle raged during the last week of May. In this Armenian Verdun the Turkish advance was not only checked, but the Turks were worsted by the ramshackle, improvised but determined Armenian force. Then the Armenian leaders, emboldened by this signal success in battle, proclaimed Armenia's independence on May 28. But Turkey was not crushed; she had only suffered a setback, and the large force in its rear was still in being. In the ensuing peace treaty (signed at Batum on June 6) the Turks imposed crippling terms, by the sheer numerical superiority of their fighting force, upon the fragile Armenian Republic barely a week old, thereby reducing it to the status of a helpless satellite. This situation continued until late October when the total defeat of the Turks was consummated by the Mudros Armistice.

Soon after the Mudros Armistice many parts of western Asia Minor and much Arab territory came under Allied occupation – under the British in certain Arab areas, the French in Syria, Lebanon and Cilicia, the Italians in the Adalia region in the south-west, while Constantinople was under joint Allied control. Months later Smyrna province was occupied by the Greeks. Then began a new type of activity, perhaps never experienced in that ancient land, or in other parts of the world. It was like harvesting season for the peasant except that in this case 'harvesting' involved the rescuing, retrieving and ingathering of tens of thousands of Armenians who were taken into Turkish homes at the time of the massacre in 1915 and were still being held in involuntary servitude. These were the real lost souls, living victims of the war, all but dead in spirit and only physically alive. They numbered some 200,000, in addition to an untold number of Armenian families who by some luck had lost themselves during the massacre in isolated parts of Arab lands and were still aimlessly, hopelessly, lingering on. All of them were to be retrieved and provided with a livelihood.

This stupendous task would of course have been undertaken by the more fortunate Armenians, but its almost miraculous performance would not have succeeded so well without the generous and unfailing financial and material aid given by numerous internationally known relief organisations, best known among these being Britain's Lord Mayor's Fund and the American Near East Relief. More than 100,000,000 dollars was collected and spent by the latter organisation, well over 50% of that sum going to the orphanages, refugee camps and hospitals which it maintained in the Armenian Republic, in metropolitan Constantinople and in Cilicia. When the first phase of this rescue work was nearly completed, early in 1920, more than 100,000 Armenians had been brought to safety, placed in orphanages and in refugee camps; at least another 100,000 Armenian families had found their way to safety, a large number of these going to Cilicia in the fond hope of reviving there (with French aid) the long submerged Armenian state.

Armenian exodus

Late in 1920, when the French began to withdraw from Cilicia, the entire Armen-

Armenian refugees from the Turkish advance in Baku in August 1918

Imperial War Museum

ian population numbering some 150,000 migrated in a body to Syria and Lebanon. There they settled, in the Antioch region, in Aleppo and in Beirut. Years later (in 1930), when France relinquished Antioch and Alexandretta to the Turks, Armenians embarked upon a new odyssey, thousands of them sailing far away from the land held by their traditional enemies and seeking safety in distant South America. Subsequently all retrieved Armenians who had been given shelter in orphanages and in refugee camps in metropolitan Constantinople, and in the Smyrna region, were to share a similar fate. Even before the regenerated Turkish nationalist forces were able to occupy these areas (late in 1922) all Armenians were again on the move, heading for other parts of Europe. During this mass exodus more than 100,000 found their way to Greece, Bulgaria, Rumania and Yugoslavia, half of these eventually making their new homes in hospitable France. And some tens of thousands, especially those in the Smyrna region, could not escape the onrush of the Turkish force; there they were caught, thus becoming the last large group of Armenian victims of Turkish cruelty.

How many Armenians were left behind in the rescue work, unheard of and unknown to rescuers, it is impossible to say. Many of them had taken on Turkish names, had forgotten their mother tongue, and of course all had become professed Moslems (at least for the duration of the war). How many of these could recall their Armenian origin and possessed enough courage to declare it, is also impossible to ascertain with any accuracy. Their number may still be reckoned in tens of thousands, for even today an inquiring person in various parts of Turkey may meet many of these half-forgotten, spiritually stunted and almost totally lost souls in every town.

The Armenian Republic, occupying a small patch of historic Armenia in its northeastern corner, was a weak and helpless entity from the time of its birth until its death in November 1920. Enlarged after the total defeat of the Turks in the war, it was duly accorded *de facto* recognition by many European governments, and was a signatory, as a sovereign state, of the Sèvres Treaty of August 10, 1920. It was able to realise most of a 20,000,000 dollar bond issue in Armenian communities, and received much more than that from relief organisations abroad. Politically and economically, however, it was not and could not become a viable, self-sustaining state. It was a land-locked, far-away

country, beyond the effective reach of its friends and sympathisers in the west. Even the delivery of relief shipments encountered considerable difficulties, first at the Georgian port of Batum and later while in transit through Georgia to Armenia. The famine that had swept through the country, especially the towns, was still a problem. The constricted country was already overcrowded with several hundred thousand Armenian refugees from Turkey, who had been cared for since their arrival in 1915 by local authorities and by relief organisations in Tiflis, Baku and other metropolitan centres in Tsarist Russia. But the Russian Revolution had disrupted the flow of aid to Armenians in distress, for even relief shipments from Tiflis suffered long delays.

Most precarious of all were the Republic's defences. By the Mudros Armistice Turkey had renounced its conquests in Transcaucasia, and the withdrawal of its forces from the area made a great difference to the young Republic. The Armenian authorities immediately took over much of the territory thus freed and began to enlarge the tiny armed force (about 20,000 in all) for the adequate defence of its new frontiers. But the best that could be done was to raise the total of the force to about 35,000. The troops were inadequately armed, and except in some almost impregnable fort towns (such as Kars) there was a serious shortage of artillery. In late 1919 and 1920, when the aggressive and well-armed Turkish nationalist forces had vowed to eliminate (in collusion with the Soviets) the Armenian Republic, it became clear that even with a much larger and better equipped Armenian force than the existing one, the sad fate that seemed in store could not be delayed much longer. In October 1920 the Turks seemed ready for the kill, and when they attacked in late November Armenian forces found themselves caught in the jaws of a pincer-movement—between the Turks and the Red Army. In a few days the Turks overran most of the Armenian Republic and were about to take its capital city, Erivan, when the Soviets intervened as arbiters and 'saviours' of the Armenian people. They did this on two conditions: that the Armenian government resigned immediately, and that a Soviet system was to be instituted there and administered by Armenian communists. The Turkish troops were halted, the government resigned, and with the establishment of a Soviet form of government in Armenia on December 2, 1920, the Armenian Republic passed into history.

The Armenian leaders who bartered

away Armenia's shortlived independence and formally consented to the institution of a Soviet government in the country had no choice in the matter. In an age without miracles they realised that nothing else would save the Armenian people from almost total extermination by the Turks. Soon Armenian communists, under the Kremlin's directives, established the Soviet form of government and proclaimed the birth of the Armenian Soviet Socialist Republic. The Turks withdrew from certain areas, yielding a small part of their conquests but retaining many venerated Armenian landmarks, including the famous mediaeval capital city of Ani and Mount Ararat, at whose snow-capped peak Armenians in Soviet Armenia would gaze in deep sorrow while cursing their former 'friends' for their sad lot.

Chaos and turmoil, famine and misery were prevalent in the communist Armenian state. The administrative machinery had collapsed, and everything was in disorder. The only functioning group of workers not seriously affected by the cataclysmic events was the American relief organisation. More successful than the governments, it carried on its work efficiently and effectively, saving the lives of tens of thousands of Armenians. In this unhappy nation of orphans and old people this organisation maintained the largest orphanage in the world, at one time housing some 40,000 waifs, in what is today Leninakan. It had clinics and hospitals in many parts of the country. Its members worked hard in the best tradition of American missionaries. Fortunately the communist government did not interfere with the work of these people, and to the credit of Armenian communists, they even cooperated with these capitalist 'lackeys'. It was said that while the United States government declined to assume the Armenian mandate, American relief workers had taken it upon themselves. And by so doing they had even succeeded in mellowing the fanaticism of Armenian communists.

Today Armenia is still a small country, only 11,800 square miles. But its 2,500,000 citizens, working prodigiously even when Stalin's draconian decrees made life most difficult, turned their homeland into an industrialised modern state in the Soviet Union. For the first time in Armenia's turbulent history the majority of the world's 4,000,000 Armenians live and work there, while nearly another million reside in other parts of the Soviet Union (mostly in adjacent Azerbaijan and Georgia). The Armenian Diaspora numbers about 600,000. About one half of these live in the Americas; there are nearly 100,000 in Europe, while the rest still live in the Arab countries and in Iran. Turkey's Armenians, at one time totalling about 2,000,000, now number no more than 50,000.

Further Reading
Barton, J. L., *The Story of Near East Relief, 1915-1930* (New York: The Macmillan Company 1930)
Elliott, M. E., *Beginning again at Ararat* (New York: Revell 1924)
Hovannisian, R. G., *Armenia on the Road to Independence, 1918* (Berkeley and Los Angeles: University of California Press 1967)
Nansen, F., *Armenia and the Near East* (London: George Allen & Unwin 1928)

[*For A. O. Sarkissian's biography, see page 1327.*]

THE TREATY OF VERSAILLES

S. L. Mayer

In June 1919 the Allies nearly went to war with Germany again – this time over Germany's refusal to sign the peace treaty. The Treaty of Versailles was to create, in the reverse of Wilson's words, an unjust and dishonourable peace. *Above:* The Hall of Mirrors at Versailles, where the treaty was eventually signed on June 28

The most momentous treaty signed in the 20th Century was negotiated in an atmosphere of tension, propaganda, and rumours of the renewal of war, amid the guns of several minor wars and revolutions. When the Congress of Vienna convened a century before, many of the crucial decisions about what to do with Napoleonic Europe were made even as Napoleon's return from Elba made many think that the Congress was attempting to divide an empire which was being born anew. The Allies of 1815 were so confident that they drew up a treaty to partition Napoleon's empire even before the last guns of Waterloo were still. Territories were exchanged across the conference tables like chips in a casino, and the principle of national self-determination was one of the spectres raised by the French Revolution which the Congress hoped to crush. The Paris Peace Conference could not take place in such a hothouse atmosphere. Admittedly, Wilson's principle of 'open covenants openly arrived at' was ignored in favour of traditional diplomacy, conducted in secrecy, and exchanged confidences; but the negotiators of Versailles could not close their ears to the tumult around them. Germany was being block-

aded until a peace was signed; its people were starving in their millions. Revolution spread from Russia into Hungary and Germany, and many feared that the world revolution Marx and Lenin had forecast was at hand. Demobilisation was taking place everywhere, and war between Soviet Russia and Poland was threatening to nullify any decisions concerning Eastern Europe reached at the conference table. The Austro-Hungarian Empire had collapsed, and new governments clamoured for recognition and territory from the Great Powers. The German army, retreating in good order from the Western Front, seemed to disintegrate once each unit had returned to its home base. In the light of these and other problems – inflation, the separation of families, disease and the rampant influenza epidemic which was sweeping the world – decisions could not be taken over a period of a year or so. They had to be reached at once, whatever their shortcomings later. But the most important difference of all between Vienna in 1815 and Paris in 1919 was the fact that the vanquished Great Power was not represented at the Conference ending the First World War. One of the reasons that the Congress of Vienna, with all its reactionary principles, proved to be such a durable peace was that France, by the intrigue of her ingenious representative, Talleyrand, was able to bargain for her country. Germany was not given this privilege. The 32 nations which met in Paris intended to present a *fait accompli* to Germany.

By mid-January most of the national delegations had arrived in Paris, which appeared to Harold Nicolson, a member of the British delegation, as a 'riot in a parrot house'. There were too many problems, too many people – over a thousand in the upper echelon alone – and too much research to

be done in too short a space of time. Experts and specialists of every type filled every available hotel room in Paris. In addition lobbyists from every land, especially the new ones of Eastern Europe, came to plead their special problems before the various committees. The delegates had it within their power – in fact it was their most pressing duty – to remake the map of the world, and thousands of representatives from emerging nations – Ukrainians, Koreans, Indians, Arabs, Armenians and Indo-Chinese – were also there to put their case before the delegates. Woodrow Wilson, who who had proclaimed national self-determination one of the foremost objectives of the Conference, was the man towards whom all gravitated. It was Wilson who could make or break the Conference. It has often been argued that it would have been best for him to stay out of the Conference, and that he would have ultimately had more influence if he had remained a detached victor, in pristine splendour at the White House. This point is hardly tenable today. The peace would have been much worse had Wilson not been in Paris to cool French ardour and Polish greed. And he felt it an obligation to hear everyone's case in order to have the best possible chance of making the right decision. But after his glorious, if wearisome, trip round Europe before the Conference, Wilson's slender physical resources showed signs of breaking down even before the Conference convened.

First meetings

On Sunday, January 12, the four principal Powers – Great Britain, the United States, France and Italy – convened a meeting of the Supreme War Council. Each of the Powers was granted two delegates: the head of the delegation and his foreign minister. The four Powers agreed to add Japan to their number and thereafter the group became known as the Council of Ten. A secretariat for the Conference was established, and on January 18 the Peace Conference opened in the Clock Salon at the French Foreign Ministry in the Quai d'Orsay. The room was so called because of a small ornamental clock on the mantelpiece, but it was renamed the Peace Salon in honour of the occasion. The first session was ceremonial, and President Wilson, dressed in striped trousers, high silk hat and a tie with a pink pin, nominated Georges Clemenceau as President of the Conference. Smooth as the first session was, when the delegates got down to the real business of the Conference, differences arose between the various committees which were set up: over Upper Silesia, which Wilson insisted become a plebiscite

a 'missionary whose function it was to rescue the poor Europeans from their age-old worship of false and fiery gods'; he ridiculed Wilson's agonised indecision over even the minutest problems. On two points, however, Wilson left no doubt; his hatred for old enemies such as Henry Cabot Lodge and Theodore Roosevelt (who died in America during the Conference); and his support for a League of Nations. Lacking the support of the US Senate, and away in the United States for part of the Conference, Wilson's words often had not the dynamic impact they should have had upon the more crafty and cynical delegates. Wilson refused to delegate authority, and insisted on making decisions himself. By working 18 hours a day his health was further undermined, and his judgement inevitably suffered.

As time went on the press in Paris bitter-

thin French defences had been against the German onslaught in early 1918. The army and Marshal Foch were behind Poincaré in trying to force the Allies to partition Germany permanently. But Clemenceau realised that the Allies would never permit a Carthaginian Peace, and Clemenceau was overheard to have said that there were two useless organs: 'the prostate and the Presidency of the Republic'. The Anglo-American promise of a 50-year alliance against Germany was music to French ears, but when that proposal fell through, the French felt even more cheated, especially when their territorial gains were not nearly what many Frenchmen had hoped for. But Churchill's schemes to invade Soviet Russia equally fell on deaf ears at the Conference, and after a month proceedings had slowed down to the point where

Clemenceau: President of the Peace Conference and intent on crushing German militarism

General Pershing, whose military career started with the US Indian wars and reached its summit as C-in-C of the US forces in France, enters Versailles to watch the signing of the Treaty

zone, rather than being ceded directly to Poland; over which sections of Schleswig-Holstein should be given over to plebiscite and which should remain German; and so on. The official language of the Conference was accepted as being English, which infuriated the French. However, on a less formal level both English and French were spoken, most of the delegates having at least a smattering of both languages. Only the Japanese were at a disadvantage. In the first days of the Conference it was Clemenceau who dominated the proceedings. Wearing grey gloves, which concealed a skin infection, and a black skullcap, he slouched heavily in his chair and seemed to be asleep, but when aroused, usually by the interests of France being directly concerned, he became rude and pugnacious, living up to his nickname of 'Tiger'. Lloyd George, on the other hand, was always smiling, alert and well-groomed, fresh from an electoral victory in which he had promised to 'squeeze the German lemon until the pips squeaked'. This, coupled with his cheap subscription to the current cry of 'hang the Kaiser!', did not add either to the dignity of the British Prime Minister or to his ability to make a just and lasting peace. Wilson appeared to Lloyd George as

ly criticised the length of time being taken to reach decisions, and the French were astounded that a sense of obligation to France seemed to be increasingly lacking among her allies. Clemenceau begged Wilson to make a tour of the battlefields so that he could see the destruction the war had brought, but Wilson refused, knowing that the French wanted to sway his opinion in their favour. France demanded just compensation for her 6,000,000 casualties – more than those of the United States, Britain, the British Dominions and Colonies, Italy and Japan put together – and the devastation of a sixth of her country. Despite the lip service paid to the sacrifices of France, the Allies were unwilling to force Germany to pay the full cost of the war, as this would destroy a potential ally in Germany as well as a former lucrative market. Clemenceau also had an enemy in President Poincaré, who believed that France had been saved, not so much by her army, as by a miracle. Poincaré remembered the three days of waiting in early August 1914 when France had to wait on Britain's reluctant decision to go to war against Germany. He could not forget how long it had taken the United States to come to the aid of France, or how

the Big Four – Orlando (Italy), Lloyd George, Clemenceau and Wilson – decided to meet separately to make the crucial decisions.

The Council of Four met on the morning of February 19, but as Clemenceau drove off from his home in the Rue Franklin he was greeted by shots fired wildly by an anarchist, Pierre Cottin. As the chauffeur veered away, one of the shots struck Clemenceau in the back and lodged near his lung. But the French Premier's constitution was strong, even for a man of his 77 years. Within hours he was in discussions with House and Balfour, although it was extremely painful for him to lie down. When the heads of the other delegations from Italy, Britain and the United States visited him at home, it was decided that the Council of Four – which had been established so informally – should meet throughout the rest of the Conference. Then Wilson left for America, and House was left in charge for a month. However, on his return Wilson repudiated any concessions House had made in his absence, and insisted that the League of Nations be made an integral part of the final peace treaty, overriding the objections of many members of his own entourage. Orlando and Lloyd George, while Wilson was away, had left Paris, so the real business of the Council of Four began in March when they all were back in Paris. The committee reports had been submitted by this time and they suggested many of the ideas which Wilson had consistently rejected: German reparation payments, French control of the Rhineland, the Italian claim to Fiume, the Japanese claim to Germany's territory in China, and many others, almost all of which ran counter to the principles of the 14 Points upon which the truce with Germany was based. Wilson, for his part, continued the fight to include the League of Nations in the Treaty. But in order to establish the League, which met with a considerable lack of enthusiasm from Clemenceau and others, he was forced to give way slowly on many of his former principles, a process which further weaken-

ed his reputation as well as his slender hold on physical health. So the Saar, entirely German-speaking, went to France for 15 years; the Rhineland was to be occupied for 15 years and permanently demilitarised, though still within the borders of a sovereign state; despite the Chinese appeals to national self-determination, the people of part of Shantung province, entirely Chinese, were transferred from the German to the Japanese sphere of influence. Against these and other violations of the spirit and letter of the 14 Points Wilson fought almost alone, winning concessions here and there, but forced to give way to save the League. By the end of March Wilson was utterly exhausted. His left eye twitched uncontrollably from time to time. But he still refused to leave the most important work to others; the

secret Treaty of London of 1915, which had promised them Fiume and much of the Adriatic coast. The other members of the Council of Four were getting tired of Orlando's histrionics and Wilson was left to reason with the unreasonable Italians. Pale and lined, colour could only be restored to Wilson's face by standing him by an open window and forcing him to do exercises. His mind wandered at times and his concentration was failing. Orlando walked out of the Conference, and when he returned to Rome he saw portraits of Wilson being ripped down. At this moment the Japanese presented their demands for Shantung, and Wilson, his last card played, gave way. He did not want the Japanese to leave too. A week later the draft treaty was presented to the German delegation. Not one of the Allies was satisfied with it.

In Germany, meanwhile, after revolution, the fall of the monarchy, the establishment of the Weimar Republic and attempted Communist coups, the government was trying to prepare itself for the worst — a treaty which was expected to be harsh but one which they had never been invited to discuss until it was ready. The man chosen to lead the German delegation to Paris to receive the draft treaty was her new Foreign Minister, Count Ulrich Brockdorff-Rantzau. Formerly Germany's Ambassador to Denmark during the war, Brockdorff-Rantzau was a caricature of the Prussian diplomat; slender, well-dressed, wearing a monocle and a thin moustache. He helped to organise a professional study group who would be able to argue the terms of the draft treaty point by point when it was presented, but neither the committee nor Brockdorff-Rantzau himself was prepared for the harshness of the actual terms. They were convinced that at least Germany would be able to discuss the terms and believed that Germany would be allowed to join the proposed League of Nations as soon as the peace was signed. The Germans did suspect they would have to hand over Alsace-Lorraine, and hoped to press for a plebiscite; they assumed that there would be arms limitations in the treaty and that the Rhineland would have to be demilitarised; but they felt that French claims on the Saar and Polish claims on Upper Silesia and Posen would be dropped if Germany put up sufficient opposition. Annexations such as Danzig and the Polish Corridor were considered so improbable that they never were even discussed. There was even hope that Austria would be allowed to join in an *Anschluss* with Germany. And the question of reparations and colonial issues was vastly underestimated; Germany expected that it would have to pay out 50 billion marks over a long period and that even that figure could be reduced, while the Weimar government had nominated a Minister of Colonies who, at the time, had no colonies to administer; but it was felt that a compromise could be reached with regard to Germany's former overseas possessions. After studying the 14 Points with great care as well as the published statements of Allied leaders, the Germans were convinced that the Allies' quarrel had been with the German rulers, not with the German people; now that the Kaiser had been overthrown and Germany was a democracy — more than could be said of many of the Allied countries — it was thought that the Allies, especially Wilson, would not be so unfair as to penal-

Roger Viollet

Above: Foch, Allied C-in-C, follows the elderly Pichon, French foreign minister, out of Versailles. Pichon was a strong supporter of Clemenceau's far-reaching claims on German territory

Roger Viollet

The generals confer: Foch, the Allied Commander-in-Chief, and Weygand (*left*)

rupture with House left him without a single confidant, other than his wife. On April 3 he collapsed. Although the disease was diagnosed as influenza he returned to the Conference table after a few days. He gave in to the demands for reparations, although even Lloyd George was worried about the extent to which Germany was left exposed. Her armies were to be reduced to only 100,000 men, while the French commandeered the Polish army; Lloyd George, in a memorandum, feared that Germany, in this weakened and partitioned condition, might throw in her lot with the Bolsheviks, the underlying fear of the whole Conference. He warned that to weaken Germany irrevocably was impossible. 'You may strip Germany of her colonies, reduce her armaments to a mere police force and her navy to that of a fifth-rate power; all the same in the end if she feels that she has been unjustly treated in the peace of 1919 she will find means of exacting retribution on her conquerors.' Despite French bitterness at least the Saar and the Rhineland were not to be permanently severed from Germany.

Then the Italians intervened. They threatened to leave the Conference if Britain did not honour the terms of the

ise the German people who, after all, had prevented Bolshevism from taking over Germany in both Berlin and Munich. Besides, Germany had not signed an unconditional surrender in the Armistice. She had merely accepted the 14 Points and pledged to cease hostilities.

Needless to say, the German delegation met with a severe shock when it was formally invited to appear at Versailles on April 25 to receive the text of the treaty. It should be noted that Germany was asked to receive it, not to discuss it, and that this treaty was not merely a draft, but a more or less final version, not now open to debate. The Allies insisted that Germany's foremost ambassadors be sent and finally, on April 28, two special trains left for Versailles with the 180 members of the German delegation aboard, headed by Brockdorff-Rantzau. The Allies were thrown into a panic, as the treaty was not nearly ready, and divisions had split their ranks. The Italians had not returned, and China was threatening to walk out. The train passed quickly through Germany and Belgium, but as it passed the battlefields of Northern France it was slowed to a low speed. The French wanted to make sure that the Germans saw the devastation of their country in order to understand the hatred their country bore toward Germany. The only people to be seen were German prisoners of war rebuilding the railway lines under the watchful eyes of French guards. The delegation threw oranges and newspapers to the prisoners from the train and were shocked to see the guards clubbing the prisoners to force them back to work. Clemenceau and Poincaré would have been pleased. The train journey had the desired effect on the German delegation.

When they arrived in Versailles, they were taken to the Hotel des Reservoirs, where the French delegation had stayed after the Franco-Prussian War, and confined to the hotel and its park throughout their stay. The weather was cold and the hotel had no central heating, so logs were burned in the open fireplaces, to the accompaniment of loud piano passages from Liszt and Wagner. The Germans had been warned before they left Berlin that the French might plant microphones in the hotel, and they were told that the only way to counteract these bugging devices was to hold all confidential conversations in rooms where music was being played. All subordinate committees were provided with gramophones, so that their discussions took place to the tune of the Pilgrims March from Tannhäuser and the Hungarian Rhapsody. During the afternoon the hotel was a cacophony of noise. With the smoke and the music, German tempers were high, until it was discovered that no microphones were there; the Germans sheepishly abandoned the nerve-shattering cacophony a few days later.

The hastily-prepared treaty was ready for the printers on May 5. It was 200 pages long, with 440 separate articles, and some 75,000 words. On May 7 messengers ran through the Parisian dawn to deliver copies of the document to senior Allied officials. Herbert Hoover was awakened at 4 am to receive his copy, and read through it, horrified by its harshness. Unable to sleep he walked through the streets of Paris and ran into Smuts and John Maynard Keynes, who had had similar experiences. Woodrow Wilson told Ray Stannard Baker, the American press chief: 'If I were a German, I think I should never sign it.'

Like criminals in dock

The Allies had prepared the confrontation with care. It was to take place in the Trianon Palace in a room about 75 feet square. The Allied representatives would sit on three sides of a square, and a separate table was set up for the Germans, which the French newspapers called the 'banc des accusés'. The meeting was to last for five minutes. The Germans, reading of this the day before the confrontation, for the first time realised that this was to be no ordinary peace conference in the accepted sense of the word: they would be confronted like criminals before the court of victors, and, without defence or opportunity for rebuttal, found guilty as charged. They were to be spared no humiliation. Their dreams of compromise were the false dreams of the condemned. The treaty would be given to them in the same room where the German Empire was proclaimed in 1871 – the Hall of Mirrors, and on the fourth anniversary of the sinking of the *Lusitania*. But Brockdorff-Rantzau prepared a riposte. The meeting took place promptly at three in the afternoon on May 7. The Allies were already in their seats when the doors were flung open as the German delegates were announced. Dressed in a black morning coat, a high wing collar and a bowler hat, and carrying a walking-stick, Brockdorff-Rantzau entered, followed by his delegation. He bowed and was led to his seat, facing Wilson, Clemenceau and Lloyd George. Clemenceau, after a brief introduction, told the Germans that they would have 15 days to make written 'observations' about the treaty. Clemenceau then asked if anyone wished to speak. Brockdorff-Rantzau's hand went up, and Clemenceau, flustered, but no more so than the Germans, asked for translators. The Germans were stunned by the savage announcement by the 'Tiger' that no negotiations would take place, but Brockdorff-Rantzau, understandably nervous, rose to speak. He replied that he understood the intensity of hatred which faced him. 'We have heard the victor's passionate demand that as vanquished we shall be made to pay and as the guilty we shall be punished. The demand is made that we shall acknowledge that we alone are guilty of having caused the war. Such a confession in my mouth would be a lie,' he hissed. Now it was the Allies' turn to be shocked. Brockdorff-Rantzau's speech continued, interrupted by the translator and Clemenceau's mutterings, as he stated that hundreds of thousands of German lives had been lost since the Armistice due to the blockade. At 4 pm he finished, unable to stand any longer, because his knees were shaking. The Germans were ushered out, Brockdorff-Rantzau lighting a cigarette as he left.

The impression made on the Allies was most unfortunate. Lloyd George said he could not remember when he had been more angry. Lord Riddell of the British delegation called it the most tactless speech he had ever heard. Foch and Clemenceau were furious. Even the rest of the German delegation considered their Foreign Minister had gone too far. By midnight the Germans had translated the whole treaty – only one copy had been given to them – and it was worse than they ever dreamed. They felt that Germany could never survive the treaty, and stripped of her colonies, her mines, 13% of her territory, millions of people, and her armed forces, she would be prostrate before her enemies. There were even to be war criminals delivered up to the Allies. The German delegates, beginning to realise the enormity of the document, started to refer to it as a *Diktat*, a dictated treaty. They felt the Allies, especially Wilson, had betrayed them.

By May 10 thousands of copies of the treaty were published in German. Soon the Germans began to send notes to the Allies protesting every part of the treaty: Upper Silesia, Schleswig, the Saar, the Rhineland, even Alsace-Lorraine. The delegates had only 15 days to prepare their arguments, and in retrospect they prepared too many, conceding little to the Allies, even in areas where they knew beforehand that they would have to give way. When the final counterproposals were prepared and handed in on May 29 they amounted to 119 pages and 25,000 words, nearly half the length of the treaty itself. But a few concessions were allowed, in Upper Silesia and the Rhineland particularly, thanks to Wilson and, by this time, Lloyd George. But aside from the territorial losses, which were an understandably bitter blow for the Germans to take, the points which angered them the most were the reparations and war guilt clauses. Everyone was amazed at the French demands, which were far in excess of the total national wealth of Germany. In any event, reparations were finally left to be determined later, and Germany was forced to sign a blank cheque for the total which, still under argument, was not announced until after the Peace Conference was over. But, worst of all, the Germans seemed to be refusing to sign the treaty at all. The only recourse left to the Allies, in such an event, was a renewal of hostilities and an occupation of the whole of Germany. And this no one wanted.

Nor would this task be easy. British detachments at Calais had already mutinied and two divisions of British Rhineland troops had to be sent there to subdue them. The remainder of the British troops wanted to go home quickly. Most of the American soldiers had already gone. Keynes savagely attacked the treaty in *The Economic Consequences of the Peace,* and Lloyd George asked Wilson if the treaty could undergo a major revision to pacify the Germans. But Wilson was tired, and refused to give the British support. Their resolve was easily overcome. Without the Americans the British could not force the French to change their tune. When the treaty was returned to the Germans with minor alterations, written in ink on the original copy, Brockdorff-Rantzau decided to return to Germany. Caught by surprise, the French had made no preparations for a German walk-out. On their way to the train, the German automobiles were stoned, and many of the delegates were cut by broken glass as the jeering crowds bid them goodbye. Their deadline for making a final decision advanced to June 23, the Germans had but seven days to decide whether to sign the treaty or not.

The German Cabinet was deeply divided when the delegates returned from Versailles. Through the influence of Matthias Erzberger, leader of the Catholic Centre Party, Germany was talked into signing, although not without debate. The German Army had already melted away; its fleet was at Scapa Flow. Brockdorff-Rantzau refused to sign the treaty. But Erzberger did not minimise the concessions which had to be made by Germany. He realised that although the Allies' ability and willingness to invade Germany had waned considerably, they still had the power to do so; and Germany did not have the power to resist. If Germany were invaded, he predicted, it would be picked over by the international vultures until nothing was left of its prostrate body. Brockdorff-Rantzau counted on time to force further divisions within the Allied ranks. But Italy had returned to the Conference just before the German delegation was presented with the peace terms, and the Allies showed every sign of collaborating and moving into Germany if such a move was required. The German Army was aware of the accusation, already circulating, that the army, undefeated in the field, had been 'stabbed in the back' by enemies of the Reich on the home front. They knew that this could be used to advantage later. Worse, however, was their report to the government which indicated that resistance would be sporadic and futile on Germany's part and that an invasion of the whole of Germany could not be opposed successfully. Moreover, the civilian population would have been appalled if such an event took place. The government fell, and in those days of indecision, when to decide against signing the treaty meant invasion, even President Ebert was on the verge of resigning. The day after the government fell the German fleet was scuttled by its own men at Scapa Flow. Now compromise was out of the question, and two days before the Germans had to give their reply, a government was formed on June 21. The Chancellor was Gustav Bauer, but even his new government was loath to sign the *Schmachparagraphen* – the 'disgraceful paragraphs' (articles 227-231) of the treaty – which admitted Germany's guilt in starting the war, and which even some of the Allies thought to be extreme. Again the Germans were faced with a defenceless country, starved by the blockade and the war, which was crying for peace and food at virtually any price. Germany agreed to sign.

How effective were the Allied plans to invade Germany and occupy the whole of it had the Germans refused? The plans were not completed without a considerable degree of difficulty. Foch stated that his forces were insufficient to the task on June 16, and he proposed that Germany be dismembered, with separate peaces made with the south German states. Only then could Prussia be invaded and occupied. Lloyd George questioned Foch's judgement, for, as he pointed out, Germany's 550,000-man army was underarmed and undermanned. Foch yielded to Lloyd George's sarcasm, and the morning of June 23 found the army of the Western Allies poised to cross the Rhine. Czech and Polish divisions, eager for the opportunity, were even better prepared. The plan was for the advance to be made in 'bounds' of 100 kilometres each. It was expected that the operation would take no more than a fortnight, for Germany could not possibly defend herself. Ninety minutes before the troops were due to march, the German acceptance arrived. It said: 'Yielding to overwhelming force, but

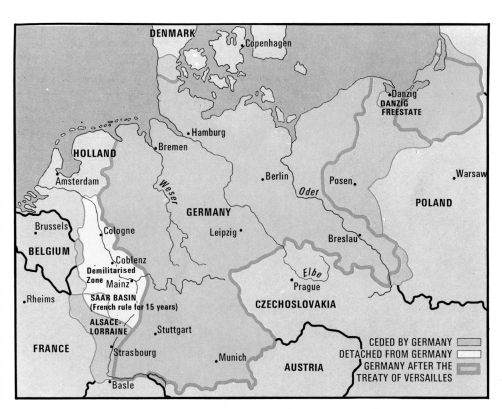

THE PROVISIONS OF THE TREATY OF VERSAILLES CONCERNING GERMANY

1. The east bank of the Rhine to be demilitarised by Germany up to a depth of at least 50 kilometres (31¼ miles) behind the river.
2. Germany to cede the coalmines of the Saar basin to France in recompense for the loss of the mines in France destroyed in the war. The Saar basin to be administered by the League of Nations.
3. Alsace-Lorraine to be retroceded to France.
4. Germany to acknowledge the complete independence of Austria.
5. Germany to acknowledge the complete independence of Poland.
6. Plebiscites to be held in the East Prussian districts of Allenstein and Marienwerder to decide their allocation either to Germany or to Poland.
7. Germany to accept the abrogation of the Treaty of Brest-Litovsk.
8. Germany to renounce all privileges, titles and rights enjoyed by herself and her allies in those parts of Europe outside the boundaries imposed upon her by the Treaty of Versailles.
9. Germany to renounce her overseas colonies in favour of the Allies.
10. By March 31, 1920 the German army to have been reduced to and after that date not to exceed a strength of seven infantry and three cavalry divisions (in total not more than 100,000 men). The Great German General Staff to be disbanded and not reformed. The manufacture of munitions to be undertaken only with the express consent of the Allies. No armoured fighting vehicles to be produced in or imported into Germany. Universal military service to be abolished. The term of enlistment to be at least 12 years for non-commissioned officers and other ranks, and 25 years for newly-appointed officers.
11. The German navy to be reduced to and not to subsequently exceed a strength of six pre-dreadnought battleships, six light cruisers, 12 destroyers and 12 torpedoboats. Germany not to build or otherwise acquire any submarines.
12. Germany to possess neither military nor naval air forces.
13. The Allies to try Wilhelm II for offences against 'international morality and the sanctity of treaties'.
14. Germany to accept responsibility for loss and damage suffered by the Allies in the course of the war of aggression launched upon them by Germany and her allies. Being unable to compensate the Allies in full, Germany to compensate Allied civilians for all damage to property and life, in a manner seen fit by the Inter-Allied Reparation Commission. Germany to make an immediate payment of 20,000 million gold marks towards such compensation.
15. As a guarantee of German compliance with the terms of the treaty, the Allies to continue their occupation of the Rhineland for 15 years.

without on that account abandoning its view in regard to the unheard-of injustice of the conditions of peace, the Government of the German Republic declares that it is ready to accept and sign the condition of peace imposed by the Allied and Associated Powers.' It was a poor omen for the future.

The German delegation, without Brockdorff-Rantzau, returned for the final humiliation in the Hall of Mirrors. The Chinese were the only ones who at last refused to sign. The German delegates were ushered in and put their names to the treaty. Most observers felt that the humiliation of being shunted in and out of the hall without the slightest dignity was extreme and brought the vanquished nation unexpected

sympathy. Colonel Edward House stated that it was 'not unlike what was done in olden times when the conqueror dragged the conquered at his chariot wheels'. At 3.50 pm on June 28, 1919, exactly five years after Sarajevo, the treaty was signed. From the forts and hills around Versailles a chorus of artillery salutes began, and the fountains in the great parks of the Palace were turned on. Bells rang throughout the town and, almost simultaneously, in Paris as well. Lloyd George, Clemenceau and Wilson appeared on a terrace to watch the fountains and were almost swamped by the crowds who broke through the lines of police and soldiers.

There are few today who defend the

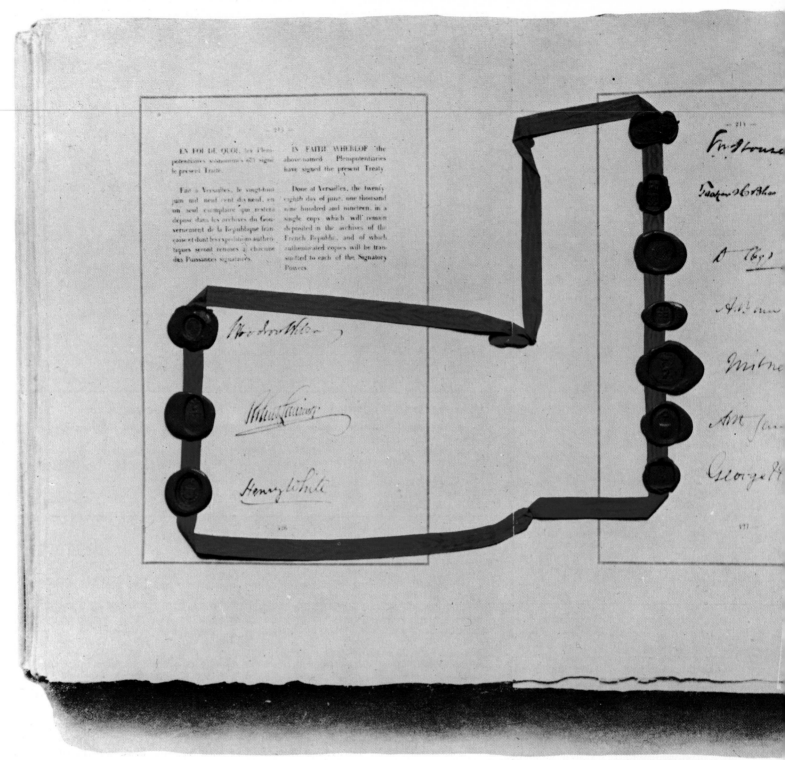

Treaty of Versailles, and there were few who defended each and every point of it even on the day it was signed. It was a bad peace. Bad because, although it did not bring Germany to its knees forever, it failed to create a climate of good will in which Germany, weak and dismembered, could return to the family of nations as an equal. It left only a feeling of bitterness and hatred which was worse than defeat. For it could, and did, only provoke revenge which the whole world paid for in the Second World War. Wilson's dreams of a 'just and honourable peace' were dashed, and he returned to the United States broken in body and in spirit, only subsequently to learn that his own country was unwilling to join the League of Nations. Lloyd George, with the Kaiser safe in Holland, was unable to keep his promise to hang him. But he was not concerned about that. He knew that the peace was not only too harsh—it

was unworkable. He told his friend, Sir William Wiseman, that the treaty was 'all a great pity. We shall have to do the same thing all over again in 25 years at three times the cost'. Apparently even this was a gross underestimate.

Further Reading

Watt, Richard M., *The Kings Depart* (Simon and Schuster 1968)

Bailey, Thomas A., *Woodrow Wilson and the Lost Peace* (Macmillan 1944)

Blum, John Morton, *Woodrow Wilson and the Politics of Morality* (Little, Brown 1956)

Temperley, H. W. V., *A History of the Peace Conference of Paris* (Oxford University Press for the Institute of International Affairs 1920)

Nicolson, Harold, *Peacemaking, 1919* (Methuen 1964)

Mayer, Arno J., *Politics and Diplomacy of Peacemaking* (Weidenfeld & Nicolson 1967)

[*For S. L. Mayer's biography, see page 19.*]

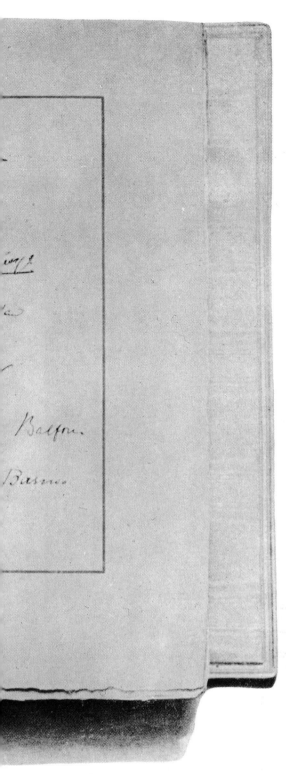

Above left: The last pages of the Treaty of Versailles, showing the seals and signatures of the American and British delegates: Wilson, Lansing, White, House, Bliss, Lloyd George, Bonar Law, Milner, Balfour and Barnes. *Left:* The treaty signed, Clemenceau, Lloyd George and Wilson (putting on his hat) leave Versailles to the sound of bells ringing in Paris and gun salutes in the Palace grounds. *Top right:* A Heine cartoon, from the German satirical magazine, *Simplicissimus,* on Germany's 'choice' of signing the treaty or not. Wilson, Clemenceau and Lloyd George, as executioners, confront a captive Germany at the guillotine: *You too have the right of self-determination. Do you want your pockets cleared out before or after you're dead?* If Germany signed the treaty she would thereby forfeit wealth and territory, formally admit guilt in causing the war and agree to reparations so far beyond her capacity as to be ridiculous. If she did not sign, hostilities would be renewed by the Allies and the end would be the same. The drawing is a bitter comment about the twisting of the 14 Points, on the basis of which Germany had originally agreed to the Armistice. *Above:* Brockdorff-Rantzau (centre, wearing light coat), German foreign minister, leaves Vaucresson Station, near Paris, where he had travelled on one of two special trains packed with the German delegation, to receive the terms of the treaty. Brockdorff-Rantzau was horrified by their harshness and in an impassioned speech said he would never agree to sign

THE LEAGUE OF NATIONS

In 1919 a Covenant for a League of Nations was included in the peace treaty. Evolved from sundry communications and welfare organisations that had grown in strength over the last 100 years it professed to be an intermediary for peace transcending nationalism—an objective then, as now, ahead of its time. *S. L. Mayer. Below:* The men who drafted the Covenant

The concept of a society of nations that would be prepared to keep the peace was a relatively new one during the First World War. The hope and desire for world peace was age-old. Yet, only after the greatest war the world had yet fought were these vague, romantic ideals put into what was hoped would be a realistic entity. Until the end of the Napoleonic wars at least hopes for a period of world peace remained merely hopes, espoused by the religious and sentimental, during an age when war was for professionals and was endemic to the settlement of European disputes. The wars of the French Revolution, however, were more comprehensive in character, involving armies of millions drawn from the masses, and ones in which civilian populations became caught up in revolutionary ideologies as well as having their land ravaged intermittently by mass armies. In medieval times war and the occasional destruction of large areas was not uncommon, but the armies which fought all over Europe were small. War was a commonplace—not considered important enough to interrupt spring planting or the autumn harvest, and in winter it was usually considered too cold to fight. Napoleon's sweep through Europe changed the nature of warfare, and although most general staffs did not universally accept it at the time, the mass army, made up of conscripts as well as recruits, was a permanent feature of life in the post-1815 period, as the Prussians

proved in mid-century. The growth of the cost and scope of war was the impetus behind the attempt to settle international disputes other than by warring. International organisations were set up throughout the 19th Century to prevent war from breaking out, even when traditional diplomacy broke down. Although these organisations did not prevent war they were a step toward breaking down international barriers in a number of ways. The internationalisation of the Danube, set up by the Paris Peace Conference which ended the Crimean War, is but one case in point. The Universal Postal Union and the International Telegraphic Union, set up a few years later, were among over 30 such bodies established between 1856 and 1914 to modify national sovereignty to a limited extent. The Pan American Union, for example, started in 1890, was organised to promote friendship and peace among the American republics—and, incidentally, to provide a medium for the influence of the United States in Latin America. The International Health Office, established in Paris in 1907, and the International Institute of Agriculture, established in Rome in 1905, were other examples of international co-operation within limited spheres. The Hague Conferences of 1899 and 1907 were, perhaps, the most ambitious attempts to limit the armaments race and to establish the laws of war; both conferences had limited success, as did all other well-

meaning attempts of this nature. The reason for their lack of success was due to the fact that sovereign nations were unwilling to limit their freedom of action in any but peripheral ways. Whatever work that was achieved was done in areas which aroused no national feelings and involved no real alteration of the political, strategic or economic situation of any participant. The Concert of Europe and the Holy Alliance, both established in 1815, were not permanent bodies and had no regular meetings. All the same, through these and other organs international disputes were, from time to time, settled by agreement among the Great Powers. This was the only way to settle any major or minor international dispute—when the Great Powers were unanimous in their opinion. When there was conflict they resorted to war in the traditional fashion, the Austro-Prussian and Franco-Prussian Wars being but two examples. But perhaps the greatest example of the failure in the attempts to disarm and create a climate of peace was in 1914. It is no wonder, then, that the horrors of the First World War caused many people in every country to try to work out a way in which such a terrible event could be prevented from ever happening again. It was in this climate of opinion that the concept of the League of Nations was formed.

This is not to imply that a movement for the abolition of war as an instrument of national policy was purely a 20th Century phenomenon. The first peace society was formed in New York as early as 1815. Others, similar in nature, were established in Paris, Geneva and London subsequently, and people like Cobden and Bright deplored the waste of money on armaments. And there were always pacifists and Quakers. But men such as Cobden and Bright were internationalists rather than pacifists, since they, and most others like them, did not rule out self-defence. Disarmament was a fringe concept, at best, until the first year of war in 1914 to 1915 indicated that the hopes of both sides for an easy, early victory were illusory. In almost every Western country peace movements of one kind or another sprang up, independent of each other at first, but aimed toward the same goal: that a society of nations be established after the First World War to prevent a repetition of the tragedy. Asquith and Sir Edward Grey gave unofficial support to the British 'League of Nations Society' when it was established in May, 1915. William Howard Taft, a former President of the United States, headed a similar society when it was founded there. In neutral America the peace movement began to gather momentum, and by 1916 President Wilson supported the so-called 'League to Enforce Peace', and he was joined by a subsequent enemy, Henry Cabot Lodge. After Wilson's re-election in that year, he appeared as the head of the peace movement throughout the world. His Peace Notes in 1916 lent further credence to this view. When the United States entered the war in 1917, Wilson's support of the peace movement took on an even greater significance, for, if the Allies won the war, Wilson would be in a position to make a reality of what once were considered the dreams of powerless idealists. But as the war dragged on, most countries demanded some sort of promise that the war would not be repeated. Lloyd George and Wilson, unknown to each other, presented such a proposal at almost the same time. On January 5, 1918 at a meeting of the TUC, Lloyd George stated that armaments must be limited after the war, that the right of national self-determination should be adhered to in the peace, and that the sanctity of treaties be re-established. Three days later, Wilson enunciated his 14 Points, which shared these views, but emphasised one more—the fourteenth, and most important, in Wilson's eyes: a 'general association of nations must be formed'. The 14 Points, with one exception —freedom of the seas, to which Britain objected—were adopted as the war aims of the Allies, and Austria and Germany sued for peace on the basis of them.

'A living thing is born'
Nonetheless, with a society of nations as a peace aim no body of individuals went further than affirming this aim other than as a general desire. No specific scheme for the formulation of a league of nations was made when the Armistice was signed except the extreme proposals made by the League of Nations Society in England and the League to Enforce Peace in the United States, and similar organisations. Immediately after the Armistice, the results of the 1918 election in America indicated serious doubts about the degree to which national sovereignty would be compromised by the inclusion of the United States in the League. Ignoring the Republican majority in the Senate, Wilson set sail for Europe a few weeks later without having made much progress toward the preparation of the Peace Conference, or his proposals for the League, which he insisted be incorporated into the final peace treaty. In the interim period after the Armistice, but before the Conference began, General Smuts of South Africa published a pamphlet: *The League of Nations: a Practical Suggestion*. The League was supposed to incorporate all the work of other international bodies already established, and a council of nine, representing all the Great Powers as well as others, was to be formed to meet at least once a year to govern the activities of the organisation; a regular conference of all the members of the League were to meet to discuss all general questions and lay down the main lines of policy; and a secretariat established on a permanent basis to maintain a close liaison with the member states. The purpose of the organisation would be threefold: to safeguard peace, to organise and regulate the growing network of international business, and to be the international centre to which every state could come for counsel and aid. It was meant to be a first step in the breaking down of international barriers to eventually reduce the absolute character of national sovereignty. Generally speaking, the League did evolve along the lines which Smuts proposed, but fell far short of his aims, largely because it was just this national sovereignty which no state was prepared to compromise except in the most peripheral way. The British, French and American schemes did not conflict too much with the Smuts plan when they were announced, and so it was with this plan that the Paris Peace Conference began with the aim of forming the League of Nations as an integral part of its task.

Once the Conference began Lloyd George drew up a resolution to be presented to the Council of Five, or Supreme Council, composed of the five victorious powers—the United States, Great Britain, France, Italy and Japan. The resolution was adopted by the 32 states and dominions gathered at the Conference on January 25, 1919. An intensive series of meetings began to draft the Covenant of the League, and the chairman of the Covenant-making committee was none other than President Wilson himself. Smuts, Colonel House, Léon Bourgeois, Orlando, and Baron Makino of Japan were other distinguished members of this committee. An Anglo-American draft proposal was quickly adopted, and in the amazingly short space of only 11 days the committee drafted a proposal to found the League. Wilson exclaimed: 'a living thing is born'. The hopes of establishing a just peace under the auspices of an international body seemed to have been fulfilled.

When Wilson returned from his trip to America, during which he had discovered mounting opposition to any curtailment of American sovereignty which his opponents felt was the heart of the League concept, he also discovered that the Conference had gone on to discuss a number of matters on which there was consistent disagreement: the Shantung question, the Italian claims, the French and Polish demands for German territory, and so on. Italy walked out of the Conference on April 23, 1919, and the importance of the League was diminished in the light of these struggles for power and territory. The French, furthermore, pressed for Brussels to be the home of the League secretariat, but this proposal was defeated in favour of Geneva, in a neutral state, Switzerland, rather than in the capital of a major belligerent. France seemed to view the League as a rather meaningless idea, but sought to please Wilson in order to gain territorial concessions from him. Most of the other states felt the same, except for Britain, which genuinely supported the League concept. Wilson therefore saw to it, despite the opposition which he faced at home, that the League Covenant was made an integral part of the peace treaty with Germany, but in order to attain this, Wilson compromised his dreams of national self-determination by giving way to those states eager for land, especially France, Italy, and Poland. Finally, on April 28, Wilson laid the final text of the Covenant before a plenary session of the Peace Conference. Since the Covenant was part of the Peace Treaty, it could not come into effect until the Treaty was effected and this did not take place until January 20, 1920. In the meantime, on the date that the Covenant was approved in April, 1919, a Secretary-General was appointed, Sir Eric Drummond, and work began at the temporary secretariat in London even before the peace itself was signed.

Cracks in the Covenant
The Covenant had set up three vital bodies to implement the work of the League: the Secretariat, to be established at Geneva, the Assembly, and the Council. The Council was to be composed of the five victorious Great Powers—the United States, Great Britain, France, Italy and Japan—as well as four other states, who would be elected from time to time by the Assembly. Brazil, Greece, Spain and Belgium were the first to join the Big Five. Its powers were deliberately left as vague and broad. The Assembly would meet at least once a year, as would the Council, and would be composed of the 32 charter members (every nation attending the Paris Peace Conference), each with one vote. The League was given authority to take whatever action seemed necessary to prevent the outbreak of war in future. Article 16 proved to be one controversial part of the Covenant. If any member of the League resorted to war, disregarding the stipulations against doing so, it would *ipso facto* be deemed to have committed an act of war against all other members of the League'. Action should be taken against the warring party, such as economic sanctions, and the Council would recommend to what extent the armed forces of each member state would contribute to the proposed international armed force controlled by the League to protect its covenants. This article was the teeth of the League, which, like the whole Covenant, could only bite if the constituent members agreed to allow it to do so. It was to this clause that many Americans objected, arguing that it would force the United States to go to war at the wish of other states, and thereby reduce America's sovereign right to decide whether or not it wanted to go to war on any specific occasion. Although this argument was spurious, since no nation could be forced to go to war or do anything else, for that matter, against its will, it illustrated the fundamental weakness of the League. It only had the power which its member states would agree

to give it, and, as it turned out, that was very little. If the American Senate in fact had nothing to fear from Article 16, neither did any potential aggressor. Other Articles in the Covenant established the International Labour Organisation, which did fine work under the League's auspices, and is, perhaps, the only body still functioning today which was established by the Covenant. The International Red Cross and other similar organisations were also placed under the League's influence, though not its authority. Bodies such as the Universal Postal Union were to be merged with the League Secretariat. The League was also given territory to administer: the Saar, for 15 years until a plebiscite was held; and Danzig, which was administered directly by the League, although it had a customs union with Poland. Furthermore, former German and Turkish colonies which were partitioned among the victorious powers were placed under the so-called mandates system, thanks to the efforts of George Louis Beer, an American historian. The

system forced Britain and France, as well as other states, to submit reports to the League about the progress each former colony was making toward self-government. There were three classes of mandates established: class A, mostly certain Arab states taken over by Britain and France, where the European power was supposed to give merely advice and assistance: in fact Iraq became independent of British authority in the 1920's after Britain's petroleum interests were secured; class B, those countries not yet considered ready for independence, and these included some of Germany's former African colonies; and class C, such as former German South-West Africa and the Pacific islands, taken by Australia and Japan, which were administered like any other colony but with annual reports made on their progress to the League. It would be splitting hairs to define the practical differences between the three classes of mandated territories. In effect, every one of them was run along colonial lines, and lip service was paid to

the principles of national self-determination for these areas. Although Wilson and Beer were sincere about the efficacy of the mandate system, Lloyd George and Clemenceau made no bones about the fact that mandates were a thin veneer behind which a colonial administration of the traditional type existed. If anything the mandate system showed that European states were only a little embarrassed about their territorial spoils, which made a mockery of principles of national self-determination.

Why it failed

The Second World War broke out just over twenty years after the Covenant was adopted. This seems to bear sufficient witness to the fact that the League failed in what it attempted to do. But the question 'why' has often been asked. Some say that since the United States refused to sign the Treaty of Versailles, in which the League Covenant was included at Wilson's insistence, it would not join the League. This assumption ignores weaknesses which the

structed Europe. But this was not the professed aim of the League, as France discovered, and overtures inviting Russia to join were made after her civil war seemed to be coming to an end. But Russia did not join until the 1930's, and Germany left the League in 1933. With the United States out of the League too, three of the world's Great Powers, more powerful together than the four others which remained League members, were unrepresented during most of the League's short history. When Japan withdrew in 1933 and Italy did the same after her Ethiopian adventure, this left the League with only Great Britain and France to support it, even though Russia, by that time, had joined the organisation. In any event, unanimity of the Great Powers on the Council was a prerequisite for the League's success. But unanimity was seldom apparent, except in cases like the Chaco War in South America, where the League did do a great deal to settle the dispute between Bolivia and Paraguay. But in Europe, the League could do little. Lithuania seized Memel, Poland grabbed Vilna, Italy seized Fiume; the League could do nothing but debate. Even the economic sanctions against Italy because of her invasion of Ethiopia, taken under League auspices, were unable to stop the armies of Mussolini and Badoglio. Italy got her oil from Britain and France through third parties. The greatest weakness of the League, then, would seem to be the lack of enthusiasm its most important permanent members, Britain and France, had for it.

Of nations, or British nations?

But the League was to be criticised in another way as well. Many Americans saw the League of Nations as a League of British Nations, and so it seemed. Whitehall had, in effect, six votes out of the original 32. British Dominions and colonies directed most of their foreign policy through the British Foreign Office, and although today Australia and Canada have independent foreign offices and often take positions counter to those of Great Britain, in the 1920's this was not the case. Whitehall controlled the votes of six states: Canada, Great Britain, Australia, New Zealand, South Africa, and India. Although the first five of these were self-governing in virtually every respect, India was still a colony, with a minimum of self-government in 1919, although this was considerably greater by 1935. With India an outright colony in 1919, Britain could certainly dictate at least two votes in the Assembly; and the other four she effectively controlled, albeit in consultation with the governments of the four Dominions. There was more than merely a considerable amount of agreement among the Dominions and the Mother Country at that time. Britain tended to modify its own policy from time to time in order to maintain this unanimity of purpose in the League. Therefore, the presumed universality of the League was a farce from the start, and as France hoped, the League often worked to maintain the status quo of 1919 which worked in France's interests. Worst of all, the League's function, to a large degree, was to maintain the territorial status quo, which Germany objected to even before she signed the Treaty of Versailles. Since the Treaty was a bad treaty — not harsh enough to permanently injure Germany and not fair enough to

make her satisfied with all its terms — if peace was to be maintained, certain territorial aspects of the Treaty of Versailles had to be changed. Since France was unwilling to allow this, and since she had many allies in Eastern Europe, as did Belgium, at least in the first years of the League's existence, the League, without teeth, was not strong enough to prevent changes, as both Germany and Italy, as well as Japan, soon learned. Unable to effectively prevent alterations in the territorial status quo when these changes were made by force (for example, when Germany marched into the demilitarised Rhineland in 1936), the League was recognised as a paper tiger in the 1930's and ceased to preserve its chief function: to maintain peace in the world. The League only had the power its member states would give it. Since it was given little power in major disputes, it followed that it could not exercise power.

It would be wrong to say, however, that the League served no useful purpose. Even debating societies allow members to let off steam publicly, and this alone is useful therapy. Furthermore, the League in its first years administered the plebiscites on the boundaries of Germany, Austria, and in the Aaland Islands dispute, and this function was carried out honourably. In the Corfu question of 1923, the League was able to prevent Italy's taking over the island, and Italian attempts to take over Albania in 1920 were denied with the help of the League. The League helped to settle the Saar question and prevented France from taking it over on a permanent basis, and despite the inherent difficulties in administering an unwilling Danzig to cooperate with its Polish neighbour, the League authority in the Free City was able to prevent either Germany or Poland from seizing it until the Second World War broke out. Perhaps it is unnecessarily cruel to criticise the League for what it did or could not do. It was, after all, an attempt at international co-operation, and any attempt, however unsuccessful, was better than none at all. Yet, even as an instrument of British and French interests, the League failed, but only because Britain and France failed to keep the peace. They failed because they themselves ceased to believe that the Treaty of Versailles was a just peace, and it was this belief which made appeasement in the 1930's seem not only wise, but an honourable policy as well; at least, that was the way it seemed to most observers at the time. It was not the American Senate which broke 'the heart of the world', as Wilson believed, when they rejected the Treaty of Versailles and the League along with it in 1920. It was the peacemakers of 1919, Wilson included, who, perhaps inevitably, did not make a just peace with Germany. It was asking too much of the League of Nations to maintain a peace, which, in the end, nobody wanted.

Further Reading
Black, C. E., and Helmreich, E. C., *Twentieth Century Europe* (Knopf 1966)
Walters, F. P., *A History of the League of Nations* (Oxford University Press 1952)
Gathorne-Hardy, G. M., *A Short History of International Affairs, 1920-1939* (Oxford University Press 1950)

[For S. L. Mayer's biography, see page 19.]

League contained from the outset, which even the inclusion of the United States could not affect. Germany complained, even before she was forced to sign the Treaty of Versailles, that since she was not included, an international society of nations, which was the League's object, was hampered from the start. This was the way it appeared to many critics of the League in the United States. There was nothing in the Covenant to prevent Germany from joining; in fact, in 1926 she did join. But the fact that the League appeared as a League of Victors rather than as a League of all nations hampered its declared intention of being the hope of the world. This was to France's advantage. With Germany and Russia excluded, France hoped to make the League a permanent instrument of alliance against a resurgent Germany as well as an instrument of the policy of a *cordon sanitaire* of French-allied states between Germany and Russia which would keep the two powers separated and thereby maintain French hegemony in a recon-

THE HALL OF MIRRORS

This eyewitness report of the signature of the Treaty of Versailles is taken from the diaries of Harold Nicolson, then a junior member of the British delegation. *Peacemaking 1919*, published by Methuen & Co Ltd

June 28, Saturday
La journée de Versailles. Lunch early and leave the Majestic in a car with Headlam Morley. He is a historian, yet he dislikes historical occasions. Apart from that he is a sensitive person and does not rejoice in seeing great nations humbled. I, having none of such acquirements or decencies, am just excited.

There is no crowd at all until we reach Ville d'Avray. But there are *poilus* at every crossroad waving red flags and stopping all other traffic. When we reach Versailles the crowd thickens. The avenue up to the Chateau is lined with cavalry in steel-blue helmets. The pennants of their lances flutter red and white in the sun. In the Cour d'Honneur, from which the captured German cannon have tactfully been removed, are further troops. There are Generals, Pétain, Gouraud, Mangin. There are St Cyriens. Very military and orderly. Headlam Morley and I creep out of our car hurriedly. Feeling civilian and grubby. And wholly unimportant. We hurry through the door.

Magnificent upon the staircase stand the Gardes Républicains—two caryatides on every step—their sabres at the salute. This is a great ordeal, but there are other people climbing the stairs with us. Headlam and I have an eye-meet. His thin cigarette fingers make a gesture of dismissal. He is not a militarist.

We enter the two anterooms, our feet softening on to the thickest of *savonnerie* carpets. They have ransacked the Garde Meubles for their finest pieces. Never, since the Grand Siècle, has Versailles been more ostentatious or more embossed. 'I hate Versailles,' I whisper to Headlam. 'You hate what?' he answers, being only a trifle deaf. 'Versailles,' I answer. 'Oh,' he says, 'you mean the Treaty.' 'What Treaty?' I say—thinking of 1871. I do not know why I record this conversation, but I am doing this section of the diary very carefully. It will amuse Ben and Nigel. 'This Treaty,' he answers. 'Oh,' I say, 'I see what you mean—the German Treaty.' And of course it will be called not the Treaty of Paris, but the Treaty of Versailles. 'A toutes les gloires de la France.'

We enter the Galerie des Glaces. It is divided into three sections. At the far end are the Press already thickly installed. In the middle there is a horse-shoe table for the plenipotentiaries. In front of that, like a guillotine, is the table for the signatures. It is supposed to be raised on a dais but, if so, the dais can be but a few

inches high. In the nearer distance are rows and rows of *tabourets* for the distinguished guests, the deputies, the senators and the members of the delegations. There must be seats for over a thousand persons. This robs the ceremony of all privilege and therefore of all dignity. It is like the Aeolian Hall.

Clemenceau is already seated under the heavy ceiling as we arrive. 'Le roi,' runs the scroll above him, 'gouverne par lui-meme.' He looks small and yellow. A crunched homunculus.

Conversation clatters out among the mixed groups around us. It is, as always on such occasions, like water running into a tin bath. I have never been able to get other people to recognise that similarity. There was a tin bath in my house at Wellington: one turned it on when one had finished and ran upstairs shouting 'Baath ready' to one's successor: 'Right ho!' he would answer: and then would come the sound of water pouring into the tin bath below, while he hurried into his dressing-gown. It is exactly the sound of people talking in undertones in a closed room. But it is not an analogy which I can get others to accept.

People step over the Aubusson benches and *escabeaux* to talk to friends. Meanwhile the delegates arrive in little bunches and push up the central aisle slowly. Wilson and Lloyd George are among the last. They take their seats at the central table. The table is at last full. Clemenceau glances to right and left. People sit down upon their *escabeaux* but continue chattering. Clemenceau makes a sign to the ushers. They say 'Ssh! Ssh! Ssh!' People cease chattering and there is only the sound of occasional coughing and the dry rustle of programmes. The officials of the Protocol of the Foreign Office move up the aisle and say, 'Ssh! Ssh!' again. There is then an absolute hush, followed by a sharp military order. The Gardes Républicains at the doorway flash their swords into their scabbards with a loud click. 'Faites entrer les Allemands,' says Clemenceau in the ensuing silence. His voice is distant but harshly penetrating. A hush follows.

Through the door at the end appear two *huissiers* with silver chains. They march in single file. After them come four officers of France, Great Britain, America and Italy. And then, isolated and pitiable, come the two German delegates, Dr Müller, Dr Bell. The silence is terrifying. Their feet upon a strip of parquet between the *savonnerie* carpets echo hollow and duplicate. They keep their eyes fixed away from those two thousand staring eyes, fixed upon the ceiling. They are deathly pale. They do not appear as representatives of a brutal militarism. The one is thin and pink-eye-lidded: the second fiddle in a Brunswick orchestra. The other is moon-faced and suffering: a privat-dozent. It is all most painful.

They are conducted to their chairs. Clemenceau at once breaks the silence. 'Messieurs,' he rasps, 'la séance est ouverte.' He adds a few ill-chosen words. 'We are here to sign a Treaty of Peace.' The Germans leap up anxiously when he has finished, since they know that they are the first to sign. William Martin, as if a theatre manager, motions them petulantly to sit down again. Mantoux translates Clemenceau's words into English. Then St Quentin advances towards the Germans

and with the utmost dignity leads them to the little table on which the Treaty is expanded. There is general tension. They sign. There is a general relaxation. Conversation hums again in an undertone. The delegates stand up one by one and pass onwards to the queue which waits by the signature table. Meanwhile people buzz round the main table getting autographs. The single file of plenipotentiaries waiting to approach the table gets thicker. It goes quickly. The officials of the Quai d'Orsay stand round, indicating places to sign, indicating procedure, blotting with neat little pads.

Suddenly from outside comes the crash of guns thundering a salute. It announces to Paris that the second Treaty of Versailles has been signed by Dr Müller and Dr Bell. Through the few open windows

comes the sound of distant crowds cheering hoarsely. And still the signature goes on.

We had been warned it might last three hours. Yet almost at once it seemed that the queue was getting thin. Only three, then two, and then one delegate remained to sign. His name had hardly been blotted before the *huissiers* began again their 'Ssh! Ssh!' cutting suddenly short the wide murmur which had again begun. There was a final hush. *'La séance est levée'* rasped Clemenceau. Not a word more or less.

We kept our seats while the Germans were conducted like prisoners from the dock, their eyes still fixed upon some distant point of the horizon.

We still kept our seats to allow the Big Five to pass down the aisle. Wilson, Lloyd George, the Dominions, others. Finally,

Bottom: Hasty repairs to the carpets of the Galerie des Glaces before the delegates assemble.
Below: June 28 – *la séance est ouverte* as plenipotentiaries and Press await the signature

Imperial War Museum

Roger Viollet

Clemenceau, with his rolling, satirical gait. Painlevé, who was sitting one off me, rose to greet him. He stretched out both his hands and grasped Clemenceau's right glove. He congratulated him. *'Oui,'* says Clemenceau, *'c'est une belle journée.'* There were tears in his bleary eyes.

Marie Murat was near me and had overheard. *'En êtes-vous sûre?'* I ask her. *'Pas du tout,'* she answers, being a woman of intelligence.

Slowly the crowd in the room clears, the Press through the Rotonde, and the rest through the Salle d'Honneur. I walk across the room, pushing past empty *tabourets*, to a wide-open window which gives out upon the terrace and the famous Versailles view. The fountains spurt vociferously. I look out over the *tapis verte* towards a tranquil sweep of open country. The clouds, white on blue, race across the sky and a squadron of aeroplanes races after them.

Clemenceau emerges through the door below me. He is joined by Wilson and Lloyd George. The crowds upon the terrace burst through the cordon of troops. The top-hats of the Big Four and the uniforms of the accompanying Generals are lost in a sea of gesticulation. Fortunately it was only a privileged crowd. A platoon arrives at the double and rescues the Big Four. I find Headlam Morley standing miserably in the littered immensity of the Galerie des Glaces. We say nothing to each other. It has all been horrible.

And so through crowds cheering *'Vive l'Angleterre'* (for our car carries the Union Jack) and back to the comparative refinement of the Majestic.

In the car I told Headlam Morley of a day, years ago, when Tom Spring Rice had dined with the Prime Minister. He was young at the time, myopic and shy. The other guests were very prosperous poli-

ticians. When the women had gone upstairs they all took their glasses of port and bunched around the Prime Minister. Tom was left out. Opposite him was Eddie Marsh, also at a tail-end. Eddie took his glass round to Tom's side of the table and sat beside him. 'Success,' he said, 'is beastly, isn't it?'

Headlam Morley agreed that success, when emphasised, was very beastly indeed.

Celebrations in the hotel afterwards. We are given free champagne at the expense of the tax-payer. It is very bad champagne. Go out on to the boulevards afterwards.

To bed, sick of life.

Below: German delegates Bell (seated) and Müller sign the treaty. A painting by Sir William Orpen

THE RHINELAND OCCUPIED

John Keegan

To the Allies it seemed vital to take over the strong German positions in the Rhineland. British, French, American and Belgian contingents marched in — with widely differing intentions. *Below:* Joffre and Foch — the French came as conquerors

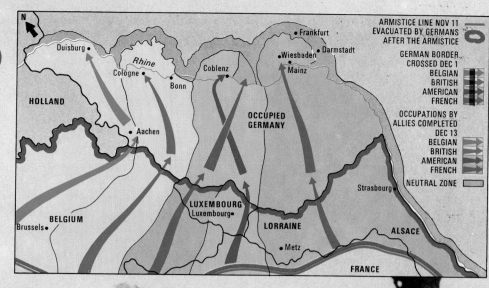

ARMISTICE LINE NOV 11
EVACUATED BY GERMANS AFTER THE ARMISTICE
GERMAN BORDER CROSSED DEC 1
BELGIAN
BRITISH
AMERICAN
FRENCH
OCCUPATIONS BY ALLIES COMPLETED DEC 13
BELGIAN
BRITISH
AMERICAN
FRENCH
NEUTRAL ZONE

The evacuation by the German army of the national territory on the western bank of the Rhine and its occupation by the Allies was one of the principal conditions imposed by the victorious Allies on the German High Command at the Armistice of November 11, 1918. The Germans were also compelled to agree to the occupation by the Allies of three bridgeheads on the eastern bank of the Rhine, each 30 kilometres in radius, with their centres on Köln, Coblenz and Mainz, to be occupied respectively by the British, the Americans and the French; the Belgians, who were to occupy the northernmost zone of the Rhineland, were not to maintain a bridgehead, since they lacked the strength to man it. In addition to surrendering all this territory to Allied occupation, the Germans were further constrained to establish a neutral zone ten kilometres deep, running parallel to the line of the Rhine and the bridgeheads along the whole distance from the Dutch to the Swiss border. All these measures were to be completed within 31 days of the Armistice coming into effect.

The Allies' insistence on these conditions, and on this precipitate timetable, cannot be explained simply in punitive terms – although a punitive element was certainly present among their motives. Of more immediate importance was simple military prudence. The German army in France and Belgium remained, in November 1918, an immensely powerful fighting force – and a force which continued to fight up to the very last moment of official hostilities. It was unthinkable that it should be allowed to retain the positions it was defending, since it would certainly seek to improve them during the truce, and it was almost as important from a military point of view that it should be made to abandon its 'Rear Area', that complex of dumps, static installations and railheads which sustained its operations. Given the logic of this judgement, the nearest line which it could be safely allowed to hold was on the far bank of the Rhine. And even then it was vital for the Allies to take possession of the principal crossing places over the river. For this reason geographical references were very clearly defined in the protocol of the November Armistice.

As it turned out, the news of the Armistice knocked the heart out of the German army and, though it preserved a splendid discipline on the march out of the area to be evacuated, it disintegrated as soon as its divisions reached their home areas. The Allies, however, were not to have foreseen this turn of events, nor did it follow immediately upon the proclamation of the Armistice. The march into the Rhineland was therefore planned and carried out as a formal military operation.

Back to Alsace-Lorraine
The exception to this rule was the French advance into Alsace and Lorraine, in legality but also very much in reality not an occupation but a repossession of a sequestrated province. The number of German-speakers in Alsace-Lorraine had been considerable before the annexation and had latterly increased, for the Imperial government had fostered immigration during the 40 years of its *Reichland* status. Nevertheless, there was undoubtedly a majority, which included many German-speakers, who genuinely welcomed the return of the French army, and enough among that majority for whom the return was a triumphal progress. The high point of the triumph was at Strasbourg, 'capital' of Alsace-Lorraine and one of the principal cities of the Rhine. The entry of the French columns into its streets marked the final stage of a *tour d'honneur* without precedent in French military history.

Very different was the form of the Allied advance into the historic German Rhine-

Roger Viollet

French military presence in the Rhineland made itself felt. *Left:* A sentry patrols a factory in the industrial Ruhr. *This page. Top:* 'Germany's river', now controlled by the French. *Centre:* Foch with Robertson in British-occupied Cologne. *Bottom:* French armoured cars in Düsseldorf

land. It had a concrete military objective, defined by Marshal Foch in a later directive as the establishment of the three bridgeheads which were to 'open and hold assured a passage to the right bank of the Rhine'. The advance to the three bridgeheads was divided into five stages, of which the second was to take the armies to the German frontier and the fifth into the bridgeheads. It began on November 17, reached the German frontier about November 29 (progress varied on the different routes), entered German territory on December 1 and ended in the bridgeheads on December 13. With all possible precautions taken—strict observance of march discipline, careful tactical deployment of the columns and thorough reconnaissance of each step of the road—no resistance or interference was encountered at any stage.

The reception each army received varied from zone to zone. In the American zone on the middle Rhine, with its centre at Coblenz, the population showed itself to be very friendly, at least to begin with, apparently on the instructions of the departing German commanders, who had persuaded civic leaders that a welcoming display would produce a favourable effect on American public opinion and perhaps persuade the American delegation to the peace conference to soften the terms to be presented to Germany. These tactics had the desired effect on the advancing Americans, who were pleasantly surprised by the lack of rancour they encountered from the defeated population. The indirect influence, however, was to be more difficult to perceive.

The British received a more indifferent reception, neither friendly nor particularly hostile. *Köln . . . went about its business as usual (on December 6). Our Hussars, our cyclist patrols . . . might almost that first day have been so many German conscripts coming in from a route march in time of peace . . . The Germans showed both dignity and control. Their mask of indifference was well carried off. They either glanced gravely at the khaki columns or didn't glance at all. There was no crowd anywhere, not even when the cavalry trotted on to the Domplatz. Here and there ex-soldiers, minus shoulder straps, sidled up and enquired politely in English, when were the infantry arriving and when were we going forward to the bridgehead perimeter? The poorer folk stopped in their tracks now and then and gazed; the middle classes appeared to be chiefly interested in our temporary officers, amateurs who had become legendary with the foe. Everyone, including the vanguard, appeared relieved at the absence of demonstrations.* The arrival of the British had, of course, been preceded by a period of lawlessness which, though neither long nor intense, had sufficed to frighten the middle classes with the spectre of revolution, which largely explained their acquiescent attitude. This was to survive even the victory parade over the Hohenzollern Bridge on November 12, when General Plumer took the salute from representatives of every unit serving in the BEF.

Tricoleur and Marseillaise
The French did not expect to be received with any warmth. Indeed their mode of advance was calculated to repel any tentative friendship that the Germans might have shown them. From the outset, they were concerned to demonstrate that they

Top: French soldier halts a Ruhr civilian at bayonet-point. The French and Germans were old enemies. *Above:* Joffre (left), on a formal visit to British-held Cologne, with General Robertson

came as conquerors, to take possession of a captive territory, as the Germans had taken possession of theirs in 1870 and 1914. It was the French who persuaded the British and Americans to promulgate an ordinance requiring German civilians to take their hats off to passing Allied officers and, unlike the British and Americans, insisted that it be obeyed. They ordered the *Tricoleur* to be flown over all public buildings and had the *Marseillaise* played in urban market-places on Sundays. In many public places, rights of way were reserved to French soldiers and, long after the British and Americans had found permanent official quarters for their officers, the French continued to billet theirs on German families, who were required to surrender their best rooms for the purpose. In so doing, the French were fulfilling the spirit of the proclamation which Foch had issued on the eve of the occupation: *The inhabitants must abstain in word and deed from any act of hostility, direct or indirect, towards the Allied authorities. They must obey the requisitions which may be made on them according to law. Every person guilty of a crime or misdemeanour will be immediately arrested and brought before a court-martial. Every infraction of the regulations, every refusal to obey, will be severely punished.* This *diktat*, appropriate enough in the immediate aftermath of hostilities, did not provide a durable basis for a permanent occupation régime. But until the signature of a peace treaty between the combatants, military government was the only means through which the occupied zone might be administered. The Allies, nonetheless, were anxious to alter that situation and indeed used the threat of their presence on the Rhine as a means to expedite Germany's acceptance of the treaty. As early as May 1919, the armies had in hand preparations to advance into Germany if the German delegation at Ver-

sailles refused to sign and the intention to do so was communicated to Berlin. The necessary force was moved up to the border of the neutral zone and would have crossed it if, after several short postponements, the German delegation had not on June 28 at last accepted the Allied terms.

These, as they affected the Rhineland, provided for its occupation for a further 15 years, but for a progressive withdrawal within that period at five-year intervals. But 'in the case of unprovoked aggression by Germany the evacuation might be delayed, and if during the occupation or after the expiration of 15 years the Reparation Commission found that Germany refused

to observe the part or whole of her obligations with regard to reparations, the whole or part of the areas would be reoccupied by the Allied and Associated forces.'

In short, the occupation, having been previously imposed as a guarantee against Germany breaking the armistice and resuming hostilities, and more recently as a means of forcing her to accept the Allies' terms, was to be continued as a measure both of military emasculation and of extracting from her the reparation payment which the Allies declared were their due. Allied policy towards Germany in these interrelated matters was to be administered through three agencies: the Com-

Both pictures: American soldiers parade through the streets of Coblenz. The Americans were outwardly welcomed—perhaps in the hope of influencing Wilson's decisions at the Peace Conference

mission of Control, which was to supervise disarmament; the Reparations Commission; and, instituted on the same day as the signing of the peace treaty, the Inter-Allied Rhineland High Commission.

High Commission: supreme authority

The Rhineland High Commission was constituted a sovereign body, with power to promulgate ordinances having the force of law. Since the power to proclaim a 'state of siege' under German state law, which conferred dictatorial rights, was specifically included, it was to be a supreme authority in theory as well as in fact. Moreover, though the German government was al-

lowed to appoint a representative, he was not given a vote and as the original choice, Starck, established a tradition of unco-operativeness, German governmental influence in the Rhineland lapsed completely.

In the immediate aftermath of the war, this situation was a matter of some satisfaction to most Rhinelanders, who recognised in the presence of the Allied administration, however arbitrarily it might act, a guarantee against the incursion of all those violent political forces which, in the name of revolution or reaction, were convulsing the life of the rest of Germany. The return of ordered ways robbed the High Commission system of that appeal. Further-

more, it shortly revealed itself as a body pursuing aims which no patriotic German could countenance.

The peculiar composition of the High Commission lay at the root of this state of affairs. Since the German representative had no vote, and the United States representative was accredited by his government only as an observer, power lay with the Chairman, who had always to be French, and the Belgian and British representatives. The Belgian voted automatically with the Chairman, who did not therefore even need to have recourse to his casting vote to ensure that the High Commission always acted, in effect, as an instrument of French foreign, military and economic policy. French policy towards the Rhineland, though at times a matter for domestic debate, was broadly consensual. It was directed towards making of it an economic colony and a military barrier. Militarily, France took advantage of the terms of the peace to station a large proportion of her peacetime army on German territory. Throughout the first five years of the occupation, she always maintained at least 100,000 soldiers in the Rhineland, excluding the very large garrisons maintained in Alsace-Lorraine. She was also able to insist on the destruction of the fortifications in the Neutral Zone on the eastern bank of the Rhine, while herself preparing to fortify massively her own eastern frontier. Economically, French policy was extortionate, as she had shown by her insistence on setting reparation payments at an almost unfulfillable level. One of her motives in so doing was to reverse the imbalance of economic power between herself and Germany. It is possible to suspect that another was to provide her with a future excuse to requisition the resources of the Ruhr to her own use. Retrospectively, at any rate, her policy may be made to bear that interpretation.

As early as 1917, France had disclosed to the Russian Tsarist government a scheme she had in mind to separate the Rhineland from Germany and set it up as an independent state. This proposal was put forward by France to her allies at the Peace Conference and forcefully argued. It was only withdrawn in return for the British and American offer to come immediately to the aid of France in the event of any renewal of German aggression. Foch was bitterly opposed to the acceptance of this compromise, arguing that a 15-year occupation, even when reinforced by the British and American guarantee, provided security 'equivalent to zero, while involving us in increased military expenditure'. Clemenceau decided nevertheless to acquiesce and the proposal for the establishment of the separate Rhenish state was withdrawn.

America's refusal to ratify the peace treaty, however, nullified her offer of military assistance to France and Britain's also, since that was contingent upon hers. France was therefore left without either her buffer state or her alliance. Hence, from 1922 onwards, her increasingly legalistic insistence upon the meticulous fulfilment by Germany of the reparation payments. Germany's failure at the end of 1922 to do so, in part brought about by the decline in the value of the mark, gave France the excuse to declare her 'in voluntary default' and to impose the sanction of an occupation of the Ruhr against satisfactory resumption.

The Allies had twice before entered unoccupied German territory for sanctional reasons, first in March 1921 in order to force the withdrawal of German government troops from the Ruhr, and again in April 1922 in order to procure German agreement to the disarmament clauses of the peace treaty. The French and the Belgians now undertook a far more extensive measure, the semi-permanent occupation of the whole of the industrial Ruhr. France at first intended only to influence production in the Ruhr to the extent necessary to make good reparation payments. But when it became clear that Germany intended to oppose the French occupation by a policy of complete non-co-operation, France imposed in retaliation a customs barrier along the whole border of the occupied zone, so depriving Germany of the greater proportion of her industrial and raw material production.

'Revolver Republic'

At the same time, France encouraged on the left-bank Rhineland (the legally occupied zone) the establishment of a separatist republic, for which there was only the most dubious local support. The leaders of this separatist movement included some men of genuine conviction, but so many of their followers were of criminal background that the state which they attempted to set up attracted the title of the 'Revolver Republic'. In one or two areas, notably the Bavarian Palatinate, the separatists were able by strong-arm methods to establish an administration to which the French government, and through it the Rhineland Commission, extended recognition. But local opposition to the separatist movement became quickly so evident that, under the threat by Britain of reference of the matter to the International Court of Justice,

France and the Commission withdrew their support and the separatist movement immediately collapsed.

By the beginning of 1924, France and Germany had both recognised the futility of the policies they were pursuing and agreed to accept, in August, a new method of reparation payment proposed by a Committee chaired by the American General Dawes. The Americans had withdrawn their residual occupation force in token of dissociation from the French action over the Ruhr in January 1924. These proposals proved nevertheless acceptable to France, as they were to Germany, and came at once into effect. In the prevailing cordial atmosphere, France, Britain and shortly afterwards, Germany were able to reach agreement at Locarno over the long-term guarantee of their frontiers and it was in this spirit that in July 1925 France completed her withdrawal from the Ruhr.

At the same time, Britain, France and Belgium agreed to evacuate the occupied area around Cologne, the British reducing their Army of the Rhine to a token force billeted next to the French at Wiesbaden. Occupation was to be sustained as an agreed policy for another four years, until the acceptance by all parties in August 1929 of the Young Plan for the settlement of reparations. In December that year the British and Belgians withdrew the last of their soldiers and on June 30, 1930, the French the last of theirs. By international agreement, the Rhineland was to remain thereafter permanently demilitarised.

[*For John Keegan's biography, see page 96.*]

Above: Not all Rhinelanders would have unhappy memories of Allied occupation. Here German children play with the driver of a Royal Army Service Corps vehicle in a back street of Cologne. *Right:* Arousing little interest, British tanks rumble through a square in front of Cologne cathedral

Imperial War Museum

THE ART OF CAMOUFLAGE

The art of camouflage, though not unknown earlier, made great strides during the First World War, at the start to disguise the terribly vulnerable entrenched front line from artillery observation officers, and later to conceal the build-up for a 'push' from prying aerial reconnaissance

Opposite page, top: *Aerodrome with Camouflaged Hangars* by Sydney W. Carline (1889-1929). The aerodrome in question is in Italy. Note how the outline of the hangar (right foreground) has been broken up by the use of a grey base with an irregular white streak across it. Opposite page, bottom: *A Camouflaged Tent* by Eric Kennington (1888-1960). The use of branches was intended to break up the outline of the bell tent and blend it into a wooded background. This page, top: *A 9.2 Howitzer under Camouflage on the Bethune Front, August 1918* by Adrian Hill (1895-   ). This page, centre: *A Camouflaged Quarry* by Charles Sims (1873-1928). This was a quarry between Cherisy and Hendicourt, and was camouflaged along its entire length of about 500 yards as a piece of typically broken ground. In the quarry walls were electrically-lit chalk caverns which had been turned into barracks by the Germans. This page, bottom: *Camouflaged Tanks, Berles-aux-Bois,* painted by John Singer Sargent (1856-1925) in 1918. While camouflage at the front was intended to deceive observers on the ground as well as in the air, behind the lines it was only important to deceive the aerial observer. Hence the tanks in the painting are under the cover of the trees and have tarpaulins over them, but no camouflage to evade detection from the ground. The same also applies to the first painting, the *Aerodrome with Camouflaged Hangars,* where it would be virtually impossible to disguise the angular shape of a hangar from a ground observer, but relatively easy to make it blend into the background to hinder, if not make entirely fruitless, the efforts of the crews of reconnaissance aircraft

BELGIUM AND THE SAAR

One of the more aggressive French claims at the Peace Conference was a bid for the Saar, an area rich in coal but strongly German in character and language. Further north Belgium was making similar claims. *S. L. Mayer. Below:* Ceuninck, Belgian Minister of War – troops were used to quell anti-Belgian protests

Cologne •

Moresnet • Aachen   Bonn •   GERMANY
Eupen •

Malmedy •   Coblenz •

BELGIUM   AREA OCCUPIED   Frankfurt •
BY THE ALLIES   Mainz •

LUXEM-
BOURG   • Trier (Trèves)

FRANCE

• Saarlouis
• Saarbrücken

▓ SAAR BASIN, MANDATE TO FRANCE
UNDER CONTROL OF THE LEAGUE
OF NATIONS
☐ AREAS FOR PEBISCITE
ASSIGNED TO BELGIUM

When Germany agreed to the Armistice terms as based on Wilson's 14 Points and the principle of national self-determination, she was in for some unpleasant surprises. First of all, as the peoples of Asia and Africa learned, national self-determination was only to apply to white and pro-Allied countries. It soon became apparent to Wilson after he arrived in Paris that he would have to defend his principles against the self-interest of the two chief victorious powers, Great Britain and France, bearing in mind the effect a punitive peace would have on Germany once she recovered from the effects of war and defeat. But Wilson had first to deal with a series of secret treaties drawn up during the war by the Allied belligerents which divided up the territory of the Central Powers long before victory was in sight. The impossible task of reconciling national self-determination

with these treaties which, in their entirety, would have partitioned Germany, was left largely to Wilson, although when British interests were not directly involved, Lloyd George came to Wilson's assistance in trying to beat off the most extreme French claims. One of the most important of these claims was for the Saar region and the Rhineland, which France wanted to annex, or at least, detach from Germany in order to form 'client' states dependent upon her. The connections between Luxembourg and Germany were to be broken, and according to a secret agreement made between Russia and France on February 12, 1917, the Saar, rich in valuable coal deposits, was to be given to France outright after the war. Whereas Wilson and Lloyd George were able to prevent a wholesale partition of Germany, and an agreement for a 15-year military occupation of the left bank of the Rhine was reached (as well as its permanent demilitarisation), the Saar question was one on which the French were unlikely to yield. The problem was that the region of the Saar was almost wholly German in

character. Until the end of the First World War the Saar had been under Germanic control of one type or another for all but two short periods. One was in the late 17th Century, when Louis XIV temporarily asserted his authority over much of the small area, but by 1697 (in the Treaty of Ryswyck) he lost all of it except Saarlouis, which remained a French military outpost until 1815. Again, during the French Revolution, the Saar, like all territory west of the Rhine, fell into French hands, but the Congress of Vienna turned all of the Saar, including Saarlouis, over to Prussia and Bavaria, with Prussia getting the lion's share.

French mandate

During the 19th Century the population of the Saar was swollen by the growing industrial power of the coal mines, and several French writers after the First World War claimed that Germans moved in to overwhelm what was once a French population. British and American authorities denied these spurious claims. There is no doubt that the region was almost wholly German. The 1910 census asserted that in the Prussian part of the basin more than 99% of the population of over 500,000 was German. Only 342 inhabitants were French-speaking, a fact not denied by French officials after the war. Even French public opinion was divided on the question of annexing the Saar outright. French socialists and many republicans were opposed

to the annexation. When the French claim to the Saar was brought up before the Council of Four at the Paris Peace Conference on March 28, 1919, Lloyd George was prepared to accept French ownership of the coal mines as just compensation for the destruction of Northern France, but was thoroughly opposed to actual annexation of the region. Clemenceau stated that there were 150,000 Frenchmen in the Saar who had written letters to President Poincaré asking him to annex their land, a figure which was unquestionably false and which did not coincide with the opinion of French experts who had accepted the population figures of 1910. The next day, March 29, Clemenceau backed down very slightly. He would accept ownership of the coal mines for France, but would agree to leave the question of sovereignty in abeyance. The region would be placed under the protection of the League of Nations (which pleased Wilson) while France had a mandate to occupy the area. German officials were to be withdrawn and France would nominate local officials and control local administration. The inhabitants retained their German nationality but could take no part in German political life, such as elections to the *Reichstag.* The proposal that Saarlouis should be annexed outright was rejected by Wilson, however, and on March 31 it was agreed that the inhabitants could choose, through a plebiscite supervised by the League, whether they wanted to become either part of France, part of Germany, or to continue with the special provisional administration. The Germans bitterly protested these terms, arguing that to tear away undisputed regions of the *Reich* purely for economic purposes demeaned the nature of the League itself. Nonetheless, in a modified form the Saar, in effect, went into French hands at the Treaty of Versailles, and on January 18, 1920 France took possession of the property assigned to her. The League of Nations set up a Governing Commission for the territory, made up of five members, one French, one Saarlander, and three who were neither French nor German. There were no Germans on the governing council and within five years the Saar was brought almost completely within the French customs system. In addition the Germans had to deliver quantities of coal to France in addition to the sums which the French were to extract from the Saar mines. As it turned out the Germans delivered only a fraction of what they were supposed to turn over at a fixed price, and hoped that when the 15-year period was up, the people of the Saar would reassert their desire to join Germany. Germany, under the provisions of Versailles, could then buy back the mines from France.

Luxembourg: a special case
The Treaty of Versailles also broke the special relationship Germany had established with the Grand Duchy of Luxembourg. For decades Luxembourg had maintained a customs union with Germany, and the Grand Duchess Adelaide's pro-German tendencies kept this small, ore-rich state safely within the *Reich's* sphere of influence, especially important during the First World War because of Luxembourg's strategic location and its proximity to Lorraine. Toward the end of the war, however, a plebiscite was held within the

Grand Duchy to decide if Adelaide should continue to occupy the throne in the light of her co-operation with Germany. There was even a question of whether or not the monarchy should be abolished entirely. The plebiscite indicated that few Luxembourgers objected to the connection with Germany being broken, and Adelaide's younger sister, Charlotte, took the throne. In the plebiscite almost three-quarters of those voting opted for a customs union with France, and the Luxembourg government stated that economic affiliation with France depended on the terms France offered. Belgium, however, was upset by the decision against union with her, and suspicious of French mastery in the area. Belgium suspended diplomatic relations with the Grand Duchy to show her disapproval of the result of the plebiscite. All the same, Luxembourg was a Germanic state of the Lotharingian variety, not too dissimilar from Alsace. The language of the peasants, the press, and the primary schools was German, while the language of the *haute bourgeoisie,* the law courts, and the public administration was French. Almost exclusively Roman Catholic, the 250,000 inhabitants of the Grand Duchy produced over 1,000,000 tons of steel annually before the war, as well as over 2,500,000 tons of pig iron and over 7,000,000 tons of iron ore. Its strategic importance was not lost on Germany, and in exchange for her guarantee of Luxembourg's neutrality, promised not to use Luxembourg's railways for the shipment of war material, a promise broken during the First World War. For these reasons Article 40 of the Treaty of Versailles forced Germany to renounce all previous rights she had held in the Grand Duchy, but the future of the small territory was left in abeyance.

By the spring of 1920 France desperately needed Belgian friendship, as the United States had again withdrawn from European affairs, and by this time French troops

were across the Rhine, temporarily occupying Frankfurt, Darmstadt and other cities. Therefore, France deliberately renounced her claims in Luxembourg in order to win over the Belgians. There being little doubt that the sentiments of most Luxembourgers, by this time, was pro-Allied, France was not overly concerned about transferring her rights over to an ally and co-belligerent like Belgium. On July 25, 1921, a Belgo-Luxembourg economic treaty of union was signed. In it Belgium and Luxembourg established a customs union, in which a progressive withdrawal of Luxembourg currency to be replaced by Belgian and a unified railway system with Belgium were immediate aims. The treaty was soon ratified by both countries and was to last for 50 years from May 1, 1922. Even today Belgian money is used interchangeably with the few notes Luxembourg still prints, and the gradual predominance of France in the territory has continued. But a German patois is still commonly spoken throughout Luxembourg.

Eupen, Malmedy and Moresnet
The question of Eupen, Malmedy and neutral Moresnet was raised at the end of the war. Eupen, a suburb of Aachen, was almost entirely German-speaking, and the area of Malmedy was largely German-speaking, although over 28% of the population spoke French in a total of just over 60,000 people in both areas. However, in the town of Malmedy 94% of the people were French-speakers. In any event, neither territory ever belonged to Belgium. Moresnet had only about 3,000 inhabitants, and only 250 were in neutral Moresnet. Most of them spoke German too. Why, then, were these small areas raised at the Paris Peace Conference? Belgian socialists during the war had raised the point that certain border areas ought to be able to choose between Belgian and German nationality, and Belgium wanted

Above: British transport passes through Malmedy. Provisionally ceded to Belgium, registers were opened in the town for the citizens to record their preference for either German or Belgian nationality. Few people dared register. *Right:* One of the few monarchs to survive the war, Albert, King of the Belgians, went into the battle area during the war to boost his troops' morale

some sort of compensation for the occupation and the destruction, especially in south-western Belgium, which the war brought. Apparently the addition of Ruanda and Urundi, taken from German East Africa, to add to the Belgian Congo, was insufficient. On February 11, 1919, the Belgian Foreign Minister claimed the *Kreis* ('district') of Malmedy and the region of Moresnet, but made no mention of Eupen. The Germans argued that Moresnet, both the neutral and Prussian sections, were entirely German, but their complaints only succeeded in losing Eupen as well. The Commission of Belgium and Danish Affairs at Paris, at first willing to cede Moresnet and Malmedy to Belgium, hesitated about Eupen, which was so thoroughly German and whose economic ties were with nearby Aachen. The American and British members of the delegation later withdrew their objections when it was pointed out that the zinc mines of Eupen would be a useful form of compensation to Belgium. Furthermore, it was agreed that during the six months after the Treaty of Versailles came into effect, registers would be opened by the Belgian authority in occupation of these areas in Eupen and Malmedy in which the inhabitants would be entitled to record, in writing, their desire to see a whole or part of the areas remain under German sovereignty. No such expression of opinion was provided for neutral and Prussian Moresnet, which was to be ceded outright. When Germany complained that this was unfair, and that both areas were predominantly German in the first place, it was argued by France and Belgium that this was because the Prussians had deliberately Germanised the regions since 1815 and that a free plebiscite would be useless and unrepresentative. In 1920 the registers were opened under Belgian military authority. By the end of January, 1920 all the areas were placed firmly under Belgian control and by March only 27

people had dared place their names on the register in Malmedy and not more than 50 had done so in Eupen. Germany complained that the registers were never open more than five hours a day, and that the process took so long, that few, even if they wanted to, could register their opinion, In mid-April a general strike broke out in Eupen in protest, but it lasted only two days, due to the energetic measures taken by Belgian troops. German protests went unheeded, and the League of Nations was told in September that only 271 registered out of about 30,000 qualified to vote. Needless to say, there was great pressure placed by the occupation troops to prevent a citizen from going to the town hall of each area to register. It was hardly an expression of free choice and a poor substitute for a formal plebiscite, but the areas passed into Belgian hands officially. Today most of the people of these areas still speak German, forming a third language group in Belgium, to add to the continuing problems existing between the French-speaking and Flemish-speaking groups. Street signs in Eupen are still in German, and the population supports the local football club—in Aachen. National self-determination in Eupen, Malmedy and Moresnet was ignored as it was in so many parts of Europe after the First World War.

It is ironic to note that the 14 Points, which, after all, were the basis for the Armistice in 1918, did not mention these cessions of territory and influence. It is, perhaps, not surprising that these cases, in addition to the case of Alsace-Lorraine, remained bones of contention with Germany after the war, and only intensified the feelings of revenge most Germans felt after the defeat. The Saar eventually returned to Germany in 1935 and the other areas became German once more in 1940. But at least a semblance of self-determination was applied in these cases. Most Germans felt more strongly about alleged injustices on their eastern frontiers than anything which took place on her western borders, accepted by the Weimar Republic at Locarno in 1925.

Further Reading

Mattern, Johannes, *The Employment of the Plebiscite in the Determination of Sovereignty* (John Hopkins Press 1920)
Temperley, H. W. V., *A History of the Peace Conference of Paris,* volume II (Oxford University Press 1920)
Survey of International Affairs, 1920-1923 (Oxford University Press 1927)
Black, C. E. and Helmreich, E. C., *Twentieth Century Europe* (Knopf 1966)

[*For S. L. Mayer's biography, see page 19.*]

Imperial War Museum

THE BELGIAN ARMY 1914-1918

Although most of Belgium was lost to the Germans in the opening months of the war, the Belgian army was not completely destroyed, but pulled back and formed a part of the Allied line north of Ypres. Re-equipped by the French, it held an important sector, around Dixmude, for the rest of the war and contributed greatly to the final Allied offensive in 1918. *Top left:* Belgian infantry establish a machine gun position in August 1914 and *(right)* as part of the defensive perimeter around Malines. *Centre left:* Belgian infantry on the march. *Centre right:* A Belgian armoured car unit near Houthem on September 9, 1917. *Bottom left:* Part of the well-built Belgian line, on September 11, 1917. Visible in front is one of the areas flooded in 1914. *Bottom right:* Belgians on parade at an American Independence Day march past in 1918

Imperial War Museum

WILSON AND THE LEAGUE

Wilson, the autocratic Democrat, completely failed in his advocacy of the League of Nations to take into account the limitations placed on his actions by the American constitution and the isolationism of his countrymen. With his head in the clouds of international co-operation, he was bound for defeat. *Thomas Keiser. Below:* Uncle Sam, unconcerned, refuses to insert the USA, keystone of the President's multi-national bridge over the abyss

President Wilson arrived home from Europe in July 1919 and began his final fight for the Treaty of Versailles, embodying the League of Nations. On July 10 he personally delivered the 264-page bound volume of the Treaty to the Senate of the United States. If the document were to become law the Senate would have to approve it by a two-thirds vote. 'Dare we reject it and break the heart of the world?' the President asked the law-makers.

In March 1920 the fight was over, and the Treaty had been rejected. Whether the heart of the world was broken is arguable, but there is no doubt about the breaking of Wilson. 'I am a broken piece of machinery,' he said four years later, two days before he died. He had dared to ask the Senate for the Treaty and the League or nothing, and it had dared to give him nothing.

'The stage is set, the destiny disclosed,' Wilson told the Senate. 'It has come about by no plan of our conceiving, but by the hand of God, who led us into this way.' But the President's faith was given a different interpretation by an American newspaper editor who said, 'God made the world in seven days, but he didn't have a senate to deal with.'

Yet it was not his enemies in the Senate alone who defeated Wilson and the Treaty. Wilson was his own worst enemy. He did not observe the political maxim which says that politics is the 'art of the possible'. He attempted the impossible and would not compromise, and, as much as anyone, killed the League he wanted the world to love.

Wilson began his fight confidently enough. Just after he addressed the Senate he told a reporter, 'The Senate is going to ratify the Treaty.' He was certain of it because he believed that if moral issues, among which he counted the question of the League of Nations, were clearly presented to the judgment of the masses they would decide correctly. He also had great faith in his ability to appeal to the masses and lead them into the 'paths of right thinking'. Public opinion—polls, resolutions, mass meetings, editorials, letters to the editor—showed that a majority of the people probably wanted some kind of league.

But no doubt Wilson was too contemptuous of his enemies. 'Senators do not know what the people are thinking,' he said. 'They are as far from the people, the great mass of our people, as I am from Mars.' There is reason to believe, however, that the Senators were at least on the near side of Mars and Wilson on the far side, for the Senate was *not* 'going to ratify the Treaty'.

If originally most Americans seemed to want the League there were still many who opposed it. Influential liberals, even more idealistic than Wilson, broke with him because, in their opinion, he had made too many unprincipled concessions at the Peace Conference. Former progressives warned against internationalism apparently because they feared it might interfere with reform at home.

Many 'hyphenates' were anti-League—immigrant German-Americans, Italian-Americans and Irish-Americans. There were about 7,000,000 German-Americans, a tremendous political force in the Midwest who hated Wilson for persecuting them while prosecuting a war against the Fatherland. In the East, particularly in New York and Massachusetts, Italian-Americans were anti-League because of Wilson's efforts to wrest the Yugoslav port of Fiume from the grasp of Italy.

Irish-Americans were natural opponents of the League if only because the English were proponents of the League. This was more serious for Wilson than the opposition of German-Americans who normally voted Republican anyway, because the Irish were natural Democrats. Eamon de Valera toured America in 1919 during the fight over the League, 'stirring up fresh hate' and reminding former sons of Erin that Wilson had failed to secure self-determination for Ireland. There were also Hibernian mutterings about Perfidious Albion and her Dominions having obtained six votes in the Assembly of the League while the United States had only one.

Other hyphenates—Japanese, Jews, Chinese, Czechs and Poles—wished the

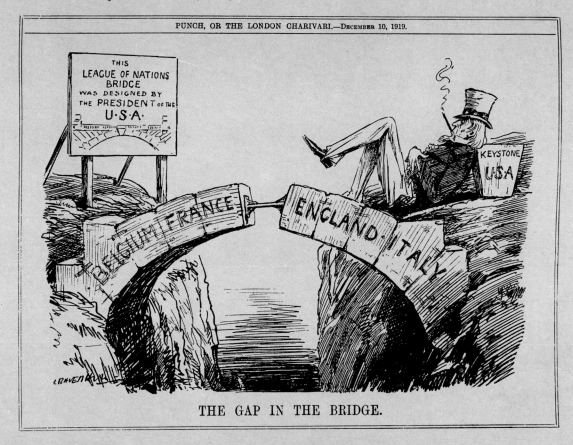

PUNCH, OR THE LONDON CHARIVARI.—December 10, 1919.

THIS LEAGUE OF NATIONS BRIDGE WAS DESIGNED BY THE PRESIDENT OF THE U·S·A·

KEYSTONE USA

BELGIUM FRANCE

ENGLAND ITALY

THE GAP IN THE BRIDGE.

League ill because of various objections about national aspirations not given sufficient attention by the Conference. Such dissidence recalled the sneer of a British ambassador who said that the Americans were 'no nation, just a collection of people who neutralise one another'.

Professional Anglophobes

Professional Anglophobes allied themselves with the anti-League faction. They were certain that wily British diplomats had 'put one over' on honest but naïve Americans, and they pointed to the six-votes-to-one provision as an example of political dishonesty. If England and her Dominions required extra votes, asked Anglophobes, why couldn't America claim 48 votes, one for each state? Fair play demanded it.

The most formidable opposition to Wilson's League, however, was American nationalism and isolationism. Millions of Americans were simply not internationally orientated, and the war fought in far-off lands had not converted them. George Washington's policy of keeping out of Europe's 'broils' was ingrained in American attitudes, as well as similar injunctions of Thomas Jefferson and James Monroe. Wilson would have to fight not only living men, he would also have to contend with the ghosts of American heroes. And pride was another factor, for Americans as League members would have to subordinate themselves to the overriding authority of a superstate. Membership, said a New York newspaper, would mark the 'sunset of our independence'.

Yet another factor weighing heavily against ratification of the Treaty was 'the slump in idealism'. The high wartime aspirations of Americans, who were probably the most optimistic people in the world, were bound to flag sooner or later. They had been promised by the 'prophet' a postwar heaven but all around them they saw the prewar hell. 'Where is Wilson's millennium?' they asked. There was no certainty that the war which was to end war and make the world safe for democracy had accomplished either objective. Disillusioned Americans like Senator Hiram W. Johnson of California learned that the British and French had negotiated secret treaties to make the world safe for the spoils of colonialism whereas the United States had asked for nothing and got nothing except, said the Socialist Victor Berger, influenza and Prohibition.

Last, there was the anger which arose from the ingratitude of America's so-called Allies. Even after the war the British and French were condemning America while still accepting American dollars and food. When would the complaints and begging end? The 'Yanks' were certain that they had won the war and were therefore enraged when they heard that Field-Marshal Sir Douglas Haig, one of the chief manipulators of the Western Front mincing-machine, had said that Britain was in fact responsible for the Allied victory. 'This seemed like an intolerable insult to the American dead.'

Despite all these factors, opponents of the Treaty seemed to be in a minority at the outset, and Wilson could be confident – but by no means certain of victory. Ratification was not going to be easy.

The basis of Wilson's support in the Senate was of course his own Democratic party. Of 96 Senators 47 were Democrats, 49 Republicans. For the Treaty to be ratified, Wilson needed the votes of two-thirds of the Senators present on the floor of the Senate at the time of the final vote. Although the President had promised to punish defecting Democrats, four had already broken with him, leaving him 43 loyalists. Thus he needed the support of some enemy Republicans. But this would mean compromise, which Wilson seriously opposed.

The unhappy burden of leading the fight on the floor of the Senate fell upon Senator Gilbert M. Hitchcock of Nebraska. He was the acting Democratic minority leader, since the regular leader was too ill to attend the debates. Having protested against going to war with Germany, Hitchcock did not enjoy the complete confidence of Wilson, but the President had grown more friendly towards the Senator when Hitchcock pronounced himself firmly behind the Treaty. A man of moderate ability, the gentleman from Nebraska fought the good fight, and probably as well as any other available Democrat would have, against the master parliamentarian of the Republicans, Henry Cabot Lodge from Massachusetts.

De-Wilsonising

The 49 Republicans of the Senate were not as united as the Democrats but they were agreed on two points. One was their opposition to the Treaty in its un-amended form. Second, party politics dictated that they 'de-Wilsonise' the Treaty and make it an 'Americanised' Treaty or, better still, a 'Republicanised' Treaty. As always in American politics, 'an election was coming up' in 1920, and Wilson already had the credit for winning the war and could not be given the further advantage of winning the peace too. Enough was enough.

Beyond these two rallying points the Republicans were in disarray. The Grand Old Party was split into three grand factions. There were 'Strong Reservations'; there were 'Mild Reservations'; and there were 'Irreconcilables'. 'Strong Reservations', led by Senator Lodge, numbered about 20 who demanded alterations in the Treaty which Wilson considered not only unnecessary but crippling. For example, Strong Reservations would not be bound by the provision which gave Britain and her Dominions six votes to America's one. They also insisted that the major signatory powers of the Treaty should formally accept their reservations.

As chairman of the Senate Foreign Relations Committee, through which the Treaty had to pass before it could be submitted to the entire Senate for debate, Lodge was an extremely important Strong Reservationist. So great was his power and prestige that he was called the 'ambassador from Massachusetts to the United States'. Nor was his intellect to be despised, despite his enemies' view that his mind was like the landscape of his native New England – 'naturally barren, but highly cultivated'. Lodge and Wilson hated each other. A Harvard PhD and an author, Lodge had been known as the 'scholar in politics' until Wilson, a former President of Princeton and an author, arrived on the scene and usurped the title. A zealous partisan, the Senator from Massachusetts believed that the virtues of the American Republic were indistinguishable from the virtues of the Republican Party.

About 12 Republicans were Mild Reservationists. They included the ablest and most liberal-minded members, such as Frank B. Kellogg of Minnesota. This faction favoured harmless reservations which would not undermine the Treaty or require further action by signatory powers. If Wilson dealt carefully with the Mild Reservationists and compromised he might make allies of them and add their numbers to those of his 43 loyalist Democrats. In the summer of 1919 these Republicans were still in a mood to be bargained with. But when Wilson later rebuffed them they reluctantly fell in behind Lodge. Senator Kellogg turned against Wilson and wished 'the Treaty was in Hell'.

The Irreconcilables were the last Republican faction. Numbering about 14 Senators remorselessly opposed to the Treaty and dedicated to killing it in any form, they were also known as the 'bitter-enders' and the 'Battalion of Death'. Some of them sincerely believed that the infamous League imperilled the life of the Republic and they fought in every possible way to defeat it. Senator Lawrence Y. Sherman of Illinois called the Covenant of the League an 'international homicide club' and he appealed to religious prejudice by asserting that as Catholics would predominate in the League the Pope would rule the new superstate.

The Irreconcilables were not all crude demagogues. Some had intellect, wit, personality and rabble-rousing eloquence. Philander C. Knox of Pennsylvania was 'the brain' of the 'bitter-enders'; the sardonically witty Frank B. Brandegee of Connecticut was 'the tongue'. Hiram Johnson of California was 'the noise' of the Irreconcilables. Johnson spoke with a 'rip-saw' voice which commanded widespread attention despite the fact, said his enemies, that it came from an eternally open mouth at the base of a head which contained an inexorably closed brain. The 'soul' of the 'Battalion of Death' was William E. Borah, the 'Idaho lion', the 'original Irreconcilable'. Probably more than any other man, including Lodge, Borah crystallised public opposition to the League. For eloquence and inspiration, he had no peer in the Senate debates. He declared that if he had his way the League would be 'Twenty Thousand Leagues under the Sea'. It was a 'treacherous and treasonable scheme', and Borah insisted that he would not change his mind even if Jesus Christ himself reappeared and pleaded for the Covenant. Few doubted his sincerity, and he was neither mean nor petty. After he had largely contributed to the defeat of the Treaty, Wilson still respected Borah.

Thus the battle lines were drawn in the Senate. About 75 members – Democrats loyal to Wilson, and Strong and Mild Republican Reservationists – wanted *a* League. The question was, whose League, if any, would emerge – Wilson's or the Republicans'?

Delay was the strategy of the Strong Reservationists and Irreconcilables – delay until pro-League sentiment became confused or evaporated, or preferably both. The Republican factions together constituted a majority on the Foreign Relations Committee and they mounted a campaign of attrition in July 1919, first with Lodge reading all 264 pages of the Treaty Wilson had presented to the Senate. This consumed two weeks. Few of the committee's 17 members attended Senator Lodge's readings; they knew all they wanted to know of the

Treaty. Only a clerk kept Lodge company on some occasions, and at one point he left the room while Lodge droned on alone.

Then, from the end of July until the middle of September, the committee conducted public hearings. Senate hearings are designed to educate and uplift ill-informed Senators, and there is no doubt that they achieved this to a certain extent, but the real purpose was to consume more time in order to confuse more people. Under attack for his obvious subterfuge, Lodge retorted that the President had taken nearly six months to compose the Treaty; surely pro-League enthusiasts would not grudge his committee a mere month or so to examine it.

1,297 pages of printed testimony record the proceedings of the six-week marathon. As Professor Thomas A. Bailey says: 'In a very real sense the League of Nations was drowned in a sea of words.' The only rule the committee imposed was that witnesses had to be American citizens; otherwise any foreigner from any part of the world with a grievance might descend upon Washington to testify. About 60 witnesses testified, mostly against Wilson or the League. Anglophobes were given their chance when the committee sought to uncover evil Albion's interest in the League. Irishmen bellowed for Hibernian liberty. Equally irrelevant, American Negroes cried racialism. A man who spoke no Swedish spoke on behalf of Sweden. A lady with an Irish name attacked Italy in support of Yugoslavia's claim on Fiume.

The absurdities of the hearings notwithstanding, it was clear by early September that Wilson was losing the fight. His enemies were emboldened, his friends

Below: White crosses mark the new graves of American soldiers in a US cemetery in France

impatient. Public opinion seemed to be turning against him. He would not compromise with the Reservationists. He would 'go to the country'.

Wilson chose to appeal directly to the masses over the heads of the obscurantist Senators, with their 'bungalow minds' and 'pygmy minds', as he called them. The people would understand high idealism if presented to them plainly and honestly. The 'prophet' would bring the word from the Potomac to the Pacific. It was the most fateful decision of his life, and he almost lost his life as a consequence.

The 63-year-old President was a sick man. He had already suffered a stroke, and he also suffered from indigestion and frequent headaches. His personal physician, Dr Cary T. Grayson, urged him not to go. Edith Wilson, his wife, attempted to dissuade him. 'The boys who went overseas did not refuse to go because it was dangerous,' Wilson said. 'If I do not do all in my power to put the Treaty in effect, I will be a slacker and never be able to look those boys in the eye. I must go.'

He was scheduled to make 40 speeches within 25 days, from September 4 to September 29, in the Mid-West and the West. The Deep South would be passed by—it was safely behind him. The East would be avoided—it was squarely against him. Isolationist centres like Chicago would also be avoided; there 'hyphenates' already hissed the name of the President.

In the Mid-West, which was German-American country, the audiences were generally cool or merely respectful when Wilson addressed them. Then the President's train crossed the Rockies and entered Irreconcilable country. Instead of facing the coolness of the Mid-West, however, Wilson transported his auditors; the enthusiasm of Western crowds was boundless. Even in

Idaho, the home of Borah, the reception was tumultuous. So, too, in Washington, the province of the 'bitter-ender' Miles Poindexter. The West had re-elected Wilson in 1916 and was seemingly still with him.

But the physical and nervous strain on Wilson was telling. If anything, the headaches were worse. Dr Grayson and Edith looked on apprehensively.

Oregon was another triumph—and then California, the bailiwick of Hiram Johnson. Berkeley, San Francisco, Los Angeles—all were taken in his stride. Wilson knew he was winning; the people were listening as he knew they would. Reporters accompanying the tour thought that Wilson carried California two to one for the League without reservations. The great difficulty was that the people would not be voting directly on the Treaty. Hiram Johnson would be, and he, like other Irreconcilable Western Senators, was as unmoved as if Wilson had never left Washington, DC.

In Colorado, on the way back, Edith noticed how thin and tired her husband was, and she suggested a few days' rest. 'No,' said Wilson, 'I have caught the imagination of the people.'

In Pueblo he made his most moving speech. He remembered the graves of American soldiers in France—'those dear ghosts who still deploy upon the fields of France'. He stopped, unable to continue because he was crying. Then he recovered and concluded: 'We have accepted that truth [of justice] and we are going to be led by it, and it is going to lead us, and through us the world, out into the pastures of quietness and peace such as the world never dreamed of before.'

Next morning after Wilson had spent another excruciating night with the usual headache and insomnia, Dr Grayson spoke to him and saw that the end had come. Saliva dripped from the left side of Wilson's

mouth and the left half of his face was fallen and unmoving when he talked. Grayson told him he must stop. Wilson said he could not quit, that he must fight on, but Edith convinced him that he must give it up. Grayson told the press, 'The President has suffered a complete nervous breakdown.' The blinds of the train were drawn and the engine sped back to Washington. There, a few days later, Wilson suffered a severe stroke that paralysed part of his body. He remained an invalid during the remaining year and a half of his administration.

Meanwhile the Foreign Relations Committee had concluded its hearings and filed a report. The committee offered 45 amendments to the Treaty and four reservations. The amendments would safeguard American sovereignty and freedom of action. Article X of the League Covenant was found to be the most objectionable. It obligated a member state to guarantee the territorial integrity of any other member from 'external aggression'. The Senate committee wanted Congress to retain the right to declare war as provided by the Constitution. Wilson had said that Article X was the very heart of the League, and from his sick-bed he ordered Hitchcock and the Democratic loyalists to vote down the amendments and reservations.

When the whole Senate debated the Covenant, the loyalists and Mild Reservationists joined forces and then voted down the proposals. To have passed them would have meant re-negotiation in Europe, which of course Wilson opposed. But during the first week of November Lodge struck back with 14 reservations.

The preamble of what became known as the 'Lodge Reservations' required that they would have to be accepted by three of the four principal signatories before Senate approval of the Treaty would come into effect. One reservation provided that in case of withdrawal from the League the United States would be the sole judge of whether it had fulfilled the obligations required under the League. As for Article X, Congress would have to approve the use of American armed forces abroad. Another reservation held the Monroe Doctrine to be beyond the jurisdiction of the League and capable of interpretation only by the United States. Another paved the way for American action on immigration control. The fourteenth and last struck at Britain and her Dominions' votes in the Assembly: America would not be bound by any League decision in which any one member cast more than one vote.

An old man, but obstinate
Events were rushing toward a climax. Mild Reservationists, who had offered interpretative amendments, had been rebuffed by Wilson and were now with Lodge. Hitchcock had his own interpretative reservations to parts of the Treaty, but he acted too late—the Mild Reservationists were gone. As the vote approached, the issue was a treaty with the Lodge Reservations or no treaty at all.

Hitchcock hastened to the White House where Edith and Grayson had insulated Wilson from the world. The President was prone to weeping spells now, and his wife and doctor censored his mail so as not to distress him. Hitchcock was allowed to enter the room but his conversation with the invalid was carefully supervised by the guardians, Edith shaking her finger at the

Senator if his questions seemed too probing.

At his bedside Hitchcock found Wilson propped up, his paralysed arm concealed beneath the covers. The Senator was shocked to find that in a few weeks the President had become a white-bearded old man. But the Scottish Presbyterian in him was as strong as ever. He would accept some of the minor Lodge reservations, but he would not change his position on the preamble or on Article X.

Hitchcock was wary of mentioning Lodge's name in fear of disturbing Wilson, but he managed to say: 'Mr President, it might be wise to compromise with Lodge on this point.' 'Let Lodge compromise,' replied Wilson. 'Well, of course,' said the Senator, 'he must compromise also, but we might well hold out the olive branch.' 'Let Lodge hold out the olive branch.' Hitchcock left the room.

With the vote hours away others urged compromise. Herbert Hoover sent a long telegram. He believed the Lodge Reservations were insignificant when compared with Europe's need of peace and the League. Close friends like Bernard M. Baruch urged compromise, arguing that 'half a loaf is better than no bread'. When Wilson learned of this friend's discouraging advice, he replied, 'And Baruch too.'

Edith pleaded, 'For my sake, won't you accept these reservations and get this awful thing settled?' Wilson said, 'Little girl, don't you desert me; that I cannot stand.' He spoke of the honour of the nation: 'Better a thousand times to go down fighting than to dip your colours to dishonourable compromise.'

At noon on November 19, 1919, the Senate convened to vote on the Treaty. The galleries were packed and there were long queues in the corridors. The Democrats had just met in secret caucus and been read their fallen leader's last-minute instructions—no compromise, vote against the Treaty with the Lodge Reservations.

They followed instructions. After five and a half hours of debate, cries of 'Vote!' arose from all over the chamber. The roll was called and the votes counted—39 ayes, 55 nays. The Treaty with reservations had lost.

The Republicans, except for the Irreconcilables, voted in favour. So did a few Democrats. The Irreconcilables voted against with Wilson's loyalists because if they had voted with their Republican brethren their ballots might have tipped the scales in favour of the Treaty with the Lodge Reservations. They had agreed to vote with any coalition which would defeat any kind of League.

Hitchcock sprang to his feet and moved an adjournment. He evidently hoped to ally his forces before they could go over to the Republican fold and agree to some kind of compromise. Only 42 Senators voted to adjourn. 51 voted against. The difference was made up by the Irreconcilables who 'crossed the aisle' again and voted with their Republican brethren. They opposed any kind of adjournment which might rally the necessary votes for any kind of Treaty. The Irreconcilables were the only faction in the Senate which was 'above party'.

Then Hitchcock moved that the Treaty be reconsidered with his interpretative reservations. But it was now too late to appeal to the Mild Reservationists and the motion was defeated, 41-50, the Irreconcilables standing with them and Lodge's Strong Reservationists.

Then Lodge, who had been in command all day, permitted Democratic Senator Oscar W. Underwood of Alabama to move approval of the Treaty without any reservations. Loyal Wilsonites could muster only 38 votes. Seven defecting Democrats joined Republican Strong and Mild Reservationists and Irreconcilables, casting a total of 53 votes against. Thus the Treaty had lost, without, as well as with, reservations.

The door closes
The Democrats had followed their leader's instructions. They voted against a Treaty with reservations which would have passed with their support. Then they voted for a Treaty without reservations which had no chance of being passed. Wilson and the Democrats killed the Treaty in the only form in which it could have passed the Senate. Just before the Senate adjourned, Senator Claude A. Swanson, a Democrat, left his seat and walked over to Lodge and pleaded: 'For God's sake, can't something be done to save the Treaty?' 'Senator,' Lodge replied, 'the door is closed. You have done it yourself.'

But the door was re-opened four months later. The Senate had re-convened and in March 1919 there was a final vote on the Treaty with the Lodge Reservations substantially intact. The British had given signs of their approval of a treaty with reservations—but not so the President. Again, from his 'Olympian seclusion' came the familiar edict—no compromise. And again, on March 19, 1919, Wilson's supporters, or at least enough of them to defeat the Treaty, followed instructions. With 84 Senators present, 56 were needed for the resolution of ratification. Lodge mustered 49 votes for the Treaty with reservations, including 21 Democrats. 23 loyalist Democrats voted against the Treaty and were joined by 12 Irreconcilables who 'crossed the aisle' again, still 'above party'. So the final vote in the United States Senate on the Treaty embodying the League of Nations was 49-35, seven votes short of ratification. If only seven more Democrats had bolted, America would have become a member of the League. But Wilson would not permit it. Just after the final vote, Senator Brandegee, 'the wit' of the Irreconcilables, turned to Lodge and said: 'We can always depend on Mr Wilson. He never has failed us.'

Next morning the secretary of the Senate delivered the bound volume of the official 264-page Treaty to the White House. It was the same one which the President had personally presented to the Senate in July 1919. The Senators had not been able to agree on the resolution of ratification, and so they were sending it back. The volume was wrapped in brown paper and tied with an excessive amount of red tape.

Further Reading
Bailey, Thomas A., *Wilson and the Peacemakers* (New York: Macmillan 1947)
Houston, David F., *Eight Years With Wilson's Cabinet*, Vol. II (New York: Doubleday 1926)
Smith, Daniel M., *The Great Departure* (New York: John Wiley 1965)
Smith, Gene, *When the Cheering Stopped* (New York: William Morrow 1964)
Walworth, Arthur, *Woodrow Wilson* (New York: Longmans 1958)

[*For Thomas Keiser's biography, see page 2916.*]

'We can always depend on Mr Wilson. He never has failed us'

Above: Senator Gilbert W. Hitchcock, acting Democratic leader in the Senate, won Wilson's favour by supporting the Treaty incorporating the League. The Republican opposition— *Left:* 'Irreconcilable' Senator Borah caricatured as a phonograph uttering mindless slogans. *Below left:* Hiram Johnson, the 'noise' of the 'bitter-enders'. *Centre:* Frank B. Brandegee, the 'tongue'. *Right:* Henry Cabot Lodge, Strong Reservationist and Wilson's rival

'The world wants
peace. The President
wants his League.
The world will have
to wait'

When peace came in November 1918 the United States seemed an extraordinarily fortunate nation. The American economy had not yet gone over to war production on anything like the European scale. Only about 100,000 American soldiers had died in the conflict—one-tenth of the British losses, one-twentieth of those of Germany or Russia. The United States was the richest country in the world, physically intact and apparently united in mood as well as in name. Elsewhere societies might be crumbling under the impact of national or radical drives: in the United States patriotic fervour seemed to indicate an almost excessively conformist spirit. 'Americanism', in fact 'One Hundred Per Cent Americanism', was the slogan of the day. The two major middle-of-the-road political parties had together secured nearly 17 million votes in the 1916 presidential election, as against a mere 600,000 for the Socialist Party.

A comfortable land then, to all appearances. Yet that was hardly the feeling of contemporaries. 'This country is still suffering from shell shock,' said Senator Reed of Missouri in August 1919. 'Hardly anyone is in a normal state of mind. . . A great storm has swept over the intellectual world and its ravages and disturbances still exist.' Or in the words of A. G. Gardiner, an English journalist writing a few years later, 'No one who was in the United States, as I chanced to be, in the autumn of 1919, will forget the feverish condition of the public mind at that time. . . Property was in an agony of fear, and the horrid name "Radical" covered the most innocent departure from conventional thought with a suspicion of desperate purpose. "America," as a wit of the time said, "is the land of liberty—liberty to keep in step".' There was a marked discrepancy between the outward prosperity and stability of the United States and its inner fears and divisions.

Some of these fears bordered on the pathological. Other causes for disquiet were, however, quite rationally based, even if they were by European standards not very grave. There was, for instance, a good deal of confusion over issues of governmental authority. Woodrow Wilson's administration had assumed war powers that controlled the nation's life to an unprecedented degree. Railroads and merchant shipping, for example, had been in effect nationalised. In the wartime atmosphere of nationalism such expedients were accepted and even welcomed as proofs of leadership, the will to win, and national unity. With the sudden end of the fighting contradictory impulses revealed themselves. There was still a demand for firm, centralised direction, especially to correct whatever was felt to be wrong with America. The President and his officials were urged to *do* something, do it quickly, and do it boldly, to solve such-and-such a problem. Large numbers of Americans took it for granted that their President should be taking the initiative to work out a peace settlement. Moral activism was an American characteristic; and the President was the nation's chief moral activist.

On the other hand there was a large and growing number of Americans who convinced themselves that federal, presidential authority had reached out too far and must be curbed. One sign of the swing was the outcome of the mid-term Congressional

AMERICA 1919

The United States was not exempt from the social and political upheaval suffered after the war by the nations involved. *Marcus Cunliffe. Below:* Troops returning

elections of November 1918, which, despite the pleas of President Wilson, confronted him with hostile Republican majorities in both houses. His personal involvement in the Paris peace-making was condemned by his critics both as an abuse of presidential power and as an indication that he was neglecting pressing domestic problems. When Wilson, worried by the threatened defeat of his peace proposals, decided to go on a Western speaking tour in September 1919 to bring his case to the people, *Harvey's Weekly* published a scathing editorial on the President's non-government. He had spent about six months of the previous twelve, the magazine claimed, in sailing between Europe and the US or in 'administration, or attempted administration, of his high office by transfer of our executive seat of government from the banks of the Potomac to the banks of the Seine. . . The day of peripatetic American Presidents is ended. From the end of the Wilson Administration on, they will stay in Washington and mind their own and the American people's business. . . .'

This prophecy was soon borne out for Wilson himself, with a cruel irony. He collapsed during his speaking tour, suffered a stroke from which he never fully recovered, and to the end of his term in March 1921 was more or less confined to the White House. From August 1919 to April 1920 he never called a cabinet meeting, though he rebuked Secretary of State Lansing for trying to bring department heads together informally. In these difficult months there was no proper discussion at cabinet level of any domestic issue. The President's wife decided whom he should see and what he should be told. In the 1920 presidential campaign Republican orators inveighed against Wilson and his officials for 'usurpation' of authority. Congress had made plain its attachment to private enterprise by returning the railways and the merchant navy to their former operators. But, in fact, the country still with part of its mind craved for strong government, and Wilson's breakdown, even if the nation as a whole was unaware how far this had gone, left something of a vacuum. In 1919-20 the United States was arguably undergoverned rather than over-governed, if by government we mean the formulation and implementation of decisive policies.

Licence and Prohibition

These considerations do not take us very far toward an explanation of the 'shell shock' symptoms of the era. Nor perhaps do the two constitutional amendments, the 18th and 19th, which were ratified by the necessary number of states in January 1919 and August 1920 respectively, after having first passed through Congress. The 18th Amendment stipulated that by January 1920 the 'manufacture, sale, or transportation of intoxicating liquors', or their import or export, should cease in the United States. In October 1919 the enabling legislation known as the Volstead Act defined 'intoxicating' as anything over $\frac{1}{2}\%$ of alcohol by volume. America was about to embark on the 'noble experiment' of Prohibition, under a law soon to be resented, derided and evaded. Prohibition offered a fine new field to gangster enterprise in the shape of 'bootlegged' liquor; early in 1920 came a significant shift of residence, when 'Scarface' Al Capone moved from New York to the more promising milieu of Chicago. But the full effects of Prohibition upon the nation's life were not yet discernible. Nor did the majority of Americans feel that something entirely new was about to happen. Prohibition was an old campaign in the United States. Local or state regulations had already turned large areas 'dry'. By 1918, 32 of the 48 states had introduced Prohibition on their own initiative. The big cities and industrial towns were 'wet' in a desert of abstainers. Chicago alone, it was said, had more saloons than could be found in the entire South. Production of alcohol had been drastically reduced during the war to conserve grain for foodstuffs, and this emergency legislation had not yet been repealed when the 18th Amendment came in. So national Prohibition was merely a new application of an idea already widely accepted.

The 19th Amendment, guaranteeing female suffrage, had been passed by Congress in June 1919. Votes for women had once been a controversial issue. But the American suffragette movement had never taken the militant form practised in Britain, and since the 1870s a number of states had given the vote to women for state purposes. None of the major political figures, including Woodrow Wilson, had been eager to extend the franchise to women. In private, such men were still apt to grumble that politics would spoil women and women would spoil politics. 1920 was the first presidential election in which women would be able to vote. But the prospect was more a theme for light journalism than for serious speculation. The 19th Amendment was seen—correctly, in the light of later developments—as an evolutionary and not a revolutionary step.

Prohibition and women's suffrage could be regarded as minor items on a long list of postwar innovations and dislocations, whose collective effect was substantial. Another problem was the demobilisation of the four million men who were in uniform at the time of the Armistice. Several hundred thousand were released almost immediately. The remainder were nearly all back in civilian life by the end of 1919. Their grievances were various and understandable. They complained that the army had been quicker to draft them than it was to liberate them. They resented the civilian 'profiteers' and the factory workers who had—according to the soldiers' mythology—prospered from emergency conditions. Some servicemen felt obscurely cheated because they had not been sent overseas. Those who had gone to France tended to come back with a low opinion of European standards of morality and hygiene. A sort of querulous bellicosity typified the outlook of a fair number of American 'veterans'—an attitude enshrined in the pronouncements of the new American Legion.

Peace and no peace

Soldiers and civilians alike found peacetime conditions a disappointment. Prices doubled between 1915 and 1920. Bonus and overtime payments during the hectic war years had disguised this trend. With the end of the wartime boom such payments disappeared and there was a sharp though temporary recession, with pockets of unemployment. The federal government was simultaneously urged to terminate its far-reaching wartime controls over the economy and to use these powers to

Above top: A Negro being stoned to death during the Chicago race riots of 1919.
Bottom: A rioter being search for arms in the street during the Pittsburgh steel-workers strike

reduce the cost of living. The mushrooming of defence industries had accelerated the movement of Negroes out of the mainly rural South: about 180,000 went north between 1910 and 1920. They were the first, both to suffer from the postwar recession, and to be blamed for it by white workers. Demobilised black soldiers were in no mood to return to their old caste-subordination. The consequence was a wave of race riots during the summer of 1919. At the end of 13 days of shooting and burning in Chicago, there were 38 dead and over 500 injured – the majority were Negroes. There were similar ugly scenes in Texas, Arkansas and Washington, DC. In Omaha, Nebraska, a Negro accused of molesting a white woman was riddled with bullets; the mangled corpse was strung up at a busy corner in the centre of the city. There were 83 lynchings in the United States in 1919, nearly all of Negroes, and 65 in 1920. A new black protest was voiced by Marcus Garvey, a Jamaican who claimed to speak not only for the 15 million Negroes in America but for the 400 million all over the world. In a speech at Carnegie Hall, New York, in August 1919, Garvey proclaimed: 'It took the black man to whip the Kaiser's soldiers. . . The first dying that is to be done by the black man in the future will be done to make himself free. And then when we are finished, if we have any charity to bestow, we may die for the white man. But as for me, I think we have stopped dying for him.' Garvey's militancy alarmed and enraged sundry bodies of self-styled patriots, among them the revived Ku Klux Klan, like the Negroes no longer confined to the South.

There was profound unrest also in the ranks of American white labour. There had been occasional strikes, especially in the Pacific coast shipyards, in 1917-18, which had angered the authorities. But organised labour, as represented by Samuel Gompers (President of the American Federation of Labour), had as a whole kept its morale high and showed the same demonstrative patriotism as the rest of the population. In the favourable conditions, union membership had rapidly expanded. In 1919 things turned sour. There were more than 3,600 strikes in the 12 months, involving over 4 million workers – figures vastly exceeding those of recent years. They were influenced to some extent by radical rhetoric stimulated by the Bolshevik revolution in Russia. But the main motive for the strikes was domestic discontent, over-inflation, and antagonism to the manifestos of big business. The businessman in the United States had been on the defensive since the beginning of the century. By the end of the war the tide of progressive reform legislation seemed to have spent itself. American victory was interpreted as, among other things, a vindication of the doctrines of free enterprise. Old public suspicions of labour were re-awakened, even among American liberals who had hitherto sympathised with the masses rather than the bosses. The *New Republic* now argued that: 'Between organised labour . . . and organised capital . . . the large class which lives by rendering services to both stands an excellent chance of being crushed as between the upper and nether millstones.' With each successive strike public opinion became more and more hostile to the nether millstone.

The process began for postwar America early in February 1919, with a general strike in Seattle in support of the city's shipyard workers, who were already on strike. 60,000 workers answered the call. The Mayor of Seattle called in troops from a nearby army camp. Like the average citizen in these nervous days, Mayor Ole Hanson was convinced that the general strike – an 'un-American' tactic, repudiated even by Gompers – was the beginning of an effort by unscrupulous radicals to 'take possession of our American government and try to duplicate the anarchy of Russia'. In four days the strike collapsed ignominiously, and Hanson was hailed as a national hero, a man (according to one newspaper) 'with a backbone that would serve as a girder in a railroad bridge'.

The year's second spectacular strike occurred in September on the other side of the country, in Boston. It involved the city's miserably underpaid police force who formed a union, affiliated to the AFL, to present their case. But the Boston police commissioner regarded this as an act of outrageous indiscipline and tried to punish the ringleaders. As in Seattle, public opinion was overwhelmingly on the side of authority, and ready to believe that revolution was on the way. When Gompers tried to plead the policemen's case with the Governor of Massachusetts, Calvin Coolidge, Coolidge responded with a long telegram in which he said: 'There is no right to strike against the public safety by anybody, anywhere, any time.' Here too the strikers lost; and, like Hanson, Coolidge was suddenly in the limelight as a national hero – just the kind of figure to appeal to the American Legion, which was sworn 'to maintain law and order; to foster and perpetuate a hundred per cent Americanism'.

In the same month a third of a million steelworkers walked off their jobs. The same pattern of action and reaction was evident. The largely foreign-born mass of steelworkers were ill-paid and ill-treated; the average working week was nearly 69 hours. Attempts to unionise met with punitive disapproval, and attempts by the unions to negotiate with the employers were ignored. Once the strike began there was violence on both sides. Troops were summoned. Little by little the strikers caved in, though not finally until January 1920. And yet another national hero of iron backbone emerged, in the person of General Leonard Wood, who had directed the operations of the federal troops. As in Seattle and Boston the strikers gained nothing. 20 men were dead in clashes between strikers and strike-breakers (the latter in some instances Negroes, a circumstance that heightened race prejudice). The American public was convinced that yet another threat of revolution had been staved off.

These events were part of the postwar economic and social dislocation. But they were also shaped by the bizarre phenomenon of the 'red scare'. A Senate committee formed to investigate the steel strike announced that behind it 'there is massed a considerable element of IWWs, anarchists, revolutionists, and Russian Soviets'. This was untrue, and it was not true of the unrest among railroad workers and coalminers that immediately followed the steel walk-out. But it was believed. There was a pervasive fear of revolutionary conspiracy. And this fear had roots in war-time and prewar experience. The 'IWWs' or Industrial Workers of the World were a militant left-wing group who had scored some successes before 1914 in organising low-paid casual and immigrant workers. They condemned American intervention in the European war, as did the larger and less militant Socialist Party led by Eugene V. Debs. Once war was declared, in April 1917, a furious over-simplification took place. In the words of ex-President Theodore Roosevelt, 'He who is not with us, absolutely and without reserve of any kind, is against us, and should be treated as an alien enemy.' The IWWs were assailed as 'Imperial Wilhelm's Warriors', and, in less jocular vein, their offices were raided, their meetings broken up and their leaders assaulted and jailed. These licensed mob activities were carried out under the protection of various state laws against 'criminal syndicalism' and the like.

'Liberty connected with order?'
At the national level three wartime laws epitomised America's passionate conformism, and gave wide sanction for repressive gestures. The first was the Espionage Act of June 1917, which made it a crime for a person to 'convey false reports . . . with intent to interfere with the operation or success of the military or naval forces of the United States or to promote the success of its enemies . . . or attempt to cause insubordination, disloyalty, mutiny, or refusal of duty . . . or . . . wilfully obstruct recruiting or enlistment service. . . .' The second was the Sedition Act of 1918. Even more sweeping, it provided heavy penalties for 'any disloyal, profane, scurrilous, or abusive language about the form of government of the United States, or the Constitution of the United States, or the uniform of the Army or Navy of the United States, or any language intended to . . . encourage resistance to the United States, or to promote the cause of its enemies. . . .' The third, of October 1918, revealed the deep distrust of unconventional foreign-born residents. It attempted to exclude from admission any aliens who were anarchists or believers in assassination or in the violent overthrow of the government. The reason perhaps for this seemingly naïve clause was that the act then went on to stipulate that any aliens already admitted to the United States could be deported if they could be shown to profess any such insidious doctrines.

Under the first two laws more than 1,500 people – IWWs, Socialists, and some conscientious objectors – were arrested. Debs, who continued to denounce the war as a capitalist enterprise, was sentenced to 10 years in gaol. President Wilson refused to pardon him when the war was over. Convict 9653 of the Atlanta Penitentiary, the Socialist Party's presidential candidate in 1920, was not released until the following year. In August 1917 Charles T. Schenck and other Socialists had been charged under the Espionage Act with mailing anti-war leaflets in Philadelphia to men who had already been summoned for military service. In 1919 their case was heard on appeal by the US Supreme Court, which was unanimous in upholding the original conviction. The defendants argued that the First Amendment protected freedom of speech and assembly. Justice Oliver Wendell Holmes, presenting the decision for the Court, conceded that *some*

Above: Poverty, and discontent among the workers, threatened the stability of post-war American society. *Inset top*: American women welcome home the returning troops. Many of the soldiers were deeply dissatisfied with the conditions they found. *Centre*: Negroes being searched for arms in a Chicago police station. *Bottom*: Prohibition in operation—police looking for hip flasks

3403

freedom of speech was constitutionally guaranteed, and that in peacetime the statements in the leaflets might not have been objectionable:

But . . . the most stringent protection of free speech would not protect a man in falsely shouting fire in a theatre, and causing a panic . . . The question in every case is whether the words used are used in such circumstances . . . as to create a clear and present danger that they will bring about the substantive evils that Congress has a right to prevent.

The 'clear and present danger' criterion was invoked by the Court soon afterwards to reject Debs's appeal. A year or so later Holmes, sometimes in association with Justice Louis D. Brandeis, began to dissent in favour of freedom of speech. In the atmosphere of 1919, however, anti-war manifestos were still being construed as grave offences against the state, even though the war was over.

To relatively cool-headed men such as Holmes the war was of course not over. It had entered a new and potentially deadly phase; and so the draconian legislation of 1917-18 seemed highly relevant. In 1919 even respectable newspapers like the *New York Times* complained that 'un-American' activities were not being countered with sufficient energy and severity. Even Woodrow Wilson on his last speaking tour now and then turned aside from expounding the Treaty of Versailles to warn his audiences of the 'poison of revolt' that was seeping into 'the veins of this free people'.

There were numerous examples of the hysteria. In February 1919 a man was shot dead for shouting 'To hell with the United States'. This was in Hammond, Indiana. The jury took two minutes to acquit the killer. In May, at a victory pageant in Washington, DC, a man who refused to rise for the playing of the national anthem was shot in the back by a patriotic sailor. The crowd is said to have 'burst into cheering and hand-clapping'. A few months later, in the milder climate of Connecticut, a salesman escaped with a six-month jail sentence for remarking to a customer that Lenin was among the 'brainiest' of the world's political leaders. One reason for the tremendous enthusiasm for deportation of 'enemy' aliens in 1919 was that many were guilty of no indictable offence, or at least none that could be proved under American law. Deportation got round the difficulty. Some public figures thought deportation too lenient a measure. 'If I had my way', cried the evangelist Billy Sunday, 'with these ornery wild-eyed Socialists and IWWs, I would stand them up before a firing squad and save space on our ships.'

Shortly before Christmas, 249 deportees were despatched to Russia aboard the *Buford,* a ship dubbed the 'Soviet Ark' by the press. The majority were members of a probably harmless organisation known as the Union of Russian Workers. To the Boston *Evening Transcript* the departure of the *Buford* was 'as epoch-making as the immortal voyage of Columbus'. The *Saturday Evening Post* said: 'The *Mayflower* brought the first of the builders to this country; the *Buford* has taken away the first destroyers.' Another 300 or so aliens were deported in the next 18 months. A senator from Tennessee, worried about native-born radicals who could not be disposed of so neatly, suggested that they

might be sent to a new penal colony that could be located on the American-held Pacific island of Guam. Plots were detected or suspected everywhere. Clergymen were denounced and schoolteachers sacked. Senator James F. Byrnes of South Carolina asked for federal aid to forestall a Negro uprising in the South which he asserted was being planned by 'the Reds'. By 1921 more than 30 states had enacted peacetime sedition laws or laws against 'criminal syndicalism'. A similar number, and various cities, passed 'Red flag' laws and ordinances to punish any display of the offending symbol of Bolshevism. When the American Communist Labour and Communist parties were established in August and September 1919, Illinois, New York and California were especially zealous in indicting and sometimes imprisoning such radical spokesmen as 'Big Bill' Hayward, Benjamin Gitlow and Mrs Anita Whitney.

Reds, radicals and revolution

Why did all this happen? For one thing, because the fear of revolution, although absurdly exaggerated, was not entirely imaginary. The Bolshevik seizure of power in Russia was violent and ruthless, and for those not in sympathy the ideology of overthrow was terrifying. Believing that the Bolshevik revolution had been inspired by the Germans, Americans, in common with many in western Europe, transferred their hostility, with Red Russia supplanting Imperial Germany as the real enemy. World revolution seemed an insidious possibility in the opening months of 1919, with the formation of the Third International (the Comintern) and with the spread of 'Spartacism' in Germany and the rise of Bolshevism in Poland and Hungary. Inspired by the success of revolution in Russia, some American radicals convinced themselves that they could achieve the same results in the United States. After all, the Bolsheviks too had only been a handful of resolute men: spirit was what counted, not numbers. Romantic radicalism in America led to a vogue for Communist slogans ('All power to the Soviets', 'Workers of the world unite, you have nothing to lose but your chains').

More disturbing to the average American were actual manifestations of violence. Cartoonists usually associated Communists and anarchists with the image of a round bomb whose fuse was lit. At the end of April 1919 the postman brought a small package to the office of Mayor Hanson in Seattle. Some acid was leaking from the parcel, which proved to be a home-made bomb. The next day a parcel of the same type arrived at the Georgia home of a former senator who had once proposed legislation to keep out alien agitators. It exploded when opened by a maid and blew off her hands. A New York postal worker, reading of these incidents, remembered seeing a number of packages which fitted the newspaper description. The post office was able to intercept another 34, all containing primitive bombs. The 'Bomb Honour List' included the multi-millionaires John D. Rockefeller and J. P. Morgan, Justice Holmes, Judge K. M. Landis, who had sentenced Hayward, Senator Overman, chairman of the Senate Bolshevik Investigation committee, and a number of other oddly selected candidates. The bombs had obviously been intended to coincide with

radicalism's traditional First of May. The culprit or culprits were never found. A few moderate newspapers maintained that the bombs were much more likely to be the work of an isolated fanatic than of any coherent movement. But a more typical reaction was that of Mayor Hanson: 'I trust Washington will buck up and . . . hang or incarcerate for life all the anarchists . . . If the Government doesn't clean them up I will.'

Another of the intended recipients of the May Day bombs was Attorney-General A. Mitchell Palmer. He, in fact, as Hanson complained, had not yet reacted pugnaciously to the 'red scare'. He still cherished his reputation as a good Wilson Democrat who had steered reform legislation through Congress. The disturbances that took place on May Day were nearly all inspired or condoned by local law-enforcement officers: radicals were the victims not the aggressors. Palmer hesitated to bring federal authority to bear. What helped to change his mind was a simultaneous set of bomb attacks a month later against the homes of mayors, judges and businessmen in eight different cities. Palmer's own house in Washington was among those dynamited. Though he and his family were unhurt, the house was badly damaged. Fragments of a human body were discovered in the débris—evidently the remains of a dynamiter who had set the bomb off prematurely and blown himself to pieces. An anarchist pamphlet found nearby declared: 'There will have to be bloodshed . . . there will have to be murder . . . there will have to be destruction . . . We are ready to do anything and everything to suppress the capitalist class . . . THE ANARCHIST FIGHTERS.' The radical press, probably with justification, disclaimed all responsibility. With less plausibility it claimed that these bomb attacks were staged by officialdom to discredit dissenters.

Palmer's personal safety had been threatened. Despite his progressive, Quaker antecedents he became infected with the general panic. Like many of his countrymen, he surrendered to 'nativist' emotions: the fear that alien, foreign-born, un-American conspirators were undermining the nation. Police experts who studied the bits of clothing among the wreckage around Palmer's house deduced that the bomber had come from Philadelphia and was an Italian alien. Aliens simply could not be trusted. That, at any rate, was the main assumption of the Bureau of Investigation—the germ of the later FBI—which Palmer threw into action under the auspices of the Justice Department. Inside the Bureau, directed by a young sleuth named J. Edgar Hoover, the key section built up a huge card-index of American radicals and distributed warnings to newspapers and magazines of the evil extent of Communist activity. This material was in turn widely disseminated by the press. The US Department of Justice thus helped to foment the hysteria of 1919. The extremism of the bomb incidents and of left-wing propaganda had by mirror-effect produced a comparable extremism of repression within the public mind. And, being a politician, Palmer was eager to give the public what it wanted.

Hence, in November 1919, the famous 'Palmer raids', when agents of the Bureau of Investigation rounded up about 1,000 suspect aliens—some of whom were later deported. Hence, too, Palmer's delighted

A police officer supervises the unloading of a cargo of whisky captured after a chase

land. So it was a prey to aberrant phobias. Indulging in them brought a glow of fellowship, a sense of unity through combat (it has been remarked that the most fraternally bound of all human groups is a lynchmob). But, happily for America, such fevers soon burn out. By the end of 1919 the hyperbolic language of Palmerism was beginning to sound slightly absurd, and then repellent. The rest of the world had *not* gone Communist. In an America palpably committed to private enterprise, prices became stable, jobs more plentiful. The doughboys disappeared into civilian life. The dreadful warnings of the hyper-patriots grew stale through repetition. Attorney-General Palmer over-reached himself by predicting a gigantic terrorist demonstration planned for May Day 1920. The day passed without the least sign of trouble. Palmer was suddenly revealed as a foolish, self-seeking jeremiah. 'We can never get to work', said one newspaper, 'if we keep jumping sideways in fear of the be-whiskered Bolshevik'. Palmer had lost his chance for the Democratic presidential nomination. On the Republican side, Coolidge was still enough of a hero to secure the vice-presidential nomination; but he was admired as much for his reticent coolness as for his firmness. The new mood was nicely expressed in the person of Senator Warren G. Harding, the Republicans' presidential nominee. Handsome and affable, he was perfectly sincere when he declared in his acceptance speech of July 1920 that 'there is no hate in the American heart'. The Americanism of the booster had replaced that of the witch-hunter.

Further Reading
Coben, Stanley, *A. Mitchell Palmer: Politician* (New York: Columbia University Press, 1963)
Draper, Theodore, *The Roots of American Communism* (New York: Viking, 1957)
Higham, John, *Strangers in the Land: Patterns of American Nativism, 1860-1925* (New York: Atheneum, 1963)
Leuchtenburg, William E., *The Perils of Prosperity, 1914-1932* (Chicago: University of Chicago Press, 1958)
Murray, Robert K., *Red Scare: A Study of National Hysteria, 1919-1920* (Minneapolis: University of Minnesota Press, 1955) and *The Harding Era* (Minneapolis: University of Minnesota Press, 1969)
Nash, Roderick, *The Nervous Generation: American Thought, 1917-1930* (Chicago: Rand McNally, 1970)
Schlesinger, Arthur M., Jr., *The Age of Roosevelt: Crisis of the Old Order, 1919-1933* (Boston: Houghton Mifflin, 1957)
Slosson, Preston W., *The Great Crusade and After, 1914-1928* (New York: The Macmillan Co., 1930)
White, William Allen, *A Puritan in Babylon: The Story of Calvin Coolidge* (New York: The Macmillan Co., 1938)

MARCUS CUNLIFFE was Professor of American Studies at the University of Sussex until 1980. Born in 1922, he read history at Oriel College, Oxford. After wartime service as intelligence and reconnaissance officer in a tank battalion (Normandy-Germany, 1944-1945), he returned to Oxford for postgraduate work in military history. He spent two years in the United States as a Commonwealth Fellow at Yale University, and returned to teach American history at Manchester University, where he later became a professor. He has been a visiting professor at Harvard and other universities in the United States. He has published many works on the United States, including *American Presidents and the Presidency*.

discovery, in the wake of similar discoveries by Mayor Hanson, Governor Coolidge and General Wood, that a man could become a public hero, a presidential possibility, by denouncing public enemies. Newspapers lauded Palmer as 'a tower of strength' whose red-hunting brought 'thrills of joy to every American'. Wilson was a helpless invalid; if anyone was running the government Palmer was, and the more he thought about replacing Wilson as the next Democratic President the more he began to impose repressive 'hundred-per-center' tactics upon the rest of the Wilson administration. For a while the logic of repression was self-fulfilling. Since the foe was cunning and depraved he was liable to appear in the unlikeliest of disguises, and his depravity could only be countered with ruthlessness. To those who insisted that the numbers of genuine extremists were very small, Palmer and his supporters could answer that fanaticism mattered more than numbers, and that anti-radicalism had prevented the contagion from spreading.

So, into 1920, the Palmer system of sudden raids and arrests and threatened deportation seemed to pay dividends. The public appeared to admire his harsh use of the injunction to compel striking coal-miners to return to work. Defending himself against criticism of his methods, in 1920, he no doubt still spoke for a great many Americans when he commented: *If there be any doubt of the general character of the active leaders and agitators amongst these avowed revolutionaries, . . . an examination of their photographs . . . would dispel it. Out of the sly and crafty eyes of many of them leap cupidity, cruelty, insanity, and crime; from their lopsided faces, sloping brows, and misshapen features may be recognised the unmistakable criminal type.* Crude xenophobia of this sort denied a fair trial in Massachusetts to Nicola Sacco and Bartolomeo Vanzetti, Italian aliens and declared anarchists, arrested in May 1920 for robbery and murder. Reviews of the evidence half a century later have suggested that Sacco may actually have been guilty. But in 1920-21 liberal Americans had good reason to believe that the two men were being tried for their beliefs, not for their acts — and that the biased judge in the trial could not perceive the distinction.

The America of the 1920s remained ponderously anti-radical. The right-thinking businessman supplied the national ethic. But gradually the hysteria of 1919, itself a continuation of the fevered emotions of wartime, was dissipated. The tribalist conformity of the era attested to a deep inner uncertainty, an alarmed suspicion that the United States was a *dis-*united

THE ARMOURED HERITAGE
The last tanks of the war

By the end of 1918, the design philosophy of the first tanks of 1916 had reached its culmination: its zenith, the Allied Mk VIII, was about to enter production. But the new designs about to see fruition were of more significance: track runs were lower, hull profiles more compact and the idea of a superimposed turret reintroduced. Thus the formula for future vehicles was laid down. It only remained to be seen if the tactical lessons had been learnt

Above: The last word in British tank design philosophy, the Anglo-American **Mark VIII** heavy tank, the International. This was the heaviest tank produced in the war, and also set new standards in crew comfort. Only four prototypes had been finished by the Armistice. *Weight:* 37 tons. *Crew:* 8. *Armament:* two 23-calibre 6-pdrs with 208 rounds and seven .3-inch Browning machine guns with 13,484 rounds. *Armour:* 16-mm front, 12-mm and 10-mm sides, sponsons and turret and 6-mm roof. *Engine:* Ricardo V-12 (British) or Liberty V-12 (American), 300-hp each. *Speed:* 7 mph max. *Step crossing:* 4 ft 6 ins. *Trench crossing:* 16 ft. *Range:* 50 miles. *Length:* 34 ft 2½ ins. *Height:* 10 ft 3 ins. *Width:* 12 ft 4 ins. *Left above:* The **Carro Armato Fiat 2000**, Italy's first venture into the design of heavy tanks. Only two were built. *Weight:* 40 tons. *Crew:* 10. *Armament:* one 65-mm gun and seven machine guns. *Armour:* 15-mm minimum, 20-mm maximum. *Engine:* Fiat 6-cylinder, 240-hp. *Speed:* 4½ mph.

Left below: The French **Char de Rupture 2C**. Designed in 1918, ten of these monsters were built between 1920 and 1922. *Weight:* 70 tons. *Crew:* 13. *Armament:* one 75-mm gun with 125 rounds and four machine guns with 10,000 rounds. *Armour:* 13-mm minimum, 45-mm maximum. *Engines:* two Daimler or Mercedes 6-cylinder, 250-hp each. *Speed:* 8 mph. *Range:* 107 miles. *Length:* 43 ft 2 ins. *Height:* 12 ft 8 ins. *Width:* 10 ft. *Below:* Germany's equivalent of the British Whippet, the **LK II**. *Weight:* 8¾ tons. *Crew:* 3. *Armament:* one 57-mm gun (another version had two machine guns). *Armour:* 8-mm minimum, 14-mm maximum. *Engine:* Daimler 4-cylinder, 55-hp. *Speed:* 8 mph. *Range:* 40 miles. *Length:* 18 ft 8 ins. *Height:* 8 ft 2 ins. *Width:* 6 ft 5 ins. The LK II was decidedly underpowered, and the limited traverse of its armament would have been a liability; but in the event, only prototypes had been built before the Armistice. Similar in design to the British medium tanks, it had no all-round protection

John Batchelor

THE CORDON SANITAIRE

The ravages of the war were political as well as human and economic. With the breaking up of Austria-Hungary and the temporary retirement of Russia, a major casualty was the balance of power which had existed in Europe before the war. As the conflict, and inevitably also the peace negotiations, developed into a 'Germany versus The Rest' struggle, France increasingly felt anxious about her prospects of future security. Her policy was to acquire the new states as satellites so that, with support, they could isolate the undamped German aggression from the nation who had most to fear from it, and act as buffers against the threatening surge of Bolshevism. It was a solution unlikely to succeed in practice. *John Keegan. Below:* Germany 'quarantined' – the intended effect of the *Cordon Sanitaire*

CORDON SANITAIRE

Unlike Britain and the United States, who had entered the First World War as a deliberate act of policy and always retained the possibility of retiring behind their seaward frontiers, France could not count her own place in the world secure simply by the fact of Germany's defeat. Isolationism is the prerogative of a maritime power. Even in victory, France was forced to look, and if necessary to scrabble, for territorial concessions and treaty guarantees which Britain and America could ignore. It was peculiarly humiliating and profoundly galling to France, who felt with reason that she had borne an unequal burden of suffering, that she should have been forced to solicit these concessions and guarantees from her allies (though not, of course, at their expense). By far the most important, in French eyes, was the resettlement of Germany's western border. Foch, the Allied generalissimo, was adamant that France should gain from victory in 1918 the frontier on the Rhine which she had lost in the wars of Louis XIV. It was not enough, in his judgement, that the Allies should occupy the Rhineland for 15 years, even with the option to return should Germany misbehave. Foch felt that France had won the right to keep the *Wacht am Rhein* herself.

Neither Britain nor the United States, both of whom were committed to re-shaping the map of Europe on the basis of national self-determination, could accept either the equity or the feasibility of separating the Rhineland from the rest of Germany, whether it be set up as an autonomous state or annexed to France. Both countries were nevertheless sympathetic to French anxieties for the future. By way of compensation President Wilson, with British agreement, proposed a Treaty of Guarantee, by which Britain and the United States would undertake to come instantly to France's aid in the event of future German aggression. In March 1919 Clemenceau reluctantly accepted this offer.

Within eight months the Treaty of Guarantee had become a dead letter, through the United States Senate's refusal to ratify it. France was deprived of the only military alliance of value which was open to her in the west and she became again, as she had been in 1914, an isolated power enjoying a military understanding with Britain. True, through the League of Nations, she would in future have recourse to sanctions in face of aggression, but in 1919 the machinery was still untried. In 1914 she had at least had an eastern alliance to throw into the balance against Germany and, though the Tsar's soldiers had not defended the frontiers of France directly, they had exerted decisive influence on the campaign of 1914. Now the Tsar was dead and the shreds of his armies, whether under white or red cockades or neither, were fighting each other as well as

Allied invaders for his empire. There was nothing to be hoped for from Russia.

Yet this confusion in the east offered French diplomacy an intriguing range of initiatives, as the Quai d'Orsay had been quick to realise. Ever since Richelieu had set the Protestant Swedes on the Catholic Austrians in the Thirty Years War, France had pursued with some consistency a policy of seeking allies among the states of eastern Europe, small as well as large, in order to maintain a balance against which ever power was controlling the centre. The

'Divide and avoid being ruled' was the theory which the French could now practise again in eastern Europe

The French general Pellé (saluting, left) reviews Czech troops with Beneš (centre) in Prague

consolidation of eastern Europe during the previous century and a half into the three empires of Romanov, Habsburg and Hohenzollern had progressively reduced the scope for this sort of divisive diplomacy. Their defeat and collapse in 1917-18 revived the prospects for a successful French eastern policy.

The application of the principle of national self-determination had created out of the débris three new states, Poland, Yugoslavia and Czechoslovakia, and greatly enlarged the existing state of Rumania. All had as yet to establish their diplomatic horizons and identify their friends and none more urgently than Poland. In open conflict with the Bolsheviks on her eastern frontiers, which had not yet been demarcated, she was also in effect at war with an illegal German army to the west. And since a fear of revolution had an even stronger hold on the French official imagination than the spectre of a resurgent Germany, there was perhaps no other state with whom she had such strong common interest. Already established as an enthusiastic sponsor of the cause of Polish nationhood, France had determined by the end of 1919 to secure a firm alliance.

Poland's protector
She had already done much to further Poland's ambitions. A Polish army nearly 100,000 strong, under the command of General Haller, had been raised by France from among the Poles of German nationality taken prisoner on the Western Front and in February 1919 it was despatched to the Baltic. At the Paris Peace Conference Clemenceau had endorsed Polish proposals for the demarcation of her frontiers. If these had been accepted Poland would have gained relatively more from the peace than any of her associates – an enviable outcome, as Lloyd George was to point out, for a people who had fought longer and harder for the defeated enemy (in a variety of puppet 'legions') than they had for the Allies. The frontiers to which Poland laid claim in her original deposition to the Peace Conference in January 1919 were those of 1772, before the first of the Partitions between Prussia, Russia and Austria. The historical and demographic case for this apparently reasonable proposal was brilliantly argued by the chief Polish representative, but its adoption would nevertheless have been grossly unjust, in terms of national self-determination, to many

Hungarian leader Béla Kun faced Czech and Rumanian invasions in his few months in power

millions of Germans and Ukrainians and to a considerable number of Lithuanians. In answer to British and American misgivings France had the matter referred to a sub-committee. Her two Allies apparently failed to notice that this was controlled by Frenchmen and other supporters of the Polish cause. The Poles for their part pointed out that most of the territory they claimed was already under their military control. When German *Freikorps* began an advance to recapture Poznan province in February, Foch threatened not to renew the Armistice in the west unless Berlin ordered their withdrawal.

Poland gained much by her policy of simultaneous diplomatic and military offensives. For although she was eventually awarded much less than she had originally claimed, many of the disputed areas to which she laid claim came her way in the end because she was able by maintaining a military presence there to gerrymander plebiscites or wear out the patience of international boundary commissioners.

This policy failed completely in her relations with Russia, the only one of her neighbours who was something like a match for her militarily, while being quite immune to her diplomatic manoeuvres. Between them, things came in the end to a straight fight, culminating in a remarkable Polish victory outside Warsaw, which a British observer, Lord d'Abernon, was to characterise as the 18th decisive battle of the world. If this was exaggerated, the battle was certainly crucial not only for the future of Poland but for the whole of eastern Europe, and its outcome fully justified the hopes France had invested in Pilsudski. It also justified the very considerable military investment with which France had supported those hopes and the risk she had taken in associating a leading French soldier, General Weygand, with the direction of Polish strategy. The successful outcome of the campaign and the extremely favourable boundary settlement which Poland achieved as a result in March 1921 was consolidated by a treaty, signed in

February by France and Poland, which bound the two governments to take 'concerted measures for the defence of their territory and the protection of their legitimate interests'. This would allow France to intervene in eastern European affairs in the future if it suited her to do so, and at the same time it would entitle her, if necessary, to call on Polish assistance against Germany. It is doubtful, however, whether the treaty was in the best interests of Poland. But the same could be said of the policy Poland had pursued since the end of the war, of which this treaty was only one of the consequences. To profit from the temporary weakness of a big neighbour is always dangerous. Poland had profited extortionately from the misfortunes of her two big neighbours, Germany and Russia. That did not augur well for her future, nor did it lay a firm foundation for France's eastern policy.

A Little Entente

But while Weygand had been working the Miracle of the Vistula, and for some time before that, France had been cultivating relations with the southern group of successor states that became known as the 'Little Entente'. Their willingness to entertain French overtures was determined in part by sentimental reasons, but more strongly by their need to secure a strong protector against the *revanchisme* of the states at whose expense they had come into existence. Their situation has been graphically described as bearing 'upon the map . . . a suggestive likeness to the jaws of a hungry dog closing upon an already well-gnawed cutlet, which was following another morsel down the animal's throat: the cutlet represented the meagre remains of Austria, Hungary was the meat already swallowed, the upper and lower jaws were respectively Czechoslovakia and Yugoslavia, while the muscle which worked them was comprised in Rumania.'

Between 1920 and 1921 Czechoslovakia, Yugoslavia and Rumania completed a triad of treaties binding themselves to uphold the Trianon Treaty imposed on Hungary by the Allies at Paris, and providing for mutual defence in the event of Hungarian attack. They realised that they would have to fight their own battles, diplomatic if not military, in order to gain credibility with friends and enemies alike.

When the Emperor Charles, now excluded from his Austrian empire, attempted in March 1921 to return to his kingdom of Hungary for the first time since the war, he was induced to leave largely through the efforts of the major powers. On the second occasion, in October, it was the powers directly concerned, the 'Little Entente' states, who brought about his departure by threatening joint military action against Hungary if Charles were not expelled and debarred from ever again setting foot in Hungarian territory. In face of this threat, which had the approval of the great powers, Hungary acceded to all the demands made of her.

This outcome conferred the seal of success on the Little Entente, in the eyes of its own members and of the outside world. It confirmed, in particular, the rightness of Benes' idea, as opposed to Ionescu's inflated views of the sort of diplomatic rôle that the successor states should try to play. Benes opposed any attempt to weld out of them a monolithic buffer zone stand-

Above: Admiral Horthy, Regent of Hungary, the country most feared by the Little Entente

Above: Hungarian President Count Károlyi, forced out of office by Béla Kun's Communists

ing between Russia and Germany, which, with western support, would seek to influence their policy. That, in his view, was a dangerous policy, which could lead, sooner or later, to another major conflict. For that reason he was opposed to the Little Entente entering into too close a relationship with France, of whose *cordon sanitaire* solution for her own international difficulties he was well aware, or with Poland, whom he regarded as being too closely committed to France. The Little Entente states nevertheless entered into treaties with France—Czechoslovakia and Yugoslavia in 1924 and Rumania in 1926—and all three modelled their armies on hers. One by one they settled their differences with Poland. But the vision with which France had comforted herself after the First World War of an anti-German and anti-Bolshevik buffer zone of fifty million people never materialised.

[*For John Keegan's biography, see page 96.*]

THE 'STAB IN THE BACK'
GERMANY'S FACE-SAVING MYTH

When Germany finally capitulated on the basis of the Fourteen Points during the negotiations of October and early November 1918, there was little doubt on anyone's part, especially those in the military, that Germany had been defeated — by the blockade, by the American entry into the war, by the failure of the Ludendorff offensive — but above all by the inevitably superior force of arms of the Allies. As the troops marched back to the Fatherland the poverty and degradation of the German people made an indelible imprint upon those who witnessed it. During a period of more than six months in which Germany's desperate economic plight was prolonged by the blockade, it became imperative that Germany should sign a peace treaty as soon as possible or face not only continued economic deprivation, but a complete Allied occupation as well, a contingency which appeared very real during the week before the signing of the Versailles Treaty. Nevertheless, as time passed the myth arose that the German military machine headed by the Kaiser did not lose the war and that the war was only lost because of the disloyalty of traitors at home. Eventually even Ludendorff and Hindenburg themselves — the very men who suggested surrender because it was impossible to fight on — supported this view. The origin of the 'stab-in-the-back' myth is especially important when one considers that it was primarily this interpretation of recent history which helped Adolf Hitler's rise to power in the early 1930s. Who created the myth? And why did it have such widespread appeal?

According to the terms of the Treaty of Versailles no group had more to lose than the German armed forces. The navy was to be scuttled (rather than turning it over to the Allies), the manufacture of most arms prohibited and the army itself reduced to little more than a glorified police force. It was not surprising that the Cabinet viewed the attitude of the army with a certain suspicion during the last days before Germany signed the Treaty. General Gröner, for one, recognised the fact that a Socialist government under the Weimar régime would not consider the maintenance of a large standing army a vital objective in its postwar plans, and even conservative figures such as Brockdorff-Rantzau, who was a vital figure in the early stage of the negotiations with the Allies, did not trust the General Staff. Ludendorff was in an especially suspect position, since it was his attitude as well as the attitude of many members of the officer corps which hindered the government's attempts to negotiate a rapid settlement with the Allies.

Before Brockdorff-Rantzau left for Versailles General Gröner appeared before the full Cabinet to explain the position of the General Staff. He urged that a large German army should be maintained after the peace, and that universal conscription be made an integral part of German diplomacy at the Conference. Furthermore, it was proposed that Germany should offer the Allies a united front against Bolshevism — that Germany, in concert with the Allies, should act as a bulwark against westward spread of Communism — and that the officer corps, commanding a strong German army, should stand in the front line of this crusade. This position was later adopted not only by Hitler, but even by the officers who engineered the plot of July 20, 1944, which narrowly failed to overthrow the Führer and negotiate a settlement of the Second World War on this basis. In short, this was an attractive proposal for western liberals and conservatives, and Gröner knew it. He also recognised that this manoeuvre would enable the Germans to keep a large army and general staff with the blessing of the victorious Allies. Brockdorff-Rantzau, however, rejected this proposal. He could not easily argue to the victors that it was in their immediate interests to maintain a large German army, particularly since any enthusiasm which existed for the invasion of Soviet Russia was quickly dwindling away. The Cabinet realistically rejected Gröner's view, and in subsequent private conversations Gröner suggested to Brockdorff-Rantzau that the German government was in danger of 'showing the white feather'. Nothing could have been more infuriating to a conservative patriot such as Brockdorff-Rantzau, and mutual recriminations between the two men were not quickly forgotten.

Peace with dishonour

The confrontation between Gröner, representing the General Staff, and the government came at a time when the *Dolchstoss* ('stab-in-the-back') theory was just beginning to gain wider acceptance. Immediately after the war, with famine and military exhaustion still problems, only military figures who had seen little action or who were politically reactionary even by the standards of the General Staff held the view that cowardly civilians, probably socialists or Jews, had stabbed the loyal German army and people in the back by creating an atmosphere of pacifism and defeatism on the home front. Nevertheless as time passed more people came to share the convenient view that the German army would have won the war had it not been for the left-wingers, often led by Jews, who had urged an end to the war on any but the most oppressive terms. The slogan 'peace without victory', which was urged by many realistic Germans during the war, was increasingly a slogan thrown in the faces of those who (often patriotically) felt that it would have been best for

Germany to have left the war before the summer of 1918. After that point, Germany was forced to make peace on Allied terms. But a scapegoat for Germany's failure had to be found to ease the consciences of many who had supported the war until the bitter end. The origin of the expression *Dolchstoss* and the legend which surrounded it is somewhat unclear. One version, perhaps apocryphal, had it that Ludendorff was dining with the head of the British military mission in Berlin, General Sir Neill Malcolm, when Ludendorff started a tirade blaming traitors and revolutionaries for having betrayed Germany at the crucial moment in 1918 when victory was at hand. Malcolm asked him, 'Do you mean, General, that you were stabbed in the back?' 'Yes, yes,' Ludendorff was said to have exclaimed, 'that's it exactly. We were stabbed in the back!' From about that time onwards, or at least from the time when the German delegation first went to Versailles to learn of the peace terms, it became an article of faith among German officers that no less an authority than a British general had suggested that Germany was forced to surrender because of betrayal at home.

There was, of course, a certain amount of evidence to support this theory. After all, the Allies had not occupied German territory until the very last days of the war, and even then the area was not large. When the war ended the Germans were still in occupation of most of Belgium and a good part of France, as well as all of Luxembourg and huge territories on the Eastern Front gained after Brest-Litovsk. On the other hand the claim that the Germans had left the battlefield unvanquished was absolutely false. Their retreat was not, as the officer corps suggested, merely a withdrawal to more defensible positions. Had the Armistice not been negotiated, there was little in November 1918 to prevent the occupation of the Rhineland, if not the whole of Germany. But with the occupation of only a portion of Germany having taken place after the Armistice, the officer corps was joined by a large section of the German public in assuming that the occupation was a direct result of the Armistice, rather than its being a *sauve qui peut* affair which in fact spared Germany even greater humiliation.

The sequence of events which took place at the end of the war gave further credence to the *Dolchstoss* legend. The Kaiser had been overthrown; a Republic, somewhat socialist in character, replaced it; the Armistice was signed. A communist *Putsch*, led by two Jews, Luxemburg and Liebknecht, followed, and was put down by the army soon afterwards. Thus, it was easy for simple minds and those who were less simple but were seeking a scapegoat to place the blame for the capitulation on Jews, socialists, and traitors who desired a

In wartime it is important not to rock the boat. Not only pacifists, but those who disagree with the cause or the conduct of the war, may find themselves stigmatised as traitors. If the war is won, dissenters may be forgiven, but not if it is lost. A nation that loses a war desperately needs an excuse, and the search for scapegoats can become obsessive. In 1918 and 1919 Germany did not have far to look. *S. L. Mayer. Below:* The English version of the myth, from *Punch,* October 1918. 'The Traitor', Bernard Partridge's uncompromising cartoon of the sly-faced British worker sneaking up to stab courageous Tommy in the back

German defeat all along. The fact that the leaders of the General Staff, Hindenburg and Ludendorff, had suggested an armistice to the Kaiser two months before the revolution and capitulation was conveniently forgotten even by those who had proposed it. Rather than assuming that the imminent defeat had been the cause of panic and revolution, it was strongly suggested that the revolution forced defeat upon a still viable, still loyal German army. The stab-in-the-back legend

quickly gained adherents and this view was expressed by Ebert and Gustav Stresemann, two of the strongest supporters of the Weimar régime. On the whole, the majority Socialists chose to ignore the *Dolchstoss* thesis and they made little or no effort to counteract it, although the legend eventually helped to bring about the Socialists' (and indeed the Republic's) own destruction. It became a generally accepted view that served both the General Staff, in the subsequent years of covert

military build-up, and the National Socialists, who later used the *Dolchstoss* legend to whip up support for Adolf Hitler during the Depression. When the military clauses of the Treaty of Versailles became known the officer corps determined to avenge their honour at some future date. At the same time the German people were unable to come to terms with the shock of the Versailles settlement. It was a disastrous way to begin the democratic experiment of the Weimar Republic.

By the autumn of 1919 it became clear to the Social Democrats that the *Dolchstoss* legend implied that they were a part of the 'back-stabbing' cabal which had caused the defeat. The leaders of the government were being blamed for having signed the *Versaillerdiktat* and having lost a war they had sought to end. Charged by many extremists with being 'November criminals', the government established a parliamentary commission to investigate the details of the responsibility for the Armistice and the circumstances leading to it. They invited Hindenburg to come to Berlin to testify. When he arrived he was greeted by a huge popular demonstration of support. Crowds of Berliners cheered him wherever he went, and the army greeted him with a guard of honour at the railroad station when he arrived. The hearing was a disaster. Hindenburg, who commanded great respect even among those charged with interrogating him, ignored the questions posed and read out a lengthy statement based on the 'stab-in-the-back' theory. The initiative had been lost to the ageing general, and when the hearing broke up the *Dolchstoss* legend had been more firmly implanted than ever. He was not called to testify again. The government could not get him out of Berlin fast enough. Their strategy had backfired, and the situation was not improved when Hindenburg, in his dotage, became President of the Weimar Republic in 1925. He was its second and last President. When he died in 1934 he had succeeded in presiding over the collapse of the Weimar régime and its replacement by the dictatorship of the Nazi Party and Adolf Hitler. The *Dolchstoss* legend was raised to an article of faith, and a national policy, including rearmament, the persecution of the Jews and war, was based largely on public support of the theory. In the long run, however, the Weimar Republic was destroyed, not by a stab in the back, but by the ineptitude of its creators.

Further Reading
Carsten, F. L., *The Reichswehr and Politics, 1918 to 1933* (Clarendon Press 1966)
Watt, Richard M., *The Kings Depart* (New York, Simon and Schuster 1968)

[*For S. L. Mayer's biography, see page 19.*]

crats and Social Democrats perpetrated the original 'stab in the back' by inciting the soldiers at the Front to desert. The poster warns that to re-elect them would be to inflict a second wound and make the German people slaves of the Entente. Dated 1924, it shows the persistence of the myth. *Opposite:* A cartoon showing the departure of the German POWs. This illustrates the French view that, victors or not, they had suffered far more intensely than the Germans, who they thought were getting off much too lightly

Wer hat im **Weltkrieg** dem deutschen Heere den Dolchstoß versetzt? Wer ist schuld daran, daß unser Volk und Vaterland so tief ins Unglück sinken mußte? Der Parteisekretär der Sozialdemokraten **Vater** sagt es nach der Revolution 1918 in Magdeburg:

„**Wir** haben unsere Leute, die an die Front gingen, zur Fahnenflucht veranlaßt. Die Fahnenflüchtigen haben wir organisiert, mit falschen Papieren ausgestattet, mit Geld und unterschriftslosen Flugblättern versehen. **Wir** haben diese Leute nach allen Himmelsrichtungen, hauptsächlich wieder an die Front geschickt, damit sie die Frontsoldaten bearbeiten und die Front zermürben sollten. Diese haben die Soldaten bestimmt, überzulaufen, und so hat sich der Verfall allmählich, aber sicher vollzogen."

Wer hat die Sozialdemokratie hierbei unterstützt? Die Demokraten und die Leute um Erzberger. Jetzt, am 7. Dezember, soll das Deutsche Volk den

zweiten Dolchstoß

erhalten. Sozialdemokraten in Gemeinschaft mit den Demokraten wollen uns

zu Sklaven der Entente machen,

wollen uns für immer zugrunde richten.

Wollt ihr das nicht,
dann
Wählt deutschnational!

3415

'VOTES FOR WOMEN'

Brown Brothers

AMERICAN STYLE

During the war, American women had the opportunity to prove themselves. They worked in munitions factories and made various contributions to the war effort. After this, the prewar level of male domination could not be allowed to return. In January 1918 women's suffrage passed through the House of Representatives. The end was in sight. *Judith Holmes.*
Left: A purposeful band of suffragettes demonstrates in New York in 1912. *Below:* Members of the American Woman's League for Self Defence receive military training in 1918

At a stormy session in Nashville on August 18, 1920, Tennessee became the 36th state to ratify the 19th Amendment to the United States Constitution. This provided the majority of states necessary to adopt the amendment and to give American women national suffrage well ahead of their sisters in, for example, Great Britain (where they were not granted equal suffrage until 1928), France (1944) and Switzerland, where women could not vote until 1970.

This victory was the result not only of a long and arduous political campaign but of a whole series of social and political changes which, precipitated by the First World War, produced a new world where women could at last be considered the intellectual and political equals of their husbands, brothers and sons.

The roots of the changes which led women to demand and finally to get the vote stretch far back into the 19th Century, when, with the coming of the Industrial Revolution, there was a great improvement in the standard of living for middle-class women, leaving them with more leisure to devote to things outside the home. Many of the housewife's traditional jobs found their way into shops and factories and the work that was left was made easier by the development of machines. By 1900 American women were much more independent than their contemporaries in England and France; they were respected and spoiled in their own country and many foreign visitors felt that they were regarded as 'superior beings'. Most state universities had been open to women from the late 1870s and several women's colleges had been founded at about the same time. The number of women in industry and commerce had rocketed from 2,500,000 in 1800 to 5,300,000 in 1900.

Women who did not go to work found diversion in the clubs that seemed to spring up like mushrooms and ranged from Browning and Shakespeare 'circles' to 'Ladies' High Jinks'. In many communities the local women's club was the only organisation devoted to civic improvement. As these women tried to cope with the evils of drink, prostitution, corrupt politicians and employers who exploited their workers (often women and children) many became convinced that the reforms they wanted could be carried out much faster if only they had the vote themselves. Increasing confidence in their ability to work effectively outside their homes and the example of women in Wyoming, Colorado, Utah and Idaho who were already voting in state and local elections spurred them on.

The National American Woman Suffrage Association (NAWSA) had been active since 1890, but things went slowly until 1910 when the movement was given a new impetus by the addition of Washington to the list of states granting women suffrage. In 1911 California followed suit by the narrowest of margins after a dazzling campaign. Women got the vote in Arizona, Kansas and Oregon in 1912 and in Illinois in 1913. But by this time the anti-suffragists were on guard and the movement facing severe opposition; liquor interests especially, rightly fearing that votes for women meant votes for prohibition, spent huge sums of money to counteract suffragist propaganda. In these circumstances, on the eve of war in Europe, the suffragist leaders decided to re-group their forces and concentrate on pushing through an amendment to the Federal Constitution. Their ranks had grown with the influx of millions of immigrants into America after the mid-1880s; at about the same time as southern women were beginning to tell their husbands how humiliating it was to be ruled by their former slaves, northern women were saying that the descendants of the great men of 1776 should not have to submit to laws made by men from every corner of the earth. It required a delicate sense of balance to reconcile

these views with the claim that women deserved the vote because all human beings were equal.

As the NAWSA settled down to map out their plans for assailing the Capitol they were joined by a young, well-educated Quaker named Alice Paul who arrived from England in January 1913. Miss Paul had been fired with the evangelical spirit of the radical English suffragettes and was determined to inject some of their passion and drama into the American movement. To this end she organised a march of 5,000 women through the centre of Washington on the day before Woodrow Wilson was inaugurated as President. There had been suffrage marches before, but this was the first to become a riot. As the procession approached the White House it was blocked by a hostile crowd and the women were spat on, slapped, tripped up, pelted with burning cigar stubs and insulted. In the end troops had to be brought in from Fort Meyer to restore order. Comparing this with the English demonstrations there were relatively few casualties, but there had been enough victimisation for the women to appear martyrs; and a touch of martyrdom was just what was needed. Money and recruits poured in.

The NAWSA welcomed the rebirth Miss Paul had stimulated, but they were embarrassed as well. Apart from everything else, she was determined to use the political tactics of the English movement by holding the party in power responsible for the delay in granting women's suffrage. This tactic was entirely inappropriate in America where the administration's control of Congress was never very secure and where votes from both parties would be needed to push the amendment through. Within a few months Miss Paul had broken away from the NAWSA and formed her own Congressional Union (later to become the Woman's Party), a dynamic organisation that was operating in all 48 states within two years.

The NAWSA wobbled along until December 1915 when Mrs Carrie Chapman Catt was elected President. The 'Big Boss', as she was affectionately known, was affable, witty, and possessed a singular gift for administrative leadership. In less than two years she had pulled the NAWSA together, appointed a board of wealthy women with time to spare, employed a professional staff for them to work with and set up a six-year plan for them to work for.

There were two challenges that had to be faced right away: America's entry into the First World War and the growing militancy of the Woman's Party. American women, like most of their countrymen, were horrified by the carnage in Europe and did not believe that the United States had anything to gain by becoming a party to it, although they were more sympathetic to the Allies than to the Central Powers.

But once war was imminent a combination of prudence and patriotism led to rapid changes of heart. Mrs Catt suppressed her own pacifist tendencies and, although the NAWSA continued to put votes for women first, it pledged aid and support to the President more than a month before America joined the war. Its war aims were to protect women workers from exploitation, to increase food production, to help in Red Cross work and to Americanise the alien. But the suffragists always remembered the experiences of Susan B. Anthony and Elizabeth Stanton during the Civil War; they had dropped all suffrage agitation in favour of war work on the promise that when the war was over they would be 'taken care of'. Of course the promise proved hollow. And so for the next three years the NAWSA kept a complete file of politicians indicating which of them was favourable to, doubtful about, or opposed to women's suffrage. They kept constant pressure on them, and cultivated Congressmen — and their wives. Their tepid attitude towards the war did not go unnoticed, especially by the anti-suffragists who, due to the

Below: Aggressive masculinity—the Cavalry Corps of the American Woman's League for Self Defence holds a public drill on Broadway. *Opposite top:* The traditional rôle persists— patriotic Red Cross workers knitting socks for the men at the Front. *Bottom:* Equality at last? Heavily muffled in protective clothing, women workers weld the fins on to bombs

National Archives

Brown Brothers

passions of war and their own rapidly receding prospects, were getting more antagonistic by the day. Much of their hostility was neutralised, however, by Dr Anna Howard Shaw who, as former president of the NAWSA and Chairman of the Women's Committee of the Council of National Defence, did enough patriotic cheer-leading to persuade doubters of the NAWSA's sincere desire for victory. She was also fighting her own private war with the Federal bureaucracy, trying to see that women were not exploited during the emergency, although there was not much she could do to prevent it.

'Democracy Begins at Home'

The militant Woman's Party did no war work at all and its activities soon threatened to halt all progress and to destroy what had already been achieved. The White House had been picketed since January 1917 and at first nothing happened. War was declared in April, but the picketing continued; the Woman's Party included many Quakers who were opposed to all war, and a number of radical socialists like Crystal Eastman and Emma Goldman who were opposed to this war in particular. By June their actions were beginning to strike many Americans as unpatriotic; banners referring to 'Kaiser Wilson' and suggesting that 'Democracy Begins At Home' made things worse. Mob violence erupted, the pickets were mauled and their banners

National Archives

torn down, often with official encouragement. They were arrested and, when they refused to pay their fines, were given prison sentences of up to six months. Poor gaol conditions and the brutality to which they were subjected led them to go on hunger strikes in imitation of English suffragettes. Eventually the government was forced to back down and they were released at the end of 1917.

Many other American women went all out for the war effort. They knitted socks, saved fuel, collected peach stones. Flower-sellers filled the streets in support of Belgian babies (whose hands, as most children knew, had been cut off personally by the Kaiser). Many suddenly found themselves making grenades, collecting street-car fares and engaging in scores of tasks hitherto forbidden by convention. When the navy ran short of clerks and had no appropriation for more civilian help Secretary Josephus Daniels asked 'Is there any law that says that a yeoman must be a man? Then enroll women!' and before long there were 11,000 smartly uniformed 'yeoman-ettes'. A few daring souls—ambulance drivers, nurses and Salvation Army and YWCA workers—even got to France where they were received with warm camaraderie, as equals, by the troops.

The call for women and girls to enter the munitions factories in 1917-18 had far-reaching effects in breaking down any lingering Victorian ideas about the rôle of females in society. The actual number of women employed was not large, but they demonstrated their ability to do the job. When the men came home, of course, many women lost their jobs and had to return to their traditional occupations, at a wage scale lower than that for men, simply because they were women. They felt the injustice deeply and that heightened their sense of their own cause.

Down with corsets!

If, in the long run, the American woman's economic status was not materially affected by the war, it caused a revolution in her social status. Even before the war the stiff corsets of 1910 had been going out of fashion and girls with conservative parents had been forced surreptitiously to discard them in cars and dressing-rooms or risk being called 'Old Ironsides' by the boys. But when young women had to cut off their hair and don overalls and goggles to work in factories, the last bonds were broken and the way was clear for short skirts, bobbed hair, sports clothes, and ultimately shorts and slacks.

The young men who went to the Continent had their eyes opened, as did the nurses, Red Cross and YWCA girls. They all returned to a country where there was more of everything—leisure, cars, movies, dance halls, jazz—even liquor, for Prohibition only made drinking more exciting. In 1910, at a White House dinner, the wife of the Russian Ambassador asked President Taft for a cigarette. It took his military aide some time to locate one—he finally got it from one of the musicians—and the shocking story was hushed up. Ten years later cigarettes were everywhere and girls were being exhorted to 'Be nonchalant—smoke a Murad'.

But all this freedom was to come later. In 1917-18 there was a war to fight, at home as well as abroad. The first great victory came on January 10, 1918 (the day that

'You were born the companion of man and became his slave . . . you grew to like the condition and think it natural.' Laclos, 1783

Top: Pillars of the movement—Mrs Catt (left) and Dr Shaw at a suffrage meeting. *Bottom:* Alice Paul, who imported English-style tactics

Great Britain granted suffrage to some of her women), when President Wilson called for women's suffrage as a war measure; the bill passed the House of Representatives by the narrowest of margins. But the Senate refused to act before Congress adjourned for the summer, and the lobbying had to begin all over again.

The suffragists were fighting opposition from the South and from a group centred in Massachusetts headed by several rich influential woman anti-suffragists. On October 1, 1918 the amendment failed to pass the Senate by two votes. More intense lobbying followed, and the next time it was before the Senate (on February 10, 1919) it only failed by one vote. By this time Wilson was at Versailles and the Woman's Party was ostentatiously burning any and all of his speeches that referred to 'freedom' in front of the White House. The suffragists' card files showed one Senator Harris of Georgia as being the opponent who could most easily be persuaded to change his vote; finally, under personal as well as public pressure from Alice Paul, Wilson summoned Harris to France. On his return to America Harris announced that he would support the amendment. 12 other Senators jumped on the band-wagon once victory was certain, and the amendment was passed on June 4 by a vote of 66 to 30.

But the fight was not yet over: under the American system the amendment had to be ratified by 36 of the 48 states before it became law. Since only 13 states needed to vote against it to block its adoption and the 11 southern states could practically be abandoned as hopeless, the suffragists needed a clean sweep in the rest of the country.

Wisconsin was the first to ratify the amendment on June 10, with Michigan a close second. Kansas, Ohio and New York followed on June 16 and Illinois on June 17. And so it went, state by state, until by March 1920 35 states had agreed to the suffrage; there was only one to go. The remaining opponents included eight southern states where there was absolutely no hope, Maryland and Delaware who had already tabled the amendment, and Vermont, Connecticut and Tennessee. In Vermont and Connecticut the governors were last-ditch fighters against both Prohibition and suffrage, so that left Tennessee where soon every element which had ever opposed votes for women rallied for the last battle. The politics were not of the cleanest; every member of the Tennessee Legislature marked 'bribable' in the NAWSA card file eventually voted against ratification. But the amendment scraped by the Senate and then, in a dramatic climax, passed the House by one vote. The final campaign for women's suffrage had cost millions of dollars, and some two million women had in some way contributed to the effort.

Further Reading
Breckinridge, S. P., *Women in the 20th Century*
Kraditor, Aileen S., *The Ideas of the Woman Suffrage Movement, 1890-1920*
Sinclair, Andrew, *The Emancipation of the American Woman*
Steinson, B. J., *Female activism in World War I: the American women's peace, suffrage, preparedness and relief movements, 1914-18* (Michigan: University Microfilms International 1982)

JUDITH HOLMES was educated at the University of Michigan and Yale and earns her living as a freelance writer; among her books is a history of the 1936 Olympic Games.

THE RUSSO-POLISH WAR

The apparent consolidation of Bolshevik rule in
Russia revived the old struggle over the balance of
power in the peripheral states to the west. Speeches
of Communist leaders contained the same expansionist aims that Eastern Europe had so
recently escaped under the former Tsarist Empire.
But Joseph Piłsudski, leading Polish statesman,
was determined to resist Soviet tutelage: his
alternative was for the threatened states to pool
their forces in order to stave off this new brand of
imperialism. *M. K. Dziewanowski. Above:* Strewn
with flowers and armed with scythes, grave Polish
recruits march off to the war with Russia

In order to understand the Russo-Polish War of 1920 one has to bear in mind that it formed the climax to a series of events unleashed in Eastern Europe by the Bolshevik Revolution. The Revolution, with its millennial dreams of a European Communist Federation, constituted a grave danger to the multi-national western fringe of the former Tsarist Empire, which had been gradually moving towards freedom. Should Bolshevik objectives be achieved, the string of newly-emerged states on the western periphery of the former Tsarist Empire—Finland, Estonia, Latvia, Lithuania and Poland—would be drawn back into Russia as Soviet republics. This was well understood by the Polish statesman, Piłsudski, an old socialist fighter and a keen student of ethnic problems in Eastern Europe. By mid-November, 1918, when Piłsudski established himself in Warsaw as head of state of the reborn Polish Republic, Eastern Europe was in turmoil. German rule was disintegrating and a political power vacuum existed as a result; the pressure of Soviet revolutionary forces could be felt everywhere. Civil war in Finland was already in full swing and its outcome was far from decided, despite the vigorous support of a crack German auxiliary force, commanded by Count Rudiger von der Goltz. On November 29, 1918, Estonia and Latvia had been overwhelmed by native Bolsheviks supported from Moscow; an Estonian Workers' Council was set up in the Communist-occupied area which claimed authority over the entire country. By December 10 more than half of Estonia was in Communist hands. In a last-ditch effort the Estonian people, supported by the En-

tente, managed to stave off the immediate threat to the existence of their tiny country. But in Latvia things were different. There, because of the existence of numerous large estates and a huge rural proletariat, the Bolsheviks could command much more substantial popular support. In January 1919, Riga, the capital, was captured by the Red Army which was hailed by mutinous local workers.

Closer to Poland, the Lithuanian capital, Vilna, after being evacuated by the Germans, was taken by the Bolsheviks on January 5, 1919. By the middle of January, a large slice of Lithuania and three-quarters of Latvia was already under Communist rule. The national government of Latvia sought refuge in Courland, protected chiefly by German volunteers and

by the Baltic militia. This retreat gave the Russian Bolshevik régime a precious foothold on the Baltic Sea, the only access to the Baltic south of Petrograd. As the Moscow paper *Izvestia* announced triumphantly on December 25, 1918, 'the Baltic Sea is now transformed into the Sea of Social Revolution'. But the westward drive of the Russian Communist forces had far more distant objectives, clarified in a speech by Trotsky on October 30, 1918: 'Free Latvia, free Poland and Lithuania, free Finland, and, on the other side, free Ukraine will not be a wedge, but a uniting link, between Soviet Russia and the future Soviet Germany and Austria-Hungary. This is the beginning of a European Communist Federation—a union of the proletarian republics of Europe.'

Right: Although discipline in the Red Army had come a long way, under Trotsky's command, since the chaos of 1917 the Communists were still hampered by inexperience and disorganisation. Here a soldier is prosecuted at an impromptu court-martial at Louza, 1920. *Below:* Soviet outpost outside Warsaw. After the first flush of victories the Polish army was beaten back to the capital, worn down by lack of arms and failing allies

Hulton Picture Library

The Communist successes in the Baltic area must be viewed against the upsurge of revolutionary trends throughout Central and Eastern Europe. In March of 1919 Béla Kun seized power in Hungary, a Soviet republic was set up in Bavaria, and a *coup d'état* attempted in Berlin. There was also mounting Spartacist ferment in Westphalia and Württemberg, and revolutionary fervour was on the increase in Austria. The Soviet government, conveying its congratulations to the two newly-established Communist republics of Hungary and Bavaria, expressed the hope that 'the proletariat of the whole world, having before its eyes the striking examples of the victorious uprisings of the workers in three countries of Europe, will follow them with complete faith in victory'.

At stake – independence

The issue at stake was whether Eastern Europe would become a conglomeration of national, independent, democratic states or be absorbed by Bolshevik Russia into a quasi-federation of Soviet republics led by Moscow. Piłsudski in particular was aware of the Communist alternative; he was determined to oppose the Bolshevik plan by maintaining his military strength and by political manoeuvring. He argued that a pooling of forces by the peoples recently liberated from Russia under the Tsars and now threatened by a new brand of imperialism was a vital necessity if they were to survive. Consequently, he sought co-operation with Poland's neighbours, lending them maximum assistance in their struggle for freedom; he hoped that by supporting her weaker neighbours Poland would strengthen herself, and that

in exchange for Poland's assistance the Lithuanians, Belorussians and Ukrainians would enter into alliances with Warsaw. This was especially true of Lithuania, to which he was sentimentally attached because of his origins and upbringing and which he wanted to see closely associated with Poland by means of federal ties. But the axis of the future balance of power in Eastern Europe was the Dnepr region in the Ukraine, rich in natural resources and strategically situated on the northern shores of the Black Sea. It had belonged to the Polish-Lithuanian Commonwealth for 200 years before the partition of the Commonwealth. Unfortunately for Piłsudski's plans, on November 1, 1918, the Ukrainians, encouraged by Austria, staged a coup in the capital city of Galicia, L'vov. The city, and then the entire eastern segment of the province, was captured and made an independent Ukrainian state.

Thus, when Piłsudski returned to Warsaw on November 10, the Polish-Ukrainian war in Eastern Galicia had been going on for ten days and French help had been enlisted in putting an end to the struggle. The available evidence indicates that Piłsudski wanted to safeguard for his country a minimum of interests in Galicia: this included the then largely Polish city of L'vov, and the oilfields of Borislav and Dorogobuzh. Piłsudski would be willing to trade the rest of Eastern Galicia in order to win over the Ukrainians of both the Galicia and the Dnepr regions to his concept of co-operation against Russia. He repeatedly expressed his doubts as to the wisdom of Poland incorporating all of Eastern Galicia with its troublesome Ukrainian majority. Piłsudski's views

about Eastern Europe may also be gauged from the letter which he wrote on May 31, 1919, to the chief Polish delegate at Versailles, Ignacy Paderewski. In the letter, Piłsudski mentioned the instructions which he had just given to another Lithuanian Pole, Eustachy Sapieha, then minister to the Court of St James. The instructions, stressed Piłsudski, were a key to his Eastern European policy. They made two points, which constituted the main goals of his policy in the area: firstly the necessity of neutralising the Russian influence in England and the importance of discrediting the idea of a Greater Russia with her western frontier on the River Bug; and secondly, the urgent need to support the idea of co-operation with Poland by all the nations situated between Poland and Russia proper, on the basis of a federation if possible. Piłsudski urged Paderewski to reach an understanding with the Lithuanians over Vilna and to hasten formal recognition of Estonia and Latvia, with whom Poland should be in close co-operation.

Nationalist preoccupation

This was a policy designed to promote *rapprochement* and co-operation among the nations of Eastern Europe. The trouble was that most Eastern Europeans, including Poles, were preoccupied with purely nationalistic objectives and ethnic vendettas. Consequently they were far from ready to accept a policy of moderation and mutual compromises and concessions. Some of the Galician Ukrainians were bent on an intransigent policy of everything or nothing; some would rather have thrown in their lot with the White Russian Army of

3423

Left: Polish women volunteers. *Right:* German caricature, entitled *The Great Allies (Entente communiqué, August 10),* of Allied failure to give practical help to the Poles in their war against the Bolsheviks. The message runs: *Rest easy, dear Pole, we are following your fate with the liveliest sympathy!* The Allied Mission to Warsaw looks on while Russia beats a helpless Poland. Despite its anxiety, the West gave no aid to the Poles

Denikin, than to strike a bargain with Poland. For most Poles of Galicia, on the other hand, the idea of partition amounted to treason. They were entirely absorbed by one thought: that of winning the struggle and incorporating the whole of Eastern Galicia. But, for Piłsudski, the fate of a few counties was not of crucial importance: beyond Galicia there loomed the Dnepr heartland, so vital, according to him, for the balance of power in Eastern Europe.

A calculated gamble

While in the case of Lithuania Piłsudski's objective was to share the controversial city of Vilna and thus make the Lithuanians accept the idea of a federal union with Poland, in the case of the Ukrainians the plan provided for splitting the disputed province of Eastern Galicia and striking a bargain with the moderate Ukrainian nationalists in order to attract the Dnepr Ukrainians to the idea of an alliance with Poland. Only by eliminating, or at least diminishing, the friction between the two nations could such an alliance be made possible. His partner was the Commander-in-Chief of the Ukrainian Directorate, Simon Petlyura, the main antagonist to Bolshevik rule on the Dnepr. After the defeat of his forces in the autumn of 1919, Petlyura had sought refuge on Polish territory, and soon entered into negotiations with Piłsudski for close co-operation against Soviet Russia in an effort to establish an independent Ukraine west of the Dnepr. The terms of co-operation were embodied in the Piłsudski-Petlyura agreement of April, 1920. In exchange for acceptance of the Polish possession of Eastern Galicia, Piłsudski promised Petlyura military aid for the reconquest of Ukraine on the right bank of the Dnepr and political as well as economic co-operation in the future.

The agreement was a calculated gamble. It represented a supreme effort to redress the balance of forces between Poland and Russia by means of a preventive war to forestall the imminent Soviet attack. It was an attempt to stop and at least partially reverse the continual process of Russian expansion over the adjacent non-Russian areas. The Muscovite-Russian Empire had originally grown in the west largely at the expense of the Polish-Lithuanian Commonwealth which from the middle of the 17th Century was in retreat. On the eve of partition, the Commonwealth numbered between twelve and thirteen million inhabitants while the Empire of Catherine II had comprised over twenty million people. At the end of the First World War the reborn Poland of about twenty-five million inhabitants had to face a vastly enlarged Russia consisting of about one hundred and fifty million people. Piłsudski's policy was not new. Unity against the aggressor had long been the policy of smaller but more compact states toward their larger, heterogeneous neighbours, and was in fact simply a political expression of the instinct for self-preservation on a national scale. Piłsudski's primary objective was to force, at a moment chosen by him, a showdown with Soviet Russia, which in his opinion was inevitable sooner or later. The contest should take place while Russia was weakened and Poland strengthened by the shift in the balance of power resulting from the deal with Petlyura.

The Piłsudski-Petlyura agreement was also an attempt to open up a new phase in Polish-Ukrainian relations. It was a bid to overlook, as far as possible, the past, to start a partnership and to seek co-operation on the basis of a close alliance against a mutual enemy. A common war effort would, with luck, extend into the postwar period, and cement the possibility of alliance between the two nations. In such an atmosphere, territorial issues might lose some of their rancour and the flow of population from one country to another attenuate them still further. The pact represented an attempt to transcend the bitter feud over Eastern Galicia and reconcile the two neighbouring peoples.

The Kiev campaign

With the agreement as a background a lightning offensive was launched against Soviet Russia on April 25, 1920, by Piłsudski and Petlyura. By the next day the Polish-Ukrainian forces had occupied the city of Zhitomir and the capital of the Ukraine, Kiev, was captured on May 8. The Polish-Ukrainian successes made a profound impression throughout the world. Despite the worsening of the economic situation, by the early spring of 1920 the military situation in Soviet Russia was, on the whole, settled. In Siberia the White forces had been liquidated; Denikin had also been beaten. Flushed with victories over the White generals, the Red leaders were full of confidence. In the Crimea, Wrangel was still reorganising the remnants of the battered White forces. In the north and north-east, on the Baltic front, military operations were over, and peace treaties were already signed with Estonia and Latvia. Now even the most natural and obdurate of Piłsudski's foes, the Galician-Ukrainians, were for a moment swayed by the capture of Kiev. Just before the Polish-Ukrainian offensive, on April 23, two Galician brigades composed of volunteers who had previously fought against the Poles in Eastern Galicia revolted and went over to the side of Petlyura. And after the first successes of the campaign, the guerilla leader, Nestor Makhno, also joined his peasant partisans to the Polish-Ukrainian forces.

A United States diplomat sent from Warsaw to report on the situation in Kiev concluded his report with the following words: *An independent Ukraine appears as the formula best suited to sap the Bolshevik tyranny in the richest part of Russia, and so prevent the restoration of Russian imperialism. From the point of view of the Ukrainians it affords the hope of a favourable solution of the agrarian question and a guarantee against foreign domination, Polish and Bolshevist. . . . Whether an independent Ukraine is to remain more than a temporary expedient, remains to be seen.*

According to the report, although the broad masses of the Dnepr Ukrainians were on the whole passive, they were not altogether uncaring. The report did not notice any tendency on the part of the Poles to entrench themselves permanently in the Ukraine or turn the country into a satellite: 'The Poles have expressed their intention not to remain in occupation of the Ukraine a moment longer than is necessary to assure the proper organisation of the country.'

Retreat to Warsaw

While the political situation was undoubtedly in a state of flux, much depended on the military outcome of the campaign. The initial success had theoretically allowed Petlyura to consolidate his position in the Kiev region, but Petlyura needed several months at least to recruit an army and organise its administration. The country, however, ravaged by civil war and eroded by the traditional scourge of the land—anarchy—did not budge. Despite the exhortations of Petlyura, Ukrainian forces expanded rather slowly, and altogether no more than a few thousand volunteers joined Petlyura during the four weeks of his stay in Kiev. Moreover, the Poles, themselves short of weapons, were also slow in providing arms and equipment for the

„Moralische Unterstützung für Polen"

Zeichnung von A. Kraska

(Ententemeldung vom 10. August)

Die großen Alliierten: „Sei ruhig, lieber Pole, wir verfolgen dein Schicksal mit lebhafter Sympathie!"

3425

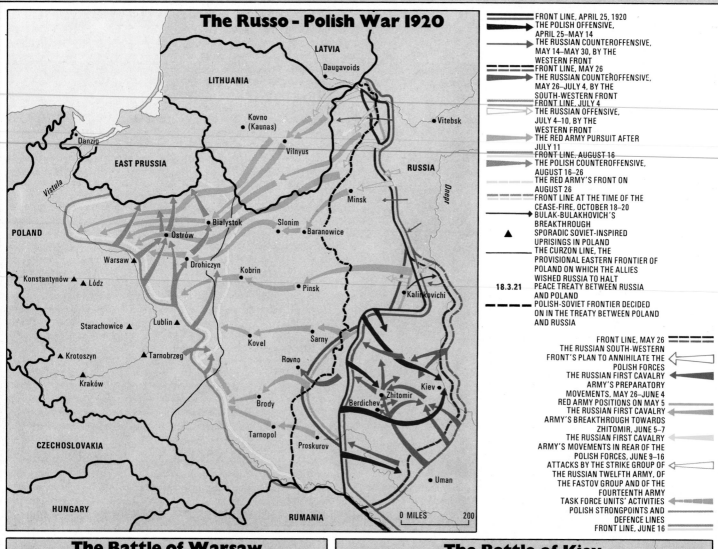

The Russo - Polish War 1920

LATVIA

Daugavoids

LITHUANIA

Kovno
(Kaunas)

Vilnyus

Danzig

EAST PRUSSIA

Vitebsk

Vistula

RUSSIA

Minsk

POLAND

Bialystok

Slonim

Baranowice

Dnepr

Ostrów

Drohiczyn

Kobrin

Warsaw ▲

Pinsk

Kalinkovichi

Konstantynów ▲ ▲ Łódź

Lublin ▲

Kovel

Sarny

Starachowice ▲

Rovno

▲ Krotoszyn

▲ Tarnobrzeg

Zhitomir

Kiev

Kraków ▲

Brody

Berdichev

CZECHOSLOVAKIA

Tarnopol

Proskurov

Uman

HUNGARY

RUMANIA

0 MILES 200

FRONT LINE, APRIL 25, 1920	
THE POLISH OFFENSIVE, APRIL 25–MAY 14	
THE RUSSIAN COUNTEROFFENSIVE, MAY 14–MAY 30, BY THE WESTERN FRONT	
FRONT LINE, MAY 26	
THE RUSSIAN COUNTEROFFENSIVE, MAY 26–JULY 4, BY THE SOUTH-WESTERN FRONT	
FRONT LINE, JULY 4	
THE RUSSIAN OFFENSIVE, JULY 4–10, BY THE WESTERN FRONT	
THE RED ARMY PURSUIT AFTER JULY 11	
FRONT LINE, AUGUST 16	
THE POLISH COUNTEROFFENSIVE, AUGUST 16–26	
THE RED ARMY'S FRONT ON AUGUST 26	
FRONT LINE AT THE TIME OF THE CEASE-FIRE, OCTOBER 18–20	
BULAK-BULAKHOVICH'S BREAKTHROUGH	
▲ SPORADIC SOVIET-INSPIRED UPRISINGS IN POLAND	
THE CURZON LINE, THE PROVISIONAL EASTERN FRONTIER OF POLAND ON WHICH THE ALLIES WISHED RUSSIA TO HALT	
18.3.21 PEACE TREATY BETWEEN RUSSIA AND POLAND	
POLISH-SOVIET FRONTIER DECIDED ON IN THE TREATY BETWEEN POLAND AND RUSSIA	

FRONT LINE, MAY 26	
THE RUSSIAN SOUTH-WESTERN FRONT'S PLAN TO ANNIHILATE THE POLISH FORCES	
THE RUSSIAN FIRST CAVALRY ARMY'S PREPARATORY MOVEMENTS, MAY 26–JUNE 4	
RED ARMY POSITIONS ON MAY 5	
THE RUSSIAN FIRST CAVALRY ARMY'S BREAKTHROUGH TOWARDS ZHITOMIR, JUNE 5–7	
THE RUSSIAN FIRST CAVALRY ARMY'S MOVEMENTS IN REAR OF THE POLISH FORCES, JUNE 9–16	
ATTACKS BY THE STRIKE GROUP OF THE RUSSIAN TWELFTH ARMY, OF THE FASTOV GROUP AND OF THE FOURTEENTH ARMY	
TASK FORCE UNITS' ACTIVITIES	
POLISH STRONGPOINTS AND DEFENCE LINES	
FRONT LINE, JUNE 16	

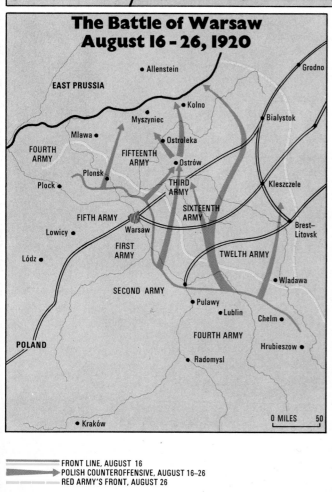

The Battle of Warsaw
August 16 - 26, 1920

EAST PRUSSIA

Allenstein

Grodno

Kolno

Myszyniec

Bialystok

Mlawa

Ostroleka

FOURTH ARMY

FIFTEENTH ARMY

Ostrów

Plonsk

THIRD ARMY

Kleszczele

Plock

SIXTEENTH ARMY

FIFTH ARMY

Lowicy

Warsaw

Brest-Litovsk

FIRST ARMY

Łódz

TWELTH ARMY

SECOND ARMY

Wladawa

Pulawy

Lublin

Chelm

FOURTH ARMY

Hrubieszow

POLAND

Radomysl

0 MILES 50

Kraków

FRONT LINE, AUGUST 16	
POLISH COUNTEROFFENSIVE, AUGUST 16–26	
RED ARMY'S FRONT, AUGUST 26	
RAILWAYS	

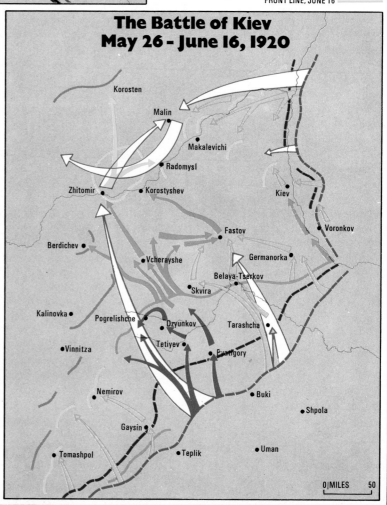

The Battle of Kiev
May 26 - June 16, 1920

Korosten

Malin

Makalevichi

Radomysl

Zhitomir

Korostyshev

Kiev

Voronkov

Berdichev

Fastov

Vcherayshe

Germanorka

Belaya-Tserkov

Skvira

Kalinovka

Pogrelishche

Dzyunkov

Tarashcha

Tetiyev

Pyatigory

Buki

Nemirov

Shpola

Gaysin

Uman

Tomashpol

Teplik

0 MILES 50

3426

Below: Three anti-Polish propaganda posters put out by the Bolsheviks; *left: Poland, the last dog of the Entente. Polish landowners want to smother the Russia of workers and peasants. Death to the landowners!* With French and British intervention in Russia ended Poland is represented as the last associate of the Entente to dispute Russian authority; *centre: Paris-trained pig.* Poland, in the arms of France — a reference to Poland's association with the Allies, in particular with Clemenceau's hopes of a *cordon sanitaire* as protection against Communist expansion; *right: Throw the Polish landlord out of the Ukraine.* The Russian peasant kicks the discredited Polish land-owner off his land. *Bottom:* Polish cavalry mount an attack against Russian guns

'The history of contemporary civilisation knows no event of greater importance than the Battle of Warsaw, 1920 . . . Had the battle been a Bolshevik victory, it would have been a turning point in European history, for there is no doubt that the whole of Central Europe would at that moment have been opened to the influence of Communist propaganda and a Soviet invasion, which it could with difficulty have resisted'

Olivova

3428

'By August 21 the rout of Tukhachevsky's right wing was complete . . . As they broke eastward in panic, the whole countryside became the scene of pandemonium . . . while Piłsudski's bare-footed and tattered men pressed the pursuit mile after mile'

Roger Viollet

Opposite page. Top right: Officers and, *top left,* men of the Red Army. The Russian 'horde' was as ill-equipped as the Polish peasant army. *Bottom:* In the wake of the Bolsheviks — results of a massacre at Jelgava, in Latvia. It was just such devastation that the Poles hoped to avoid by fighting to define their territorial boundaries. *This page, right:* General Weygand, left, with Lord d'Abernon, French and British observers in Warsaw during its attack by Tukhachevsky's army

Ukrainians. While the Ukrainians, with Polish assistance, were groping for a solution to their many problems, the Red Army was licking its wounds and preparing a counteroffensive. At the beginning of June a Soviet attack was launched: it was spearheaded by a sudden attack of Büdenny's First Cavalry Army composed of four mounted divisions. At the head of 12,000 horses, with 300 machine guns and 50 guns, he suddenly hit the Polish front south of Kiev. On June 5, after a murderous struggle the Polish lines near Zhitomir were broken. Stalin, who at that time was Political Commissar of the Büdenny Army, described the operation in an interview with a Moscow correspondent:

The breakthrough effected by our cavalry in the Zhitomir area was undoubtedly the decisive factor in the radical change at the front. The breakthrough began at dawn on June 5. On that day, our cavalry units, compressed into a tight fist . . . breached the enemy's positions in the Popelnya-Kazatin area, raced through the Berdichev area, and on June 7 occupied Zhitomir. The resistance of the Poles was so desperate that our cavalry literally had to hack their way through, the result being that the Poles left on the field not less than 8,000 wounded and killed by shot or sabre. For a moment the Polish-Ukrainian Third Army was nearly surrounded in Kiev, but on June 13 the army broke through the encirclement and effected an orderly retreat to the West. A fresh line of defence was taken up, but could not be held. The Polish-Ukrainian forces had to abandon the Dnepr Valley. By the middle of June the Red Army was pushing westward victoriously.

It is obvious that the Kiev campaign was undertaken with inadequate and insufficiently equipped military forces. In the spring of 1920, the whole Polish army numbered not more than 700,000 men and only a part of it was used in the East. The lines of communication were dangerously overextended. Piłsudski gambled on an upsurge of Ukrainian patriotism which never materialised; although Petlyura's troops fought bravely throughout the campaign their numbers were small. The main cause of the failure of the Kiev campaign was the passivity of the Ukrainian people, exhausted by six years of war and easily deceived by various propagandistic slogans. The Bolsheviks once more proved supreme masters in manipulating mass loyalties. They successfully aroused both the latent fears of 'Polish landlords', and hopes for

Great Russian nationalism.

While arousing chauvinistic emotions in the Russian masses, the Bolsheviks did not neglect the cosmopolitan tenets of their doctrine. At the time of the spectacular Soviet successes the Second Congress of the Communist International opened in Moscow on July 19. The Congress exhorted the Soviet government to march on Warsaw and not to lay down its arms until Poland had become a member of a world federation of Soviet republics. The Congress summoned the Communists of the world to help 'the first Socialist state' to achieve its goal. Thus, the Red armies were to bring with their bayonets not only a new social order but also a new conception of statehood. When the Soviet counteroffensive began, the Soviet People's Commissar for Nationalities, Stalin, was already exchanging letters with Lenin concerning a future Communist Eastern Europe. On June 19 he wrote to Lenin about the problem of the future status of the nations of the area, suggesting confederation as the most appropriate form by which to link Eastern European countries with Russia. Lenin agreed with Stalin's proposed solution of the problem. These were days of great expectation for the delegates to the Second Congress of the Comintern. They eagerly watched the large military map hanging in the hall of the building where the Congress was taking place, a map which showed the advance of the Red Army toward Warsaw. Comintern propaganda represented Poland as the epitome of both feudal and bourgeois vices, and the willing tool of greedy, perverted and bloodthirsty western capitalists. This was, according to Moscow, 'the third campaign of the Entente' against 'the first Socialist state' of the world.

Alarm in the West

The swift advance of the Red Army terrified Paris and London. Germany, on the other hand, was torn between fear and hope, for the penetration of the Soviet armies into Poland offered Germany a chance to liquidate the barely established status quo completely. The spectre of a possible Russo-German collaboration began to haunt the French. The very survival of Poland and of all newly-created states was now at stake. While Paris was for military assistance to Poland, London hesitated. Moreover, much of the help which the French were dispatching was paralysed by the strikes organised by Communist parties in England, France, Italy and

Czechoslovakia, as well as by the dock workers in Gdańsk. So, at this critical moment, the Poles were for all practical purposes alone.

Meanwhile, the Soviet army was pushing toward Warsaw. All of Europe was breathless with suspense watching and waiting for the result of the contest, the outcome of which would settle the fate of Eastern Europe. By August 13, the Soviet troops advanced to within six miles of Prague, the north-eastern suburb situated on the right bank of the River Vistula. The fall of the Polish capital was expected any day, and rumours were spread by Soviet propaganda that Warsaw had actually fallen. But it was obvious that the real goal of the Red Army was not Poland but Germany, seething with social unrest.

Day and night the roaring of the guns could be heard in the streets. Most of the Diplomatic Corps left the capital and sought shelter in Poznan. The panic of the western diplomats, however, was not shared by the bulk of the Polish people. In fact, most foreign observers in Warsaw were puzzled by the calm and self-confident attitude of the Polish people.

While Polish diplomacy was vainly attempting to enlist some western aid, Piłsudski, who was not only head of state but also Commander-in-Chief, was trying to stem the tide. His opponent, Tukhachevsky, Commander on the Soviet western Front, had massed three of his four armies in the region north of Warsaw and planned an encircling manoeuvre from the north. The next Soviet army, advancing on War-

Popperfoto

'Tukhachevsky had the soul of Genghis Khan . . . Autocratic, superstitious, romantic and ruthless, he loved the open plain lands and the thud of a thousand hoofs, feared the orderliness of civilisation.' *Fuller*

torn in two but profoundly dislocated by the deep Polish penetration to the rear of the north-central sector. By August 17, the Soviet retreat had turned into a rout and the dreaded First Cavalry Army of Büdenny was stopped and beaten by the Poles at Zamość and Komarow, in two great cavalry battles. The defeat had struck the Soviet leaders like a bolt from a clear sky. They had taken the capture of Warsaw for granted. A Communist Provisional Revolutionary Government for Poland had even been set up in anticipation.

The significance of the Battle of Warsaw was immediately grasped by the British ambassador in Berlin, Lord d'Abernon, who declared in a press interview: *The history of contemporary civilisation knows no event of greater importance than the Battle of Warsaw, 1920, and none of which the significance is less appreciated. Had the battle been a Bolshevik victory, it would have been a turning point in European history, for there is no doubt at all that the whole of Central Europe would at that moment have been opened to the influence of Communist propaganda and to Soviet invasion, which it could with difficulty have resisted. It is evident from speeches made in Russia during the war against Poland that the Soviet plans were very far-reaching. In the more industrialised German towns plans were made on a large scale to proclaim a Soviet régime a few days after Warsaw had fallen. Several times Poland has been the bulwark of Europe against Asiatic invasion, yet never had Poland's services been greater, never had the danger been more imminent.*

Contrary to a widespread rumour General Weygand did not play any significant rôle in the planning of the Battle of Warsaw. His personal relations with Piłsudski were strained from the beginning, and his advice was largely disregarded. In fact Weygand's plan for the battle of Warsaw was to abandon the city. Here Lord d'Abernon's evaluation coincided with that of Lenin who declared soon after the war: 'If Poland had become Soviet, if the Warsaw workers had received from Russia the help they expected and welcomed, the Versailles Treaty would have been shattered, and the entire international system built up by the victors would have been destroyed. France would not then have had a buffer separating Germany from Soviet Russia. It would have no hope of getting back its milliards. . . .' While adopting various purely technical

saw from the east, was to launch a frontal attack on the Polish capital. But between this army and the next large Soviet force, the ill-co-ordinated advance created a gap, thinly covered by the small Mozir group. Polish military intelligence quickly spotted the gap and, consequently, Piłsudski's main objective became its exploitation. He decided to withdraw six of his most reliable divisions to the triangle formed by the Vistula, south of Warsaw and the River Wieprz. There, he secretly assembled and reorganised them into a strong, mobile army, 'the shock group' as he called it, under his personal command. While the northern and central sectors would oppose the bridgeheads east of the city, this sector of the front would draw the enemy as far to the north-west as possible without surrendering the city. The rôle of the crack 'shock group' would be to wait. At an

appropriate moment they would pounce on the Mozir division, destroy it and drive a deep wedge between the northern front centred on Warsaw, and the southern segment of the Soviet drive focused on Lemberg. By this means the Soviet offensive would be split in two. The army would then be able to penetrate the rear of the northern sector and destroy it in a broad, enveloping sweep.

The Polish counteroffensive was launched on August 13. After the first day of fighting it became clear that the offensive had surprised the enemy and that the place and timing of the drive had been judiciously chosen. The Russian advance was first checked, and then, when its momentum was lost, forced into retreat.

Overnight, the Poles regained their confidence. By August 16 it was already evident that the Bolshevik front was not only

Piłsudski—'an ardent patriot and a man of immense courage . . . he loves danger, his pulse only beating at a normal rate when he is in imminent personal peril . . . Next to danger he is said to love intrigue . . .' *D'Abernon*

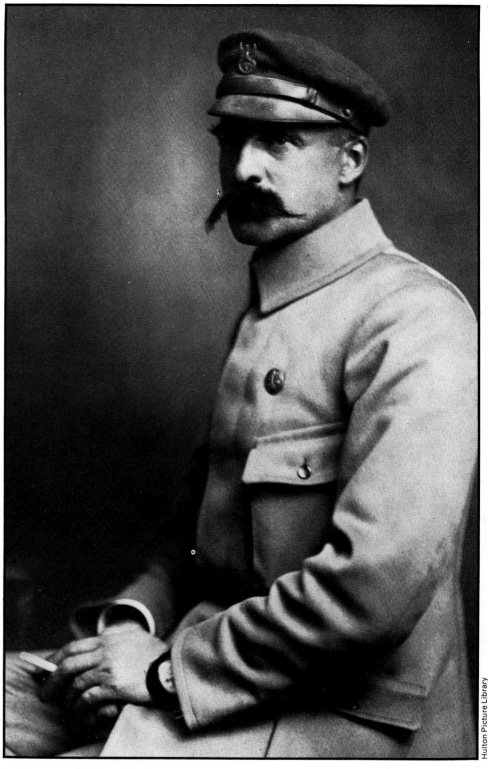

Hulton Picture Library

improvements suggested by the French general, Piłsudski rejected his plan for the decisive battle which Weygand wanted to wage west of the Polish capital. In an interview with a correspondent of a Paris paper, *Information,* published on August 21, 1920, in reply to the remark that some Poles proclaimed him the 'saviour of Warsaw', General Weygand declared: 'That is not the case, and I beg you to fix French opinion on that important point. The victory which is being celebrated in Warsaw is a Polish victory; the military operations were executed by the Polish generals in accordance with a Polish plan.'

There is little doubt that a victory of the Red Army in the Battle of Warsaw would have had radical consequences. For the Soviet revolution might well have inundated the Baltic States, Rumania, Hungary, Czechoslovakia, Austria, and eventually probably Germany. And from there the Soviet drive would have had its way open to the west. The Polish victory now barred this possibility. The Battle of Warsaw was followed by another test of strength, the Battle of Neman, at the end of September. This second Polish victory compelled the Soviet government to seek for peace. The preliminary peace treaty was signed on October 12 at Riga, the capital of Latvia. The two belligerents pledged neither to interfere in one another's internal affairs, nor to support armed bands aimed at destroying the peace and welfare of the other party. Minority rights were to be respected on both sides of the new frontier. Poland was assured the return of the numerous libraries, archives, art treasures and historical monuments which the Russians had seized since the partition of the Polish Commonwealth. Both sides now recognised without any qualifications the independence of the Ukrainian and Belorussian Soviet Republics. The frontier fixed by the Treaty of Riga ran south from the River Swine, that is, from the Russian-Latvian border, with Minsk remaining on the Russian side of the border, down to the River Zbruch, which it followed to its junction with the River Dnestr.

Thus, the Treaty of Riga ended Soviet-Polish hostilities. The bulk of the Ukrainian and Belorussian lands went to Russia and were soon linked with the Soviet Union by quasi-federal ties, while their western fringes were allotted to Poland.

By the Treaty of Riga Poland regained only about one third of the territories she had possessed before the first partition of 1772, while Russia kept the bulk of the lands belonging to the pre-partition Polish-Lithuanian Commonwealth. Poland obtained less than what the Polish delegate, Dmowski, claimed for her at Versailles, but more than what the Great Powers considered 'undisputed Polish territories'. In 1923 the frontiers of Poland were officially recognised by the Council of Ambassadors.

From the perspective of half a century the Russo-Polish War of 1920 appears as an event of considerable importance; one may argue that in 1918 to 1920 two schemes for organising Eastern Europe confronted each other: Lenin's plan aimed at splitting 'capitalistic encirclement' by the axe of proletarian revolution. The class war would atomise 'bourgeois' states along horizontal lines and prepare them for an easy absorption by Russia. By this means a belt of satellite states eventually comprising practically all of Central and Eastern Europe would be created; this Communist bloc was meant to be a jumping-off ground for a further march through Germany to the west. Lenin's stratagem was shattered by the Polish victory, and by the failure of his plans for a social revolution in Poland. There is no doubt that the Russo-Polish War of 1920 largely determined the balance of power in Eastern and Central Europe for almost two decades.

Further Reading
Dziewanowski, M. K., *European Federalist: Joseph Piłsudski* (Hoover Institute 1969)
Wandycz, Piotr, *Polish-Soviet Relations, 1917-1921* (Oxford University Press 1969)

[*For M. K. Dziewanowski's biography, see page 1834.*]

3432

PILSUDSKI

Above and left: The legendary Piłsudski. He said: 'To be vanquished and not surrender is victory, to vanquish and rest on laurels is defeat'

CAF/Warsaw

Joseph Piłsudski was born on December 5, 1867 on the family estate at Zulow, near Vilna, the second son of an impoverished Polish-Lithuanian family of ancient lineage. The dominant figure of his childhood was his mother, Maria Bilewicz, who inspired in him love of Polish history and literature and hatred of the oppressive Tsarist régime. These sentiments were confirmed by the young Piłsudski's own experiences at the Russian school in Vilna, where speaking Polish was forbidden and native history was treated with contempt by the haughty and often brutal Russian teachers.

After leaving school in 1855, Piłsudski studied medicine at the University of Khar'kov but was dismissed in the following year for his political activities. Returning to Vilna he drew closer to the local revolutionary circles and began to study the works of Karl Marx and other socialist writers. In 1887 he was arrested and charged with plotting an attempt on the life of Tsar Alexander III. Despite the fact that he was innocent of the accusations Piłsudski was banished for five years to Eastern Siberia. He used the years of the Siberian exile for further study of socialism, history and politics.

In 1892 he returned to Vilna with the belief that socialist ideas, in order to be effective in captive Poland, should be combined with patriotic slogans. He was determined to work for the liberation of Poland and for her reconstruction as an independent democratic republic, a stepping stone toward a fully socialist state. He joined the newly-established Polish Socialist Party (known in Poland as PPS) and by 1894 had become one of its leaders.

Soon Piłsudski set up a clandestine newspaper called *Robotnik ('The Worker')* and edited it until 1900 when its operations were accidentally discovered by the Tsarist police. Piłsudski, arrested with his first wife, Maria Janoszkiewicz, was imprisoned in the Warsaw Citadel. There, in order to secure a transfer to a hospital he feigned insanity. Soon after the transfer occurred he escaped in May 1901.

He settled at Kraków in Austrian Poland, which since 1867 had enjoyed a fairly mild, autonomous existence, within the framework of the Habsburg Empire. In July 1904 he visited Japan to solicit Japanese assistance for his anti-Tsarist activities. There he clashed with his political rival, the leader of the Polish National Democratic Party, Roman Dmowski, who attempted to persuade the Japanese authorities that his opponent's plans for an insurrection in Russian Poland were impractical. Dmowski's arguments prevailed over those of Piłsudski. There was no large-scale uprising in Russian Poland, but this did not prevent Piłsudski from taking an active part in the revolution of 1905. He set up the Military Organisation of the Polish Socialist Party, which was responsible for numerous acts of terrorism and sabotage directed against the Russian authorities in Poland. But on the whole it was the National Democratic Party that was in ascendence up until the outbreak of the First World War.

After the failure of the Revolution of 1905, a split occurred within the PPS; its left wing, which proposed dropping from the Party platform the slogan of Poland's independence, seceded from the Party, and formed the PPS-Left, bent upon close collaboration with the Russian revolutionaries. In 1918 this splinter was to merge with the Social Democratic Party of Poland and Lithuania and set up the Communist Party of Poland.

After the split, Piłsudski, still the acknowledged leader of the right wing of the PPS, known as the Revolutionary Faction, settled in Galicia and began systematically to study military subjects: strategy, tactics and organisation of armed forces. Anticipating a conflict between the Central Powers and Russia, he concluded that it would be imperative to form Polish military units in order to be ready to take advantage of the opportunities that the future war would provide. In 1908 he began secretly to organise such units in L'vov (Lemberg), then the capital of Galicia. Soon he received approval from the Austrian authorities for his military preparations.

Piłsudski believed that in the first stages of the future war the Central Powers would beat Russia, while ultimately France and Great Britain, supported by the United States, would defeat the Central Powers. He tailored his political and military plans in accordance with these theories.

During the first two years of the war the three brigades of the Polish legions, organised and trained by Piłsudski, fought alongside the Austro-Hungarian troops with bravery and distinction against the Russians. On November 5, 1916, Germany and Austria, short of manpower, proclaimed the independence of Poland under their joint protectorate, hoping that this move would attract recruits to the Polish army. Piłsudski, appointed head of the Military Department of the Polish Council of State, accepted the idea of an enlarged Polish army provided it would be under the command of a sovereign Polish state.

While the Central Powers hesitated the Tsarist régime collapsed in Russia. The new Provisional Government proclaimed Poland's independence. When Germany and Austria refused to commit themselves to Poland's future and insisted that the Polish army units should swear 'fidelity in arms with the German and Austrian forces' Piłsudski refused. In July 1917 he was again arrested and imprisoned by the Germans in Magdeburg on the River Oder.

After the German collapse, Piłsudski was released and returned to Warsaw on November 1918 as a popular hero. On November 19, the Regents' Council entrusted him with the office of Head of State and Commander-in-Chief of the Armed Forces of reborn Poland. In this dual task he devoted himself to laying down the democratic foundation of the Republic and to protecting its frontiers, mainly in the east, from the menace of Bolshevism. A convinced federalist and always conscious of his mixed ancestry, he tried to carry out the programme of his native Polish Socialist Party, and achieve some form of association with the Lithuanians, Belorussians and Ukrainians. These plans brought Poland into a war with Soviet Russia, in which the Soviet régime tried not only to regain the lands that the Tsars had once ruled, but to spread the proletarian revolution to the west. The Russo-Polish war continued with varying intensity from February 1919 until October 1920, when the Russian advance was checked and turned at Warsaw. A compromise peace treaty was drawn up at Riga in March 1921.

In May 1923 Piłsudski ceded his place as Head of State to an elected President of the Republic and retired to a country home, dissatisfied with the functioning of the Polish parliamentary system. He returned to power as a result of a *coup d'état* in May 1926 and ruled Poland as a virtual dictator until 1935. He died of cancer of the liver in Warsaw on May 12, 1935, and was buried in the cathedral of the royal castle in Kraców alongside former Polish kings.

Snark

Imperial War Museum

LOCOS AT WAR

It is hard to see how the First World War could have attained the enormity and length it did if there had been no railways. For on these were moved the whole paraphernalia of the war— men, casualties, ordnance, munitions, rations and all higher army staffs

Left: A German troop transport *en route* from Russia to France. The fact that Germany possessed an efficient internal communication system based on her railway system made it possible to switch troops rapidly from one front to another.
Right: Marshal Foch's command train. In this mobile HQ Foch was transported to Spa to discuss the landing of General Haller's troops in Danzig in 1919. *Below:* A German 0-4-0 tank locomotive

Opposite page, centre: A British light railway engine made from motor parts operating near High Wood, on the Somme, in October 1916. As each side's front moved backward or forward, the light railways fanning out from the main railheads to the front had to be altered very extensively to meet the new requirements.
Left: British troops moving up on a light railway near Elvertinghe, in the Ypres area, in February 1917. *Right:* Maricourt, September 1916—an 0-6-0 railway goods loco on loan to the Railway Operating Division from the North British Railway off the rails

In the summer of 1918 the struggling Soviet régime was forced to contend with a large-scale civil war, for the revolt of the Czechoslovak Legion (originally Czech prisoners of war organised by the Tsarist government to fight the Germans) had brought into the conflict all the White forces opposed to Bolshevism. The running of the war on both sides was haphazard: on the White side there was too large a bulk of officers and, while better equipped, much of their energy was turned to intrigue and private ends; the various anti-Soviet strongholds were completely unable to co-operate and much of the time that could have been spent in fighting their common enemy was used in political manoeuvring and rivalry between themselves. The Red Army, its shortage of specialists and maltreatment of its officers a severe handicap, had at least numerical superiority, although there was an abnormally high desertion rate because of the lack of food, clothing and ammunition. The peasantry at first had no affiliations, one side seeming as bad as the other, but towards the end of the war the increasingly reactionary attitudes of the Whites and the drunkenness, looting and violence suffered by the peasantry at the hands of White forces swayed most of the rural proletariat in favour of the Bolsheviks.

The first major confrontation occurred in September 1918 between the Czechs, and the Whites who had joined them, and the Red Army in the mid-Volga region. Trotsky, as War Commissar, took personal command and launched an offensive against Kazan, which had been captured some months earlier by the White 'government' at Samara. Outflanked and badly supplied, the Whites were forced to retreat through Simbersk, Samara and then up to the Urals before winter conditions stopped military operations in the region. The Samara Directorate had to take refuge, as unwelcome visitors, in Omsk in Siberia. At this point the British government, ironically enough, decided to recognise the Directorate as the All-Russian government, but by September 18 it had ceased to exist: Admiral Kolchak had been proclaimed Supreme Ruler, after a *coup d'état* in Omsk. Russian and Siberian Social Revolutionaries, who predominated in the region, accepted Kolchak's leadership only reluctantly, and despite initial successes on the front during the early part of 1919 Kolchak proved incapable of reconciling the interests of the various nationalities under his command, of appointing the right subordinates or of controlling the excesses of his army. In June 1919, at a crucial stage of the battle, two brigades mutinied and then deserted to the Bolsheviks; by October, after a string of defeats, Kolchak's empire was crumbling. On November 10, with Bolshevik forces only 40 miles away from Omsk, Kolchak's army escaped over the frozen River Irtysh and on November 14 Kolchak left in an armoured train. The next day Omsk was occupied by the Red Army.

The death of Kolchak

Having been refused protection by the cities in which the Social Revolutionaries had a majority Kolchak was forced to throw himself on the mercy of the Czech Legion, who were at the time in control of a large section of the Trans-Siberian railway. But the Czechs were reluctant guardians: Kolchak had early alienated them by the brutality and incompetence of his régime and his ingratitude for their support against the Bolsheviks. As soon as

VICTORY FOR THE BOLSHEVIKS

From 1918 the most immediate threat to the Bolsheviks lay in the counter-revolutionary armies that were gathering strength in far-flung areas of Russia; the success or failure of the Soviet régime rested on its ability to annihilate opposition. In a series of bitter campaigns all over Russia the White leaders were destroyed or forced to flee abroad. But with Soviet military and political power established the economy remained in a state of chaos: famine, drought and disease wasted the land. *J. F. N. Bradley. Left:* As the diminutive Whites rush up to challenge the mighty Red horseman they are impaled on his lance — Soviet propaganda poster

the Czechs had to fight to get out of Siberia they disclaimed any connection with the fallen régime or its leader, Kolchak. With the desire to leave Siberia at any cost outweighing any other consideration, they actively supported the Social Revolutionaries and even concluded an armistice with the Bolsheviks. In January they handed Kolchak over to the socialist régime at Irkutsk, but soon afterwards the régime collapsed and Kolchak, along with his Premier, Pepeliaev, was captured by the Bolsheviks. On February 7, 1920 the two prisoners were executed and their bodies pushed under the ice of the River Angara, on which Irkutsk stands. In March the Red Army occupied Irkutsk and from there gradually took over the Eastern provinces. With the exception of a few regions, which under Japanese protection survived as the Far Eastern Republic until 1924, the Bolsheviks overran the whole of Siberia. By the end of 1920 the White movement in Siberia had ceased to exist, while the western Allies, chiefly represented by the Czech Legion, withdrew in disorder.

The progress of the White movement in the Baltic provinces was equally short-lived. After a year of confused partisan fighting

General Yudenich tried to organise all the White forces into an effective fighting force under his command. But although it was clear that disunited they would all fall to the Bolsheviks one by one, while united they could still be victorious, the various factions never managed to co-operate. The Estonians, Latvians and Lithuanians insisted on the separateness of their causes and would only join together as a temporary expedient. The Finns, also previously part of the Russian Empire, never joined even as a temporary ally. Even the Russians themselves were deeply divided: the area contained pro-German and pro-Allied Russian armies who were prepared to quarrel at a time when this could be fatally dangerous for them. Thus the Bermondt-Avalov Corps, organised and financed by the Germans, began to move up the front in support of Latvian and Estonian troops; however, instead of joining battle with the Bolsheviks it attacked the Whites and their allies. General Yudenich's offensives, supported by the British naval forces in the Baltic Sea, were at first extremely successful, and in their second major effort the soldiers of the North-Western army penetrated into the suburbs of Petrograd. However, the Bolsheviks, seeing the danger on this front, reorganised their defences, transferred reinforcements and by December 1919 the North-Western army, let down by their Baltic allies, disintegrated, fled in chaos across the border of Russia and was disarmed and interned by their former allies.

Once again disunity among Bolshevik opponents caused the destruction of their movement and all that was left was diplomatic tying-up in the area. After the destruction of General Yudenich's army the British squadron was recalled, the Baltic Corps disarmed and disbanded, and individual nations came to terms with the Bolsheviks. Peace negotiations started early in 1920 and during that year peace treaties were signed establishing Estonia, Latvia and Lithuania as independent states. This was only a qualified success for the Bolsheviks, for these minute Baltic republics and Finland, parts of the defunct Russian Empire, were lost until the Second World War.

Novosti

Russo-Polish conflict
In the west the Bolsheviks had to struggle against the newly-independent Poland and the nationalist Ukrainians. Poland became independent finally after the Western Armistice in November 1918, but to establish her frontiers her head-of-state, Piłsudski, realised that a clash with the Soviet régime would be inevitable and when the Bolsheviks seized power in the Ukraine and occupied Belorussia in 1919, Poland and Bolshevik Russia were locked in conflict. The threat of Soviet expansion brought together even those historic opponents, the Poles and Ukrainians, and in April 1920 they undertook a common offensive against the Soviet menace. Within a month the Polish army occupied the Ukrainian capital, Kiev, and the Ukrainian leader, Petlyura, appealed to the Ukrainians to join the Poles against the Bolsheviks, who were massing their armies to strike against them. But the appeal failed and when the Red Army struck the Poles were forced to retreat. Warsaw was almost surrounded, but by a piece of clever military strategy the Bolshevik armies were checked and routed. An armistice was agreed and peace terms settled in the Treaty of Riga, giving the Poles large chunks of Russian territory. However, the peace represented for the Bolsheviks one more front on which their boundaries were settled, leaving the Red Army free to combat the remaining White resistance.

Challenge from the south
It was the Don Cossacks in the south who had constituted the first opposition force against the Bolsheviks as early as November 1917. While tough and well organised they were necessarily isolated from the other White forces, and would have been no problem for the Bolsheviks had not their ranks been swollen by opposition Russians, especially officers. General Alexeyev tried to build up this movement, renamed the Volunteer Army, throughout 1918 and when he died the task fell to another general, Denikin. After the Armistice in the west Allied aid arrived and Denikin also brought under his control the separatist movements of the Cossacks of Don Kuban and the tribesmen of the Caucasus. Early in 1919 the French army landed in Odessa and attempted to provide a protective shield round Denikin's army until it organised itself and was able to strike hard at the Bolsheviks. However, from the beginning General Denikin had a difficult task to tackle. The nature of Allied assistance and recognition was never clearly defined and he had to quarrel constantly about policy matters with the Allies, local separatists and various political groups within the movement itself. In June 1919 his armies were, nevertheless, ready to strike against the Bolsheviks and their immediate success was

Far left: Yudenich, Commander of the north-western Whites. Although his army nearly reached Petrograd he failed to make contact with Denikin in the south and, after disputes with their Estonian allies, the army was forced to retreat to the Baltic.
Left: Denikin, Commander of the White forces on the southern front, described by the Soviet Politburo as 'the most difficult, dangerous and important of the fronts' in mid 1919. Denikin was one of the luckier White leaders—he fled to the United States where he died peacefully in 1947.
Below: Kolchak, ironically named 'Supreme Ruler' of Omsk for a short time, with generals Gaida, left, and Bogoslowsky, right. Formerly an admiral, Kolchak was executed by the Bolsheviks on February 7, 1920

Ullstein

Ullstein

immense. The Volunteer Army drove the Bolsheviks before them, destroying them in pincer-like cavalry manoeuvres. Kharkov, Tsaritsyn and Kiev fell to the advancing Whites and in October 1919 they reached Orel, a town 80 miles from the Bolshevik capital: Moscow. However, when Soviet counterattacks came the Volunteers collapsed and their advance rapidly turned into a rout. The unresolved problem of the Makhno peasant movement backfired; the peasants turned against the Whites, attacked them from behind, cut their lines of supply and communication and helped the Bolsheviks to destroy the movement, although they themselves were destroyed by the Bolsheviks when their turn came. However, by February 1920 the Volunteer Army and their local allies were destroyed and driven out of Russia. The remnants concentrated in the Crimea.

After this catastrophe General Denikin was replaced as commander by General Wrangel. He took advantage of Soviet preoccupation with other problems to reorganise and re-equip his movement and armies. He even tried to revive resistance among his Cossack allies, but failed: the Cossacks were exhausted. Although it was obvious that the movement would be finished when the Bolsheviks could concentrate all their forces against him, he prepared the defences of the Crimea and also made plans for the evacuation of his soldiers and their families. In November 1920 the final battle for the Crimea was launched. After some determined fighting on both sides the Reds burst into the peninsula and the Whites put into operation their evacuation plans. Without panic and in co-operation with the French navy this immense operation was smoothly carried out; some 150,000 Whites left Russia, leaving the Bolsheviks firmly in control.

This was the greatest Bolshevik triumph over the toughest opponents. Throughout 1919 and 1920 they also had to deal with a large number of smaller, isolated opponents. In the far north, for instance, White régimes established themselves after the landing of Allied troops at Murmansk and Archangel. However, when in 1919 it was decided to evacuate the Allied forces the White movements fell almost immediately and the Bolsheviks took over. In the Ural Mountains Cossacks rose against the Bolsheviks but when attacked retreated into Central Asia, where they were liquidated together with other local resistance movements. In the Caucasus the Georgian Republic lasted until February 1921, when it was finally declared a Soviet Socialist Republic; the last to fall to the Bolsheviks was the Far Eastern Republic. Militarily the Bolsheviks were absolute masters of the former Russian Empire in 1920; politically shortly afterwards.

After war, the problems of peace

In a sense the Civil War solved certain political problems for the Bolsheviks. The revolution of November 1917 suppressed the Liberals; the coalition partners, the Left Social Revolutionaries, were soon to follow suit. When the Social Revolutionaries organised a series of uprisings at Vladimir, Rybinsk, Kazan, Simbirsk and Moscow, they were mercilessly crushed and their movement outlawed. In the Volga region, under the protective umbrella of the Czechoslovak Legion, the Social Revolutionary majority convened the Constituent Assembly to Samara in June 1918. Soon this government collapsed and with it the rival government of Russia, the Directorate at Omsk. All the other White movements disintegrated under the impact of military defeat and the Bolsheviks were left single-handed to mould the policies of Russia. Because of the demands of the Civil War it was vital that they should retain firm control over industry and agriculture and this they did by using the doctrine of 'war communism'. For the time being no industrial unrest was possible and any occurring was ruthlessly repressed. In the country war communism meant that armed squads appropriated wheat from the peasants and supplied the towns. Everything was geared to the needs of the fronts.

By the winter of 1918 to 1919 a watering down of the more extreme applications of war communism occurred and above all smallholders gained some relief after the sixth Congress of the Soviets in March 1919. But the peasants' problems were far from solved, for the Bolsheviks could offer nothing in return for grain and requisitioning had to continue. By the autumn of 1920, while victorious against the Whites, the Bolsheviks faced their greatest danger yet in the form of rebellious peasants. The demobilisation of the armies led to banditry, and since the armies could no longer live on the land, the level of grain production had to be raised to feed them. A new state plan for compulsory sowing was prepared, but it soon became evident that it would not work.

Industry was also utterly disorganised as a result of the Civil War. At first it was thought that the soldiers could be turned into labourers and labour armies began to work the mines, forestry and other sections of industry. But this 'militarisation of labour' seems to have lost its significance when the White enemy was defeated and as a solution was far from efficient. Strong disagreements occurred on the resolution of these problems: Trotsky favoured 'mobilisation', others wanted the Trade Unions to make policy decisions, while Lenin wanted the state organs to function properly. Everything else needed reshaping; new trading relations had to be established to abolish shortages.

The Kronstadt uprising

By March 1921 the country was in economic chaos and for pragmatic reasons a solution had to be sought. As if to emphasise the urgency of these new measures the sailors of the Baltic fleet rose against the Bolshevik régime at the naval base in Kronstadt. What sparked off this uprising was a strike by Petrograd workers. The Labour Army, an organisation of strike breakers, became the target of the strikers; the workers also demanded the freedom of choice of their own representatives on trade union and soviet bodies. The sailors' representatives attended all these meetings and then themselves passed a political resolution demanding a general election by secret ballot, freedom of the press and speech for the workers and peasants and all the left-wing groups as well as the release of all left-wing political prisoners. It further called for the freedom of individuals to bring food to towns without the fear of its confiscation, the right of peasants and artisans to organise their own production and the abolition of extra rations for privileged persons. It also wanted the withdrawal of Bolshevik guards from factories and the abolition of the Propaganda Department.

On March 1, 1921, Kalinin, a Party steward, tried in vain to calm angry sailors at Kronstadt. Instead, he was ignored and the following day the sailors began to organise a new election for the Kronstadt Soviet. Bolshevik commissars were arrested and the naval base made ready for a rebellion. On March 3 the government responded by arresting and shooting out of hand a naval airman at a base south of Kronstadt in anticipation of a rebellion there. Two days later Trotsky, as War Commissar, sent a threatening ultimatum to Kronstadt itself and on March 7 the young commander Tukhachevsky led an infantry assault on the fortress across the frozen Gulf of Finland. However, this first assault failed, for despite Tukhachevsky's exertions the troops were reluctant to fight with determination against the sailors of Kronstadt.

It was obvious that the rebellion would have to be put down quickly, after thorough military preparations. If the base was not taken almost immediately, before the ice broke, it would be inaccessible to the infantry which Tukhachevsky controlled, and in turn rebellious ships could get out of the base and bombard Petrograd. In Petrograd itself the situation was tense and if fighting was started in the city it was possible that the population might rise up in revolt as well. Tukhachevsky first handpicked the troops for the operation; he stiffened them with Red officer-cadets (who had just passed out of the Soviet military academy) and Party delegates. On March 16 preliminary bombardment of the fortress was begun.

The next day two columns of infantry made a dash across the frozen bay. The first one ended ingloriously in a minefield, but the

Below: Red infantry pursue Wrangel's fleeing 'Russian Army'. *Right: Enrol on command courses; you must learn how to lead for the defence of the workers' and peasants' republic* — a stern Soviet poster

ИДИ НА КОМАНДНЫЕ КУРСЫ,–
НАДО УЧИТЬСЯ, КАК РУКОВОДИТЬ ЗАЩИТОЙ
РЕСПУБЛИКИ РАБОЧИХ И КРЕСТЬЯН!

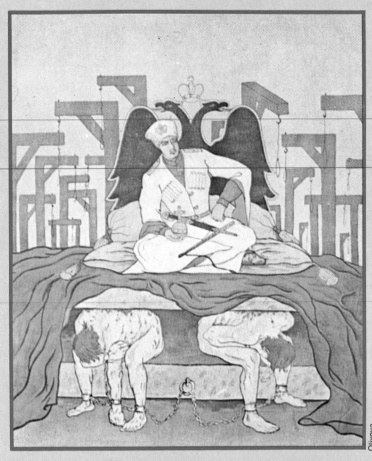

Left: German caricature of Trotsky, as War Commissar. Trotsky had been responsible for the moulding of the Red Army after the revolution. *Right:* Soviet propaganda poster sees Wrangel as Khan of the Crimea and usurper of Russia, threatening a return to slavery and feudal injustice. *Below:* Uniform of a soldier of 'the workers' and peasants' republic' — a Red Guard during the Civil War

second one broke through into the fortress. Fighting went on all day and only on March 18 did the Red Army manage to capture and immobilise the battleships. The clearing-up operations included public shooting of carefully selected minor offenders and imprisonment of the genuine leaders (they were shot quietly some months afterwards). Lenin still wanted to demonstrate to the people that the uprising was started by counterrevolutionaries; at the same time he announced his new economic policy (NEP).

The economy stabilised
The new policy was a series of economic measures to break the vicious circle set in motion by war communism. Population had been drained away from industrial centres by shortages of food and as a result industrial production was brought practically to a standstill. The most important measure to be taken was to increase food supplies to the towns and this had to be done by offering greater inducements to the peasants. Next, trade had to be encouraged and a stable currency re-established. All these measures would finally lead to increased industrial productivity which was the prerequisite for the building of the new soviet order.

These economic measures were dependent on political concessions. Since Russia was still predominantly a peasant country (80% of the population were smallholders) the policy had to find favour with the peasants. A grain tax replaced the brutal requisitions and the peasants were free to sell their surplus. Even then the measures came too late to avert a natural catastophe. For the second successive year the Volga grain basin suffered from a drought. Millions suffered in a famine resulting from the drought and millions would have died had not Russia been aided by international relief agencies. In December 1921 the Party decided to take extreme measures to remedy the famine and all members were mobilised into agriculture. NEP measures began to be applied and the 1922 harvest was the largest since the revolution. Lenin took it as a sign of vindication of his policies, although the Party still remained split on the peasant and agricultural problem.

In industry NEP encouraged the revival and establishment of small rural industries, whether as co-operatives or private enterprise, while larger industrial enterprises were de-nationalised and leased to private individuals. Other nationalised enterprises changed their principles: they were run on precise economic accountability and were encouraged to form trusts. In all the element of profit was emphasised. Even then the progress of industry was much slower than that of agriculture and 'Bolshevik victory' on this front proved hollow in Lenin's lifetime.

[*For J. F. N. Bradley's biography, see page 99.*]

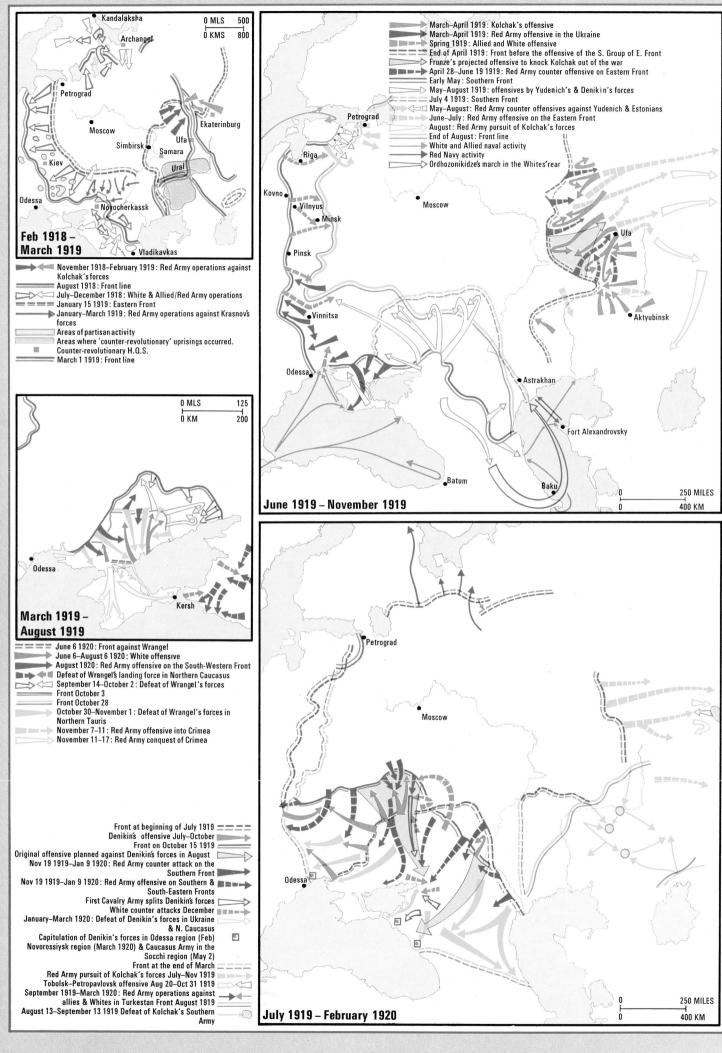

Feb 1918 – March 1919

0 MLS 500
0 KMS 800

Kandalaksha, Archangel, Petrograd, Moscow, Kiev, Odessa, Simbirsk, Samara, Ufa, Ekaterinburg, Ural, Novocherkassk, Vladikavkas

November 1918–February 1919: Red Army operations against Kolchak's forces
August 1918: Front line
July–December 1918: White & Allied/Red Army operations
January 15 1919: Eastern Front
January–March 1919: Red Army operations against Krasnov's forces
Areas of partisan activity
Areas where 'counter-revolutionary' uprisings occurred.
Counter-revolutionary H.Q.S.
March 1 1919: Front line

March 1919 – August 1919

0 MLS 125
0 KM 200

Odessa, Kersh

June 6 1920: Front against Wrangel
June 6–August 6 1920: White offensive
August 1920: Red Army offensive on the South-Western Front
Defeat of Wrangel's landing force in Northern Caucasus
September 14–October 2: Defeat of Wrangel's forces
Front October 3
Front October 28
October 30–November 1: Defeat of Wrangel's forces in Northern Tauris
November 7–11: Red Army offensive into Crimea
November 11–17: Red Army conquest of Crimea

Front at beginning of July 1919
Denikin's offensive July–October
Front on October 15 1919
Original offensive planned against Denikin's forces in August
Nov 19 1919–Jan 9 1920: Red Army counter attack on the Southern Front
Nov 19 1919–Jan 9 1920: Red Army offensive on Southern & South-Eastern Fronts
First Cavalry Army splits Denikin's forces
White counter attacks December
January–March 1920: Defeat of Denikin's forces in Ukraine & N. Caucasus
Capitulation of Denikin's forces in Odessa region (Feb) Novorossiysk region (March 1920) & Caucasus Army in the Socchi region (May 2)
Front at the end of March
Red Army pursuit of Kolchak's forces July–Nov 1919
Tobolsk–Petropavlovsk offensive Aug 20–Oct 31 1919
September 1919–March 1920: Red Army operations against allies & Whites in Turkestan Front August 1919
August 13–September 13 1919 Defeat of Kolchak's Southern Army

June 1919 – November 1919

March–April 1919: Kolchak's offensive
March–April 1919: Red Army offensive in the Ukraine
Spring 1919: Allied and White offensive
End of April 1919: Front before the offensive of the S. Group of E. Front
Frunze's projected offensive to knock Kolchak out of the war
April 28–June 19 1919: Red Army counter offensive on Eastern Front
Early May: Southern Front
May–August 1919: offensives by Yudenich's & Denikin's forces
July 4 1919: Southern Front
May–August: Red Army counter offensives against Yudenich & Estonians
June–July: Red Army offensive on the Eastern Front
August: Red Army pursuit of Kolchak's forces
End of August: Front line
White and Allied naval activity
Red Navy activity
Ordhozonikidze's march in the Whites' rear

Petrograd, Riga, Kovno, Vilnius, Minsk, Pinsk, Moscow, Vinnitsa, Odessa, Ufa, Aktyubinsk, Astrakhan, Fort Alexandrovsky, Batum, Baku

0 250 MILES
0 400 KM

July 1919 – February 1920

Petrograd, Moscow, Odessa

0 250 MILES
0 400 KM

KRONSTADT
Singeing the Bolsheviks Beard

The main danger to the small British naval mission to the new states in the Baltic was posed by the Soviet Baltic Fleet. In a daring raid on the latter's well-fortified base at Kronstadt, a group of British CMB's operating from Finland disabled all the major units of this fleet. *Brigadier Michael Calvert. Below:* The scene of the Kronstadt operation. *Bottom:* The loss of the British submarine *L55,* sunk by two Russian destroyers.

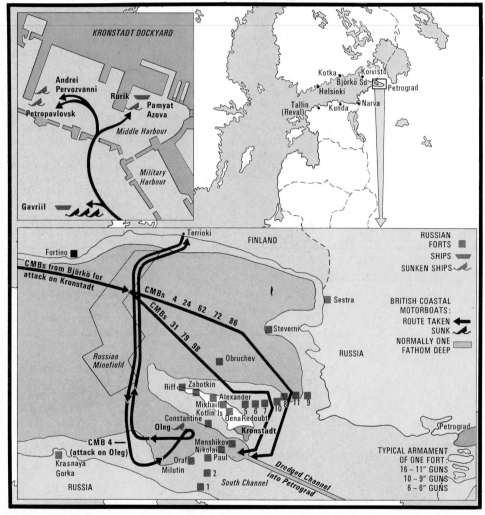

In 1919 Britain was at war with the revolutionary Bolshevik régime in Russia and was blockading Petrograd, the former capital city of Russia situated at the head of the Gulf of Finland.

At 0100 hours on August 18 eight British Coastal Motor Boats (CMB's), each armed with machine guns and one or two 18-inch torpedoes, and each manned by two young Royal Naval officers and a chief motor mechanic, crept out of the British base at Björkö Sound in south Finland. Their aim was to penetrate the almost impregnable naval base of Kronstadt on Kotlin Island, which barred the entrance to Petrograd harbour. Their target was the Soviet Russian capital fleet and especially the two battleships *Petropavlovsk* (23,370 tons) and *Andrei Pervozvanni* (17,680 tons), and also the submarine depot ship *Pamyat Azova* (12,000 tons), the destruction of which would seriously hamper the Russian submarine flotilla.

The CMB attack was to be assisted by a bombing raid of 12 Sopwith Camel biplanes of the RAF under the enthusiastic command of Major David Donald. These were to swoop down and deliver their bombloads in the darkness just before the naval attack, as a diversion.

As soon as the bombing was over, and in the confusion created by it, the leading torpedo boats swept into the harbour of Kronstadt, 'the strongest naval fortress in the world', at 0420 hours. They had passed by 20 forts each armed, nominally, with 16 11-inch guns, ten 9-inch guns and six 6-inch guns. In fact, at least two of the forts had only rifles and machine guns. There was no adequate protective boom defence as had been anticipated.

By 0425 hours the *Petropavlovsk*, the *Andrei Pervozvanni* and the *Pamyat Azova* had all been torpedoed and sunk, and the floating dock very slightly damaged by a bomb. Three CMB's had been destroyed by coast defence artillery and by the Russian destroyer, *Gavriil,* anchored at the entrance to the harbour.

Brilliantly successful

The operation had fulfilled its purpose. Of the Bolshevik fleet only a handful of destroyers and submarines remained. At a cost of three CMB's sunk, six officers and nine ratings killed, and three officers and six ratings made prisoners-of-war, Rear-Admiral Sir Walter Cowan, Commander of the British Baltic Force, had the satisfaction of knowing that the Russian battle fleet opposing him had ceased to exist.

Two Victoria Crosses were awarded and all the surviving members of the crews were decorated for bravery. Commander C. C. Dobson, who commanded the CMB flotilla and whose boat torpedoed the *Petropavlovsk,* and Lieutenant Gordon Steele, who had sunk the *Andrei Pervozvanni* after the captain of his boat had been shot through the head, were the recipients of the Victoria Cross.

The Royal Navy, who, with the RAF, had been running this theatre of war throughout the Baltic almost singlehanded, was jubilant. But not so the vacillating British Cabinet, who were engaged at the time in secret negotiations with the Bolsheviks for the withdrawal of the considerable British land forces in Archangel. This brilliant naval success embarrassed them.

There was another counterproductive result. The Russian Baltic Fleet and the no

Above left: Zelanoy, Bolshevik C-in-C, hampered by superiors ignorant of naval strategy. *Above right:* Cowan, Baronet of the Baltic. *Below:* British convoy carrying arms to the Baltic allies

less confined Kronstadt garrison had been openly and riotously critical of the Bolshevik command in general, and of Lenin in particular. This disastrous raid threw them back into the arms of the Bolsheviks whom, for a time, they supported. However, by 1921, when the pressure from without had ceased, they again mutinied against the policies of Lenin.

How did this all come about?

It is not possible here to trace the long drawn out and eventful history of the continued clashes between Russia, Poland and Germany (and at times Sweden) over the ownership of the Baltic coastline between the Gulf of Finland and Prussia, except to say that the struggle was always bloodstained, ruthless, relentless and with varying success and failure by each contestant. But, as we have seen, by the middle of 1917 Russia had been knocked out of the war by the Germans and had relapsed into revolution, civil war, chaos and ignominy. In the negotiations for the Treaty of Brest-Litovsk, between imperial Germany and revolutionary Russia, the Bolshevik government under Lenin, beset on all sides by the counter-revolutionary forces of Denikin, Kolchak, Yudenich, Savinkov and others, granted independence to the states of Poland, Finland and the Baltic States of Latvia, Lithuania and Estonia.

Renewed German aggression

The Germans, who were achieving great success in their 1918 March offensive against the Allies, were quick to take advantage of the new state of affairs on their Eastern Front and, besides transferring massive reinforcements to the west, started to pick the fruits of their victory over Russia. General Count Rüdiger von der Goltz, with 12,000 men, was sent to Finland to support their newly-fledged

government. Lithuania was still occupied by German forces and the Kaiser planned that Lithuania, as well as Latvia and Estonia, should become Grand Duchies within his Empire. At that time Britain and her Allies were too busy fighting desperately on the Western Front to heed the cries of the Baltic States for help. However, the Allies had occupied the ports of Archangel, Murmansk, Vladivostok and Odessa to prevent the huge supplies of arms and equipment, which they had sent to support Tsarist Russia, being passed on to central Russia where it might fall either into the hands of the Germans or their Bolshevik quasi-allies with whom they had made a treaty.

But the German armies collapsed under the Allied autumn counteroffensive from the west and in November appealed for an armistice which was signed on November 11, 1918. The British High Seas Fleet could now enter the Baltic and attempt to enforce the conditions of the Armistice, some clauses of which included: *Article XII: the Germans are to withdraw from the territory that was formerly part of the Russian Empire* (the Allies had given all the Baltic States de facto recognition of independence). Article XXIII covered the transfer and the internment of the German Fleet into Allied ports. Article XXV gave freedom of access to and from the Baltic to the naval and mercantile marine of the Allies. Article XXVI stated that the existing blockade conditions [of Germany] set up by the Allies were to remain unchanged.

It must be remembered that Lenin had proclaimed 'world revolution' and Trotsky's armies, although fighting desperately against their own countrymen and former comrades all over Russia and parts of Siberia, were also trying to reoccupy the Baltic States in the face of a new German

threat; von der Goltz had crossed over from Finland and joined his compatriots occupying Lithuania and parts of Latvia.

The Balt governments' appeal to Britain for troops to sustain their newly-won independence was in vain as, after four years of slaughter on the Western Front, the British army was in no condition now that peace had been celebrated, either physically or morally, to embark on new ventures in the Baltic for a cause which was unintelligible to the citizen soldier.

So the whole Baltic situation was handed over to the reliable Royal Navy, ably assisted at times by units of the RAF. The Admiralty chose the aggressive and intrepid Rear-Admiral Sir Walter Cowan (who was later, in the Second World War, to win a bar to his Distinguished Service Order at the age of 72 while serving as a commando in the Western Desert). Cowan eventually had 88 ships of all kinds under his command including auxiliaries, minesweepers, submarines and coastal motor boats. He lost 17 ships, mainly to mines as a result of the extensive and uncharted minefields which littered the area. His ships and crews had to be relieved frequently (about every six weeks) as a result of the severe conditions in which they operated. A few French, American and Italian naval vessels also formed part of his navy.

One meteorological factor must also be emphasised which affected all campaigning. From the beginning of December to April the Gulf of Finland was frozen and naval operations throughout the remainder of the Baltic were severely limited.

At first it was not considered politic to treat the Russian navy as an 'enemy force' and sink on sight. Two of their ships had already surrendered to the Royal Navy. But when Lenin stated that the Baltic must be made a 'Russian Lake' and ordered his

submarines to attack British ships (which they successfully did), British policy gradually hardened.

The *cul de sac* at Kronstadt

By July 1919, after some Russian ships had been sunk, what remained of the Russian fleet was bottled up in Kronstadt harbour. The Baltic fleet had originally consisted of approximately 30 warships, including two battleships, one cruiser and eight destroyers. The British had no battleships in the Baltic, and therefore it was essential to eliminate the two Russian ones before the Baltic States could consider themselves safe when the British withdrew.

Also, at this time, a White Russian army under General Savinkov, assisted by Latvian and Estonian patriot forces and militia, was driving on Petrograd from the west. Savinkov did not appear to appreciate the importance of sea-power since he could not be persuaded to capture the ports of Reval, Kunda and Narva en route and so receive support from the sea. One way to reduce Kronstadt was for a combined army-navy operation against the forts along the south coast of the harbour. If these fell their guns could nullify those on Kotlin Island and the British navy, supported by the Russian White Army, might capture Petrograd by assault and so destroy this last Red wasps' nest in the Baltic. This was Cowan's bold plan but he could not obtain the co-operation of Savinkov, so he sought around for other ideas.

Kronstadt had long been legendary in European history. Peter the Great had captured Kronstadt from the Swedes in 1703 and first constructed the forts and docks. Between 1875/85 a 23-foot-deep canal had been dredged to St Petersburg and Kronstadt lost its commercial value and became a lonely, introspective garrison town. Its

Inset. Right: Lying at Björkö Sound, the British base in south Finland, three CMB's await orders to set off for Kronstadt. *Centre:* The pre-dreadnought *Andrei Pervozvanni* and, below, the dreadnought *Petropavlovsk,* both sunk by the British. *Bottom:* The submarine depot ship *Pamyat Azova* lists after being torpedoed by the British in Kronstadt Harbour.

sailors and garrison troops always formed the most disgruntled and revolutionary part of the Russian armed forces.

A Kronstadt officer led the mutiny of the Decembrists in St Petersburg in 1825. A Kronstadt sailor called Sukhanov led the Marodnaya Volya revolutionary group in 1881. He was shot in 1882. In 1905 and 1906 further mutinies broke out in Kronstadt but were suppressed brutally. In February 1917 the Kronstadt garrison, after drinking the blood of their officers whom they had killed, formed a 'soviet' which opposed the moderate provisional government of Kerensky and declared a 'Kronstadt Republic'. Hitched to Lenin's star they took a major part in the July mutiny. During the Bolshevik revolution of October the same year the Baltic Fleet bombarded Petrograd and its Winter Palace. After the events related here this same garrison and navy was to mutiny once more against the Soviet government in 1921, but the rebels were eventually crushed by Trotsky's armies advancing across the ice amidst scenes of almost mediaeval carnage and rapacity.

Advance base at Björkö

In June 1919 Cowan had first established a base at Björkö Sound some 30 miles east of Kotlin Island on the Finnish shore. On June 4 the two British destroyers HMS *Vivacious* and *Voyager* engaged the Russian destroyers *Azard* and *Gavriil*. In a second attempt to keep the Russians busy while the base at Björkö was being installed, the two British destroyers accompanied by a third, HMS *Walker*, again opened fire over the barrage protecting the harbour but this time the battleship *Petropavlovsk*, well out of range of their own guns, answered their fire and quickly drove them off. But two British submarines on patrol tried also to join in with a torpedo attack. One of them, the *L55*, after firing its torpedoes, broke surface and was rammed and sunk with all hands by the *Gavriil*.

Cowan had complained to the Admiralty of the difficulty of his set task of blockading Petrograd in the face of an opposition consisting of two battleships armed with 12-inch guns. The Admiralty replied that while the present policy of the government remained in force Cowan was precluded from taking offensive action against Kronstadt by monitors, coastal motor boats or by bombing aircraft. But he would be reinforced with minelayers in the hopes that he could bottle up Kronstadt with mines. The Admiralty realised the unsound nature of the whole situation and would again try to make the Cabinet understand.

But whilst these messages had been passing, a Lieutenant Agar had formed a secret base for his *CMB No 4* at Terrioki on the Finnish shore just north of Kronstadt. From there he operated a ferry service to and from Petrograd for secret agents, and thereby came to know well the waters between Kronstadt and Petrograd. During part of his secret operations he hoisted the White Ensign and torpedoed and sank the cruiser *Oleg* (6,650 tons), for which he was awarded a VC, before resuming his more clandestine rôle. But he put forward ambitious ideas to Cowan for an attack on Kronstadt from the north, in the course of which he would lead the attackers into the harbour.

But the Russians countered with several attacks, some successful, on Cowan's base at Björkö. Cowan was told by the British Cabinet to ask the Russian Fleet to surrender. An unarmed patrol boat, the *Kitoboi*, was the only one to do so. Later she was recaptured in Estonia and her captain was crucified by the Bolsheviks. The British Prime Minister, reluctantly lifted the ban on offensive action in the middle of July. By this time Cowan was mining the approaches to Kronstadt, and also to his own base for protection against some nearly successful Russian submarine attacks. The sinking of the *Oleg* by Agar had convinced the Admiralty of the usefulness of CMB's, and eight more of the larger 55-foot craft were sent out under command of Commander Dobson.

Several air attacks against Kronstadt had proved fruitless since, in spite of the pilots pressing home their attacks with great valour, their bombs were too puny and light to do any major damage to heavily armoured naval vessels or shore installations.

Hit and run raid

It was, therefore, finally decided to stake all on a bold CMB attack into Kronstadt Harbour in order to sink the two Russian battleships whose existence endangered the naval balance of power in the Baltic. The scope and success of the attack has been briefly recounted. It would be opportune now to fill in some of the gaps in the story and name some of the participants. The map shows better than a long description the routes the CMB's followed to attack their targets and the obstacles which lay in their way. The garrisons of the forts were somnolent and when they did wake up found that if they fired on the CMB's they would hit their own ships or that they could not depress far enough to fire on the nimble CMB's. Besides its crew, each CMB had on board a Finnish smuggler who knew these waters at night. These latter deserve great credit for their resolution in guiding the boats in. Some of the boats missed the planned way in so the smuggler pilots guided them in by other routes. Agar, in his boat, led the way as far as the harbour entrance, where he waited as a sort of master of ceremonies, but Dobson in *No 31*, commanded by Lieutenant MacBean, led his flotilla into the depths of the harbour and pressed home the attack. Three boats had been detailed to sink the destroyer *Gavriil* which was guarding the entrance, but their torpedoes ran too low and all passed underneath her. The *Gavriil*, aided by the searchlights from the forts, was to sink three of the CMB's. The cruiser *Rurik* had also been detailed as a target since she was supposed to be carrying 300 mines, whose detonation might destroy the whole dockyard and another cruiser tied up nearby. But Sub-Lieutenants Howard and Bodley, commanding *Nos 86* and *72* respectively, and detailed for this task, both had bad luck. Howard's engines broke down just as he was about to attack and a shell splinter damaged the mechanism of Bodley's torpedo firing apparatus. But Bodley did not forget Howard, who was drifting aimlessly in the harbour among all the hail of Russian shellfire. He took Howard's boat in tow and brought him back all the way to Björkö.

Lieutenant Bremner, whose task it was to destroy the boom and carried much explosive for this purpose, on finding no boom continued into the harbour and sank the submarine depot ship *Pamyat Azova*.

Lieutenant-Commander Brade, RNR, in *No 62*, found that his task of sinking the *Petropavlovsk* had been completed by Commander Dobson, and therefore made top speed to the entrance of the harbour to attack the *Gavriil*, which was doing so much damage. But in the darkness he hit Bremner's boat, nearly cutting it in two. But by keeping at top speed he kept the two boats locked together until Bremner and his crew transferred to *No 62*, but not before Bremner had coolly ignited his explosive charges so that after his boat was allowed to part company it blew up.

As already related, after his commander, Dayrell-Reed, had been shot through the head Lieutenant Steele took over and successfully torpedoed and sank the battleship *Andrei Pervozvanni*. Lieutenant Napier in *No 24* was sunk after attacking the *Gavriil*.

As soon as the naval raid was over, Major Donald, with his twelve Sopwith Camels, carried out a further raid to increase the damage and add to the confusion. Air photographs of the sunken ships were also taken at first light. These showed three vessels lying on their side in the shallow water. Although the London *Times* and other reputable British papers printed the naval despatch of the action in full (later Intelligence proved the despatch to be accurate), some left-wing papers, with their reporters in Finland, tried to smear over the whole affair and say the Russian Fleet had suffered no damage.

But the Russians themselves carried out a Commission of Enquiry into the raid, an account of which appears in *Cowan's War* by Geoffrey Bennett, which confirmed the Royal Navy's claim of ships sunk:
The Commission of Enquiry reached the following conclusion on the reasons for the success of the attack:
(a) The complete unexpectedness of the idea of a CMB attack on Kronstadt.
(b) The complete confidence in the impossibility of any sort of naval operation by way of the North Channel.
(c) The complete distraction of the attention of the forts, batteries, signal stations and ships, by aircraft.
(d) The shallow draught of the boats which allowed them to proceed on the surface at 40 knots.

Thus culminated one of the most brilliant actions of the Royal Navy whose memory has sadly been blurred or forgotten as a result of the complex political disputes of that period of history.

Further Reading
Bennett, Geoffrey, *Cowan's War: the Story of British Naval Operations in the Baltic, 1918-1920* (Collins 1964)
Churchill, Winston S., *The World Crisis: the Aftermath* (Butterworth 1931)
Coates, W. P. and Z. K., *Armed Intervention in Russia* (Gollancz 1935)
Marder, A. J., *From the Dardanelles to Oran* (OUP 1974)

MICHAEL CALVERT is a Civil Engineer and Hallsworth Research Fellow in Military Studies at the University of Manchester. As an instructor in guerilla warfare he served in Scotland, Australia, New Zealand, Burma, China and throughout Europe from 1939 to 1952 and was appointed a brigadier in Burma at the age of 31. He is a Member of the International Institute of Strategic Studies and of the Royal United Services Institution in London and the author of a number of books, including *Prisoners of Hope* and *Fighting Mad*.

Imperial War Museum

THE END OF THE HIGH SEAS FLEET

The nadir of dishonour and low cunning, or a noble action in the face of defeat? And was the demise of the German High Seas Fleet a blessing in disguise for the Allies? *Paul Kennedy. Above:* The royal progress of the HMS *Queen Elizabeth,* Beatty's flagship, with the Grand Fleet on November 21, 1918

'The German fleet has assaulted its jailor, but it is still in jail', observed a New York newspaper immediately after the battle of Jutland. Through her geographical position, Britain dominated the exits from the North Sea; and this fact, together with the superiority of her Grand Fleet, meant that she could implement a policy of 'wide blockade' and wait until the High Seas Fleet ventured out to challenge this mastery, which was not likely to happen, given the disparity in numbers and the Kaiser's caution. Though not a very exciting policy, it was extremely effective.

While this was undoubtedly the correct strategy, the Royal Navy's unadventurous rôle attracted much criticism in later years

and even at the time was hard to justify in the face of the army's great exertions on the Western Front. Moreover, the prolonged periods of inaction led to acute frustration in the Grand Fleet, with Beatty confessing himself to be 'War-weary. Scapa-weary, weary of seeing the same old damned agony of grey grey grey, grey sky, grey sea, grey ships.' Nevertheless, morale was high compared with that of the High Seas Fleet, where the situation was very serious indeed. Aware of the superiority in size and numbers of the British warships, the German crews were deeply pessimistic about the outcome of any large-scale action. Confined to their cramped quarters on board ship, subject to fierce discipline without much sport or entertainment, given very poor food rations, and seeing all the best young officers taken away for U-Boat service, the sailors became daily more distrustful and bitter against the leaders. 'What a shame that we cannot lay down our arms for at least a day and allow the Indians and the New Zealanders to run amok upon the estates of the Junkers,' wrote one of them, Seaman Richard Stumpf, in his diary.

This gloom and frustration was merely deepened by the news that Germany's allies were collapsing on all sides and that the government had asked for an armistice on October 4, 1918. Two

3449

weeks later, with the bases at Ostend and Zeebrugge abandoned, and Scheer forced to agree to Wilson's demand that all U-Boats should be recalled, it seemed that the war at sea was at last over for Germany. In fact, Scheer and Hipper (now Chief of Admiralty Staff and C-in-C, High Seas Fleet, respectively) were planning upon one final sortie, which was to redeem the navy's reputation and perhaps affect the Armistice terms. This scheme was quickly abandoned after the Wilhelmshaven mutinies on October 29. The German challenge to the Royal Navy's supremacy had ended, as no-one would have dared to forecast even a few months previously, with a whimper rather than a bang.

A more humiliating event was to follow, however. Throughout October, the Allies had been discussing the demands they would present to the Central Powers as conditions for granting an armistice. Beatty and the Admiralty, naturally crestfallen at the receding chances of a great naval battle, pressed for the complete surrender of the German navy; but Lloyd George, influenced by the army and by the French and American governments, refused this demand out of fear that it might provoke Berlin into continuing the war to gain better terms. Eventually, the Supreme War Council decided that the enemy vessels should be interned in a neutral harbour until the peace terms were settled, and during the Armistice negotiations with Germany between November 8 and 11 it was agreed that this force should include ten battleships, six battle cruisers, eight light cruisers, 50 destroyers and all the U-Boats. While this decision appalled the British admirals, it was even more shocking to the Germans themselves; even the revolutionary sailors at Wilhelmshaven were chilled by the terms. By this stage, though, peace was essential for Germany and the government was determined to accept the conditions.

Neutral countries, perhaps understandably, declined to allow the High Seas Fleet to be interned in their harbours and thus the Allies decided on November 13 that, while the U-Boats would be directed to English ports, the surface ships should be interned in Scapa Flow. Two days later, the cruiser *Königsberg* brought Rear-Admiral Meurer to the Firth of Forth, where the final details were worked out with Beatty and his staff; the U-Boats would surrender to Tyrwhitt at Harwich and the High Seas Fleet would come to the Forth before sailing north to Scapa.

'Der Tag'

November 21, 1918 was *Der Tag,* as the Germans called it. Despite the activities of the rebel sailors and the uncertain political situation, those ships which were to be interned were prepared for the journey. Only the minimum crews necessary to run these vessels were to be used, which meant about 400 men in the capital ships and the rest in proportion. Gloomily, Seaman Stumpf described the scene at Wilhelmshaven a few days earlier and uttered the feelings of many: 'At this moment *Friedrich der Grosse* and *König Albert* are in the locks and the other ships are ready

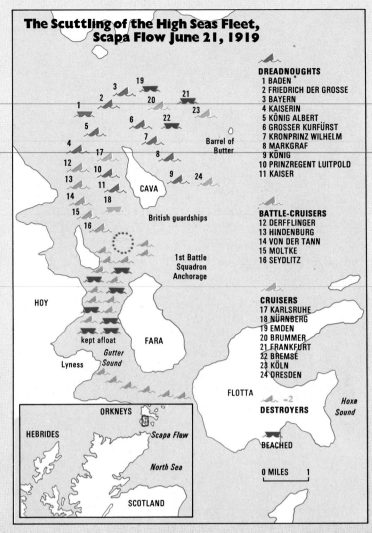

The Scuttling of the High Seas Fleet, Scapa Flow June 21, 1919

DREADNOUGHTS
1 BADEN
2 FRIEDRICH DER GROSSE
3 BAYERN
4 KAISERIN
5 KÖNIG ALBERT
6 GROSSER KURFÜRST
7 KRONPRINZ WILHELM
8 MARKGRAF
9 KÖNIG
10 PRINZREGENT LUITPOLD
11 KAISER

BATTLE-CRUISERS
12 DERFFLINGER
13 HINDENBURG
14 VON DER TANN
15 MOLTKE
16 SEYDLITZ

CRUISERS
17 KARLSRUHE
18 NÜRNBERG
19 EMDEN
20 BRUMMER
21 FRANKFURT
22 BREMSE
23 KÖLN
24 DRESDEN

DESTROYERS

BEACHED

0 MILES   1

Barrel of Butter

CAVA

British guardships

1st Battle Squadron Anchorage

HOY

kept afloat

Gutter Sound

Lyness

FARA

FLOTTA

Hoxa Sound

ORKNEYS

HEBRIDES

Scapa Flow

North Sea

SCOTLAND

Below: German battleships in line on their way to be interned, SMS *Bayern* nearest the camera. *Inset above right:* German submarine *U 126.* One of the U 117 class built for general service and minelaying off the coast of the United States. U-Boats were not interned at Scapa, but surrendered at Harwich. *Right:* The dreadnought SMS *König.* One of a class of four completed in 1914, the first German battleships to have all main armaments on the centre-line and the last with 12-inch guns. They were all scuttled at Scapa Flow and never raised

to follow. They are assembling at Schillig Roads for their final difficult voyage. The submarines will also go along. It is like a funeral. We shall not see them again. Impassively holding their sea-bags, the men who are being left behind stand at the pier. At the last minute they feared for their lives and threw down their weapons. I, too, feel too disgusted to remain here any longer. I wish I had not been born a German.'

On the other side of the North Sea, the greatest naval force in the world had sailed from Rosyth early on the morning of the 21st. Two days earlier, the U-Boats had begun to surrender at Harwich without much of a reception, but now the British were determined to put on as spectacular a display of might as possible. Apart from the Grand Fleet itself, there were detachments from the Channel and other stations: 90,000 men in 370 warships, flying as many white ensigns as they could, as if they were going into action. The Americans were represented by the 6th Battle Squadron and the French had sent an armoured cruiser and two destroyers. In one immense line, they had steamed in single file to the rendezvous 40 miles east of May Island, where they divided into two long columns, about six miles apart, and waited for the German fleet. The light cruiser *Cardiff* and the destroyer flotillas were sent forward to make contact and to lead in the German ships. At 0930 hours these could be spotted in single line ahead. Admiral von Reuter in the *Friedrich der Grosse* was followed by the other eight battleships, five battle cruisers and the smaller warships. (One destroyer had been sunk by a mine on the way; the battleship *König* and a light cruiser were in dock and came over later; while the battle cruiser *Mackensen* was still in the builder's yard.)

Silently, almost eerily, the *Cardiff* led the German fleet down the line formed by Beatty's two columns, which promptly reversed course and shepherded their enemies towards the Forth. Fearing a desperate last-minute, blow, all the British ships were at action stations but, as the minutes ticked by and nothing untoward occurred, the tension diminished. Nevertheless, there was no cheering, no jubilation, until this vast assembly of warships had anchored, Reuter's vessels and their escorts halting at Inchkeith, while the Grand Fleet proceeded to its customary berths higher up above the Forth Bridge. By this stage, the Forth was full of small boats, packed with journalists and sightseers, and the atmosphere was far more relaxed. Beatty himself was repeatedly cheered by the crews of the Grand Fleet, and he announced his intention of holding a service of thanksgiving on the *Queen Elizabeth* 'for the victory which Almighty God has vouchsafed to his Majesty's arms'.

Despite all this, an air of unnaturalness persisted on board the ships throughout that historic day. That there had been no great Trafalgar-style battle, no real chance to re-fight Jutland, was due, as everyone realised, to the immense superiority of the Royal Navy; that the Kaiser's navy had not dared to challenge Britain's control of the North Sea was an acknowledgement of defeat; that the German fleet had voluntarily surrendered instead of seeking a last battle was, in some ways, a victory even greater than Trafalgar. Yet there was on the British side a feeling of incompleteness mixed with disgust and incredulity that the Germans had not chosen to fight. Beatty expressed some of this when he said: 'It was a pitiable sight, in fact I should say it was a horrible sight, to see these great ships . . . come in, led by a British light cruiser, with their old antagonists, the battle cruisers, gazing at them.' On the German side, there was nothing but bitterness and shame at their ignominious surrender. It was, wrote Ludwig Freiwald, a sailor on the battleship *Nassau*, 'the most shameful deed in all the history of the sea'.

On the next day, the interned ships were searched for ammunition before being moved up to Scapa Flow in smaller groups during the following week. The destroyers were then moored in pairs off Hoy, while the larger vessels anchored around the small island of Cava. When the warships delayed by repairs eventually joined the force, it consisted of 11 battleships, five battle cruisers, eight light cruisers and 50 destroyers, the fleet flagship *Baden* having also been added to the list in December in place of the unfinished battle cruiser *Mackensen* to make up the number of capital ships specified in the armistice conditions. The wireless equipment on all the interned ships was removed and the guns were put out of order by the confiscation of the breech-blocks. Nor would the Germans be able to make a surprise escape, for very little fuel was allowed on board. These precautions having been taken, the British permitted a steady reduction in crew numbers on these vessels, so that only enough were left for care and maintenance; the rest of the men were shipped back to Germany.

The German fleet was originally guarded by the Battle Cruiser Force but in May 1919 these duties were taken over by Vice-Admiral Fremantle's 1st Battle Squadron: to assist him, armed trawlers and drifters were posted near the anchorages, with instructions to report immediately if the Germans attempted to scuttle the interned ships. The position of these vessels in international law was a rather special one. When the original intention of internment in a neutral harbour fell through, it was too late for the British to change the Armistice conditions. Under these, it would clearly be a breach of the agreement to place armed guards on board each ship, since Reuter's fleet had not been legally surrendered. There was always a danger, therefore, that the Germans might try to scuttle their fleet, even though this would also constitute a violation of the Armistice; Article XXXI stipulated: 'No destruction of ships . . . to be permitted.' However, although contingency plans had been drawn up by the authorities at Scapa Flow — and some of these involved seizing the interned vessels even *before* a peace treaty was signed — the Admiralty was too concerned with the negotiations in Paris to pay any attention to such suggestions.

Disposal problem

While the pride of the German fleet rusted at their anchors at Scapa, Allied politicians and admirals argued over what to do with the warships. It was difficult enough to find a solution for the U-Boats, 176 of which either sailed or were towed into Harwich harbour. While the British and American admiralties, who had regarded these vessels as being in some way 'uncivilised', pressed for their destruction and the complete banning of submarines by all countries, this was opposed by both France and Italy, who, as weaker powers, could appreciate their uses. By March 1919 it had been decided that the U-Boats should be divided among the Allies and then either sunk or broken up, while those under construction in Germany would be destroyed under supervision, since she was not to be allowed such weapons in the future. Even so, the exact disposal of the captured vessels was still under discussion after the Versailles Treaty had been signed. In December 1919 it was decided that the French should be allowed to keep ten U-Boats, all the rest to be broken up within a year.

It was equally difficult for the Allies to decide on the future of the German surface fleet, both at Scapa and in the home ports (the latter included eight dreadnoughts, six pre-dreadnoughts, 14 light cruisers, 54 destroyers and 62 torpedo-boats). Once again, it proved easier to deal with the German side first and to decree that the defeated foe's navy would be restricted to 15,000 personnel and to the six pre-dreadnoughts, six of the light cruisers, 12 destroyers and 12 torpedo-boats. But what of the remaining ships, which constituted the second-largest navy in the world? The Americans wanted them all to be sunk, particularly if the alternative was for them to be distributed to the Allies on the basis

Below: Some of the 50 destroyers moored in pairs in Gutter Sound. Isolation and excess of leisure, no less than dirt and shortage of food, contributed to the demoralisation of the German crews.

of war losses, which would mean that they would get very few and the British would obtain the lion's share. While the British shared the Americans' preference, they were prepared to argue for sharing out the ships of the High Seas Fleet among the Allied powers if the Americans persisted in their own vast warship construction programmes. The French and Italians were, as ever, eager to augment their own naval forces with captured vessels. Fortunately for the British, and perhaps for all concerned, the decision was taken out of their hands.

The long months at Scapa had not been happy ones for Admiral von Reuter or his crews. The latter were in a sullen and bitter mood, particularly on board the capital ships. They were cut off from home by the lack of wireless communications and the inadequacy of the postal service. Food, though sufficient, was very poor and the sailors often bartered their decorations and binoculars with the British seamen in return for chocolate and cigarettes. At the same time there was an excess of alcohol in the German vessels, resulting in many cases of drunkenness. The interned crews were not allowed ashore, so they had little recreation or relief from the sheer monotony of their lives. Added to all this was the fact that many of the men had been influenced by the naval mutinies and were no longer amenable to discipline; in any case, most of the officers were too demoralised to enforce the

normal regulations. As a result, the ships were neither polished nor cleaned out, and soon became very shabby and stinking, causing further deterioration in morale. On the anniversary of the battle of Jutland on May 31, red flags as well as the Imperial ensign were hoisted on many ships. Reuter encountered so much trouble with the crew of the *Friedrich der Grosse* that he was allowed to transfer his flag to the light cruiser *Emden*. To his British captors, however, the Admiral was polite and reasonable, and always extremely efficient in carrying out instructions. In these circumstances, the prospects of the Germans taking decisive action and scuttling their vessels appeared to grow less and less.

In the event, the British greatly under-estimated Reuter and his fellow officers. As soon as it became clear from the press reports that the discussions in Paris concerned only the question of whether the German warships should be sunk or retained by the Allies and that there was no chance of them being returned to the Fatherland, plans were begun for scuttling the interned force. As Reuter wrote afterwards, 'It was unthinkable to surrender defenceless ships to the enemy'. Scuttling in these circumstances was expected by his superiors, although it seems very doubtful indeed whether specific instructions about this were sent from Wilhelmshaven. After the event, Reuter claimed full responsibility and initiative, and there is no reason to dispute this.

Ironically, the hoisting of the red flag by the rebel sailors on May 31 gave Reuter the chance to further his plans; for he suggested that the crews' numbers should be cut by about 40% to forestall future troubles. Although the Admiral had earlier insisted that the existing numbers were necessary to look after his warships properly, the British agreed to this request, not recognising until too late the implication that Reuter had decided that he no longer needed to keep his vessels in good running order. On June 17, certain that the German fleet would be seized as soon as the Armistice expired at noon on the 21st, he ordered preparations on all ships for the scuttling, which would begin about two hours before the deadline. Since Reuter was allowed the privilege of communicating with the vessels under him and his suggested action was welcomed by every officer, there were few difficulties of co-ordination and co-operation.

What of the British side? On June 16, Fremantle submitted to Admiral Madden, the new C-in-C, Atlantic Fleet (as the Grand Fleet was now called), a plan for seizing the ships at midnight on the 21st. This action would have been too late in any case, but other factors intervened to change the British schemes. Fremantle was eager to take his 1st Battle Squadron to sea to practise a large-scale tactical exercise, and the weather prospects for this seemed good for June 21, the only drawback being the political uncertainty about the ending of the Armistice. However, on the evening of the 20th he learnt that the deadline had been postponed two days by the Council of Four in Paris, and he therefore had no qualms about postponing his planned action until the evening of the 23rd and taking his ships to sea on the following morning. Though there is still some doubt about whether Fremantle informed Reuter of the extension of the Armistice, this does not alter the German Admiral's responsibility in the matter, since he planned to violate it in any case.

Loyal or dishonourable?

After the 1st Battle Squadron had departed, the only British warships left in the huge anchorage were several destroyers and trawlers. At 1120 hours, Reuter gave the fateful order to scuttle, having prepared for this by an earlier signal at 1000 hours. At once, the sea-cocks and watertight doors were opened, while the small boats were prepared for the evacuation. By noon the *Friedrich der Grosse* and many others were already beginning to list, and all the German warships had broken out the Imperial ensign. Only at this stage did the British realise that something was amiss and at 1220 the message 'German battleship sinking' was flashed to Fremantle, then in the Pentland Firth, some eight miles away. The fleet exercise was swiftly cancelled but the ships of the 1st Battle Squadron, arriving back at 1430 hours, were too late to do anything but watch. It is difficult to see how, even if they had been there, they or anyone else could have prevented the scuttling once the sea-cocks were opened. Certainly, the few small British vessels and launches already in Scapa Flow were helpless, although they did fire at the German fleet in an effort to compel the evacuating crews to go back and save the listing warships. The captain of the battleship *Markgraf* and nine others were killed in the shooting, which added to the picture of utter confusion, with dozens of vessels sinking all over the vast bay.

All five battle cruisers went down, as did ten out of the 11 battleships; only the newly-completed *Baden* failed to sink and was beached in shallow water. Half of the eight light cruisers sank, while the other half were beached. Of the 50 destroyers, four were only partly flooded, 14 were beached, and the remaining 32 sank. Reuter's scuttling operation had been almost completely successful. As Professor Marder notes: 'It was all over by 5 pm: 400,000 tons of metal and machinery worth £70 million had been sent to the bottom of the Flow.'

The immediate British reaction was one of sheer disgust and fury. Fremantle ordered the 1,800 German officers and men to be treated as prisoners of war since they had broken the Armistice; before Reuter was taken away, the British Admiral insisted on publicly scolding him for adding 'one more to the breaches of faith and honour of which Germany has been guilty in this war'. The Admiralty itself considered (and abandoned) the idea of trying Reuter by court-martial, and requested that more ships be taken as compensation from Germany, although the government in Berlin declared that they had not ordered the scuttling and knew nothing about it. On the other hand, Admiral Scheer openly rejoiced that 'the stain of surrender has been wiped from the escutcheon of the German fleet', and the German press was as full of praise for the act as the British newspapers were of scorn.

A short while afterwards, however, the mood of British official circles began to change. After all, they had always wanted to sink the German fleet in any case, and the question of its redistribution was leading to tedious and irritating discussions with the French and the Italians. By June 1919 much of the heat had gone out of the Anglo-American naval rivalry, and the Admiralty felt that it no longer needed to employ the threat of taking over large numbers of German dreadnoughts for the Royal Navy. For these reasons, therefore, the First Sea Lord, Wemyss, privately informed his Deputy: 'I look upon the sinking of the German fleet as a real blessing. It disposes once for all of the thorny question of the distribution of these ships and eases us of an enormous amount of difficulties.' Indeed, the scuttling was so fortuitous for the British that certain members of the French and Italian governments believed that it might have been connived at: the absence of the entire 1st Battle Squadron on that very morning seemed too much of a coincidence to be accidental. Yet the official and private correspondence of those authorities concerned both at London and Scapa Flow reveals no evidence for this assertion. The Admiralty were very quick to refute American and French suggestions that an armed guard should have been placed on the German ships by pointing out that it was precisely the insistence of those two governments that the German fleet should be interned rather than surrendered which had made this precaution impossible.

In an effort to reach a compromise between the American determination to have all the remaining German fleet sunk except

Imperial War Museum

those allowed her in the Versailles settlement, and the Franco-Italian desire to obtain some good vessels (or at least the scrap metal), the great powers finally agreed, on December 9, 1919, that the surviving German surface warships were to be distributed according to war losses; but they were then to be broken up within five years, except for some light cruisers and destroyers which France and Italy were to be permitted to incorporate into their own navies. By this decision, Great Britain obtained 70% of the German total, but with one proviso: that the ships scuttled at Scapa Flow be included in her share. This proposal, made by Lloyd George in an effort to avert a deadlock, proved acceptable to all. Of the larger vessels remaining of Reuter's fleet, only the light cruisers *Emden* and *Frankfurt* passed into other navies, the rest becoming the property of the British Admiralty, along with a number of older warships in Germany. The one battleship not scuttled at Scapa, the *Baden,* was subjected to various trials and then sunk in 1921. As for the many vessels lying on the bottom of that vast and gloomy anchorage, a private salvage firm was given the contract to raise them for scrap, a task which was still being carried out at the start of the Second World War. Seven warships (three battleships and four light cruisers) were too deep to be salvaged. They are still there, a hidden and almost forgotten memorial to the dramatic end of the German High Seas Fleet.

Further Reading

Bennett, G., *Naval Battles of the First World War* (Batsford 1968)

Freiwald, Ludwig, *Last Days of the German Fleet* (Constable 1933)

Gladisch, Admiral Walther, *Der Krieg in der Nordsee,* Volume 7 (Official German Naval History; Berlin: E.S. Mittler und Sohn 1965)

Horn, Daniel (ed.), *War, Mutiny and Revolution in the German Navy: The World War I Diary of Seaman Richard Stumpf* (Brunswick, New Jersey; Rutgers University Press 1967)

Marder, A. J., *From the Dreadnought to Scapa Flow,* Volume 5: *Victory and Aftermath* (London: Oxford University Press 1970)

Newbolt, Sir Henry, *Naval Operations,* Volume 5 (Official British Naval History; Longmans 1931)

Reuter, Vice-Admiral Ludwig von, *Scapa Flow: The Account of the Greatest Scuttling of All Time* (London: Hurst and Blackett 1940)

Schubert, Paul, and Gibson, Langhorne, *Death of a Fleet 1917-1919* (Hutchinson 1933)

[*For Paul Kennedy's biography, see page 633.*]

Below: June 21, 1919 – the end of SMS *Bayern.* Her sister ship, the flagship *Baden,* was the only one of the 16 capital ships not to sink

LETTOW-VORBECK: a hero's homecoming

The proliferation of traitors, or scapegoats, in a defeated Fatherland immediately after the war only increased the need for heroes. The triumphal return of Lettow-Vorbeck, universally admired for his East African campaign, provided an emotional focus for people starved of glory.
D. R. Shermer. Below right: Lettow-Vorbeck. *Opposite:* The *Ostafrikaners* welcomed in Berlin on March 2, 1919

In 1919 Berlin, the elegant city of the kings of Prussia, was a major industrial centre as well as the capital of the defeated German Empire. The workers were acutely class-conscious and sensitive to social injustice, and many who had supported the Social Democrats before the war had joined the Spartacists, the Revolutionary Shop Stewards and Communists.

General Paul von Lettow-Vorbeck, hero of the East African campaign, made his triumphal entry to a city in turmoil. On March 3, the day after his arrival, a ten-day strike began, and when the government forces finally succeeded in breaking it they were aided by volunteer corps including the Lettow Division, which had been raised by Lettow-Vorbeck himself.

Both in Rotterdam and in Berlin, the welcome accorded to Lettow-Vorbeck was a psychological release for those Germans who regretted the passing of the old Imperial order and who were left desperate and confused by the mutiny of the German fleet at Kiel, by the German revolution of November 9, 1918, by the abdication of the Kaiser and, above all, by the Armistice. Lettow-Vorbeck's disbelief and incomprehension when he himself learned of these events on November 13, in East Africa, was typical of their reaction: 'All this news seemed to me very improbable, and I did not believe it until it was confirmed.'

In a sense, these Germans substituted Lettow's return for the triumphal victory parade which they had confidently expected at the conclusion of hostilities. Inexplicably defeated, short of food because of the blockade, surrounded by revolutionary ferment, the German burghers fêted one of their own, a stalwart who for over four years had held down a large number of British troops in East Africa, had cost Great Britain £72,000,000 in precious currency, and had inflicted three times as many casualties as Britain suffered in the Boer War. In his *Reminiscences,* Lettow-Vorbeck rightly attributed the enthusiasm for his homecoming to the fact that 'everyone seemed to think that we had preserved

some part of Germany's soldierly traditions, that we had come home unsullied and that the Teutonic sense of loyalty had kept its head high' so far from home.

Colonel Lettow-Vorbeck, as he then was, had assumed command of German forces in German East Africa in January 1914. At the outbreak of war, he determined to follow a diversionary campaign which would bring glory to Germany and siphon off Allied troops needed in the European campaigns. His efforts were brilliantly successful, and he was awarded Germany's highest military decoration, the *Pour le Mérite,* in the latter part of 1916.

An example of Lettow's success was the four-day battle of Mahiwa (Nyangao) in October 1917. Here his *Ostafrikaners* inflicted 2,700 casualties on a British infantry force of 4,900. By November, General Jan Smuts, commander of British Empire forces in East Africa, had driven Lettow out of German East Africa itself, but he had crossed into Moçambique with 278 Europeans, 16,000 Askaris and 400 porters. For the next ten months Lettow conducted a troublesome campaign of evasion before returning to Tanganyika. Next he invaded Northern Rhodesia, but was halted by news of the Armistice. His formal surrender was accepted by General

Edwards at noon on November 25, but Lettow was secure in the knowledge that his campaign had resulted in 62,220 British casualties, excluding porters, with a high proportion of deaths among these. At one time or another 300,000 officers and men, using 140,000 horses and mules, had been pitted against him. A. J. Barker has described Lettow-Vorbeck as 'one of the great guerrilla leaders of the century'.

After many delays, Lettow and his entourage of 114 German soldiers, 107 women and 87 children set sail from Dar-es-Salaam on January 17, 1919, travelling via Cape Town on board the steamer *Feldmarschall.* 200 British soldiers escorted them. It was the fifth anniversary of Lettow's arrival in East Africa.

After reaching Plymouth on February 24, a few days later they entered the port of Rotterdam. There the Germans encountered a reception which was a foretaste of the welcome they were to receive in Berlin. On the quay to greet them were about 400 German residents of the city, and, as Lettow remarked, 'many Dutch also gave us proofs of goodwill'. Prince Henry of the Netherlands, President of the Dutch Red Cross and consort of Queen Wilhelmina, was there to greet the general, as were members of the German diplomatic

corps and the personal representative of the Imperial Family. In an excess of enthusiasm, the German Military Attaché told Lettow-Vorbeck that his name was now the most popular in the world!

'A cheer for the Fatherland'
Amid cheers and acclamations, the party landed and made its way to a beer-drinking celebration organised by the *Deutsche Verein*. There the German Minister at The Hague told Lettow and his men that 'those who had come to welcome them were deeply moved' by the occasion. In a highly emotional atmosphere, Lettow replied with a call for 'a cheer for the German Fatherland as it was and as it will be'. The clamour of the reception quickly resolved itself into a manifestation of sympathy for the rejected Kaiser. The chairman of the reception paid tribute to 'the noble and unfortunate Kaiser, whose reign was the period in which Germany became one of the first nations in the world and won a leading position in the domains of science and art'. To deafening cheers and applause, the president of the *Verein* reached a crescendo: 'Prussia to lead the German Empire, Germany to lead the world!' Lettow now passionately declared that Germans should remember 'all that the Hohenzollern dynasty has done for Germany . . . we must firmly keep the principles of the former army if we wish the German Fatherland to recover its ancient power. Men, not fate, make history.' The celebration ended in renditions of *Deutschland über Alles* and *Die Wacht am Rhein*.

On March 2 Lettow-Vorbeck arrived at the *Lehrter Bahnhof*, Berlin. He and his men were met at the station by Colonel Reinhard of the *Freikorps*, members of the Colonial Office and the German Officers' League. Present was a guard of honour from Lettow's old regiment, the *4th Regiment of Guards*, and from Wilhelmshaven had come a deputation of the *2nd Marine Battalion*. To the delight of onlookers, General von Winterfeld 'tendered warm thanks in the name of the General Staff'. Referring to Lettow's achievements the Colonial Secretary remarked that these 'refuted the fable of Germany's colonial inability', while the War Minister acclaimed the *Ostafrikaners* as 'the bravest of the brave'. Vice-Admiral Rogge and the Burgomaster extended a welcome on behalf of the navy and the city of Berlin.

To the accompaniment of military marches, Lettow-Vorbeck proceeded in triumph through the Brandenburg Gate to the *Pariser Platz*. Thousands of enthusiastic Berliners thronged the streets, and several women fainted with excitement. Instead of the banners of the new Republic, Imperial flags fluttered everywhere, and 'patriotic songs of the old régime rang out in quite the old way'.

An incident during the festivities was symbolic of the feelings of injured national pride given free rein that day. The crowd suddenly noticed some American officers who were observing the celebrations at the Brandenburg Gate from the windows of the Hotel Adlon. A number of onlookers started jeering, hissing, shaking fists, waving sticks and abusing the Americans, and the hotel was obliged to bar its doors for fear that the demonstrators would break in. For some time a hostile mob seethed outside the hotel, which was also the headquarters of the French mission in Berlin, because of an unfounded rumour that the French had hissed the triumphal procession. In the end, German troops had to be 'lined up in front of the hotel to prevent possible violence'.

The importance of this footnote to the troubled history of Germany between the Armistice and the Treaty of Versailles lies in the insight it affords into the recalcitrant sentiments of a section of the German populace. Long afterwards, for many Germans, Lettow-Vorbeck continued to symbolise that valour and daring which gave them consolation in defeat and hope in the future.

Further Reading
Barker, A. J., *The War in East Africa, History of the Twentieth Century,* Volume 2, Number 18 (Purnell 1968)
Lettow-Vorbeck, General Paul von, *Mein Leben* (Munich: Koehlers Verlagsgesellschaft, Biberach an der Riss 1957)
Lettow-Vorbeck, General Paul von, *My Reminiscences of East Africa* (2nd Edition, Hurst and Blackett 1922)
Watt, Richard, *The Kings Depart* (Weidenfeld and Nicolson 1969)

[*For D. R. Shermer's biography, see page 407.*]

Ullstein

NAVAL AVIATION:
the first aircraft carriers

At the end of the war, Britain led the rest of the world in the development of naval aviation, possessing the only true aircraft carrier. Here *Captain Donald Macintyre* traces the carrier's evolution from the early gun turret take-off platforms. *Above:* The world's first carrier-operated wheeled torpedo bomber, the Sopwith Cuckoo, which entered service in 1918

Imperial War Museum

Right: The humdrum aspect of naval flying, convoy escort, portrayed in *A Convoy, North Sea, 1918. From NS 7* by Sir James Lavery. *Below:* The hazards of over-water flight — the crew of a ditched FBA flying boat about to be rescued by their patrol companions in a similar boat

National Archives

The wide-spread and varied nature of the tasks undertaken by the RNAS during the first 18 months of the war was partly described in a previous article (in Issue 83). In addition to demonstrably naval aspects of aviation, naval aviators had been engaged on strategic bombing operations, home air defence, army support, the manning of airships and kite-balloons, while the RNAS also operated 15 armoured car squadrons and three armoured trains and manned a large anti-aircraft gun and searchlight force as part of the home defences.

Little of this contributed to development of a system that would give the Grand Fleet the aerial scouting capability required and offer opposition to the Germans' scouting Zeppelins. Even the fast carriers such as HMS *Ben-my-Chree* and *Campania* failed in this respect as a result of the continued reliance placed upon floatplanes. A high proportion of these were always damaged when they tried to take off from the open North Sea; only the smallest could be launched from the deck and, though demonstrations of the technique had been made, it had never been used operationally.

When Mr Balfour took over from Mr Churchill as First Lord of the Admiralty in May 1915 this continued shortcoming of naval aviation led him to a suspicion that funds were being misapplied to support the RNAS's numerous sideshows. He arranged for them to be taken over by the War Office including, in February 1916, the responsibility for Home Air Defence. In the last of these the navy retained the responsibility for intercepting and attacking approaching hostile aircraft over the sea. Nevertheless, the new arrangement released a large number of aeroplanes and pilots and they, together with others thrown up by the abandonment of the Gallipoli campaign, were sent to reinforce the Dunkirk air command. This was rapidly expanded to comprise three wings at Dunkirk and additional satellite airfields. The fighter element was composed of Nieuport Scouts and the new Sopwith two-seater known as the '1½ Strutter', though the latter was also used for bombing and for spotting; for bombing there were also the French Breguet and the Caudron twin-engined aircraft.

German aeroplanes and seaplanes had been raiding the Kentish coast; in reply a bombing offensive against German airfields by the Dunkirk force and by seaplanes from the carriers HMS *Riviera* and *Vindex* was mounted. These in turn brought retaliation in the form of German air raids on Dunkirk, against which the first homogeneous RNAS squadron, known as 'A' Squadron and composed of Nieuport Scouts, was formed and deployed at an advanced airfield. New fighters became available to the RNAS — the Sopwith Scout (more familiarly the 'Pup') in May 1916, and the Sopwith Triplane in June.

Thus, during 1916, the Dunkirk wings, besides their more maritime responsibilities for co-operation with and protection of the units of the Dover Patrol — spotting for bombardments, providing defensive fighter patrols and anti-submarine patrols — became steadily more involved in the air war over the Western Front. In August a heavy programme of bombing raids on German airfields, gun batteries and ammunition dumps was undertaken, mainly with the object of drawing German air strength away from the area of the great Battle of the Somme that was raging. In October the first of a number of naval air fighter squadrons (No 8) that were to build up a brilliant record on duty with the hard-pressed RFC for the rest of the war was detached from the Dunkirk wings and, equipped with Sopwith Pups, was stationed at Vert Galand.

Bold but ineffective
Few of these operations, studded with gallant exploits and deeds of airmanship and valour as they were, contributed anything to the fighting efficiency of the fleet, the primary aim of a Naval Air Service. As mentioned before, desultory efforts towards such an aim had been made at intervals since 1913, when HMS *Hermes* operated an amphibious plane flown off a platform while under way. When next such a platform was used — by the *Campania* in June 1915 — instead of using any of the land-planes available to the RNAS, such as the little Nieuport Scout, and accepting, as was done later, the need to 'ditch' the machine at the end of its

Sopwith Camels on HMS *Furious'* flying-off deck. Note the RNAS stripes on the elevators and the downward-swinging palisaded wind-break

flight if out of range of an airfield, an obsession with floatplanes led to the tiny Sopwith 'Schneider' being selected. A seaplane was inevitably handicapped in performance as compared to a land plane. Nevertheless when the new fast (22 knots) seaplane carrier *Vindex* took the *Campania's* place when she went back into dockyard to have a larger platform fitted, Schneiders or the improved version, the Sopwith 'Baby' seaplanes, continued to be carried. Furthermore, although in November 1915 a Bristol Scout aeroplane was successfully flown off the *Vindex's* deck, when operations against Zeppelin sheds in north Germany were mounted in March and May 1916, the *Vindex's* Babies were not so launched but were hoisted out. On the second of these occasions, 11 Sopwith Babies were hoisted out from the *Vindex* and HMS *Engadine,* of which eight failed to get into the air, one crashed after fouling a destroyer's wireless aerial, one came down with engine failure and only one carried out its mission – unsuccessfully.

The *Campania* rejoined the fleet in April 1916; operation of her Short scouting seaplanes so that they could be hoisted out and re-embarked while the ship was under way was successfully practised; her Babies could be launched from the deck. Subject to the limitations of the Shorts, the fleet had, for the first time, its own integrated air element. At the end of May the opportunity presented itself for aviation to establish its place firmly in the Grand Fleet's fighting organisation. On the evening of the 30th, Admiral Jellicoe led it to sea from Scapa Flow headed for the one great sea battle of the war off Jutland.

By a calamitous oversight the sailing signal did not reach the *Campania* until two and a half hours later. She weighed at once and followed at full speed; but in the absence of any escort for her during the long chase to catch up, the C-in-C was unwilling to expose her to submarine attack and ordered her to return to harbour. Had Jellicoe been certain of the momentous encounter about to take place, he would surely have accepted the risk. Whether or not the reconnaissance difficulties which snatched decisive victory from the British admiral's hands would then have been resolved must remain speculation. The Short seaplane sent up from the *Engadine,* accompanying Admiral Beatty's Battle Cruiser Fleet, came down with a broken petrol pipe after making two enemy reports to the parent ship. These never got through to the flagship. No further aerial reconnaissances were attempted, a rising swell in the otherwise calm sea being considered too much for the flimsy aircraft.

Three days after the Battle of Jutland, a Short seaplane was flown off the *Campania's* deck and this then became standard practice; but unfortunately when the High Seas Fleet next came to sea in August 1916 the *Campania* was immobilised at Scapa with defective machinery.

Flight-deck take-off

Nevertheless the essential requirement, arrangements for launching aircraft from the deck, had become firmly established. In the same month the Admiralty commandeered the unfinished hull of a liner, the *Conte Rosso,* and commissioned Beardmore's to complete her with a flush deck covering her whole length, on which aeroplanes could both land and take off, a conversion which was to take two years to complete. It was in August 1916, too, that a fighter was first launched from a carrier's deck to attack a Zeppelin – a Bristol Scout from the *Vindex,* flown by Flight-Lieutenant C. T. Freeman. The airship escaped though damaged by the Ranken darts dropped on her envelope, but the episode inspired the equipping of the converted Isle of Man packet HMS *Manxman* with the new Sopwith Pup fighter to operate from the deck in place of the Baby seaplanes originally carried.

Flight-Commander F. J. Rutland, senior flying officer of the *Manxman,* who had piloted the *Engadine's* seaplane during the Battle of Jutland, added to a mounting rôle of flying adventures by an unsuccessful chase of a Zeppelin with one of these Pups in April 1917, a flight which ended in the sea off the Danish coast, whence he was rescued by Danish fishermen.

Meanwhile the take-off performance of the Pup, which, with a wing-loading of only 5 lbs. per square foot, required only a 20-foot run into a 20-knot wind to get airborne, had led to experiments with a platform built forward of the bridge of the light cruiser HMS *Yarmouth.* From this Rutland made the first flight in June 1917. On August 21 the *Yarmouth,* with the 1st Cruiser Squadron, was covering a minelaying operation off the Danish coast when the Zeppelin *L23* was sighted. The force steered out to seaward for an hour, luring the shadowing airship further from the coast before turning into wind to launch the *Yarmouth's* Pup flown by Flight Sub-Lieutenant B. A. Smart.

At 7,000 feet Smart set off in chase of the Zeppelin which, on sighting him, turned to escape. For any seaplane at that date the

Top: Squadron-Commander E. H. Dunning landing his Sopwith Pup on the flying-off deck of HMS *Furious.* On his third attempt on August 7, the right-hand tyre of his Pup burst and the machine fell over the side. Note the rope toggles. *Above:* A Pup being swayed out of its hangar

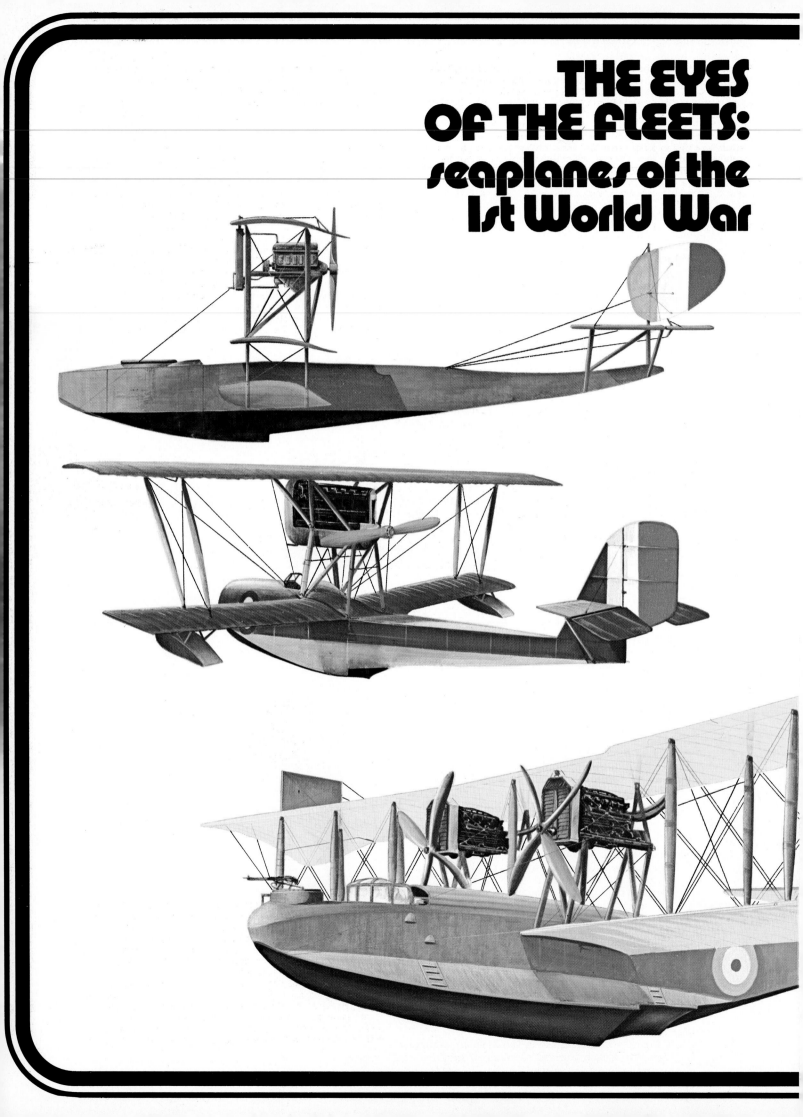

THE EYES OF THE FLEETS: seaplanes of the 1st World War

Opposite page, top: The **Franco-British Aviation Type H** flying boat. Despite its name, the FBA concern was almost entirely French, and built a series of excellent flying boats for the air services of the Allies, starting with the Type B in 1915 and culminating with the Type S in 1918. Illustrated is the first model to be powered with an inline engine, the Type H anti-submarine and coastal patrol flying boat. This model was built in great numbers (at least 982) in Italy, and had the distinction of being produced in larger quantities than any other such machine in the First World War. *Engine:* Hispano-Suiza inline, 150- or 170-hp, Lorraine inline, 160-hp or Isotta-Fraschini inline, 180-hp. *Armament:* one machine gun (Lewis or Revelli) and a small bomb load. *Crew:* 3. *Speed:* 90 mph at sea level. *Climb:* 3,280 feet in 8 minutes. *Ceiling:* 16,000 feet. *Range:* 373 miles. *Weight empty/loaded:* 2,170/3,218 lbs. *Span:* 46 feet 7 inches. *Length:* 33 feet 2 inches. *Centre:* The Italian **Macchi M 7** fighter flying boat of 1918. Only three had been delivered before the Armistice, but they would have been more than a match for the Austro-Hungarian fighters of the same configuration. *Engine:* Isotta-Fraschini V-6B, 250-hp. *Armament:* two Fiat machine guns. *Speed:* 130 mph at sea level. *Climb:* 16,400 feet in 22 minutes. *Ceiling:* 16,400 feet. *Range:* 522 miles. *Weight empty/loaded:* 1,710/2,381 lbs. *Span:* 32 feet 8 inches. *Length:* 26 feet 7 inches. *Bottom:* The **Porte-Felixstowe F 3,** one of Britain's best boats of the war, developed from a Curtiss design by Commander J. Porte RN. The design was for an anti-submarine and patrol bomber, and was built mainly in 1918. *Engines:* two Rolls-Royce Eagle VIII, 345-hp each. *Armament:* four Lewis guns and four 230-lb bombs. *Crew:* 4. *Speed:* 93 mph at 2,000 feet. *Climb:* 10,000 feet in 24 minutes 50 seconds. *Ceiling:* 12,500 feet. *Endurance:* up to 9½ hours. *Weight empty/loaded:* 7,958/13,281 lbs. *Span:* 102 feet. *Length:* 49 feet 2 inches. *This page, below:* The German **Hansa-Brandenburg FB** patrol flying boat. Only six were built for the German navy, though the type was used in some numbers by the Austro-Hungarian navy in the Adriatic between 1915 and the end of the war. *Engine:* Austro-Daimler inline, 165-hp. *Armament:* one Parabellum machine gun. *Crew:* 3. *Speed:* 87 mph at sea level. *Climb:* 3,280 feet in 8½ minutes. *Range:* 683 miles. *Weight empty/loaded:* 2,513/3,571 lbs. *Span:* 52½ feet. *Length:* 33¼ feet

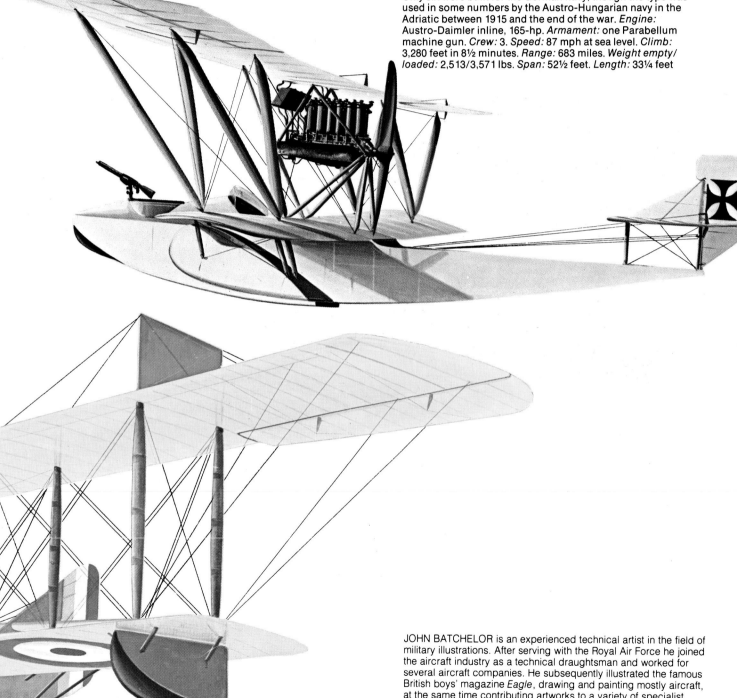

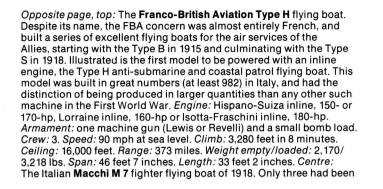

JOHN BATCHELOR is an experienced technical artist in the field of military illustrations. After serving with the Royal Air Force he joined the aircraft industry as a technical draughtsman and worked for several aircraft companies. He subsequently illustrated the famous British boys' magazine *Eagle*, drawing and painting mostly aircraft, at the same time contributing artworks to a variety of specialist trade and technical publications.

Besides the Purnell reference histories of World Wars I and II, John Batchelor illustrated the *Weapons and Warfare* set as well as the hugely successful Ballantine *World War II* pocket book series.

He has produced a series of illustrated books both in the U.S. and Britain showing the development of tanks, armoured vehicles and aircraft and has illustrated a number of Time-Life publications.

situation would have been hopeless; but, unencumbered by floats, the Pup overhauled the airship and gained a position 1,500 feet above it. Putting his machine into a dive, Smart opened fire with his machine gun, firing incendiary bullets along the whole length of the envelope. A sheet of flame flashed out from end to end and the whole structure fluttered seawards, blazing fiercely. The triumphant pilot alighted alongside the destroyer HMS *Prince* and was picked up, though his aircraft could not be salved in those submarine-infested waters.

This success was to have an electrifying effect upon naval opinion with regard to the air arm. Even while it was in progress, important discussions as to the naval air policy to be pursued were taking place between Sir David Beatty, commanding the Grand Fleet, and the Third Sea Lord. The former, with considerable justification, complained that as far as he knew no firm policy existed, though several decisions destined to be epoch-making had been taken by the Admiralty. In March 1917, following on a suggestion by the Grand Fleet Aircraft Committee, it had been decided to convert into a carrier HMS *Furious*, one of 'Jacky' Fisher's three brain-children—HMS *Courageous* and *Glorious* were the others—a fast cruiser of 19,100 tons with a main armament of two 18-inch guns in two single turrets. That the precedence due to air power was not yet fully understood was shown when Beatty came out in opposition to this plan unless the *Furious* could also retain both her 18-inch turrets. But he was over-ruled by the Admiralty, and the *Furious* was taken in hand for the fitting of a flying deck forward, 228 feet long and 50 feet wide, with a hangar to house ten aircraft underneath it. So fitted and carrying three Short reconnaissance seaplanes and five Sopwith Pups, she joined the fleet in July 1917.

Though the provision of the means to carry aircraft with the fleet was thus going ahead, the type of aeroplanes needed was still a matter for argument. News of the brilliant little exploit from the *Yqrmouth* thus made a considerable impact. It led to Beatty coming down on the side of aeroplanes as opposed to seaplanes for all fleet aircraft. At the same time the Admiralty asked for the Commander-in-Chief's views on a proposal to fit one light cruiser in each squadron with a flying-off platform in the manner of the *Yarmouth*. The gun was still the queen of battles to the naval officer of that day—and indeed was to remain so too long in the British navy—with the result that Beatty gave only qualified approval to this scheme, agreeing with it, provided that no gunpower was sacrificed for it. This proviso was met by the erection of a rotatable platform amidships in place of the one forward. This had the added advantage of giving the aircraft some shelter from the sea spray when the ship was heading into the wind.

While this was under consideration, there came another development designed to give the fleet its own, ship-borne air element without sacrificing gunpower. Lieutenant-Commander C. H. B. Gowan, an enthusiast in his conception of the importance of the air weapon, who had been associated with the experiments in the *Yarmouth*, suggested a platform on the roof of a gun-turret in capital ships, running out along the top of the 15-inch guns themselves. This would not only preserve the full gun armament of any ship carrying it but, by training the turret into the 'felt' wind, would reduce the hitherto large alterations of course necessary for flying off. Once again it was Rutland who tried it out against the pessimistic opinions of many. He was successful, taking off from the turret of the battle-cruiser HMS *Repulse* in October 1917 in a Pup, without any difficulty.

Soon afterwards the platforms were enlarged by portable, planked extensions running along the big guns, giving a take-off run sufficient for the two-seater Sopwith 1½ Strutter reconnaissance machines, making use of a quick-release device to allow them to develop full power before beginning their run. By the beginning of 1918 nine battle-cruisers and the *Courageous* and *Glorious* were fitted with turret platforms carrying 1½ Strutters, Sopwith Pups and, later, the very successful Sopwith Camel fighter.

Prior to this, however, the problem of launching fighter aircraft from the fleet had been solved by the arrival of the converted *Furious*, whose Sopwith Pups were operated regularly from her flight deck. To get them back was a different matter. It was one which challenged the flying skill of the pilots in the *Furious*.

While she was in harbour her pilots, working from the near-by naval airfield, practised flying slowly up her side and then, on passing the mast and bridge, side-slipping inwards to the centre-line of the flying-off deck. Given a strong wind along the deck such as would be produced by the ship steaming at high speed into the wind, it seemed feasible to land-on, and Flight-Commander E. H. Dunning, the senior flying officer, got permission to attempt it when the ship was next at sea.

This took place on August 2, 1917. Dunning brought his Sopwith Pup in with great skill. As he straightened up over the deck

and cut his engine, a party of officers ready and waiting rushed out, caught hold of the rope toggles which had been attached for the purpose to wing tips, tail skid and fuselage, hauled the aircraft down and held it on the deck. It was a sweet little piece of flying. Dunning took off and repeated it successfully. But that it was a stunt could not be denied; and though stunts were the breath of life to many of those early fliers, it was not a manoeuvre which could be regularly relied upon. Five days later Dunning proved this, giving his life in the process, when his aircraft fell over the bows of the ship.

Further trials were forbidden; some better arrangement had to be devised. The correct solution, of course, was that being sought in the conversion of the *Conte Rosso*—a continuous deck free of obstructions. In addition, a contract had been placed with Messrs Armstrong for an ocean-going aircraft carrier of 10,850 tons to be called HMS *Hermes*. This was the first of such ships to be designed expressly for the purpose. A few months later the *Almirante Cochrane*, a battleship of 28,000 tons, lying uncompleted for the Chilean government since the beginning of the war, was bought and plans made to complete her also as an aircraft carrier. Renamed HMS *Eagle*, she was launched in June 1918.

The problem of disposing of the furnace gases of the *Conte Rosso* without a vertical funnel was proving difficult. As a short-term solution, therefore, it was decided to withdraw the *Furious* again for a landing deck 285 feet by 70 feet to be constructed, extending from her stern to her funnel. When she came to sea again in March 1918 with this addition she also had additional accommodation for aircraft, extra workshops and lifts from the hangars to the flight decks. Her initial complement of aircraft was 14 Sopwith $1\frac{1}{2}$ Strutters and two Pups in accordance with Admiralty policy that scouting aircraft should be mainly provided by carriers, while fighter aircraft should be operated from fighting ships.

Stopping

To arrest the aircraft landing on the *Furious'* after deck and prevent them running into the funnel, a primitive arrester system was fitted which had been tried out on land at the Isle of Grain air station, where it had been quite successful. Fore and aft along the deck were stretched wires held nine inches above it by ramps. Projecting from the undercarriage of the aircraft, fitted with skids instead of wheels, were a pair of horns which were expected to engage in the wires, the primary purpose of which was to keep the aircraft straight after touchdown. Across these wires were laid ropes with sandbags at each end which, caught up by a hook on the aircraft, would bring it to a halt. Finally a vertical curtain of manila ropes was stretched across the deck to catch an aircraft if all else failed.

Captain Wilmot S. Nicholson of the *Furious*, backed by the expert advice of his pilots, had foretold that it would be difficult, if not impossible, to bring an aircraft reasonably gently on to the deck through the turbulent air flow set up by the ship's superstructure ahead of it and the hot gases from her funnel. The advice was ignored, but proved only too well founded. The aircraft were bumped and buffeted as they made their approach and rarely arrived straight and level over the deck. Furthermore the arrester gear usually failed to achieve its purpose and, as the head wind disappeared in the lee of the funnel and superstructure, even correctly landed planes often ended up in the rope barrier, suffering some degree of damage. Throughout the trials only three safe landings were made, all other attempts ending in broken aircraft. Even so experienced a flyer as Rutland went over the side and nearly lost his life.

As a result of these trials, attempts to use the *Furious'* landing deck were abandoned. For the rest of the war she operated her flying-off deck only, from which on July 19, 1918 seven Sopwith Camels took off and led by Captain B. A. Smart, RAF, attacked the Zeppelin sheds at Tondern, destroying two with *L54* and *L60*, which were housed in them. That naval aviation, using single-seater fighters for this sort of operation, was still not properly equipped is obvious from the fact that four of the seven planes were unable to find their way back to the ship, three landing in Denmark, the fourth suffering an unknown fate.

It will be noted that B. A. Smart, who featured earlier as the hero of the episode resulting in the destruction of Zeppelin *L23*, had given up his rank in the RNAS to become a Captain, Royal Air Force. The RNAS, in fact, had ceased to exist, absorbed into the newborn RAF on April 1, 1918 as the result of a government decision on the advice of a committee dominated by the South African statesman, General Jan Smuts.

The origin of this administrative upheaval arose out of a complex situation. The Admiralty and War Office had been in competition for the best fighting aeroplanes and aero engines—a competition in which the former had held a marked advantage resulting in the navy acquiring far more of these types than could be used in a maritime rôle. A number of naval squadrons had, therefore, been attached to the RFC to reinforce them in the stern struggle for air superiority being fought out over the Western

The world's first true aircraft carrier, HMS *Argus*. She was completed in September 1918, could make 21 knots, had a displacement of 15,775 tons and could accommodate up to 20 aircraft in her hangars

Imperial War Museum

Front. In addition, the divided responsibility for combating the German air attacks on London, whereby the navy was expected to intercept over the sea, while the RFC did the same over land, had failed to achieve any success.

Taken in conjunction with Smuts' foresight of the day when operations such as those by the German Gotha heavy bombers he had witnessed over London would become a regular feature of war, the situation plainly called for an independent air force and a central air staff to administer it and to plan its operations. And so he advised.

Unfortunately for the efficiency of the navy, however, Smuts went further and recommended that all air operations of every kind and the provision of all types of aircraft should be the responsibility of the new service. Thus the control of its own air element which had just come to be appreciated as an integral part of the Fleet was taken out of the Admiralty's hands, only to be restored in 1937.

The first aircraft carrier

Returning to 1917, however, the lessons learnt from the fiasco of the *Furious'* landing-on deck had not been ignored. At Beardmore's yard the *Conte Rosso*, now renamed HMS *Argus*, was taking shape as the world's first true aircraft carrier. Her original design had incorporated a flush deck but divided into a landing and a takeoff area by a navigating bridge carried on a girder construction some 20 feet above the deck joining narrow superstructures on either side which contained radio offices, cabins and crane machinery spaces.

It was largely as a result of the insistence of Commander Gerard R. A. Holmes, an early enthusiast for the carrier concept and, during the *Argus'* conversion, liaison officer between the Air Department of the Admiralty and the Director of Naval Construction, that this was all swept away. The fittings for navigating and working the ship were rehoused below the flight deck, while a small chart house was mounted on a hydraulic ramp so that it could be lowered during flying operations and raised as necessary at other times.

The problem of disposal of the furnace gases had been solved by two horizontal ducts running below the deck to discharge them over the stern in place of a vertical funnel. So, at last, there had emerged the proper solution to the problem of provision of air support to the fleet—a ship with an unobstructed flush deck for aircraft to land on and take off from, connected by lifts with the hangar below it.

Not until October 1918, however, did the *Argus* go to sea for flight trials. A modified arrester gear was fitted. The athwartships

Above: The extraordinary HMS *Furious*, designed as a light battle-cruiser or large light cruiser at 'Jacky' Fisher's instigation. After her completion in July 1917, but before her commissioning, the forward of her two 18-inch guns was removed and replaced by an aircraft flying-off platform. The after gun was removed in 1918, and a landing-on platform was fitted. This latter did not prove successful, however, as the turbulence set up by the superstructure made it impossible to land aircraft with safety. Only the flying-off platform was then used until the *Furious* was reconstructed between 1921 and 1925 with a single uninterrupted flight deck, the superstructure being moved to an 'island' on the starboard side. In this guise she served until 1949. *Displacement:* 22,000 tons. *Length:* 786½ feet. *Beam:* 88 feet. *Power/speed:* 94,000 hp/32½ knots. *Armament:* ten 5.5-inch, five 3-inch AA and 20 aircraft. *Protection:* belt 2-3 inches, deck 1-3 inches and torpedo bulges. *Crew:* 737. *Right:* A line up of redoubtable Sopwith Triplanes of No 1 (Naval) Squadron, which had received its full complement of 'Tripehounds', as they were nicknamed, by the middle of February 1917. The squadron moved into action on April 22, and between that date and May 5 engaged 175 German aeroplanes, destroying four of them and driving 12 down out of control. Another famous unit to use the Triplane was No 10 (Naval) Squadron, whose 'Black Flight' of five men between them sent down 87 German aircraft between May and July 1917. The Triplane was obsolete by the end of the year, but it had led to the development in Germany of the famous Fokker Dr I triplane. *Right:* A Sopwith Camel on the flying-off platform over one of the 6-inch guns on a light cruiser. Though this afforded naval units at sea with protection against German Zeppelins, it was expensive and hazardous for the pilot, as it was impossible to land-on. The pilot had to ditch as close to his parent ship as possible and wait to be picked up. Only if there was no chance of U-Boats lurking in the vicinity could the aeroplane be recovered from the sea

sandbagged ropes were eliminated; the fore and aft wires were stretched between the upper edges of a pair of ramps so that the aircraft, which had their normal wheeled undercarriages, fell into a sort of shallow pit where hooks on the axle engaged the wires. When the plane reached the forward ramp and ran up it, the increased friction between the hooks and the wires acted as a brake and brought it to a halt.

Although this system worked quite satisfactorily in the trials with the lightly loaded 1½ Strutters, Pups and Camels, which had quite low landing speeds, further reduced, of course, by the wind down the carrier's deck as she steamed at 20 knots into wind, it proved more of a menace than a help when heavier postwar aircraft arrived, and it was abolished. Thereafter, for many years, until the belated development of an arrester system of athwartships wires engaged by a hook hanging below the aircraft, British naval aircraft landed on the decks of carriers relying upon the slowest possible touch-down and the wind down the deck to bring them to a halt.

The *Argus* had come to sea too late for the accumulated expertise acquired during the First World War to be applied. A carrier-borne torpedo plane, the Sopwith Cuckoo, was available and Admiral Beatty was pressing the Admiralty for an opportunity to use this on the High Seas Fleet where it lay inactive behind its harbour defences when the war ended in November 1918.

[For *further reading see* page 2317, and for Captain Macintyre's biography see page 1413.]

KAPP PUTSCH

The 'stab-in-the-back' myth and the frustration and resentment of the militarists were evidence that the revolutionaries of the Left were not the only threat to Ebert's government. *A. J. Nicholls*

Top: President Ebert, forced to depend for the security of his government on a largely hostile army. *Above:* General Walther von Lüttwitz launched the coup in defence of the Ehrhardt Brigade. *Right:* Dr Wolfgang Kapp, as political leader, did not control Lüttwitz

Ullstein

Bundesarchiv

3468

The Kapp *Putsch* of March 13, 1920 was at once symptomatic and decisive. On the one hand, it illustrated the extent to which the new German Republic, founded after the fall of Kaiser Wilhelm II in November 1918, depended for its security on soldiers, policemen and judges who were either actively or passively disloyal to it. On the other hand, it initiated a shift in the distribution of political power away from those moderate political parties which, in January 1919, had won a majority in the National Constituent Assembly at Weimar. This shift enabled the nationalist and largely anti-Republican forces on the right to exercise far more influence on German political life than would have seemed possible shortly after the revolution.

The *Putsch* itself was not an isolated or unheralded event. It had been a possibility ever since the spring of 1919, when the Allies had presented Germany with the peace terms they intended to impose on her, terms which provoked nation-wide indignation and which were especially repugnant to the German army. That army was in any case unsympathetic to the Republican régime. The decision by Republican leaders like President Friedrich Ebert and Defence Minister Gustav Noske to rely for protection on the remnants of the old German army and *Freikorps* formations recruited and led by Imperial officers meant that most army men were monarchists at heart and regarded the Republic as at best a necessary evil. In June 1919 some officers had been ready to defy the Republican government in order to organise resistance to the Allied peace ultimatum, and although more cautious counsels prevailed, the apparent submissiveness of the government to Germany's foreign enemies was a constant source of bitterness in the army.

Apart from Allied demands for the extradition of Germans accused of war crimes – a demand successfully evaded by the Berlin government – the most important consequence of the peace treaty from the military point of view was the enforced reduction in the size of the army. In January 1920 the *Reichswehr* and associated *Freikorps* formations numbered 250,000 men. The Allies required that by July 10 this figure should be cut to 100,000. At a time when the German economy was making the difficult adjustment from war to peace production there was no guarantee that the soldiers thus dismissed would find work on the civilian labour market. Some of the *Freikorps* troops had already been angered and disillusioned by events in the former Baltic provinces of Russia in spring and summer 1919, when they had been encouraged to volunteer to fight against the Bolsheviks in the erroneous belief that they would be given land for settlement in the Baltic region. After a confused campaign the government was forced by Entente pressure to withdraw these formations. Some were disbanded; others remained as a particularly discontented element within the army.

Early in 1920 the *Freikorps* were especially vulnerable to government measures to reduce the army. The Defence Minister, Noske, and the head of the *Reichswehr*, General Walther Reinhardt, were not unhappy to see these units disbanded, because they seemed politically unreliable. The chief of the army's *Truppenamt* (the successor to the General Staff), General

Hans von Seeckt, took a similar view, though he disliked the *Freikorps* simply because he regarded them as undisciplined. His aim was not to build an army loyal to the Republic, but to keep the *Reichswehr* aloof from politics, retaining the spirit of the old Imperial officer corps.

'Father of the *Freikorps*'

Yet it was clear that to disband the *Freikorps* would arouse fierce opposition. Many officers were prepared to resist army reductions, despite Allied pressure. The most important among these was General Walther von Lüttwitz, the officer in charge of Army Group I. Lüttwitz was responsible for all German forces east of the Elbe, as well as those in Saxony, Thuringia and Hanover. He was known as the 'Father of the *Freikorps*' and he realised that his own

Matthias Erzberger, hated by the nationalists for signing the Armistice on Germany's behalf

position in the army was strengthened by *Freikorps* support. He had no intention of allowing it to be undermined by letting the government erode his forces. Like many in his profession he was largely ignorant of politics. He simply hated the weakness and confusions of Republican Germany and thought that the army should use its power to impose a 'strong' government on the country. By March 1920 the threat of troop reductions seemed to him to be forcing his hand. The situation in the German army had reached a point of crisis.

On the political front matters were also looking very bleak for the Republican government. The shock of the Versailles Treaty had combined with serious economic problems to create an atmosphere of disillusionment and hostility. The national debt was more than 30 times as great in June 1919 as it had been six years earlier, and national expenditure had increased seven times in the same period. To deal with this situation the German finance minister, Matthias Erzberger, imposed a variety of new taxes, many of which weighed most heavily on the wealthier sections of the community. Erzberger was already widely hated in nationalist circles as the man who had signed the Armistice in November 1918, and he now became the object of a virulent smear campaign accusing him of treason and corruption. In January 1920 he was forced to sue one of his leading traducers for libel. The proceedings were conducted in such a manner that by the time the trial ended on March 12 his career was in ruins. Government prestige thereby sustained another blow.

At the same time the right-wing opponents of the régime, the German National People's Party (DNVP) and Gustav Stresemann's German People's Party (DVP) were demanding that the National Constituent Assembly, having fulfilled the task of drawing up a constitution, should be dissolved, and that elections for a new *Reichstag* be held. Since these would obviously be damaging to the government parties, this demand was resisted. However the opposition did not always confine itself to lawful measures. Many impatient monarchists were prepared to use force. The activities of such men centred on the *Nationale Vereinigung* in Berlin, sponsored by General Erich Ludendorff and led by Dr Wolfgang Kapp.

Kapp was a Prussian civil servant and landowner who had been elected a Con-

Gustav Stresemann tried to arrange a compromise when Kapp was seen to be losing ground

servative member of the *Reichstag* before the war. In 1917 he joined with Admiral von Tirpitz in setting up the Fatherland Party to press for an annexationist peace. After the November Revolution he became chairman of the DNVP organisation in East Prussia. Since the summer of 1919 he had been making intensive preparations for a counter-revolutionary coup. His *Nationale Vereinigung* was used to disseminate anti-Republican propaganda and build up contacts with politicians and civil servants sympathetic to the cause of reaction. It paid particular attention to the armed forces, stressing the claim that Republican leaders had stabbed Germany in the back during the war. Its business manager was a former army captain, Waldemar Pabst, who had played a leading part in suppressing the so-called Spartacist rising in Berlin in January 1919, when troops from his brigade had killed Rosa Luxemburg and Karl Liebknecht. Subsequently Pabst retired from the army, having tried to instigate a military *Putsch* against the Republican government. In the *Nationale Vereinigung* he worked closely with Ludendorff in drawing up plans for a coup.

Kapp, Pabst, and Ludendorff, as well as the latter's indefatigable aide, Colonel Max Bauer, collected money from landowners and industry, selected ministers for a new government and dreamed of rebuilding German power. But their chances of success depended on the army and, in particular, on General Lüttwitz. Lüttwitz sympathised with them, and was ready to install Kapp as Chancellor. But he was not a man to be led by others. When he decided to move it was on his own initiative and as the result of the crisis within the army itself.

Time to act?

The immediate spur to Lüttwitz was Noske's decision to disband one of the most powerful *Freikorps*, the Naval Brigade commanded by Captain Hermann Ehrhardt. Ehrhardt's force was a very effective fighting unit and its members, some of whom had fought with other *Freikorps* in the Baltic, were highly politicised and hostile to the civilian government. Their barracks at Döberitz were within a few hours' marching distance of Berlin. Ehrhardt, a tough and ruthless naval officer, had no intention of obeying Noske's order to disband and on March 1 held a parade at which General Lüttwitz himself announced that he would not tolerate the Brigade's dissolution. During the parade a service was conducted by the Protestant chaplain, who called on the Almighty to restore the German monarchy.

Noske's order was due to come into effect on March 10. At 6 pm on that day Lüttwitz presented President Ebert and Noske with an ultimatum. The government must dissolve the National Assembly, appoint non-party 'experts' to head key ministries, dismiss General Reinhardt, give Lüttwitz himself supreme control over the army and rescind all orders to dissolve *Freikorps* units. For Lüttwitz control of the army was of paramount importance; his political claims were merely the common currency of the Nationalist opposition. He seems genuinely to have thought that Ebert and Noske would give way to his demands, and was prepared to retain both of them in office — at least temporarily — if they did so. To his evident surprise and confusion they refused. Early the following morning, Noske and Reinhardt agreed to dismiss Lüttwitz, who was ordered on leave. His staff officers were, however, reluctant to take over his command. Some of them doubted the wisdom of his actions, but were unwilling to oppose him.

Lüttwitz himself ignored Noske's orders and went to Döberitz. He commanded Ehrhardt to march on Berlin that night. The *Freikorps* leader was taken by surprise at such haste; his troops were not ready and the operation had to be postponed for 24 hours. It was only one example of the lack of co-ordination which characterised the *Putsch*. There were many more. Kapp and his colleagues in the *Nationale Vereinigung* were unhappy at Lüttwitz's sudden decision. Kapp had

talked with the General of a coup at the end of the month; now he had little time to make his preparations. Yet urgent action was necessary once Lüttwitz's confrontation with the government had precipitated the crisis. Noske issued orders on March 12 for the arrest of Kapp, Pabst and other *Nationale Vereinigung* members, but thanks to contacts in the Prussian police headquarters the conspirators escaped.

In Berlin Noske pooh-poohed fears of an impending *Putsch* when they were raised at a cabinet meeting. Rumours of such action had been current for weeks and nothing had happened. The Minister of the Interior in Prussia, Heine, was lulled into a false sense of security by reports from police officials sympathetic to Kapp. No defensive measures were taken until the evening of March 12, when Reinhardt realised the danger and ordered the regiment guarding the government quarter of Berlin to resist Ehrhardt's men, an order which the regimental commander accepted.

Reinhardt's determination was not shared by most of his senior colleagues in the *Reichswehr,* who preferred to avoid any action which might bring their men into conflict with the Naval Brigade. A remarkable number of them, including Seeckt, had social engagements that evening, and could not be contacted for several hours.

At 1 am Reinhardt, Noske, Seeckt and a number of other officers met in the Defence Ministry. They were told that Ehrhardt, with whom several officers had been in contact, had reiterated Lüttwitz's ultimatum — and that he would await an answer at the Brandenburg Gate at 7 am that day. Noske and Reinhardt both demanded that military action be taken against the insurgents. But the commander of the Berlin garrison, Lieutenant-General von Oven, claimed that his soldiers would not shoot their comrades-in-arms. He was sup-

ported by Seeckt, who curtly declared it impossible for the army to stage 'a field exercise with live ammunition between Berlin and Potsdam'. Noske and Reinhardt were isolated. The *Reichswehr* officers had put their corporate solidarity before the defence of the Republic. Since the security police also declined combat, Ehrhardt's men marched into Berlin unopposed.

Below: March 1920, and the soldiers are back in the streets of Berlin. Here, an armoured car in position on the Wilhelmstrasse, with guards manning a barricade. But the people had their own weapon, the general strike

On orders from Lüttwitz, but a day late, the Ehrhardt Brigade marches into Berlin. Lüttwitz's suddenness took his associates by surprise

Nevertheless, Ehrhardt's decision to await the answer to his ultimatum caused a delay which damaged Kapp's plans. The latter felt it essential to seize the legal government. Instead the Republican ministers were given a vital period of grace in which to make good their escape. At 4 am the cabinet was called together and after some hesitation decided to flee Berlin. It left Vice-Chancellor Schiffer of the Democratic Party behind to represent the legal régime and negotiate on its behalf. Shortly after 6 am President Ebert, the Chancellor, Gustav Bauer, and other cabinet ministers left Berlin by car for Dresden. Before their departure the Social Democratic members of the government issued a press statement calling for a general strike against the *Putsch*. One of the senior civil servants in the Chancellery thoughtfully pocketed as many official rubber stamps as he could find and sent the telephonists on a week's holiday. This was accepted after the operators had confirmed that it would not be taken out of their annual leave.

Meanwhile, Ehrhardt's men, bearing the old Imperial colours of black, white and red, and with swastikas on their helmets, marched through the Brandenburg Gate singing *Deutschland über alles*. They were watched by Kapp, Lüttwitz, and General Ludendorff, who, as he subsequently explained in court proceedings, had happened 'by chance' to be passing by in uniform at that hour. Kapp proclaimed himself Chancellor and Lüttwitz Defence Minister, and a former Berlin police president, Traugott von Jagow, was made Prussian Minister of the Interior. The Ehrhardt Brigade was given an enthusiastic reception by the middle-class citizens of Berlin's more fashionable quarter; this was taken by the *Putschists* as proof of their popularity.

Yet once Kapp had established himself in the Chancellery, the weakness of his position became apparent. He was unable even to find enough volunteers to fill vacant posts in his cabinet. He had no effective personal staff and senior administrative officials discreetly avoided contact with him. His public relations were abysmal. He banned all newspapers in Berlin, including those sympathetic to the *Putsch*. This meant that the legal government, which was energetic in its use of the press and news agencies outside Kapp's control, was able to put its case far more effectively to the German public than Kapp had done. By the time he realised his mistake a general strike was paralysing Berlin newspapers. Kapp's reaction to the strike, which had been called by Social Democratic and liberal trade unions and proved very effective, was typically indecisive. At first he tried to persuade the workers that the *Putschist* régime would defend them against the rapacity of finance capital. When they declined to believe this he announced that strike leaders would be arrested. Ehrhardt wanted to cut off water supplies to working-class districts and shoot down anyone who tried to resist the *Putsch*, but Kapp and Lüttwitz lacked the stomach for a really violent counter-revolution. No effective measures were taken to deal with the strike, which in any case extended far beyond Berlin.

The only real power behind Kapp and Lüttwitz was that of the army, but even this proved unreliable. It was one thing for officers to avoid fratricidal conflict, quite another to risk their careers in an adventure which seemed unlikely to succeed. At first Lüttwitz could hope that the favourable reaction of *Reichswehr* troops in Berlin to his coup would be matched by the support of army formations elsewhere. In northern and eastern Germany army commanders generally accepted the new régime. But in the west and south the situation was much less favourable. Lüttwitz had hoped, for example, that the commander of *Reichswehr* forces in Saxony, General Ludwig Maercker, would arrest President Ebert and his ministers when they arrived in Dresden. Maercker did nothing of the kind. Instead he tried to mediate between the two sides. This caused the legal ministry to move once again, to Stuttgart, where the *Reichswehr* was completely loyal. In Bavaria the *Reichswehr* commander sympathised with the *Putsch* but did not commit himself to supporting Kapp. As days went by, and the credibility of the new régime oozed away, army commanders outside Berlin became less inclined to associate themselves with it.

In the capital too, the *Putschists* were having difficulty with the army. On the one hand Ehrhardt was contemptuous of the régime's weak attitude towards its opponents. On the other the officers in the Defence Ministry refused to accept orders from Lüttwitz.

The 100 hours
It soon became clear that Kapp lacked both the nerve and the ability to fill the rôle of a German dictator. The right-wing parties, DNVP and Stresemann's DVP, which had at first seemed inclined to give the *Putsch* discreet *de facto* recognition as a means of achieving new *Reichstag* elections, now sought to negotiate a compromise between Kapp and the legal government in order to gain at least something from the *Putsch*. But Chancellor Bauer and his colleagues were rapidly growing in confidence and insisted on unconditional surrender. Pressure on Kapp to yield became more intense as the threat of a left-wing insurrection in Berlin increased the nervousness of both political and military leaders there. On March 17, it became known that the security police in Berlin had turned their coats once again and were now against Kapp. In some army units there was the prospect of serious trouble: a Guards Engineer battalion overthrew its officers and declared its allegiance to Ebert. That afternoon Kapp, having achieved just 100 hours of ignominiously unsuccessful counter-revolution, fled the Chancellery and disappeared. Shortly afterwards he escaped to Sweden in an aeroplane. He had handed over his

The counter-revolution fails ignominiously. The Baltic troops leave Berlin on March 18, 1920, disposing of some of the citizens en route

authority, such as it was, to General von Lüttwitz. Although the General was made of sterner stuff than Kapp, he soon saw that his position was untenable. He was visited by a group of senior officers from the Defence Ministry led by Colonel Heye, who had been acting under discreet instructions from General von Seeckt since the *Putsch* began. Heye told Lüttwitz respectfully that he had lost the confidence of the army and would have to step down. Lüttwitz blustered and threatened him with arrest, but the *Putsch* was virtually over. At a meeting in the Ministry of Justice with some political party leaders—including Stresemann—Lüttwitz got them to promise that they would try to arrange for an amnesty to cover the *Putschists*. He then wrote out his resignation and returned to the Defence Ministry in time to dissuade Ehrhardt from arresting senior officers there as mutineers. Lüttwitz had stayed on for only a few hours after Kapp's departure. He too left Germany, choosing Hungary as his place of exile. The Ehrhardt Brigade marched out of Berlin, pausing only to shoot down some jeering civilians who were rejoicing at their departure.

With the end of the *Putsch* the Republican government had apparently triumphed. Certainly the parties of the Right were in considerable embarrassment over their behaviour and it was expected that retribution would overtake the mutineers. Bauer and his colleagues in Stuttgart were in a mood to take firm action of this kind, but were dismayed to discover that representatives of government parties in Berlin had been treating with Lüttwitz before his fall and that Vice-Chancellor Schiffer had apparently participated in negotiations for a settlement with the rebels. This embarrassed the government in Stuttgart—although it had never compromised with the *Putsch*—since it could less easily adopt stern measures against the followers of Kapp and Lüttwitz once the *Putsch* was over. Yet the Social Democratic trade unionists who had led the

resistance to Kapp were insisting on decisive action. They continued their general strike and tried to impose political terms on the government, demanding that unreliable ministers must be dismissed, that the armed forces and civil service be democratised, and a start made with the socialisation of industry. In this the trade unions had overreached themselves. The only result of their pressure was the fall of Bauer's cabinet on March 27; the government which replaced it was even less capable of implementing radical reforms.

Meanwhile in some parts of Germany, especially the Ruhr, left-wing opposition to the *Putsch*, led by Independent Social Democrats and communists, had escalated into an attempt to create a new, socialist Republic. The *Reichswehr,* including Ehrhardt's Marine Brigade, was ordered to perform the congenial task of suppressing red revolution.

Aftermath

From the Republican point of view the army leadership had changed for the worse as the result of the *Putsch*. Noske had been quite discredited and his career as a minister was finished. General Reinhardt resigned after his failure to defend the constitution. He was replaced by Seeckt, who had refused even to try. Seeckt was determined not to allow the *Reichswehr* to be republicanised in the aftermath of the *Putsch*. Although some officers who had disobeyed orders were relieved of their posts, many involved in the affair were allowed to remain. On the other hand soldiers dismissed for refusing orders from Kappist officers were not reinstated, despite—or because of—their loyalty to the constitution. The army in Berlin never again attempted a *coup* against the Republic, but remained uncommitted to it.

The fact was that, despite its failure, the Kapp *Putsch* had undermined the Weimar Coalition. The use of the general strike to oppose the rebels had shocked many in the

middle-class Democratic and Roman Catholic centre parties. Subsequent clashes with armed workers led by radical socialists and communists confirmed fears that the government had led the country to the brink of revolution. As the result of the conflicting pressures on the régime it was felt impossible to postpone any longer elections for a new *Reichstag*. Hence one of the major objectives of the right-wing parties had been achieved. At these elections, held in June 1920, the middle-class parties which supported the Republican system lost heavily to the DNVP and DVP. The working-class vote was split by recriminations over the *Putsch* and its aftermath. The result was that, less than a year after creating the Republican constitution, the Weimar Coalition parties had lost their parliamentary majority. They never regained it.

The weakness of Republican authority was shown in the treatment of those who had participated in the *Putsch*. Most were able to make their escape with the help of friendly police officials in Berlin, to the eastern districts of Prussia or Bavaria. Precisely three were brought to trial for their actions, of whom only one, Traugott von Jagow, was punished. He received five years relatively comfortable fortress imprisonment and emerged after serving three of them. He then successfully sued the Prussian government for the payment of his pension. Kapp returned to Germany in 1922 but died before he could be called to account before the law. In death, as in life, he was the master of anticlimax.

ANTHONY NICHOLLS was born in 1934. He gained his degree at Merton College, Oxford. He is a Fellow at St Antony's College, Oxford, where he works in the field of recent German history. He has published *Weimar and the Rise of Hitler* and is co-editor of *German Democracy and the Triumph of Hitler*.

THE 'WAR GUILT' QUESTION

It was difficult enough for the Germans to accept the humiliation of losing the war, and in retrospect the inclusion of a war guilt clause in the Versailles Treaty seems unrealistic and insensitive. *S. L. Mayer*

Perhaps the most shocking provisions of the Treaty of Versailles as far as the German government was concerned, and certainly the most controversial section of the treaty, were the 'war guilt' clause and the reparations payments attached. The Allies had prefaced the section on reparations with a short paragraph which to them seemed simple enough. This famous article – Article 231 of the Treaty of Versailles – stated: 'The Allied and Associated Governments affirm and Germany accepts the responsibility of Germany and her allies for causing all the loss and damage to which the Allied and Associated Governments and their nationals have been subjected as a consequence of the war imposed upon them by the aggression of Germany and her allies.'

Although Article 231 was not drafted casually, it is fair to say that no one realised how important it was to become in the fate of the treaty as a whole. The Peace Conference's committee dealing with reparations had not even thought of including it until the French suggested that it might be well to introduce this clause before the subject of reparations was discussed so as to establish the moral justice of the claims. The other Allies agreed, and the clause was drafted and soon forgotten. Thus, when Germany received the draft treaty, many of the Allies were surprised to find that this paragraph was the most violently disputed article in the entire treaty.

The violent protests of the German delegates to this 'war guilt' clause were repeated and sincere. The German people were convinced that they had been attacked by Tsarist Russia and that France and Belgium were only invaded to forestall an invasion of Germany. In any event, Germany felt the war had been brought on by a policy of encirclement undertaken by France and her allies as part of a giant conspiracy to prevent Germany from taking her rightful place in the world. More sober opinion within Germany only disagreed slightly with this view, and the most reputable scholars within the Reich were convinced that the war was a terrible historical accident for which Germany shared the guilt with many others, such as Russia, whose mobilisation set off the final events in the July Crisis of 1914 which finally led to war. Generations of historians have debated the causes of the First World War and no conclusion has been generally accepted. But there is no doubt that, at least in part, Germany was responsible for the outbreak of the war. No one nation or politician was responsible. The so-called 'war guilt' clause, of course, did not state that the Germans were 'guilty' of starting the war – the word was 'responsible' – but from the outset the Germans, and eventually everyone else, referred to Article 231 as the 'war guilt' clause of the treaty. Articles 227-230, immediately preceding it, dealt with penalties, such as bringing the Kaiser to trial as well as handing over to the Allies all those whom the Allies judged to have committed acts in violation 'of the laws and customs of war'. This made it seem as if Article 231 was merely a continuation of the 'penalties' section of the treaty and therefore could be considered an indictment of the whole German people as war criminals. By the time the Germans were handed the treaty to read, most Allied diplomats felt that the 'penalties' section should not have been included at all, but it was too late to change it at that stage, and the effect on the Germans was devastating. Not that the Allies doubted that Germany was responsible for the war. But if the question were taken to some neutral court, the Allies would have been placed in the position of common litigants pleading their case. It became clear that the moral status of the whole treaty, not merely the accompanying reparations clauses, rested on the validity of this single clause. Perhaps the Allies might have been willing even to drop it in the final treaty; but the Germans made sure, by vociferous protests to the press as well as to the diplomats, that the world public was aware of Article 231, and after a short time it became clear that if the Allies abandoned Article 231 it would imply that the Germans were not responsible for the war after all. No Allied government could hope to face its electorate after making that admission. So the clause stayed in.

Desperate as the German situation was in June 1919, just before the ultimatum which would have meant the occupation of the whole of Germany by the Allies was to take effect, the German government was still unprepared to accept the so-called *Schmachparagraphen* (or articles of shame, 227-231), even though it knew that it had to accept the rest of the treaty. The parties of the centre and the left only approved the signing of the treaty if these clauses were removed, and the National Assembly approved of the treaty without these clauses by a margin of almost two to one. The dissenters disapproved of signing the treaty at all. But the Allies insisted that Germany should sign the treaty as it stood or suffer occupation, and so the two German ministers sent to Versailles to sign on June 28, 1919, Hermann Müller and Johannes Bell, accepted humiliation because they had no choice. And, in signing, they put their names to a blank cheque for reparations, for which the bill had not yet been presented.

Certainly one of the most hotly debated sections of the treaty was that dealing with reparations payments to be made by Germany. Article 231 had been included only as an introduction to the section which discussed Germany's postwar payments of compensation to some of the Allies. The Germans pointed out that on February 11, 1918, Woodrow Wilson had stated that there would be 'no annexations, no punitive damages, no contributions', a statement modified to mean that the invaded portions of France and Belgium were to be 'restored' and that was supposed to include Alsace-Lorraine as well.

Wilson's limitations had never really been accepted by many of the Allies, who saw no moral problem at all: the victors were entitled to divide the spoils as they saw fit. Germany, up until 1918, saw it the same way. They had intended to exact reparations and indemnification from the French if they had won, and the Treaty of Brest-Litovsk indicated that Germany was not planning an easy peace for her enemies. But the French, especially, felt that Germany ought to pay for the whole cost of the war, which had been ruinous for northern France. French politicians had failed to mention to their impassioned electorate how they proposed to extract the money from the Germans, who could not possibly pay the whole cost of the war, even if it were paid out in instalments over several generations. It was simply too much.

Realistic idealism

At the Peace Conference, the Americans on the committee dealing with reparations, led by Bernard Baruch, Thomas Lamont and the young John Foster Dulles, fought hard to prevent punitive reparations from being presented to Germany, but they were outvoted: by the British, led by Lord Sumner, a distinguished legal expert, and Lord Cunliffe, governor of the Bank of England, who were savage in their demands, asking for repayment by Germany of all of Britain's wartime expenditures; and by the French, who were prepared to wait up to 100 years to collect what they demanded, with the Germans paying interest on the principal throughout the century, which, even at low rates, would roughly treble the original sum. As the French Chamber of Deputies and British Parliament demanded even more, the demands mounted to incalculable heights. The only limiting factor seemed to be Germany's capacity to pay. Some experts felt that Germany could pay up to 120,000 million dollars. The entire German national wealth at that time was estimated to be only 75,000 million. But the French did not care. The Germans, they felt, ought to pay every penny of the cost of the war, no matter how long it took and no matter how Germany was impoverished.

The Americans kept pointing out that the most that could be extracted from the German economy, even over a period of 30 years at the most, was far less than what the French and British, as well as the Belgians and Italians, wanted them to pay, while at the same time other committees at the Conference were stripping away Germany's colonies, overseas investments, ships, chemicals and coal, in addition to about 13% of her home territory. How could the Germans pay if they were to lose all this as well? John Maynard Keynes pointed out that Germany's only alternative would be to dump her manufactured goods on the world market at ridiculously low prices for as long as her raw materials held out, thereby ruining the trade of the victors. Finally Lloyd George admitted that Germany could not

Below: The remains of Albert Church, in Belgium. Since the Germans had been compelled to accept responsibility for the results of the fighting, they were technically liable for all damage, whether caused by their own or the Allies' forces. The 'war guilt' idea only added insult to the injury which was done to Germany by the massive sums demanded in reparation. It was impossible to exact payment at the levels set by the Reparation Commission in 1920, but there was great pressure for compensation in individual instances. As well as private property, many buildings of religious, social or historical importance had been damaged or left in ruins by the war

ECP Armées

3475

pay such huge debts, but that he had to defend himself against the hysterical demands of Parliament. To come home with small reparations payments would force Lloyd George from office; to come home with none would be worse.

It was finally decided by the Conference that no set figure would be determined at that time, and that a final sum would be worked out later – presumably, when the immediate postwar fever had cooled. The draft treaty compelled Germany to pay 5,000 million dollars in gold to the Allies before May 1, 1921, along with virtually the whole of the German merchant marine and large deliveries of coal, chemicals and other items. An Allied Reparation Commission was established to calculate the total of reparations owed, and by May 1921 it was to meet with representatives of the German government to arrange for payments to be spread out over a 30-year period. Although the Germans made various counterproposals, they fell on deaf ears, except for those of the Americans, who could do little.

As it turned out the Germans did not have to worry about imminent financial ruin. However, they protested vehemently when, on February 3, 1920, the Allies submitted to them a list of 900 persons to be handed over to them for trial. On the list were most of Germany's wartime leaders, including Hindenburg, Ludendorff and three Hohenzollern princes. The charges ranged from murder to petty theft. The matter was negotiated with the Allies, who agreed that the Germans could try their own 'war criminals'. Only six obscure Germans were actually tried and convicted, and then for short sentences. The matter was dropped by the Allies, who could only enforce the demand by resuming the war, which was unthinkable in the 1920s. Similarly, perfunctory attempts to extradite the Kaiser from Holland were dropped, especially after the Dutch had been secretly informed by the Allies that they did not really want to hang the Kaiser. Again the outrageous demands for reparations payments could never have been met, for as the American financial experts pointed out, the only way Germany could have hoped to meet the Allied demands was by maintaining a very favourable balance of payments by exporting far more than she imported, which would have taken place at the expense of Allied exporters. Otherwise, Germany could have made vast payments in kind over a number of years, which would have ruined the manufacturers of similar products in the Allied countries.

Billions in baskets
Britain gradually lost interest in the question of reparations, leaving only France and Belgium to press the matter further. When the Reparation Commission announced their decision in 1920, in which Germany was to pay 269,000 million gold marks over a 35-year period, Germany announced that this was not possible (at that time, 1,000 million gold marks was roughly equivalent to £50 million). In January 1921 Germany told the Commission that she had already paid out the equivalent of 21,000 million marks. The final sum owing was reduced to 132,000 million marks, but the Allies insisted that only 12,000 million had been paid in so far. The San Remo, Boulogne and Spa Conferences had been

an exercise in futility, and the Germans, on every occasion, including the London Conference of March 1921, tried successfully to whittle down the terms. An ultimatum was issued on March 3, which was followed on the 8th by the occupation of Ruhrort, Düsseldorf and Duisburg, as well as further sanctions taken against Germany. But even the lowered payments proved too much for Germany to bear, and with rampant inflation accelerating in Germany, and Germans forced to shop for bread with wheelbarrows and bushel baskets full of billions of marks, the German economy ground to a halt. The French and Belgians occupied the Ruhr in 1923, and the German people answered by passive resistance to the Allied policy.

In the end the Americans came to the aid of Germany with the Dawes Plan, by helping to reorganise the German financial system and financing, through (mostly American) loans, the resumption of reparations payments and consequently Allied war debts to the United States. Over the period 1924-1931 Germany borrowed about 18,000 million marks, paying out only about 11,000 million. But the German economy soon prospered, and another scheme, similar to the Dawes Plan, called the Young Plan, was put into action. But Germany could not pay off both the loans and the reparations payments, and the world depression intervened. A conference at Lausanne in 1932 reduced the balance of reparations to a token of 3,000 million marks, and after Hitler came to power in 1933, even this sum was not paid.

In all Germany paid about 36,000 million marks in reparations, but she borrowed about 33,000 million. It is safe to say that the reparations payments, a poor idea from the outset, motivated largely by wartime propaganda, had little or no effect upon the German economy in the immediate postwar years. But the worst effect of the reparations-war guilt issue was political. A periodical called *The War Guilt Question* was circulated in Germany throughout most of the 1920s and early 1930s, which numbered among its contributors many of the leading historians through-

out the world. The research published in the journal supported the German argument that the Second Reich could not be exclusively blamed for the war. The German diplomatic documents, released in the mid-Twenties, gave historians the intellectual evidence they needed to sustain their arguments. And if Germany did not really cause the war, then why should she pay reparations? Indeed, why should Germany have been partitioned or penalised at all? Or so it was argued. One of the most convincing proponents of this view during the Weimar period was Adolf Hitler.

Even if the Treaty of Versailles was not the 'Carthaginian Peace' which Keynes thought it was, it was sufficiently suspect morally to allow the enemies of democracy in Germany to use it for their own ends. Saddled with reparations and the responsibility of the war in which it had played no part the Weimar Republic never really stood a chance, and the occupations of the Ruhr and the Rhineland, combined with inflation in the Twenties and depression in the Thirties, made things worse. It is easy today to say that the reparations clauses as well as Articles 227-231 should have been removed from the Treaty of Versailles. But public opinion in the Allied countries in 1919 did not see it that way. It was wartime propaganda which helped to create a revanchist atmosphere in many of the victorious states, and, in the long run, to create the conditions which led to the Second World War.

Further Reading
Gathorne-Hardy, G. M., *A Short History of International Affairs 1920-1939* (London: Oxford University Press, 1964)
Holborn, Hajo, *A History of Modern Germany 1840-1945* (New York: Alfred A. Knopf, 1969)
Mayer, Arno J., *Politics and Diplomacy of Peacemaking* (London: Weidenfeld & Nicolson, 1967)
Walters, F. P., *A History of the League of Nations* (London: Oxford University Press, 1965)
Watt, Richard M., *The Kings Depart* (New York: Simon & Schuster, 1968)

[*For S. L. Mayer's biography, see page 19.*]

German inflation. With banknotes almost worthless, a pound of butter could buy almost anything

THE CHANAK CRISIS

In September 1922 Turkish and British armies faced each other across the Dardanelles, once again on the brink of war. Despite an Allied decision to cede Constantinople to Kemal, the British alone refused to leave. The crisis was averted by the British Commander on the spot but the unpopularity of Cabinet policy brought down the Coalition government — and with it Lloyd George. *David Walder. Below:* War debris — a dockyard arsenal in Constantinople, with the 1894 pre-dreadnought HMS *Caesar* in the background

Left: The Allied Fleet in Constantinople, a painting by F. H. Mason

The complete defeat of the Greek army in Anatolia in the autumn of 1922 removed a wall of men from between the exultant Turks and the Allied garrisons which occupied both sides of the Dardanelles, the Sea of Marmara and the Bosporus and Constantinople (Istanbul). Originally, in 1918, the British, French and Italian troops had occupied a rather loosely drawn 'neutral zone' on both sides of the Straits. Later, by the Treaty of Sèvres, new lines had been drawn on the map defining a rather wider 'international zone'. These zones were, however, luxuries for the Allies, insulated from the Turks by the Greek army engaged in its eastwards march into Anatolia. With the Greeks killed, captured or swept into the sea the zones were meaningless. The reality was that Allied troops would soon face Turks intent on reclaiming all Turkish territory in Asia Minor plus Constantinople and Eastern Thrace.

To regain Constantinople and Eastern Thrace Mustapha Kemal would have to cross the Straits so that the first confrontation was bound to occur on the Asian side. The question was—what would the Allies do? Very soon that question became —what would the British do, as the French and Italian governments made plain their intention to get out of an awkward situation as quickly as possible. Their attitude was in many ways a reasonable one, for neither the French nor the Italians had ratified the Treaty of Sèvres and in any event the document promised the Turks the ultimate return of their capital, Constantinople.

What then were the British preparing to fight about? Lloyd George, the Prime Minister, provided many answers, but the truth was probably—pride. That the Turks, vanquished four years ago, should now, after defeating the Greeks and destroying one of his foreign policy dreams, regain their former territory at gun point was to him completely unacceptable. Once again, as in the Graeco-Turkish war, and it may have bolstered his determination, he made an over-optimistic military assessment. Talk of neutral and international zones had blurred realities in the mind of the Prime Minister and his Cabinet colleagues.

On the ground the military situation was stark, simple and dangerous. Mustapha Kemal, in Smyrna, had declared himself to the British Consul General, Sir Harry Lamb, as being still at war with the British. Lieutenant-General Sir Charles Harington, the Allied C-in-C in Constantinople, was consequently ordered to hold the Straits against the Turks. Unfortunately the resources at his command were woefully inadequate. In Anatolia there were two defensive areas linked by a narrow strip of coastline: opposite the Gallipoli peninsula the southern area, comprising the district of Chanak and the town of the same name, and opposite Constantinople the area of the Ismid peninsula. A strong British fleet was available in the Sea of Marmara but on land the forces at Harington's disposal were puny: a squadron of the 3rd Hussars, a battery of field artillery, some engineers and one battalion of infantry, the Loyals, plus an extremely unreliable battalion of Turkish gendarmerie, still notionally loyal to the Sultan and the Allies. For a few days Colonel

Shuttleworth, at Chanak, also had under command small detachments of French and Italian troops sent to assist him by Harington's deputies in Constantinople, Generals Charpy and Mombelli. However, when the Paris and Rome governments heard of the generals' decision their orders were rapidly countermanded and the troops withdrawn. In the meantime, however, two more infantry battalions, the Gordon Highlanders and the Royal Sussex from Malta, had been landed at Chanak as reinforcements.

Luckily, however, it was not until September 23 that the British troops, behind their hastily improvised barbed wire and trench defences at Chanak and Nagara Point, further to the north, actually saw Turkish troops within rifle range. The cavalry patrols seen on that day were the advance guard of a force estimated at about 5,000 men. South of the Ismid peninsula it was thought there were another 20,000 men with 40,000 still in the Smyrna area. In Eastern Thrace there was an irregular, but armed and equipped, force of about 6,000 Turks. The total Allied force in the area, including French and Italian elements, with the garrison in Constantinople amounted to 7,600 men, 28 guns, 12 tanks and armoured cars, 12 aeroplanes and 5 seaplanes. Even this disparate balance represented an optimistic calculation, for if the situation escalated into war there seemed little chance that the French and Italians would support the British.

'I have incessantly been working for peace here, which I thought was the wish of HM Government'— Harington

Eight days before the first Turkish soldiers were seen by the British, on September 15, the Cabinet met in Downing Street. General Harington had made it plain that if the Straits were to be defended it could not be done piecemeal—there would have to be soldiers in strength on both shores backed up by naval and, if possible, air support. (In this, of course, he was quite right, the failure of unco-ordinated action had been one of the lessons of Gallipoli.) More or less the Cabinet accepted Harington's view, but the real interest of the meeting was to be found in the fact that by their other decisions Lloyd George and his colleagues revealed almost completely the hopes and fears which they harboured throughout the crisis.

The Prime Minister was quite adamant in his determination 'not to run away before Mustapha Kemal'. Lord Curzon, the Foreign Secretary, was prepared to use his diplomatic arts upon Raymond Poincaré, the French Prime Minister, to persuade him to co-operate with the British, while in Paris Curzon would also try to bring in the Yugoslavs, as their King and Prime Minister were there at the moment. Perhaps he would also extend an invitation to an international conference to the Rumanians and Bulgarians. Winston Churchill, now Secretary of State for the Colonies, wanted British reinforcements to be sent out at once and also had hopes that

Greece, Yugoslavia and Rumania might send a military contingent. This idea appealed to Lloyd George who said that 'by combining the Greek, Rumanian, Serbian and British forces a considerable army would be available. If Mustapha Kemal crossed the Straits with 60,000 rifles then he would be met by 60,000 plus the British fleet.' Together Lloyd George and Churchill drafted a telegram to the Dominions, South Africa, Australia and Canada, New Zealand and Newfoundland, asking for military assistance in the event of war with Turkey. In fairness to him, Lord Curzon was worried and a trifle confused but it was only Austen Chamberlain, the Lord Privy Seal, who sounded a note of real caution. When the idea of an international conference was mooted he said he did not want the British 'to make a stand for something which was not of any great value'.

In the event, none of these things came to pass. Curzon's trip to Paris was a complete waste of time and a personal humiliation. The Yugoslavs were virtually indifferent, likewise the Rumanians and the Bulgarians. British approaches to the Greeks had infuriated the French and Poincaré was ready to accede to Mustapha Kemal's demands there and then. Indeed his attitude was so abrasive that he reduced Curzon, literally, to tears. Count Sforza, the Italian delegate, found the Foreign Secretary in that embarrassing state but his own attitude was not softened; he was even less willing to help the British than were the French.

Churchill's telegram was attended with calamities from the start. He released the news to the British press prematurely, forgetting the difference in time between Britain and the Dominions. As a result the first intimation of the request received by the Prime Ministers of Canada, Australia and New Zealand was via their own newspapers.

Reaction to the telegrams was cooled by this muddle but in any case the Dominions regarded his request as peremptory and imperialistic. The replies he received were not encouraging. Mackenzie King, the Canadian Prime Minister, had no intention of embroiling his countrymen in a new war and said so. The Australian response was less abrupt but no less firm. The South African Prime Minister, perhaps tactfully, never sent an official answer at all. The Newfoundland government made no offer of military help; only New Zealand produced a reply which could be published in the British press—a battalion would be sent and perhaps a brigade if necessary.

'Stop the War!'

By the time the Turks were in sight from Chanak plainly the British were on their own. Indeed from Lloyd George's point of view the situation was rather worse than that, for in many ways the British government was on its own. A few days before, Churchill had issued an official communiqué to the British people. Curzon, not consulted on its contents beforehand, called it a 'flamboyant manifesto'. He was right: there were wildly inaccurate purple passages which suggested that the whole of the Balkans was about to go up in flames, coupled with regrets over the imminent 'loss of the whole results of the victory over Turkey in the last war'.

As Churchill himself admitted later, but

without repentance, the communiqué was not a success; it was 'censured for being alarmist and provocative in tone and certainly it was ill received in important quarters'. One of these quarters was the British press; the *Daily Mail's* reaction was the strongest, but its headline, 'Stop This New War', pinpointed a great deal of popular feeling. No newspaper supported the government and only the *Daily Express* was prepared to offer somewhat lukewarm concern for 'the freedom of the Straits'. Protest meetings began to be held all over the country and the TUC sent a delegation to remonstrate with the Prime Minister.

Nevertheless, however unpopular, the government was determined: what Churchill called 'a small group of resolute men', largely consisting of the Prime Minister, the Lord Chancellor Lord Birkenhead, and himself, was prepared to adopt a tough line with the Turks. No other government was prepared to do so and the only result of a great deal of diplomatic activity was that the French and Italians were prepared to sign a joint note to be sent to Ankara inviting the Turks to send a representative to a conference to negotiate a final treaty

of peace between Turkey, Greece and the Allies. The other nations invited were Japan, Rumania and Yugoslavia. The Allies 'viewed with favour' the desire of Turkey to recover Thrace as far as the Maritsa and Adrianople but the 'provisional neutrality' of the area was meanwhile proclaimed. No Turkish troops were to be sent there until the conclusion of the peace treaty. Similarly, the Turks could have Constantinople after the peace had been signed. With regard to the Straits the document was considerably more vague. The Greeks should retire to a line fixed by the Allied generals in agreement with both Greeks and Turks. In return the Turks must undertake not to send troops into the neutral zone nor to cross the Straits or the Sea of Marmara. It was finally suggested that Allied generals might meet Mustapha Kemal to discuss these matters at Mudania or Ismid. The note was dispatched on September 23.

Three points are noteworthy. First, that the 'neutral zone' was still regarded as being in existence and of importance, second that Mustapha Kemal was expected to deal with generals, not heads of state—

he was still not recognised for what he was, the ruler of Turkey—and third, most significant of all, the note in effect granted Mustapha Kemal all that he was asking.

The Allied note was the best that Lord Curzon could persuade the French and Italians to accept. He himself called it 'abject surrender', but knew in his heart that, short of war, there was no other course but a face-saving operation. Unfortunately it is doubtful if the Prime Minister and his fiery lieutenant, Winston Churchill, saw things in that light at all. They were now the two most militant members of the government and it is interesting to examine how they each came to their respective positions.

Originally Lloyd George had enthusiastically espoused the Greek cause and encouraged their invasion of Turkey. In those days Churchill had been very cautious indeed and had on more than one occasion predicted disaster for the Greeks and difficulties for Britain. The Greek defeat and the present crisis had proved him right. Nevertheless, faced with the possibility that Mustapha Kemal might now threaten British troops, and get away

Far left: A battalion of British 28th Division lands *(top)* at Constantinople while French sailors look on and, *below,* marches into the city. Lloyd George was determined 'not to run away before Mustapha Kemal' even though pleas for aid had been coldly rejected both by the European allies and by all the Dominions except New Zealand. *Left:* Part of the Allied Fleet in the Bosporus. *Below:* Kemal Ataturk – Mustapha Kemal. A highly respected military commander, he was unanimously voted Turkey's first president in 1923

with it, all Churchill's natural pugnacity came to the fore. In consequence he became the energetic chairman of a committee consisting of himself and the three Service chiefs, Beatty, Cavan and Trenchard, the purpose of which was to co-ordinate all measures necessary to wage war against the Turks if they continued to press round the British positions in Asia Minor. The Prime Minister was happy to hand over the naval and military details to his deputy. Unlike Churchill he had never been interested in the details of ships and men and guns. Broad strategic concepts captured his mind but logistics bored him, as did most naval and military commanders. Kemal and the Turks had to be resisted; how it was done or indeed who did it and with what was a matter of little concern.

The rest of the Cabinet was, for the moment, content to follow rather reluctantly in the wake of Lloyd George and Churchill, with Lord Curzon acting out the semi-independent rôle of trying to paper over the cracks of Allied disunity. For this task the Foreign Secretary got no thanks and scarcely any acknowledgement from

either the Prime Minister or the Secretary of State for the Colonies.

In London all was preparation for hostilities. In the newspapers there appeared photographs reminiscent of the autumn of 1914. The Guards, back to khaki again, were ready to leave Windsor, and the Rifle Brigade, weighed down by Field Service Marching Order, were preparing to leave Winchester. The Highland Light Infantry and the King's Own Scottish Borderers were being shipped from Egypt. The Mediterranean Fleet was steaming eastwards.

Harington's dilemma

Curiously, perhaps, little was known at this stage of what was actually happening in Turkey. There in fact the situation for Harington was as difficult as can be imagined. He himself was as determined as a man could be in his position that a war should not break out. At the back of his mind he was convinced that Mustapha Kemal did not want war with Britain and he had considerable reservations about the attitude of the British government. Nevertheless he was a soldier with a duty to obey orders. Therefore he prepared for

action while at the same time using every endeavour to prevent war breaking out because of some chance incident or accident.

By September 26 at Chanak the scene was set for war. On that day Major-General Marden took over command from Colonel Shuttleworth. All the British troops were now in entrenched positions protected by barbed wire. Outside, considerable numbers of Turkish cavalry and infantry were assembled. They did not attack, but plainly their numbers were increasing.

In Constantinople, which was also rapidly being reinforced, all was quiet but there were disturbing rumours of the Turkish population preparing to welcome their compatriot liberators. In the Ismid peninsula, opposite Constantinople, there was little activity and it was assumed that if the Turks were going to provoke hostilities it would not be there but at Chanak that they would strike. This assumption was probably a correct one, because a Turkish advance in the Ismid peninsula would directly threaten Constantinople, where in addition to the still remaining French and Italian garrisons there was a considerable foreign population, plus a large Greek colony swollen by recent refugees. Mustapha Kemal did not want another Smyrna, especially as Constantinople was promised to him in any event, nor did he want trouble with the French and the Italians. Correctly he saw the British as his principal opponents. What however he perhaps failed to appreciate was the degree of resolution of the British government which, rightly or wrongly, in Lloyd George's words: 'intended to force the Turk to a negotiated peace before he should set foot in Europe'. Kemal had seen the British let down the Greeks, he had seen British warships, static and impotent, in the harbour at Smyrna. He knew that a large part of the British press and public was opposed to war. Perhaps therefore he thought that Lloyd George was playing a gigantic game of bluff despite the massing of troops and warships.

If this was his view, and if it was not he was deliberately playing a very dangerous game, it was quite wrong. True, Parliament had not been recalled. The King, George V, was at Balmoral but his train was ready at Ballater station to whisk him to London. There his private secretary, Lord Stamfordham, had in his custody the necessary proclamations for the King's signature to declare a state of emergency. Those items in 'the War Book' designed to alert the Army, Navy, Air Force and Intelligence departments for the outbreak of hostilities had been adopted by the Cabinet. At the same time, because of the reinforcements flowing into Constantinople, the military odds were rapidly lengthening against Kemal's chances of a hastily snatched victory.

General Harington by now was confident that he could hold the Turks at Chanak for three or four weeks, at least into October, by which time five more infantry battalions, a considerable quantity of artillery and three RAF squadrons would have arrived. The Cabinet digested Harington's views and prepared itself for the situation after the first Turkish attack had been repulsed. Orders would be given for 'the mobilisation of an Interim Expeditionary Force of two divisions and a cavalry brigade, and their dispatch to the Dardanelles for the purpose of driving back the Turks and re-establishing control of the neutral zone'.

Panic in the Cabinet
At this stage, September 28, it will be seen that at least the Cabinet had realised that the neutral zone no longer existed and therefore that the British troops only possessed a small toe-hold in Anatolia. However, the realisation by the politicians of the realities of the military situation proved even more dangerous than their previous ignorance. For, influenced by an unconfirmed rumour that the Turks were preparing to attack on September 30, on the morning of September 29 the Cabinet sent General Harington an order to impose an ultimatum—if the Turks did not withdraw from the neutral zone, a broad band of territory outside the defensive positions, then 'all the forces at our disposal—naval, military and aerial—will open fire'. Harington and the soldiers at Chanak, under considerable stress, had kept their heads, but the statesmen in Downing Street had decided to pull the trigger.

The Cabinet ultimatum was not to be

delivered to Ankara, only to the Turkish commander on the spot, although the basic reason for the Cabinet's decision was Kemal's failure to reply to the joint Allied note suggesting a peace conference. Although the Turks had infringed the proposals of the note by sending troops into the provisional neutral zone, they had offered no violence to the British. There they were, as Harington put it, 'grinning through the wire', but they had not fired a single shot. Militarily too, it was a curious time to decide on action. No more reinforcements would be arriving in Turkey until the first week in October and the Turks would be well prepared for the British attack by the very fact of the ultimatum. This, it was thought, should contain a 24-hour time limit, taking the point of expiry up to the day on which it was rumoured the Turks would themselves attack.

Still, whatever the inconsistencies of government action, General Harington had been given an order. It only remained for him to carry it out. From the time of the dispatch of the signal to the Commander-in-Chief the Cabinet was in almost continuous session, waiting for acknowledgement and confirmation—even for reports of the commencement of hostilities. None arrived. Lord Curzon used the time profitably to talk to Nihad Rechad who was one of Kemal's representatives in Paris, now in London at Curzon's request. His colleagues denigrated his last-minute

'We cannot alone act as the policemen of the world' — Bonar Law in a letter to *The Times*, 1922

efforts for peace and waited for war.

By the late evening of September 30 it began to dawn on the Cabinet that there was not going to be a war because General Harington had disobeyed orders and not sent the ultimatum. Eventually a long telegram arrived in which Harington said that he was within an ace of arranging a peace conference with the Turks with the agreement of Sir Horace Rumbold, the High Commissioner in Constantinople, and Admiral Brock, the naval Commander-in-Chief. Therefore would the Cabinet leave him to exercise his own judgement. On the subject of his non-delivery of the ultimatum perhaps his most trenchant comment was: 'I have incessantly been working for peace here, which I thought was the wish of His Majesty's Government.' Lord Curzon later confided to Harington that there had been at least a suggestion of censuring the General for his disobedience which he (Curzon) had opposed. If it had happened, the Cabinet would have been in a very curious position, for on October 1 Harington learnt that Mustapha Kemal would meet him and other Allied generals at Mudanya, on the Sea of Marmara, to discuss peace terms. The General's restraint had paid off and his disobedience had been sanctioned by success.

The conference at Mudanya lasted from October 3 until October 11. In fact Kemal did not attend but sent Ismet Pasha, the victor of Inönü, in his place. The sub-

stitution was irrelevant, for in many ways the proceedings were a formality. Admittedly there were difficult moments, especially when Harington had to suppress another Cabinet telegram which recommended his opening of hostilities unless agreement was reached with some speed. As he wrote later: 'I did not think of the telegrams in my pocket. I only thought our nation did not want another war so soon.'

The Mudanya Convention signed on behalf of Britain, France, Italy and Turkey, and agreed to, but not signed, by the Greeks, came into force on October 15, 1922. By its terms hostilities between Greeks and Turks came to an end. The Greek forces would retire to the left bank of the Maritsa from its outlet in the Aegean to the point where it met the Bulgarian frontier. The Allies would occupy the right bank and the Greek civil administration would then hand over to Allied military commissioners. Allied troops would stay in Thrace for 30 days to preserve law and order during the Greek evacuation. At Chanak the Turks would retire 15 kilometres and not increase the number of their troops; they would do the same in the Ismid peninsula. The Allies would remain at Constantinople and in the Gallipoli peninsula until a formal peace treaty was made.

The Chanak crisis was over. The final peace terms were agreed at Lausanne in November 1922 and the Treaty formally signed in July 1923, by which time the last Sultan had fled from Constantinople, with Harington's help, on a British warship. Henceforth there would only be Kemal's Turkey.

Before Lausanne, however, the crisis had had its effect in Britain. It proved to be the last nail in the coffin of Lloyd George's Coalition Government. On October 19 at the Carlton Club the Tories who kept the Coalition in office voted against its continuance by 187 votes to 87. Stanley Baldwin and Bonar Law both made powerful and telling speeches. The latter had already written to *The Times* criticising Lloyd George's foreign policy, using the phrase: 'We cannot alone act as the policemen of the world.' When he heard the results of the voting at the Carlton Club, Lloyd George said simply: 'That's the end.' Bonar Law was appointed Prime Minister and confirmed his position in the General Election of 1922.

The series of events which had been put in motion when Greek troops had landed at Smyrna and which had involved two Greek kings and a prime minister, a Turkish general who became a national leader and a British general who saved his country from war, and thousands of dead Greeks and Turks, had ended in bringing down one of the most renowned statesmen in Europe.

Further Reading
Blake, Robert, *The Unknown Prime Minister: A Life of Bonar Law* (Eyre & Spottiswoode 1955)
Harington, General Sir Charles, *Tim Harington Looks Back* (Murray 1940)
Lloyd George, David, *The Truth about the Peace Treaties* (Gollancz 1938)
Nicolson, Harold, *Curzon: The Last Phase* (Constable 1934)
Walder, David, *The Chanak Affair* (Hutchinson 1969)

[*For David Walder's biography, see page 1789.*]

The Graeco-Turkish War

Left: King Alexander of Greece. His unexpected death in 1920 plunged Greece into political turmoil.
Below: A Turkish field gun unit. Greek equipment was far better.
Bottom: King Constantine, accompanied by Prince Andrew, right, and General Papoulas, left, arrives in Smyrna. Papoulas, C-in-C in Anatolia, was quite unable to control the rivalries and intrigue between Constantinists and Venizelists that split the Greek army

Since 1863 Greece had been extending her borders, often at Turkey's expense, and, emerging on the winning side in 1918, there seemed every chance of securing Anatolia. But the Greek Prime Minister, Venizelos, had underestimated the resilience of the Turks under their distinguished commander, Kemal. And he could not have possibly foreseen the constitutional crises or his own fall from power which plunged the Greek army into dissension and lost them vital British aid. *David Walder*

Less than a year after landing at Smyrna the Greek army began to advance eastwards into Turkish Anatolia. It was a decision to embark upon a general war and in the last analysis was made by Venizelos, the Greek Prime Minister, aided and abetted by the British Prime Minister, Lloyd George. The two men were personal friends, each admired the other as politician and statesman, and in this matter each deceived the other, with disastrous results for both.

Their first and gravest mutual mistake was in their estimate of the Turks. Both allowed themselves to be over-influenced by the situation in Constantinople. There a compliant Sultan and his Ministers administered an apparently indifferent population and seemed to set a model of co-operation with their conquerors. In fact they had little alternative, as British, French and Italian troops occupied the city in strength and a considerable combined fleet lay off the Golden Horn. In these circumstances it is not difficult to see how a Cabinet was found by Damad Ferid, the Sultan's brother-in-law, to ratify the Treaty of Sèvres by which a large part of Turkey in Asia was parcelled out among the Allies.

However, Constantinople was not Turkey. At Sivas and Erzerum, far from the influence of Allied troops and warships, Mustapha Kemal was turning a resistance movement into a nation. In essence his argument was Turkey for the Turks. The old Ottoman Empire had gone and the tough peasants of the Anatolian uplands were quite willing to be shown by their new military leader that they were in no ways bound by decisions in favour of Greeks forced upon a captive Sultan by the British, the French and the Italians.

To this emergence of a new type of nationalism, Turkish nationalism, both Lloyd George and Venizelos managed to turn very blind eyes indeed. Venizelos also succeeded in giving the British Prime Minister an inflated idea of Greek military strength and capabilities and of the real possibility of his establishing a new Hellenic Empire based on the 'unredeemed Greeks' of Asia Minor. At the same time Lloyd George, more by winks and nods than firm undertakings, seemed to assure the Greek Prime Minister of British support for his ambitions. This Lloyd George did against the opinion of his own military advisers and the judgement of some of his government colleagues, notably Winston Churchill, the Secretary of State for War, who with Field-Marshal Sir Henry Wilson, the CIGS, had attempted unsuccessfully to cross-examine Venizelos on a number of precise military matters when he visited London.

On March 24, 1920 Churchill wrote to Lloyd George as follows: *With military resources which the Cabinet have cut to the most weak and slender proportions, we are leading the Allies in an attempt to enforce a peace on Turkey which would require great and powerful armies and long, costly operations and occupations. On this world so torn with strife I dread to see you let loose the Greek armies—for all our sakes and certainly their sakes.*

The Prime Minister ignored the plea, Venizelos was not restrained and at first, as if to confound his critics and confirm Lloyd George's judgement, the Greeks added success to success. Their army cleared Eastern Thrace of Turkish soldiers and then occupied Adrianople (Edirae). Two divisions moved north from Smyrna (Izmir) and quickly neutralised the bands of Turkish irregulars which had been giving considerable trouble to the British and French in the Ismid peninsula. Bursa was captured and the Greeks came to the conclusion that the Turks possessed little discipline and less inclination to stand and fight. Further to the east, however, long-term plans were being made. Among its more impossible provisions, the Sèvres treaty had established an Armenian state on the borders of the new Soviet Union and Turkey. Kemal sent his representatives to Moscow and the resultant agreement between the two revolutionary governments

enabled him to occupy Armenia and capture Kars on September 28.

His flank with his country's traditional enemy secured, on the basis of mutual advantage, henceforth Kemal could concentrate on repelling the Greeks, who, almost at this moment, suffered their cruellest and strangest stroke of fate.

Alexander, King of the Hellenes, now 27 years old, had succeeded to the throne when his father Constantine had gone into enforced exile with his eldest son, Paul. Naturally enough, Alexander's relations with his Prime Minister, who had ousted his father, had not at first been of the best. By the autumn of 1920, however, they were steadily improving, not least because Venizelos favoured recognition of the King's morganatic wife, Aspasia Manos, as Queen. Aspasia was in fact expecting her first child when her husband was bitten by a pet monkey belonging to the royal vineyard keeper. The wound, disregarded at first, grew serious; blood poisoning set in and after 11 emergency operations Alexander died.

Greece was plunged into political turmoil. Even if Aspasia's unborn child were a boy and entitled to succeed there would have to follow a lengthy period of regency. Venizelos wanted Prince Paul to return as

'Full of eagerness, faith, and self-sacrifice, the Greek soldier threw himself into the age-old struggle of his race — the struggle of civilisation against Asiatic barbarism' — Prince Andrew of Greece

king, but the latter argued that he could not do so unless his father was formally rejected. Eventually the issue was put to a general election which quickly resolved itself into a contest between the two old rivals, Venizelos and Constantine. To his own utter astonishment, and that of his British and French friends, Venizelos lost — and lost decisively, even losing his own parliamentary seat in the process.

'It is enough to make one despair of democracy' wrote Lloyd George to the admired Venizelos as he was replaced by the disliked and distrusted Constantine, the man who had refused to bring his country into the war to aid the Entente, and who had been pushed off his throne by the British and French in consequence.

The return of Constantine to Athens was not the only surprise the wartime Allies had to suffer. Their interpretation of the election result was that the Greeks must be tired of Venizelos' warlike expansionist policy. It was confidently assumed therefore that the returned Constantine would now bring the war to a close. In fact he did nothing of the sort, but began a wholesale advance with Ankara, the Turk-

Below: Turkish cavalrymen in Anatolia. Rarely used in the First World War, Turkish cavalry was held together under Kemal's experienced command

ish Nationalist capital, as his objective.

Recovering from his surprise at this 'mad outbreak of regal vanity', as he called it, Lloyd George realised that the King's action released the British government from an ever-increasing dilemma. As Churchill put it, 'for the sake of Venizelos much had to be endured, but for Constantine, less than nothing'.

The Greeks were now on their own. Their former allies had all deserted them. The Italians had never looked with favour on Greek expansion, the French had no intention of antagonising a new Turkish state if it came into being, and now the British, reverting to their old distrust of Constantine as an excuse, withdrew their military and naval advice and assistance and also their diplomatic support.

So the foundation on which Venizelos had laid his political and military plans, that of Allied co-operation, was removed from under Constantine's feet. That, in the circumstances, the King proceeded may seem surprising, but there were three reasons. First, the advice of his generals who were confident of success; secondly, the fact that the Greek people expected him to overtop the achievements of Venizelos; and thirdly, a feeling that as the French, the Italians and particularly the British were still involved with one part of Turkey, they could not remain indifferent to what the Greeks were doing in another. There was still a feeling in Greece that the British, and especially their Prime Minister, would not let them down.

An ally or not?
So the Greek army was still referred to as 'the Allied Army in Anatolia', not entirely as a mere propaganda boost to morale. In fact, as well as losing its allies, that army had also suffered in another respect. With the return of the King there had been a complete purge of all those who owed their positions and offices to Venizelos, including army officers. General Paraskeropoulos, the Commander-in-Chief in Smyrna, anticipating some such action, left for France as the King entered Athens. It is doubtful, however, if he anticipated the scale of the changes on their way. Over 1,500 officers, from generals to subalterns, previously dismissed by Venizelos, were reinstated and promoted. At the same time a large number of Venizelist senior officers were dismissed or demoted. Their juniors who remained in the service found that preferment went to the returned Constantinists. The army in Anatolia was in effect turned upside down. It may have been straight political tit-for-tat, but it was military madness for an army which was taking on new and increased responsibilities.

In one appointment, however, the King and his new Prime Minister, M. Rhallis, did show some wisdom. General Papoulas, the new Commander-in-Chief in Anatolia, was by no means a brilliant general, but he was a straightforward, loyal and non-political soldier, something of a rarity in Greece at the time. From the day of his appointment he gave himself the task of re-establishing unity. He himself set an

Above left: Turkish artillery on the move through the stony slopes of Anatolia. The entire Turkish nation was behind the war effort, the army united under one command. *Above right:* Greek infantry in retreat, 1922, demoralised and exhausted

example of impartiality and concern with military efficiency only, but unfortunately his subordinates, whether Venizelists or Constantinists, seemed quite incapable of following it. Throughout its sojourn in Anatolia the Greek army remained a force riven by political rivalries, jealousies and dissension.

At first, however, whatever its internal state, the tasks which the army carried out were of obvious military advantage. Under Venizelos there had been no particular strategic pattern in its movements. It had spread out from Smyrna, it had taken Bursa, but overall it had merely responded to the resistance offered by the sporadic and irregular warfare of the Turks. Allied advice, too, had not always been helpful. The British and the French in the last days of Venizelos had expressed their concern as to just how far his troops intended to go. So they had been pulled back, but the line then taken up had been neither offensive nor defensive, extending from Smyrna on three virtually disconnected fronts.

Now at least in the January of 1921 there was military logic in the plans of the Greek army. The ultimate aim was the capture of Ankara and the short term objectives were the taking of Eskişehir and

Afionkarahisar, key junction towns on the main Smyrna-Ankara railway line.

The army was divided into two groups, a northern group composed of four infantry divisions, a total of 18,000 men, and a southern of seven infantry divisions and a cavalry brigade totalling 33,000 men. Between the two concentrations there stretched a front of about 40 miles which was comparatively lightly held, as was the rest of the Greek line which ran from the Sea of Marmara in the north down to the south of Smyrna.

When the clash came with the Turks there was little subtlety about it. Against the Greek northern group the Turks had assembled about 23,000 men to the west of Eskişehir. To protect Afionkarahisar to the south they concentrated another 25,000. Overall, the Greeks had a slight superiority in numbers, but as the main Greek thrust was made on the northern front the disparity in numbers was in fact of little significance.

The Greeks did have a definite advantage so far as equipment was concerned. They were superior to their opposition in field artillery and had more than twice the number of machine guns per battalion. In fact, where technical and mechanical equipment of all sorts was concerned, in transport, aircraft and weapons, the Greeks were better off than their opponents. The Turks would admittedly be fighting a defensive battle in difficult terrain over which the Greeks would have to advance. Nevertheless, there were no doubts in the minds of the officers of the Greek General Staff that the operations would be successful.

The battle when joined, on January 10, was by First World War standards a small affair. Nevertheless, the Turks accord it its rightful importance and celebrate it as the First Battle of Inönü. For a day, fighting in snow and slush, they held their ground under their commander Ismet Pasha. (When the Turks adopted surnames he was to take his from the river valley he defended.) On the second day the Turks counterattacked with great persistence and courage. Greek confidence turned to surprise and consternation. The new Royalist commanders were forced to admit defeat and order a retirement to Bursa.

The First Battle of Inönü was the first in which a properly led and disciplined Turkish army had met the Greek invaders on anything like equal terms and its result was a portent for the future. Three months later the Greeks tried again. In the south they captured Afionkarahisar comparatively easily and advanced along the road to Konya, nearly due south of and less than 200 miles from Ankara. In the north however they once again reached Inönü and once again were held by Ismet. This time, however, the battle lasted a week and the Greeks committed all their available forces, casualties were heavy and the exhausted Greeks were unable to resist the inevitable Turkish counterattack. After the First Battle of Inönü the Greeks re-

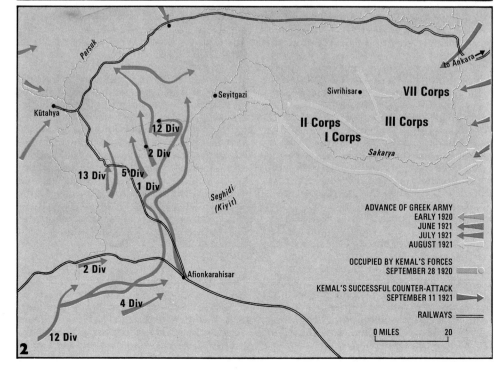

It was not only the Greek and Turkish armies that suffered heavily during the war. *Above:* A village left in flames by the Greek army

tired, after the second they retreated, beaten and in confusion. Two very different foreign observers, Ernest Hemingway and Arnold Toynbee, both discerned the beginning of defeatist attitudes in the Greek army.

Interposed between the two battles of Inönü had been the London Conference, convened by Lloyd George as an attempt to find some solution both to the war and the problem of postwar Turkey. It was a disaster. Representatives of both Turkish governments, the Sultan's and Mustapha Kemal's, plus the Greeks, the French and the Italians attended. No worthwhile agreement was reached but somehow Lloyd George gave the impression, by his anti-Turk and pro-Greek attitudes, that in the last resort even Constantine's government could rely upon British assistance.

Nothing could have been further from the truth. Lloyd George, a Liberal, presided over a Coalition Government which was kept in office by a Tory majority in the House of Commons. That majority was pro-Turk in sentiment, and opposed to foreign adventures, especially those which seemed likely to arise from Lloyd George's individualistic conduct of foreign affairs. In Beaverbrook's phrase, Lloyd George was 'a prime minister without a party'. Consequently any assurances he might seem to give to Greece were almost bound to be worthless.

To what extent the Greek government did rely on the often expressed pro-Hellenic sentiments of the British Prime Minister it is difficult to say, but it is certain that the British government never gave any clear indication that it had in effect washed its hands of the whole Greek affair. Rather the reverse: military observers were sent to report on the state of the Greek army and the exiled Venizelos was frequently con-

sulted as to his views.

The situation angered both Churchill and Sir Henry Wilson, and the former again bombarded Lloyd George suggesting a realistic solution including the eventual evacuation of Smyrna by the Greeks as part of a general peace agreement with Kemal.

There was in fact in the early summer of 1921 considerable diplomatic activity between the three wartime Allies and the Greeks, but nothing as definite as Churchill's tough realistic terms was ever put to the two belligerents. Understandably, perhaps, in all this confusion, the Greeks decided once more to put the issue to the test of battle and the offensive was resumed once again on July 10.

The passage of both time and events had wrought its changes on the two opposing armies in Anatolia. The Greek army's internal difficulties had not been diminished by the unexpected reverses it had suffered. Numbers in Anatolia had been increased, but there were immediate problems among the officers promoted to command the new formations. Papoulas had tried to strike a balance between Venizelists and Constantinists but finished up with what Prince Andrew, who commanded the 12th Division, called 'a plethora of generals and colonels'. Lower down the scale inexperienced NCO's were promoted to fill the junior commissioned ranks. Even the increase of the army from 110,000 men to 200,000 was a mixed blessing, as many of the new units were formed almost entirely of untried young recruits.

As some attempt to improve morale the King himself took charge and was proclaimed Supreme Commander of the Greek Forces in Asia. He landed at Smyrna to a tumultuous reception and was well received elsewhere by the rank and file. The

trouble with the Greek army was however not in the quality of its tough, courageous private soldiers, but in the higher reaches of command. Constantine was Supreme Commander in name, but he still had to take the advice of his generals and that was often conflicting, and frequently motivated by intrigue and self-interest.

The Turks, on the other hand, had the advantage of the clear monolithic authority of their political and military leader, Mustapha Kemal. His abilities had been shown at Gallipoli; once more he was asking the Turks to repel an invader and this time the nation was united behind him. Every little factory in Ankara was turning out war equipment, each household provided one sheet for bandages, Turkish women for the first time in their history served as nurses and auxiliaries. Every man and boy was used in an attempt to redress the balance of the Greeks' numerical superiority. However, once again the Greeks scored an initial success and captured Eskişehir and again Afionkarahisar, but they lost 8,000 killed and wounded in the process. King Constantine returned from Athens to witness the Turkish counterattack, which was repulsed. The Turkish army began to retreat beyond the Sakarya river, their final position being only 50 miles from Ankara.

The Greeks too ambitious
The Greeks were elated and the capture of Kemal's capital was seen not as a military objective but as a method of destroying Kemal himself and his Nationalists. Papoulas himself was cautious and wanted to take up a different position west of the

Sakarya. His advice was overborne and on August 10 the Greeks advanced again, over the most difficult terrain they had yet encountered. By August 23, when they met the Turks, the conditions of near desert warfare had taken their toll. Supplies ran short, motor transport broke down, horses died and heavy equipment had to be abandoned.

The battle of the Sakarya river raged for 22 days and nights. Countless times the Greeks were hurled at the well-supplied and well-sited Turkish defensive positions. The two armies fought each other to a standstill, the Greeks losing 18,000 men, the Turks nearly as many. The Turks were, however, capable of the last counterattack; unable to resist it, on September 11 the Greek army, on the orders of its King, began its retreat westwards.

For another year the Greek army remained in Anatolia, but it was a defeated army, just managing, despite incredible hardships and declining morale, to maintain a defensive position.

Papoulas and his whole staff resigned in May 1922 after many disputes with the Ministry of War. Prince Andrew, after a disagreement with the General Staff, returned to Greece. General Hajianestis, who succeeded Papoulas, was 58 years old, mentally ill, and decided to command his army from a yacht moored in Smyrna harbour. His only show of vigour was when he moved two divisions by sea to Thrace to threaten Allied-held Constantinople. It was a gambler's last throw, and the occupying powers were unyielding. They would not give up the Turkish capital to the Greeks as compensation for their lost war in Anatolia. Sir Nevile Henderson, the British High Commissioner in Constantinople, wrote later, 'I have always hated my action on that occasion.'

When the end came it came swiftly. On August 26, 1922 Mustapha Kemal launched his long prepared offensive. Their goal, he told his soldiers, was the Mediterranean. On September 9 the Turks entered Smyrna. 'Here's a bloody mess,' said Lloyd George, when told the news.

The aftermath of the war was for the Greeks more terrible than the war itself. The army had collapsed. On September 13 Smyrna went up in flames, whether by accident or design it is virtually impossible to tell. To this day the Greeks blame the Turks and the Turks the Greeks. Three days later three-quarters of the town was a smouldering ruin. Nearly 220,000 refugees were evacuated by foreign warships and merchantmen, and taken to Greece and the islands of the Aegean. This figure was in addition to the 50,000 POW's held by the Turks and 30,000 counted dead.

On September 23 what had begun as a military mutiny erupted into a full-scale revolution in Athens. On September 27, for the second time, King Constantine was forced to abdicate, in favour of Crown Prince George. The actual government was taken over by a clique of colonels with Colonel Plastiras at their head. He was, he declared, prepared to resist the Turks' demand for Eastern Thrace, the province of mixed Greek and Turkish population on the Constantinople side of the Sea of Marmara.

Before Mustapha Kemal gained both Eastern Thrace and Constantinople he was to come into collision with the British, still occupying both the capital and the neutral zone at Chanak. For a few days Britain and Turkey were nearly at war. In the aftermath of the crisis Lloyd George fell from power, one of the gravest counts against him being his foreign policy.

Technically the state of warfare between Greeks and Turks was not brought to an end until the signature of the Treaty of Lausanne in July 1923 which ended the Allied military occupation of Constantinople and recognised both the territory and status of the new Turkish Republic.

By then, however, Mustapha Kemal had seen most of his opponents cast down. Lloyd George's Coalition Government had been destroyed. Constantine died in exile in 1923. General Hajianestis, along with five former Cabinet Ministers, had been shot by firing squad in Athens. In the same year as his father died King George II was compelled to leave Greece, which then entered into a prolonged period of military dictatorships. Venizelos was subsequently in and out of office but died in 1936 in exile, a discredited conspirator. Kemal himself remained President of the Turkish Republic until his death in 1938, when he was succeeded by Ismet Inönü.

Further Reading

Alastos, D., *Venizelos* (Lund Humphries 1942)

Andrew of Greece, Prince, *Towards Disaster: the Greek Army in Asia Minor in 1921* (John Murray 1930)

Beaverbrook, Lord, *The Decline and Fall of Lloyd George* (Collins 1963)

Bierstadt, E. H., *The Great Betrayal* (Hutchinson 1925)

Bujac, Colonel A., *Les Campagnes de l'Armée Hellenique 1918-1922* (Paris: Ch. Lavazelle et Cie 1930)

Cosmetatos, S. P. P., *The Tragedy of Greece* (Kegan Paul 1928)

Pallis, A. A., *Greece's Anatolian Adventure — and after* (Methuen 1937)

Toynbee, A. J., *The Western Question in Greece and Turkey* (Constable 1922)

[*For David Walder's biography, see page 1789.*]

Südd Verlag

From Gay Hussar

The range of uniforms worn by the Austro-Hungarian army during the First World War. *This page, left to right. First left:* A *Wachtmeister* (Warrant Officer) from the Honved Hussar Regiment, 1914 to 1915. *Second left:* A *Stabswachtmeister* (Warrant Officer 1st Class) from the 3rd Ulane Regiment, 1914 to 1915. *Third left:* Trooper of the 15th Dragoon Regiment, 1914 to 1915. *Fourth left:* A *Gefreiter* (Lance-Corporal) of the 4th Infantry Regiment, 1914 to 1915.

to Storm Trooper

This page, left to right. First left: An officer of less than staff rank in an artillery regiment, 1915 to 1918. *Second left:* A rifleman from a rifle regiment, carrying alpine equipment and dressed for mountainous conditions, 1917 to 1918. *Third left:* A rifleman from an infantry regiment, 1916 to 1918, with an Austrian steel helmet and full winter equipment. *Fourth left:* A Stormtrooper of 1918, kitted out with German steel helmet, light equipment, respirator and grenades

The Allies quit Russia

Below: Murmansk Harbour, Northern Russia. A British base for over a year, it was evacuated in mid-October 1919, by which time it had become obvious that the White forces were failing. *Right:* March past of soldiers of the Slavo-British Legion at Archangel. As in Murmansk British forces there were withdrawn in the autumn of 1919

Imperial War Museum

In December 1918 the French ambassador to
Russia, Joseph Noulens, boldly declared that
'France and her allies will not abandon the
Russian people to the Bolsheviks'. Less than
six months later the French had made their
first withdrawal from Russia, having foundered
on the problems of co-operation with Denikin's
Volunteer Army and of agreement with the
British. It was a pattern that was to be
repeated throughout Russia and by the end of
1920 the Western Powers had withdrawn all aid
from the failing White armies. *J. F. N. Bradley*

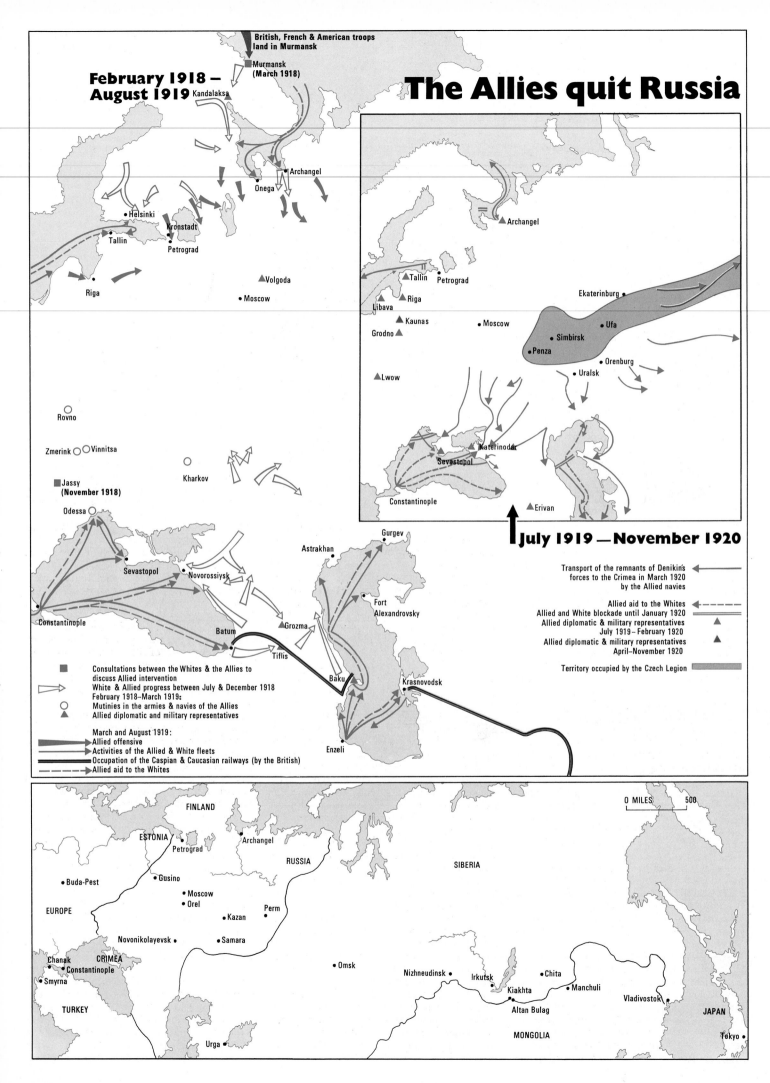

The Allies quit Russia

February 1918 – August 1919

British, French & American troops land in Murmansk

Murmansk (March 1918)

Kandalaksa

Archangel

Onega

• Helsinki

Kronstadt

Tallin

Petrograd

Riga

• Volgoda

• Moscow

July 1919 — November 1920

▲ Archangel

▲ Tallin   • Petrograd

Libava

▲ Riga

▲ Kaunas

Grodno ▲

• Moscow

▲ Lwow

Ekaterinburg •

• Ufa

• Simbirsk

Penza

• Orenburg

• Uralsk

○ Rovno

Zmerink ○ ○ Vinnitsa

■ Jassy
(November 1918)

Kharkov

Odessa ○

Sevastopol

• Novorossiysk

Constantinople

Batum

Tiflis

Grozma

Astrakhan

Gurgev

Fort Alexandrovsky

Baku

Enzeli

Krasnovodsk

Katerinodar

Sevastopol

Constantinople

▲ Erivan

Transport of the remnants of Denikin's
forces to the Crimea in March 1920
by the Allied navies

Allied aid to the Whites

Allied and White blockade until January 1920

▲ Allied diplomatic & military representatives
July 1919 – February 1920

▲ Allied diplomatic & military representatives
April–November 1920

Territory occupied by the Czech Legion

■ Consultations between the Whites & the Allies to
discuss Allied intervention

⇨ White & Allied progress between July & December 1918
February 1918–March 1919:

○ Mutinies in the armies & navies of the Allies

▲ Allied diplomatic and military representatives

March and August 1919:

Allied offensive

Activities of the Allied & White fleets

Occupation of the Caspian & Caucasian railways (by the British)

Allied aid to the Whites

FINLAND

ESTONIA

Petrograd

• Archangel

RUSSIA

SIBERIA

• Buda-Pest

• Gusino

• Moscow

• Orel

EUROPE

• Kazan

Perm

• Novonikolayevsk

• Samara

0 MILES 500

Chanak   CRIMEA

• Constantinople

• Smyrna

TURKEY

• Omsk

Nizhneudinsk •

Irkutsk •

• Chita

Kiakhta •

• Manchuli

Vladivostok •

JAPAN

Urga •

Altan Bulag

MONGOLIA

Tokyo •

3494

'We remember the grim days when ... all the capitalist countries of Europe and America marched on our country to strangle the new revolution' — Khrushchev

Above: Vladivostok. The last convoy of Czechs was evacuated from the port in 1920

In June 1918 Allied intervention in Russia was launched for the declared purpose of continuing the war against the Central Powers inside Russia. After the Armistice in November 1918, although there was no longer either an agreed principle or a common Allied policy towards Russia, it was still felt necessary to curtail German influence there. Since, in Allied eyes, the Bolsheviks had been linked with the Germans, it was thought that they also would have to be removed. The problem was how far the victorious Allies would have to go to achieve this.

From the beginning the Allies proved immeasurably stronger in words than in deeds. On leaving Russia, on December 18, 1918, Ambassador Noulens declared: 'France and her allies will not abandon the Russian people to the Bolsheviks', while Lord Balfour had told the House of Commons on November 18: 'The Bolsheviks followed a deliberate policy of exterminating their political opponents ... we shall therefore not strengthen this government.' On November 13, 1918 France and Britain had reaffirmed the Zonal Convention of December 1917, but this was the end of co-ordination. Henceforth each Ally would look after its own interests.

The British were determined to hang on to their Murmansk and Archangel bases until Bolshevik collapse but the Balfour memorandum of November 1918 made it clear that they would not get directly involved in Russian affairs. The French, on the contrary, evolved the theory of a *cordon sanitaire* stretching from Odessa to Riga. Pichon, the Foreign Minister, formulated it

and General Berthelot, on his arrival in Bucharest on November 15, 1918, was ordered to interpret and implement it. French forces were in control of Serbia and southern Hungary and were co-operating with Rumania who had just re-entered the war. This was to be the ground force of the policy. French naval forces received orders for transportation of French troops to Odessa, where they would be joined by two Greek divisions. Direct French intervention was launched. Before the expeditionary forces arrived, the French consul Henno convoked a conference to explain 'Allied' plans of intervention to pro-Allied Russian delegations. 'Allied' divisions were being sent to Odessa to restore order, supervise German withdrawal and provide the Volunteer Army with a protective shield, so that it could reorganise in peace and prepare its anti-Bolshevik strike. The Russians agreed that they would support the Allies in order to reconstitute Russia in its pre-1914 borders (with the exception of Poland) and that this struggle would be waged under General Denikin's leadership. They dispersed, assuming that the Allies had undertaken to support them in their struggle with the Bolsheviks. But it soon became clear that strong words would not be followed by equally forceful actions. Events in the French zone took an unexpected turn when Ukrainian nationalists seized power on November 17, 1918. The Ukraine was declared independent and Clemenceau instructed Consul Henno to deal with this complication and prepare Odessa for French landing. But all Henno could do was bluff and threaten. Nevertheless he scored a concrete success when he stopped Petlyura, Ukrainian C-in-C, from issuing the final orders for his troops to take Odessa. Even the plans for inter-

vention were becoming complicated: obviously intervention itself would be a labyrinthine affair.

The French had originally taken on themselves to police southern Russia in the hope that soon there would be a common policy towards Russia which would be defined at the Peace Conference. But on January 22, 1919 the five Allied Powers rejected the plan drawn by Marshal Foch for a military intervention. The aborted Prinkipo Conference, which would have benefited no one but the Bolsheviks, was the last commonly agreed idea for the solution of the Russian problem. Henceforth the Allies reverted to the old unsatisfactory zonal arrangements. Actions were unco-ordinated; duplicated efforts and useless rivalry continued to bedevil the Russian situation and even endanger Franco-British relations, which by March 1919 reached a point of crisis.

Evacuation of Odessa

Even before the French landed in Odessa they sensed that military co-operation with the Russians would be difficult. Russian officers were also politicians and would judge French generals from a political point of view which was incomprehensible to them. After landing, General Borius appointed a Siberian, General Grishin-Almazov, as military governor of Odessa. Grishin-Almazov considered himself under General Denikin's command and applied to him for approval, which was granted. Unknowingly, General Denikin and his army operated in the British zone and strictly speaking had no authority over Odessa. However, neither Denikin nor Grishin-Almazov were enlightened on this point and immediately a dangerous bone of contention arose among the Allies. Henceforth Denikin considered his 'interference' in the French zone as entirely natural, to the great annoyance of the French commanders.

When in March 1919 a Franco-Ukrainian agreement became publicly known (it made nonsense of the White Russians' 'one, indivisible Russia') General Denikin vehemently protested to Colonel Corbel, Head of the French Mission, at his HQ, and was told quite truthfully that the coup at Odessa had been necessary in order to save the situation there. The French were in desperate straits. Ataman Grigoriev, a Cossack anarchist from the Ukraine, threatened and could take the city without much struggle after he had routed Allied forces at Berezovka. He even captured two French tanks. Early in April 1919 the French Command, hearing of an open mutiny in the fleet, decided to evacuate Odessa. The French, disillusioned with the Russians, left behind most of the Russian refugees who wanted to evacuate with them. On April 5, 1919 Grigoriev's partisans arrived in the city and took it on behalf of the Bolsheviks. This was the tragic result of the bitter quarrel between the French and the Volunteers which had serious repercussions on Franco-British relations.

The Allies: continued disagreement

The British differed very strongly from the French in their application of the zonal arrangement. They stuck to it in the strictest sense: for them intra-zonal factors became British factors, with disastrous effects on Franco-British relations. Two

British missions, one under Colonel Blackwood, the other under General Poole, were sent to Ekaterinodar, General Denikin's headquarters, to report on his forces; both urged London to recognise Denikin as Supreme Commander-in-Chief in southern Russia. Within a month Denikin received the first shipments of British aid and a powerful military mission led by General Briggs, consisting of some 500 officers and men, arrived to help him. The French recognition of an independent Ukraine roused the Volunteers and alarmed the British. General Briggs sent a message to London in which he forecast disastrous consequences. The French Ambassador, Cambon, was called by Lord Curzon on March 21 to explain his position. The French explained themselves satisfactorily and the Allies made another effort at reaching an agreement *vis-à-vis* Russia. On April 4 a conference was held in Paris to try to resolve the differences between Generals Denikin and Berthelot. Military moves were to be co-ordinated and troops and supplies would be permitted to cross or be taken over the zonal borders. No political negotiations would be entered into with other Russian or Ukrainian factions without Denikin's representatives, and Russian ships would be allowed to fight for General Denikin.

Beginning of the end

The protocol of April 4 became the cornerstone of Franco-British co-operation in southern Russia. Nonetheless, it was the beginning of the end. Pichon once again stated that zonal agreements were still in force and hinted that France would probably reappraise her policy in southern Russia. Britain was also ready for a reappraisal. On June 11, A. Selby, who so successfully ironed out the April agreement, wrote a memorandum which dealt with the whole of Russia. He pointed out the still prevalent dissatisfaction with the zonal agreements and stressed the disproportionate financial burden which Britain had to bear. He recommended comprehensive zonal and financial agreements, or the end of intervention. But nothing constructive followed this proposal; and, with the increasing military failures of the Whites, withdrawal became inevitable.

In June 1919, after the success of the

Top: Finn ski company near Murmansk in 1919. Having sided with the Tsarist Russian forces throughout the First World War the Finns seized the chance, after the revolution in Russia, of gaining national autonomy. As a result they were unwilling to associate themselves with the aims of Yudenich's North-Western Army or with Allied intervention. *Above left:* In the frozen north special transport and equipment was a necessity. Here troops with reindeer sleighs wear arctic dress. *Above right:* British and Slav troops set up camp in a clearing. *Right:* Cossack and British troops man an armoured train south of Archangel. *Far right:* In the piercing cold of northern Russia heavy snow shoes, mittens and fur hats were usually worn

Bolshevik offensive in the East, it became clear that Admiral Kolchak was beaten. Even if he recovered from the capture of Omsk his régime would no longer be the decisive factor, as it once was, in the struggle against the Bolsheviks. After the successful Soviet offensive the long-sought junction of anti-Bolshevik forces in north Russia and Siberia had become militarily impossible. But even previously, General Janin, the French Commander of the Czech Corps, had refused to allow his troops to fight their way through to Archangel and join up with Allied and White forces there. When this became obvious the British government decided on the evacuation of its forces: the Archangel White government would have to be abandoned

but the British had not much choice. In July 1919 mutinies among Russian troops in the North convinced General Ironside that the White forces could not hold out on their own and their weakness only accelerated British departure. It was decided to withdraw all Allied forces from Archangel before October 1, 1919. The safety of the evacuation was assured by Ironside's successful attack against the Red Army, astride the River Dvina. But the British had first to destroy guns, motor lorries and millions of rounds of ammunition to avoid their capture by the Reds or use by the Whites. By September 27, 1919 the last British soldier had left Archangel; on October 12, exactly as planned, the evacuation of Murmansk was completed.

In Siberia, after the fall of Chelyabinsk in July 1919, it was decided to bring home the two British battalions in the area. It became clear that Kolchak's rule was unpopular, both in Russia and with British public opinion, although he had initially been a source of hope to the British. The Admiral was eventually to die at the hands of the Bolsheviks at Irkutsk, on February 7, 1920. When his régime and army collapsed, he had placed himself under Czech protection. But in order to get out of their own difficulties with the Bolsheviks and the Social Revolutionaries, who had revolted against Kolchak, the Czechs handed the Admiral and his Prime Minister, Pepeliaev, over to the Irkutsk socialists. The two White leaders were executed by a Bolshevik firing squad when the Red Army moved into Irkutsk, but the Czechs at least gained time and were able to save themselves, as well as the French and British Allies, by concluding an armistice with the advancing Bolsheviks.

British and French involvement in Siberia did not survive Kolchak: by early March 1920 the military missions were withdrawn and all Britons and French evacuated. The evacuation of the Czech Corps went on safely and the last convoy left Vladivostok on September 2, 1920.

Rout of the Volunteer Army

In June 1919, after the reverses in Siberia, the Volunteer Army and its Cossack and Caucasian allies stood poised for a massive offensive—their objective was the Bolshevik capital, Moscow. It was therefore natural that Clemenceau's attention should shift from Siberia to southern Russia. At the time when Britain began to feel the economic strain of supporting Denikin, 'the Tiger' prepared for a bid for French influence in the British zone. He sent his own observer to Denikin's Russia, Captain Widhoff, to report on the Volunteers and find out whether they were worth French support. On the strength of Widhoff's report and because the Volunteer Army had thrust deep into Russia, the French decided to take over from the British. The British in a sense had forced the French to act in this way, by establishing a White naval base in the Crimea, which was a part of the French zone, and implying a British takover. Thus Clemenceau decided to send a new, more powerful mission to General Denikin, under the command of General Mangin; he was also prepared to assume the financial burdens of military aid. But by the time these decisions were made the Volunteers were in deep trouble and retreating rapidly from Central Russia. By

November 1919 the British came to the painful conclusion that they had backed the wrong horse: Lloyd George made a public allusion to the possibility of negotiations with the Bolsheviks and of withdrawal of British aid from the Whites. However, France was now too deeply committed to follow the British example or to learn from British failure. Clemenceau realised full well that the Russian Whites could achieve nothing on their own, but combined with other nations, especially the Poles on the fringes of Russia, they could achieve much. General Mangin's mission now amounted to selling this idea to the parties concerned. He tried to reconcile the Volunteers and the Poles, but in vain. Mangin also urged Clemenceau to give Denikin an important rôle to play in his plans for Eastern Europe in the struggle against the Bolsheviks but this advice was also ignored. The Volunteers' fate was finally sealed in London, where Clemenceau met Lloyd George in December 1919 and agreed to concentrate Allied support on the border states rather than on the 'discredited' Whites.

Early in 1920, General Wrangel succeeded General Denikin as the White leader. He was not slow in exploiting Franco-British differences, and even hoped for a revival of White military fortunes. On June 11, 1920, under the pretext of Wrangel's ignoring a British ultimatum to drop plans for an offensive, Lord Curzon instructed the British High Commissioner in Istanbul, Admiral de Robeck, to withdraw the military mission and break off all relations with the Volunteers. By June 1920 Britain and France were disagreeing deeply about the handling of the situation in Russia and Eastern Europe: the former wanted peace negotiations with the Bolsheviks, while the latter wanted to stop the Polish retreat, and then, by a combined operation, defeat the Bolsheviks before talking peace. President Millerand of France needed General Wrangel's co-operation for this plan, and recognised his government on August 11, 1920. But it was too late, for by then communications were in chaos. Supplies from Rumania did not arrive in the Crimea in time or in sufficient quantities to prevent the Kuban offensive undertaken by the Whites from collapsing. By September 1920 the French had reluctantly to recognise that the whole Volunteer movement and the Wrangel government would disintegrate under the next Bolshevik attack. They could only promise help with the evacuation of the White army and their families. When the Bolsheviks finally launched an offensive against the Crimea the French faithfully carried out their promise and evacuation was completed in November 1920.

The Baltic: no further help

Since October 20, 1919, the day on which General Denikin started retreating from Orel,. 80 miles from Moscow, the White North-Western Army also stopped its advance, having gone as far as the suburbs of Petrograd. General Yudenich, in command of this front, was in the eyes of Lord Curzon thoroughly reactionary and ineffective, and the British had no confidence in either him or his troops. It had been made clear to General Gough, head of the British military mission to Finland and the Baltic provinces, that the British government's policy was of non-interference and

limited support. Thus when Admiral Kolchak started retreating and asked the Finns to attack Petrograd, in July 1919, the Allies were requested to provide support for the North-Western Army and the Finns. In August 1919 limited supplies began to arrive for the Whites but it became clear that Finnish help was out of the question. The Estonians had to be courted instead and an agreement was signed between them and the North-West Russian government which had been formed under the pressure of Allied representatives on the spot. The Baltic states asked for official recognition by the Allies, in return for continuing their fight against the Bolsheviks, so putting the full burden of continuing White resistance squarely on to the Allies, but when the Yudenich movement wavered the Allies stuck to their policy of limited support and failed to deliver recognition, so the Balts withdrew their offer of military aid. This was really the final blow for General Yudenich who had been planning an offensive for September 15: Estonian detachments were to play an important part in it. However, Yudenich launched his offensive nevertheless: some 17,000 White troops began their advance on Petrograd in October and though the Bolshevik forces outnumbered the Whites the advance at first went well. But soon Trotsky reorganised the front and with reinforcements made a determined stand before Petrograd. Yudenich's army was forced to retreat. A terrible epidemic of typhus struck the routed army and the surviving remnants crossed into Estonia where they were disarmed and interned.

On October 31, 1919 the British Cabinet decided to withdraw the Baltic Fleet and a month later Lloyd George told the House of Commons: 'it is not proposed that the British fleet should undertake the patrol of the Baltic in the spring.' British and French military missions were also withdrawn and the Baltic states left to fend for themselves against the Bolsheviks.

Armed resistance against the new Russia had failed, due to bad Intelligence on the spot and international rivalry, which vitally affected the local situation. When one by one the Russian White movements failed to defeat the Bolsheviks, the Allies turned to Poland. But the Poles had their own aims in Eastern Europe and while they ultimately scored a decisive victory which enabled them to conclude an advantageous peace treaty, they failed to fall in with Allied plans.

Another reason for the failure of Allied intervention was that Russian national interests were completely ignored. This led the Whites to oppose Allied policies, especially in the lower echelons. of the White movements. The Allies also failed to proclaim clearly their aims in Russia. Thus Britain advocated different policies in different parts of Russia, in one area favouring national separatism and in another opposing it. France could not decide either whether the Russian element or the separatist ones would help her most in her pursuance of national interests and her support fluctuated accordingly.

So intervention failed, having been of no benefit to the Allies, but having helped to weld the Bolsheviks together, and inspired Soviet leaders with deep mistrust towards the Western Powers.
[*For J. F. N. Bradley's biography, see page 99.*]

RUSSIA
The White armies defeated

In December 1917 the British Foreign Office was surprised by a message from their ambassador in Tokyo: a Russian admiral, Alexander Kolchak, had offered his services, 'as a private soldier if necessary'.

It was a strange but timely offer. The newly-established Bolshevik government had that same month concluded an armistice with the Germans. If it was a lasting peace – as Lenin was determined it should be – millions of German soldiers would soon be free to reinforce the Western Front. Both Britain and France rapidly agreed to support any Russian groups willing to go on fighting the Germans. A fateful, if well-intentioned decision, it engendered Allied support of anti-Bolshevik leaders round the edge of Russia and Allied involvement, with America and Japan, in the events which over the next four years led to the total defeat of anti-Bolshevism and the establishment of the first Soviet satellite, Mongolia.

The most successful anti-Bolshevik challenges came in Siberia and the Far East, spearheaded by Kolchak. He seemed at first ideal for the Allied purpose. Noted as an Arctic explorer, he had given gallant service in the Russo-Japanese War in 1904 and had become, in 1916, Vice-Admiral of the Black Sea Fleet at the early age of 44. On the outbreak of the Revolution he had been invited to America to advise on a possible American attack on the Dardanelles. His sincerity was beyond question, his integrity unblemished. Frugal, taciturn and authoritative, he inspired the belief that here was a self-possessed leader who could be relied upon.

But relied upon to do what? The British War Office was not quite sure. At first they ordered him to Mesopotamia, but he had only reached Singapore when he was sent back to Manchuria, as a member of the board of the Chinese Eastern Railway, a Russian-administered subsidiary stretch of the Trans-Siberian which ran through Manchuria to Vladivostok. By the time Kolchak reached Peking in April, 1918, the situation to the north was one of baffling complexity. Every regional or national group in Siberia and Manchuria had its own claims to authority: Bolsheviks, Social Revolutionaries, Buryat Mongols, Tsarists, Muslims and predominantly the Cossacks, the officer-landlords, by origin mostly Ukrainian, who were to play a prime rôle in the coming years.

Semenov: snub for the Allies

Though the Bolsheviks had nominal control of most important centres – those on the Trans-Siberian, the life-line of Central Asia and the Russian Far East – their authority already faced a two-fold challenge. At Manchuli, on the Russian-Chinese border, ruled Grigori Semenov, a 28-year-old Mongolian with a black moustache and puffy lips who liked to ape Napoleon, with one arm stuck inside his jacket. His reputation soon became appalling. Travelling by armoured train, he shot his prisoners, robbed banks, customs stations and passing trains, and was renowned for merciless and indiscriminate attack and torture.

The Civil War in Russia was for the Whites an essentially piecemeal resistance, their ultimate failure due to lack of co-ordination and inefficiency, anxiously observed by the Western Powers. But in Admiral Kolchak, 'Supreme Ruler' of the Omsk 'All-Russian Government' in Siberia, the Allies thought they had found a man of integrity and action, one capable of providing a strong challenge to Soviet encroachment. At the same time, with their original reasons for intervention obscured by political change, the Allies were becoming increasingly uneasy about their exact status and motives in post-war Russia. On the death of Kolchak the British, somewhat thankfully, pulled out, leaving the anti-Communist struggle to be carried on in Outer Mongolia, soon to become the first Soviet satellite.
John Man. Above: Kolchak

With a diminutive force of 600 men, Semenov had already made a 10-day foray into Bolshevik territory. His activities so impressed the British military attaché in Peking that for the first six months of 1918 they paid him £10,000 per month. This was nothing, however, to the amount he was receiving from the Japanese, who supported him to the tune of perhaps 20 million yen a year. It was in fact the Japanese who were the real challengers to the extension of Soviet power in the Far East, and their aims were long-standing ones: they wanted their own empire in the area, to control the vast industrial potential of Manchuria and maritime provinces to the north. For them Semenov's ambition of creating a united Mongolian state was a means to this end: his state could perhaps be a foundation for their own.

The Allies at first had high hopes of Semenov, and it was with this power-seeking young thug that Kolchak was improbably meant to co-operate. On May 15, he arrived at Manchuli, a little walled town surrounded by a huddle of Mongolian tents, set in the midst of a barren plain. Semenov deliberately refused to meet him and when Kolchak eventually traced his supposed colleague to a railway carriage in a siding, Semenov rejected out of hand any suggestion of co-operation. Rebuffed, Kolchak returned to Tokyo. It looked like the end of his brief career with the Allies, and it certainly highlighted Semenov's attitudes. From now on, he asserted his independence, operating as a bandit with impunity. Far from menacing the Bolsheviks, as the Allies originally intended, his major historical importance was the ease with which he could – and did – hold up Allied and White supplies.

Complexity followed on complexity. Travelling along the Trans-Siberian were the Czech echelons, deserters and prisoners of war originally organised to fight their one-time Austro-Hungarian rulers on the Eastern Front and now on their way round the world to fight in the West. At the end of May, the tenuous thread of confidence between Czechs and Bolsheviks snapped and the Czechs seized much of the central section of the Trans-Siberian. They eradicated the Bolsheviks, who then began to form forest-based partisan groups. In the vacuum left by the Czech action, two main anti-Bolshevik committees sprang up – in Omsk and Samara – and Semenov moved up to Chita, where the Trans-Siberian meets the Chinese Eastern. The French and British now had a better justification for intervention – to help the Czechs. Japan, too, committed 72,000 troops to the mainland, more than all the other Allies put together, and the United States, though dubious of such involvement, entered the fray.

Allied disunity

But there was neither community of Allied interest, nor clear thinking by the three Western governments. Neither the French nor the British could afford an all-out anti-Bolshevik crusade—yet they were anxious to support anti-Communists, whether White or Czech. America was as much concerned to limit Japanese expansion as to crush Bolshevism. And Japan herself had aims at total variance with all three Allies: set on creating her own empire in the Far East, she had no interest in involvement beyond Lake Baikal, and would thus never agree to plunge into Siberia to aid the Czechs; nor had she any interest in creating an independent, anti-Bolshevik régime which would undermine her own chances of expansion. Indeed, as they advanced, the Japanese sponsored yet another petty empire builder, who in his turn promised his devoted service when he came to absolute power. He too was a Cossack Ataman: Ivan Kalmykov, and he based himself on Kharbarovsk where he rapidly carved out a reputation rivalling Semenov's, gathering round him sadists who shared his obsessive hatred of Germans and Bolsheviks.

Meanwhile, the Czechs, promised aid by the Allies, began to stave off the Bolshevik advance. They took Ekaterinburg (Sverdlovsk) in July, and the following month Kazan. Here they captured the imperial gold reserve, worth some eighty million pounds, a glittering jackpot for the victors in the coming struggle. Behind the defensive Czech shield, a provisional anti-Bolshevik—mostly Social Revolutionary—government was set up. Known as the All-Russian Directory, it was based on Omsk. The same month, September 1918, Kolchak's wheel came full circle. He was recalled to Russia on the initiative of the British commander, General Alfred Knox, who had met Kolchak in Tokyo, and been impressed by his formidable temper, which kept discipline, and his 'disinclination to talk for the sake of talking'. Kolchak was forthwith despatched to breathe life into the Omsk Directory.

Arriving on October 13, after a 3,000-mile train journey, he found that the five-man Directory was little more than a farce. It had no popular support and no liaison with the Czechs who were in effect its defence. Kolchak, though an outsider, was offered the ministries of war and the navy (which consisted mainly of officers).

No sooner had he taken office than events took another twist: the war in the West ended. Czechoslovakia was recognised and the Czechs had even less to hold them in Siberia. The Allies, with no need to create an Eastern Front, were still committed to aiding the Czechs and Kolchak. They were thus left in the strange position of upholding a committed anti-Bolshevik while at the same time considering recognising the Soviet régime. Allied commitment was, in these circumstances, bound to be confused and half-hearted.

The Omsk coup: Kolchak in power

It was clear at least to Kolchak's commanders that something would have to be done to inject some authority and power into the Omsk régime. On the night of November 17, 1918, a small group of Cossacks arrested some of the Directory. The next day at a meeting of officers and politicians, Kolchak was declared 'Supreme Ruler of the All-Russian Government', though he insisted—probably sincerely—that he was a fighting man reluctant to assume the burdens of statecraft.

Who organised the coup? Kolchak himself was no intriguer by nature and had anyway arrived too recently to set up the contacts. Soviet historians have since pointed at the British: there were strong British mining interests in the area, Kolchak looked to the British for his strongest support, and British troops did indeed keep peace in Omsk that day. But London would never have approved direct support: the coup was in direct opposition to Britain's diplomatic interests, for a few days later she recognised the Soviet government. The only ones with a real interest in the establishment of a right-wing dictatorship were the officers of the White High Command, the *Stavka*, and they were the only ones with the organisation capable of bringing it off.

Militarily indeed the position did im-

Above: Unnoticed by his fellow soldiers the body of a White Russian lolls over the front of an armoured train. *Above right:* A despatch rider in the Red Army delivers new orders to the infantry. Since Trotsky had taken command of the army as Commissar of War, organisation had steadily improved until the Reds formed a relatively single-minded fighting force—unlike the scattered, divided armies of the Whites. *Below:* A Cossack cavalry formation in Rostov Don territory in the south. The Cossacks, well known for their brilliant horsemanship, nearly always fought on the side of the Whites. *Right:* Budenny (right), the Bolsheviks' distinguished cavalry commander, with Mikhail Kalinin, a prominent revolutionary in 1917 and in 1923 President of the USSR.

prove. In December the Whites took Perm. Knox reported one general as saying he was 'afraid of being late for the capture of Moscow'. There seemed a real chance to outsiders that Kolchak would succeed in joining up with anti-Bolshevik forces at Archangel. No wonder Kolchak, who could call on forces of some 250,000, angrily rejected President Wilson's suggestion in January 1919 of a conference to discuss peace terms between Whites and Reds. In Omsk itself such optimism would have struck the casual visitor as misplaced. Its broad dusty avenues of wooden houses and occasional brick buildings were crowded with refugees, many living in holes in the ground roofed over with leaves. Though there was a façade of stability – the occasional ball, to the sound of a Rumanian orchestra – the administration was riddled with profiteering. Military supplies were either waylaid before they reached the front or were distributed via black market rings. Many troops were literally in rags; there was even a report that in one area the only equipment received by the officers in six months was 1,000 pairs of braces. And the railway workers were not paid – an unforgivable piece of inefficiency considering that the railway was Kolchak's life-line from the outside world.

'Cowardice, greed and treachery'

But besides all this, Kolchak's reputation was destroyed almost immediately by the brutality of his officers. In December, the unhappy railway workers planned an uprising. It was betrayed and crushed, and drumhead court martials had some 200 people shot. One of the White generals, Sergei Rozanov, when a village refused him guides to seek out partisans, would burn it to the ground, and if resistance continued, would shoot every fifth male. In July, 1919, there was a purge of Jews in Ekaterinburg: over 2,000 died. To the sturdily independent Siberians, such manifestations of arbitrary dictatorship were worse than both Tsarism and Bolshevism. Kolchak himself was quite unable to control his officers, though he was shocked at the way in which they acted. 'I am surrounded by moral cowardice, greed and treachery,' he complained pitifully. 'Many of the Whites are no better than Bolsheviks.' But he did nothing about it, apparently hoping that his austere example of 'grit, pluck and honest patriotism' – the words of a British officer – would rub off on his subordinates. As the historian Bernard Pares has written: 'It may be questioned whether Kolchak ever ruled Siberia at all. It was living its own life without him and apart from him.'

Military organisation was appalling. 'Not one of his subordinates,' wrote a British colonel, 'could I trust to manage a whelk stand.' Officers at the front would base themselves in trains to guarantee a rapid retreat, and the chief-of-staff, Lebedyev, was, according to a member of the British Military Mission, an extreme Right Cossack 'who believed that men will fight, provided they are beaten and flogged sufficiently'. A war correspondent commented laconically on the Whites' 'Immortal Regiment' that it had indeed done everything possible to achieve immortality –'by withdrawing without casualties from the field of honour' at every opportunity. There were no real attempts to boost the local economy by organising harvesting or trade, and to complete the picture, the Whites insisted on wearing epaulettes, which for the Bolsheviks – and the peasants – were symbols of the officer-landlord class, of the alienation of rulers from the ruled.

The Red Army meanwhile gathered strength and advanced under Trotsky's dynamic, centralised leadership. In October the foreign missions and the Omsk government – plus gold reserve – pulled out. Kolchak, who had banked everything on military victory, refused to retreat until the last possible moment, and when he finally did so, on November 14, one day before the Red Army moved in, large numbers of his troops and trainloads of supplies fell to the Red Army.

The retreat towards Irkutsk was a four-month catalogue of catastrophe. Both lines, one of them reserved for priority traffic, were clogged with trains – Kolchak and his staff alone filled seven of them. Fuel was scarce, and when no wood was available engines froze to a standstill on sidings. Passengers in the fireless carriages, threatened with frostbite, joined the thousands who jammed the stations waiting for space on the next train, often leaving notes for family or friends fluttering hopefully from the station walls. Along the *Trakt*, the road which ran parallel to the railway, dragged the remnants of an army – soldiers, horses, peasants, cattle. Typhus raged. Whole trainloads, shunned by all, perished. Corpses, frozen solid, were piled like logs beside the track.

Moreover, the railway – and thus the retreat itself – was firmly in the hands of the Czechs, who speeded their own trains to the front. With 500 miles to go to Irkutsk, Kolchak's trains were switched to the slow line, where they made just 20 miles a day; and at Nizhneudinsk, 300 miles out, they were brought to a complete halt. In fury, Kolchak telegraphed Semenov to cut off the Czech withdrawal – a virtual declaration of war against the Czechs which throws light on his state of mind: if the Czech line of retreat was cut, he too would be immured in Siberia at the mercy

'The retreat towards Irkutsk was a four-month catalogue of catastrophe . . . Typhus raged. Corpses, frozen solid, were piled like logs beside the track'

Above: The battle for Omsk, before Kolchak's disastrous retreat. *Right:* Whites in transit, wearing the epaulettes that aroused the hatred of the peasants as symbols of the officer class

of the Reds. The Czechs, not the Bolsheviks, now seemed the principal enemy.

But he had other enemies as well. In Irkutsk itself, his rump government was challenged by a combination of Social Revolutionaries and Mensheviks known as the Political Centre. Several were imprisoned by the Whites, a fact which in a roundabout and peculiarly grisly way contributed to Kolchak's downfall. For in one of their bandit raids along the railway, a group of Semenov's men, in January, 1920, managed to acquire as hostages the 30 political prisoners taken by Kolchak's agents. Semenov's men then embarked on the ice-breaker *Angara* into Lake Baikal, and on January 6 the hostages were brought up on deck one at a time, battered to death with a long-handled mallet used for chipping ice off the decks and thrown overboard. In Irkutsk, people remembered bitterly that it was Kolchak's men who had handed over the Irkutsk townsmen and that Kolchak and Semenov were, at least theoretically, on the same side.

The same month, Kolchak's man in Irkutsk fled, abandoning power to the Political Centre. The Allied commissioners – French, British and American – prepared to leave, and their trains were hacked free of the icicles which locked lavatory and kitchen carriages to the ground. Though the Allies drafted a directive that Kolchak should be protected, the Czech and Allied C-in-C's made little effort to do so.

On January 6 – the same day as the *Angara* atrocity – Kolchak announced his resignation from 'supreme power throughout all the Russias', and although parts of the White army fought on under the able and brilliant General Kappel, Kolchak was allowed to proceed eastwards under Czech guard. Everywhere, pro-Bolshevik partisans, originally organised in self-protection against Kalmykov, Semenov and Kolchak's generals, were closing in. All along the line crowds, now incensed at news of the *Angara* massacre, demanded that Kolchak be handed over. He reached Irkutsk on January 15, and was immediately handed over to the Political Centre. 'So the Allies have abandoned me,' he remarked calmly, before he was led off to gaol with a mistress, who had remained unwaveringly faithful, and his cowering Prime Minister, Victor Pepeliaev, who had spent most of his term of office impotently in a railway carriage.

Six days later, a Soviet Military Revolutionary Committee took over Irkutsk. Kolchak and his two companions were not molested for the time being. Indeed, one Soviet visitor noted that he was addressed as 'Your High Excellency' by his warders, who went in awe of the trim, lean figure — 'like an Englishman'. But the Bolsheviks did begin an interrogation. Their aim was to establish the facts of his life and rule before his execution. Though there was no trial, no witnesses and no defence, the approach was leisurely, even respectful. Kolchak answered with dignity, and once again he displayed those qualities of assurance and authority that had so misled his sponsors two years before.

Meanwhile, Kappel was still battling back towards Irkutsk. There was a chance he would take it. In increasing panic, the local Soviets applied for Red Army approval to proceed with Kolchak's execution, and set about finding solid ground on which to convict him. They found it in the reprisals in Omsk taken after the railway-workers' uprising at the end of 1918. Kolchak could give only the lamest answers: 'Nobody reported. . . . This is the first time I have heard of this.'

Early on February 7, while it was still dark, Kolchak and the abject Pepeliaev were marched down a tributary of the Angara river. Lorries lit a hole in the ice. Kolchak remained calm, again 'like an Englishman' in the words of the official report. He refused a blindfold. There was a ragged volley — Kolchak's mistress heard it from her cell — and the bodies slid down the bank into oblivion.

In Siberia at least, White and Allied opposition was at an end. The last British troops had left in November, 1919. Kalmykov had fled to Manchuria where he was captured and shot by the Chinese in January, 1920. The Americans went in April. The same month, the puppet Far Eastern Republic came into existence as a Soviet-sponsored buffer state between Bolshevik-controlled Russia and Japanese-held areas. The last Czechs left in September.

But Kolchak's death was not quite the end of the White challenge. Kappel's forces were yet to be destroyed. He himself died, but 16,000 of his forces arrived in Chita in February, 1920, from where the Japanese took them to the coast. Here they joined the remnants of Semenov's forces in the final campaign in the Russian Far East. A long stalemate ended with Japanese withdrawal in October, 1922. Semenov himself fled to Peking in April 1921. After a brief stay in America, from which he was deported, he surprisingly survived in a remote Manchurian rural community until 1945, when he was found by Soviet troops, taken back to Moscow, tried and shot.

The Mad Baron: Mongolia in revolution

But even as Semenov fled, his aims received a new lease of life. Further south, in Outer Mongolia, one of his accolytes, Baron Romanov von Ungern-Sternberg, set about realizing his commander's dream of an anti-Bolshevik Mongol empire. Ungern-Sternberg, whose staring eyes and murderous habits earned him the nickname of 'The Mad Baron', reached the Mongolian capital, Urga, in October 1920, was driven off, and finally took it on February 2, 1921.

He could not have chosen a better time to take over the country. Mongolia, comprising less than a million people, mainly herdsmen, in an area approaching that of western Europe, was ripe for revolution. Traditionally under Manchu control, it was at the turn of the century under the two-fold grip of a feudal Buddhist church, which absorbed a third of the male population, and of extortionate Chinese money-lenders. In 1911, taking advantage of China's revolution, Mongolia broke away under her monarch, the Mongolian 'Living Buddha', the Jebtsun Damba Khutukhtu, turning to Russia for support. In 1917, the situation was reversed, and China reimposed her control. Under this stimulus, there formed in Urga an embryo People's Party, headed by the two foremost revolutionaries, Sukhe Bator and Choibalsan. Both of humble origin, they made a strange pair: Sukhe, 26, had only learned to read at 18, knew no Russian and was never truly Communist. He died three years later, ensuring himself a still unchallenged place in Mongolian hearts as the ideal of revolutionary heroism. Choibalsan, on the other hand, spoke good Russian and knew Boris Shumyatski, the President of the Far Eastern Republic. Even then, at 25, his leather jacket and jackboots made him a sinister figure, aptly so for one who was to become Mongolia's Stalin-figure.

The aims of these two were at first purely nationalistic: to break the Church but to

'At Manchuli ruled Grigori Semenov, a 28-year-old Mongolian with a black moustache and puffy lips who liked to ape Napoleon . . . His reputation soon became appalling'

Grigori Semenov *(left)*, a power-seeking terrorist renowned for indiscriminate violence, was at first backed by the British and the Japanese in his anti-Bolshevik activities. But the Allies soon discovered that, fired by dreams of establishing an independent Mongolian state, he was a law unto himself. *Below:* Soldiers of the White Russian army. With the death of Kolchak and Kappel the remains of the army, starving and typhus-ridden, began the slow haul across Siberia to the Far East, gradually disintegrating into small bands of *Kappelevtsy.* Some clung together until 1922, by which time Soviet authorities had more or less full control of the area

Südd Verlag

defend the religion, the state and the law. Nor were their methods particularly revolutionary: one of their declarations, which were all couched in the remote terms of Manchu bureaucracy, accused the nobles of 'abandoning the three bonds and the five eternals,' and was even addressed directly to the Chinese governor. And when they decided to appeal to Shumyatski for help, Sukhe took along a covering letter from the Khutukhtu by way of authorisation! (His lone ride past Chinese border guards, with the letter hidden in his whip handle, has since become legendary for Mongolians.) Shumyatski imposed a more revolutionary approach, and the party set off to see Lenin in Moscow.

At this point the Mad Baron arrived. To the Mongolians, it seemed at first a heaven-sent deliverance from Chinese oppression, a view quickly dissipated by Ungern's campaign of looting to acquire the financial backing for his crusade into Russia. He followed this with an atrocious persecution of 'suspected Bolsheviks' and

Jews. He was supported by the Khutukhtu, who issued orders to reject Communism. 'It is opposed to God, princes and true virtue,' ran one directive, 'and deadly to the great purpose of creating a Mongol state.'

But in March, the Mongolian revolutionaries held their first party conference in the border town of Kiakhta, formed a 400-strong army, and on March 18 took the first step in liberating their country by seizing Altan Bulag from the 10,000 disorganised Chinese who had fled Ungern. In April, the Provisional Government requested Soviet help, in May it arrived and in July Urga was retaken. Ungern, who had fled northwards, was finally defeated at Gusino on Russian soil in August. At his trial he expressed no regrets at any of his actions and was duly shot in Novonikolayevskiy on September 14, 1921. All remaining White forces, some 4,000 scattered throughout Sinkiang and western Mongolia, were mopped up by December. The White threat was over. When the Japanese left the coastal area of the Far

East the following year, the Communists ruled from Europe to the Pacific, and had their first satellite into the bargain.

Further Reading
Bawden, Charles, *The Modern History of Mongolia* (Weidenfeld & Nicolson 1968)
Fleming, Peter, *The End of Admiral Kolchak* (Hart-Davies 1963)
Lattimore, Owen, *Nationalism and Revolution in Mongolia* (New York 1955)
Rupen, Robert, *Mongols of the Twentieth Century* (Indiana University Publications 1964)
White, John, *The Siberian Intervention* (Princeton University Press 1950)

JOHN MAN studied Mongolian at the School of Oriental and African Studies after reading languages at Keble College, Oxford. He was with Reuters in Germany before joining Purnell's *History of the 20th Century*, for which he wrote on the Nuremberg Trials and the Berlin Wall. He also contributed to the BBC/Time-Life publication *The British Empire*.

THE WASHINGTON CONFERENCE
America Rules the Waves?

After the Treaty of Versailles, it would have been understandable if the world had lost its faith in international
conferences. But Britain, the United States and Japan
needed to examine the changed situation in the Far East
and a large-scale conference did seem to be the answer, with
the United States once again playing the lead. *S. L. Mayer*

The Treaty of Versailles had realigned the balance of power in
Europe, Africa and the Middle East, and it had also changed the
balance of power in the Far East. Indeed, the power configurations
in East Asia had been changing perceptibly for almost two decades
since Britain abandoned her policy of 'splendid isolation' and had
made an alliance with Japan. At the turn of the century Britain
and Russia were the greatest powers in Asia. Even by 1914 this
had ceased to be the case. After the Japanese decimated Russian
naval and land forces in the war of 1904-5, Russia was no longer
a significant power in East Asia. The revolutions of 1905 and 1917
made her turn inwards. As a European war became imminent,
Britain was obliged to leave the protection of her vast Far Eastern
interests to her ally, Japan. The United States, by this time in
possession of the Philippines and Guam, was both unwilling and
unable to fill the void.

When the First World War broke out Japan sought to consolidate
her hegemony in North-East Asia by seizing the German concessions in China as well as the German islands north of the
Equator. Britain was not terribly pleased to witness the relative
decline of her power in the Pacific at the start of the war, but
the Western Front and the Middle East took preference. By the
time the war was over, Japan was in every respect the more
authoritative partner in Britain's Far Eastern alliance. The
Treaty of Versailles confirmed Japan's conquests, and although
Australia and New Zealand were also able to expand in the
Pacific, it was Japan who received the lion's share of the German
imperial spoils. Britain's economic interests in China, her possessions in Hong Kong, Malaya and elsewhere in the Pacific,
as well as America's Philippine colony, were effectively pawns in
the hands of the Emperor of Japan. Both the Anglo-Saxon states
realised that their wartime ally had to be contained if they were
to protect their far-flung interests. Furthermore, while the United
States began to retreat into isolationism in 1919, Japan's naval
programme swept forward. Immediately after the war Japan increased her spending on naval armaments to almost $250,000,000,
a sum which, in 1921, represented almost one-third of the entire
budget of the Imperial Government. This figure was gradually
increased to about $400,000,000 by 1927, at a time when neither
Britain nor the United States was willing or able to match this
sort of expenditure. In fact the naval budget of the United States
matched that of Japan, but the government was almost as in-
capacitated as Woodrow Wilson himself in 1919-20, and the
Harding Administration which replaced the Democrats in 1921
was more isolationist than its predecessor. The fact that their
former ally was a potential threat came as a slow shock to the
Anglo-Americans.

Perhaps the greatest blow was to the British. Before the war
they had tried to adhere to a so-called two-power standard, meaning that the British intended to keep their naval strength greater
than that of the next two largest fleets in the world combined.
In 1919 this policy was no longer practicable. Not only had Britain

spent much of her wealth in helping to win the war; she was
heavily over-committed, with new mandates to administer, a war
still going on in Ireland, and insurgency mounting all over
her Empire. The British could not afford to build up their fleet
to a two-power, prewar standard; over a period of years Britain
could not even hope to keep pace with America. On the other
hand, Britain did not want to see her interests overseas held to
ransom by others. What made it all most embarrassing was that
the United States had only recently fought side by side with
Britain against Germany, as Japan had done, and Japan was
Britain's longest standing ally. How could Britain arrange to
break agreements with Japan and tacit understandings with
America without thoroughly antagonising both and thereby
making the situation even worse?

Changing partners
From October 1920 to January 1921 a Foreign Office Committee
reviewed the question of the renewal of the Anglo-Japanese
Alliance, which was to expire at the end of that year. It was decided that the absence of any alliance with Japan would remove
all restraints on Japanese economic and territorial expansion in
the Far East which might have been placed on her in the past;
but the Committee also realised that the Alliance had never
seriously hampered Japan. It was finally suggested that the
Alliance should be replaced by an entente between Britain, Japan
and the United States. This would discourage all three from naval
competition in the Pacific and would at the same time help to
cultivate the Anglo-American relationship, which had undergone
great stress since the Paris Peace Conference. In short, it was
hoped that America's power, added to that of Britain, might
restrain Japan in the Pacific. At the root of the trouble was the
inherent weakness of China, which was divided against herself
and would be helpless if attacked. Japan had made no bones about
her interest in North China when she presented the 21 Demands
a few years before, and it was generally recognised that without
certain restraints being imposed on Japan, she had carte blanche
to do what she liked with China now that America was rapidly
retreating into isolationism. However, it was almost as bad for
Britain if the United States decided to undertake a massive naval
building project, since in the context of a continued Anglo-Japanese Alliance it would be directed against both Japan and Britain.
In short, Britain was caught between unpalatable alternatives
due to over-commitment in an Empire which, alone, could not be
properly defended against either external attack or internal
revolt. The British Imperial Conference held in 1921 debated
the issues and came to the conclusion that an entente with both
the other Far Eastern powers was a necessity.

The United States found relations with Japan almost as embarrassing as did the British. Both American and Japanese troops
were in Siberia, and in this operation America was the junior
partner. The Japanese were displeased about Wilson's attempts

to thwart the extension of their interests in South Manchuria, and also about discrimination against Japanese-Americans on the West Coast of the United States. At the Paris Peace Conference the question of Yap had been raised, and this tiny island in the Pacific became a bone of contention between the two powers.

Yap was a crucial cable centre, through which American communications with the Philippines and other points in the Far East were directed. In Paris in 1919 Wilson had insisted that the island should be internationalised, since, being within the pre-war German sphere of influence, it would otherwise go to Japan. Few Americans outside the government could take the Yap issue seriously. One humorist parodied a popular war song which did strike a certain mood:

> 'Give us Yap! Give us Yap!
> The Yanks have put it,
> The Yanks have put it,
> The Yanks have put it
> On the Map!'

But provisionally Yap went under a League mandate to Japan, and the Americans continued to be worried in case the Anglo-Japanese Alliance might be directed against the States or her possessions in the Pacific. Although London informed Washington that it would not consider the Alliance binding in the event of a war between Japan and the United States, the Americans were still not satisfied. They could not understand what purpose it had, if it was not directed against the United States. Canada, placed in an awkward situation in view of her relationships with both Britain and America, could see no good coming from the Alliance and asked the British to terminate it. They did not want to be forced to take sides in a possible Anglo-American conflict. Therefore, both Britain and the United States were anxious for a change but did not know how to achieve it.

Japan, on the other hand, was concerned that the British and Americans would thwart her efforts to extend her sphere of influence in North-East Asia. Time and again, the disunited European powers had managed to move together to contain Japanese expansion in Asia. The humiliation Japan suffered in 1895 at the hands of Russia, Germany and France was not forgotten, and the Japanese felt that the United States had loaded the dice in Russia's favour at the 1905 Peace of Portsmouth which brought the Russo-Japanese War to an end. Theodore Roosevelt had offered the good offices of the United States to settle the war; he won the Nobel Peace Prize for his efforts. But the Japanese felt they should have done better. Subsequent events had not brought Japan and America closer together, and it was recognised by both sides that the Lansing-Ishii Agreement, signed between the two powers during the war, had only deferred a possible conflict of interest between the two wartime allies. Japan wanted to make sure that her islands and interests were protected and that she could extend her economic and political hegemony in North-East Asia without Western interference. Japan too wanted to end the British alliance, but saw no way to do this without forcing Great Britain to lose face. When the idea of a Far Eastern Conference was raised, Japan leaped at the chance to resolve her dilemmas.

America's own conference

The calling of a Far Eastern Conference was the act of the new Republican government which came into office early in 1921. It was the Republicans who had rejected the Treaty of Versailles and who refused to allow the United States to join the League of Nations. Once Harding was elected, the Republican Party began to modify their views, especially when they learned of the seriousness of the naval arms race as well as its cost to the American exchequer. The League of Nations was supposed to reduce armaments, and the Harding Administration felt a moral obligation to do something which would be effective and look good, without involving it in joining the League. The Republicans supported a low-spending, low-taxing and balanced national budget, and a costly arms race in the postwar period would not have won them votes from their political enemies or their agrarian supporters. Thus, a month after Harding's election, in December 1920, Senator Borah, one of the fiercest isolationists, introduced a resolution designed to bring about a tripartite disarmament conference. Although Harding resented Borah's initiative, the press and public were enthusiastic. Mass meetings were held in support of the idea and in St Louis a huge petition was drawn up and a great dial erected in a public square, on which a hand moved forward a notch with each thousand signatures. The bill was passed

Right: US representatives at the Washington Conference. Left to right, Elihu Root, Henry Cabot Lodge, who disliked 'foreign entanglements', Charles Evans Hughes, Secretary of State, and Oscar Underwood

3507

unanimously by the Senate, the House of Representatives only had four dissenting votes, and the new Secretary of State, Charles Evans Hughes, sent out informal inquiries to Britain and Japan. The British suggested that the conference should include other issues as well, so that Britain could gracefully extricate herself from the Japanese alliance and replace it by something multi-lateral and vaguer. Hughes sent out invitations to a conference to be held in Washington. It was agreed that the entire China question should be discussed, so Portugal and the Netherlands were invited as well as France. Italy, with few Asian interests, was invited because to ask France and to ignore the other Latin great power would have given offence. Belgium insisted on going because Holland was going. An invitation was even sent to China, however reluctantly, as it was felt that the Chinese might want to have something to say about their own future. The only one of these powers to decline the invitation was Japan, whose naval building programme was under way, and whose government and people were suspicious that anything so popular in Europe and America could not be good for Japan. Lloyd George saw the Japanese reticence as being racial in character: *They are getting suspicious of us in Japan, and they think we are doing something. They say, 'Well, they are white races, they are the cousins of the Americans. They quarrel amongst themselves, but when trouble comes they act together.' That is true, the last war showed it . . . The people who govern in America are our people. They are our kith and kin. The other breeds are not on top. It is the men of our race who govern in America.*

Some of the most distinguished representatives of the various countries came to Washington for the conference. For the United States there was the Secretary of State, Hughes, as well as the former Secretary of State under Roosevelt, Elihu Root, Henry Cabot Lodge and Oscar W. Underwood, both presidential hopefuls with large political followings in the States. A former Prime Minister, Arthur James Balfour, led the British team which included Sir Auckland Geddes, the Ambassador to Washington, and Baron Lee of Fareham, First Lord of the Admiralty. Canada, Australia, India and New Zealand were also independently represented, although Balfour spoke for their interests in most cases. Baron Tomosaburo Kato, Minister for the Navy, represented Japan with Japan's Ambassador to Washington, Shidehara, as well as Masanao Hanihara, Vice Minister for Foreign Affairs, and Prince Iyesato Tokugawa, whose presence was an indication of the great importance attached to the conference. The Tokugawa family led the shogunate for over two and a half centuries prior to the Meiji Restoration. Little more than 50 years before the conference a Tokugawa was second only to the Emperor and second to none in terms of real authority. The appointment of the Prince to the conference delegation was a signal honour which was duly noted. Among the other delegates were Wellington Koo, Nationalist China's most famous diplomatist, Aristide Briand and Albert Sarraut, Deputy Minister of Colonies, for France, whose interests in Indo-China were well-established; for Italy, Carlo Schanzer and Luigi Albertini, both Senators of the Kingdom, the latter of whom was to become one of Italy's most distinguished historians with his book on the origins of the First World War.

Sacrifice
The delegates assembled in the beautiful Memorial Continental Hall in Washington three years after the Armistice, and the day after the Tomb of the Unknown Soldier was dedicated in Arlington National Cemetery across the Potomac. America had denied herself a place in the League, but the Republicans were determined to recreate the atmosphere and grandeur of the Paris Peace Conference in their answer to Versailles. The hall used was the head-quarters of the Daughters of the American Revolution, and in the simple majesty of the hall a square, green-covered table was placed to seat the delegates, while the gallery was packed with members of Congress and their families. The portraits of George and Martha Washington looked down upon President Harding, who welcomed the delegates briefly in the first session of November 12, 1921. His soothing words were followed by a speech from Hughes, who astounded the delegates with his candour and dynamism. He declared that the only way to disarm was to do so at once – not in the distant future. He called for the scrapping by the United States, Britain and Japan of 66 existing battleships totalling almost 2,000,000 tons. Furthermore he suggested that there should be a ten-year moratorium on the construction of capital ships, defined as those exceeding 10,000 tons, which included battleships and battle cruisers. He suggested that the US should scrap 30 of these, two of which had just been launched and six of which were under construction. Britain was to abandon the four new 'Hood' class battleships which she had not yet laid down, but

on which money had already been spent, and also to scrap 19 older battleships – in all, over half a million tons. Japan was to abandon her plan to construct four battleships and four battle cruisers. She was to scrap three new capital ships, one just launched and three which were under construction, as well as ten older ships – 17 in all, totalling almost half a million tons. One British observer stated that what Hughes proposed would sink more ships than all the admirals of the world had sunk in centuries. The non-Americans at the Conference were overwhelmed by Hughes' forthright approach, which, however, though criticised by many at the time, gained more than it lost. It set the Conference off in high gear, in contrast to the other, lack-lustre, postwar conferences which had followed on the heels of the Paris Peace Conference of 1919, and saved weeks of time which might otherwise have been lost in preliminaries. He mobilised world public opinion behind the Conference, and those who listened to the speech, particularly the audiences in the galleries, cheered wildly.

But when the hard bargaining began the applause died away, particularly on the Japanese side. The proposal to limit capital ships to a 5:5:3 ratio, with Britain and the United States having the larger shares and Japan the smaller, was met by Japanese opposition. Not that Japan demanded parity. She recognised that America had two coasts to defend and Britain a world-wide Empire. But it was felt in Japanese circles that Japan should have a 10:10:7 ratio, which would protect Japan against any possible attack on her exposed island position. The United States argued that she had the greatest potential capacity for building capital ships. Japan finally backed down, and the Hughes proposal was adopted almost as written, with certain additional stipulations: that a ten-year holiday on capital ship building be observed, that fortifications would not be built on any of America's Pacific possessions with the exception of Hawaii, and that Britain and Japan would refrain from fortifying their Pacific islands, excluding, of course, Australia and New Zealand and the Japanese

Below: Senator William E. Borah, opponent of the League of Nations, instigator of the Washington Conference. *Above right:* Charles Evans Hughes's practical introduction impressed delegates at the opening session. *Below right:* Theodore Roosevelt, whose efforts to achieve a Russo-Japanese settlement in 1904-5 won him the Nobel Peace Prize

Brown Brothers

home islands themselves, as well as Hong Kong. The non-fortification issue was a crucial factor, since Japan need not fear attack if American and British ships remained thousands of miles distant.

France and Italy, the other naval powers at the Conference, were not expected to obstruct this agreement, but France objected to being relegated, with Italy, to a 1:7 ratio. The ignominy of being ranked with Italy as a naval power was insult enough. But France was security-conscious almost to the point of paranoia. Fearing a revival of German sea power, France also was forced to face the fact that during the war she had neglected her navy to the point that, from being a formidable sea power, she had already sunk to the second rank. She demanded twice what was allowed in the Conference provisions, even though she had no plans for building a navy anywhere near so large. The British leaked the French demands to the press, and soon they were made an object of criticism and even ridicule. Reluctantly the French accepted the 1:7 ratio, but they would not agree to any limitation on the number of cruisers, destroyers or submarines. This opened the flood-gates later on to Japanese naval rearmament.

When the Five-Power Pact was signed by Britain, Japan, the United States, France and Italy on February 6, 1922, they agreed that these terms should stand until 1936, after which any power could terminate after having given the others two years' notice. When Japan announced her intention of leaving the Pact in 1934 the Depression was on, and Britain and America were late in beginning to rearm in a totally altered political and economic climate.

RIP

The corpse of the Anglo-Japanese Alliance was laid to rest when the Four-Power Pact of December 13, 1921 was signed. In it, Britain, France, Japan and the United States agreed to respect each other's rights in the Pacific, and refer all disputes in the area to a joint conference. If the rights of the signatories should be threatened by another power, they were to communicate and consult each other about what to do. Who this other power was to be was anybody's guess, and the Four-Power Treaty was trivial compared with the guarantees which Japan had had under the Anglo-Japanese Alliance, which was now formally terminated.

THE WASHINGTON TREATY (LIMITATION OF NAVAL ARMAMENTS), CONTRACTED BETWEEN THE UNITED STATES, GREAT BRITAIN, FRANCE, ITALY AND JAPAN ON FEBRUARY 6, 1922.

1. Capital ships specified in the Treaty to be retained; all other capital ships, built or building, in the United States, Great Britain and Japan, to be disposed of.
2. Subject to the above, capital ship building programmes to be abandoned, and no new capital ships to be built or acquired, except as replacement tonnage as specified below. Ships replaced to be disposed of.
3. Total capital replacement tonnage to be (in tons standard displacement): United States and Great Britain, 525,000 tons each; France and Italy, 175,000 tons each; and Japan, 315,000 tons.
4. No capital ships exceeding 35,000 tons standard displacement to be built, acquired or within the jurisdiction of the contracting powers.
5. No capital ship to have guns in excess of 16-inch calibre.
6. Total aircraft carrier tonnage not to exceed (in tons standard displacement): United States and Great Britain 135,000 tons; France and Italy, 60,000 tons; and Japan, 81,000 tons.
7. Replacement of aircraft carriers to be effected only as prescribed below, provided that all aircraft carrier tonnage in existence or building on November 12, 1921 be considered experimental and replaceable within the tonnage limitation without regard to age.
8. No aircraft carriers exceeding 27,000 tons standard displacement to be built, acquired or within the jurisdiction of the contracting powers. Provided that the total tonnage limitation is not exceeded, however, each power may build not more than two carriers, each not exceeding 33,000 tons standard displacement, using if it so wishes the hulls of ships built or building otherwise to be scrapped. Armament of any carriers exceeding 27,000 tons standard displacement to be in accordance with the requirements stated below, except that the total number of guns to be carried (in the event of their being over 6-inch in calibre, except anti-aircraft guns and other guns not exceeding 5-inch calibre) not to exceed eight.
9. No aircraft carrier to be armed with guns of over 8-inch calibre. If armament carried is over 6-inch calibre, the total number of guns carried (excluding anti-aircraft guns and weapons of less than 5-inch calibre) not to exceed ten. If all armament is below 5-inch in calibre, no limit on the number of guns to be imposed. In either case, anti-aircraft guns and guns of less than 5-inch calibre not to be limited.
10. No warship of more than 10,000 tons standard displacement, other than a capital ship or aircraft carrier, to be built, acquired or within the jurisdiction of any of the contracting powers. Vessels not specifically built as warships nor impressed in time of peace, but used on fleet duties, as troop transports or for any other military purpose, not to be subject to this limitation.
11. No ship, other than capital ships, to carry guns exceeding 8-inch in calibre.
12. Except as is permitted in 8. above, no ship designated in the Treaty to be scrapped to be reconverted into a warship.
13. No preparations to be made in time of peace to merchant ships for the purpose of converting them into warships, other than the stiffening of decks to accept the mounting of guns not exceeding 6-inch in calibre.
14. None of the contracting powers to build for a non-contracting power any warship exceeding the limitations established for the contracting powers themselves. And in the case of aircraft carriers, none exceeding 27,000 tons standard displacement to be built for a non-contracting power.

15. In the event of one of the contracting powers building a ship for a non-contracting power, it shall communicate to the other contracting powers details of the ship, the date of the signing of the contract and of the laying of the keel.
16. In the event of war, none of the contracting powers to take over warships building for or awaiting delivery to another power.
17. Each contracting power not to dispose, by way of gift, sale or any other mode of transfer, of any warship in such a manner that it enter the navy of any other contracting power.

REPLACEMENT

1. Capital ships and aircraft carriers may be replaced 20 years after the date of their completion, within the limitations of 3. and 6. above. The keels of such new construction not to be laid down less than 17 years after the date of completion of the vessel to be replaced. No capital ship to be laid down, except as provided for in the Treaty, before November 12, 1931.
2. The contracting powers to inform the others of:
   (a) the names of any capital ship or aircraft carrier to be replaced by new tonnage.
   (b) the date of authorisation of new tonnage.
   (c) the date of the laying down of the keels of replacement tonnage.
   (d) the standard displacement of such ships in tons and metric tons, and also the principal dimensions.
   (e) the date of completion of replacement tonnage, together with standard displacement and principal dimensions.
3. In the event of loss or accidental destruction of any capital ship or aircraft carrier, it may be replaced immediately so long as it conforms to the Treaty limitations.
4. No retained capital ships or aircraft carriers to be reconstructed except to provide defence against submarine or air attack. To that purpose, existing tonnage may be provided with water-line bulges and deck armour, provided that total tonnage is not increased by more than 3,000 tons per ship. No alteration of side armour or in the mounting, calibre or number of guns comprising the main armament to be permitted except:
   (a) France and Italy to be permitted to increase armour protection up to a weight of 3,000 tons in existing ships and also the calibre of their main armaments up to 16-inch.
   (b) Great Britain to be permitted to complete HMS *Renown*.

DEFINITIONS

A capital ship is defined as a ship exceeding 10,000 tons standard displacement or carrying guns exceeding 8-inch in calibre. An aircraft carrier is defined as a ship exceeding 10,000 tons standard displacement and designed for the specific and exclusive purpose of carrying aircraft. It must have provision to fly off and land aircraft, and an armament not exceeding 8-inch in calibre. Standard displacement is defined as the displacement of a ship complete, manned, fully engined, equipped for sea, including all armament and ammunition, equipment, outfit, provisions and fresh water for crew, miscellaneous stores and implements of every description that are intended to be carried in war, but without fuel or reserve feed water.

Japan was not fooled and her feeling of distrust for the West was not removed by this compromise. One Japanese diplomat commented, 'we have discarded whisky and accepted water'. The treaty was left purposely vague for the sake of Senator Lodge, who had fought Wilson so long to keep America free of 'foreign entanglements'. The pact was hardly a substitute for membership in the League of Nations, but it seemed adequate to many Americans at the time.

Finally the delegates turned to the 'sick man of Asia', China. The signatories of the Nine-Power Treaty of February 6, 1922, which included all those who attended the conference, hypocritically pledged themselves to respect the 'sovereignty, independence, and the territorial and administrative integrity of China'. This agreement was transparently insincere, since none of the signatories was prepared to give up the vast holdings, concessions and extra-territorial rights which they already possessed in China. The same could be said of the agreement to maintain the 'open door' in China and to assist her in establishing a stable government. Britain's position in China south of the Yangtse was dependent on a weak China, and any show of strength in the north would have been (and was) opposed by Japan, who only signed this pact reluctantly after heavy Anglo-American pressure.

One issue which was outstanding from the Paris Peace Conference was finally settled. Wilson had strongly opposed Japan's takeover of the German rights in Shantung in 1919 before he finally yielded. In a separate agreement between Japan and China, signed on February 4, 1922, Japan agreed to return to China the leasehold of Kiaochow in Shantung Province. This was completed by 1926, by which time the Japanese had secured their economic interests in the province. Japan complained that if she withdrew, Britain ought to do the same in nearby Weihaiwei. When Britain finally agreed, Lord Curzon noted bitterly that a part of the Empire had been given away. Britain's small port was of little value in comparison with the territory retroceded by Japan, and in any event Britain hung on to Weihaiwei long after Japan withdrew from Kiaochow, dragging her heels even at this minor concession. In another agreement Japan yielded special cable rights to America in the island of Yap and Japan further agreed to withdraw her remaining troops in Siberia. Japan also had to consent to the annulment of the Lansing-Ishii Agreement, which conflicted with the spirit and the letter of the Nine-Power Pact in that it guaranteed her special position in Manchuria. In short, Japan had to make concessions all along the line, and left the Conference dissatisfied.

Japan was not the only one. The French were still bitter about the agreement, and, at the last, refused to sign the treaties unless the word 'French' was placed before the word 'English' in the clause stating that both texts were authentic. The usually unflappable Elihu Root lost his temper and said, 'To hell with them! Let the whole business go to pot – I wouldn't care.' The point was conceded, of course, but the pettiness of the French, Anglo-American intransigence vis à vis Japan, and the vagueness of so much of what was agreed soured the international atmosphere for years after.

The Washington Conference, with all its drawbacks, did accomplish a first step in disarmament that might have led to other, more substantial reductions in other spheres. These never materialised because, as the French logic insisted, security must precede disarmament. Since there was no real security in the paper-thin guarantees of the League, the Four and Nine-Power Pacts and other even less substantial agreements, how could the great powers disarm? Other attempts throughout the 1920s proved even less successful than the Washington Conference, which did, at least, have some specific results, however limited in scope. Both Britain and America bought a temporary containment of Japan on the cheap, and in the climate of American public opinion that was something. The Four-Power Pact passed through the Senate by only four votes with Democratic support, and even then the Senate attached to the treaty a rider declaring that there would be no American commitment to armed force, alliance or joint defence of the Pacific. In the light of American isolationist sentiment, the Washington Conference could be construed as a sort of victory. After all, there would have been no disarmament at all had there been no Washington Conference, but, on the other hand, even the participants had few illusions.

The termination of the Anglo-Japanese Alliance marked the end of an era and the beginning of a new one. To the old school of prewar diplomatists, the alliance of 1902 had been a turning point in British and world history, the end of the period of 'splendid isolation' and the beginning of a series of alliances and ententes which ultimately led the British into the war with Germany. When the treaty was finally abandoned at the conference table,

As an ex-Prime Minister, veteran of an earlier British mission to Washington and signatory of the Treaty of Versailles, Balfour (centre foreground) was chosen to lead the British delegation at the conference

almost 20 years after it had been created, Mr Balfour's head, according to one journalist, 'fell forward on his chest exactly as if the spinal cord had been severed . . . The head of stereotyped diplomacy had fallen forward – the vital cord severed – and new figures hereafter would monopolise the scene.' Britain publicly acknowledged her changed rôle in the Far East. From then on it was to be dominated by the Japanese and the Americans. But Wilson's dream of a world without war seemed a good deal closer after the Washington Conference than before it. The Conference and the Kellogg-Briand Pact of 1928, which outlawed war as an instrument of national policy, were the high-water marks of the idealism which the war and Woodrow Wilson had engendered. The system of collective security proved unsuccessful, but the attempt was worthwhile. The Second World War came about because the postwar solutions in general lacked the necessary enforcement. The Washington Conference could not be criticised on these grounds. The resulting provision for disarmament was one of the few postwar agreements that actually worked for the period it intended to cover. The Five-Power Pact, like the Versailles Treaty, was denounced in the 1930s and in the meantime Japan built up her fleet with ships below the 10,000 ton limit. But at least it was a step in the right direction. Unfortunately the will to go further was not sufficiently widespread. The Washington Conference achieved a measure of success in both security and disarmament, even if the effects lasted for little more than a decade.

Further Reading
Bailey, Thomas A., *A Diplomatic History of the American People* (New York: Appleton-Century-Crofts 1958)
Buell, Raymond Leslie, *The Washington Conference* (New York and London: D. Appleton and Co 1922)
Griswold, A. Whitney, *The Far Eastern Policy of the United States* (New Haven: Yale University Press 1938)
Ichihashi, Yamato, *The Washington Conference and After* (Stanford: Stanford University Press 1928)
Louis, William Roger, *British Strategy in the Far East, 1919-1939* (Oxford: Clarendon Press 1971)

[*For S. L. Mayer's biography, see page 19.*]

THE ORIGINS OF NAZISM

Was Germany's slide into Nazism a mass psychosis which could have overtaken any nation, or was it a natural, perhaps inevitable, development of the Teutonic character and German institutions? The Germans recovered from the burden of guilt which had been imposed on them after the First World War only to be branded indelibly with the responsibility for the Second. *Imanuel Geiss*

By the middle of 1914 Imperial Germany had become a powerful bulwark of conservatism by a remarkable coalescence of the feudal-monarchical principle with industrial power. The hard core of the Reich had been Prussia, originally an agrarian monarchy, run by a military-minded lower gentry, the *Junkers,* east of the River Elbe. In 1815 Prussia had acquired the valuable Rhine provinces, where the Industrial Revolution was just beginning. The growing industries in the west and the secondary industrial district, Upper Silesia, in the east provided the material basis for Prussia's emergence as the founding state of the new German Empire in 1871.

But Prussia's political and military leadership still came from the agrarian *Junkers* living east of the River Elbe. The *Junkers* owned fairly small holdings, the *Rittergüter* (knights' holdings), a distant echo of the *Junkers'* medieval military origins. Their economic stability and political power were threatened in many ways by the Industrial Revolution. The rise of modern industries made the proportion of the national income derived from agriculture dwindle. At the same time, the growing population in the new cities could not be fed by German agriculture alone. From the 1870s onwards food was imported from Russia, America and later also from Australia. The result was a serious crisis in German agriculture. Intermarriage with new-rich families of the emerging industrial bourgeoisie and far-reaching rationalisation did not help the *Junkers* in the long run because of the increasing rate at which the economic emphasis within Germany was shifting from agriculture to industry. It also meant that fewer people were directly subject to the *Junkers'* political influence. Nevertheless, they clung to their political power and tax immunity. In the end, they even succeeded in gaining the support of most of the middle-class and the peasantry.

The aristocracy and the middle classes had a common aim in the preservation of the Reich and the fight against socialism. Most Germans retained an attachment to a highly romanticised concept of the mediaeval Empire. The idea of the Reich was associated with German hegemony in Europe. The middle class was largely prepared to leave political power where it was, with the aristocracy and the Crown.

Weltpolitik

The central position of Prussia in the new German Empire was neatly illustrated by official heraldry: in the heart of the Imperial eagle perched the Prussian eagle. Prussia, the new Empire's seat of wealth and power, was also the source of its structural deficiencies, which the passage of time did little to remedy. The predominance of pre-industrial values in a modern industrial society was bound to produce, in the long run, dangerous instability both internally and externally. The German Empire was a strange anachronism in the age of nationalism and democracy. Bismarck and Kaiser Wilhelm II, the leading personalities of the Reich, were avowed enemies of the democratic principle, and in that they reflected the interests and ideology of Germany's ruling classes. The idea of Empire plus growing economic power plus military power plus authoritarian ruthlessness of the *Junkers* made Germany a dangerous neighbour, once she tried to become a world power in her own right. The moment had come with the inauguration of German *Weltpolitik* in 1897/98, which provoked Germany's isolation by a policy of what could be called 'containment'. The Triple Entente

Right: The *Stosstrupp Hitler,* Hitler's body-guard and forerunner of the SS, took over the *Münchener Post* offices in the 1923 *Putsch*

STOSSTRUPP·HITLER
MÜNCHEN

of 1907 grouped together the two more democratic imperialist powers, France and Britain, with reactionary Tsarist Russia, whose middle class, however, was western-orientated and whose reactionary aggressiveness had been broken by the Revolution of 1905. This left only the German Empire to defend the principle of monarchy against democracy. Her major allies, Austria-Hungary and the Ottoman Empire, were themselves political anachronisms left over from the Middle Ages, and were threatened from within and from without by national movements.

German *Weltpolitik,* carried to its logical end, made world war inevitable. German leaders saw and accepted the harsh facts of life, at least in private, while they prepared the German public for war by raising the spectre of *Einkreisung* ('encirclement') by vicious and envious enemies.

Germany's drive for world power status made for a world war which, if won, would have propelled the Reich to world domination. In July 1914 the situation leading up to the war was carefully manipulated so as to leave Germany in the most advantageous position, and Germany's war aims, both official and private, reflected the views of highly-placed Germans, who were ready to take on the world.

The First World War brought into the open two basic elements of traditional German statesmanship since Bismarck: the use or threat of violence internally and externally. In times of political crisis Bismarck always played with the idea of a *coup d'état* from above, dissolving the constitution of 1871. In fact, he achieved a

disguised coup when he came to power in 1862 to obtain for the Crown the increase of the army despite objections raised by the Prussian parliament on the grounds of their constitutional budgetary rights. And he created the new German Reich with the help of a very Prussian army, which was victorious in three local wars. One generation later, German *Weltpolitik* was based on the concept of an imperialist, anti-socialist common front against enemies both inside and outside the Reich.

The Right in disarray

The common front appeared to have become a reality on August 4, 1914, but it cracked under the stress of four years of a war that was lost. The lack of rational and honest analysis in German politics, the system of lies, illusions and self-deception coupled with the traditional 'arrogance of power' backfired on German society. It split into three major groups who were to shape Germany's future course: the extreme Right; Catholics, Liberals and Social Democrats of the Centre; and the revolutionary socialists.

The traditional Right fell back on the most rigid and reactionary interpretation of Bismarckian statecraft—more repression inside and more and better warfare outside. Its hard core was provided by the Pan-Germans, who, with the blessings of ex-chancellor Bismarck, had inaugurated propaganda for an expansive and aggressive *Weltpolitik* as early as 1894. In their bitter determination to win the war at any cost, the Pan-Germans practically won over most of the conservatives, a large part of the middle-class bureaucracy and most of

the officer-corps both in the army and in the Imperial navy. In the latter part of the war, they gained additional influence through General Ludendorff's unofficial dictatorship after Chancellor Bethmann-Hollweg had fallen in July 1917.

In reaction to the moderates' peace resolution in the *Reichstag* of July 19, 1917, the extreme Right formed the *Vaterlandspartei* (Fatherland Party) under the leadership of Admiral Tirpitz, the father of the German battlefleet, and Kapp, the later *putschist* of 1920. The *Vaterlandspartei* rose quickly to a million members. It was the first political mass-organisation of the proto-Fascist and extreme reactionary elements in Germany. They stood for the maintenance of the status quo inside Germany, but modified by some kind of military Caesarism with or without the complication of traditional monarchy. Their foreign policy was to win this war if possible and to prepare for the next if the present war could not be won. When military defeat became certain, in September 1918, Ludendorff, the most important representative of the extreme Right, made the moderates shoulder formal responsibility for concluding the Armistice by introducing parliamentary government and suing for peace at his command. At the same time, the extreme Right concocted the legend of the 'stab in the back' and, even in the hour of defeat, quietly thought of conserving and rebuilding Germany's military power.

The second group, consisting more or less of the Catholic Centre Party, and most of the Liberals and Social Democrats, also wanted, in principle, to preserve the social

and economic status quo, but they were prepared to admit limited social and political reforms. This had the additional advantage of making the western democracies more willing to help Germany in the struggle against Communism and against smaller Slav national states in the east who were in a position to prevent the rebirth of the Reich as a great power in Europe.

The moderate groups left and right of the centre had openly come together for the first time in the parliamentary majority that carried the Peace Resolution of July 19, 1917 and they carried, more or less sullenly, the Weimar Constitution. Under pressure from the Right, however, they gave way to nationalist agitation from 1929 onwards: the Liberal voters were practically absorbed by rising Nazism; the Catholic Centre Party accommodated by a return to authoritarian government by decrees under Heinrich Brüning; the Social Democrats, isolated once again as they were before 1914, were paralysed and helpless between Communists to the left and the bourgeois parties, overtly or covertly deserting the Weimar Republic in 1932/33, to the right.

The third group, the genuinely revolutionary one, was the weakest of all. It was represented by the extreme left wing of the old Social Democratic Party, which, after

Below left: Ludendorff (centre, helmeted), Hitler's figurehead; Göring (second from right); and von Epp, Bavarian *Freikorps* commander. *Below:* George Grosz's comment on the *Freikorps'* Baltic ravages of 1919. *Below right:* The government needed the army's support against insurgents

bitter controversies and much confusion, broke away early in 1917 to re-emerge as the Communist Party led by Rosa Luxemburg and Karl Liebknecht on January 1, 1919. At the beginning, they were a mere handful, more of a nuisance value and providing a welcome excuse for another turn to the right soon after the 'Revolution' of November 1918. The Communists remained a minority party with fluctuating support in the Weimar Republic. Even at the peak of their voting strength, in November 1932, they mustered no more than 16%. They represented largely the weakest section economically, and the most powerless, of German society, the jobless masses in the industrial cities, whose only effective weapon—the strike—had been blunted in the Great Depression by mass-unemployment.

In the agonies of the Weimar Republic the KPD appealed above all to the unemployed. From 1928 the increase in the numbers of Communist voters was about parallel with that in the numbers of unemployed: both figures had reached, in November 1932, their peak with about six million. The alleged Communist threat served as a perfect pretext for the takeover by the Nazis and the passive acceptance of the German middle class.

Aftermath

The failure of Germany's bid for world power in 1914-1918 thus had the overall effect of destroying the superficial yet powerful 'national' consensus within the German Reich. The frustrated energies blocked off from outward expansion turned inward. The so-called Revolution of Novem-

ber 1918 was the natural and swift reaction of German society. Yet, once the first revolutionary turbulence was spent, it soon became clear that hardly more than the façade of the Wilhelmine edifice had collapsed, leaving the apparently more solid Bismarckian structure almost intact. Parliamentary democracy had been introduced in October 1918 more to appease the victorious Allies and to prevent impending revolution than from inward conviction and the ruling classes of the German Empire survived more or less unscathed. Once they realised, by the time of the elections of the National Constituent Assembly in January 1919, that nothing serious had happened to threaten their traditional privileges and powers, the conservative forces regained their confidence again, at best tolerating for the moment the abhorred Republic. Once the Crown had fallen away, a powerful barrier to the spread of Fascism in Germany had disappeared as well. On the other hand the notorious sympathies of Crown-Prince Wilhelm, both for the Pan-Germans before 1918, and for the extreme right-wing conservatives, make it conceivable that Nazism could have risen in Germany under a Kaiser Wilhelm III, just as Fascism did in monarchical Italy and Rumania.

The First World War, the mystical *Kriegserlebnis,* became the emotional background to the New Right. Nazism, the German brand of Fascism, rose to power in reaction to the Revolution, the emergence of Communism and the inclusion of Social Democrats and Liberals in the new national consensus of the Weimar Republic. The massive continuity from the Imperial

German establishment is undeniable: Pan-Germans, conservatives, officers and generals, the clergy of both great Churches, judges and most of the university and high-school teachers remained loyal to their old ideal of a powerful Reich. They were united, despite their many shades of political opinion, in their hatred of the weakling bastard Republic. The Weimar Republic did carry on the name and some of the emblems of the Reich, and it tried to change the Reich into a modern nation. In vain, the mystique of the Reich, the traditional social structures and the desire to have a dominant government proved too powerful to obliterate by reforms.

The *Vaterlandspartei* (Fatherland Party), it is true, was quietly disbanded in November 1918, but its proto-Fascist elements looked for new forms of organisation. By January 1919 most conservatives and chauvinists found themselves members of a new party, the *Deutschnationale Volkspartei* (DNVP). This was the more respectable wing of the New Right—many small groups of former anti-semites and chauvinists of the pre-war era remained outside. The workers' section within the *Vaterlandspartei,* for example, stayed in isolation, and became the nucleus of another party, the NSDAP, the Nazi Party, as early as 1919. It quickly rose above the chaos of rival organisations on the extreme right, thanks to its new leader Adolf Hitler.

Hitler

Hitler had absorbed his political ideas from writings of obscure chauvinist and anti-semite authors and sects in pre-war Austria and Germany. In early August 1914, then in Munich as an Austrian draft-dodger, he participated in the orgiastic mystique of the *Augusterlebnis,* which seemed as if it must unite Germans for all time in the service of a powerful Fatherland. Four years of active warfare at the Western Front sharpened his political consciousness, the breakdown and Revolution of November 1918 gave it a clear direction: he was against Communism and Socialism, against Jews and liberal democrats, for the resurrection of the power and glory of the German Reich. Hitler started his political career as an undercover political agent of the Bavarian *Reichswehr* Division that drowned in blood the Munich Commune or *Räterepublik* of spring 1919. Sent to the newly founded Nazi Party, a minuscule group in Munich, to observe it for the Bavarian military command, he quickly sensed that it could serve his own political purposes. Hitler became the leader of the young party, but remained in contact with his former military superiors, who continued to finance and protect Hitler and his new party. His direct military superior, Captain Ernst Röhm, was to become the first and most important organiser of Hitler's SA *(Sturmabteilung)* after the relationship between Hitler and Röhm had been reversed.

Nazism found in Bavaria extremely favourable conditions for its start and rise. Monarchists in the agrarian, backward and conservative state deeply resented the loss of the monarchy. The leading political forces stood well to the right within their respective national parties, and during most of the Weimar Republic Bavaria was ruled either by openly authoritarian oligarchies or by a parliamentary majority of the *Bayerische Volkspartei* (Bavarian People's Party), an extreme right-wing Catholic party, and the Bavarian DNVP which had close affinities with Nazism. Gürtner, the Minister of Justice of the DNVP in Munich, discreetly did his best to protect Hitler in the early part of his political career, and Hitler's gratitude allowed Gürtner to carry on as Minister of Justice for the Reich after 1933.

Vexation of a dream

The Nazi Party was only the best organised and most extreme expression of the widespread refusal in German society after 1918 to analyse rationally the causes of Germany's failure in the First World War and the true causes of Germany's isolation. Inside Germany the spell of the Reich remained unbroken. The ruling class began to dream of another powerful Germany, the Third Reich, which Nazism promised to create. The gap between the industrial foundation and the agrarian-influenced ideology of the Reich, already the main structural deficiency of Bismarck's Germany, was to be carried by Nazism to the point of absurdity. While the modernisation and expansion of German industries rapidly progressed both in the Weimar Republic and in Hitler's Third Reich, the Nazis regressed to the crudest type of ideology, extolling the Teutonic tribes in their barbarian phase of development as the great ideal of German society. The widening gap between reality and these ideological fantasies was to produce even greater and more dangerous emotional and political instability in German society under the Führer than under Bismarck or the Kaiser. The Nazis' wild dreams showed them a Pan-Germanic Empire of the Germans over Europe. This would be achieved by cultivated brutality and studied barbarism with the help of the most mechanised military machine, which in its turn was based on a highly modernised industry. As a national aim it was bound to produce even more violent conflicts with the rest of the world, and the Second World War was only the logical consequence.

Some of the most devastating arguments of the extreme right, Nazis and others, were directly traceable to the outcome of the First World War. The myth of encirclement, Germany's denial that her actions were the cause of the outbreak of war in 1914, the stab-in-the-back legend, the *Diktat* of Versailles and its consequences. The refusal to accept Germany's share of the blame for the First World War became one of the most effective ways of preparing German society for the Second. In 1929 one of the few clearsighted people in Weimar Germany, Professor Hermann Kantorowicz, pointed out the danger to both the German Foreign Office (in protest against its suppression of his penetrating study on the origins of the First World War) and the general public, in a book on the same subject. But his warnings were useless and Kantorowicz was among the first German intellectuals whose books were burned in 1933. He emigrated from Nazi Germany and died in Oxford in February 1940, shortly after the beginning of the Second World War.

The Second World War can best be understood as a German war of revenge for the defeat of the First World War, with Nazism representing a supreme effort to organise German society for the renewed attempt to challenge most of the rest of the world. The Weimar Republic, seen in this perspective, appears as a muddled interlude between the Second Reich and the Third Reich, between the Kaiser's Germany and the Führer's Germany. It is more than a formality that the obscure lance-corporal of the First World War became the military and political leader of the Third Reich in the Second World War. The exiled Kaiser and his son became more or less enthusiastic spectators. The lieutenants and captains of the First World War, like Rommel, became the generals and field-marshals of the Second. The battlefields of 1914-18 were fought over again in the Second World War, this time at lightning speed, with German armies storming out victoriously and reeling back again defeated.

Even more impressive is the striking similarity between German aims in the two conflicts: the leaders in both wanted to achieve a combination of direct annexation and indirect domination through economic power and satellite régimes. One great difference was that in the later war the Reich dared to implement, even if only for a short time, the plans which had been made after Germany's victories in the First World War. Large Polish areas were incorporated in the Reich, roughly comparable with the planned annexations of the First World War. This time, the Nazis were bold enough to fulfil the dreams of their predecessors (Ludendorff, the Pan-Germans and the Imperial Government) and expelled large parts of the Polish population and even killed off practically all Jews to make room for Germans from minority enclaves in Eastern Europe. Again, there was the sinister disparity between German actions in the West and in the East. While, in the West, German administration and troops kept roughly to the code laid down in international law, in the East they flung aside all inhibitions to open a brutal campaign of extermination against Slavs, Jews and Communists which recalled the barbaric era which the Nazis idealised.

The Reich fails

Once again the German Reich failed to subdue most of the world. In 1945 the Reich perished in the attempt and today only hopeless reactionaries still dream of resurrecting it. The imposing national consensus, partly voluntary, partly imposed by the Third Reich, collapsed in 1945. This time, the split in society divided Germany into two states along the lines laid down by the Cold War. The western one is ruled by elements of the Centre and the Right, the eastern one by the equivalent of extreme Left of the Weimar Republic. The political balance between the two modern German states may help to avoid the danger of a new militarist society rising to threaten the security of Europe.

Further Reading
Rothfels, H., et al., *Road to Dictatorship. Germany 1918-33* (Wolff 1963)
Taylor, A. J. P., *The Course of German History* (Methuen University Paperbacks)
Vogt, H., *The Burden of Guilt. A Short History of Germany 1914-45* (New York: Oxford University Press 1965)
Wiskemann, E., *The Europe of the Dictators 1919-1945* (Fontana 1966)

[*For Imanuel Geiss's biography, see page 68.*]

The Offspring of Versailles

Hitler, Adolf: Born 1889, Braunau, Austria. Became fervent German nationalist while still at school. Despite nationality, at outbreak of war joined *16th Bavarian Reserve Infantry Regiment.* Served throughout War as a runner. Gained first fighting experience at First Ypres. Wounded in leg at Bapaume, after the Somme. Took part in 1918 spring offensive. Injured in gas attack near Ypres, October 1918; in hospital when War ended. Awarded Iron Cross, Second Class, December 1914; First Class, August 1918; never promoted. Spent April-May 1919 in Munich during Bavarian Revolution. Responsible for indoctrinating soldiers against left-wing subversion, came into contact with the 'German Workers' Party', a working-class nationalist group which he joined. Built up the Bavarian party which took title 'National Socialist German Workers' Party', developing propaganda methods and turning membership into mass following for himself. From 1919 to 1923 tried to plan large-scale German coup, which ended in the failure of Munich *Putsch* of November 8-9, 1923, and Hitler's subsequent imprisonment

Göring, Hermann Wilhelm: Born 1893. After various schools, where he was unable to settle, went to military academy. Served in *112th Prinz Wilhelm Infantry Regiment* in Alsace-Lorraine, but became a pilot in the War. Won Iron Cross, 1st Class, in 1915. Shot down by English airman in same year, but landed behind German lines and spent next four months in hospital. 1917 shot down 20th enemy aeroplane and received the *Pour le Mérite,* Germany's highest award for valour. After Richthofen's death in 1918 took command of the 'Circus of Death'. Never accepted that Germany had lost the War, taking the line that the military had been betrayed by the politicians. Spent the years immediately following the War in Sweden, first as a commercial pilot, then as a mechanic, later in a shop Married a Swedish girl, Karin, whose money and moral support helped him to go back to Germany and re-establish himself in Bavaria. He met Hitler in Munich in 1922 and joined the National Socialist Party. Soon became leader of the SA (Storm Troopers). Took active part in 1923 *Putsch*, and was seriously wounded

Röhm, Ernst: Born 1887. In 1906 joined *Royal Bavarian 10th Infantry Regiment König.* At beginning of War was adjutant of *1st Battalion.* Wounded after two months by grenade splinter in the face, but returned to regiment at Front before fully recovered. Again seriously wounded east of Verdun in June 1916, at head of his *10th Company.* While still unfit to return to the Front worked in Bavarian War Ministry. Became General Staff Officer of *12th Bavarian Infantry Division* and retained this position until the War ended. One of the first to join the *Freikorps* set up by Major-General Ritter von Epp at Ohrdruf. Took part in overthrow of Spartacist rising in Munich and Ruhr. Met and became friends with Hitler. Helped enlarge National Socialist Party with ex-*Freikorps* members and ex-servicemen. In October 1923 took under own command local groups of the *Reichsflagge,* one of the Bavarian patriotic leagues. Largely responsible for bringing about alliance between these leagues and National Socialists. In 1923 *Putsch* occupied Munich War Ministry with Storm Troopers. Forced to capitulate under siege

Above: Göring, one-time air ace and early adherent to the Nazi Party. *Below left:* Hitler. *Below right:* Ernst Röhm, SA leader and one of Hitler's earliest victims

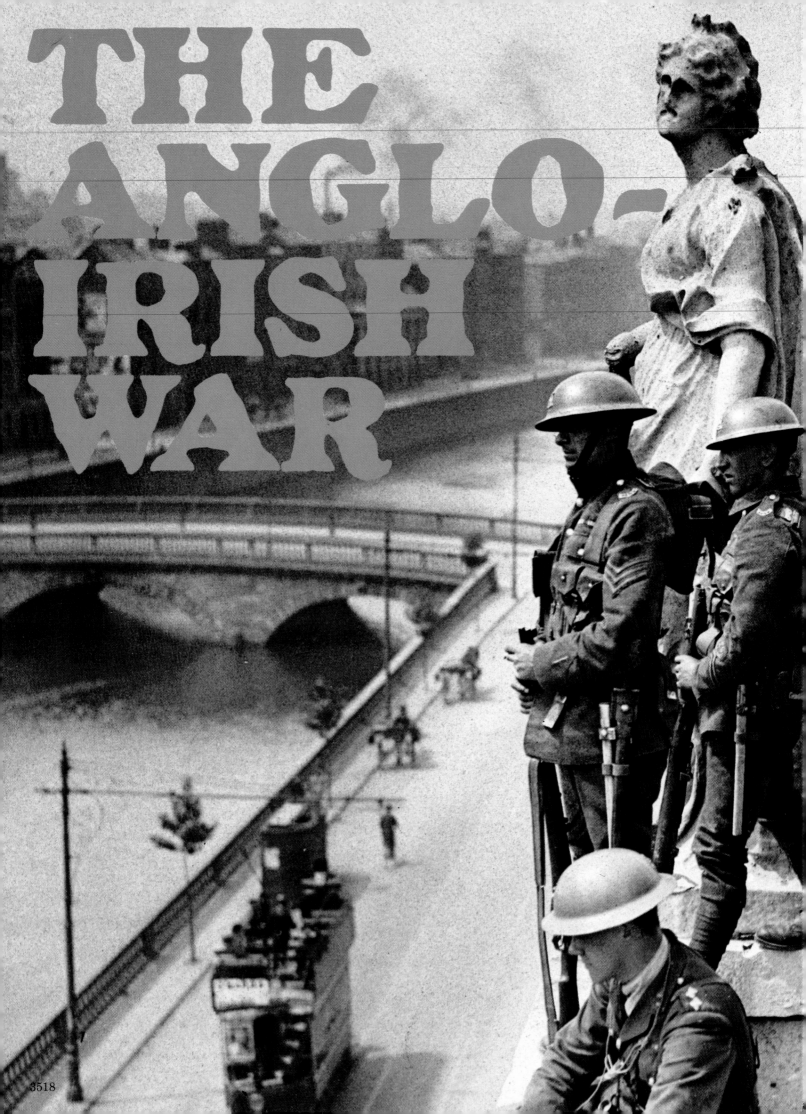

THE ANGLO-IRISH WAR

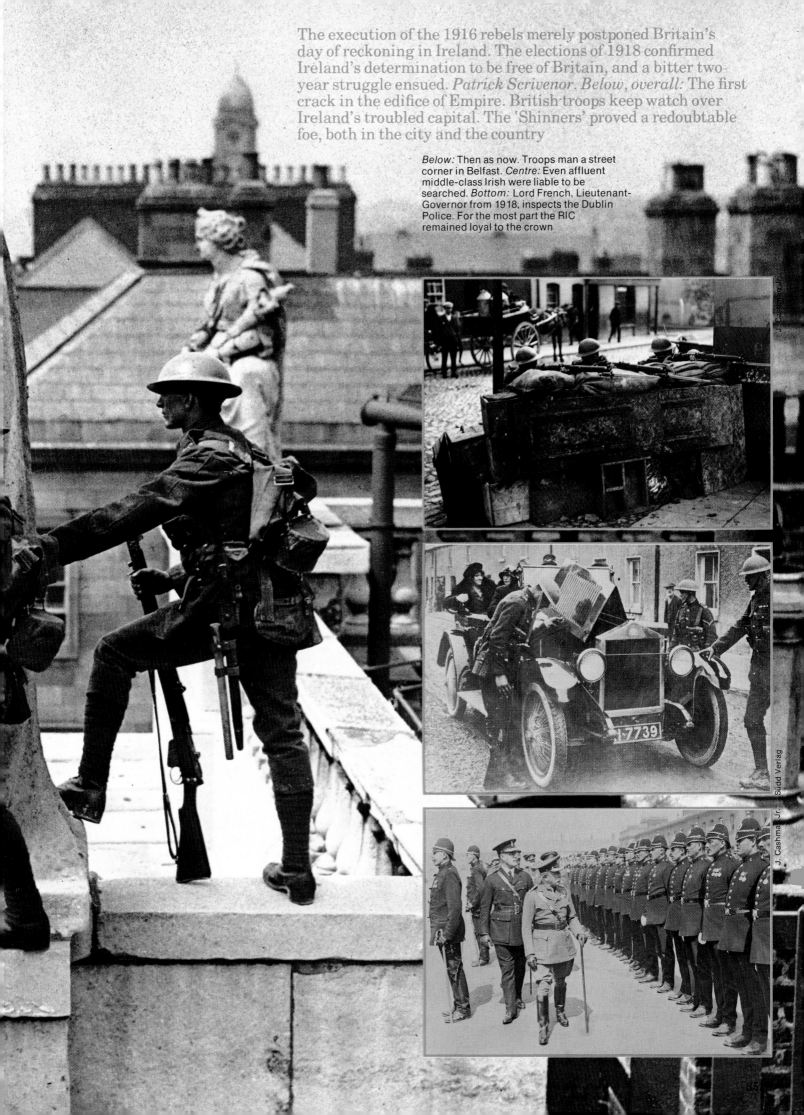

The execution of the 1916 rebels merely postponed Britain's day of reckoning in Ireland. The elections of 1918 confirmed Ireland's determination to be free of Britain, and a bitter two-year struggle ensued. *Patrick Scrivenor. Below, overall:* The first crack in the edifice of Empire. British troops keep watch over Ireland's troubled capital. The 'Shinners' proved a redoubtable foe, both in the city and the country

Below: Then as now. Troops man a street corner in Belfast. *Centre:* Even affluent middle-class Irish were liable to be searched. *Bottom:* Lord French, Lieutenant-Governor from 1918, inspects the Dublin Police. For the most part the RIC remained loyal to the crown

During 1917 and 1918 both sides in the Irish question were awaiting the end of the war and the outcome of probable peace talks. The involvement of America from early 1917 onwards made an Allied victory nearly certain, and the known attitude of the American President gave both sides to hope that the question would be settled to their advantage without further bloodshed. Lloyd George and the British government hoped that their Home Rule proposals would satisfy the President's demands for national self-determination. The republicans hoped that, in view of his intentions declared in the Fourteen Points, Wilson would scarcely be able to ignore their demand for independent nationhood.

If, however, Lloyd George ever entertained a hope that the Irish themselves would accept Home Rule, it was to be rudely shattered. Three events during 1917 and 1918 had served to harden anti-British feeling in Ireland. The death of Thomas Ashe, a hunger-striker, in Mountjoy Jail; the threatened imposition of conscription in Ireland; and the re-arrest of the republican leaders in May 1918. Nor was the appointment of Lord French as Lieutenant-Governor very tactful, as he represented a type of British soldier, of Irish ascendancy extraction, most distasteful to the republicans.

The only republican leader of any note to escape arrest was Michael Collins, and from this moment until the escape or release of the other leaders he ran both the political and military arms of the republican cause virtually singlehanded, earning for himself the nickname 'the big fellow', and becoming the most outstanding personality on either side in the Anglo-Irish war. Much of the groundwork of his later success was laid during the last months of the World War, establishing his Intelligence network, transforming the Irish Volunteers into what was to become the Irish Republican Army (IRA), and setting up the organisation by which the movement was to be financed.

In December, 1918, Great Britain went to the polls. Lloyd George had gone to great lengths to ensure victory for his coalition government, but in Ireland matters stood otherwise. Of the 105 Irish seats, *Sinn Fein*, the republicans, won 73. Twenty-six, in Ulster, went to the Unionists, and six to the old Irish Party. The republicans had been at even greater pains than Lloyd George to make certain of victory, and there is evidence of republican supporters voting twice, and even of dead men's names appearing in the ballot! Nonetheless, the republican landslide reflected the true state of Irish opinion.

Events now began to move fast. Of the 73 elected republicans, 47 were in jail. On January 7, 1919, the 26 remaining members met in the Mansion House, Dublin, and appointed a time and place for the meeting of the Dail Eireann, or Irish Parliament. On January 21, the Dail met, adopted a republican constitution, and heard read the Irish Declaration of Independence. As the name of each absent member was read out, an official intoned in Irish 'imprisoned by the foreign enemy'. The press gallery was full of correspondents from all over the world, and the whole proceedings constituted a

public and solemn avowal of the Irish Republic. There could be no going back on it, and equally, no way of ignoring it. Surprisingly, the British did not immediately declare the Dail an illegal organisation, and indeed, on March 8, 1919, they released the political prisoners, and the Dail was able, for a time, to function normally. And it was during this time that a remarkable phenomenon appeared. All over Ireland, in response to the enactments of the Dail, separate republican courts and organs of government sprang up alongside the parallel institutions of the crown, and the people of Ireland started to use them in preference to their British counterparts. British-appointed Resident Magistrates suddenly found their courts unattended, and increasing numbers of them resigned.

Quietly and unobtrusively *Sinn Fein* was taking over the running of the country.

What was the British response to all this activity? The 1914 Home Rule Bill was still on the statute book, and Lloyd George was determined to enforce partition, separating the six counties of Ulster from the rest of Ireland. But the events of 1916 had taught him caution, and he had no wish to weaken his position at the Paris Peace Conference, or with his American allies, by acts of coercion in Ireland. For this reason French had been sent to Ireland in April 1918 with strict instructions to 'let *Sinn Fein* fire the first shots'.

On January 21, 1919, the same day as the meeting of the Dail, the Tipperary County Council moved a consignment of gelignite for quarry blasting to the vil-

J. Cashman Jr.

lage of Soloheadbeg. It was escorted by two armed members of the Royal Irish Constabulary (RIC). Near Soloheadbeg it was intercepted by a local IRA figure, Dan Breen, and nine men. The two constables were killed, and the gelignite appropriated for purposes other than quarrying. These are generally accepted as being the first shots of the Anglo-Irish war. Tipperary was declared a military area, and a reward of £1,000 was offered for information leading to the arrest of those responsible. Although the IRA campaign did not get under way fully until after it became clear that Ireland would not even be listened to, much less represented, at the Peace Conference, this incident marks the start of the 'Troubles'.

The Troubles. This very Irish euphem-

ism is used to describe the period from January 1919 to June 1921 during which the British government struggled to retain its ever-loosening grip on Ireland. The scale of the fighting between the forces of the crown and the IRA was not large, and the nature of it decidedly unglamorous. The majority of the casualties are accounted for by executions by the IRA and reprisals, often wholly indiscriminate, by the forces of the crown. The direct encounters that did take place between the two sides involved small numbers, and were of the ambush and counter-ambush type. It was a classic guerrilla war in which an un-uniformed force used a sympathetic civilian population as cover from which to harass, pin down, and eventually totally discredit the regular forces of the government.

As in all operations of the same kind, far more important than the actual fighting was the silent battle between the Intelligence organs of each side, and the psychological battle for the sympathy of public opinion both in Ireland and all over the world. The crown forces lost both these battles, and, as in the case of the Boer War 20 years before, they resorted to measures of coercion that were nothing short of barbarous.

The forces that confronted each other in 1919 were sharply unequal. In one of his wilder despatches to Westminster French estimated the IRA strength at 100,000. It was, in fact, no more than 15,000, with arms for only 5,000. Throughout the war shortage of arms and ammunition was to hamper the IRA. The republican forces were organised on a regional basis, each district brigade, or column, being answerable direct to Dublin. 'Brigade' was a relative term, and the columns in the field often numbered only 100 men.

The crown forces in Ireland in 1919 consisted of the RIC and a garrison of British troops. The nominal roll of the RIC was 10,000, but their position and task was very nearly impossible. They were grouped in police barracks in detachments of five or six. Tactically, they were hopelessly vulnerable to attack, and psychologically they were vulnerable as well, all of them being Irish, and many having been born in the areas where they worked. They remained loyal to the crown; but, placed in an impossible situation, obvious and easy targets for the IRA, the RIC suffered from a growing rate of resignations, and eventu-

J. Cashman Jr.

Far left: Lord French with General Macready, the Commander-in-Chief in Ireland. Both believed in putting down rebellion with a strong hand. *Left:* A heavily armed 'Auxie' stands by as Liberty Hall is looted. A paramilitary force of ex-officers, the 'Auxies' were trigger happy and ill disciplined. *Below:* Dwellings gutted in reprisal by the crown forces can still be seen in Ireland. In 1920 a large part of Cork was thus destroyed

J. Cashman Jr.

ally had to be reinforced from England. The British garrison in 1919 consisted of territorial troops; the first regular troops did not arrive till half way through the year. Compared with the armies that had been fighting in France these troops were of a poor quality. The veterans of the war had been demobilised, and the new recruits were young, and under-nourished and ill-educated as a result of four years of war. Few, if any, of their officers or NCOs had any experience of the type of warfare in which they were about to be engaged.

During the period May to December 1919 the initiative in the fighting came entirely from the IRA, and it took the form of attacks on isolated police barracks and individual policemen with the aim of obtaining arms and ammunition. No republicans were killed, and many who were still imprisoned made spectacular escapes. The IRA was gradually building up its strength. During the same period 18 RIC constables were killed, and one British soldier. This last death sparked off an incident that was to set the pattern for the next 18 months of violence. On September 7 a patrol of the KSLI was ambushed on its way to church in Fermoy, Co. Cork. One soldier was killed. At an inquest the jury refused to return a finding of murder, and on the same day 200 soldiers ran amok in Fermoy doing £3,000 worth of damage. No disciplinary action was taken against them.

Three days after this event, on September 10, the Dail was declared by the British authorities to be an illegal institution. In November, the *Sinn Fein,*

Above: The funeral of the Mayor of Limerick and Michael O'Callaghan, shot by the 'Tans' in their homes in 1921. *Right:* Britain's answer to terrorism—terrorists. Members of the Auxiliary Division, RIC. *Below:* A target for the IRA. A heavily guarded British ammunition train is destroyed

the Volunteers, and the Gaelic League were similarly banned. Although these moves effectively disrupted the slow *Sinn Fein* takeover of the functions of government, it also ensured that Ireland entered 1920 more than ever united behind the republican cause. On December 19, 1919, an attempt was made on the life of Lord French. It failed, and one IRA member was killed, a fitting end to the sporadic action of 1919.

1920 opened with a further demonstration of the hold of the republicans on the country. In January the municipal elections were held, and of the 127 corporations in Ireland, *Sinn Fein* won 72. Of the 12 major cities of Ireland, only one, Belfast, did not fall to *Sinn Fein*. It seemed that all the coercive measures of the previous year, the raids on private houses, the meetings broken up, the arrests for petty offences like singing republican songs, had done nothing but harden opposition to British rule.

By the beginning of 1920 there were 43,000 British troops stationed in Ireland. Officially they were there to help and protect the police, but more and more they came to take over the police's duties and tasks. As always when regular troops are used in this rôle, their conduct deteriorated. On January 20 the town of Thurle was 'shot up'. The windows of private houses were fired into, grenades were thrown into a local newspaper office, and premises were broken open and looted. All this was in reprisal for the death of a constable that morning. Clearly the British campaign was to be intensified during 1920. In January alone over 1,000 raids were carried out and 220 arrests

were made. In February 4,000 raids and 296 arrests were made. But this activity and an increase in the number of troops to 45,000 seemed to have little effect. The killing of policemen still continued, and by Easter more than 300 police barracks had been evacuated. The morale of the RIC, and indeed their usefulness, was clearly wearing thin. Resignations were frequent, and recruiting in Ireland had virtually ceased. As early as January 1920 recruiting for the depleted RIC had begun in England. A year of peace had thrown plenty of demobilised soldiers out of work, and the offer of 10/- per day all found for RIC 'special' constables (later to be nicknamed the Black and Tans) brought in more recruits than could be coped with. The allegation that violent criminals were released from jail to serve in the 'Specials' is unfounded. Unfortunately the far more damaging fact is that large numbers of 'normal' citizens were prepared to do the work involved.

The first Black and Tan reinforcements for the RIC arrived in March 1920. In the same month General Sir Neville Macready took over as Commander-in-Chief in Ireland, Lord French remaining as Lieutenant-Governor. Macready was in close contact with Sir Henry Wilson, the CIGS. Both believed in 'putting down rebellion with a firm hand'. At the same time senior RIC officers were removed, and General Tudor became Chief of Police.

It would be impossible to catalogue in an article of this length all the incidents and cruelties of the ensuing year. A full account will be found in Dorothy Macardle's *Irish Republic,* but here a few ex-

amples will have to suffice to show the kind of policy inaugurated by the British to coerce Ireland into accepting partition. The crown forces, finding themselves attacked by an unseen enemy, reacted with indiscriminate reprisals. On March 19, 1920, men with blackened faces burst into the home of Thomas McCurtain, Lord Mayor of Cork (and also Commandant of the Cork IRA Brigade), and shot him dead. The incident followed a series of threats on his life, and at the time of the killing the streets around his house were cleared and cordoned off by the police and military. A coroner's jury returned a verdict of wilful murder against the crown forces, naming three of them. No action was ever taken against these men. Between January and June 1920 a total of 15 reprisals against towns and villages was made by the crown forces, mostly in counties Limerick and Tipperary. The unhappy town of Thurle was 'shot up' four times in addition to the occasion already mentioned.

Perhaps the most famous outrage by the crown forces took place on November 21, 1920 – Bloody Sunday. It is an incident that points very neatly the difference between the methods of the British and the IRA. Neither side used honourable methods, and murder is a word that can be used accurately to describe both sides' tactics, but where the IRA were reasonably careful to kill only participants in the struggle, the crown forces quite frequently killed at random.

Living in Dublin in plain clothes was a group of British officers whose task it was to locate and kill Collins. They had made considerable progress, and had

J. Cashman Jr.

become the main threat to his safety, when they blundered by releasing two suspects they had questioned. Both were Collins' men, and immediately he was able to locate and identify his enemies. At 0900 hours on Sunday, November 21, members of the Dublin IRA Brigade executed fourteen British officers at their hotels and lodgings. Of the fourteen only one man was innocent, a RAMC officer shot in error. That afternoon a crowd of 8,000 was gathered at Croke Park to watch a football match. Suddenly the ground was surrounded by crown forces looking for arms which, it was believed, had been brought by IRA members of the visiting team. Just after this a detachment of the Black and Tans arrived in lorries and, without warning or reason, opened fire on the crowd. Twelve people were killed, and 60 wounded. On the same day two IRA suspects were shot by their captors in the guardroom of Dublin Castle. No disciplinary action was taken as a result of either of these incidents.

1920 was marked by two other complications of the Irish scene. The first was Ulster. This province had never been as homogeneously Protestant as the Unionists would have liked. But during 1920 the Orangemen did their best to make it so. What can only be described as a pogrom against the Catholic population of Ulster took place. Roman Catholics were driven out of employment in the shipyards, and Catholic minorities in mainly Protestant areas were driven out. To refer to the activities of an Orange 'mob' would be misleading. It could more accurately be described as an Orange 'army'. Protestants, armed and organised along the lines of the 1914 Ulster Volunteers, attacked Catholic homes, and drove out the occupants. Catholic homes and churches were burned, and witnesses spoke of scenes similar to the evacuation of Belgium in 1914. The consequences of these events need no elaboration.

The second complication was the recruiting of a second 'special' force by the British. The Auxiliary Division, RIC, unaffectionately known as the 'Auxies', was first established in July, 1920. One thousand five hundred strong, it consisted of ex-officers many of whom had known no other way of life than the trenches. Their own commander, Brigadier Crozier, who was to resign in protest against the methods they used, described them as 'insubordinate, dishonest, sadistic, drunken'. They were also a formidable fighting force, reckless and ruthless. Collins said that the garrisoning of an area by the Auxiliaries was the best compliment that could be paid to the local IRA commander. Perhaps their most dangerous feature, however, was their complete immunity from criticism and discipline. They were not under military discipline and could not be brought before a civil court. On occasions when their misdeeds did catch up with them, they were able to blackmail their superiors by threatening to publicise their activities. They specialised in raids, reprisals, and straightforward murder, and in execution of these 'duties' they were frequently drunk. Their dark blue uniform became the most hated and feared in Ireland. Although, because of their small numbers, their impact was not as widespread as that of the 'Tans', the recruitment and conduct of the 'Auxies' remains the most discreditable incident in the history of the British Empire. Throughout 1920 the level of violence in Ireland increased. Except in a small area of Co. Cork, where *Sinn Fein* held complete sway and maintained a praiseworthy degree of law and order, normal life became impossible. Local fairs and markets were banned by the crown forces, completely disrupting the economy of the countryside, and raising the cost of living by almost 100%. A further election in June, 1920, this time for County Councils, showed *Sinn Fein* still had the complete support of the Irish electorate outside Ulster. Nonetheless, the crown forces still continued to behave as if they were dealing with a minority revolt. Raids on private homes were by now a nightly occurrence. If the raid were conducted by regular troops, it might be no more than an orderly search. If by the police or 'Tans' in concert with the military, abusive and violent behaviour was likely. If by the 'Auxies' any male occupant of the house ran the risk of being shot out of hand. These raids accomplished little, and provoked the most intense fear and hatred.

Much of the trouble stemmed from the extraordinary way in which the crown forces were being used. Lloyd George was determined to preserve the polite fiction that he was suppressing an entirely minority rebellion, and throughout 1920 he resolutely refused to declare →

martial law. This meant that outside the martial law areas in the south, the police acted on orders from Dublin Castle, and not from the local military commander. The British were, in effect, trying to suppress a guerrilla insurrection with a police force, a task that no police force could possibly undertake.

But to preserve Lloyd George's fiction, something more than police action was needed. In April 1920 he presented the 'Bill for the Better Government of Ireland' to the Commons. Under the terms of this bill, two Irish parliaments, in Belfast and Dublin, were to be set up. They were to be subordinate to Westminster, and were to elect representatives to an All Irish Council. Under this provision the six northern counties were to elect the same number as the 26 southern counties. These terms, which offered rather less than the Liberals' Home Rule Bill of 1914, were wholly unacceptable to *Sinn Fein,* and, as one observer pointed out, the bill was more an attempt to satisfy foreign opinion than a serious attempt to govern Ireland. The bill was eventually passed in December 1920, with the added provision that if it were not in force and operating by May 1921 martial law would be declared, and the whole of Ireland would be administered as a Crown Colony.

Even when the bill was presented to the Commons, it was an absurdity, and as 1920 progressed it became more so. In addition to raids and arrests in the attempt to come to grips with the IRA, the forces of the crown also adopted the policy of wrecking instalments of

importance to the economic life of Ireland. The main targets were the co-operatively owned creameries of such importance to Irish dairy produce, but mills, bacon factories and other targets were attacked as well. Eventually over 100 centres of this kind were destroyed. Reprisals, both against property and persons, were now an admitted part of the crown's policy. To lend this a semblance of legality further legislation was passed through Westminster during August. An extension of the Defence of the Realm Act, the Restoration of Order in Ireland Act, was passed, granting the military in Ireland immunity from almost all the restraints of law. They were empowered to imprison suspects without trial for an indefinite period. Secret courts martial replaced the normal courts, and military enquiries, also secret, replaced coroners' inquests. In effect a servant of the crown guilty of killing someone no longer had to fear that his action would be punished, or even criticised.

Naturally the bloodshed increased. Ambush and counter-ambush were regular events in areas where the IRA was strong enough to mount such operations. This was mainly in the south and west, particularly in west Cork, where an IRA brigade under Tom Barry was extremely active. In November, at Kilmichael, Barry's column ambushed a convoy of 'Auxies', killing 17. The crown forces, who depended for their mobility on vehicles, were hampered by the appalling roads and wet weather. Reprisals also escalated, and far too many sackings and

shootings took place to be chronicled fully here. A few examples must suffice.

On September 20, 1920, a 'Tan' was shot dead and another injured in a pub brawl in Balbriggan. That night about 150 'Auxies' from the nearby barracks descended on the town. Twenty-five houses were destroyed, two men were bayoneted by the 'Auxies', many were beaten up and taken off to the Auxiliary barracks for the night. In Mallow, in Co. Cork, 'Auxies' sacked the town hall, doing damage of about £20,000 and shooting and wounding two men.

One event more than any other drew world sympathy to Ireland during 1920. After the murder of Thomas McCurtain, Terence MacSwiney had become Lord Mayor of Cork. Almost immediately, on August 12, he was arrested and imprisoned. He went on hunger-strike. His strike lasted 74 days while all the world watched. No attempt was made at forcible feeding as it was supposed that he would die resisting it. At last, on October 25, he died. MacSwiney had enjoyed a considerable reputation as a poet, scholar, and dramatist. It was no murdering hobble-dehoy or gunman who had chosen to make this sacrifice. World opinion was awakened to what was happening in Ireland.

Another event in 1920 fired Irish imaginations, and is indeed still remembered. On November 1, in Mountjoy Jail, a young Volunteer, Kevin Barry, aged only 18, was hanged. Previous to his hanging he had been tortured to extract information. The maltreatment of suspects by the crown forces was common, and some units had a particularly bad reputation. The

Far left: IRA prisoners are escorted into captivity. *Left:* Mrs Despard, French's sister, sits outside Mountjoy Jail in protest against the treatment of IRA hunger-strikers. *Below:* Another scene outside Mountjoy Jail, a British tank patrols the street. *Right:* A sympathetic crowd awaits news of the prisoners on hunger-strike

IRA have persistently alleged that Major Percival of the Essex Regiment ran a 'torture' squad at Bandon Barracks in Co. Cork. This has never been substantiated, but two IRA members, called Hale and Harte, were captured by the Essex Regiment in July 1920. On release Harte was insane, and never recovered his sanity, remaining a helpless patient in Cork Mental Hospital until his death two years later. Whatever the truth of these allegations, there can have been few tears shed in Co. Cork when, some years later, Percival rounded off his military career by surrendering Singapore to the Japanese.

By the end of 1920, all Ireland was in chaos. In the south particularly, the crown forces were finding it increasingly difficult to come to grips with the IRA, and on December 10 the whole of Cork, Kerry, Tipperary and Limerick was placed under martial law. On December 11 the whole centre of the city of Cork was mysteriously burnt down, doing damage estimated at £3,000,000. Thousands were thrown out of work. Responsibility for the event has never been ascertained, but the burning took place after crown forces had cleared the streets at gun point. There is a strong suggestion that the burning was the work of the crown forces in reprisal for a successful IRA ambush at Dillon's Cross that morning.

With the end of 1920 the 'Troubles' entered their bloodiest phase. Wexford, Waterford, Kilkenny and Clare were now added to the martial law area. Both sides were getting desperate. The British, in spite of the measures to which they had resorted, seemed no nearer a solution, and the IRA, in spite of an appearance

of success, were incurring heavy casualties and were increasingly hard pressed. The troops that had seemed so raw when first sent to Ireland, now had a year's experience, and their officers were developing some of the techniques of counter-insurgency warfare. Casualties mounted. During the first three months of 1921 174 members of the crown forces were killed and 288 wounded. During the same period 317 Volunteers and civilians were killed and 285 wounded. In addition about 73 'spies' were executed by the IRA. These 'spies' were informers who had given information against the IRA. Many were citizens who, because of government pensions or former service to Britain, remained loyal and did what they saw as their civic duty in spite of the real risks they ran. Both sides now executed informers, and many an Irishman or Anglo-Irishman must have found himself in an impossible situation of split loyalties and divided sympathies. One of these was a Mrs Lindsay, held as a hostage by the Cork IRA. She had given information that led to the arrest of five IRA members, and when these five were executed, her captors shot Mrs Lindsay.

But although the methods of the IRA were ruthless, and in many other circumstances would have alienated public support, they continued to be less harsh than those of the crown forces, and, more important still, the IRA was still backed by the organisation of the republican government. This, it is true, had been driven underground and harassed by the crown forces, but it continued where possible to operate. One of the policies it adopted that was vital in keep-

ing the Irish public behind the *Sinn Fein* movement was the payment of compensation to victims of the crown forces and dependants of IRA members. In all, by April 1921, the republican government had paid out £4,317,318 in this way.

In March 1921 IRA reprisals were extended to England, mainly in the form of arson. During March and April upwards of 50 premises were destroyed by fire, mainly in the north and midlands. The physical effect of these raids was little, but their moral impact, by bringing the Anglo-Irish conflict home to the English public, was immense.

In May, Lloyd George's Better Government of Ireland Act came into force. As a conciliatory gesture Lord French was replaced as Lieutenant-Governor by the Catholic Lord Fitzalan. The Irish reaction was that they would as soon have a Catholic hangman. Elections were held for the two parliaments, and again in the south the republicans swept the board. Of 128 constituencies in the south, 124 returned republicans unopposed. The four remaining seats were safe Unionist seats elected by Trinity College. In the north the elections were again the signal for anti-Catholic outbursts. Republican electors were intimidated, their election offices smashed up, and again Catholic homes and houses were attacked, their owners driven out, beaten up, and in some cases killed. But the elections had one very important result. They defined and created Ulster. With a parliament of its own, and its boundaries indicated by the electing constituencies, the province of Ulster was a *fait accompli*. Partition, though *Sinn Fein* might still oppose it,

had been achieved, and the British had gained a tremendous tactical advantage.

The background to all this political activity was continued fighting. British military leaders increasingly urged a declaration of martial law through the 26 southern counties, and it was agreed that unless the southern parliament were operating effectively by July 12, martial law would come into effect. This was tantamount to declaring martial law as from July 12, as it was clear that no one except the Trinity College members would take their seats in the southern parliament as constituted under Lloyd George's Act.

Even without military law, it was clear that the summer of 1921 would bring more than normal troubles to the IRA. As from May the weather, in a most un-Irish way, became hot and dry, developing into one of the finest summers in Irish memory. The waterlogged mountain roads dried out and became passable to the Crossley tenders and other lorries used by the crown forces. As before mentioned, the British regular troops were becoming more experienced. They formed their own flying columns—patrols of up to company strength lightly equipped in gym shoes and shorts, and carrying only weapons and ammunition, that were able to move fast into cut-off positions after any ambush or raid. It became increasingly difficult for the IRA to carry out major operations.

In Dublin, however, the IRA achieved one major success. On May 26 the Dublin brigade of the IRA surrounded the Customs House, evicted the staff, and set the building on fire. Other IRA members thwarted the efforts of the fire brigade, and the building was totally destroyed. This operation, carried out right under the noses of the Dublin Castle authorities, had a tremendous moral effect, but its practical value was high as well. The Customs House was the centre of nine departments of the British administration. The records of these departments were now completely destroyed. But the operation was costly. About eighty members of the Dublin IRA brigade were captured.

Throughout the first half of 1921 Lloyd George made attempts to contact the rebel leaders. Secretly various emissaries offered them every imaginable variant of Dominion Home Rule, but they would consider nothing less than full republic status. These clandestine overtures show that in his own mind Lloyd George had abandoned the idea that *Sinn Fein* was a minority movement, and show also that he was worried by the increasing hostility in England to the methods he was using in Ireland, but they help to explain the suddenness with which peace came.

As the summer wore on the success of the crown forces mounted. Desperately short of ammunition, the IRA was forced to rely increasingly on bombings and arson. Suddenly, on June 22, a man was arrested during a raid on a house in Dublin. Later his captors identified him as de Valera. Thus, on the same day as King George opened the Ulster parliament, the crown forces captured the President of the illegal republic. They were jubilant. For the first time there seemed to be clear evidence that they were winning.

Then, to their amazement, they were ordered to release their prisoner. On June 25, de Valera received a letter from Lloyd George proposing a truce and peace talks. The Anglo-Irish war was over. Between January 1919 and June 1921, 752 Irishmen lost their lives, 866 were injured, and a further 24 were officially executed as traitors. The sequel to the talks in London is not the subject of this article, but it is fitting to mention that the agreement reached between Lloyd George and the Irish delegates for a southern Irish Free State with Dominion status was not accepted by a sizeable faction in *Sinn Fein* and the IRA, and that the next two years were to witness a civil war in Ireland far more bloody than the war of liberation just described.

Today the Anglo-Irish war is looked back on as the first of the guerilla campaigns for colonial freedom. Certainly it has been widely studied and imitated, particularly by the Jews in Palestine. But the would-be freedom fighter could learn at least as important a lesson from its sequel as from the war itself.

Further Reading
Butler, Ewan, *Barry's Flying Column* (Leo Cooper, London, 1971)
Churchill, Winston, *The World Crisis: The Aftermath* (Butterworth 1929)
Crozier, Brig-Gen Frank, *Ireland For Ever* (Cape 1932)
Macardle, Dorothy, *The Irish Republic* (Victor Gollancz 1938)
Taylor, Rex, *Michael Collins* (Hutchinson 1958)

[*For Patrick Scrivenor's biography, see page 353.*]

Left: After a long and unglamorous struggle the crown forces and the IRA arranged a truce. Then the treaty and partition. Here General Macready takes the salute as British troops leave southern Ireland for ever in 1922. *Right:* After two years of struggle former enemies meet. British troops hand over Portobello Barracks in Dublin to the Free State army—hastily recruited from the pro-treaty faction in the IRA

J. Cashman Jr.

THE HARDING ELECTION
Wilson Repudiated

'Where do we go from here?' 1920 was election year in the United States. The Democrats and Wilson had led the nation through the war; now the people were tired and the President sick. Everything pointed to a change, but who was to replace the present administration? America (and the world) watched as the contenders fought it out between them. *Wesley M. Bagby*

The Presidential election of 1920 in the United States, the first following the First World War, marked important changes in both domestic and foreign policies. It provided answers to two leading questions of the day, both of which had arisen as results of the war: would the prewar Progressive Movement be resumed, and would the movement towards more international co-operation, which had contributed to America's entry into the war and creation of the League of Nations, be continued?

The 'Progressive Movement' is the name given to the wave of reform that dominated the American scene from about 1901 until 1917. Its leaders wanted to make the government more democratic, to use it to protect the common man from exploitation by the growing corporations and to make it an instrument of social justice and social welfare. They were remarkably successful in winning public support and pushing through political, economic, and social reforms at all levels of government. Also, after the outbreak of the First World War President Woodrow Wilson set America on a course of broader participation in international politics. Both these policies had opponents, and the outcome of fights within and between the parties in the election year would determine who would be in charge for the next four years.

In 1919, as interest in the coming election intensified, conditions seemed favourable to the Republicans. Dissatisfaction with the Democratic administration of Woodrow Wilson seemed to be increasing. Some commentators attributed this discontent to the shortages, high prices, regimentation, and dislocation that had accompanied the war. Demobilisation had brought an economic slow-down, widespread strikes and soaring inflation. Tensions between left-wing and right-wing extremists, natives and aliens

and whites and blacks were high and produced a wave of violence. Senator Warren G. Harding said that America's present need was 'not heroics, but healing, not nostrums, but normalcy, not revolution, but restoration . . . not surgery, but serenity.' The Republicans won decisively in the mid-term Congressional elections of 1918 and, with the Bull Moose bolters of 1912 back in the ranks, they looked forward to 1920 with confidence.

In both parties the contest for the Presidential nomination seemed to be open. President Woodrow Wilson was in his second term, and a well-established two-term tradition stood in the way of his seeking a third nomination. He was also seriously ill. Former President Theodore Roosevelt, who, according to many political observers, held a commanding lead for the Republican nomination, died in early 1919. Immediately a number of Republican contenders entered the field.

Republican rivalry

Usually, after a victorious war, the United States had elevated its leading general to the Presidency. However, General John J. Pershing who led the American Expeditionary Force, seemed cold and forbidding and had little political appeal. The rôle of military candidate was assumed by General Leonard Wood, who, although the army's ranking officer, had been kept out of the fighting by the Wilson Administration for what his partisans insisted were political reasons. Wood had commanded the 'Rough Riders' in the Spanish-American war, was a close friend of Theodore Roosevelt, and after Roosevelt's death became the Roosevelt family candidate. John King, who had been Roosevelt's manager and his link with the 'regular' politicians who controlled the party organisation, assumed the

management of Wood's campaign, and it appeared that the party leaders would give Wood the nomination.

However, Wood was unwilling to accept the military man's traditional rôle of front man for machine politicians. Many of the businessmen and political amateurs who had followed Roosevelt urged him to build an independent political base and campaign for delegates in the Presidential preferential primaries. Dismissing John King, he gave the direction of his movement to millionaire soap manufacturer William Cooper Procter, and rejected offers of bargains from Boies Penrose, the national Republican 'boss', and from oil producers, to support him in return for the nomination of cabinet members. These moves alarmed regular politicians who feared that as President he might prove to be difficult to control, and they combined to deny him the nomination.

The second most noted candidate for the Republican nomination was Senator Hiram Johnson of California. He had been a militantly progressive governor and a liberal senator, but he was now campaigning as an uncompromising opponent of United States membership of the League of Nations, the only leading candidate to take so strong a stand on this issue. Such extremism, and his 'bolting' the party to run as vice-presidential candidate on the 'Bull Moose' ticket of 1912, made him unacceptable to the politicians who controlled the Republican convention. However, impressed by his popularity in the primaries, they repeatedly offered him the vice-presidential nomination, which he indignantly refused.

Governor Frank O. Lowden of Illinois was also among those prominently mentioned and he launched a vigorous and expensive campaign for the nomination. However, he was somewhat too independent to be an ideal nominee from the regular politicians' point of view and, when one of his political lieutenants was caught bribing delegates, they dropped him.

20 states held Presidential preferential primaries between March and June 1920. General Wood's campaign was much better financed than those of his rivals, and he won 124 instructed delegates. To do so, however, he had to enter the home states of 'favorite son' candidates which offended the party organisations in those states. With an expenditure of much less money, Hiram Johnson won 112 delegates and more popular votes than Wood. Lowden ran a poor third while Harding was unable even to win all the delegates in his home state of Ohio. However, most convention delegates were not chosen in primaries and even when they were they were inclined to be responsive to their states' regular party leaders.

The dark horse

With the three leading candidates, Wood, Johnson, and Lowden, disqualified in one way or another in the eyes of the regular politicians who controlled the convention they turned for a nominee to the handsome, serene, kindly and pliable Senator Warren G. Harding who, one of their own kind and a 'second McKinley', had the qualifications they desired in a candidate

Right: Senator Warren G. Harding, chosen by the Republicans as their Presidential nominee in preference to more obviously suitable rivals

Brown Brothers

3528

3530

to an almost ideal degree. After a few ballots had demonstrated that neither Wood nor Lowden could garner the necessary votes for nomination they fed votes to Harding who won on the ninth ballot.

The public was astonished that the convention had rejected the three men who had been considered in the lead and had chosen, instead, a relatively unknown senator who had run poorly in the primaries. In explanation, some political reporters in overdramatised accounts attributed his nomination to the secret machinations of Senator Boies Penrose, to the oil interests, and to a 'smoke-filled room' of back-stairs manipulators. However, in the circumstances of the convention, the nomination of Harding was the logical outcome and can be explained as a movement as well as a plot.

When convention leaders sought to 'balance the ticket' by nominating liberal Senator Irvine L. Lenroot of Wisconsin for the Vice-Presidency, the rank and file of the delegates, throwing off all control, 'bolted' to name Calvin Coolidge, the diminutive Massachusetts governor who had won national fame by taking a firm stand against re-hiring policemen who had gone on strike in Boston. The delegates had proved to be more conservative than their leaders.

In their platform, the Republicans condemned 'Wilson's League' as un-American, unjust and powerless, calling, on the other hand, for the establishment of an 'international association of nations' based on justice to meet in immediate conference whenever peace was threatened. Other planks favoured limitations on the right to strike, a high protective tariff, education for 'a sense of patriotic duty', a tougher policy toward Mexico, military preparedness, restriction of immigration, exclusion of Asians, and punishment of those who advocated 'resistance to the law or violent overthrow of the government'. The platform was conservative with overtones of the exaggerated nationalism that had been generated by the war.

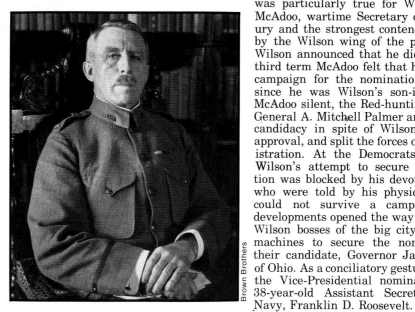

Left: The 1920 Chicago Republican convention which nominated Harding for President and Calvin Coolidge as his running-mate. *Above:* General Leonard Wood was not prepared to be a political stooge. *Above right:* Senator Hiram Johnson, rejected as Presidential candidate, refused to stand for Vice-President

In the Democratic camp, campaigning for the party's Presidential nomination was inhibited by uncertainty as to whether President Wilson would stand a third time. The Democratic party was the smaller of the two major parties in voter registrations and required a particularly appealing candidate or issue to draw the independent and Republican votes needed to win. Only two Democrats, Grover Cleveland and Wilson, had succeeded in capturing the Presidency since 1856. Wilson remained the towering leader of this party. He was in the midst of great enterprises and there was widespread speculation that he would challenge the third-term tradition.

Wilson outworn

However, after his disabling cerebral thrombosis in September 1919, party leaders considered his nomination undesirable and his failure to withdraw as a candidate increasingly embarrassing. This was particularly true for William Gibbs McAdoo, wartime Secretary of the Treasury and the strongest contender produced by the Wilson wing of the party. Unless Wilson announced that he did not want a third term McAdoo felt that he should not campaign for the nomination, especially since he was Wilson's son-in-law. With McAdoo silent, the Red-hunting Attorney-General A. Mitchell Palmer announced his candidacy in spite of Wilson's testy disapproval, and split the forces of the Administration. At the Democrats' convention Wilson's attempt to secure the nomination was blocked by his devoted followers who were told by his physician that he could not survive a campaign. These developments opened the way for the anti-Wilson bosses of the big city Democratic machines to secure the nomination for their candidate, Governor James M. Cox of Ohio. As a conciliatory gesture, Cox gave the Vice-Presidential nomination to the 38-year-old Assistant Secretary of the Navy, Franklin D. Roosevelt.

On the Versailles Treaty issue, the Democratic platform, while not opposing 'clarifying' reservations, called for ratification without reservations which would impair the League of Nations. Otherwise less conservative than the Republicans, the Democrats were also still influenced by wartime nationalism. They represented a firm policy toward Mexico, no toleration of advocacy of the overthrow of the government, and the exclusion of Asian immigrants.

Control of both parties had shifted to the right. Wilson progressives had lost control of the party machinery to anti-Wilson Northern bosses, while Republican Old Guard regulars had shown scant consideration to the views of the Progressive wing of their party.

The campaign opened with Harding apparently far in the lead. The Wilson Administration had amassed a formidable number of bitter enemies. The President's illness and the secrecy that surrounded it, his arbitrary firing of Secretary of State Robert Lansing and his refusal to compromise on the League issue created an autocratic impression and undermined public trust and confidence. Many of the groups which had contributed to Wilson's narrow 1916 victory were now alienated. Labour was offended by the anti-strike injunctions secured by Attorney-General Palmer. German-Americans, Irish-Americans, and others were determined to punish the Democrats for betraying their promise to stay out of the war and for negotiating a treaty which they regarded as unjust to their countries of origin.

Cox was forced to wage an uphill fight under severe handicaps. Wealthy Democrats who had backed Wilson were slow to contribute to his funds. Although a gallant campaigner, his stage presence was not as impressive as that of Harding. As Governor of Ohio, Cox had not participated in the fight on the ratification of the Treaty, and was reported to have shown some reluctance to make it his leading issue. However, his use of old Progressive themes met with slight public response. In his strenuous speaking tour of the country he leaned increasingly on the League issue and became its strong champion.

However, Harding, whose speech, at best, was no model of clarity, found it easy to prevent the election from developing into a referendum on the League issue. His standard address combined equal parts of denunciation of 'Mr Wilson's League' with warm advocacy of an 'association of nations' designed by the 'best minds' and including what was best in the League and the World Court. This so successfully obscured the League issue that both leading opponents of the League and outstanding advocates of the League actively campaigned for his election.

At first it was said that the Republicans planned to confine Harding to a front-porch style of campaign, but he proved to be such a captivating campaign orator that he later made several major speeches in the larger cities. Cox and Roosevelt toured the country, making several speeches each day.

The Republican resurgence
The Republicans were confident, but the magnitude of Harding's victory exceeded their expectations. Receiving 16.1 million votes to 9.1 million for Cox, he won 404 electoral votes to 127. The Democrats carried only 11 states and, of these, only Kentucky was outside the South. Harding even captured Tennessee to break the 'Solid South' for the first time since the post-Civil War Reconstruction era. Boston voted Republican for the second time in history.

Governor Frank O. Lowden of Illinois, here with his family, was too independent to succeed

Only in South Carolina and Mississippi did Democrats win as large a share of the vote as they had in 1916. German-Americans, Austrian-Americans, Irish-Americans and Italian-Americans who had voted Democratic in 1916, now voted heavily Republican. Republican majorities were larger in cities than in rural areas. However, in states that gave women the vote for the first time in 1920 Republican gains were less than average.

Except for the League's most extreme opponents, few newspapers or politicians viewed the election as a popular verdict on American membership of the League of Nations, and many insisted that it was not. The general view was that it expressed a massive repudiation of 'Wilsonism', chiefly the Administration's domestic record and a demand for change. President Harding nevertheless announced that the League was dead.

Domestically, the election represented a crushing defeat for Progressives. Some liberals had feared that Progressivism would be undermined by the war. Woodrow Wilson had predicted that it would brutalise our society: 'To fight you must be brutal,' he had said in 1917, 'and the spirit of ruthless brutality will enter into the very fibre of our national life, infecting Congress, the courts, the policeman on the beat, the man in the street.' Apparently the war required the inculcation of principles contradictory to the philosophical foundations of Progressivism, such as humanitarianism, the social gospel and the sanctity of the individual, and the postwar years were characterised by nar-

row nationalism, violence, intolerance, crime, cynicism and materialism. Hiram Johnson said that 'war and the things that go with war have extinguished the spirit of Progressivism', and William Allen White called war 'the Devil's answer to human progress'. A victory in the name of Progressive ideals had set in motion forces that undermined Progressivism and produced a social climate that could not support progressive leaders.

Further Reading
Bagby, Wesley M., *Road to Normalcy: The Presidential Campaign and Election of 1920* (The Johns Hopkins Press 1968)

Cox, James M., *Journey Through My Years* (New York: Simon & Schuster 1946)

Hagedorn, Hermann, *Leonard Wood* (New York: Harper & Brothers 1931)

Murray, Robert K., *The Harding Era: Warren G. Harding and His Administration* (Minneapolis: University of Minnesota Press 1969)

Russell, Francis, *The Shadow of Blooming Grove: Warren G. Harding in His Times* (New York: McGraw Hill 1968)

Sinclair, Andrew, *The Available Man: The Life Behind the Mask of Warren Gamaliel Harding* (New York: Macmillan 1965)

Smith, D. M., *War and Depression: America 1914-1939* (St Charles, Mo: Forum 1974)

WESLEY M. BAGBY, born in 1922, is Professor of History at West Virginia University. He is a specialist in the diplomatic history of the United States and 20th-Century US history. He graduated from the University of North Carolina and gained his PhD at Columbia. He has several publications to his name, and has been a delegate to two national party conventions.